Upstream Law and Regulation

A Global Guide

Consulting Editors **Dr Eduardo G Pereira** and **Professor Kim Talus**

Consulting editors
Eduardo G Pereira
Kim Talus

Publisher
Sian O'Neill

Editor
Carolyn Boyle

Production
Paul Stoneham

Publishing directors
Guy Davis, Tony Harriss, Mark Lamb

Upstream Law and Regulation: A Global Guide
is published by
Globe Law and Business
Globe Business Publishing Ltd
New Hibernia House
Winchester Walk
London SE1 9AG
United Kingdom
Tel +44 20 7234 0606
Fax +44 20 7234 0808
Web www.globelawandbusiness.com

Printed by CPI Antony Rowe Ltd

ISBN 978-1-905783-89-2

Table of contents

Part V Asia and Pacific

Upstream regulation: an introduction

Eduardo G Pereira
STR Holding
Kim Talus
University of Eastern Finland

I. Introduction

The petroleum industry has undergone significant changes in recent decades. As the industry has developed, it has become progressively more regulated, competitive, expensive and challenging. The balance of power has shifted from international oil companies to host governments; the changes in government take over the decades illustrate this shift. Another trend is increased concern about the environmental and social impact of petroleum operations, coupled with tightened enforcement mechanisms and heightened international interest. This trend has already changed the ways in which the petroleum industry operates. The perception of international oil companies as powerful entities beyond the control of host governments, with little or no care for the environmental or social impact of their operations, is outdated. In addition, the definition of 'international oil companies' today is much wider, as more and more companies engage in international operations to fill the gaps where the majors could not develop.

The movement from onshore to offshore, and from shallow waters to deep, represents one of the challenges that the industry has been forced to address. This has also increased the risks involved. The movement from traditional producing areas to the farthest corners of the world, such as the Arctic, has further heightened the risks involved and the need to cope with new operating environments. Development has also become even more closely linked to demand for hydrocarbons, as exploration in frontier areas tends to be far more costly.

In recent years, new types of resources – unconventional oil and gas – have additionally been harnessed, and new exploration and production areas are being examined at many levels. Consider shale gas and tight gas in Poland or other EU member states, which would not typically be regarded as petroleum-producing countries. Consider also the Eastern Mediterranean – Greece, Turkey, Cyprus, Lebanon and Israel: once again, not exactly traditional producing countries. New regulatory frameworks are being adopted to respond to new situations. Sometimes, this is a response to changes in national borders or even to the emergence of new countries, as in the case of Sudan and South Sudan. Other times, it is a response to the discovery of new potential reserves.

For international oil companies, all of this translates into new challenges. The era of easy oil is over. Companies must scrutinise the applicable regulatory frameworks with increasing care and take considered decisions on where to engage in petroleum activities.

This book is a response to the need to understand and compare new and changing regulatory frameworks for upstream petroleum. It examines the main components of more than 30 regimes in various jurisdictions around the globe. These include both established oil and gas jurisdictions (eg, the United States, the United Kingdom, Norway and Nigeria), and new jurisdictions, or jurisdictions that have recently revised their regulatory frameworks or their approach to specific significant issues (eg, Poland, Brazil and Mexico). For these and other petroleum-producing countries, the book explains the nuts and bolts of their regulatory frameworks for upstream petroleum activities. It also highlights recent changes that may affect the operational and other types of risk that the industry faces.

2. Regulatory framework: objectives

The regulatory framework of an emerging petroleum-producing country has several objectives. From the host government's perspective, the aims are:

- to attract international oil companies to explore and exploit potential resources;
- to develop a well-functioning petroleum industry – in both a technological and human resources sense; and
- to develop the economy more generally, both short term and long term.

Sustainability has also become a key objective of most petroleum-producing states and will be of importance to any new petroleum-producing country. Underpinning these objectives are the principles of national revenue maximisation and exercise of sovereignty, which have informed the approaches of petroleum-producing countries for decades. In order to achieve its objectives, the host government needs to acquire capital, information, know-how, assets, control, human capacity and similar.

The objectives of an international oil company differ quite significantly from those of the host government. Its chief objective is revenue maximisation. However, the emergence of certain national oil companies as international players has triggered certain changes in this regard. For national oil companies, the objective of revenue maximisation is sometimes trumped by objectives relating to national energy security: the need to secure future supply in the national oil company's home country may play a more significant role than short and long-term revenue maximisation. In case of an internationally active national oil company, there may also be other politically motivated objectives. However, the trend towards internationalising national oil companies, such as Statoil and CNPC, might have implications for international agreements such as bilateral investment treaties and double tax treaties, as the host government will need to consider how best to protect international investments.

Other revenue-related objectives of international oil companies often include the ability to book reserves, reduce investment and operational risks and so on.

In order to induce an international oil company to invest, it is therefore essential to include internationally accepted regulatory and contractual provisions in the regulatory framework for upstream petroleum. In order to stimulate foreign direct investment, host governments must establish terms that reasonably assure investors that their investments will yield the expected profits. This translates into requirements of transparency, predictability and stability. A natural balance between risk and reward must be struck. More favourable terms should apply to more challenging areas than to well-established areas. Most of all, however, any investor will be anxious to secure its investment over the long term, so stability is crucial.

The regulatory framework for upstream petroleum operations typically – though not always – has its roots in the national constitution, which will generally provide that the ownership of natural resources rests with the people of that country. The state's role is to manage those resources on behalf of the people. The national system often includes a specific regulatory framework for petroleum development. In addition, it includes a myriad of other legislative instruments that affect or relate to petroleum operations, such as general import and export regulations, tax regulations, environmental regulations, general administrative law and practice, and international legal instruments protecting foreign investment.

The following sections briefly examine these various levels of regulation. Typical provisions of the national constitutions of petroleum-producing states, common clauses in petroleum legislation and the main models of host government contract are analysed. The objective is to provide the necessary tools to understand the content and discussion in the country-specific chapters of this book.

3. National constitutions and petroleum

With the exception of the United States and certain parts of Canada (excluding federal lands), the ownership of subsoil resources either is shared between the people of a given country or rests with the state. These resources are then managed by the state or the national oil company on behalf of the state.

Typically, the national constitution provides for state control and state ownership. The constitution also sets out certain rights and obligations of private actors; these include some degree of ownership, with exceptions, and the right to engage in commercial activities. The state's right to expropriate privately held assets is also among the constitutional provisions of relevance for these purposes, provided that fair compensation is secured.[1]

4. Petroleum legislation

Petroleum-producing countries can choose between a regime in which most issues relating to petroleum operations are fixed in statute, or a regime which leaves a wider range of issues to be agreed in the granting instrument. Under the extreme form of the first option, no issues are negotiable at all and the only bidding parameter is a bonus or work programme. The regimes in the United States and Brazil follow this approach. At the other extreme, there is no petroleum law in place and upstream operations are based entirely on negotiated agreements between the international oil company and the host state. Most states have adopted a regime that lies somewhere

1 For details, see C Duval, H Le Leuch, A Pertuzio and J Weaver, *International Petroleum Exploration and Exploitation Agreements: Legal, Economic and Policy Aspects* (New York: Barrows 2009), pp 13–23.

between the two. Typically, the more mature areas are closer to the US system.

The petroleum legislation will typically include a number of provisions. In some cases these can then be further specified in the granting instrument; in other cases, the legislation itself will be comprehensive and leave much less to be agreed in the granting instrument. Essentially, many of the non-negotiable elements should be included in the petroleum legislation, with the granting instrument restricted to essential and negotiable provisions.

Issues that may be regulated through petroleum legislation include:

- the institutional organisation of the sector (eg, the powers and roles of various public entities, including ministries, sector-specific agencies and regulators; the existence and role of the national oil company);
- qualification requirements;
- management of areas;
- exploration and relinquishment;
- granting instruments and decisions on licences or contractual schemes;
- development and production (permits and licences, work programmes);
- decommissioning and abandonment and related issues; and
- government take and fiscal provisions.

A myriad of other issues – such as health, safety and environmental protection, local content, procurement, access to information, national reservation and emergency supplies – are also typically regulated through upstream legislation and related regulations.

5. Granting instrument

'Demise and let' all the lands owned or held under lease by said company in the Country [sic] of Vanango, State of Pennsylvania, "To bore, dig, mine, search for and obtain oil, salt water, coal and all materials existing in and upon said lands, and take, remove and sell such, etc., for their own exclusive use and benefit, for the term of 15 years, with the privilege of renewal for same term. Rental, one-eighth of all oil as collected from the springs in barrells furnished or paid for by lessees. Lessees may elect to purchase said one-eight at 45 cents per gallon, but such election, when made, shall remain fixed. On all other minerals, 10 per cent of the net profits. Lessees agree to prosecute operations as early in the spring of 1858 as the season will permit, and if they fail to work the property for an unreasonable length of time, or fail to pay rent for more than 60 days, the lease to be null and void."

– First lease (1857) between Pennsylvania Rock Oil Company and EB Bowditch and EL Drake

The petroleum industry has come a long way since the now-famous lease issued in 1857 to Colonel Drake in Titusville, Pennsylvania. Despite significant developments in the scale, value, complexity and nature of petroleum transactions, the 1857 lease included many of the basic features of today's granting instruments.[2]

Host government contracts are contracts between a host government authority and an exploration and production company that allow the international oil company to operate in the country and that set out the parties' rights and obligations. In addition to provisions on division of production or revenue, host government contracts typically include provisions on work commitments and other obligations of the international oil company, which could include local content obligations and obligations to transfer certain information and assets to the host government. These contracts may variously be categorised as concessions, production sharing agreements (PSAs), service agreements and risk service agreements. In practice, however, the final, executed contracts do not follow these rough categorisations. Specific host government contracts thus do not always fall neatly under these headings. As such, a hybrid model is widely used, containing elements from two or more of these general categories.[3] In essence, contracts should be categorised by the nature of their terms, rather than by the name used.[4]

5.1 Concession agreements and licences

Under a concession, the international oil company is granted the exclusive right to explore, develop and produce petroleum in a specific block, but the state maintains ownership of the petroleum *in situ*. The ownership of hydrocarbons passes over to the international oil company only once the resource has been produced at the wellhead or at some other defined delivery point, such as a national export point. The duration of concessions is typically 20 to 30 years, with options to extend this term based on specific negotiated conditions, such as production in paying quantities or other ongoing development. Concession areas or blocks are relatively small and are highly dependent on the specifics of the exploration area, such as maturity or prior exploration and development. Additionally, onshore exploration blocks are typically smaller than offshore blocks. Under modern concessions, the international oil company is under a minimum work obligation and must relinquish parts of the block within certain timeframes. State or national oil company participation, royalties, bonuses, income taxation and local content requirements are other typical features of modern concessions. In essence, a concession is a licence to produce hydrocarbons from a block, whereas a PSA – which is examined below – is an agreement to share production from a block.

5.2 Production sharing agreements

Under a PSA, the state retains ownership of the petroleum and production is shared between the international oil company and the state – through a ministry or other authority, or through the local national oil company – at a certain contractually agreed stage of the production process. Typically, the international oil company has the right to take 'cost oil' for cost recovery purposes and the rest of the production

---

2 Similarly, see C Duval, H Le Leuch, A Pertuzio and J Weaver, *International Petroleum Exploration and Exploitation Agreements: Legal, Economic and Policy Aspects* (New York: Barrows 2009), p 42.

3 E Smith, J Dzienkowski, O Anderson, J Lowe, B Kramer and J Weaver, *International Petroleum Transactions* (Colorado: Rocky Mountain Mineral Law Foundation 2010), p 501.

4 For an overview of various issues on host government contracts, see S Otillar and J Sonnier (eds), "Host Government Contracts in the Upstream Oil and Gas Sector", OGEL 4 (2010). See also, K Talus, S Looper and S Otillar, "*Lex Petrolea* and the internationalization of petroleum agreements: focus on Host Government Contracts", *Journal World Energy Law and Business* (5) 3 (2012), pp 181–193.

is shared. The international oil company is still obliged to pay taxes and sometimes even an additional royalty. If the international oil company is unsuccessful, it assumes all of the costs associated with its exploration efforts, including a bonus or similar payment that is typically due at the inception of a PSA.[5] Not necessarily, but quite often, a PSA will provide a carry for the national oil company. This approach aims to bring more experience and technology into the country as a whole.

5.3 Service agreements

Under a service contract, ownership of the petroleum remains with the host state at all times, including after production. Where the international oil company is compensated by a royalty in kind from the produced oil, the distinction between the service contract and the PSA is less clear. For the purposes of this discussion, two types of service agreement may be distinguished: pure service contracts and risk service contracts. The former – under which the exploration risk is borne by the state – is a pure service contract, and the international oil company is paid according to agreed terms notwithstanding the discovery or production of oil and gas. Under the latter, the exploration risk is borne by the international oil company, which is compensated for its services through payments that are dependent on and limited by the amount of proceeds derived from hydrocarbons produced in the contract area. This is a more typical risk service contract model, where the international oil company assumes all exploration risk and is entitled to only limited reward.

Generally, service contracts are well suited to states that have sufficient capital but need the expertise of international oil companies, or for fields where there is little or no exploration risk. Risk service contracts have traditionally been used in countries such as Iraq, for fields that have been producing for many years with limited exploration risk; and more recently in jurisdictions such as Mexico, where technology and resources are in high demand, but the exploration risk is relatively low (such jurisdictions are becoming increasingly popular for secondary and tertiary recovery).[6] These contracts tend to favour oil service companies such as Schlumberger and Petrofac. This issue raises a competition concern between oil and gas companies and service companies. However, it is important to remember that pure service contracts are commonly utilised for a development stage where reserves have been proved. An oil and gas company might argue that a service company is not going to take exploratory risks. Without exploratory work, there cannot be proven reserves; and without new reserves, production is likely to decline.

While host government contracts may be categorised under these general headings – each of which provides for different concepts and different levels of control – they all produce very similar end results, and the choice between the different contractual regimes has much to do with historical developments in the

---

5 The nature and details of the PSA are simplified here. A more detailed examination of division of the risk and financial implications between the state and the international oil company would require examining issues like development costs, participation of a national oil company partner at the stage of production in commercial quantities and so on.

6 For example, the service contract signed by BP and CNPC for the old Rumaila field in Southern Iraq provides for a US$2 per barrel fee for the companies for producing oil from the field. See http://www.bp.com/genericarticle.do?categoryId=2012968&contentId=7061109.

country. Further, the content of host government contracts is often similar, because the parties "borrow terms and conditions" from other pre-existing contracts.[7] Specific contractual language tends to vary only in relation to jurisdiction or time-specific factors such as oil prices, the global economic situation or internal political forces. However, this is not to say that there are no differences between the various contract types, or that it makes no difference which system is adopted; on the contrary, there can be significant consequences. For example, the international oil company's ability to book reserves is different under a concession, a PSA and a service contract. Ultimately, however, it is not possible to judge the attractiveness of a contract by its type, but only by its content.

6. Conclusion

The issues explored in this introduction are just some of those addressed in the country-specific chapters. Issues such as division of revenue, industry organisation, government supervision, tender proceedings, work obligations and assignment are examined in detail in the following chapters. This book should provide readers with a sound understanding of international trends in upstream oil and gas, and serve as a basis for comparisons between different regimes and their respective pros and cons.

7 E Smith, J Dzienkowski, O Anderson, J Lowe, B Kramer and J Weaver, *International Petroleum Transactions* (Colorado: Rocky Mountain Mineral Law Foundation 2010), p 501 and K Talus, S Looper and S Otillar, "*Lex Petrolea* and the internationalization of petroleum agreements: focus on Host Government Contracts", *Journal World Energy Law and Business* (5) 3 (2012), pp 181–193.

Angola

Paolo Esposito
RAGA Advogados, Studio Legale Esposito
Patrícia Rosário
RAGA Advogados

1. Introduction

Angola, a member of the Organisation of Petroleum Exporting Countries (OPEC) since 2007, is a major oil producer: according to the 2012 OPEC Annual Statistical Bulletin, Angolan proven crude oil reserves amount to 10.47 billion barrels, while crude oil production is at 1.618 million barrels per day.[1]

As "one of the fastest-growing economies places on earth",[2] Angola is rivalling "Nigeria as prodigious source of crude".[3] Against this background, which is almost totally dependent on oil,[4] it is perfectly logical that the stream of investments that have been directed to this country calls for political and economic stability and, what is more, legal protection and certainty with regard to Angolan oil rights.

2. Upstream activities

Upstream is the major oil sector in Angola. The downstream sector, limited to one refinery only, located in Luanda, has been recently developed with the construction of one of the largest refineries ever built in Africa, the Lobito refinery, which is designed to increase the overall production up to 200,000 barrels per day by end of 2014, and the liquefied natural gas (LNG) project located in Soyo, with a processing capacity of 5 million tons per year.

Exploration and production in Angola is essentially developed offshore, where the majority of Angolan oil reserves are located: indeed, almost 97% of the current

1 See OPEC's data available at www.opec.org/opec_web/en/about_us/147.htm. According to the OPEC's forecasts, global oil demand was expected to grow by some 900,000 barrels per day in 2012, and then by some additional 800,000 barrels per day in 2013. OPEC's most recent world oil outlook, published in November 2011, foresaw an equivalent figure close to 360 million barrels per day by 2035, ie an increase in oil production of almost 50%.
In addition, in 2011 Angola succeeded in achieving a remarkable increase of some 82% in exports to China, being the second largest importer for China, after Saudi Arabia: see International Energy Agency's data available at www.eia.gov/countries/cab.cfm?fips=CH. For data concerning oil production and the effect of petroleum activities on the Angolan GDP, see 2012 *African Economic Outlook*, available at www.africaneconomicoutlook.org/en/countries/southern-africa/angola/.

2 *Financial Times*, Special Report on Angola, Wednesday July 18 2012, p 2.

3 *Financial Times*, Special Report on Angola, Wednesday July 18 2012, p 4.

4 "[E]xportation of oil is by far the most important element in the Angolan economy. It constitutes 90% of the country's exports and 80% of its government revenue" ("Oil Rules All", in *African Business*, June 2012, no. 387, p 54).

5 The Angolan civil war, which began in 1975 and continued, with some interludes, until 2002, has had a negative impact on onshore oil activities: to date, despite recent discoveries of reserves in the Soyo and Zaire provinces, offshore operations still dominate the local industry, with Block 0 (located in shallow waters offshore Cabinda and in operation since 1955) being the main production block, accounting for half of Angola's crude production.

national oil production is generated from offshore activities.[5] Angola's continental shelf is divided into three bands: shallow-water (Band A – blocks 0-13), deep-water (Band B – blocks 14-30) and ultra-deep (Band C – blocks 31-40). At present, blocks 0, 14, 15, 17 and 18 are at the forefront of the Angolan production and expansion.

Since the discovery of the Girassol field (block 17) in 1996, when the Angolan upstream sector started moving from onshore and shallow waters to deep waters, the Angolan government has been developing consistent legislation in order properly to accommodate the expansion of the oil sector and make it compatible with the protection of the environment. Under the umbrella of the Angolan Strategic Energy Policy Act,[6] a modern set of laws is in place, which is applicable to both the onshore and offshore sectors[7] and aims at implementing efficient governance of the oil industry.[8]

3. Petroleum legal regime

Oil exploration in Angola commenced in 1910, when the first concession was awarded in the offshore area within the Congo and Kwanza basin. Later, in 1955, the first commercial discovery in the Benfica field occurred, with production starting in 1956. In 1962, after conducting the first seismic survey, traces of oil were also revealed in Cabinda. By the end of 1974, total national oil production had reached 172,000 barrels a day.[9]

In 1976, Sonangol – Sociedade Nacional de Combustíveis de Angola, EP, was established as a national public company and sole concessionaire for the exploration of oil and gas on the subsoil and continental shelf of Angola,[10] where it operates with foreign companies primarily through joint ventures and production sharing agreements, in which it is the majority shareholder.[11] Sonangol also operates outside Angola, having overseas interests in Brazil, Iran and Iraq.[12]

3.1 Petroleum legislation and relevant provisions

The Angolan legal framework governing upstream petroleum activities is formed mainly of:

---

6 Presidential Decree 256 of September 29 2011, integrating a strategic plan conceived to respond effectively to the challenges of developing infrastructure and supplying-capacity in Angola, recognises the energy sector as one of the priorities for the promotion of Angolan economic and social development.

7 Decree 1 of January 27 2009, Article 2(1).

8 See, for example: the new private investment law (Law 20 of May 20 2011), setting out the conditions and incentives granted to investors; Presidential Decree 141 of June 21 2012, establishing the regime on prevention, surveillance and control of pollution in national waters by pollutants from ships, vessels, platforms and industrial facilities; the regulation on the management of operational discharges applicable to the oil sector (Executive Decree 224 of July 16 2012) aimed at establishing control in national waters and preventing pollution; the new foreign exchange law applicable to the oil and gas sector (Law 2 of January 13 2012; discussed below at paragraph 4.3). In addition, of particular interest is Presidential Decree 297 of December 2 2010: in order to avoid the entrance, into the Angolan upstream sector, of companies without the necessary financial capacity, the government approved a set of regulations on limited tenders for the upstream sector.

9 See official data provided by the Angolan national concessionaire, available at www.sonangola.co.ao.

10 Law Decree 52 of June 9 1976.

11 Law 10 of November 12 2004, Article 15(1). In exceptional circumstances the government may authorise a lower level of participation in the stock capital (Article 15(2)).

12 See data provided by US Energy Information Administration, available at www.eia.gov/countries/cab.cfm?fips=AO.

- the 2010 Constitution of the Republic of Angola;
- Law Decree 52 of June 9 1976 (establishing Sonangol as a state-owned company responsible for managing hydrocarbons in Angola);
- Decree 39 of October 10 2000 (on environmental protection in the course of petroleum activities);
- Order 127 of November 25 2003 (establishing a general regulatory framework for the contracting of goods and services from national state and/or private companies by companies in the oil sector);
- Law 10 of November 12 2004 (the Petroleum Activities Law);
- Law 11 of November 12 2004 (on the customs regime applicable to the petroleum sector);
- Law 13 of December 24 2004 (the Law on the petroleum activities tax);
- Decree 69 of September 26 2005 (on the allocation of mining rights regarding prospecting, exploration, development and production of liquid and gaseous hydrocarbons to Sonangol);
- Decree 48 of September 1 2006 (on the regulation of bids for oil concessions and tenders for the supply of goods and services);
- Decree 1 of January 27 2009 (on the regulation of petroleum operations);
- Law Decree 17 of June 26 2009 (on the recruitment and development of the workforce in petroleum activities);
- Presidential Decree 297 of December 2 2010 (establishing limited tender procedures for the award of exploration and production contracts);
- Presidential Decree 194 of July 7 2011 (on liability for environmental damage);
- Law 2 of January 13 2012 (on the foreign exchange regime applicable to the oil and gas sector).

Recently, efforts have been made for further regulating and consolidating the energy sector by establishing a uniform national energy policy. This is intended to implement the goal set out in Presidential Decree 256/2011 (the Angolan Strategic Energy Policy Act)[13] of establishing a new framework to meet the challenges arising from the expansion of the energy sector, by bringing forward regulatory and legislative initiatives intended primarily to promote Angolan national energy independence through the development of renewable energy sources and the implementation of measures relating to security, cost efficiency and environmental sustainability.

(a) *Regulatory bodies*

The Ministry of Petroleum is the public authority responsible for regulating and supervising the oil sector in Angola.[14] The Ministry's most significant task consists of formulating the general basis of Angolan national oil policy, proposing the

---

13 See footnote 6 above.

14 Article 1 of Law Decree 10 of October 18 1996. This approved and endorsed the organic statute of the Ministry of Petroleum.

development plan in accordance with the national strategic plan, and ensuring supervision and control over its implementation.

In practice, the national concessionaire[15] also plays an important role as co-regulator: other than fulfilling commercial activities (eg, managing support services for petroleum operations and the export of crude oil), Sonangol's tasks include overseeing and supervising oil operations conducted by foreign oil companies and submitting recommendations to the Ministry of Petroleum about new areas that should be opened up for prospecting; most importantly, it is the institutional body in charge of public procurement and negotiations concerning concession licences.[16]

In order to ensure the impartiality of the national concessionaire, there are plans underway to create a National Oil Agency in Angola acting as an independent regulator and concessionaire separate from Sonangol.[17]

(b) *Types of agreements*

The Law on Petroleum Activities[18] establishes that petroleum operations may only be carried out under a prospecting licence or petroleum concession.[19]

While prospecting activities[20] can be developed by national or foreign companies autonomously, all other petroleum operations "outside the scope of a prospecting licence" can only be carried out in partnership with the national concessionaire.[21]

The Law on Petroleum Activities sets out the types of association and risk services agreement that, "[s]ubject to the prior consent of the government",[22] can be entered into by the national concessionaire with "Angolan or foreign entities of recognised capacity, technical knowledge and financial capability".[23] These are:

---

15 See, for example, Law Decree 52 of June 9 1976 and Law 13 of August 26 1978. The state concessionaire is a distinct department of Sonangol, through which the government manages its oil and gas rights and its contractual relationships with other oil companies.

16 "Sonangol plays a dominant role in the Angolan oil economy as both concessionaire and regulator, overseeing all of the operators' major financial and technical decisions and directing a web of subsidiaries that carry out sub-contracts for services ranging from shipping to platform manufacturing to insurance." See information available at www.revenuewatch.org/countries/africa/angola/extractive-industries.

17 See US Energy Information Administration data available at www.eia.gov/countries/cab.cfm?fips=AO.

18 Law 10 of November 12 2004.

19 Law 10 of November 12 2004, Article 6. According to Law 10 of November 12 2004, Article 2(18), prospecting operations are those "conducted through the use of geological, geochemical or geophysical methods, with a view to locating petroleum deposits, excluding the drilling of wells ...". All other petroleum operations, instead, have to be carried out under a concession:

> *...including the running, servicing, maintenance and repair of completion wells, as well as of the equipment, pipelines, systems, facilities and plants completed during development, including all activities related to planning, scheduling, controlling, measuring, testing and carrying out of the flow, gathering, treating, storing and dispatching of petroleum from the underground petroleum reservoirs, to the designated exporting or lifting location, and furthermore, the operations of abandonment of the facilities and petroleum deposits and related activities.*

20 Prospecting licences allow the licensee to carry out, among other operations, magnetic and gravity surveys, resistivity surveys, seismic surveys, heat flow mediation, radiometric mediation, geochemical surveys, soil sampling and magneto-telluric surveys (Decree 1 of January 27 2009, Article 8).

21 Law 10 of November 12 2004, Article 13. Petroleum concessions are published in a concession decree that is the formal legal instrument of assignment to the national concessionaire, containing the following information: (i) allocation of mineral rights; (ii) definition and description of the concession area; (iii) duration of the concession and the different phases and periods; and (iv) identification of the operator (Law 10 of November 12 2004, Article 48).

22 Law 10 of November 12, 2004, Article 14(1).

23 Law 10 of November 12, 2004, Article 14(1).

- corporation;
- consortium;
- production sharing agreements;[24] and
- risk services agreements.[25]

As further analysed below, each type of contract has a different tax regime.

(c) *Acquisition of acreage*

The Law on Petroleum Activities provides for acquisition of concessions by means of tenders and direct negotiations. Which system is actually adopted depends on the interests of the national concessionaire in its association with other entities for the purpose of carrying out petroleum operations.

The general rule established by the Law on Petroleum Activities clearly states that any joint association with the national concessionaire shall be open to tender and granted by means of a concession decree.[26] The creation of an association with the national concessionaire through direct negotiation is therefore the exception.[27] The exceptional nature of direct negotiations is confirmed by the legislative restrictions imposed on those allowed to negotiate with the national concessionaire[28] and the necessary precondition of a recommendation to the supervising ministry from the national concessionaire.[29]

Public tenders are regulated by Decree 48 of September 1 2006.[30] This decree,

---

24 A production sharing agreement (the most common form of arrangement) is a contract between an oil group and the national concessionaire under which the contracting group bears all the expenditure for exploration and extraction of substances in the contract area together with related losses and risks. 'Profit oil' is the difference between the total oil produced and oil required for cost recovery (cost oil). 'Cost oil' is the share of oil produced that is allocated for recovery of exploration, development, production and administration and service expenditure.
Profit oil is shared between the national concessionaire and its partners, based on the accumulated production or on the contracting group's rate of return. The computation of tax charges for each petroleum concession is carried out on a completely independent basis. In a production sharing agreement, the assessment of taxable income is independent for each area covered by the production sharing agreement, except for the expenses provided for in Article 23 (2)(b) of Law 13 of December 24 2004: common revenues and costs associated with distinct development areas and concessions are then allocated proportionally, based on the annual production. For the purposes of assessing taxable income, crude oil is valued at the market price calculated on the free on board price for an arm's length sale to third parties. Bonuses may be due from the contracting group to the national concessionaire in compliance with the Law on Petroleum Activities, and cannot be recovered or amortised. Furthermore, a price cap excess fee may also be payable under a production sharing agreement whenever the market price per oil barrel exceeds the price fixed by the minister of oil. In both cases, the amounts are ultimately due to the Angolan state. A contracting group may also be requested to make contributions for social projects to improve community living conditions, which also cannot be recovered or amortised.

25 Risk service agreements are applicable only to certain partnerships set up in the 1960s and 1970s, such as Block 0 and FS/FST.

26 Law 10 of November 12 2004, Article 44(3).

27 Use of the direct negotiation procedure is limited to the following cases: (i) Immediately following an open tender procedure which has not resulted in the award of the status of associate of the national concessionaire because of the lack of bids; (ii) Immediately following an open tender procedure which has not resulted in the award of the status of associate of the national concessionaire due to the supervising ministry, after consulting with the national concessionaire, considering the submitted bids to be unsatisfactory in view of the criteria specified for the award (see Law 10 of November 12 2004, Article 44(4)).

28 Law 10 of November 12 2004, Article 47(1).

29 Law 10 of November 12 2004, Article 47(2).

30 This decree represents another government initiative to improve transparency in the contracting procedure.

among others, lists the pre-qualification requirements, sets out disclosure obligations, and establishes a committee responsible for reviewing and evaluating bids (Juror, composed of a representative of the National Concessionaire, a representative of the Ministry of Petroleum and a representative designated by the Ministry of Finance). According to this secondary instrument, blocks are to be attributed to companies presenting the best offers, while the terms of the production sharing agreements are to be negotiated subsequently, to accommodate, in particular, the possibility of simultaneous bids for multiple blocks and to shorten the negotiation period.

More recently, Angola approved a new piece of legislation[31] specifically conceived to regulate the pre-salt sector. Among other things, it allows the regulatory body (the Ministry of Petroleum, upon request of the national concessionaire) to solicit tenders from a number of pre-selected oil companies only, whenever this is justified by imperative strategic reasons.[32]

(d) Qualification requirements

Prospecting licences can be obtained by any Angolan or foreign company of recognised capacity, technical knowledge and financial capability upon application to the supervising ministry. In addition, applicants must clearly state the objectives, the intended area, their technical and financial resources and the provisional budget, and reveal any other information deemed relevant. The supervising ministry, once it has received the recommendation of the national concessionaire and reviewed the application, shall issue the prospecting licence.[33]

In order to obtain the status of operator associate of the national concessionaire in a petroleum concession, companies shall demonstrate "the technical and financial

---

31 Presidential Decree 297 of December 2 2010.

32 These limited tenders are restricted to the following circumstances: (i) minor risk and low capital areas reserved for small/medium oil companies; (ii) areas reserved to Angolan investors; (iii) pre-salt areas intended to be explored by large, highly specialised and financially sound companies; (iv) strategic areas aiming at the development of Angola; (v) direct negotiations (Presidential Decree 297 of December 2 2010, Article 2).
De facto, this news tender regulation will allow access to the recently discovered pre-salt basins only by the largest global oil multinationals.

33 Law 10 of November 12 2004, Articles 34, 37, 38 and 45.

34 Law 10 of November 12 2004, Article 45(1). Less stringent requirements are required of "non-operator associates of the national concessionaire", who shall "show capacity and financial capability" Law 10 of 12 November 2004, Article 47(2).

35 Decree 48 of September 1 2006.

36 In the relevant part, it is requested that operators should, for the purpose of complying with tendering pre-qualification, be able to provide: (i) the firm's name and registered place of incorporation and the address of its registered office; (ii) the most important activities carried out; (iii) details of the company capital structure; (iv) references from reputable banks, to prove their financial capacity; (v) annual activity reports and balance sheets; (vi) details of experience in exploration and production of oil; (vii) number of employees and professional experience of management staff in the field of oil research and production; (viii) details of litigation and arbitration proceedings initiated against the company in the last five years; (ix) details of future policies of the company that may have an impact on the work programme; and (x) details of business activity developed in Angola to date. In addition, an oil concession operator should also be able to provide evidence of expertise and experience in the management and execution of petroleum operations, of technical and operational proficiency as well as of efficient organisational structure. Furthermore, in evaluating an operator's application, consideration is given to elements concerning safety, environmental protection, prevention of pollution, employment, integration and training of Angolan personnel (see Decree 48 of September 1 2006, Articles 4 and 5).

capacity and capability to carry out petroleum operations in the relevant concession area."[34] Additional requirements are set out in secondary legislative instruments[35] complementing the Law on Petroleum Activities and further specifying the rules and procedures applying to public bidding in the petroleum sector.[36]

(e) *Duration*

The contract term as determined in the licence is established in the concession decree.[37] On the one hand, the law provides that the maximum duration of a prospecting licence shall be three years;[38] on the other, no maximum term is predetermined for concessions, which is instead established in the relevant concession decrees on a case-by-case basis.[39]

The duration of the prospecting licences or of each of the concession periods may, exceptionally, be extended, upon the request of the licensee or the national concessionaire to the supervising minister, provided that the concession holder has performed its contractual obligations.[40]

(f) *Minimum work programme*

During the exploration period, when activity is aimed at discovering commercially exploitable resources, any activity undertaken shall be duly scheduled and carried out on a regular timescale.[41]

During the production phase, the national concessionaire and its associates shall draw up a general development and production plan, which shall be submitted by the national concessionaire to the supervising ministry for revision and approval.[42] Further annual development and production plans, detailed with reference to works to be undertaken and budgets, has to be submitted by the national concessionaire to the supervising ministry for approval.[43]

Once the plan is approved, an obligation arises to carry out the works in the approved plan within the time frame established. The national concessionaire[44] and the licensees[45] shall therefore "carry out the obligatory work programmes and other approved work plans within the time frames established therein, under sound

---

37 Law 10 of November 12 2004, Article 12(1) and Decree 1 of January 27 2009, Article 6.

38 Law 10 of November 12 2004, Article 12(2) and Decree 1 of January 27 2009, Article 10(1).

39 Duration is an essential term of the concession decree (see Law 10 of November 12 2004, Article 48(2)(c) and Decree 1 of January 27 2009, Article 6. The duration of the concession covers two periods, usually divided into phases: the research period (which includes research activities and evaluation); and the production period, which includes the development and production phases. However, concessions may cover the period of production only (Law 10 of November 12 2004, Article 10).
See also Decree 69 of September 26 2005 (on the allocation of mining rights in respect of prospecting, exploration, development and production of liquid and gaseous hydrocarbons to Sonangol), Article 3, stating that the duration of the concession is divided into two separate periods: a five-year research period and a 20-year production period).

40 Law 10 of November 12 2004, Article 12(3) and (4).

41 "During the exploration period, the national concessionaire shall carry out prospecting operations and exploration drilling throughout the concession area on a regular basis, in accordance with the annual plans and relevant work programmes" (Law 10 of November 12 2004, Article 59(1)).

42 Law 10 of November 12 2004, Article 63(1).

43 Law 10 of November 12 2004, Article 65(1). Failure to comply with this obligation constitutes a breach that is subject to a fine of Kz3,700,000 (Decree 1 of January 27 2009, Articles 50(d) and 51(1)(a)).

44 Law 10 of November 12 2004, Article 30(1)(b).

45 Law 10 of November 12 2004, Article 28(2).

technical rules and in accordance with the oil industry practice." Failure to comply with these obligations may result in termination of the concession.[46]

(g) *Assignment and encumbrance*

In view of the qualification requirements imposed on operators and associates of the national concessionaire, the law provides that an assignment of part or all the contractual rights and duties[47] can only take place in favour of "third parties of recognised capacity, technical knowledge and financial capability,"[48] subject to prior approval by the national concessionaire and the consent of the supervising minister in the form of an executive decree.[49]

The prior consent of both the Ministries of Finance and Petroleum, in the form of an executive joint decree, is required where the national concessionaire and/or its associates raise funds through a transaction involving the assignment of rights over the petroleum production to third parties.[50]

(h) *Local content*

The requirement for Angolan local content has two aspects, relating to both the employment of Angolan human resources (Angolanization) and to the procurement of Angolan goods and services. The necessity of such local involvement is clearly stated, both in the Law on Petroleum Activities and in several other pieces of legislation.[51]

As to the first aspect, the law aims at imposing integration, recruitment and training of Angolan workers, thus requiring that all oil companies operating within the national boundaries hire Angolans.[52] With regard to the second aspect, all entities carrying out petroleum operations are required by law to acquire national materials, equipment, machinery and consumer goods where these are of the same (or approximately the same) quality and are available for sale and delivery in due time, at prices that are no higher than 10% above those of imported items, inclusive of transportation, insurance costs and any customs charges due.[53] To that end, consultation of Angolan companies, on the same terms as those used for

---

46 The government, acting on a proposal from the supervising ministry, shall terminate the concession for "unjustified failure to carry out petroleum operations under the terms of the approved plans and projects" (Law 10 of November 12 2004, Article 53(1)(a)) or "abandonment of any petroleum deposit without the prior consent of the supervising minister" (Law 10 of November 12 2004, Article 53(2)).

47 The transfer to third parties of shares representing more than 50% of the share capital of the assignor is deemed to be equivalent to the assignment of contractual rights and duties (Law 10 of November 12 2004, Article 16(2)).

48 Law 10 of November 12 2004, Article 16(1).

49 This authorisation is not required if the assignment is to be executed in favour of an affiliated company, and provided that the assignor remains jointly and severally liable for the duties of the assignee (Law 10 of November 12 2004, Article 16(3)).

50 Law 10 of November 12 2004, Article 85.

51 For example, Decree 20 of May 27 1982 (regulating the mandatory hiring and training of Angolans by foreign companies operating in the Angolan oil industry), later reformulated by the Law Decree 17 of July 26 2009 (establishing the rules and procedures to be observed in recruitment, integration, training and development of workers in the oil sector); Order 127 of November 25 2003 (setting out the general regulatory framework for hiring of services and goods from national companies by companies operating in the oil industry); and Law 14 of July 18 2003 (regulating the promotion of the Angolan private business community).

52 Law Decree 17 of July 26 2009, Article 1.

53 The same requirement applies to the provision of services (Law 10 of November 12 2004, Article 27(1)).

international companies, is mandatory,[54] and oil companies should always hold competitive tenders to contract the supply of goods and the provision of services.[55] Only in cases of urgency or unavailability of goods or services on the domestic market, may oil companies resort to direct hiring from foreign companies. This local preference is further strengthened by the fact that any contract entered into in breach of these provisions is "deemed to be null and void."[56]

The promotion of Angolan involvement is further shown by fiscal incentives and privileges granted to Angolan investors[57] and by benefits offered for promoting Angolan entrepreneurship.[58]

(i) ***National reservation***

A concession holder may freely dispose of the oil to which it is entitled under the law.[59] However, in order to meet the needs of domestic consumption:

> *the government may request the national concessionaire and its associates, to supply to an entity appointed by the same at the delivery point, from their respective share in output, a quantity of petroleum aimed at satisfying the domestic consumption requirements of the Republic of Angola.*[60]

The Law on Petroleum Activities sets out the limit of the participation required of the national concessionaire and its associates in satisfying the country's internal consumption needs[61] as well as the costs of any such acquisition.[62]

(j) ***Environment***

Angola has in force a particularly stringent set of regulations[63] aimed at safeguarding

---

54 Law 10 of November 12 2004, Article 27(2).

55 Order 127 of November 25 2003, Article 1. In addition, Angolan companies have the exclusive right to provide services and goods that do not require substantial investment or expertise; while services and goods that require a reasonable level of investment and know how may be performed by either Angolan companies or by joint ventures between foreign and Angolan companies (Order 127 of November 25 2003, Article 2).

56 Law 10 of November 12 2004, Article 27(3).

57 Law 14 of July 18 2003.

58 Decree 39 of June 23 2008.

59 Decree 1 of January 27 2009, Article 30.

60 Law 10 of November 12, 2004, Article 78(1).

61 It shall not exceed the proportion that the annual output derived from the concession area represents of the total annual output of petroleum in the Republic of Angola, nor shall it exceed 40% of the total output from the relevant concession area (Law 10 of November 12 2004, Article 78(3)).

62 Law 10 of November 12 2004, Article 78(4).

63 For example, Law 5 of June 19 1998 (general environmental law); Resolution 18 of April 20 2001 (Convention on Civil Liability and Damages Related to Maritime Transport from Pollution by Noxious and Potentially Dangerous Substances); Resolution 22 of May 11 2001 (International Convention on the Prevention of Marine Pollution by Dumping of Wastes and Other Matters); Resolution 29-A of October 5 2001 (Convention on Intervention on the High Seas in the Event of Accidents Causing Hydrocarbon Pollution), Resolution 30 of October 26 2001 (the Funds Convention); Resolution 32 of November 1 2001 (International Convention on Civil Responsibility for Losses Caused by Pollution of the Sea by Hydrocarbons); Resolution 33 of November 9 2001 (International Convention on Preparation, Control and Cooperation against Pollution by Hydrocarbons); Resolution 41 of December 21 2001 (International Convention on Prevention of Pollution); Decree 51 of July 23 2004 (environmental impact studies); Executive Decree 11 of January 11 2005 (spill notification regime); Executive Decree 8 of January 5 2005 (regulation of procedures on the management, removal, and disposal of waste); Decree 59 of July 13 2007 (environmental licences); Executive Decree 1 of January 13 2010 (environmental audits); Decree 39 of October 10 2010 (on environmental compliance in the oil industry); Presidential Decree 194 of July 7 2011 (on liability for environmental damage); Executive Decree 224 of July 16 2012 (on the regulation of operational discharges management).

and protecting the environment,[64] including a national oil spill contingency plan (in force since 2008)[65] and several international conventions such as the International Convention on Oil Pollution, Preparedness, Response and Cooperation[66] and the 1992 International Convention on Civil Liability for Oil Pollution Damage,[67] which governs the liability of shipowners for oil pollution damage.

It is a general principle that petroleum operations shall be conducted in a prudent manner in order to safeguard "the protection of the environment and the conservation of nature."[68] In conformity to international standards, the national concessionaire and its associates, through the operator, are requested to prepare a detailed environmental impact assessment for approval by the Ministry of Petroleum.[69] Among other measures, the government has set up strict controls over the execution by oil companies of their environmental obligations and over operational discharges,[70] and it has put in place a national major spill emergency response plan.[71]

In order to impose sanctions on any breach of the obligations imposed by the relevant legislation, the Angolan government has established a liability regime essentially based on the 'polluter pays' principle.[72]

(k) *Governing law and dispute resolution*

Any dispute arising between the supervising ministry and licensees, or between the national concessionaire and its associates, which relates to strictly contractual issues

---

64 Since the Macondo incident of 2010 in Gulf of Mexico, Angola has amplified the scope of environmental protection by implementing a modern and increasingly more sophisticated environmental regime adapted to the new reality.

65 *National Official Gazette* (*Diário da República*), I series – 240, of December 22 2008.

66 Adopted on November 30 1990 and in force since May 13 1995.

67 The International Maritime Organisation Convention on Civil Liability for Oil Pollution Damage has been in force since 30 May 1996, and has been implemented in Angola by means of Resolution 32 of November 1 2001 (International Convention on Civil Responsibility for Losses Caused by Pollution of the Sea by Hydrocarbons). See data available at www.imo.org/About/Conventions/ListOfConventions/Pages/International-Convention-on-Civil-Liability-for-Oil-Pollution-Damage-(CLC).aspx.

68 Law 10 of November 12 2004, Article 7(2). Specifically, environmental protection aims at protecting and preserving "health, water, soil and subsoil, air, the preservation of biodiversity, flora and fauna, ecosystems, landscape, atmosphere and cultural, archaeological and artistic heritage" (Law 10 of November 12 2004, Article 24(1)). The wording of this provision reflects that of Decree 39 of October 10 2010, imposing on oil companies an obligation to develop measures aimed at minimising the environmental impact inherent in petroleum activities (the latter are defined in Article 1(a) as "all the activities related to the prospecting, exploration, appraisal, development, production, transportation, refining, processing, storage, distribution and sale of oil and its by-products, as well as the use and storage of chemical products for the performance of the petroleum activities").

69 The opinion of the Ministry of Fisheries and Environment also has to be sought before the assessment is approved (Decree 39 of October 10 2010, Article 6(4)).

70 Executive Decree 224/12 prohibits all discharges resulting directly from petroleum activities onshore or in interior and coastal waters, except in cases of duly justified safety reasons. Under Article 5 the operator must elaborate an operational discharges plan identifying the main and collateral wastewater discharge points, listing the chemical products in use and their inherent risk to the environment, and setting out mechanisms aimed at replacing the chemical products in use, an environmental monitoring plan and the procedures in place in order to minimise gas emissions harmful to human health.

71 Decree 39 of October 10 2010, Article 14.

72 Presidential Decree 194 of July 7 2011, Article 1. The same principle applies also by operation of international convention: for example, under the Convention on Civil Liability for Oil Pollution Damage, compensation for pollution damage suffered in the territory, territorial sea and exclusive economic zone or equivalent area as defined in the United Convention on the Law of the Sea is always available irrespective of where the incident itself occurred.

shall be resolved by agreement between the parties, according to the principles of good faith and equity and balance between the interests of the parties.[73]

In the event that no agreement is reached, disputes shall be resolved by arbitration under the terms set out in the prospecting licences and the relevant contractual agreements entered into by the parties.[74] The arbitral tribunal shall have its seat in Angola and apply Angolan law, and arbitration shall be conducted in the Portuguese language.[75]

The language of the relevant provision, which refers only to "strictly contractual issues", leaves open the possibility of additional protection granted by applicable international instruments available to the foreign investors. Angola is not a signatory to the United Nations New York Convention[76] or the World Bank's International Centre for Settlement of Investment Disputes. Angola is, however, a member of the Multilateral Investment Guarantee Agency, which provides private sector investment guarantees and dispute settlement assistance. Angola is also party to Bilateral Investment Treaties with Cape Verde,[77] the United Kingdom,[78] Italy,[79] Germany,[80] South Africa,[81] Spain[82] and Portugal,[83] each of them setting out specific dispute resolution mechanisms through arbitration.

---

73 Law 10 of November 12 2004, Article 89(1).

74 Law 10 of November 12 2004, Article 89(2).

75 Law 10 of November 12 2004, Article 89(3). The Angolan Voluntary Arbitration Law (Law 16 of July 25 2003 published in the *Official Gazette* (*Diário da República*) on July 25 2003, has been in force since September 25 2003) is the main framework for settling conflicts on issues arising from commercial contracts and asset rights, avoiding the overburdened public judicial system (the World Bank's Doing Business 2010 report estimates that commercial contract enforcement, measured by time elapsed between filing a complaint and receiving restitution, typically takes 1,011 days in Angola). The Voluntary Arbitration Law provides a general legal framework for faster, non-judicial arbitration of disputes, except for cases expressly excluded by the law. To this end, "the arbitration procedure established under the new law offers an expeditious mechanism, which also ensures judicial safety and predictability that investors require for the settlement of the disputes arising from internal and external commercial relations" (the Public-Private Infrastructure Advisory Facility and the World Bank, Private Solutions for Infrastructure in Angola, 2005, p 34).

76 Signing the New York Convention is considered to be "[o]ne immediate measure Angola could take to boost investor confidence" (the Public-Private Infrastructure Advisory Facility and the World Bank, *Private Solutions for Infrastructure in Angola*, 2005, page 103). In general, as to the African continent, the New York Convention has been applied on only a few, and not very prominent, occasions by courts in Africa, their practical experience of the New York Convention being very limited as opposed to the situation in Europe, US and Asia (see UNCITRAL Report of the Secretary General, *Study on the application and interpretation of the Convention on the Recognition and Enforcement of Foreign Arbitral Awards* (A/CN.9/168) of April 20 1979). Some African states are yet to accede to the New York Convention and, in those that have acceded, questions have arisen concerning the unfamiliarity of judges and legal practitioners with the New York Convention as a result of the general lack of relevant information and materials on arbitration in Africa. Subsequently questions have also arisen as to the proper interpretation of its provision by African courts. In particular, some possible negative implications of the commercial and reciprocity declarations which the convention's contracting states are allowed to make are of concern to the business community (in general, see Amazu A Asouzu, *International Commercial Arbitration and African States*, 2001 CSICL).

77 Signed on September 30 1997; in force since December 15 1997.

78 Signed on July 4 2000 (not yet in force).

79 Signed on July 10 1997; in force since May 21 2007.

80 Signed on October 30 2003, in force since March 1 2007.

81 Signed on February 17 2005 (not yet in force).

82 Signed on November 2 2007 (not yet in force).

83 Signed on February 22 2008 (not yet in force).

3.2 Government take

The Angolan Constitution of 2010 endorses the principle of national ownership of natural resources,[84] thus transforming the concession system previously in place whereby investors were recognised as the owners of the installations located within the concession area, and of the petroleum they extracted, while the state collected the tax revenue provided for by law.[85]

As a consequence, it was necessary to adapt existing contracts and the tax regimes applicable to their respective concessions, which had already been previously amended on a number of occasions.[86] Law 13 of December 24 2004 on the taxation of petroleum activities is therefore "the result of an effort to systematise the different tax regimes that were spread across various pieces of legislation, which meant that for taxpayers they were difficult to access, consult and apply."[87] It is of paramount importance, and conforming to international best practice, that tax obligations shall be assessed on an independent basis.[88]

Currently:[89]

all entities, whether Angolan or foreign, performing petroleum operations in Angolan territory, as well as in other territorial or international areas within the tax levying

---

84 Angolan Constitution 2010, Article 16:

> *The solid, liquid and gaseous natural resources existing in the soil and subsoil, in territorial waters, in the exclusive economic zone and in the continental shelf under the jurisdiction of Angola shall be the property of the state, which shall determine the conditions for concessions, surveys and exploitation, under the terms of the Constitution, the law and international law....*

To this end, "Mineral deposits, mineral and medicinal water sources, natural subterranean cavities and other natural resources existing in the soil and subsoil ... constitute property in the public domain" (Angolan Constitution 2010, Article 95(1)(d)), being property that is "non-transferable, imprescriptible and immune from attachment" (Angolan Constitution 2010, Article 95(2)). The principle is also endorsed in Law 10 of November 12 2004, Article 3: "Petroleum deposits [in surface and subsurface areas of the Angolan national territory, inland waters, territorial waters, exclusive economic zone and the continental shelf] are integral part if the public property of the state".

The legal doctrine governing state powers over petroleum resources is rooted in the classic doctrine of territorial sovereignty (Jennings and Watts (editors), *Oppenheim's International Law*, Oxford University Press, 1996, volume 1, p 386). "The principle of ownership of oil and gas *in situ* depends, in most jurisdictions, on an assumption of state sovereignty over petroleum reserves, an exclusive (although often sub-licensable) right of the state to extract those reserves or both. The more commonly discussed issue is not who owns the petroleum, but rather how the state allows companies to exploit petroleum" (Hammerson, *Upstream Oil & Gas: Cases, Materials and Commentary*, Globe Law & Business, 2011, page 16). International materials endorse this principle, for example the Charter of Economics Rights and Duties of States, United Nation General Assembly Resolution 3281 adopted on December 12 1974, Article 2: "[Every] state has and shall freely exercise full permanent sovereignty, including possession use and disposal, over all its wealth, natural resources and economic activity", and the Energy Charter Treaty, Article 18(1): "The Contracting Parties recognise state sovereignty and sovereign rights over energy resources."

85 Decrees 41356 and 41357 of November 11 1957.

86 For example, Decree 52 of September 8 1989.

87 Law 13 of December 24 2004, Preamble.

88 Law 13 of December 24 2004, Article 5(1):

> *In corporations, unincorporated joint ventures or any other type of business association, and in risk service contracts, the assessment of taxable income and the computation of tax charges for each petroleum concession shall be carried out on a completely independent basis, with the tax obligations pertaining to a given petroleum concession being entirely independent from the obligations pertaining to any other concessions.*

The same criteria apply to production sharing agreements, except as to exploration expenses, which shall be recovered according to Article 23(2)(b) (Law 13 of December 24 2004, Article 5(2)).

89 The current oil and gas taxation regime applies to concessions granted on or after January 1 2005, as well as to profits or capital gains from assignment of an interest in an earlier concession.

90 Law 13 of December 24 2004, Article 3.

jurisdiction of the Republic of Angola, as recognised by international law or agreements[90] are subject to payment of:

- petroleum production tax;
- petroleum income tax;
- petroleum transaction tax;
- surface fee; and
- levy for the training of Angolan personnel.[91]

(a) *Petroleum production tax*

Petroleum production tax, which is the sole tax deemed to be a "royalty" in the traditional sense, is imposed on the net quantity of crude oil or natural gas as measured at the wellhead.[92] Petroleum production tax is applicable exclusively to partnerships[93] at a tax rate of 20%, which may be reduced by up to 10% by the government at the request of the national concessionaire in specific circumstances, such as when oil exploration occurs in marginal fields, in offshore depths exceeding 750 metres or in onshore areas that the government has previously defined as "difficult to reach".[94] This tax is deductible for the computation of petroleum income tax.

(b) *Petroleum income tax*

Petroleum income tax is calculated on a taxable net income basis[95] for activities carried out in:

- exploration, development, production, storage, sale, exportation, processing and transportation of petroleum;
- wholesale trading of any other products resulting from such operations; and

---

91 Law 13 of December 24 2004, Article 4(1). The levies referred to in Article 4(1) do not exempt entities from other taxes, duties or fees to which they are subject as result of their statutory or corporate activity, supplemental or incidental to those relating to petroleum activities (Law 13 of December 24 2004, Article 4(2)).
General corporation tax applicable to companies operating in sectors other than the oil and gas is outside the scope of this chapter. However and in general terms, entities engaged in business activities in Angola that are not subject to the special oil and gas taxation regime are subject to industrial tax on business profits. Resident companies are taxed on their global income at a rate of 35%; while the branch of a non-resident company is taxed only on the revenues generated in Angola, at the same rate of 35%. A lower tax rate of 20% applies to companies whose profit derives from agricultural or similar activities. No specific tax regime applies to capital gains, which are taxed as regular business income.

92 Law 13 of December 24 2004, Article 12(1). The net quantity is the overall quantity of crude measured at the wellhead "deducted from the quantities consumed in natura by petroleum operations". Any such deduction "shall only be accepted upon a favourable opinion from the state concessionaire" (Law 13 of December 24 2004, Article 12(2)) and if, "as a result of negligence and serious fault", crude or natural gas is lost in an operational accident, "the quantities which technically could have been produced if such an accident or deficiency had not occurred, shall be considered as having been produced for the purposes of this tax" (Law 13 of December 24 2004, Article 12(3)).

93 Petroleum production tax is not imposed under a production sharing agreement ("Petroleum and other substances referred to in Article 1 produced under Production Sharing Agreements shall not be subject to Petroleum Production Tax provided for herein" (Law 13 of December 24 2004, Article 12(4)). The agreement between Sonangol and Cabinda Gulf Oil Company, a subsidiary of Chevron Texaco, in Cabinda (Block 0) is the only offshore block subject to the concession model, and thus liable to pay production tax.

94 Law 13 of December 24 2004, Article 14.

95 Taxable income is fixed by an assessment committee on the basis of the tax return submitted, validating the amounts reported and determining the taxable income (Law 13 of December 24 2004, Article 28(1)). The finding of the committee may be challenged by the taxpayer before a reviewing committee (Law 13 of December 24 2004, Articles 34–39).

- other occasional or incidental activities of entities primarily engaged in carrying out such operations, provided that such activities do not represent a different business.[96]

The standard rate is of 50% if the company operates under a production sharing agreement, otherwise a rate of 65.75% is applicable.[97] Articles 21 to 23 of Law 13 of December 24 2004 provide detailed guidelines on taxable revenues, deductible costs and non-deductible costs.[98] Incentives may be granted by the government, upon a duly justified application from the Ministries of Petroleum and Finance, by means of investment allowances, which shall be included and regulated in each concession statute.[99]

(c) ***Petroleum transaction tax***

Petroleum transaction tax is levied at a rate of 70% and is computed on taxable

---

96 Law 13 of December 24 2004, Article 18(1).

97 Law 13 of December 24 2004, Article 41. Petroleum income tax does not apply to the receipts of the national concessionaire, premiums, bonuses and the price cap excess fee received by the national concessionaire under the terms of the relevant contracts (Law 13 of December 24 2004, Article 18(2)).

98 Under a production sharing agreement, tax deductible costs should comply with the following general rules:

- Cost oil is limited to a maximum percentage of the total amount of oil produced in each development area, in accordance with the relevant production sharing agreement (generally 50%, but it may be increased up to 65% if development expenditure is not recovered within four or five years from the beginning of commercial production or from the year costs are incurred, whichever occurs later).
- Exploration expenditure is capitalised, and is recognised up to the amount of cost oil (with the same limits mentioned above). It does not include the recovery of direct production and development expenses or indirect administration and service expenses.
- Development expenditure is capitalised and the amount is increased by the investment allowance (uplift) defined in the respective production sharing agreement and amortised at an annual rate of 25% up to the cost oil amount (from the year incurred or upon commencement of oil exportation, whichever occurs later).
- Production expenditure is deductible up to the cost oil amount.
- Administration and service expenditure is either capitalised and amortised (in the same way as development expenditure) or immediately deducted up to the cost oil amount and allocated to exploration, development and production costs.
- Inventory is allocated to exploration, development, production and administration and service activities in proportion to its utilisation or consumption within oil operations.
- Strategic spare parts are allocated to exploration, development, production and administration and service expenses in accordance with the relevant production sharing agreement.
- Costs incurred in assignment of a participating interest (the difference between the acquisition price and recoverable costs plus the net value of remaining assets/goodwill) are considered as development expenditure (but do not benefit from uplift), provided such difference has been taxed at the level of the transferor.
- Should the cost oil amount not be enough to recover allowable expenses, the balance can be carried forward within the same concession.

For partnerships and risk sharing contracts, tax-deductible costs should comply with the following general rules:

- Costs incurred in the course of exploration operations, drilling costs of development wells, costs incurred for production, transportation and storage facilities, as well as costs incurred in the assignment of a participating interest (the difference between the acquisition price and the capitalised costs plus the net value of remaining assets/goodwill, provided this difference has been taxed at the level of the transferor), are recognised at an annual rate of 16.666% as of the beginning of the year in which they are incurred, or the year in which oil is first commercially produced, whichever occurs later.
- Costs incurred before production are capitalised and recognised over a four-year period (25% per year) from the first year of production.
- If the costs exceed the revenues in a given year, the excess can be carried forward up to five years.

99 Law 13 of December 24 2004, Article 43.

income, taking into account adjustments under the applicable tax regime.[100] This tax is deductible for the computation of petroleum income tax, while petroleum production tax, the surface fee and the training tax contribution and financing costs are not deductible in computing the taxable basis.[101] Concession agreements can provide for deduction of a production allowance and investment allowance.

(d) ***Surface fee***

The surface fee is computed on the concession area or on the development areas and is payable under Law 13 of December 24, 2004 whenever provided for in the relevant agreement. The charge is equivalent in Angolan currency to US$300 per square kilometre and it is payable by partners of the national concessionaire.[102] This surcharge is deductible for petroleum income tax purposes.

(e) ***Training tax contribution***

A levy for the training of Angolan personnel (known as the 'training tax contribution')[103] is imposed[104] on the national concessionaire's associates, oil and gas exploration and production companies and on service companies that contract with these entities for more than one year.[105]

Angolan companies owned or controlled by Angolan nationals (that is, those whose capital is entirely or more than 50% owned by Angolan nationals) are not subject to this levy. Also excluded from this levy are:

- foreign companies supplying materials and equipment;
- services providers and entities engaged in the construction of structures, which perform the entire or most of work outside Angola; and
- entities whose corporate activities are not strictly connected with the oil and gas industry.

(f) ***Bonuses***

Although excluded by the Law on Taxation of Petroleum Activities and not specified by the Law on Petroleum Activities, bonuses may be due to the national concessionaire under the relevant contractual agreement entered into for the carrying on of petroleum operations. These bonuses "shall revert in their entirety" to

---

100 Law 13 of December 24 2004, Article 48. Petroleum transaction tax is not imposed under a production sharing agreement (Law 13 of December 24 2004, Article 44).

101 Articles 21 and 45–46 of Law 13 of December 24 2004 provides guidelines on deductible and non-deductible costs.

102 Law 13 of December 24 2004, Article 52.

103 Law 13 of December 24 2004, Article 57.

104 Rates are as follows:
- US$0.15 per barrel for production companies and companies engaged in refinery and processing of petroleum;
- US$100,000 a year for companies owning a prospecting licence;
- US$300,000 a year for companies engaged in exploration.

105 For those companies the levy is calculated on the gross revenue generated from any type of contract, at the rate of 0.5%.

If a clear distinction exists between goods and services, it may be possible to exempt the portion relating to the goods and, in some circumstances, it may also be possible to exempt part of the services for work entirely performed abroad. The 0.5% rate also applies to the revenue obtained by entities engaged in the storage, transport, distribution and trading of petroleum.

the Angolan State.[106] A portion of such bonuses funds regional and local development projects, in order to support the Angolan private business community.[107]

(g) *Customs duties*

The customs law applicable to the oil and gas industry is laid down by Law 11 of November 12 2004, which details a special regime applicable to the national concessionaire and its associates[108] operating in the petroleum sector that is different from the regime applicable to the other industries. The law provides for a customs-free regime applicable to "importation of goods to be exclusively and directly used in carrying out petroleum operations",[109] provided that any such imported item is not available on the Angolan market[110] or is for re-sale to workers.[111] A similar exemption applies to the "exportation of petroleum produced in each petroleum concession, either in its natural state or after having been processed."[112]

4. Current issues

Angola is expected to increase its oil production during the forthcoming decades, especially given the recent studies undertaken on pre-salt layers, concentrated particularly in the Kwanza basin and lower Congo.[113] Facing the challenges of ultra-deep water oil exploration, which has already proven to be highly technical and capital intensive, will require a focus on straightening out Angolan upstream legal regime (including addressing additional environmental concerns).

At present, on the one hand, upstream activities are centralised and can only be carried out with the participation of the national concessionaire[114] by a limited number of operators,[115] while regulation of the downstream sector, on the other hand, is being driven by an attempt to liberalise its activities, favouring a competitive market (for instance Law 28 of September 11 2011 on crude oil refining and storage, transportation, distribution and marketing of refined products establishes the principles of competition for downstream activities, free access to such activities and

---

106 Law 13 of December 24 2004, Article 55(2), Law 10 of November 12 2004, Article 84(1).
107 Law 10 of November 12 2004, Article 84(2).
108 Law 11 of November 12 2004, Article 2.
109 The exclusion refers to equipment, machines, apparatus, instruments, utensils, raw materials and products utilised in petroleum operations as detailed in the annexed list to the law, and does not extend to "Stamp Duty, the statistical tax of one per thousand and '*ad valorem*' and other fees for the provision of services associated with the import and export of goods" (Law 11 of November 12 2004, Article 4(1)).
110 Law 11 of November 12 2004, Article 6.
111 Law 11 of November 12 2004, Article 7.
112 Law 11 of November 12 2004, Article 8.
113 Following the conclusion of a competitive limited international bidding round organised by Sonangol for access to the offshore pre-salt acreage in the Kwanza Basin, Statoil has been awarded the righ to operate in blocks 38 and 39. See data available at www.sonangol.co.ao.
114 Sonangol is the holder of all mining rights: "The national concessionaire is Sociedade Nacional de Combustível de Angola, Empresa Pública – (Sonangol, EP), as the holder of mining rights" (Law 10 of November 12 2004, Article 4 (1)). These rights cannot be alienated or transmitted (Law 10 of November 12 2004, Article 5).
115 For example, Presidential Decree 297 of December 2 2010 further develops the principle that a tender can be restricted to pre-approved companies by Sonangol and the Ministry of Petroleum whenever it is justified by national strategic reasons.

non-discrimination between operators, together with transparency and objectiveness in the applicable rules). The target is to improve access to capital for the construction and operation of large-scale infrastructure, of which Angola is still lacking.[116]

With an eye on the expected additional investment in the downstream sector, the Angolan government has attempted to boost the financial and banking sector by introducing a new foreign exchange regime: the Foreign Exchange Law for the Petroleum Sector[117] has modified the foreign exchange regime previously applicable to the petroleum industry in Angola.[118]

Under the new regime, oil and gas companies are required to transfer the funds necessary to pay for all petroleum operations into Angola and to process these transfers through local banks and in local currency.[119] This new regime – which will have a massive impact on international companies operating in the oil and gas sector, and which will certainly depend on the ability of the Angolan banks to ensure available means and resources consistent with international banking standards – is obviously aimed at favouring the development of the banking and financial sectors in Angola in the medium and long term.[120]

5. Conclusion

"Angola has emerged from more than four decades of war to become Africa's second largest oil exporter and its third largest economy."[121] The prospects for the Angolan oil industry are promising. The legislative efforts made by the government over the

116 Taking into account that the country has only one refinery in Luanda and does not have enough crude oil processing capacity to cover internal consumption, the government has made plans for a new refinery, SonaRef, in the coastal city of Lobito.

117 Law 2 of January 13 2012; in force since May 12 2012.

118 Under the previous regime, oil and gas companies were subject to a special foreign exchange regime detailed in an annex to the concession decree governing the block. Under this regime, foreign oil and gas companies were entitled to make payments as non-resident entities from offshore bank accounts. Although payments to Angolan resident entities had to be made into bank accounts domiciled in Angola (unless a special authorisation was obtained), any such payments could be made in foreign currency. The new law has revoked the previous special regime.

119 To this end, the Banco Nacional de Angola (BNA), the Angolan Central Bank, issued Order 20/2012 (in force since May 12 2012) detailing the procedures, deadlines and mechanisms that must be adopted under the new foreign exchange law, and setting out a schedule for their phased implementation. In a nutshell, the effect of the new regulation is as follows: (1) as from October 1 2012, oil companies (including operators) are requested to make all payments for goods and services supplied by residents through an Angolan bank account, whether in national or foreign currency; (2) as from July 1 2013, oil companies (including operators) will be required to make all payments for goods and services provided by residents in Angolan Kwanzas; (3) from October 1 2013, operator companies will have to make all payments for goods and services provided by non-residents out of bank accounts domiciled in Angola; (4) operators shall submit on a quarterly basis to BNA a list of the agreements entered into with non-residents (detailing the names of all counterparties, the scope and terms of the agreement, the amount at stake, the currency, and the countries where money will be cashed); (5) during the time payments in foreign currency to residents are still permitted, operators shall submit on a quarterly basis to BNA a list of the agreements entered into with residents (which shall include the information set out in point (4)); (6) each company operating in the sector shall also individually submit to BNA a budget forecasting its foreign exchange revenues and expenditures for the following year.

120 "The new foreign exchange law for oil companies will involve the shift of a large share of their financial transactions from offshore to domestic banks. This is expected to increase the scope for domestic financial intermediation and serve as a channel to promote increased competition and financial innovation" (International Monetary Fund, press release 12/183 of May 17 2012, available at www.imf.org/external/np/sec/pr/2012/pr12183.htm).

121 International Monetary Fund, Public Information Notice 12/79 of July 16 2012, available at www.imf.org/external/np/sec/pn/2012/pn1279.htm.

last decade, underpinned by the Constitutional principles, are providing the oil sector with a modern legal framework.

Nonetheless, the attractiveness to business of the Angolan oil industry, driven by substantial deposits and the possibility of making large profits, is limited by the need for additional legal protection. Implementation of bilateral investment treaties, as well as of international conventions offering investors the possibility to arbitrate disputes and have the award recognised and enforced in Angola[122] would be a major achievement for the country. What is more, it would likely be a manner of reducing favouritism and of supporting the fight against corruption.[123] A real contribution to this latter goal could also be achieved through the implementation of real competition in the upstream sector, which is centralised and only open to those companies selected by the national concessionaire.[124] Separation of the national concessionaire from Sonangol would, in the eyes of foreign observers, reinforce the idea of the national concessionaire's independence, and would provide an independent decision-making process.

Last but not least, reduction of the scope of the principle of confidentiality[125] and unveiling the stream of money generated in the upstream process would be most welcome: public disclosure and transparency in oil operations would satisfy democratic expectations and earn the trust of national and international investors. What is more, it would earn the trust of Angolan citizens, the majority of whom are still being affected by poor living conditions. After all, it is an accepted principle of international law that the natural resources of a country should be exploited to the benefit of its people.[126]

---

122 See above at paragraph 3.1.11 and footnote 73.

123 See for example, Hodges, *Angola: Anatomy of an oil state* (Fridtjof Nansen Institute (Lysaker, Norway), 2nd edition, 2004). See Transparency International's data and corruption perceptions index available at cpi.transparency.org/cpi2011/results/.

124 See above, para 3.1(k).

125 See Law 10 of November 12 2004, Article 77, and Law 13 of December 24 2004, Article 68(1).

126 "... in the interest of their national development and of the well-being of the people of the state concerned", United Nation General Assembly Resolution 1803 adopted on December 14 1962 (Permanent Sovereignty Over Natural Resources), Article 1(1).

Chad

Anselme Patipéwé Njiakin
Ernst & Young Chad

---

1. Introduction

Since the 1970s, Chad has seen exploration of its soil and subsoil for 'black gold'. The first oilfields were discovered by the American Continental Oil Company, in partnership with other oil companies, and the first basins to be explored were those of Doba and Lake Chad. However, it was not until 2003 that a consortium made up of Exxon Mobil (through Esso, its subsidiary), Chevron Texaco and Malaysian Petronas began to exploit the Doba basin – the largest oil basin located in the southern area of the country.

In order to allow the transportation of Chadian oil, this consortium has constructed a pipeline measuring approximately 1000 kilometres (km), enabling its export via the port of Kribi in Cameroon. The total cost of this oil project was $4 billion.

The Doba fields will produce about 950 million barrels over 25 to 30 years. Current production is running at 120,000 barrels a day.

After the Doba basin, the Bongor basin which is located in the southwest of the country is the second largest basin. It is being exploited by China National Petroleum Corporation (CNPC). The site started to produce in June 2011 and will be able to produce 60,000 barrels a day. Other basins, such as those of Lake (licensed to CNPC), Dosséo (licensed to Esso), Logone Birnie (licensed to CNPC) and Erdis are not yet in production.

The oil-bearing fields currently in exploitation are those of Komé, Miandoum, Moundouli, Nya, Maikeri and Bolobo. They have an estimated capacity of 977 million tons of oil and are located in the south of Chad, in the department of Eastern Logone. In addition, oil reserves have been discovered in Séguidi, which is in Kanem in the west, and in Mougo which is in Chari Baguirmi, 300km southwest of N'Djamena. According to most of the exploratory studies, basins could potentially exist in the areas of Doseo and Am Timam, both located in the south. Should the existence of these basins be confirmed, it would in the long-term mean that Chad would hold one the largest oil reserves in Africa whereas now it ranks ninth.

According to the International Monetary Fund's forecasts, Chad should experience growth of 7% in its gross domestic product in 2012, as against 3% in 2011. This growth has come about not only thanks to an increase in oil productivity, with the first complete year of operation for Chad's first refinery, but also thanks to the development of new infrastructure allowing an increase in electricity production and a new cement factory. However, the country is not completely safe from a potential slowing down of its growth because the economy still relies too much on oil. Activities such as agriculture, breeding and fishing represent only 2% of the gross domestic product. Companies interested in exploiting Chadian oil must obtain the necessary authorisations or licences from the Chadian government through either a concession agreement or a production sharing contract.

2. Upstream activities

Upstream oil activities in Chad are of four types:

- prospecting;
- research and exploration;
- exploitation;
- transport and storage of crude.

Prospecting for petroleum is defined by Article 8 of Law 006/PR/2007 relating to hydrocarbons as:

Preliminary activities for detecting indications of the existence of hydrocarbons by the use of geological, geochemical or geophysical methods, other than drilling ...

Prospecting for petroleum requires an authorisation granted by a decree of the minister in charge of hydrocarbons. Such an authorisation may be granted to any legal entity that has shown its technical expertise and its financial ability, and after having paid the necessary fees to the Treasury. The duration of the authorisation is for two years. This authorisation gives to its holder a non-exclusive right to undertake prospecting activities inside the perimeter defined in the authorisation.

Research or exploration in respect of petroleum is defined as:

The whole of the activities of prospecting, as defined above, as well as works of geological, geochemical or geophysical surveys and drilling allowing the description of hydrocarbons fields.

Research is therefore the advanced phase of prospecting, making it possible to describe the fields detected in the previous phase. Research or exploration is carried out under a licence or an exclusive authorisation granted by a decree of the minister in charge of hydrocarbons. This licence or authorisation is attached to a petroleum contract and gives the holder an exclusive right within a defined perimeter.

'Exploitation' is defined as:

Studies and works, especially of drilling and completion of the wells, as well as the realisation of necessary installations, in order to develop and set a field of hydrocarbons in production, the operations of the first preparation of produced hydrocarbons, aiming at marketing them, the transportation of these hydrocarbons notably by pipeline, their marketing and most generally all other operations related to the preceding ones and leading to the same objectives.

Exploitation is undertaken under an exclusive exploitation authorisation or an exploitation licence issued by a decree of the president made during a meeting of the Council of Ministers.

As regards petroleum transportation, this activity relates either to upstream or downstream operations, depending on whether it concerns crude oil or refined oil.

'Petroleum transportation' is defined by Article 8 of Law 006/PR/2007 as:

The whole of the activities of transporting by pipeline hydrocarbons and extracted oil products up to the delivery point, except the collection and service networks on the fields ...

Transportation of hydrocarbons is carried out through pipelines or other lines duly approved by the Chadian state. The construction of pipelines or the use of any other means of transportation requires a joint authorisation from the minister in charge of the environmental matters and the minister in charge of hydrocarbons.

3. Petroleum legal system

3.1 Petroleum law and relevant provisions

Regulation of the oil industry in Chad began with Ordinance 7/PC/PT/MH of February 3 1962, relating to prospecting, exploitation and transportation of hydrocarbons by pipeline and to the taxation of these activities, and its decree of application of May 10 1967, modified by Law 006/PR/2007 of May 2 2007 relating to hydrocarbons, which was itself modified and supplemented by Ordinance 001/PR/2010 of January 7 2010, concerning approval of the standard production sharing contract for the prospecting for and exploitation of liquid or gas hydrocarbons.

Decree 796/PR/PM/MPE/2010 establishes the procedures for enforcement of Law 006/PR/2007 and Ordinance 001/PR/2010.

With a view to ensuring the transparency of oil resource management, a number of texts were adopted, particularly Law 001/PR/99 of January 11 1999, which has been amended by Law 016/PR/2000 of August 1 2000.

The whole of this regulatory framework enables the state of Chad better to inform investors of its desire for an open market.

(a) Regulatory bodies

Various official organs play a role within the framework of the regulation of oil operations.

The minister of energy and oil, is responsible for the design, coordination implementation and supervision of government policy in the field of hydrocarbons (see Article 3.1 of Law 006/PR/2007). He is also responsible for the control and supervision of oil operations and for ensuring respect of the Chadian regulations on the matter (see Article 41.1 of Law 006/PR/2007). In the same way, he is the representative of the state in all oil operations, especially during the signature of oil contracts. Finally, he is empowered to grant the licences and authorisations necessary for undertaking oil activities, except for production licences and exclusive authorisations.

The minister of finance can examine, or have examined by auditors of his choice, the registers and the account books relating to oil operations as well as records relating to the tax obligations of oil contract holders.

The tax and customs authorities are, within their respective remits, in charge of carrying out the necessary checking in order to ensure that the tax and customs obligations of oil operators are strictly respected.

Another official organ intervening within the framework of oil regulation is the National Assembly. This body intervenes in upstream activities by passing the laws governing such activities and oil resources management. As regards downstream activities, it approves in their legislative form, all oil contracts before their implementation (see Article 9.2 of Law 006/PR/2007).

The Ministerial Council is in charge of approving, or not, endorsement of oil contracts. In the event of approval, the Ministerial Council makes a decree which is published in the *Official Journal of the Republic of Chad.*

Finally, the president intervenes in the sphere of the oil activities by promulgating the laws passed by the National Assembly. He is also in charge of granting, by decrees taken in the Ministerial Council, production licences or exclusive authorisations.

(b) *Types of agreement*

Under Chadian law, there are two types of petroleum contract:

- concession contracts; and
- production sharing contracts.

A concession contract is defined by Article 2 of Decree 10-796/PR/PM/MPE of September 30 2010 specifying the procedures for the enforcement of Law 006/PR/2007 as:

The oil contract attached to a licence by which the state or the national company confers on a qualified legal entity, which assumes all the risks relating to it, the exclusive right to undertake hydrocarbons research and exploitation inside a defined perimeter.

It can be seen from this that there are two main characteristics:

- the concession contract is attached to a licence, that is to say that the holder must already hold a prospecting licence for the area within the perimeter of the contract; and
- the concession contract confers to its holder, the exclusive rights of research and exploitation in the event of discovery of hydrocarbons, within a given perimeter.

A production sharing contract is defined by Ordinance 10-001/PR/2010 of September 30 2010 as:

The oil contract in which the holder commits himself to carry out oil operations, at his expense and risk, on behalf of the state, in exchange for a share of hydrocarbons produced in the dependent contractual zone as remuneration in the event of exploitation.

Three main characteristics emerge from this definition:

- the holder commits himself to carry out the oil operations at his own expense and risk;
- the oil operations are carried out on behalf of the state; and
- the holder is remunerated for his work by a share of the production.

(c) *Acquisition of acreage*

Article 9.2 of Law 006/PR/2007 provides that:

Unless the minister in charge of hydrocarbons decides otherwise, concession and production sharing contracts are awarded according to a procedure of international invitation to tender ...

In the same way, Article 13 of Decree 10-796/PR/PM/MPE provides that:

the minister in charge of hydrocarbons can, for the granting of a licence or an authorisation, proceed to an invitation to tender which states the conditions, the criteria for the award, the handover date of the offers and the blocks that are the subject of the invitation to tender ...

As a result of these provisions, petroleum contracts (concession contracts or production sharing contracts) may be concluded either according to the procedure resulting from an invitation to tender, or by direct negotiation.

(d) Qualification requirements

Applicants are required to establish their technical and financial ability, which is justified by the objectives of optimising recovery, conservation of hydrocarbons and environmental protection.

To this end, Article 4 of Law 006/PR/2007 states:

The activities of prospecting, research, exploitation, transport by pipeline and refining of hydrocarbons can be carried out in the territory of the Republic of Chad only by the public or private, national or foreign companies, which have and provide evidence of sufficient technical and financial abilities enabling them to fulfil their obligations ...

This law provides for regulations to define the concept of technical and financial abilities. Accordingly, Decree 10-796/PR/PM/MPE provides that the holders of a licence or an exclusive authorisation for research or exploitation should be Chadian companies. In addition, in order to make it possible to assess the technical and financial abilities of applicants for a licence or an authorisation, the application must be supported by a file including among other things:

- evidence of the applicant's share capital and the extent to which this is paid up;
- financial statements for the last three fiscal years;
- in the case of a consortium, notification of which oil company has been appointed as the operator and documents showing this company's qualifications as regards the management of oil operations; and
- all documents demonstrating the technical and financial abilities of the applicant company, or the companies who are members of the consortium, in regard to the carrying out of oil operations.

(e) Duration

A prospecting authorisation is granted for a period of two years, renewable once (see Article 26 of Law 006/PR/2007). There is a contradiction here between this provision and Decree 796/PR/PM/MPE which provides for a one year duration. However, the provision of the law is applicable.

Prospecting licences and exclusive authorisations for research are granted for an initial duration of five years at the most, renewable once for a period of three years at the most (see Article 27.3 of Law 006/PR/2007 and Article 4(3) of Ordinance 10-

001/PR/2010). In the event that a discovery is recorded in the last year of the validity of a prospecting licence, a two-year extension can be granted for a discovery of oil, or one of three years for a gas discovery, in order to enable the holder to assess the discovery.

An exploitation licence is granted for a duration of 25 years for liquid hydrocarbons and 30 years for gas. It can be renewed for an additional ten-year period at the request of the contractor and on the condition that he has fulfilled all his contractual obligations.

An exclusive authorisation of exploitation is granted for a period of 25 years whether for liquid or gas hydrocarbons. There is no express provision for the possibility of renewal (see Article 4(4) of Ordinance 10-001/PR/2010). However, the practice is to include in the production sharing contract the possibility of renewal for a maximum 10 years, provided that the contractor has fulfilled all of its obligations under the contract.

(f) Minimum work programme

In accordance with Article 10 of Law 006/PR/2007, a petroleum contract (concession or petroleum sharing contract) fixes among other things, the minimum work programme for exploration and the corresponding financial commitments that the holder has agreed to make in the initial period of validity of the licence (or exclusive authorisation) to undertake research, and in the period of renewal. In the same way, a programme of works to be undertaken and the corresponding budget, as well as the way in which their execution will be supervised, are provided for the event that an exploitable discovery is made.

The nature and the extent of the minimum work programme to be executed by the holder of the licence or the exclusive authorisation are specified within the petroleum contract (concession or production sharing agreement). They generally consist of geophysical and geochemical analyses, drilling and all necessary works for the discovery and exploitation of hydrocarbons.

A holder of a prospecting licence or of an exclusive authorisation to undertake research must present the programme of work for the following year to the minister in charge of hydrocarbons within a month following the grant of such licence or authorisation, and before October 31 of each year thereafter. This is a descriptive document detailing the tasks to be undertaken in the calendar year concerned.

Total or partial non-execution of the works' programme provided for in the petroleum contract gives rise to the payment of penalties.

(g) Assignment and encumbrance

Article 21 of Law 006/PR/2007 provides that:

> *Subject to the fulfilment of his works and budgetary commitments, the contractor can yield and/or transfer, with the preliminary authorisation of the minister in charge of hydrocarbons, his interests deriving from the oil contract, to people having the technical and financial abilities to properly carry out the oil operations.*

From this provision it is clear that surrendering or transferring oil rights is conditional on the prior agreement of the minister in charge of hydrocarbons. It is the same for any operation involving a change of control in the contractor.

To this end and in accordance with Article 62 of Decree 10/796/2010 of September 30 2010, the contractor must address to the minister a request for approval containing information relating to the assigned rights, the grantor and the assignee as well as the nature of any existing relationship between them. He must also attach to his request the draft deed of transfer, all covenants agreed between the grantor and the assignee and the draft adoption of the oil contract in question.

The minister in charge of hydrocarbons has a deadline of 90 days as from the submission of the request to approve or refuse the surrender or the assignment. If he does not reach a decision within this deadline, the minister's approval is deemed to have been granted.

Any rejection of a request for approval of a transfer or change of control must be duly explained and notified to the holder. In such a case, the contractor can either continue to carry out his contractual commitments or give up the oil contract.

If he approves the proposed transfer and adoption of the petroleum contract, the minister in charge of hydrocarbons informs the holder, and may ask the assignee to rectify or supplement the file during the transfer or the change of control, if it is necessary.

Then the minister submits the proposed adoption of the oil contract for the approval of the Council of Ministers.

The proposed adoption of the oil contract is then approved by a decree made during the Council of Ministers and the transfer of the title is then authorised by an ordinance of the minister in charge of hydrocarbons. The decree and ordinance are published in the Official Journal of the Republic of Chad. Notification is made to the assignee within 15 days following the respective dates of their signature.

A non-deductible tax at the rate of 1% is applied to the amount of the transaction, payable by the assignor. In addition, cessation or transfer of oil rights is subject to a fixed fee of ??CFAfr.

In the event that the transfer is approved by the Chadian authorities, all profits resulting from the transfer of assets relating to an authorisation, are subject to an exceptional deduction of 25% payable by the vendor according to the terms provided in the standard production sharing contract (see Article 17 of Ordinance 10/001/PR/2010 of September 30 2010).

(h) Local content

There are no requirements laid down by law as to the use of local goods or supplies.

(i) National reservation

All oil contracts (whether concession or of production sharing agreements) include provisions relating to supplying the local market. Thus, Article 20.1 of the standard production sharing contract provides that:

> *If the state cannot satisfy the Republic of Chad's internal needs for consumption of crude oil from its own share in all the quantities of crude oil produced in the territory of the Republic of Chad, the contractor agrees, from his own share of the crude oil production, to sell to the state the share necessary to satisfy the country's internal consumption needs.*

The result of this provision is that in the event of shortage resulting from the failure of the state to fulfil local demand for oil products from the quantities of oil that belong to it, the state has a pre-emption right over the quota of oil products belonging to the contractor.

Application of this pre-emption right by the state is strictly constrained and must in no case affect the principle of equality between the oil contractors operating on Chadian territory. Therefore, the quantities of hydrocarbons that each contractor can be required to supply for the needs of the domestic market should not exceed the total of the Chadian domestic market's needs, reduced by the total of the production of hydrocarbons which belongs to the state under the terms of its various oil contracts (including its production royalty), the whole multiplied by a fraction in which the numerator consists of the share of hydrocarbon production allocated to the contractor and the denominator consists of the total production of hydrocarbons extracted from Chadian territory. This calculation is made every quarter (Article 20.3 of the standard production sharing contract).

In addition, the state must notify the contractor of its desire to buy its production for the purpose of supplying the domestic market, at least six months in advance. It must specify in its notification the quantities necessary to satisfy the needs of the domestic market during the next six months up to the expiry of the notice. This notification constitutes a firm purchasing commitment by the state in respect of the quantities notified for each of month at issue (Article 20.2 of the contract).

The contractor can substitute its obligation of supplying the domestic market by buying hydrocarbons produced in Chad or abroad. However, such a decision is subject to the condition of acquiring prior written authorisation from the state.

The crude oil sold to the state under the obligation to supply the domestic market is paid for in US dollars and is delivered the state at the measuring point.

To receive its payment, the contractor invoices to the state at the beginning of each month for the price of the deliveries carried out during the previous month. Payment by the state must occur within 30 days following the date of invoicing. In the absence of payment within the deadline, the sums due accrue interest at rates laid down by law. Nevertheless, the contractor must continue the deliveries for the six-month period covered by the notification.

(j) ***Environment***

Under Article 10 of Law 006/PR/2007, an oil contract provides among other things:

> *... obligations regarding environmental protection, according to precautionary principle, and supplementing those provided by the legislation and the Chadian regulations in force.*

The standard production sharing contract stipulates the obligations of the contractor as far as environmental protection is concerned. These obligations, which are also applied by extension to concession contracts in the absence of specific regulations, consist of:

- providing environmental impact studies as required by the contract and by legislation;

- instituting a rigorous system of prevention and control of pollution resulting from oil operations, particularly through the treatment and control of toxic emissions resulting from oil operations that are likely to cause harm to people, goods or the environment;
- instituting a system for the collection of waste and used material resulting from oil operations; and
- all other usual measures tending to prevent, avoid or minimise damage being caused to the environment by oil operations.

An environmental impact study is, according to Article 8 of Law 006/PR/2007:
... a document that the holder of an oil contract must present to the qualified Chadian authority including: identification, description and evaluation of the effects of oil operations projects on human beings, fauna and flora, the ground, water, air, climate and the landscape, including the interactions between these factors, cultural heritage and other tangible properties as defined by law, as well as suitable corrective measures.

An environmental impact study can be carried out either by the contractor himself or by an expert appointed by him and approved by the state. It must necessarily contain the following information in accordance with the combined provisions of Law 14/PR/98 of August 17 1998 defining the general principles of environmental protection and of the production sharing contract:

- a non-technical summary of the information provided under each of the points below, including the main findings and recommendations; this summary being in a separate document from the report supporting the document;
- a complete description of the project, including information relating to its site and the criteria used for its selection, to its design and its dimensions, the targeted aims, the justification for the project, the various phases of the project (research, development and exploitation) and any additional projects, if applicable;
- an analysis of the initial state of the area covered by the authorisation and the locations necessary for the activities concerned and their environment; this analysis relating in particular to the effects on the species concerned, the landscape, resources and natural environments, the biological balance, cultural heritage and, if applicable, any inconvenience to neighbouring communities (noise, vibrations, odours, light output), or effects on hygiene and public health;
- the reasons for the choice of site;
- the opinion of the local population, if applicable;
- a description of the legal framework of the environmental impact study;
- identification of the environmental impacts and the damage that will result from the oil operations and any related activities being carried out, within the area concerned, including an analysis of the toxicological risks and the risks of a technological accident, if applicable;
- a statement of the measures planned by the contractor to eliminate or compensate for the detrimental consequences of oil operations on the

environment, with an estimate of the corresponding expenditure and the estimated timeframe for achievement of these measures, and of any emergency measures in the event of an accident;

- a presentation of other possible solutions and reasons for which, from the environmental protection point of view, the option or the solution suggested by the contractor was adopted;
- a plan of environmental monitoring and follow-up;
- proposals for guidelines to follow in order to minimise environmental damage.

The environmental impact study produced in accordance with these requirements must be submitted by the oil contractor to the administration in charge of the environment in exchange for a receipt.

Once the administration in charge of the environment has received the study and has considered it to be acceptable after an evaluation, it publishes its decision in an official advertisement and opens the study to public consultation for a period of 45 days. During this period, it keeps a public record of all observations relating to the project and the environmental impact study. The expenses of advertisement are covered by the applicant.

Any licence or authorisation to carry out a petroleum operation granted by the appropriate authorities must aim to implement measures suggested in the environmental impact study as approved by the administration in charge of the environment.

Failure to produce an environmental impact study can lead to the cancelling of the licence or of the authorisation granted.

In addition, the oil contractor must submit to the state at the latest on October 31 of each year, a waste management plan in accordance with the provisions of Law 014/PR/98 of August 17 1998 defining the general principles of environmental protection and its implementing texts.

(k) Governing law and dispute resolution

In accordance with the provisions of Article 104 of Law 006/PR/2007:

Any disputes between the parties to a petroleum contract relating to the interpretation or the execution of the aforesaid contract that cannot be solved by mutual agreement will be submitted to the arbitration of the International Chamber of Commerce (ICC) of Paris.

In this case, the dispute will be resolved according to Chadian law and, if necessary, supplemented by the principles and practices recognised by the oil industry.

This means that the ICC of Paris is the competent jurisdiction in the event of any dispute concerning a petroleum contract, while Chadian law remains the applicable law. However, international law and in particular the general principles applicable in the international oil industry can be applicable, subject to mutual agreement of the parties.

Law 006/PR/2007 favours mutual agreement for the settling of any disputes.

Thus, when a dispute arises, the parties must endeavour to resolve amicably. It is only after failure to achieve this that it is necessary to call for arbitration by the ICC of Paris. If such arbitration is required, each party designates an arbitrator and the ICC designates the third arbitrator who acts as the president of the arbitration tribunal.

In addition, the standard production sharing contract contains a stabilisation clause, by which the state promises that it will not be apply to the contractor, without his prior agreement, any modification to the laws in forced that has the effect of:

- making more onerous the obligations and charges imposed on him under the oil contract; or
- reducing its economic rights and advantages resulting from the oil legislation and the contract.

3.2. Government take

Oil operations are subject to tax and non-tax levies as provided by various regulations in force. The most significant are listed below.

(a) Royalties

Royalties are levies made by Chadian government on the production of hydrocarbons.

The royalties, which are also called the 'fee on production', are imposed on all hydrocarbons produced as measured after treatment at the field. Hydrocarbons consumed by the direct needs of the oil operations or reintroduced into the field within thresholds based on technical usage in the oil industry are excluded from the basis of calculation of this fee.

The rate of these fees is fixed within the framework of the concession or production sharing contract. However, this rate cannot be lower than 16.5% for liquid hydrocarbons (Article 70.4 of Law 006/PR/2007). The standard production sharing contract fixes the rate at between 14.25% and 16.5% (Article 14 of Ordinance 001/PR/2010 of September 30 2010).

As for gas hydrocarbons, the rate of the royalties is between 5% and 10%.

The payment of this royalty may be in cash or in kind, at the state's discretion. The state must inform the oil contractor of how it wishes to receive payment at least 90 days before the date of the production of the first ton of hydrocarbons. This choice is however changeable provided that the state gives notice of at least 180 days.

The royalty on production is paid in cash if the state does not make its choice within the time limit (Article 43.1 of the standard production sharing contract).

Royalty payments are made monthly before the 15th of the month which follows that of production. In the event of a delay in the payment of the royalty or the delivery of hydrocarbons where the royalty is paid in kind, the sums or quantities due are raised to 0.1% per day of delay.

These royalties are a deductible expense in the calculation of the contractor's taxable profit.

(b) *Bonuses*

Bonuses are sums paid to the state of Chad by the contractor, either at the time of the granting of an exclusive authorisation for research, or after the award of an exclusive exploitation authorisation.

The first of these, the signature bonus must be paid by the contractor on the granting of an exclusive authorisation to undertake research by the minister in charge of hydrocarbons. Its amount, the time limit and other details of its payment are agreed by the parties and specified in the contract.

In accordance with the provisions of the standard production sharing contract, the payment of the bonus is generally required by whichever of the following dates is the later:

- five working days after the delivery of the exclusive authorisation to undertake research and the completion of all the necessary legal procedures, including publication in the *Official Journa*l of the relevant ordinance; or
- 30 days after signature of the contract.

The bonus payable on the award of an exclusive authorisation for exploitation is due after the publication of the presidential decree formalising the award. The contractor must then pay to the state within five days following the publication in the *Official Journal* of the decree, a bonus whose amount is fixed by the standard production sharing contract at $2 million (Article 38.2 of the contract).

Neither of these bonus payments is recoverable in terms of oil costs.

(c) *Rental fees*

Under Article 69 of Law 006/PR/2007:

The holders of the oil contract and licence while it is in force are subject to the payment of an annual surface royalty whose amount and methods of payment are specified in the oil contract.

It can be seen from this provision that the oil contract provides the amount and the modes of payment of the surface tax. But generally it is payable annually.

The standard production sharing contract distinguishes between payments under an exclusive authorisation for research, an exclusive authorisation for exploitation, or an authorisation of inland transport.

Under an exclusive authorisation for research, the fee is:

- in first period of validity – CFAfr500 per square kilometre (km^2) per year;
- in the second period of validity – CFAfr1,500 per km^2 per year;
- in the third period of validity – CFAfr1,500 per km^2 per year; and
- in the extension period (if any) – CFAfr5,000 per km^2 per year.

Under an exclusive authorisation for exploitation, the fee is:

- in the first period of validity – CFAfr1.5 million per km^2 per year;
- in the second period of validity – CFAfr2 million per km^2 per year.

Under an inland transport authorisation, the equivalent fee is CFAfr 150,000 per year.

The surface royalty is payable annually in advance on the basis of the situation at January 1 of the current year. It must be paid to the Treasury at the latest on March 31 of the relevant year.

It is not deductible under oil costs.

(d) *Special participation*

Article 13.1 of Law 006/PR/2007 provides that "The state, by the means of the national company, is entitled to an initial participation in the research tasks."

Under this provision the state of Chad is allowed to take a participation in any oil contract, and it does this by the means of the national company (SHT). The amount of this initial participation is fixed by the oil contract.

In the same way, in the event of the discovery of hydrocarbons in commercially exploitable quantities, the state can acquire an additional participation. The national company acting on behalf of the state has a time limit of six months as from the granting of the exploitation licence or exclusive authorisation to declare its intention to take up this option.

The total participation of the state (the initial participation and, if applicable, the additional participation) cannot exceed 25% of the rights and obligations attached to the licence or authorisation. All the other parties see their participation in the licence or the authorisation automatically decreased by the percentage granted to the state, which in effect becomes a co-holder of the licence or authorisation.

When the state decides to exercise its option of participation, it pays a share of the oil costs incurred both before and after the granting of the exploitation licence or authorisation, including those incurred in exploring and developing the oilfield, corresponding to the state's participation, which will be at least 10%.

The expenditure incurred by the state is paid to the contractor by prior deduction at the field's measuring point from the share of production belonging to the state. The contractor is not subject to tax on the amounts deducted in this way.

(e) *Corporate taxes*

Article 74.1 of Law 006/PR/2007 provides:

> *The holders of oil contracts ... are subject to corporation tax on the profits that they make from the whole of their activities of research and exploitation in the Chadian territory, whether they undertake them alone or in partnership with other companies.*

However, it is advisable to distinguish the situation within the framework of a concession contract from the one within the framework of a production sharing contract.

Concession contract: According to the provisions of Article 74.1 quoted above, the holder of an exploitation and prospecting licence and his associates are subjected to corporation tax on the profits that they makes from their activities. Its rate varies from 40% to 75% according to the provisions laid down in the concession contract (Article 74.2).

In calculating the taxable profit made by the holder of the licence, the royalty or production fee is deducted (Article 73).

The taxable net profit consists of the difference between the value of the taxpayer's net assets at the closing and the opening of the fiscal year, which is the basis for the tax, decreased by supplementary contributions and increased by deductions made during the fiscal year by the company or its associates. 'Net assets' for these purposes means the total value of assets reduced by liabilities to third party creditors, depreciations and other authorised or justified provisions.

In the event of a deficit during a fiscal year, this deficit is carried over to the next fiscal year and deducted from the profit made in that fiscal year.

A deficit can be carried forward for a maximum of three fiscal years following the deficit year. Accountancy must conform to the accounting rules in force within the Organisation for the Harmonisation of Business Law in Africa (OHADA).

Production sharing: Unlike the position under a concession contract, where the contractor's operating profit is subject to corporation tax, any profit resulting from a production sharing contract is tax free.

Article 15 of Ordinance 001/PR/2010 of September 30 2010 provides that: "The holder of an authorisation is subject to no other taxation than that provided for in the standard production sharing contract attached to this ordinance."

However, the standard production sharing contract expressly exempts the contractor from the payment of corporate tax (Article 47.1.2(d)). In fact the purpose of this exemption is to avoid a double charge on the oil company. In practice, the exemption from corporate tax is compensated by the share that the state holds, of at least 40%, in the 'profit oil' under the contract. A final discharge as to payment is given after the payment of the state's share by the holder of the authorisation.

Nevertheless the company has an obligation to declare annually its oil incomes no later than March 31 following the end of the fiscal year. However, any oil company or consortium companies that hold an exclusive exploitation authorisation and which also carry on an activity other than that under the authorisation must account for their earnings from that other activity separately.

4. Current issues

4.1 Cooperation between Chad and the Central African Republic

One of the most significant current developments is the cooperation between Chad and the Central African Republic for the supply of the latter with Chadian oil. This cooperation is of great importance for both Chadian government and for national or foreign investors. This cooperation will have the advantage of creating a new export point for oil. Many new companies are settling in the country as a result of this opportunity to develop the economy of Chad.

4.2 Complaint against International Monetary Fund

Peasants of the oil-bearing zone of Doba, in the South of Chad, with the help of the Group of Alternative Research and Monitoring of the Chad-Cameroon Petroleum Project (Gramp/TC), supported by the independent CCFD-Terre Solidaire organisation, have submitted a complaint against the World Bank for attacks on human rights and environmental damage arising from the project for the construction of the Chad–Cameroon pipeline, which is co-financed by International Finance Corporation of the World Bank Group.

This project, if completed, will involve extensive works requiring specific oil installations, but will also involve pollution and harmful effects on agriculture, thereby preventing some villagers from freely carrying on their activity. Furthermore, local populations consider that they are victims of the project insofar as they are no longer free to work in their fields.

The complaint was submitted to the International Finance Corporation and the Multilateral Investment Guarantee Agency of the World Bank to try and find a solution to the disputes arising from its intervention. The complaint was received on November 29 2011 and the affected population is waiting impatiently for compensation and hoping that lasting solutions can be found in respect of the resultant pollution.

4.3 Lower productivity in the Doba basin

According to information that Alwihda published on its website in June 2011 (see www.alwihdainfo.com), oil production in the Doba basin dropped from 225,000 barrels per day in 2008 to almost half that in 2011. According to the newspaper, discussions are taking place with the Chinese company CNPC-Exxon and the COTCO consortium about producing more oil in the Djarmaya refinery and to transporting it through the Chad-Cameroon pipeline.

Egypt

Loïc Conan
PICO International Petroleum
Ghada Kaptan
BG Eypt SA

---

1. Introduction

The petroleum sector has historically been an important pillar of Egypt's economy, with mining accounting for some 15% of gross domestic product.[1] Foreign direct investment plays a key role in Egypt's petroleum sector, which received 69% of the foreign direct investment in 2010;[2] the principal sources were from the European Union and the United States, followed by the United Arab Emirates and Saudi Arabia.[3] In Africa, Egypt is the second largest natural gas producer (after Algeria) and the first non-OPEC oil producer.[4] Besides the upstream segment, Egypt has significant petroleum activities because of its geographic situation. Egypt is crossed by the Suez Canal, which spans 120 miles and connects the Red Sea with the Mediterranean Sea.[5] The Suez Canal is a key route for Persian Gulf oil and liquefied natural gas (LNG) shipments: in 2010, 2.3% of the global oil supply was shipped through it and 368 LNG vessels used this route.[6] In addition, Egypt is crossed by the Suez-Mediterranean pipeline (SUMED), flowing from the Red Sea to the Mediterranean Sea.[7] In terms of consumption, Egypt is the most populous country in the Arab world (over 83 million), with increasing domestic demand for energy which is forecast to account for over 20% of total African demand by 2015 with respect to oil, and 35% with respect to gas.[8]

2. Upstream activities

2.1. Statistics

According to the BP Statistical Review of World Energy, in 2011, Egypt had proven crude oil reserves of less than 0.3% of the world total (4.3 billion barrels) and produced 0.9% of world supply (735,000 barrels a day), while it had proven natural gas reserves of 1.1% of the world total (2.2 trillion cubic metres (m^3)) and for the whole year produced 1.9% of world output (61.3 billion m^3).[9]

---

1 US Geological Survey, *2010 Minerals Yearbook*, Egypt (May 2012).
2 *Ibid.*
3 *Ibid.*
4 US Energy Information Administration, *Country Analysis Briefs*, Egypt (July 2012).
5 *Ibid.*
6 Business Monitor International, *Egypt Oil & Gas Report.*
7 *Ibid.*
8 *Ibid.*
9 *BP Statistical Review of World Energy June 2012*, available at www.bp.com/assets/bp_internet/globalbp/globalbp_uk_english/reports_and_publications/statistical_energy_review_2011/STAGING/local_assets/pdf/statistical_review_of_world_energy_full_report_2012.pdf.

2.2 Production areas

Geographically, oil production comes from five different parts of Egypt, the Eastern and Western Deserts, the Gulf of Suez, the Mediterranean Sea, the Nile Delta and Sinai, whereas over 70% of its natural gas is extracted from the Nile delta basin and offshore Mediterranean Sea blocks.[10]

2.3 Declining oil production

Egypt's oil production reached its peak in the 1990s, with production at over 900,000 barrels a day. Since then, production has declined, but with resort to enhanced oil recovery techniques, this shift has slowed down, with more being extracted from mature fields. Also, significant new finds have been made in the onshore Western Desert area.[11]

2.4 Booming gas production and domestic demand

Over the last decade, natural gas exploration has intensified, and Egypt has become a significant exporter through its two LNG projects and network of regional pipelines. However, further export development plans were halted by the government, as declining domestic oil supply can no longer meet increasing domestic energy demand, which has to rely on natural gas to compensate.[12] In 2008 the government declared a moratorium on gas exports due to this increasing domestic demand, the unpopularity of some export deals, such as the one with Israel, and the declining price levels at that time.[13]

3. Petroleum legal regime

3.1 Petroleum law and relevant provisions

(a) Regulatory bodies

EGPC:[14] Egypt's hydrocarbon activities are managed by the Ministry of Petroleum through national oil companies, the foremost being the Egyptian General Petroleum Company (EGPC), established in 1976 and tasked with managing upstream oil activities and implementing the three prongs of the government's oil policy: maximising the declining domestic oil production, obtaining additional foreign investment and operating the country's large refining system. In addition to sharing in production through partnerships with international oil companies, EGPC directly produces 20% of Egypt's output.[15]

---

10 US Energy Information Administration, *Country Analysis Briefs*, Egypt, (July 2012). See also Business Monitor International, *Egypt Oil & Gas Report.*

11 *Ibid.*

12 *Ibid.*

13 *Ibid.*

14 www.petroleum.gov.eg/en/Pages/default.aspx; see also US Energy Information Administration, *Country Analysis Briefs*, Egypt, (July 2012) and Business Monitor International, *Egypt Oil & Gas Report.*

15 Business Monitor International, *Egypt Oil & Gas Report.*

EGAS[16] **and Ganope:**[17] With respect to upstream activities, the two other important national oil companies are the Egyptian Natural Gas Holding Company (EGAS), established in 2001, which is in charge of natural gas activities, and Ganoub El Wadi Holding Company (Ganope), established in 2002, which is responsible for both natural gas and crude oil activities in Upper Egypt.[18]

(b) Types of agreement

Although still formally termed a concession agreement, the granting instrument mostly in use in Egypt is technically a production sharing agreement. The 'contractor', that is to say the international oil company, agrees that, in exchange for recovering the costs it incurs to explore and develop a specified area, together with a profit margin, it will share the future production with EGPC, EGAS or Ganope, one of which, along with the government, will be the other party to the agreement.[19] Such production sharing agreements have been in place in Egypt since the 1960s. As of 2012, around 75 international oil companies hold working interests under Egyptian production sharing agreements, and 50 of them are operators.[20]

Once the parties have finalised the production sharing agreement, there is a constitutional requirement that the agreement receive approval from the Egyptian parliament in order to be effective and have the force of law.[21] According to the Egyptian Constitution, the production sharing agreement then prevails over any conflicting laws.[22] Although production sharing agreements in Egypt have common features, they are standalone legal instruments, and the wording of the model contracts has evolved through time, having followed the transformations and shifts in the industry as a whole to become more favourable to host governments.[23] Consequently, reference to the individual production sharing agreement at issue is necessary in order accurately to assess what upstream regulations apply to a specific situation. In addition to the relevant agreement, Egypt's oil and gas sector is mainly governed by Law 66 of 1953 as amended by Law 86 of 1956 Organising Mining and Quarries and their respective executive regulations issued by Ministerial Decrees 69 of 1959 and 758 of 1972. These laws provide the legal basis for mineral exploration and exploitation in Egypt.

(c) Acquisition of acreage

Acquisition of acreage from the government is usually through bid rounds offered by one of EGPC, EGAS or Ganope, depending on the hydrocarbon or the area at stake.

---

16 www.egas.com.eg/home.aspx.

17 www.ganope.com.

18 *Ibid.*

19 Tarek Fouad Riad, "Egyptian Business and Commercial Laws", in *Yearbook of Islamic and Middle Eastern Law* Volume 12, p 41 (Brill Academic Publishers, 2007).

20 US Geological Survey, *2010 Minerals Yearbook*, Egypt (May 2012).

21 This is usually specified in Article XVIII of the agreement, on laws and regulations. Pending the new Constitution being drafted, Article 123 of the current Constitution still provides that parliamentary approval is required; see Minas Katchadourian, "Legal Safeguards in Egypt's Petroleum Concession Agreements", *Egypt Oil & Gas*, November 2010, available at www.egyptoil-gas.com/read_article_issues.php?AID=447.

22 *Ibid.*

23 Ernest E Smith and John S Dzienkowski, "A Fifty-Year Perspective on World Petroleum Arrangements", 24 *Texas International Law Journal*, p 13 (1989)).

The main terms and conditions, as well as the model contract, are usually available on the website of the national oil company that is organising the bid.[24] Direct negotiation is not common.

(d) *Qualification requirements*

According to the procedures set out in the bid rounds, inquiry is made as to the technical experience and the financial strength of the bidder.

Technical requirements: The bidder must provide evidence of any previous similar projects and activities in Egypt and abroad, including technologies mastered and reserves developed.

Financial requirements: Recent annual reports are required to prove the financial strength of the bidder. A preliminary bond is also required that will be returned to unsuccessful bidders or converted to cover a percentage of the work programme expenditure for a successful bidder. All bidders are required to purchase a data package from the national oil company organising the bid, failing which they may be disqualified.

Identity requirements: The bidder can be an individual company or a group of companies, an unincorporated consortium. The bidder is required to provide (for each company if it is a consortium) corporate documents such as the articles of incorporation, the bidder's commercial registration and all documents relevant to prove its legal existence, the identity of its shareholders and their nationalities. The company that becomes the operator will have to establish a branch in Egypt.

(e) *Duration*[25]

Exploration phase: Egyptian production sharing agreements specify an initial exploration period, which is subject to two successive extensions (depending on how challenging the geology in the area concerned is expected to be). The first initial period is usually for three or four years, and the two successive extensions are usually for two or three years each.

Development phase: When a discovery is made that is deemed to be commercially viable, this being defined either by reference to a threshold quantity or more broadly when a well is capable of producing at an economic rate, the extent of the area capable of production is agreed upon by the international oil company and the national oil company party to the production sharing agreement, and then approved by the Ministry of Petroleum. As a result, this area is covered by a development lease for a period of 20 years. An extension of five years can be granted by the Ministry of Petroleum if it is economically justified by the level of production. In the event of an

---

24 Business Monitor International, *Egypt Oil & Gas Report.*

25 Usually specified in Article III of the agreement, on the grant of rights and terms.

oil discovery in an area covered by a development lease initially granted for a gas discovery, or vice versa, the development lease will be extended for 20 years in respect of the latest substance discovered, but in no case can a lease exceed 35 years from the date of the initial discovery. A commercial discovery triggers the setting-up of an operating company, that is to say the joint venture company to be established between the international oil company and the national oil company to conduct the operations in the area of the discovery.

Relinquishments:[26] Provisions relating to relinquishment are twofold, mandatory and voluntary. As for the mandatory part, there is usually a requirement to relinquish 25% of any area that has not been converted to a development lease or leases at the end of the initial exploration period, and then an additional 25% at the end of the first extension of the exploration period, subject to the condition that if the drilling and financial obligations for the period concerned have been fulfilled, the area may not have to be relinquished, provided the contractor elects to enter into a second extension of the exploration period. The remainder of the area not converted into a development lease or leases has to be relinquished at the end of the second exploration period extension. Voluntary relinquishment is possible provided that the work programme obligations are met. Any area relinquished voluntarily may be credited toward the mandatory relinquishment.

(f) ***Minimum work programme***[27]

Drilling obligations: In Egyptian production sharing agreements, the minimum work programme consists of a set of commitments, more or less detailed depending on the features of the area at stake (such as the data already available, whether it is a new or mature field, deep water or shallow water and so on). The concession agreement contains drilling obligations such as drilling a number of exploratory wells, undertaking a number of kilometres of 2D seismic surveys and/or a number of square kilometres of 3D seismic surveys and/or reprocessing existing seismic data, and more generally carrying out technical/geological/geophysical studies.

Financial commitments: The production sharing agreement states the minimum financial amount that the contractor must spend in order to cover the exploration operations committed to. Any excess spent in the initial period can be offset against the financial commitment for the succeeding exploration period. At the end of the exploration period, if the production sharing agreement expires and the actual expenditure is less than the sum committed, the difference shall then be paid (to the relevant national oil company) by the contractor. A letter of guarantee is required to cover each of the exploration periods and the corresponding expenditure. The letter of guarantee needs to be issued by the National Bank of Egypt or any international

26 Usually specified in Article IV of the agreement, on relinquishments.
27 Usually specified in Article IV of the agreement, on the work programme and expenditures during the exploration period.

bank working under the supervision and control of the Central Bank of Egypt. The text of the letter of guarantee is annexed to the production sharing agreement.

(g) Assignment and encumbrance

Assignment:[28] In order to assign a working interest under an Egyptian production sharing agreement, the approval of the government is required, and the national oil company that is party to the production sharing agreement has a priority right to acquire the assigned interest. The language of the production sharing agreements has evolved over the time to cover both the assignment of an interest and the sale of shares in the corporation that owns the interest, as the latter manoeuvre was being used to avoid any government obstacles and delays. An assignment to an affiliated company is exempt from the need for such governmental approval. A requirement has also appeared in some agreements whereby the seller must pay an assignment bonus to the government. This assignment bonus is usually set at 10% of the deal value, or 10% of the financial commitment if it occurs during the exploration phase. A flat fee assignment bonus may also be provided for in the event of an assignment to an affiliated company.

Encumbrances: Rather than providing for encumbrances on the contractor's assets, Egyptian production sharing agreements provide for a mechanism whereby the contractor's assets become the property of the national oil company that is party to the production sharing agreement as these assets become subject to cost recovery.[29] This mechanism applies to land and to fixed and movable assets. The granting of encumbrances over the revenues generated by sales of the oil and gas produced is allowed provided that the national oil company acknowledges them.[30]

(h) Local content

Two articles in Egyptian production sharing agreements are usually devoted to local content. One deals with the employment rights and training of Egyptian personnel, while the other addresses the preference for local contractors and locally manufactured material.

Employment and training:[31] The production sharing agreements state that all alien employees needed to conduct the operations shall be granted visas, but that a certain amount of their salaries shall be paid in Egyptian currency, and that the investor has to carry out a training programme for Egyptian personnel. They also state the principle that both the international oil company and the joint venture shall give priority to the employment of Egyptian nationals.

---

28 Usually specified in Article XXI of the agreement, on assignment.
29 Usually specified in Article VIII of the agreement, on title to assets.
30 Article 305 of the Egyptian Civil Code stipulates, among other things, that, an assignment of a right has to be either notified to or acknowledged by the debtor to be effective against him.
31 Usually specified in Article XVII of the agreement, on employment rights and training of Arab Republic of Egypt personnel.

Services and goods:[32] The same principle of local priority applies in respect of services. Local contractors, EGPC's affiliate companies in particular, shall be preferred if their performance matches international standards and their prices are not more than 10% above market prices. Identical provision is made for locally manufactured material, equipment, machinery and so on. It shall be given preference if comparable to internationally available material, but import remains an option if the cost of local material, including transportation and insurance, is more than 10% above market costs.

(i) ***National reservation***[33]

The national oil company is given a right of first refusal to dispose all of or part of the contractor's share of production in order to meet local market needs.

In the event of a war or national emergency, Egyptian production sharing agreements grant the government a right of requisition over all or part of the production and the related facilities. The agreements provide for compensation in such a case, unless the damage is due to an enemy attack.

(j) ***Environment***

Environmental obligations and liabilities are addressed in Egyptian legislation and the production sharing agreement itself.

In the production sharing agreement: Egyptian production sharing agreements contain an article on "saving of petroleum and prevention of loss",[34] which imposes an obligation on the joint venture to prevent loss or waste by following proper measures and accepted methods in use in the petroleum industry. The government has the right to prevent any operation that could lead to such loss or waste. Data related to well activities have to be recorded/reported to the government for examination and/or approval (this includes well test dates, any resort to a single tubing string, amount of petroleum and water produced, type of cement used, etc). A related article in the production sharing agreement deals with and completes the duties and obligations relating to these records, reports and inspections.[35] In the event that environmental liabilities materialise as a result of drilling, production, exploration, gathering and distribution or storage activities, the agreements provide that the contractor shall entirely and solely be responsible toward third parties, and shall indemnify the government and the national oil company against all damages for which they may be held liable on account of any such operations.[36] An exception is made when the damage results from the issuance of an order, regulation or direction from the government, in which case the contractor may be exempted from the consequent responsibility and be granted the necessary period to restore the damage.

---

32 Usually specified in Article XXVI of the agreement, on local contractors and locally manufactured material.

33 Usually specified in Article XX of the agreement, on the right of requisition

34 Usually specified in Article XI of the agreement on saving of petroleum and prevention of loss.

35 Usually specified in Article XIV of the agreement, on records, reports, and inspection.

36 Usually specified in Article XV of the agreement, on responsibility for damages.

Outside the production sharing agreement: The primary law in Egypt dealing with environmental issues is Law 4 of 1994 and the consequent Executive Decree 338 of 1995. It restructured the Egyptian Environmental Affairs Agency (EEAA) and entrusted it with the mandate of both drafting environmental legislation (for air, land and water) and monitoring its compliance. With respect to the oil and gas industry more specifically, this law imposes an obligation on joint ventures and international oil companies to use safe methods which do not result in damage to the marine environment. They are also required to treat all discharged waste and polluting substances in accordance with the available state-of-the-art techniques and in line with the conditions prescribed in international treaties. Egypt is party to several international conventions regulating and controlling pollution of the environment: the 1958 Geneva Convention on the Law on the High Seas, the 1958 Geneva Convention on the Continental Shelf and the 1982 United Nations Convention on the Law of the Sea.

Decommissioning obligations: There are no regulations requiring a certain standard of decommissioning or abandonment in Egypt. The model production sharing agreement is silent on that issue. However, the 1953 Egyptian Petroleum Law states that a contractor conducting business in Egypt has statutory obligations regarding abandonment. The contractor must follow recognised standards for covering up wells. Therefore, a productive well cannot be plugged or abandoned unless it can be demonstrated that the well is not commercially viable, and upon EGPC's approval. Upon expiry of the production sharing agreement, the contractor is required to deliver the contract area to EGPC/EGAS in "good condition" with all movable and fixed property necessary for continuing the operation of the area. However, there is no definition of "good condition", leaving it open to wide interpretation. Under the Egyptian model production sharing agreement, the title to assets passes on to the national oil company as soon as the costs of those assets are recovered or upon expiry of the agreement. Therefore, ultimately, the decommissioning obligation should be that of the national oil company and the Egyptian government.

(k) Governing law and dispute resolution[37]

Governing law: Egyptian laws govern the concession agreement.

Dispute resolution: With respect to disputes, the resolution mechanism is twofold. If the dispute involves the international oil company and the government, then Egyptian courts are competent. On the other hand, if the dispute is between the international oil company and the national oil company, then arbitration is the designated mechanism. The rules of the Cairo Regional Centre of International Commercial Arbitration in effect on the date of the production sharing agreement shall apply. The number of arbitrators is usually three, the seat of arbitration Cairo[38] and the languages both Arabic and English.

---

37 Usually specified in Article XXIV of the agreement, on disputes and arbitration.

3.2. Government take

Egypt's fiscal regime for the petroleum industry consists of a combination of a royalty-based taxation, bonuses and a corporate income tax.

(a) *Royalties*[39]

Egyptian production sharing agreements provide that the government shall be entitled to a royalty in cash or in kind at a rate of 10% of the total quantity of petroleum produced and saved from the area during the development phase. This 10% royalty is borne and paid by the national oil company, not the international oil company. The payment of royalties by the national oil company does not result in any income attributable to the international oil company.

(b) *Bonuses*[40]

Egyptian production sharing agreements provide for various bonuses to be paid to the national oil company that is party to the production sharing agreement:

- signature (of the production sharing agreement) bonus;
- development lease bonus;
- development lease extension bonus;
- assignment bonus;[41]
- production bonus when the total average daily production reaches a certain rate for a period of a number of consecutive days;
- training bonus to cover the training of the national oil company's employees.

The amounts of these bonuses are negotiable when submitting the bid application and finalising the production sharing agreement (in the event of a successful bid). These bonuses cannot be recovered by the contractor. Instructions were issued by EGPC stressing the deductibility of the signature bonus and production bonuses for corporate tax purposes, but these instructions were challenged by the Egyptian tax authorities, which issued opposing instructions stressing the fact that such costs should not be deductible.[42]

(c) *Rental fees*[43]

Use of equipment owned by either the national oil company or the international oil company is subject to a charge at rental rates that are appropriate to the cost of ownership and operation of such equipment, provided that such rates do not exceed the competitive rates prevailing in Egypt. The contractor alone has to bear all direct costs attributable to the acquisition, renewal or relinquishment of surface rights acquired and maintained in the allocated area under the production sharing agreement.

---

38 The parties could mutually agree on another venue for arbitration.
39 Usually specified in Article III of the agreement, on grant of rights and term.
40 Usually specified in Article IX of the agreement, on bonuses.
41 See also paragraph 3.1 (g) above, on assignment.
42 Ernst & Young, *Global Oil and Gas Tax Guide 2011*, EYGM Limited, at p 146.
43 *Ibid.*

(d) ***Special participation***

There are no special participation provisions under Egyptian production sharing agreements. The Egyptian government retains ownership of the resources. In addition, there is no direct participation or carried interest on the part of the national oil company.

(e) ***Corporate tax***

In Egypt, the general rate of corporate tax is 20%, however, taxable income from oil exploration and production activities is subject to a corporate tax rate of 40.55% on all profits. Corporate tax is levied on taxable income. Under Egyptian production sharing agreements, the national oil company is the final tax payer. Corporate tax is paid by the national oil company after grossing up the taxable base, and the company pays it directly to the government. Tax returns prepared by the exploration entities are therefore reviewed, approved and signed by the national oil company that is party to the production sharing agreement. Egypt does not apply ring-fencing in the determination of corporate tax liability, so profits arising from one project may be offset against losses from another project, provided it is held by the same tax entity.

There is no windfall tax in Egypt.

4. Current issues

4.1 The Arab Spring and the upstream sector in Egypt

Unlike neighbouring Libya at the peak of the crisis in late January/early February 2011, international oil companies working in Egypt did not see their operations interrupted.[44] Also, no adverse regulatory measures have been enacted under either the interim military rule or the Muslim Brotherhood presidency.[45] However, international oil companies have had to cope with side effects of the transition. There have been legal issues arising from first the absence of parliament and then its election in an uncertain constitutional framework, as Egyptian production sharing agreements require parliamentary approval to amend their terms. There have also been financial consequences because of the outstanding debt owed by EGPC (and the other national oil companies) arising from the cost recovery scheme and the profit share that the EGPC has elected to take in accordance with its priority right.[46]

The alarming condition of EGPC's finances is mainly due to its subsidising foreign petroleum products (gasoline, kerosene, diesel, fuel oil etc), as it has been buying those products at international market prices but reselling them to Egyptian households, businesses, and governmental bodies at below-market prices, to meet demand and to boost the economy.[47] The extent of EGPC's debts and delays in payment have provoked international oil companies into threatening to suspend

---

44 Ed Crook and Sheila McNulty, "Oil and Gas Groups Hope Egypt Will Not Interrupt Output", *Financial Times*, February 13, 2011, available at www.ft.com/intl/cms/s/0/0885e016-37bc-11e0-b91a-00144feabdc0.html#axzz1eu1cse6r.

45 Business Monitor International, *Egypt Oil & Gas Report.*

46 Shady Ahmed, "Settlement of Outstanding Debts: The EGPC's Sole Solution Sustaining Steady Foreign Investment", *Egypt Oil & Gas*, September 2011, available at www.egyptoil-gas.com/read_article_issues.php?AID=514.

their exploratory activities. International oil companies have also been trying to obtain relief by pushing either for the right to export their share, or for the adoption of a concession royalty system. One example of the latter is the deal signed in June 2010 between EGAS and BP regarding the West Nile Delta project, according to which BP will bear the full cost of investment (there is no cost recovery scheme) but gets all the production, albeit that it is required to sell some of the output to EGAS.[48] This arrangement has sparked popular discontent. The parties have put forward the high cost of exploration in deep water to justify departing from the standard production sharing agreement approach, nevertheless there has been some controversy around these amended terms which are seen as benefitting international oil companies too much.[49] Although this deal was defended by energy professionals, there remains a public perception of an unfair bargain: that international oil companies have been given privileges by some executives of the former government who only care for their own wealth.[50]

4.2 The 2012 EGAS bid round

This is the first EGAS bid round since 2008 and it follows a round launched by EGPC in September 2011 for acreage in the Gulf of Suez, Eastern Desert and Sinai. This bid is part of the post-revolution government's actions towards attracting and encouraging international oil companies to invest in the promising but highly challenging deep waters of the Mediterranean Sea, and to overcome the current political and financial difficulties of Egypt. EGAS invited international oil companies to explore for and exploit hydrocarbons in 13 blocks offshore and a couple of blocks onshore in the Nile Delta basin, amounting to a total of over 57,300 km^2. The proposed arrangement is a standard Egyptian production sharing agreement in which EGAS's share of the oil profits (after deducting cost recovery) cannot be less than 60%. The production sharing agreement does not dictate a specific gas price, which is intended to be an incentive for international oil companies to offer aggressive exploration plans. The gas price will be agreed between EGAS and the contractor following any commercial discovery, on the basis of the technical and economic factors affecting development of the find and the prevailing price for gas being produced by similar concessions. The outcome of this bid round (the number of concessions granted, conditions, bidders awarded, parliamentary approval process

47 *Ibid.*; see also Mona El Fiqi, "Subsidising the rich?", *Al Ahram*, May 19–25 2011, available at weekly.ahram.org.eg/2011/1048/ec4.htm.

48 Daria Solovieva, "Egypt Steps on the Gas", *Business Today Egypt*, available at businesstodayegypt.com/news/display/article/artId:311/Egypt-Steps-on-the-Gas/secId:5.

49 Kate Dannies, "Egypt's Gas Agreements: Exploitative or Necessary for Growth", *Egypt Oil & Gas*, September 2011, available at www.egyptoil-gas.com/read_article_issues.php?AID=472; Olal Galal and Alaa Shahine, "BP, RWE Amend Two Gas Contracts with Egypt, to Start Paying Royalties", July 19 2010, available at www.bloomberg.com/news/2010-07-19/bp-rwe-amend-two-gas-contracts-with-egypt-to-start-paying-royalties.html.

50 Naser Gouda, "Gas and Petroleum Companies in Idku. Investment or Destruction?", *Egypt Votes.Org*, October 25 2011, available at www.egyptvotes.org/en/economy/item/181-gas-and-petroleum-companies-in-idku-investment-or-destruction.html; Nadine Marroushi, "BP Project in Idku Raises Environmental Concerns", *Egypt Independent*, September 20 2011, available at www.egyptindependent.com/node/497501; Nadine Marroushi, "BP's Controversial Gas Project Delayed by Local Distrust", *Egypt Independent*, December 13 2011, available at www.egyptindependent.com/node/546191.

and so on) will give an indication of if and how political events are still affecting the oil and gas industry in Egypt.

5. Conclusion

In terms of resources, Egypt remains an attractive location, with the Mediterranean Sea and Nile Delta being considered a world class basin for the production of natural gas, and the successful use of enhanced recovery techniques mitigating the declining production in aged oil fields in the Gulf of Suez and Western Desert.[51] In the aftermath of Mubarak's fall, the upstream sector in Egypt has received continuous political support, and legal and financial issues arising from the constitutional vacuum and the dire condition of EGPC's finances have been addressed. But the industry has also been facing public distrust. Eliminating political risk altogether in Egypt's petroleum sector will require all parties to address the problem of corruption in Egypt. Corruption is known to be endemic, the country ranking 112th out of 183 countries in Transparency International's *Corruption Perceptions Index 2011*.[52] Although anti-corruption laws exist, along with government agencies to enforce them, lack of accountability and transparency has so far largely prevented their implementation. This situation is unlikely to last. The end of corruption, which has been a bar to social justice and the introduction of a meritocracy, has been a central theme in the Egypt and Arab Spring uprisings.

The authors would like to thank Iain Campbell (BG Group) and Cyril Vock (Total) for their valuable assistance in the preparation of this chapter.

---

51 Business Monitor International, *Egypt Oil & Gas Report*; see also US Energy Information Administration, *Country Analysis Briefs*, Egypt (July 2012).

52 Transparency International, Egypt data available at http://www.transparency.org/country#EGY; 2011 ranking available at http://cpi.transparency.org/cpi2011/results/#CountryResults.

Kenya

Mwendia Nyaga
Oil and Energy Services Limited

1. Introduction

Kenya is located on the eastern coast of Africa with a population of 39.5 million according to the 2009 census. The country's gross domestic product (GDP) is estimated to be US$65 billion with a growth rate of 5.8% in 2010, 4.4% in 2011 and a projection of 5.5% in 2012. The country covers an area of 582,646 square kilometres (km^2) and enjoys a coastline that is over 300 kilometres long. The oil and gas prospecting acreage is 399,519 km^2 of which 150,000 km^2 are offshore.

The main foreign exchange earners for the country are currently tea, coffee, tourism and horticulture. There is well developed information and communications technology (ICT) infrastructure, and Kenya is identified as one of the fastest developing countries in Africa in regard to ICT usage and sophistication.

Kenya is a key focus of adventure travel in Africa and is one of the finest safari destinations in the world. It is also proud of the attractions of its rich culture and diverse environments. Its geography is marvellously varied. While much of north and eastern Kenya is a flat, bush-covered, semi-arid plain, the remainder of the country encompasses pristine beaches, scenic highlands and lake regions, the Great Rift Valley, and the magnificent Mount Kenya.

Kenya's coastal region (on the Indian Ocean) is on the southeast, and its neighbours are Somalia to the East, Ethiopia to the north, South Sudan to the northwest, and Uganda directly to the west. The western border of the country is partly marked by Lake Victoria, and southward lies Tanzania.

Although Kenya's varied environments experience a wide variety of climate conditions, the temperature remains comfortably warm year-round. Much of Kenya experiences heavy rainfall from March through to May and, to a lesser extent, from October through to December.

2. Upstream activities

2.1 History

Petroleum exploration in Kenya began in the 1950s with the first well being drilled in 1960. British Petroleum (BP) and Shell began exploring in Kenya in 1954 in the Lamu embayment where they eventually drilled 10 wells. None of the wells were fully evaluated or completed for production despite several indications of oil staining and untested zones with gas shows.

In the 1970s, several consortia acquired acreage in the upper part of the Lamu basin. Several wells were drilled by Texas Pacific, Chevron and Esso in the southern part of the Anza basin. The drilling mud of both tests was suspected of having hydrocarbons and microfossils that contaminated the geochemistry and cuttings.

A total of 13 more wells were drilled in the 1980s in different parts of the country. Although many of the wells continued to show the presence of hydrocarbons, none was declared successful in discovering hydrocarbons that could proceed to the evaluation and appraisal stage.

Kenya's petroleum exploration and production legislation was developed in 1984, and revised in 1986, to provide suitable incentives and flexibility to attract international exploration interest in the country.

By 1993, a total of 30 wells had been drilled, 21 of them showing signs of hydrocarbons. There was then a long break as oil companies gave the country a wide berth until renewed licensing activities took place from 2002 in the offshore areas.

In 2007, Woodside drilled the Pomboo 1 well in the deep offshore Lamu basin, which did not contain any hydrocarbon shows. Subsequently in 2010, CNOOC drilled the Bhogal 1-1 well onshore in the Anza basin to a depth of 5,045 metres (m) and encountered significant shows of dry natural gas. Tests undertaken to assess the flow of the gas revealed a very tight reservoir, and so the discovery was classified as not commercial.

The decade beginning 2011 is expected to be the busiest and by far the most rewarding in Kenya's search for hydrocarbons. In March 2012, Tullow Oil announced a significant find onshore in block 10BB with an estimated 143m of oil net pay. This was followed by a natural gas discovery offshore by a consortium led by Apache Corporation, which though significant, after preliminary assessment was declared not commercially viable due to the distance from the shore and deep waters in which the discovery is located. A further discovery was announced in October 2012 by Tullow Oil very near the March 2012 discovery. Neither of the oil finds has yet been tested, but the operators are optimistic about their commercial viability.

A data centre for the storage of seismic data, well logs, well reports, other oil exploration reports, and aeromagnetic and gravity data which has been obtained in Kenya to date as a result of petroleum exploration activities, has been set up by the National Oil Corporation of Kenya.

2.2 The basins

Kenya's petroleum potential is best illustrated by the four large sedimentary basins that straddle the country (see the sedimentary basins map on the following page). These are the Lamu, Anza, Mandera, and Tertiary Rift basins. The Lamu basin extends even further offshore to occupy all of Kenya's exclusive economic zone (EEZ) and beyond.

Kenya has also submitted a claim for extension of its EEZ by a further 150 nautical miles, in accordance with the United Nations Convention on the Law of the Sea (UNCLOS), based on an extensive study that revealed that the continental shelf extends beyond the current EEZ limit.

Kenya sedimentary basins

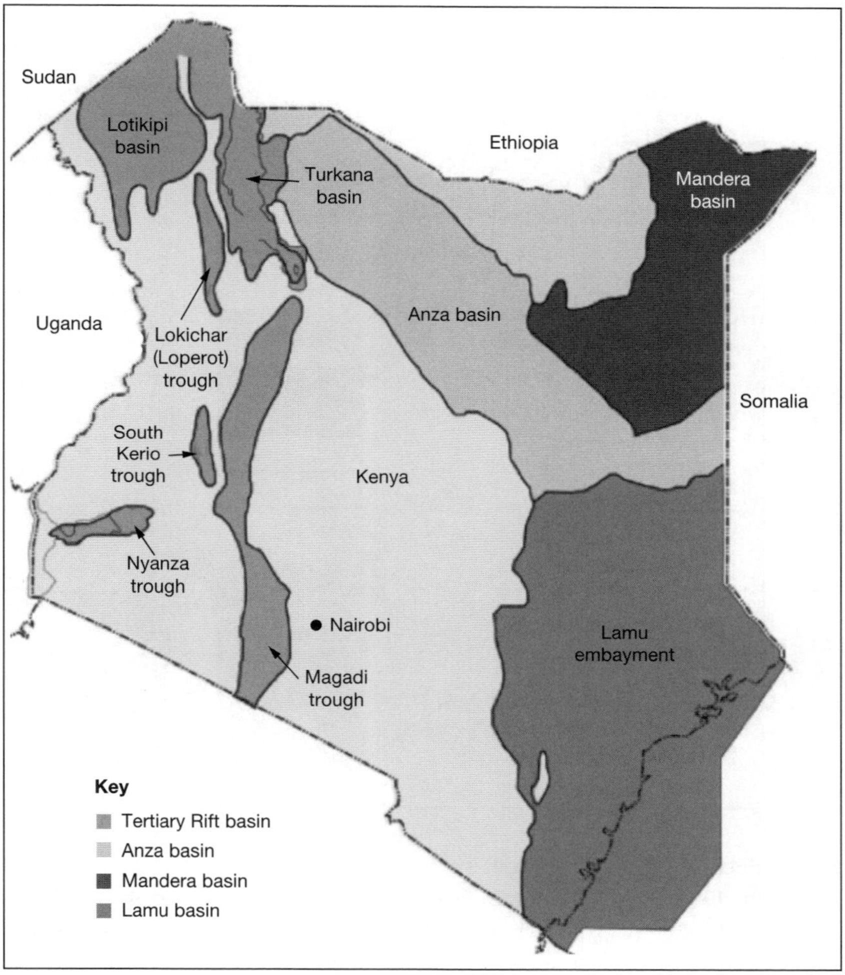

2.3 Exploration activities and blocks

Kenya is divided into 46 exploration blocks as shown in the map on the following page.

As at October 2012, 45 out of the 46 blocks were licensed for exploration. Untested oil discoveries have been made in blocks 10BB and 13T, while gas discoveries have been made in blocks 9 and L8 but both were declared as not commercial by the operators.

It is expected that exploration activities will be aggressive in the coming years following the existing oil discoveries and with companies working to fulfil their minimum work commitments.

Kenya exploration blocks

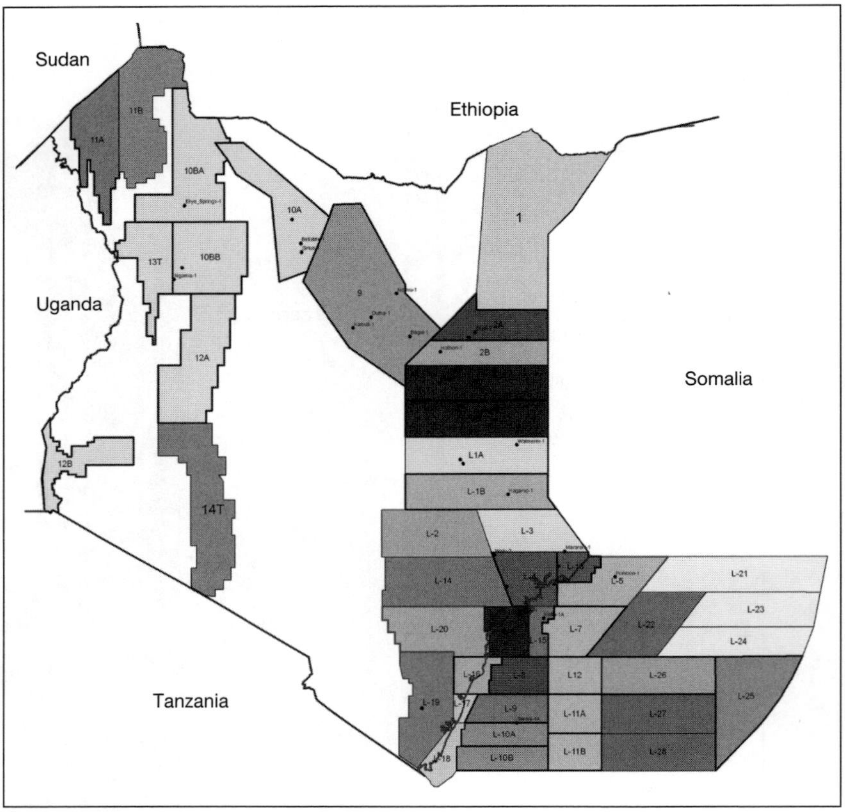

3. Petroleum legal regime

In 1984, Kenya National Assembly enacted the Petroleum (Exploration and Production) Act (Chapter 308, Laws of Kenya), which was thereafter revised in 1986. The act is meant to regulate the negotiation and conclusion by the government of petroleum agreements relating to exploration. This act is the chief legislation in Kenya so far as petroleum exploration and production operations are concerned. The act is currently undergoing a review to bring it into line with the new Constitution of Kenya that was enacted in 2010, introducing a devolved system of government among other far reaching changes in the licensing and management of natural resources.

3.1 Petroleum law and relevant provisions

As mentioned above, the relevant law in the upstream operations in Kenya is the Petroleum (Exploration and Production) Act. Its purpose is to regulate the negotiation and conclusion of petroleum agreements by the government relating to exploration, development, production and transportation of petroleum and for connected purposes.

In the act, 'petroleum' is defined as mineral oil and includes crude oil, natural gas and hydrocarbons produced or being capable of being produced from oil shales or tar sands. A 'petroleum agreement' in the act is defined as an agreement, contract or any other arrangement between the government and a contractor to conduct petroleum operations in accordance with the act.

Section 3 of the act provides that all petroleum existing in its natural condition in strata lying within Kenya and the continental shelf is vested in the government, subject to any other written law, which may vest the same to another person. The 'government' in this provision should be taken as referring to the national government, given that the Constitution of Kenya provides for regional governments, also known as county governments. The current act does not mention any mode of apportioning petroleum proceeds to the regional governments, as it was enacted in 1984 and the current Constitution was promulgated recently, in August 2010.

(a) Regulatory bodies

The upstream regime in Kenya is regulated by the Ministry of Energy, the chief authorising officer being the Minister for Energy. Section 4(1) of the Petroleum (Exploration and Production) Act provides that no person shall engage in any petroleum operation without having obtained permission from the minister in such manner, in such form, and on such terms as prescribed by the act and regulations made thereunder. Section 4(2) of the act also provides that all petroleum operations shall be carried in accordance with the provisions of the act.

Section 4(4) provides that the government may authorise a contractor to engage in petroleum operations within a specified area within the terms specified in the petroleum agreement. The act also provides that the minister may negotiate, enter into and sign petroleum agreements, and may also enter into non-exclusive exploration agreements.

The minister takes advice from a committee known as the National Fossil Fuels Advisory Committee (NAFFAC), which is chaired by the permanent secretary of the ministry and advises the minister on negotiations, regulation and evaluation. The permanent secretary is the main technical adviser to the minister and is also the chief accounting officer of the ministry's affairs.

The National Oil Corporation of Kenya manages the national data centre for exploration data. The data may be reviewed by any interested person by appointment. Only data that is not proprietary may be reviewed. Copies of data may be made on payment of a token amount to cover administrative expenses.

(b) Types of agreement

The Petroleum (Exploration and Production) Act provides that petroleum agreements are to be negotiated on the basis of the model production sharing contract. It is contained in subsidiary legislation referred to as the Kenya Petroleum Fiscal Environment, which is primarily a model production sharing contract that was developed in 1986 and has been improved over the years to incorporate recent environmental and economic developments. The most recent form of the model contract can always be obtained from the Ministry of Energy or the National Oil Corporation of Kenya.

Any application for negotiation of a petroleum agreement is required to be made in writing and addressed to the minister, specifying the name, nationality and the business of the applicant, name and nationality of every director of the applicant, the block for which the applicant is applying and the terms under which the applicant wishes to negotiate.

(c) Acquisition of acreage

Applications for licences are entertained on an open door/direct negotiation basis. Kenya has not yet adopted the licensing round approach as its frontier status has meant that it has remained without a commercial discovery despite five decades of exploration. This approach is likely to change with the first discovery having been made and reported in March 2012.

Licence applications are made to the minister through the permanent secretary who oversees analysis of the application. Details are discussed in a meeting of the National Fossil Fuels Advisory Committee after which, if deemed fit, the applicant is invited for negotiations. The National Fossil Fuels Advisory Committee is a committee appointed by the minister to advise him on upstream petroleum matters and includes representatives from the following bodies:

- National Oil Corporation of Kenya (which provides the secretary to the committee);
- the State Law Office;
- the Treasury;
- the Kenya Revenue Authority;
- the National Environmental Management Authority;
- the University of Nairobi Geology Department;
- the Department of Mines and Geology (part of the Ministry of Environment and Mineral Resources); and
- the Petroleum Institute of East Africa.

The negotiations are conducted by a sub-committee of the National Fossil Fuels Advisory Committee comprising representatives of the Ministry of Energy, National Oil Corporation and the State Law Office.

(d) Qualification requirements

The minister has the power to set any criteria or terms as qualification requirements. Under existing laws and regulations, any person intending to enter into any exploration agreement with the government must have a registered office in Kenya, under the Companies Act (Chapter 386). It is also provided that the government (in the form of the Ministry of Energy) can only enter into exploration agreements with contractors who have the financial ability, technical competence and professional skills necessary to fulfil their obligations under the agreement. However, the exact nature of these capabilities and the process of ascertaining their existence is not defined. It is left to the National Fossil Fuels Advisory Committee to review the capabilities of all applicants and make recommendations to the minister accordingly.

(e) ***Duration***

The time set for exploration is a maximum of six to seven years broken down into three periods of three years, two years and two years for deep offshore areas, and three periods of two years each for the rest of the acreage. These three periods are known as the 'initial exploration period', the 'first additional period' and the 'second additional period' respectively. In an effort to speed up exploration, the government recently reduced the initial exploration period to two years other than for deep offshore blocks, which were considered to require more time at the front end because of their frontier status. The production period in most licences is 25 years for oil and 30 years for gas. There are favourable terms regarding the period it takes for the appraisal of gas discoveries.

(f) ***Minimum work programme***

The minimum work programme is normally dependent on existing geological and geophysical surveys. If an exploration block has more existing data the contractor may be required to make early drilling commitments. The minimum work commitments are negotiated between the contractor and the National Fossil Fuels Advisory Committee.

All work commitments are coupled with minimum financial obligations that a contractor is required to secure with a performance bond in the form of a combination of a bank guarantee and a corporate guarantee.

(g) ***Assignment and encumbrances***

The Minister for Energy is the chief administrator of the Petroleum (Exploration and Production) Act. Section 6(1)(g) of the act stipulates that the minister shall make regulations relating to the procedures for the assignment of rights and obligations of contractors under petroleum agreements. While no such regulations relating to assignment have been made by the minister, Section 35 of the model production sharing contract provides for assignment, with the consent of the minister, which shall not be unreasonably withheld.

(h) ***Local content***

Under the Petroleum (Exploration and Production) Act, the contractor is obligated to give preference to the use of products, equipment and services locally available.

The current model production sharing contract provides that the contractor, its contractors and subcontractors shall give preference to Kenyan materials, supplies and services for use in their petroleum operations as long as the prices, quality, quantities and timeliness of delivery are comparable with the prices, quality, quantities and timeliness of delivery of non-Kenyan materials and supplies.

No punitive measures or penalties are defined in the act for non-compliance with these provisions. There are also no incentives that have been set to encourage contractors to use local content.

(i) ***National reservation***

The Petroleum (Exploration and Production) Act provides that the Minister for

Energy may reserve blocks to be exploited by the government. It does not, however, specify the procedure to be followed, or factors to be considered, when preserving exploration blocks for exploration by the government.

While the National Oil Corporation currently holds one exploration block, there has not so far been a clear case of reservation of blocks for exploration by the government.

The production sharing contract also provides for supply of petroleum for domestic market consumption which should be given priority over exports of crude oil or supply of crude oil to be refined for export. Under the relevant provision, the minister is obliged to advise the country's requirements on quarterly basis, and this is to be divided between all crude oil producers pro-rata based on their production as a percentage of the total crude oil produced in the country. The crude oil to be allocated for domestic production in this manner is to be the country's total requirement less the government share of crude oil produced from all licences.

(j) *Environment*

The Petroleum (Exploration and Production) Act, in Section 6(1)(k), provides that the minister may make regulations in respect of the conduct of petroleum operations, conservation of petroleum resources and measures relating to safety, environmental protection and the avoidance of waste, pollutions and accidents. No detailed regulations have been made by the minister, but there have been significant improvements in the model production sharing contract in provisions relating to the environment and abandonment of operations.

Presently environmental legislation in Kenya is found in the Environmental Management and Coordination Act, which was enacted in 2000. This is a framework law that contains provisions for the environmentally sound management of proposed and current projects in Kenya and creates the National Environment Management Authority as the regulator.

(k) *Governing law and dispute resolution*

The Petroleum (Exploration and Production) Act provides that the parties to a petroleum agreement shall be governed by the provisions of the act and any dispute shall be determined by a court of competent jurisdiction, which in this regard refers to the Kenyan courts. The jurisdictional competence of courts in Kenya is determined by the location in which the dispute arises and the value of the subject matter. The jurisdiction of courts is also now and then stipulated by the chief justice through issuance of legal notices. The High Court has original jurisdiction over matters in which the value of the subject matter is above a certain amount. Further, under the Civil Procedure Act (Chapter 21), any matter, even one pending before a foreign court, can still be tried in Kenya under a court with competent jurisdiction.

From the foregoing, it is clear that any petroleum dispute shall be determined under Kenya's civil laws, but Kenya's commercial laws allow parties flexibility, in that they can expressly in their commercial agreements agree to resolve their disputes through alternative dispute resolution and arbitration mechanisms. The current practice in Kenya is that parties may agree to be fully bound by determinations of an arbitrator, or can expressly agree to move to the court if they are dissatisfied by the decision of the arbitrator.

Under Section 41 of the model production sharing contract there are detailed provisions for the settlement of disputes amicably and then through arbitration if no amicable resolution is attained. It is envisaged that disputes shall be referred to arbitration in accordance with the arbitration rules adopted by the United Nations Commission on International Trade Law (UNCITRAL). The decision of the arbitrator is expected to be final.

3.2 Government take

The Kenyan production sharing contract is flexible, and generally the terms of the agreement depend of the parties' negotiating powers. Negotiations are held with the minister who has the assistance of the National Fossil Fuels Advisory Committee, which is chaired by the permanent secretary, the membership of which is detailed above.

Generally speaking, the production sharing contract is a simple model in which the contractor recovers its costs and the balance of the petroleum is shared between the contractor and the government according to a sliding scale, which is open to negotiation and is based on the amount of profit oil produced in a development area. The higher the amount of profit oil, the higher the government share.

The average government take in existing production sharing contracts is between 50% and 70%. It is however expected that the government take will increase in future contracts, depending on the outcome of the appraisals of the recent discoveries.

(a) Royalties

There is no provision for paying a royalty under the Kenyan production sharing contract or the Petroleum (Exploration and Production) Act. There are, however, attempts to introduce a production-based royalty through a new energy policy and bill that are currently in draft form. Whether these provisions will be approved remains to be seen, as oil companies are expected to lobby very strongly against them, especially in so far as they may apply retrospectively to existing contracts.

(b) Bonus

A signature bonus is payable once on signing the contract and is expected to ensure the seriousness of the applicant. Generally, like all other fees, the amount of the bonus is negotiable, but it is advisable to look to the most recently signed bonuses for guidance, as the government uses these as benchmarks.

(c) Rental fees

The Kenyan production sharing contract provides for the payment of surface fees, calculated per square kilometre per annum, on or before the beginning of each contract year, to the accounting officer of the ministry. The rates, which are usually open to negotiation, tend to increase with each exploration period and are highest when the contract enters the production period. As with the signature bonus, the government tends to use recently agreed fees as a benchmark for negotiations.

The surface fees are calculated on the basis of the remaining surface area of the contract at the beginning of the relevant year, are not refundable, and late payment attracts interest in accordance with the terms of the contract.

(d) *Special participation*

The option of a government participation is provided for under the production sharing contract. Under this provision, the maximum percentage participation is provided for, and it is to be carried and paid for in full by the contractor until such time as the government elects to convert its carried participation interest into a full working participation interest, in which case it becomes liable for all its costs thereafter.

The option of conversion can be exercised in respect of an approved development area only, and the government participation interest in respect of the remainder of the contract area continues to be carried and paid for by the contractor until the government elects to convert its carried interest into a full working interest.

Over and above the carried interest, the government may elect to participate in the petroleum operations in any development area and acquire an interest of up to an agreed maximum percentage.

Under the contract, the government may participate either directly or through an appointee, which would be a body corporate wholly owned or controlled by the government and appointed for the purposes of the contract.

(e) *Corporate tax*

There is no excise tax on exports in Kenya and none is provided for in the Petroleum (Exploration and Production) Act. In regard to corporate taxation, the contractor has to comply with the income tax laws in force in Kenya, which impose taxes on income or profits.

However, it is assumed in the production sharing contract that the profit oil received by the government includes all taxes on income payable by the contractor, including income tax and the dividend tax imposed by Kenya on the distribution of income or profits.

The government therefore agrees to pay the taxes to the tax authorities and furnish the contractor with the proper receipts for the purpose of tax returns for the relevant fiscal year. The contractor, however, is responsible for the preparation and filing of income tax returns.

4. Current issues

Some excitement over the upstream oil and gas industry has been caused by the discovery of oil and gas in three consecutive wells in Kenya between March and October 2012. This excitement has brought up discussions in two separate but related subjects: that of revenue distribution, and that of local content.

Local content under the current regime is not clearly defined. While the contractor and subcontractors are required to exercise preference for Kenyan materials, services and supplies, it is not clear whether this means only supplies from Kenyan-owned companies, or whether it also encompasses Kenyan-registered companies or value addition in Kenya. It is expected that discussions on local content will intensify in the coming years as has been seen in other countries with new discoveries, such as Ghana and Uganda.

On the matter of revenue distribution, there have been debates arising from communities in the areas where discoveries have taken place claiming that they would like to be beneficiaries of a significant portion of the government revenues from the petroleum operations. The current legal framework does not provide for the distribution of petroleum proceeds to local communities.

The Constitution of Kenya, however, envisages a situation where the people of the areas where natural resources are discovered and produced will benefit from the resultant revenues. The Constitution also establishes a county system of devolved governance, and creates counties which are semi-autonomous from the national government.

The ongoing review of the legal and policy framework in Kenya has attempted to address these two issues among others. Both the new energy policy and bill are currently in draft form, and it remains to be seen how they will turn out.

5. Conclusion

The Petroleum (Exploration & Production) Act was developed in 1984, and was last revised back in 1986. Among other things the act was meant to regulate the negotiation and conclusion by the government of petroleum agreements relating to exploration. The act is short in detail, and leaves the minister with the powers to determine operational rules and evaluate applicants' capabilities to undertake petroleum exploration. In addition, the energy policy which developed in 2004 included only one brief paragraph on upstream oil and gas operations that was scanty in detail and appeared to suggest that the government may not have been very serious about petroleum exploration when the policy was written and approved.

There is now an ongoing review of both the legal and policy framework for the entire energy sector. Existing drafts contain comprehensive provisions on the upstream oil and gas sector, addressing most of the gaps that have been identified over the years. This may be interpreted to mean that the government is now taking upstream oil and gas operations very seriously, and should be seen as a positive gesture by investors.

Some negative outcomes may arise, especially relating to any retroactive change of fiscal terms that may require investors to pay more to the government, especially through the proposed introduction of a royalties based on production.

Positive outcomes of the review of policy and legal framework should include the development of terms specific to gas, support in infrastructure development, clarification and enhancement of the legal and institutional framework, and positive engagement of stakeholders by the government. Other positive outcomes may include capacity development through the National Energy Institute, the clear definition of revenue-sharing mechanisms between national and county governments, and tax incentives for investments in the energy sector.

The main point to watch for investors is that of possible change to the current fiscal terms through the introduction of royalties and windfall profit taxes.

In conclusion, the Kenyan upstream oil and gas sector is a fast-growing one and currently one of the hottest spots in the world today. Some of the world's largest oil companies have been attracted to Kenya and now hold or participate in licences, ending the era of Kenya as a frontier country for upstream operations. Finalisation of the new legal and policy framework should assist in the country's transition from an exploration frontier to a producer country.

Libya

Waniss A Otman
Petroleum Economist

1. Introduction

A good grasp of the evolution and unique characteristics of the various Libyan petroleum and fiscal regulations is necessary to understand fully the current Libyan exploration and production sharing agreement (EPSA), EPSA Model IV. This chapter provides a brief yet thorough analysis of all Libyan petroleum provisions, from the Mineral Law of 1953 and Petroleum Law of 1955 linked with the concessions granted in the 1950s, to the present EPSA-IV.

The chapter outlines the key features of EPSA-IV, ranging from obligations and rights of both parties with respect to exploration and exploitation areas, signature bonuses, royalty and income taxes, ownership of equipment, abandonment, assignment, and the pre-emption rights of the Libyan National Oil Corporation. There is also an analysis of the four bidding rounds from 2005 to 2007. By critically analysing the defects of these EPSA-IV rounds, especially regarding financial commitments for exploration, the author concludes that they can be seen only as a remarkable success for the Libyan government. The salient features of these rounds, in which a points system using several criteria determines the selection of the winners, are described. The first of these criteria is allocation of production share, the second the amount of the signature bonus, and the third the value of exploration commitments.

2. Upstream activities

Because oil shows had been discovered during drilling in the Italian colonial period, many geologists, including the Italian Ardito Desio, believed that the country possessed significant hydrocarbon resources, correctly identifying the Sirte basin as a favourable area for hydrocarbon accumulation. These circumstances led to the Libyan Petroleum Law of 1955 (Law 25 of 1955), which can be described as one of the earliest, and in some ways the most comprehensive, modern pieces of oil legislation.[1] It is still in force in Libya in 2012, pending the release of the new Libyan Petroleum Law. It provided that some years after the effective dates of the commencement of petroleum concessions, the oil companies were obliged to return to the state a substantial percentage of their acreage in the process known as 'relinquishment'. This acreage could then be re-licensed to other oil companies,

1 AQ Kubbah, *Libya: Its Oil Industry and Economic System*, Baghdad, Arab Petro-Economic Research Centre (1964).

usually under much stiffer terms and conditions. By April 26 1956 the first well in Libya was spudded in the Cyrenaica basin with disappointing results, and it was not until 1958 that a commercial accumulation of oil was discovered by Esso Standard Libya Inc. This took place in Concession 6 in the heart of the Sirte basin, and it was clear that a new world-class oil province had been discovered.

Production of crude oil in Libya began in 1961, and by the end of the decade the country had become the fourth largest producer in the Organisation of Petroleum Exporting Countries (OPEC), with a share of world output in 1970 of 7.5%, when the oil companies aggregate production peaked to reach 3.7 million barrels per day. A few years later these figures had declined dramatically to 2.8% of world output, positioning the country as fifth or sixth largest of OPEC's producers. Over the past three decades Libyan crude oil production's share in all of these groupings has declined considerably.

As at the third quarter of 2012 Libyan crude oil production stoods at 1,504,000, barrels per day.[2] The major producers are Arabian Gulf with 26%, Waha Oil Company 21%, Repsol 15%, Agip (including Agip Gas) 12%, Sirte Oil Company 7%, Veba Oil Company 6%, Wintershall 6%, Zueitina Oil Companies 4% and Total with 3% of total Libyan production.

3. Petroleum legal regime

3.1 Petroleum law and relevant provisions

The first Libyan petroleum legislation was issued in 1953, two years after the country attained political independence. The 1953 Mineral Law granted international oil companies engaged in preliminary geological reconnaissance the right to gather information concerning the potential of exploiting the natural resources in the country, without any legal obligation for subsequent exploration or production. Between 1953 and 1954 nine international oil companies were granted rights for reconnaissance, but they were concerned about several issues at the time, negotiating with the Libyan monarchy's policy makers to accede to their request to give exploration and production rights for mineral resources, if discovered. This led to the issue two years later, in April 1955, of the first comprehensive Libyan Petroleum Law, replacing the Mineral Law.

The Libyan Petroleum Law (Law 25 of 1955) which introduced the Libyan concessions contract was the initial arrangement for petroleum exploration and production between the Libyan government and the international oil companies. Under this arrangement profit was divided on a 50:50 basis between the Libyan government and oil company, with the government receiving it share as royalty and tax payments.

The main objective of the Petroleum Law was to attract and encourage international oil companies to invest in Libya. The country was divided into four zones. Zone I represented the territory of Tripolitania, Zone II represented the territory north of the 28th parallel in Cyrenaica, Zone III represented the territory

---

2 *Opec Monthly Market Report*, October 2012.

south of the 28th Parallel in Cyrenaica, and Zone IV represented the territory of Fezzan. Concessionaires were granted rights that covered vast areas – in Zones I and II the maximum area was 30,000 square kilometres (km^2), while in Zones III and IV it was 80,000 km^2. With regard to relinquishment, concessions had to be reduced to 75% of their original size within five years, 50% within eight years, to 33% within 10 years for areas located in the Zones I and II, and 25% for areas located in Zones III and IV.

The duration of the concession was considerable, typically 50 years, and some of them are still in operation (eg, Wintershall). The concessionaires were given exemption from export and import duties and total control of petroleum exploitation, with freedom to explore for oil under the most flexible terms. In the event of a discovery of commercial quantities of oil, they had the right to produce and export any amount of crude oil at their own quoted prices. The government had no claim on the proceeds of oil revenues apart from the right to receive a specified royalty and taxes. No revision of the concession terms could be effected without prior consultation with the companies. In actual fact, in retrospect, the law was clearly drafted in line with the requirements of the oil companies, to ensure total control in running the petroleum sector. Effectively, the concession terms restricted the role of the Libyan government to that of a tax collector.

The Libyan Petroleum Law was subsequently amended before Libya started exporting oil in 1961. This was followed by several amendments throughout the 1960s. A major revisions in the early 1970s was the issuing the Law 30 on March 20 1971, which amended certain provisions of the Petroleum Law. Through this amendment the government's share in the profits realised by the concessionaires was boosted from 50% to 55%. After long and acrimonious negotiations with the international oil companies regarding increasing the posted price, the government achieved this through the September 1 1970 settlement, the Caracas Posted Prices Agreement on December 1970, the Tehran Agreement of February 14 1971 and the Tripoli Agreement of March 20 1971. As a result of all of these agreements the Libyan posted price was increased from $2.23 a barrel in 1970 to $3.386 a barrel by 1973.

The Libyan government was also influenced by OPEC guidelines in respect of participation agreements, highlighted in OPEC's Resolution 139 of September 22 1971, the "General Agreement on Participation" which called for its members to acquire a "sensible" level of participation in oil operations, based on two basic criteria advocated by OPEC – the host government participation should begin at 25% and to increase gradually to 51%; and compensation for nationalised assets was to be given at updated book values.[3]

Thereafter the Libyan government systematically acquired 51% of the concessionaires' assets by issuing a series of laws and regulations regarding mandatory participation. While some international oil companies agreed, including Agip, the Oasis Group (the US companies Conoco, Marathon and Amerada Hess), Esso (later Exxon), Occidental and other US oil companies (except Phillips), other

---

3 WA Otman and M Bunter, *The Libyan Petroleum Industry in the Twenty First Century: The Upstream, Midstream and Downstream Handbook*, OGEL/MARIS (2005).

companies such as Shell and BP rejected the government terms of demanding majority shares, which resulted in the government nationalising their assets at agreed compensation rates.

After its success in its participation and nationalisation initiatives, the Libyan government went even further towards increasing revenue from its upstream oil sector. It rapidly followed OPEC in increasing its share of revenue from royalties and taxes in line with OPEC's Geneva and Ecuador meetings in 1974. In fact in the period from 1971 to 1974 the Libyan government made several changes to the Petroleum Law which increased royalty from 12% to 14% and then to 16.67%, with taxes also gradually increased from their level in the original concession (50%), to 55%, then to 60% and finally to 65%.

Under Article 24 of the Petroleum Law several petroleum regulations were issued to implement of the law. From 1955 to the early 1970s the Libyan Ministry of Petroleum issued nine regulations concerning the law relating to petroleum operations. Six of these regulations have been incorporated within the amended Petroleum Law, and the remaining three regulations are still in force, Petroleum Regulations 1, 8 and 9.

Petroleum Regulation 1 was issued in August 1955 and dealt with the Libyan petroleum map which divided the country into four zones, as detailed above. Regulation 8 was issued in 1968 and dealt with petroleum operations. It aimed at regulating oil and gas production levels, and can be considered as one of the most important practical steps taken for the reformation of the Libyan petroleum industry. Finally, Petroleum Regulation 9 issued in July 1973 provided comprehensive financial, administrative and technical rules for the implementation of a rigorous management policy for the country's oil wealth.

(a) Regulatory bodies

Libyan Ministry of Petroleum: The Libyan Ministry of Petroleum was established in 1963 and a Council of Ministers' decision regulating its affairs was released in 1964. However, the decision did not specify any prerogatives for either the ministry or to any of its general departments. Because of this the ministry was not able to play its proper role in regulating the operations of the oil companies. Soon after taking power, the new government took action by amending Article 2(a) and (b) of the Petroleum Law. These two key paragraphs related to powers over licensing: the granting of licences for exploration in and full relinquishment of an operation area, the granting and cancellation of concession deeds and accepting or rejecting their relinquishment, the determining of resort to arbitration and setting the period in which applications for concessions would be opened.

Whereas in the 1964 Council of Ministers' decision these matters fell within the terms of reference of the Council of Ministers, and not the Minister of Petroleum and the Higher Petroleum Council, the new Law 120 of October 18 1970 clarified the prerogatives of the Ministry of Petroleum, entrusting it with the organisation, supervision, and control of oil wealth exploitation.

Law 120 also fixed and organised the structure of the ministry by dividing it into five specialised departments, and three offices with a branch office in Benghazi. The law authorised the Ministry of Petroleum to issue an internal organisation decision and distribute assignments. This was achieved by the Ministry of Petroleum's Decision 49 of 1971.

It was in this manner that the Libyan government, through Law 120 of 1970, reinforced the powers of the Ministry of Petroleum which, although technically in existence since the 1963 to 1964 period, had been to a large extent sidelined. This enabled it to impose effective control over oil companies, leading to the emergence of its role in achieving the systematic development of the country's oil wealth. It is also worth noting that with this reorganisation there was no place left for the Supreme Petroleum Commission, established by Law 6 of 1963, which had been vested with the powers to formulate petroleum policy and with other executive matters. These matters now clearly fell under the jurisdiction of the Ministry of Petroleum. Any duplication of work was therefore avoided with the cessation of the operations of the Petroleum Commission. In 2000 the Ministry of Petroleum was abolished and its authority and capacity passed to the Libyan National Oil Corporation.

More significantly, another piece of legislation, Law 4 of the General People's Committee (Libyan Council of Ministers) of April 2004, reaffirmed the role of the Minister of Energy in the post-sanctions period, and this, in conjunction with the Libyan National Oil Corporation's active posture, appears to have helped Libya to streamline its approach to the oil and gas sector, enabling it to formulate new policies aimed at encouraging direct foreign investment. However, in 2006 the Ministry of Energy was abolished and replaced by the Higher Council of Oil and Gas Affairs acting as the higher executive authority within the petroleum sector. In 2011 the new Libyan government reinstated the Ministry of Petroleum as a regulatory authority in this sector.

Libyan National Oil Corporation: It was during a state visit to Paris on April 4 1968 by the Libyan Prime Minister, at the invitation of the French President de Gaulle that the principles and structure of the first Libyan joint venture agreement, for utilising certain petroleum areas in Libya were discussed between the government of Libya and the French state group ERAP. Based on these initial meetings several joint venture agreements were agreed and signed in Tripoli on April 30 1968.

In order to regularise the position of the Libyan signatories to this agreement, Law 13 of April 14 1968 was issued, establishing the Libyan General Petroleum Corporation (Lipetco).[4] According to Law 13, Article 2(3), Lipetco was granted the right to perform exploration and development activities in available acreages either directly or through joint ventures with foreign partners. It was clear that Law 13 intended that any financial rewards such as bonuses and other incentives offered to Lipetco would better those provided to the government under the existing concessions. Crucially, for the future development of the oil industry in Libya, the law gave Lipetco the right to participate directly in petroleum exploitation through a share in the joint management of the company.

4 *Middle East Economic Survey*, April 19 1968.

Consequently on April 30 1968 agreements were signed between Lipetco and the two French firms Auxirap and Aquitaine under which Aquitaine was nominated as the operating company. In these agreements the Libyan share was to start at 25% of physical production when below 200,000 barrels per day (b/d), increasing gradually (by 1% for each 14,000 b/d increment) to 50% when the average daily production reached 550,000 b/d.[5] Using this sliding scale formula, the government's receipts were expected to reach over 80% of total profit in respect of crude oil exported from the agreement's area. The decision to develop an oilfield after commercial discovery was to be the point at which Lipetco would take up its share, and Lipetco was to finance the development costs of its share, but the French companies would procure finance for Lipetco at favourable interest rates.[6] The French consortium also undertook to sell the first party (ie, Libyan) share of crude oil at realised prices less a marketing allowance of 2%. The companies would be liable for income tax based on posted prices.[7]

As mentioned above, Lipetco was established hastily by Law 13 of 1968 specifically in order to facilitate the creation of the French joint ventures. As a consequence, the new government realised that there were big gaps in its application as well as in Lipetco's jurisdiction and its control by the government. The new Libyan government in the early 1970s wished to have a national oil company which could become an effective tool in supporting the national economy, by means of developing oil resources effectively for the good of all sectors of Libyan society. To this end the government, on March 5 1970, promulgated Law 24 concerning the establishment of the Libyan National Oil Corporation to replace Lipetco. Law 24 required the Libyan National Oil Corporation's share in a joint venture to be fixed at the time the contract was signed, at the same time shifting all the risk in the pre-commercial discovery period on to the foreign partner. Further it introduced, in conformity with current trends in the oil industry globally, service agreements for the first time in Libya's oil legislation. This enabled the Libyan National Oil Corporation to exploit its own areas by using a contractor with the technical competence and financial ability, for the Libyan National Oil Corporation's account and on its behalf. At the same time, it would still own all the oil produced and saved at the wellhead from the contract area, while the contractor would bear all the risk during the exploration period and would undertake to bear all development and marketing expenses against a certain fee. This model of agreement provided a large increase in the state's profits from its oil wealth, and provided additional supervision and control over its natural resources. Additionally, the Libyan National Oil Corporation was able to add substantial quantities to its oil reserves, and could develop these on its own or through a contractor. This would subsequently enable it to enter the marketing field gradually, at the same time stabilising price levels.

Subsequently, prior to the emergence of second model exploration and production sharing agreement in 1980, the Libyan petroleum industry witnessed

---

5 K Hossain, *Law and Policy in Petroleum Development – Changing Relations between Transnationals and Governments*, Frances Publishers Ltd, London (1979).

6 Frank C Waddams, *The Libyan Oil Industry*, Croom Helm Ltd, London, (1980).

7 Judith Gurney, *Libya: the Political Economy of Oil*, Oxford University Press, Oxford, UK (1996).

significant progress in what has been termed the re-construction of Libyan fiscal policy for the oil industry. In Decree 10 of 1979 of the General People's Congress, the Libyan government consolidated its plans for the further development of this sector. By this decree, the Libyan National Oil Corporation was reorganised by amending Law 24 of 1970 which had established it. Its funding was boosted, enabling it to invest both within and outside the country though its own subsidiaries or in participation with others. The amended law also empowered it to enter into new types of contracts. As a direct result of this decree, in late 1979 the Libyan National Oil Corporation introduced its second generation of production sharing contracts, known as 'EPSA-II', which became available in January 1980 to the international oil companies.

The Libyan National Oil Corporation was therefore established as a key state agency responsible for the development, administration and exploitation of oil resources at all stages, with a mandate to shape and structure all of these into an integrated industry.

The Libyan government, in setting up the Libyan National Oil Corporation on such a strong foundation, enabled it to grow into one of the major pillars supporting the national economy. By its establishment the role of the Libyan government had been changed from being a dormant collaborator and tax collector to that of an active player with the power and responsibility to formulate all policies for utilising vital national oil resources. In attempting achieving these objectives, the Libyan National Oil Corporation also secured vast areas for its own development, without the participation of the international oil companies.

(b) Types of agreement

Currently in Libya, there are several types of petroleum agreements in use in the upstream sector. The classic concession model was the initial arrangement between the Libyan government and international oil companies for petroleum exploration and production, and the granting of concessions began soon after approval of the Petroleum Law in 1955. The concession contracts took the form of a tax/royalty system, in which the oil company took full responsibility for petroleum activities and operations, with the government's role being that of a tax collector. The primary objective of the Libyan Petroleum Law of 1955 had been to attract and encourage international oil companies to invest in Libya, diverting their historical interest away from the Middle East.

Later, in 1968, through Law 13, the Libyan Petroleum Corporation (Lipetco) was established and authorised to enter into joint venture agreements with foreign (and initially in point of fact, French) partners. Two years later, during the nationalisation process, most of the existing concession arrangements were changed to participation agreements. At this period the assets of several international oil companies were nationalised with their operations taken over completely, by establishing new Libyan firms as affiliates of the Libyan National Oil Corporation, such as the 100% owned Arabian Gulf Company, formerly BP/Bunker Hunt.

However, although historically global oil prices remained low until the 1970s they took on another dimension with the sudden increase of oil prices during 1973 to 1974. The rise in prices led to massive profits for the oil companies under the classic concession agreements. This turned out to be one of the major factors driving the emergence of the first Libyan exploration and production agreement (EPSA-I) in 1974, followed by EPSA-II in 1980, the latter introduced during the second oil market shock following the Iranian Revolution in 1979.

A drop in oil prices during the 1980s had devastating effects on the Libyan economy as well as on oil companies globally. In 1983 the oil price was $34 a barrel while in 1986 it was less than $10. The decline in oil prices adversely affected the capacity of the oil companies` to invest in petroleum exploration and development in Libya. Acreage under lease and exploration rig count during the same period were also considerably reduced, resulting in a much slower tempo of exploration and development.

These market conditions and the impact of the US companies' withdrawal from the Libyan oil sector in 1986, exacerbated the Libyan National Oil Corporation's multiple problems which, because of insufficient exploration and production brought about by the strict terms of EPSA-I and II, forced a change. To reverse the situation, a new generation of exploration and production sharing agreements, the third one (EPSA-III), was announced by the Libyan government in 1988 as a response to changes in the international oil market and an attempt to attract more participants in new exploration. In this new model the Libyan National Oil Corporation adopted flexible contractual terms, including the guaranteeing of cost recovery by the international oil companies, and the achievement of a larger and earlier cash flow on investments relative to the previous generation of agreements. Despite the new attractive terms, however, the Libyan oil sector was still overwhelmed by a continuing drop in oil prices, and the political fallout from the sanctions imposed by the United States and United Nations.

The lifting of US sanctions against Libya in 2004, and drastic changes in the geopolitics of the global energy markets in the preceding 30 years made it imperative for the Libyan National Oil Corporation to re-evaluate its relationship with the international oil companies. In the 1970s and the early 1980s, the competitive environment in the industry was characterised by limited opportunities and abundant financial resources, largely because significant parts of the world were closed to direct foreign investment and because of the prevalence of high oil prices respectively. In the early 1990s, as most countries started to open up, new opportunities became available to the international oil companies at a time when the available financial resources were scarce, mainly due to relatively lower oil prices. In effect, the early 1980s and the 1990s saw fewer dollars chasing a larger number of opportunities.

Therefore, the Libyan government reacted swiftly to the lifting of the US sanctions in 2004, and the primary target for a major economic makeover was without doubt the hydrocarbon sector. Its strategy was two-pronged. The first was immediately to open negotiations with certain American international oil companies to return to their assets in Libya, abandoned in 1986 due to the application of the sanctions, while the second was the introduction of a new petroleum fiscal model represented by EPSA-IV, the fourth generation of the production sharing contract system utilised in Libya since the 1970s. The four generations of production sharing contracts vary considerably in their economic, financial, and legal terms and implications, but while there was considerable continuity and similarity between EPSA-I and II, EPSA-III was radically different and similar to EPSA-IV.

Thus, currently EPSA-IV is the only contractual form presented by the Libyan government for international oil companies wanting to invest in the Libyan petroleum exploration and production sector

EPSA-IV: Prior to the introduction of the fourth generation of production sharing contracts, there was immense debate among Libyan petroleum policy makers as to how investment by foreign oil companies in the Libyan petroleum sector could be made more attractive compared to other producer countries. This debate was driven by the basic fact that only 31% of the total area of Libya's onshore and offshore sedimentary basins had been licensed, with no exploration activities whatsoever in the remaining 69%. Despite more than half a century of exploration and production activities, it is only the Sirte basin that could be said to have been extensively explored, and even there considerable potential still existed.

Basin potential is enormous due to a combination of many factors. Libya, from the earliest development phases of its hydrocarbon industry, had been a proven, high-quality oil province that offered a wide range of oil and gas plays. It is also a low-cost environment, where operating costs are often as low as $0.60-1.50 per barrel, and capital expenditure is regularly under $2.00 per barrel.

EPSA-IV was designed and modified to replace all the previous models of the production sharing agreement, and in addition complete transparency was brought to the bidding process, as further incentives for international oil companies to invest in the Libyan upstream sector.

(c) Acquisition of acreage

The complete transparency of the EPSA-IV round public bidding procedures is unique within the Middle East and North Africa, where closed room negotiations are the norm, giving rise to many accusations of corruption and squandering of state resources, as well as preventing the international oil companies from competing on a level playing field due to political favouritism. In the actual implementation of all public rounds of EPSA-IV, the Libyan National Oil Corporation handled affairs and met schedules which were very close to its stated timetable (a minor extension was given to allow companies to continue evaluating the acreage on offer), in an efficient, transparent and professional manner. This has improved the Libyan National Oil Corporation's standing and increased international oil companies' confidence in the country.

In the EPSA-IV public round procedures all the international oil companies interested in participating in exploration and production in Libya have to meet certain criteria in a qualifying round aimed at assessing their financial and technical capabilities. This involves the submission of audited financial statements for the previous three years, as well as activity reports for the same period. If an applicant is an affiliate company, the parent company is required to submit the same qualification documents. A special evaluation committee within the Libyan National Oil Corporation investigates all applications in line with fixed guidelines on public bidding.

In cases where oil companies apply as a consortium, they have to select their operational 'director' or 'operator' which has to submit all the qualification documents of the consortium members. It has also to be qualified in both financial and technical aspects, while the other members of the consortium are required to be, at least, financially qualified. Disqualifying the consortium's operator will result in disqualifying the consortium. Members of the consortium will be individually informed on qualification status, and any change in composition of the consortium will require approval from the Libyan National Oil Corporation.

In the public round procedures the Libyan National Oil Corporation has also considered the situation where conflict might arise among consortium members or where any individual member wishes to withdraw from the consortium. Should the member wishing to withdraw have already been qualified as an operator, then it still has the right to submit a bid separately for the contract areas acquired with the other consortium members. If a withdrawing member has been pre-qualified as holding non-operator status, then it can still join another consortium, provided that this consortium is not bidding on the contract areas that the previous consortium had bid on.

Bid opening is conducted in public and in the presence of the legal representatives of the bidders on the bid opening date. The winners of individual blocks are selected on the basis of the offer with the lowest 'second party allocation', that is to say the percentage of oil allocated to the bidding company (the 'second party' to the contract) for cost recovery. Initially, the evaluation committee examines all the allocation values, and the lowest is deemed to be the winner. Should more than one winning bidder offer the same value, then the bidder offering the highest signature bonus will be successful.

However, in the event that only one offer is received for any contract area, then a 'sole bidder situation' is said to arise. In such a situation the evaluation committee can decide at its sole discretion whether or not to accept the offer and announce a winner, or declare the bid process for the area void. The committee must deliver its decision not later than a week after the bid opening day.

If more than one bidder offers exactly the same allocation value and signature bonus, the bidders concerned are required to submit new offers for both amounts after two days, and if after this there is still a tie, then the process will be repeated until a clear winner emerges.

(d) Qualification requirements

Candidates go through a qualifications process to determine that they process the necessary experience and technical and financial capabilities to perform the contractual obligations. In verifying the technical and financial capabilities of the applicants, the appointed committee (which is part of the Libyan National Oil Corporation) evaluates certain financial ratios as well as tangible assets, such as oil and gas reserves and production rates. Also intangible assets will be examined, such as the company's operational experience which is evaluated by looking at the number of years for which it has been involved in exploration and production as well number of qualified staff working in the exploration and production divisions of the company. In addition, affiliates will be judged based on the capabilities of their parent companies; and consortia will qualify if the leader of the consortium is qualified. Companies already operating in Libya are deemed to be already qualified, and do not have to go through this process.

Qualified companies that pay the data room fees and sign a confidentiality agreement are allowed to visit the data room to examine part of the geological and geophysical data, and receive copies of such data in electronic form, together with copies of the model contract, the commitment letter and the bank guarantee.

(e) *Duration*

The exploration period under EPSA-IV runs for five years, with 25 years for exploitation. However, the exploration period can be extended under certain conditions clearly stated under the agreement relating to the drilling period, the ongoing appraisal programme, establishing commerciality and gas marketing issues. Once an exploitation area has been identified, the agreement is terminated for the remainder of the contract area. The 'exploitation area' is defined as the number of sectors within the offered block covering the entire extent of the underlying structures or stratigraphic closures defining the reservoir or pay zone in the field where a commercial discovery has been made and declared.

(f) *Minimum work programme*

Before the bidding process begins the Libyan National Oil Corporation will indicate a minimum work programme for each block, on the location and size of the block and its hydrocarbon potential given the relevant basin prospectivity. The minimum programme therefore varies from basin to basin, with bidders being invited to present in their offers an incremental amount that will be used as a bidding parameter for selecting the winning bid.

The bidding oil companies compete based on the minimum work programme they offer, including a technical work programme such as 2D and 3D seismic surveys and the number of exploration wells, as well as signature bonus and the percentage allocation for cost recovery. The bid offering best value will be the winner of that block.

The terms of EPSA-IV obligate the successful oil company to complete the exploration commitments during the specified exploration period. If there are any remaining exploration commitments not accomplished in due time, then the company is required to pay penalties to the Libyan National Oil Corporation as set out in the agreement.

(g) *Assignment and encumbrance*

The EPSA-IV provisions relating to assignment of a contract are informed by three main conditions. First, no assignment will be permitted until all seismic surveys have been executed and at least 50% of the wells are drilled. Second, the operator will be jointly responsible with the assignee, unless the Libyan National Oil Corporation explicitly agrees otherwise. Finally if the assignor is the operator, it will have to continue until replaced.

After the first commercial discovery has been made, the Libyan National Oil Corporation has the right of first refusal with respect to any assignment by the contracting oil company to a third party. If the Libyan National Oil Corporation does not wish to exercise its pre-emption rights, it informs the oil company accordingly of its decision. Otherwise the parties meet to discuss the terms of the assignment to the Libyan National Oil Corporation. If no agreement is reached within 120 days from the date of notice, or any agreed extension, the international oil company has the right to go ahead with the assignment to the third party, but must first give the Libyan National Oil Corporation the opportunity to take the interest being assigned at the same terms as those agreed with the third party.

(h) *Local content*

International oil companies working under EPSA-IV as operators must hire Libyan nationals to carry out petroleum operations in the contract area, except to the extent that specialised technical personnel or key management positions are involved and suitable candidates are not available in Libya. In those circumstances, the operator may hire non-Libyan nationals to carry out those operations.

The operator has to prepare and submit an annual training programme to the management committee for approval. The objective of these programmes is to enable Libyan nationals to fill posts of higher responsibility and to replace any non-Libyan personnel in the areas of specialisation for which such non-Libyan personnel were hired. The annual budget allocated for this training programme must be sufficient to cover all costs for training in each calendar year during the exploration period, and shall not be less than 10% of manpower costs during each year of the exploitation period. For these purposes, 'manpower costs' constitute the total of all direct and indirect costs associated with the operator's employees.

In addition, EPSA-IV gives priority to local work, stating that the operator shall at all times give priority to Libyan supplies, equipment and services, provided that they are competitive in terms of performance, price and availability.

(i) *Environment*

EPSA IV imposes two main duties on the operator on the subject of the environment. First, operators must carry out an assessment of the environmental impact of each planned petroleum operation, and must submit that report to the management committee prior to the start of that operation. The report must include measures to be taken to ensure that the conduct of petroleum operations does not cause damage to the environment.

Second, under the Petroleum Law the operator is obliged to provide an adequate system for the disposal of water and waste oil, and it must securely plug all boreholes and wells made by it before they are abandoned, in accordance with good oilfield practices.

In this connection, the terms of EPSA-IV obligate the operator to abandon the field after the cessation of production, and this is dealt with in two separate phases.

Expenditure relating to the abandonment of exploration operations is borne 100% by the operator, while expenditure relating to operations during the exploitation period is borne by both parties equally (50:50). In cases where commercial exploitation is possible, the operator makes cost estimates to be approved by the management committee. If these are approved, there are a series of steps to be followed. The operator must make annual provision for its share in the current budget; the operator must update its abandonment cost estimates annually; and the operator must deposit its share of abandonment costs in a special interest-bearing account under the custody of the Libyan National Oil Corporation. If the Libyan National Oil Corporation decides to continue operations at end of the agreement, all accumulated abandonment funds are credited to it and the operator is discharged from abandonment liability in respect of future petroleum operations.

(j) Governing law and dispute resolution

EPSA-IV is governed by the Libyan Petroleum Law, as amended, and relevant Libyan regulations, except as otherwise provided for in the agreement.

The management committee scheme adopted under the earliest versions of the production sharing agreement was further developed in EPSA-III. While the foreign company was still required to act as operator, under EPSA-III it had to conduct its petroleum operations under the supervision and control of a three-member management committee. Under EPSA-IV the management committee is now composed of four members: two, including the chairman, to be appointed by the Libyan National Oil Corporation, and two to be appointed by the operator. The management committee has to be formed not later than one month after the effective date of the agreement. Each party notifies the other of the committee members it is appointing. The operations are managed on a day-to-day basis by the operator's management under the supervision of the management committee, which acts as the board of directors. All petroleum operations in the contract area must be conducted under the control and supervision of a management committee.

The operation of the management committee under EPSA-IV makes a notable departure from previous practice relating to the major issues relevant to petroleum operations, in that its decisions are no longer made by a simple majority vote but by unanimous vote of its members, including, without limitation, the approval of work programmes and budgets prepared by the operator for petroleum operations and the approval of the list of contractors and contracts above a certain value.

Settlement of differences in all disputes between the operator and any of the other parties arising in connection with operations under the agreement are referred to the management committee, which shall use its best endeavours to settle the matter amicably. Any dispute or claim arising out of the agreement itself, or any breach thereof, if it cannot be settled amicably, is to be referred for final settlement by arbitration, in accordance with the Rules of Arbitration of the International Chamber of Commerce (ICC), in Paris, France, in Arabic or English as the parties may agree, by three arbitrators. Each party shall appoint one arbitrator, and the ICC shall appoint the third arbitrator, who must be in no way related to either party and who will be the chairman of the arbitration body.

4. Government take

(a) *Royalties and corporate income tax*

Under EPSA-IV the contracting international oil companies are subject to royalties and corporate income tax imposed by the Petroleum Law. However, the Libyan National Oil Corporation agrees to meet and discharge any royalty and corporate income tax obligations imposed by the Petroleum Law in relation to the oil companies' share of production.

The oil companies have to prepare a corporate income tax declaration as required by the Petroleum Law and submit same to the Libyan National Oil Corporation for review and audit one month prior to the due date for submitting the declaration to the relevant tax authority. The Libyan National Oil Corporation notifies the oil companies of any comments thereon, and if necessary the oil companies have to prepare a revised corporate income tax declaration incorporating the comments and resubmit it to the Libyan National Oil Corporation prior to the due date. The Libyan National Oil Corporation processes the tax declaration and obtains a tax certificate from the competent tax authority in the name of the oil companies. This is promptly delivered to the oil companies.

For the purpose of corporate income tax and royalty calculations, the official selling price in Libya is used for calculating the revenue derived from disposal of crude. However, the actual selling price under gas sales agreements is used for calculating the revenue derived from disposal of the natural gas. For calculating the revenue derived from disposal of liquid hydrocarbon byproducts, the prices referred to EPSA-IV (Article 12.3.3) are used.

With regard to other issues relevant for the purposes of determining Libyan taxes and other Libyan governmental charges due from international oil companies, those companies may not offset costs incurred under one production sharing agreement against income realised under another agreement; nor may income derived from a production sharing agreement be consolidated with income from other activities.

(b) *Bonuses*

The international oil companies are obliged to pay two types of bonuses, a signature bonus and a cumulative production bonus, both of which are not recoverable. When a bid round is initiated, a minimum signature bonus is set, and the bidding companies may offer above that, these amounts being considered as a secondary bidding parameter (see the tables at the end of the chapter for the signature bonuses agreed by successful bidders in the rounds so far conducted under EPSA-IV). The cumulative production bonus is paid in three steps: US$1 million on the start of production from the first commercial discovery; US$5 million once cumulative production has reached 100 million barrels; and a further US$3 million when each further 30 million barrels is achieved.

(c) *Rental fees*

Under Article 19 of EPSA-IV the contracting international oil companies are exempt from customs duties under the Petroleum Law. They are also exempt from payment of rentals and fees with respect to the contract area.

In addition, the terms of EPSA-IV are clear on the subject of title to the oil and gas exploitation equipment and tools, and the agreement still uses the provisions stated in the Petroleum Law. During the exploration period, any material purchased by the operator shall become the property of the Libyan National Oil Corporation when it is first actually used in petroleum operations. The operator has the right to utilise this equipment for its petroleum operations without paying any charges or fees. Any equipment or materials not used in the petroleum operations by the end of the exploration period remain the property of the operator, and the cost of its purchase shall not be considered petroleum operation expenditure.

Under this rule, the equipment and tools purchased by the operator become the property of the Libyan National Oil Corporation immediately if they are purchased in Libya, or as soon as it is landed in Libya if purchased overseas.

(d) Special participation

In the past, the conservative nature of Libya's oil policies, especially in the context of the first two versions of the production sharing contract, have often adversely affected the investor's position, especially when international oil prices have been low. This, combined with Libya's political marginalisation, backfired badly in terms of the amount of investment in the Libyan upstream petroleum sector.

Fundamentally the terms of EPSA-IV are similar to those of EPSA-III, but designed to be more attractive. In summary, the international oil companies are totally responsible for finance and take the entire risk during exploration and appraisal, as well as paying for the training of Libyan nationals during the exploration period. In the event of a commercial discovery, the development expenditure and risk are shared equally with the Libyan National Oil Corporation. The operating costs are divided according to the parties' respective shares of total production (as determined during the bidding process).

The new EPSA-IV covers all sizes of discoveries, with small discoveries still able to secure an acceptable return for the international oil companies, as well as giving them a fair return in the event of major or giant discoveries. One of the elements in EPSA-IV is the use of a sliding scale in the sharing of the profit oil. This provides for exploration, appraisal, development and production costs to be recovered very quickly from a proportion of output.

The determination of the petroleum production allocation and profit split between the parties is largely dependent on three factors: the 'second party allocation', the 'base (B) factor' and the 'A factor'.

The second party allocation is the percentage of production allocated to the international oil company (the second party to the contract) for cost recovery, which varies according to offer made by the company in the competitive bidding for a given block. The terms of EPSA-IV allow the Libyan National Oil Corporation (the first party to the agreement) to receive a share of production (the 'first take') with the remainder being available for cost recovery by the investor. Once full cost recovery has taken place, the net production or profit oil ('net crude oil') is shared between the Libyan National Oil Corporation and the investor on a sliding scale that is linked to the A and B factors.

According to Article 12.1 of EPSA-IV: for any calendar year or part thereof, crude oil, liquid hydrocarbon byproducts and natural gas produced under the agreement are allocated between the parties as follows.

The Libyan National Oil Corporation receives 100% of production less the second party allocation as set during the bidding as a percentage (X%).

The remaining percentage of production is allocated to the second party (the international oil company) for cost recovery until the cumulative value of that allocation equals the cumulative petroleum operations expenditure incurred by the second party, including its share of the petroleum operations expenditure in the calendar year at issue. Thereafter, any excess of the second party allocation not required for cost recovery, referred to as 'excess petroleum', is allocated under a formula using the A and B factors.

The second party's allocation of excess petroleum is determined by applying the following formula: (B factor) multiplied by (A factor) multiplied by (excess petroleum).

For the purpose of this calculation, the B factor is a figure set according to the indicated levels of average daily production from the area during the relevant calendar year as shown in Table 1, except in the case of natural gas for which the B factor is always equal to 1.

Table 1: Base (B) factor

Average total daily production (barrels per day)	Base factor
1 – 20,000	X
20,001 – 30,000	X
30,001 – 60,000	X
60,0010 – 85,000	X
More than 85,000	X

The A factor is a figure set on the basis of the ratios of the cumulative value of the oil received by the investor from the production in such area over the cumulative petroleum expenditure incurred by the investor in respect of the area, as shown in Table 2.

Table 2: A factor

Ratio	A factor
Less than or equal to 1.5	X
More than 1.5 but less than or equal to 3.0	X
More than 3.0 but less than or equal to 4.0	X
More than 4.0	X

In addition, under the EPSA-IV model, the government has settled for a competitive and pragmatic pricing policy, pegging its crude to Brent market prices by using the same formula linked to the sliding scale of the A factor, which allows the agreement continuously to reflect market conditions without the need to review and adjust the initial terms. Thus, in line with the spirit of the new agreements, for the purpose of determining the value of crude oil received by the oil company, the official selling price is that applicable during the month of production of such crude oil. However, if the official selling price over a period of at least three months differs from prices for similar crude on the world market by more than a certain percentage of the official selling price, the parties shall, upon the request of either of them, consult with a view to agreeing on an appropriate adjustment.

Figure 1: Petroleum production allocation between both parties under EPSA-IV

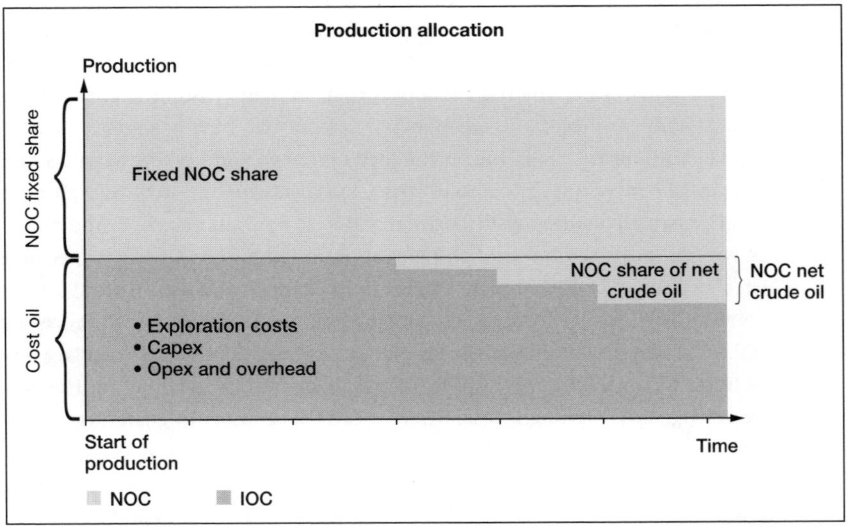

Source: Libyan Ministry for Energy, 2006.

(e) *EPSA-IV and gas development*

With regard to both associated and free gas, the provisions in EPSA-IV (Articles 13.2. and 13.3) are fairly straightforward, with regard to appraisal, commercialisation and timing of gas developments, all of which hinge on the decision of the management committee (MC) which supervises operations in the contract area, under Article 4.1. of EPSA-IV. This can be seen as acknowledging the growing importance of gas in the present and future energy market and the particular requirements of the development and marketing of gas. There is provision for a set of incentives to enable the parties jointly to develop a discovery of natural gas.

However many issues relating to natural gas are poorly dealt with in EPSA-IV. Probably the most contentious issue for international oil companies considering investing in the Libyan gas sector is contained in Article 13.5.1: "The Parties agree to give priority to supply the domestic market in Libya from all or part of the Natural Gas produced under this Agreement." In itself, this takes any decision regarding marketing of gas outside Libya completely out of the oil companies' hands. The situation is further exacerbated by Article 13.5.2. which states that:

> *The Parties (as sellers) and First Party or another local buyer (local buyer) shall proceed in good faith to negotiate a gas sales agreement incorporating the principles set forth in Article (13.4) and the price shall be stipulated in accordance with Article (13.4.3) less fifteen percent (15%).*

Until these clauses concerning priority for the local market and subsidised pricing are considerably revised, and ideally incorporated in a separate law containing a series of incentives specifically for gas, it is highly unlikely that there will be any major foreign investment in developing gas discoveries. This has been borne out by the facts: apart from the Western Libyan Gas project and the Shell Libya Sirte Gas project of 2005, there have been no major gas development projects announced in Libya since the implementation of EPSA-IV in 2004.

Additionally, the crucial linkage between the gas upstream and downstream sectors through access to infrastructure for transport and distribution of gas is dealt with in Article 13.6. The basic reality is that, in many cases, the commercial success of upstream gas projects is largely based not only on having a relatively competitive market with regard to pricing, as touched on above, but also on having some type of guarantee concerning access to downstream infrastructure such as existing pipeline.

The virtually monopolistic position of the Libyan National Oil Corporation in terms of gas transport – either through pipelines belonging to its wholly owned subsidiaries such as Arabian Gulf Company and Sirte Oil Company, or those belonging to its joint ventures with foreign companies, such as Agip or Repsol, in which it has a majority stake – places a new investor in the Libyan gas segment in a particularly vulnerable position with regard to physical market access for its gas, whether for the domestic or export markets. Although Article 13.6 of EPSA-IV appears to guarantee access to such facilities owned or controlled by the Libyan National Oil Corporation, on terms not less favourable than those granted to other shippers or users of the processing facilities (ie, presumably, the Libyan National Oil Corporation's subsidiaries and affiliates), it could have gone further by legislating for guaranteed third party access to plant and pipelines constructed for any future gas development projects by other companies.

5. Current issues

5.1 Appraising the EPSA-IV rounds

An economic appraisal of the bidding rounds conducted under EPSA-IV shows that there have clearly been both advantages and disadvantages to the Libyan National Oil Corporation and the international oil companies. To try to explain these more fully, the main features are summarised below.

(a) *Efficiency and transparency*

What is initially apparent is that the Libyan National Oil Corporation has achieved a new level of efficiency in its planning and implementation of the bidding rounds, as well as high levels of transparency in the bidding processes. This had undoubtedly enhanced not only its own reputation, but has also positively impacted international perceptions of Libya in general. The public nature of the bidding process, the transparent regulations, as well as the relatively straightforward and legally documented way in which the duties and commitments of both parties are laid out, all achieved within a specified timeframe, speak volumes about a new awareness among Libyan policy makers as to what defines a successful bidding process.

(b) *Signature bonus*

In basic financial terms, with the re-introduction of the signature bonus, which had not been applied in Libyan upstream contracts since the time of the concession agreements, the Libyan National Oil Corporation achieved considerable financial gains. These amounted to a total of US$472,383,000 for all rounds (as highlighted in Table 3). These broke down to US$132.9 million (28% of the total amount) in the first round; US$103.4 million (22%) the second round; US$88.1 million (19%) in the third round and US$148 million (31%) in the fourth round.

(c) *Exploration commitments*

With regard to the exploration commitments, in financial terms for all rounds commitments secured were US$2,291.2 million. For the first round, it was US$298.7 million (13% of the total over all four rounds) with the values divided into three types of expenditure, 2D seismic surveys, 3D seismic surveys and the number of exploration wells to be drilled. For the first round this was 24 exploration wells, 2D seismic was about 24,500 km and 3D seismic amounted 2,850 km^2. These were very low, and did not secure the real objectives of the Libyan National Oil Corporation, which wanted to extend exploration activities in the Libyan sedimentary basins greatly. For example, in the Murzuq basin the financial commitments did not match the combined size of the areas offered, with areas 177, 163, and 131 totalling 32,932 km^2 securing financial commitments of only US$1,700 per square kilometre.

But in the following rounds, starting with the second round, things were more promising, with tital commitments increasing from US$298.7 million to US$482.45 million, representing 19% of the total amount over all four rounds. Compared with the first round, 2D seismic activities increased from 24,500 km to 27,850 km, 3D seismic surveys increased from 2,850 km^2 to 7,600 km^2, while the number of exploration wells increased from 24 to 32.

For the third round the total contract value achieved by the Libyan National Oil Corporation was US$951 million, approximately 42% of the total amount for all rounds. The exploration commitments were for 35 exploration wells, 2D seismic activities covering 41,100 km, and 10,000 km^2 for 3D seismic. For the fourth round the total values was US$611 million (27% of the total), including 33 exploration wells, 13,100 km 2D of seismic surveys and 8,600 km^2 of 3D seismic.

The third round was slightly different from the previous two rounds, since this time the Libyan National Oil Corporation inserted extra provisions in the bidding process. These related to the selection of the winners by reference to three criteria. The first of these was the second party allocation (the percentage of oil reserved for cost recovery), the second the amount of the signature bonus, and the third the value of the exploration commitments. This latter condition was new, with the Libyan National Oil Corporation stipulating specific technical and financial values and minimum exploration programmes.

For each of these three bidding elements, the Libyan National Oil Corporation used a system of points which were aggregated to select the winners. Fifteen points are allocated for each additional 0.1% added to the Libyan National Oil Corporation's share of production, while 1 point is allocated for each $100,000 increment to the minimum signatures bonuses specified for each area. For seismic surveying, 10 points are allocated for each 100 km additional to the minimum requirement for 2D, 10 points for each 50 km^2 additional to the minimum 3D requirement, and finally 15 points are awarded for each US$1 million added to the minimum value of each exploration well.

In a situation where two or more bidders' points accumulated for a specific area are equal, the Libyan National Oil Corporation requested these bidders to submit new offers aimed at increasing the total points originally achieved, through a closed envelope procedure.

Applying this approach in the third and fourth rounds the Libyan National Oil Corporation achieved considerably greater financial commitments for exploration, together representing 69% of the total from all four rounds. In addition, it had realized that the size of areas in the first round were very large, and reduced the size of many of the areas before the announcement of the second round. Accordingly, the 126,639 km^2 total area offered in the first round was reduced to 101,672 km^2 in the second round, a reduction of around 25%, while the areas in the third and fourth rounds were reduced further, to 69,104 km^2 and 32,999 km^2 respectively.

It is interesting to note that most of the areas offered were previously 100% government-owned, through Sirte Oil Co and Arabian Gulf Co, and that the Sirte basins in particular offered extremely high potential.

Table 3: Summary of EPSA-IV rounds exploration and financial commitments

EPSA - IV	Total area km^2	Signature bonus (million US$)	2D seismic km	3D seismic km^2	Number of exploration wells	Total contract values (million US$)
Round – 1	126,639	132.9	24,500	2,850	24	298.7
Round – 2	101,672	103.383	27,850	7,600	32	430.5
Round – 3	69,104	88.1	41,100	10,000	35	951
Round – 4	32,999	148	13,100	8,600	33	611
Total	**330,414**	**472.383**	**106,550**	**29,050**	**124**	**2291.2**

Second party allocation: The bidding levels with respect to the second party allocation which were achieved during the first round were higher than those of the other rounds (see the tables below), which demonstrated that more international oil companies were willing to compete much more strongly in the second round, in for example the Murzuq basin. In the first round the lowest share offered was in the Sirte basin, block 24, with a second party allocation of 10.8%, whereas in the second round the lowest offered allocation was in the Murzuq basin, block 176, with 6.8%. On the other hand, the highest allocation in the first round was in the Cyrenaica basin, block 59, with a percentage of 38.9%, while in the second round it was in the offshore basin block 17, where the allocation was 28.5%.

Additionally, from the following tables it can be seen that, in the first round, the most attractive basins to bidders, those for which they were willing to offer the lowest second party allocations, were the Sirte, Murzuq, Ghadames, offshore and Cyrenaica basins in that order. However, in the second round, the Murzuq basin came first with the oil companies bidding at a very low second party allocation, followed by Ghadames, Sirte, offshore, Kufra and Cyrenaica. In the third round the Murzuq basin obtained the lowest value with 7.8% offered by Chinese Petroleum Corp in block 162, followed by the offshore basin with Gazprom bidding a value of 10% in block 19, followed by the Ghademes basin blocks 82 and 98 with offers of 10.4% for each by Tatneft Co. In the last round, which was meant for gas blocks and where all the participating companies were targeting gas, Gazprom offered 9.8% in block 64 in the Ghademes basin, followed by Polskie with 11.8% for block 113 in the Murzuq basin.

5.2 Comments on all EPSA-IV rounds

Many industry observers had noted that, prior to the announcement of the first EPSA-IV round, the political manoueverings underpinning the lifting of the US sanctions against Libya in 2004 would inevitably mean that the lion's share of new exploration and production contracts would somehow go to US companies. While this view may have seemed justified by the results of the first round – although, as is analysed above, this was due more to Occidental's intimate knowledge of the Sirte basin acquired during its pre-1986 operations in Libya – it is emphatically not the case if all the rounds are analysed together. The tables below, which show that companies from virtually every continent won areas, convincingly illustrate this point. This again underlies the transparency and competitiveness of the EPSA-IV bid process.

In the brief critical analysis of the defects of the bidding rounds, especially regarding financial commitments for exploration, securing which was after all one of the main objectives of the Libyan government in order to reverse the negative trends of almost 30 years in reserves and production, has shown that the bidding rounds can only be seen as a partial success from the Libyan standpoint. Undoubtedly this was one of the main reasons underlying the appointment of the petro-economist Dr Shukri Ghanem as the new head of the Libyan National Oil Corporation in March, 2006. The corporation hoped that, by fine-tuning the third round bidding process, and introducing a points system aimed at increasing financial commitments for exploration, crucial issues would be addressed, resulting in a much more rapid exploration of the Libyan basins, leading in turn to significant future increases in both production and reserves.

The following Tables 4–11, containing the list of winning bidders, reads like a summary of the world's leading oil companies, signifying the extremely high level of interest of global players in acquiring Libyan acreage. The interest of top US and Russian producers such as BP, ExxonMobil and Gazprom indicate their intentions to become key players in a Libyan context.

Regarding the eastern European companies, there were two new aspirants to the Libyan scene in INA Industrija Nafte, the former Croatian state oil company privatised in 2002, and Polskie Gornictwo Naftowe, a major vertically integrated Polish oil and gas group involved, among other things in the import, transmission, distribution and storage of natural gas, and the operation of the Polish domestic natural gas distribution system. Libya has, of course, previously had dealings with the national oil companies of countries such as Romania (Rompetrol) and Bulgaria (BOCO): it was Rompetrol's discovery in block NC-115 in the Murzuq basin in the mid-1980s which led to the eventual exploitation of the El-Sharara field by Repsol, who acquired this discovery from Rompetrol in 1993.

The presence of Far Eastern firms, including the Japanese Mitsubishi and Itochu Corporations and Japan Petroleum Exploration Co Ltd, as well as the Chinese Petroleum Corp and Sinopec, and Indonesia's PT Medco Energi International, again demonstrates their desire not to be left out of the latest offer of Libyan acreage, while Indian and Pakistani firms were also bidders.

From the point of view of the Libyan National Oil Corporation, the situation is extremely favourable, and the timing could not have been better. Underlying the high level of interest are of course two factors – the current high price of crude and a renewed affirmation by the international business community that Libya is undoubtedly perceived as a safe haven for investment. By ensuring that the list of prequalified bidders is geographically diverse, the Libyan policy makers are also emphasising that the days of Libya's historical reliance on a handful of US and

European oil companies are over – a painful lesson learned from the application of the US/UN sanctions against Libya from 1986 to 2004, which the country's leaders are unlikely to forget.

A comparison of the EPSA-IV terms with terms on offer elsewhere appears to highlight how tough the Libyan terms were in all four rounds compared with other countries, both regionally and in a global context. This has led many analysts to comment negatively about the Libyan EPSA-IV terms. However, healthy oil market conditions coupled with low production costs, the high prospectivity of the Libyan sedimentary basins and their proximity to European markets are all very positive factors which, combined, undoubtedly encourage international oil companies to invest in Libya.

Undoubtedly, should oil prices return to certain historical levels, like the 1999 levels when they were less than $10 per barrel, the position of oil companies under EPSA-IV would become alarming, especially in the frontier basins with limited infrastructure and more geological complexity. However, in such a situation, the EPSA-IV contractual terms could still be modified by the Libyan National Oil Corporation with regard to the A and B factors, to secure the companies a reasonable return for their investments.

Considering, however, the very high potential and massively under-explored status of the Libyan basins, as well as the locational advantages and low production costs, the commercial reality is that the four EPSA-IV bidding rounds have shown that the Libyan policy makers have achieved major successes in terms of foreign investment, exploration commitments and a new awareness of international production sharing contract conditions. More than this, they have unequivocally demonstrated that the international rehabilitation of Libya's image is virtually complete.

In terms of Libya's hydrocarbon resources, the lessons learned in these bidding rounds should mean that Libya is well on its way to increasing its proven reserves to a level much more in line with its true potential.

6. Conclusion

The traumatic events and civil disruptions in Libya in the months following February 2011 originally led to a severe dislocation of the oil and gas industry. However, as can be seen from the *OPEC Monthly Oil Market Report* for October 2012, the country has succeeded in bringing production up again, to over 1.5 million barrels per day – virtually the level it was at before the Libyan revolution started.

As stated in this chapter, the Libyan National Oil Corporation has since its inception managed and dominated the Libyan oil and gas sector. It appears that there will be little structural change in the sector in the immediate future, although, as stated earlier, the Libyan Ministry of Petroleum was revived in 2011. Existing concessions, joint ventures and exploration and production sharing contracts will continue to operate as originally agreed and signed.

There are certain issues that need to be addressed, however, before Libya can yet again meet its true potential as an oil and gas producer. The first is to ensure, through collaboration between the Ministry of Petroleum and the Libyan National Oil

Corporation, that the new draft Libyan Petroleum Law, which has been on ice for many years, is finally put on the statute book. The second is for the government to ensure that internal security and the rule of law are reinstated. This will encourage future investment and ensure that new investors and key service contractors such as Schlumberger and Halliburton can safely return.

Table 4: EPSA-IV, first round: bidders and winners

Number	Basin	Area	Number of blocks	Areas (km²)	Number of bids submitted	Winners (IOCs)
1	Sirte	106	4	6,520	15	Occidental (90%), Liwa (10%)
2	Sirte	123	3	6,113	4	Occidental (90%), Liwa (10%)
3	Murzuq	131	4	10,381	10	Occidental (90%), Liwa (10%)
4	Murzuq	163	4	11,236	9	Occidental (90%), Liwa (10%)
5	Cyreneica	59	2	5,298	1	Occidental (90%), Liwa (10%)
6	Offshore	35	4	9,070	3	Woodside (55%), Occidental (35%), Liwa (10%)
7	Offshore	36	4	10,414	8	Woodside (55%), Occidental (35%), Liwa (10%)
8	Offshore	52	4	6,182	6	Woodside (55%), Occidental (35%), Liwa (10%)
9	Offshore	53	4	8,047	8	Woodside (55%), Occidental (35%), Liwa (10%)
10	Murzuq	177	4	11,317	6	ChevronTexaco (100%)
11	Offshore	54	4	9,769	15	Amerada Hess (100%)
12	Sirte	86	4	7,078	5	Oil India (50%), Indian Oil (50%)
13	Ghadames	47	4	10,531	9	Verenex (50%), Medco Energi (50%)
14	Ghadames	65	2	4,374	4	Sonatrach (100%)
15	Offshore	18	4	10,307	2	Petrobras (70%), Oil Search (30%)
Total				126,639	105	

Table 5: EPSA-IV first round: financial and exploration commitments by company and area

Number	Winners (IOCs)	Area	Financial commitment (million US$)			Exploration commitment		
			Signature bonus	Company share %	Contract value	2D seismic (km)	3D seismic (km^2)	Number of wells
1	Occidental & Liwa	106	25.6	14.6	32	1,000	750	3
2	Occidental & Liwa	124	15.3	10.8	25.8	600	400	3
3	Occidental & Liwa	131	25.6	13.3	16	1,200	0	2
4	Occidental & Liwa	163	15.3	15.9	20	3,000	0	1
5	Occidental & Liwa	59	1.1	38.9	15	1,200	0	1
6	Woodside, Occidental & Liwa	35	5.2	20.4	18	2,000	0	1
7	Woodside, Occidental & Liwa	36	16.1	17.4	21.5	1,500	500	1
8	Woodside, Occidental & Liwa	52	10.5	17.9	18	1,000	500	1
9	Woodside, Occidental & Liwa	53	8.1	19.8	19	2,000	0	1
10	ChevronTexaco	177	0.6	22.8	20	3,000	0	1
11	Amerada Hess	54	6.2	12.4	23	3,000	0	1
12	Oil India & Indian Oil	86	0	18.4	17	1,000	0	2
13	Verenex & Medco Energi	47	0.3	13.7	19.4	1,000	200	3
14	Sonatrach	65	2.0	25	13	1,000	0	2
15	Petrobras (70%), Oil Search (30%)	18	1.0	31.8	21	2,000	500	1
Total		**15**	**132.9**		**298.7**	**24,500**	**2,850**	**24**

Table 6: EPSA-IV, second round: bidders and winners

Number	Basin	Area	Number of blocks	Areas (km^2)	Number of bids submitted	Winners (IOCs)
1	Offshore	2	1, 2	4,650	10	Nippon / Mitsubishi
2	Offshore	17	3	2,010	6	PT Pertamina
3	Offshore	17	4	2,535	1	CNPC
4	Offshore	40	3, 4	4,540	10	Japex/Nippon/Mitsubishi
5	Offshore	44	1, 2, 3, 4	10,290	1	Exxon Mobil
6	Cyreneica	42	1, 3	4,564	–	–
7	Cyreneica	42	2, 4	3,352	1	Total/Inpex
8	Cyreneica	94	1, 2, 3, 4	10,001	1	Statoil
9	Ghadames	81	1	1,900	1	Ongc Videsh
10	Ghadames	81	2	2,650	8	Teikoku/Mitsubishi
11	Ghadames	82	3	2,500	6	Teikoku/Mitsubishi
12	Ghadames	82	4	2,306	4	Tatneft
13	Sirte	102	3	2,750	–	–
14	Sirte	102	4	2,750	4	Oil India/Indian Oil
15	Sirte	121	2	1,830	–	–
16	Sirte	123	1	2,750	1	British Gas
17	Sirte	123	2	2,000	2	British Gas
18	Sirte	123	3	2,030	8	PT Pertamina
19	Murzuq	146	1	2,444	8	Hydro
20	Murzuq	147	3, 4	2,270	4	Turkish Petroleum
21	Murzuq	161	1	2,750	2	ENI North Africa
22	Murzuq	161	2, 4	3,900	6	ENI North Africa
23	Murzuq	176	3	2,750	5	ENI North Africa
24	Murzuq	176	4	2,750	5	Japex
25	Kufra	171	1, 2, 3, 4	11,000	1	Statoil/BritshGas
26	Kufra	186	1, 2, 3, 4	8,400	2	ENI North Africa
Total		**26**	**44**	**101,672**	**97**	

Table 7:EPSA-IV second round: financial and exploration commitments by company and area

Number	Winners (IOCs)	Area	Number of Blocks	Financial commitment (million US$)			Exploration commitment		
				Signature bonus	Company share %	Contract value	2D seismic (km)	3D seismic (km^2)	Number of wells
1	Nippon / Mitsubishi	2	1, 2	2.500	8.0	21	1,000	1,000	1
2	PT Pertamina	17	3	8.009	11.7	30	0	1,000	2
3	CNPC	17	4	6.080	28.5	18	1,000	500	2
4	Japex/Nippon/Mitsubishi	40	3, 4	1.700	8.0	32	1,000	500	2
5	Exxon Mobil	44	1, 2, 3, 4	1.500	28.3	22	1,000	1,000	1
6	–	42	1, 3	–	–	–	–	–	–
7	Total/Inpex	42	2, 4	1.801	27.8	21.5	2,500	0	1
8	Statoil	94	1, 2, 3, 4	2.950	24.9	24	3,000	0	1
9	Ongc Videsh	81	1	6.00	11.8	12.5	500	500	1
10	Teikoku/Mitsubishi	81	2	6.00	7.5	12.5	500	500	1
11	Teikoku/Mitsubishi	82	3	6.00	7.5	10	1,200	0	1
12	Tatneft	82	4	6.00	10.5	16.5	500	500	1
13	–	102	3	–	–	–	–	–	–
14	Oil India/Indian Oil	102	4	3.001	10.5	17	1,000	500	1
15	–	121	2	–	–	–	–	–	–
16	British Gas	123	1	7.501	10.9	15.5	700	500	1
17	British Gas	123	2	7.501	14.2	14.5	500	500	1
18	PT Pertamina	123	3	7.009	8.8	19.1	700	300	2
19	Hydro	146	1	7.068	7.0	13.8	750	0	2
20	Turkish Petroleum	147	3, 4	7.262	9.7	16.1	500	300	2
21	ENI North Africa	161	1	3.100	8.5	12.5	1,500	0	1
22	ENI North Africa	161	2, 4	4.000	7.8	20	2,000	0	2
23	ENI North Africa	176	3	3.300	9.8	15	2,000	0	1
24	Japex	176	4	3.000	6.8	15	2,000	0	1
25	Statoil/BritshGas	171	1, 2, 3, 4	1.001	19.8	26	2,000	0	2
26	ENI North Africa	186	1, 2, 3, 4	1.100	15.4	26	2,000	0	2
Total		26	44	103,383		430.5	27,850	7,600	32

Table 8: EPSA-IV, third round: bidders and winners

Number	Basin	Area	Number of blocks	Areas (km²)	Number of bids submitted	Winners (IOCs)
1	Offshore	19	1,2,3,4	10,288	2	Gazprom (100%)
2	Offshore	20	1,2,3,4	10,294	1	ExxonMobil (100%)
3	Offshore	43	1,2,3,4	7,449	1	ONGC (100%)
4	Sirte	69	1,2,3,4	8,114	2	Tatneft (100%)
5	Ghadames	82	1	2,704	8	Tatneft (100%)
6	Ghadames	98	2,4	5,218	2	Tatneft (100%)
7	Murzuq	113	3,4	4,272	1	Inpex (85%) / Mitsui (15%)
8	Sirte	137	3,4	5,440	2	Petro-Canada (50%)/ Repsol-YPF (50%)
9	Murzuq	162	1,2	3,757	7	Chinese Petroleum Corp (100%)
10	Kufra	201	1,2,3,4	11,566	4	Wintershall (65%) / Mitsui (35%)
Total		**10**		**69,104**	**30**	

Table 9: EPSA-IV third round: financial and exploration commitments by company and area

Number	Winners (IOCs)	Area	Number of Blocks	Financial commitment (million US$)			Exploration commitment		
				Signature bonus	Company share %	Contract value	2D seismic (km)	3D seismic (km²)	Number of wells
1	Gazprom	19	1, 2, 3, 4	10.1	10	182	4,000	2,000	6
2	ExxonMobil	20	1, 2, 3, 4	10	22.3	288	20,000	1,000	4
3	ONGC	43	1, 2, 3, 4	10	28	61	1,000	4,000	1
4	Tatneft	69	1, 2, 3, 4	10	12	113	5,000	750	6
5	Tatneft	82	1	10	10.4	75	2,000	750	5
6	Tatneft	98	2, 4	10	10.4	75	2,500	500	5
7	Inpex / Mitsui	113	3, 4	10	12.9	38	1,000	500	3
8	Petro-Canada / Repsol-YPF	137	3, 4	10	18	28	1,000	500	1
9	Chinese Petroleum Corp	162	1, 2	5	7.8	34	1,600	0.00	3
10	Wintershall / Mitsui	201	1, 2, 3, 4	3	13.5	57	3,000	–	1
Total		**10**		**88.1**		**951**	**41,100**	**10,000**	**35**

Table 10: EPSA-IV, fourth round: bidders and winners

Number	Basin	Area	Number of Blocks	Areas (km²)	Winners (IOCs)
1	Cyreneica	58	1, 2, 3, 4	10,289	RWE
2	Ghadames	64	1, 2, 3	3,936	Gazprom
3	Sirte	89	1, 3	1,740	Shell
4	Ghadames	95	1, 2	6,629	Sonatrach / Oil India / Indian Oil
5	Ghadames	96	2, 4		
6	Sirte	103	1, 2, 3, 4	4,911	Occidental & Liwa
7	Murzuq	113	1, 2	5,494	Polskie
Total		7		**32,999**	

Table 11: EPSA-IV fourth round: financial and exploration commitments by company and area

Number	Winners (IOCs)	Area	Number of Blocks	Financial commitment (million US$)			Exploration commitment		
				Signature bonus	Company share %	Contract value	2D seismic (km)	3D seismic (km²)	Number of wells
1	RWE	58		5	30	76	4,600	0	2
2	Gazprom	64		10	9.8	110	1,500	1,750	6
3	Shell	89		103	15	95	0	1,750	6
4	Sonatrach / Oil India / Indian Oil	95		10	13	152	2,000	2,600	8
5		96							
6	Occidental & Liwa	103		10	18	70	2,000	1,000	3
7	Polskie	113		10	11.8	108	3,000	1,500	8
Total		7		**148**		**611**	**13,100**	**8,600**	**33**

Mozambique

Jose de Barros
National Petroleum Institute

1. Introduction

During the Third Mozambican Mining and Energy Conference, the minister of mineral resources of Mozambique stated that:

> *Mozambique is a nation with great economic development potential, for many reasons including the growing market and good business environment. There is a steady increasing interest for both domestic and foreign companies in investing in the petroleum and mining sector. The sector contributes approximately 5% of the GDP, but the minister responsible for the sector believes that this will increase ...*

Despite this positive outlook, the country remains poor, with *per capita* income below the average levels for the sub-Saharan region and other low income countries; social indicators are low, infrastructure is inadequate and the business environment remains challenging.

In response to increasing interest in the country's natural resource potential, the government is developing strategies on the best use of petroleum resources in order to promote inclusive and sustainable development of the economy, and to ensure that production is developed in such a way as to secure revenue collection and be for the long-term benefit of all Mozambicans.

Looking at the Rovuma Basin discoveries, it is a fact that the country cannot consume internally the volumes discovered. Export may be an alternative use of the available resources.

For this purpose the government is undertaking studies in several legal, economic and social fields in order to prepare the country and the national economy for the future. The government is seeking to implement its policy through the continued evolution of its petroleum administration capabilities, the petroleum regulatory framework and the decisions for its implementation. The drivers for this approach have their roots in five main policy approaches which are aimed at making the country a business destination and investor-friendly:

- optimising recovery of all offshore petroleum resources;
- maximising the evaluation of petroleum potential in sedimentary basins and consequently exploration and production activities (in order to increase government revenue);
- securing for the state a substantial portion of the income from petroleum operations;[1]
- allowing for increased national industrial development based on the use of the country's petroleum resources, creating improved business conditions for

local industry, with the aim of at creating jobs for nationals, training the national workforce and transferring technology;

- establishing of an efficient and accountable petroleum regulatory and administrative regime, together with a predictable and secure legal framework for investments, particularly with regard to taxation and legal certainty, to encourage investment and reduce the cost to the state by limiting its actions to setting policy and strategy and leaving room for innovation by the private sector; and
- ensuring that production projects actually happen and that they operate in a way that will secure revenue for the long-term benefit of all Mozambicans.

2. Upstream activities

Upstream petroleum activities in Mozambique first took place back as far as the early 20th century, between 1927 and 1937, when seven unsuccessful wells were drilled in the Mozambique Basin. During the 1960s several contracts were signed with international oil companies such as Hunt International Petroleum, Mozambique Gulf Oil, Aquitane, and Sunray Mozambique Oil Co. None of these activities resulted in commercial production at the time. However, these activities paved the way for the first relevant discoveries of natural gas in the 1960s in the Buzi block, Pande and Temane field, onshore in the Mozambique Basin.

Significant exploration activities have been carried out since independence in 1975. Initially activities were conducted under the Petroleum Activities Law of 1981 (Law 3/1981, of October 3 1981), which established an institutional framework consisting of the National Oil Company and the State Secretariat of Coal and Hydrocarbons, a state organ integrated into the Ministry of Mines. This law has now been replaced by the Petroleum Law of 2001 (Law 3/2001, of February 21 2001).

Several agreements, including production sharing agreements and technical evaluation agreements were signed early on under the 1981 Petroleum Activities Law and substantial amounts of data were acquired and available to commercial companies. In 1983 the first licence round open to the international oil community was launched, and four out of 17 blocks awarded. From then on a lot of exploration activities took place until the launch of the second open bidding round in 2005. There was, however, a limited bidding round in 2000 which resulted in the award of the Zambeze Delta offshore block to Petronas Carigali Mozambique Exploration. None of the blocks offered in the limited 2000 round resulted in any commercial discoveries. After the 2000 and 2005 rounds a number of new model exploration and production concession contracts[2] were awarded through direct negotiations on the

1 This term is used in accordance with the definition it is given by the 2001 Mozambican Petroleum Law, meaning all or any of the activities related to exploration, development, production, separation and treatment, storage, transportation and sale or delivery of petroleum to the point of export, or to the agreed supply point in the Republic of Mozambique, and includes natural gas processing operations and the closure of all concluded activities.

2 The concession contracts differ from traditional production sharing agreements in that concession contracts are not governed by contract law, but by specific laws of a public administrative law nature. While production sharing agreements in principle are commercial agreements and for this reason in theory may be concluded subject to foreign law, a Mozambican concession contract is only concluded subject to Mozambican law.

basis of the new 2001 Petroleum Law. These directly negotiated exploration and production concession contracts formed the model on which the 2005 bid round and later bid round negotiations were conducted.

In 2005, Mozambique launched what can be considered the most successful bidding round, for Rovuma Basin acreage. This basin, which had previously constituted one block was divided into seven new exploration and production concession contract areas, one area being onshore and six offshore. Subsequently, in 2007 and 2009, the government offered a few additional offshore areas and also some onshore areas, in the third and fourth bidding rounds, but these resulted only in the award of one area during the third bidding round and no area during the fourth bidding round.

According to the policy in place at present, the government will continue to open areas for petroleum operations every two to three years, independently of the market or industry interest for areas. This approach may have influenced the low level of interest in the last two bidding rounds. According to an announcement in 2012, the government is currently preparing for a fifth bidding round for offshore areas in the Rovuma and Mozambique Basins.

The industry has made concerned noises regarding the reasons for announcing a new bidding round at this time. The question is whether the time is right after two unsuccessful rounds (the third and fourth), and whether the fixed timing approach should continue to be the guiding criterion for announcement of new acreage, or whether other criteria, such as industry demand, would keep exploration activities at a more desirable and relatively constant level. The responses to these and other questions will be crucial for making future bid rounds more attractive and competitive, thereby leading to a consistent level of activities and to the government obtaining more beneficial terms and conditions for those concession contracts awarded.

3. Petroleum legal regime

The legal framework for the upstream petroleum sector in Mozambique is founded on the Constitution and a set of laws, regulations and ministerial documents, called *Diploma Ministerial and Despachos* in Portuguese, including certain model documents such as the Model Exploration and Production Concession Contract and the associated standard joint operating agreement, accounting and financial procedures, the bank guarantee and parent company guarantee approved by the Council of Ministers.

The Constitution establishes the principle of ownership of resources, which means that all the resources located in the soil and the subsoil of the land territory, in the seabed of Mozambique internal waters and the territorial sea, in the exclusive economic zone and on the continental shelf, are the property of the Republic of Mozambique.

Furthermore, it establishes that natural resources constitute state public domain, and that the concept encompasses energy and hydraulic potential, mineral deposits, nature protection zones, archaeological assets, air space, the maritime zone, roads and railways and other areas as defined by law. In order to allow the exploration for and exploitation of petroleum, the state grant rights to private or public entities through concession contracts.

In terms of protection of investments, the Constitution recognises the right of property ownership, and any expropriation is subject to the condition that fair compensation be made. Despite this recognition stated in the Constitution, its legal implementation is still vague since the relevant legislation that should define in which cases expropriation should, or may, take place is yet to be approved.

The specific petroleum sector legislation currently in force comprises the following legal instruments:

- the Constitution of the Republic of Mozambique (1990);
- Law 3 of February 21 2001 (Petroleum Law);
- Decree 24 of August 20 2004 (Regulation of Petroleum Operations Decree);
- Model Exploration and Production Concession Contract;
- Resolution 279 of June 8 2009 approving the licensing strategy for petroleum operations; and
- Ministerial Diploma 271 of December 30 2009 approving the Regulation for Licensing of Petroleum Installations and Activities.

The relevant tax legislation consists of:

- Law 12 of June 27 2007 amending the tax laws, especially those relating to oil activity;
- Law 13 of June 27 2007 setting out tax incentives for mining and petroleum operations;
- Law 32 of December 31 2007, the Value Added Tax Code;
- Law 34 of December 31 2007, the Corporate Income Tax Code; and
- Decree 4 of April 9 2008 approving the Regulation on Tax on Oil Production, provided for under Law 12/2007.

The structure of the legal framework is illustrated in the pyramid shown below. An important premise in this regard is that the government has sought to work vertically through the entire regulatory chain from the Petroleum Law down to the new model documents (exploration and production concession contracts and pipeline concession contracts). The effect of this has been that core concepts and terminology are utilised throughout the chain of documents and in the provisions they contain. This should ensure better consistency between the general rules enacted and the specific rights and obligations designated in the model documents, and in other administrative decisions or agreements the government may approve for the management of petroleum operations.

The law, regulations and model documents have a hierarchal structure, and are functional rather than geographical in their regulatory approach. This structure has substantially reduced the administrative burden on the government institutions tasked with granting rights and monitoring oil and gas companies' conduct. A substantial amount of duplication in the various rules applicable to petroleum activities has been rooted out, allowing the National Petroleum Institute (INP) and other institutions to respond more quickly to industry applications and requests for permits, approvals and consents. Reducing the regulatory complexity and improving transparency has greatly reduced the response time of the administration, allowing

Fig. 1 – Petroleum Legal Regime – Petroleum Legislation Hierarchy

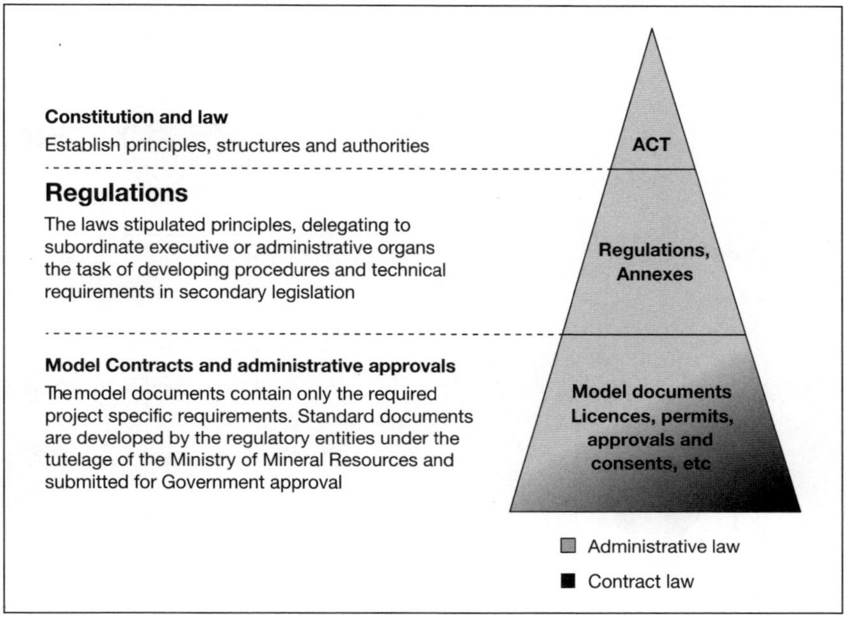

improved efficiency and enabling the administrators to focus more of their attention on core resource management issues rather than being tied up in efforts to find solutions to administrative issues.

2.1. Petroleum law and relevant provisions

(a) Regulatory bodies

At the turn of the century Mozambique introduced profound structural, economic and institutional reforms that resulted in a drastic reduction of the state's active role in the petroleum sector as an operator and owner of assets. With increased participation from private sector and semi-public entities in the economy, the government set up a new system resulting in an economy that could be adjusted to the market-oriented principles of the 1990 Constitution.

The impacts of these reforms started to be evident in the petroleum sector back in 1994, with the creation of the National Directorate for Coal and Hydrocarbons (DNCH), an entity subordinated to the Ministry of Mineral Resources and Energy (MIREME). Under the supervision of MIREME, DNCH was the entity responsible for regulatory functions relating to the regulation, promotion, negotiation and monitoring of upstream operations. While these reforms took place, until the approval of the Petroleum Law in 2001 the national oil company Empresa Nacional de Hidrocarbonetos (ENH) remained the sole holder of rights to undertake petroleum operations as a commercial entity.

Fig. 2 – Institutional framework prior to the approval of Law 3 of February 21 2001

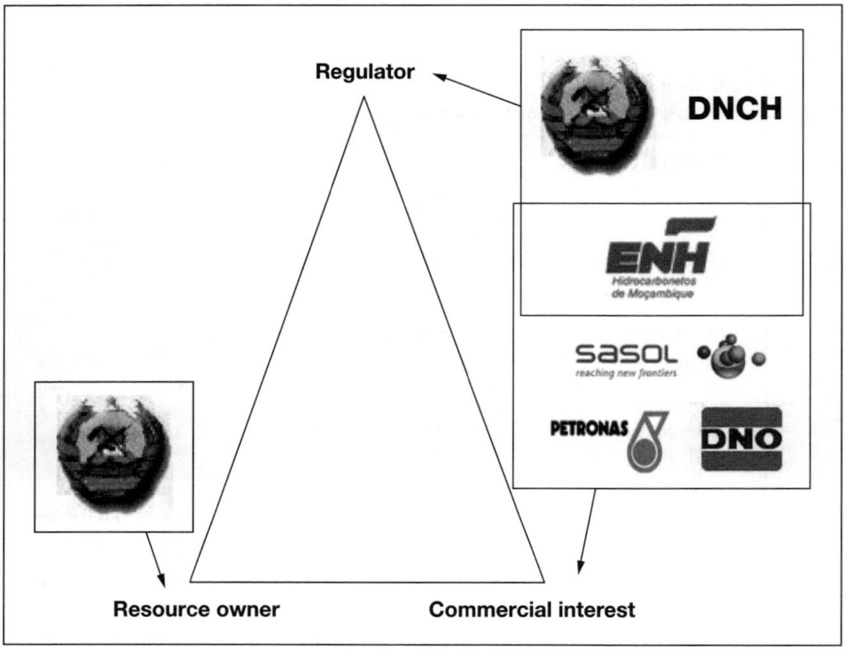

The new Petroleum Law approved by the Parliament in 2001, complemented by the Petroleum Operations Regulation approved by the Council of Ministers in 2004, represented an important step in the development of the petroleum regulatory framework. The government put in place the basic requirements necessary to implement a new petroleum policy, including the creation of the first elements of a regulatory system which enabled consistency, transparency and predictability, all of which are essential elements for the development of the petroleum sector.

At the institutional level, the new framework made the rights and obligations of administrative organs such as the INP and the commercial companies much clearer. It also had the effect of clarifying the roles and tasks allocated between government institutions and government-owned companies. Further, the legislation addressed requirements placed on national and international investors.

The new administrative structure emerged from the clarification of roles and tasks laid down by law and the nature of the roles allocated to public authority organs, on the one hand, and to companies, whether owned by the state or entirely financed through private equity, on the other. The amendment to the administrative structure enabled INP to focus on regulatory matters, and ENH as the Mozambican state oil company to function better as a commercial company.

Fig. 3 – Institutional framework after the approval of Law 3 of February 21 2001

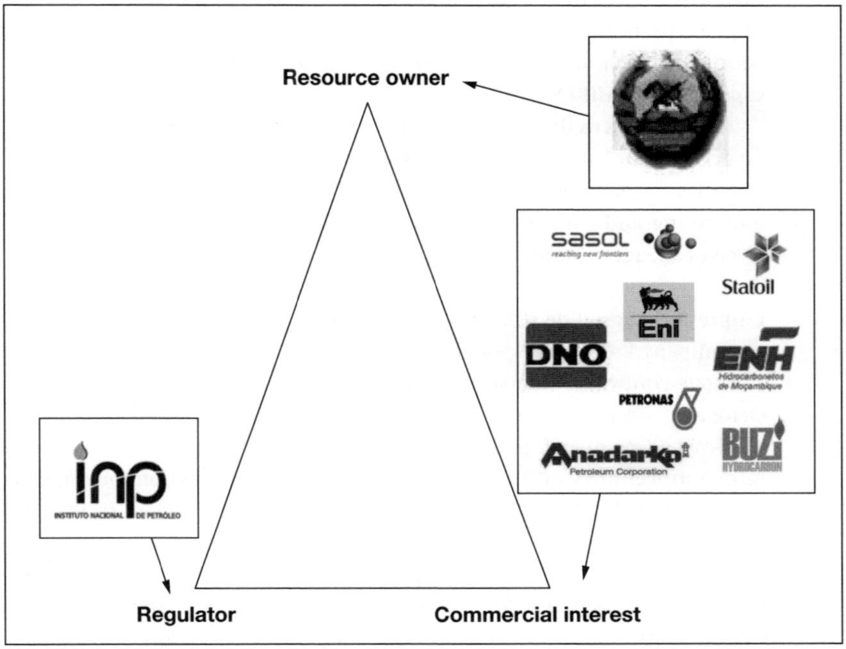

This approach to the system of governance, with a clear separation of roles and responsibilities between legal entities looking after the various interests of the state, enabled more transparency with regard to the decisions taken, assisted in rendering administrative processes more predictable, and provided increased stability to the legal and administrative process.

Parliament: In this structure, the parliament, through laws and decree-laws, authorises the government to legislate, thereby establishing the legal foundation and principles for conducting petroleum operations.

Government: The government, the Council of Ministers, has the authority to ensure the implementation of its petroleum operations policy, to approve secondary level regulations, and to formulate proposals for necessary legislative developments or amendments. In executing the petroleum operations policy some ministries have specific roles over petroleum operations, such as the Ministry of Finance (through the Tax Authority and Customs and Excise), the Ministry of Agriculture, the Ministry of Fisheries and the Ministry for the Environment.

Ministry of Mineral Resources and the National Petroleum Institute: The Ministry of Mineral Resources (MIREM), created in 2004 as a result of division of the Ministry of Mineral Resources and Energy into two ministries, namely the Ministry of Energy and the Ministry of Mineral Resources, is in charge of the upstream sector, and together with the National Petroleum Institute (INP)[3] it is the part of the executive branch of government tasked with policy development and implementation, and the public sector coordination required for upstream petroleum operations. The national oil company, ENH and its affiliates, are under the supervision of MIREM.

The INP acts as the upstream regulator and renders assistance related to technical aspects of petroleum operations to the minister, particularly as regards promotion of activities, regulation and negotiation of concession and other contracts, and monitoring and control of petroleum operations, including ensuring that MIREM receives adequate information.

Empresa Nacional de Hidrocarbonetos, Empresa Publica (ENH, EP): The national oil company Empresa Nacional de Hidrocarbonetos, Empresa Estatal was established as a state-controlled company by the Law Regulating Petroleum Activities (Law 3 of October 3 1981). By this law, the parliament created a national oil company as a state-owned company, granting rights over national basins and allowing ENH to form joint ventures with foreign companies for the exploration for and exploitation of petroleum. The law granted ENH a monopoly over petroleum sector activities.

This law recognised the rights of foreign companies to recover their investments in the event of a commercial discovery. Associations between ENH and foreign investors could be in the form of shareholding companies, joint venture production sharing contracts or service contracts. Following its creation, ENH signed several production sharing contracts with international oil companies. The other formats of cooperation were not employed, although reasons for this were never stated. Some technical evaluation agreements were also signed with oil and seismic companies for the evaluation of non-mature areas.

In 1997, as a result of structural reforms and the introduction of the market economy model in the 1990 Constitution adopted at the end of the civil war, ENH was transformed from state company into a public company, but with 100% of its shares held by the state. From this point, ENH assumed only a commercial role and the National Directorate of Coal and Hydrocarbons (DNCH), an entity integrated into the MIREM, assumed all the regulatory functions over the upstream petroleum sector that it had previously shared with ENH.

With the Petroleum Law of 2001, ENH ceased formally to have a monopoly on petroleum exploration and production and lost all its regulatory responsibilities, including licensing. Unlicensed acreage was returned to the state, and INP assumed the function of upstream regulator. Currently ENH plays a role in the upstream sector managing the state's commercial interests in upstream concession contracts, and in the downstream sector through holding participation interests in pipeline projects and the natural gas distribution network. In order to diversify its business units, ENH created three main affiliates that also play a role in the gas sector, namely:

3 The acronym INP is taken from the Portuguese Instituto Nacional de Petroleo and is used both in Portuguese and English. The INP was created in 2004, by decree of the Council of Ministers (the government of Mozambique),as an entity responsible for the supervision of petroleum operations, replacing the National Directorate for Coal and Hydrocarbons.

- Companhia Moçambicana de Hidrocarbonetos SA (CMH) – a shareholding company owned by ENH and private entities, responsible for the upstream venture in the Pande and Temane project. Presently, it holds a state participation of 25%, and the remaining 5% state participation has been allocated to International Finance Corporation to guarantee the financing it has raised to fund CMH's participation. The remaining 70% of the project is held by commercial entities.
- Companhia Moçambicana de Gasoduto SA – a shareholding company held 100% by the state. This company is responsible for managing the state participation of 25% in the Pande/Temane to Secunda (South Africa) pipeline venture.
- ENH Logistics SA – recently incorporated and registered under Mozambique laws, this company is responsible for logistic services that focus on the Rovuma Basin projects. Through joint ventures with any interested entities, ENH Logistics will, subject to the procurement rules relating to concession contracts, handle all potential services to concessionaires developing projects in the country.

(b) ***Types of agreement***

Petroleum operations since the enactment of the 2001 Petroleum Law are conducted on the basis of concession contracts. Currently, petroleum operations in Mozambique may only be conducted under one of the following types of concession:

- A reconnaissance concession contract allowing the holder the right to conduct preliminary work and assessment operations in the area subject to the concession contract. Such a contract gives an exclusive right for a maximum period of two years, and permits the drilling of wells to a depth of 100m below the surface or the bottom of the sea.
- An exploration and production concession contract[4] granting an exclusive right to conduct petroleum exploration and production activities and the non-exclusive right to operate petroleum pipelines.
- A petroleum pipeline concession contract granting the right to construct and operate an oil pipeline or a gas pipeline for the purpose of transporting crude oil or natural gas for up to 30 years in cases not already covered by an exploration and production concession contract. When it is part of an

4 The exploration and production concession contract is an administrative law based contract between the government and one or more commercial companies. The companies become concessionaires not contractors. If more than one concessionaire participates in an exploration and production concession contract, they will be required to establish an unincorporated joint venture governed by a standard joint operating agreement, and to appoint an operator to conduct the day-to-day petroleum operations and represent them as the primary contact with the government. An exploration and production concession contract is given for an initial period up to a maximum eight years, the exploration period, with a work programme that has to be performed, relinquishment provisions and guarantees to secure execution of the minimum work programme, normally a bank guarantee. If there is a discovery, the concessionaire has the right to submit a development plan for construction of facilities and production of petroleum for a period up to 30 years. Exploration and production concession contracts are awarded through competitive bid rounds launched at two to three year intervals. Exclusive exploration and production rights are granted within a geographical area delineated by coordinates stipulated in degrees and minutes as stipulated in the exploration and production concession contract.

exploration and production concession contract, the right to operate the pipeline will most likely last for the time stipulated in the development plan, or another duration, but will not exceed 30 years.

(c) *Acquisition of acreage*

By systematically implementing its policy goals through legislation the government has ensured that the criteria for the award of rights from the government to Mozambican and foreign investors alike are open and transparent.

The 2001 Petroleum Law constitutes the primary source for the licensing policy and the basic principles of the system regulating the process of granting rights for petroleum operations. The Petroleum Law, relevant regulations, in particular the 2004 Regulations for Petroleum Operations, and specific decisions and policies provide the legal basis for the granting of such rights.

According to the Petroleum Law, exploration and production rights and associated rights relating to petroleum operations are normally granted through a concession contract resulting from a bidding round. So far four bid rounds have been completed. Despite this, simultaneous or direct negotiations may take place in the cases stipulated in the Regulation for Petroleum Operations. For these purposes the regulation's provisions stipulate that acreage that was available through a prior public tender but was not awarded and acreage available as a result of termination, relinquishment, cancellation or surrender may be awarded through direct or simultaneous negotiations.

The government has, however, the prerogative to include in the package of acreage to be announced and offered in a bid round, both acreage that has been relinquished from a previously awarded concession contract area and acreage that has not been awarded during any previous bid round.

Acreage to be awarded is divided into blocks of 30 minutes of latitude and 30 minutes of longitude, unless the acreage borders on other nation states or if other circumstances so warran, as illustrated in the map reproduced below. The rights granted include the right of use and enjoyment of land and maritime areas in the awarded area for petroleum operations purposes.

Lawful occupiers or third parties holding rights to use and enjoy land included in the awarded concession contract areas keep such rights unless this interferes substantially with petroleum operations. In cases of conflicting rights the ministers with authority over such rights will decide on which right shall prevail, in accordance with the national interest. The law is not clear as to what is understood by the term 'national interest', but the discretionary powers that may be exercised by ministers in this regard are subject to legal constraint under applicable material law and the principles of public administrative law.

Fig. 4 – Map of concessions areas awarded.

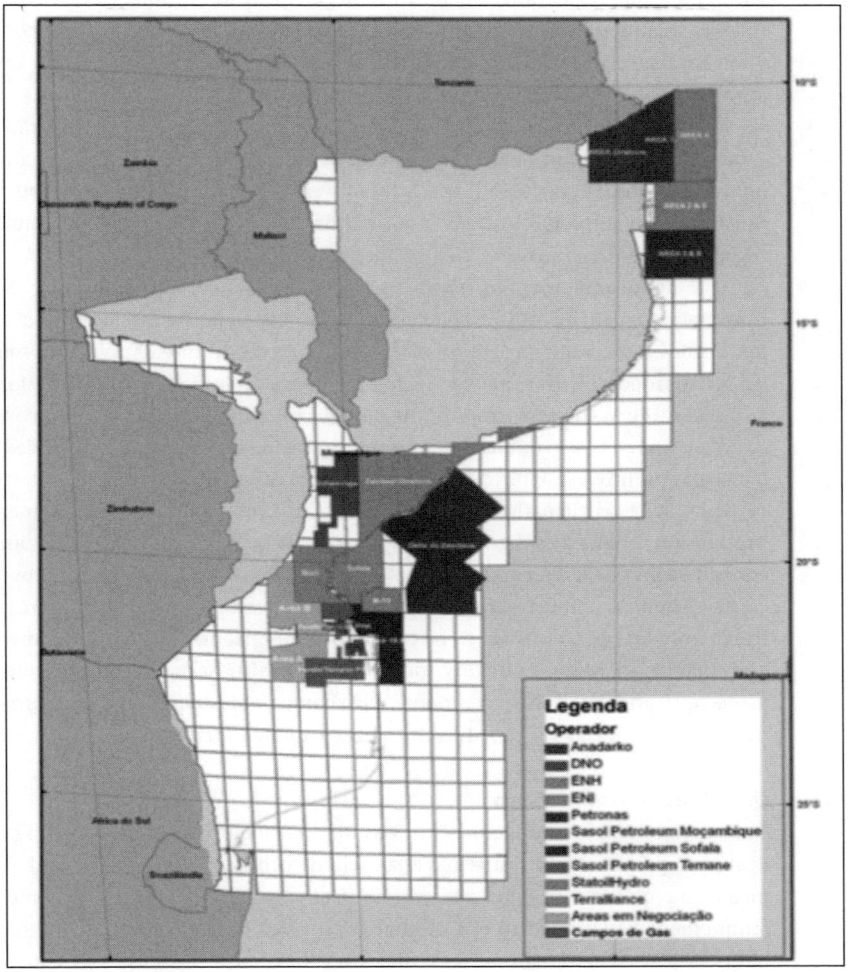

Source: INP website

Bidding round process: When a bidding round is to take place, the government, through the National Petroleum Institute (INP), initiates the process by identifying areas for which the authorities have relevant knowledge with regard to geology and the prospects for the presence of petroleum. The acreage is selected in such a way as to allow for the setting of optimum terms and the stipulation of relevant obligatory work programme commitments. INP has data available for this purpose. INP may also enter into arrangements with companies to obtain data through speculative seismic or other surveys to be licensed to interested oil companies.

When the areas have been evaluated or geological information is available, INP prepares the data packages and announces the bid invitation, publishing the terms and conditions for the blocks on offer. Application documents are in the public domain. Applications must be consistent with the requirements of the Petroleum Law, applicable regulations, such as the Regulations for Petroleum Operations, and model documents such as the model exploration and production concession contract and its standard associated documents, such as the joint operating agreement and the accounting and financial procedures.

Single companies or groups of companies may apply for an exploration and production concession contract consisting of one or more blocks. A list of companies applying is posted on the INP and MIREM websites at the closing date, and the bids must remain valid for at least six months after that date, to allow their evaluation by the government commission created for that purpose.

The applicants are requested to provide detailed corporate and financial information, plans of work to be conducted to evaluate the acreage and a proposal for a minimum work programme and related expenditure. Applicants must also submit a proposal with respect to negotiable items identified by the invitation to bid and according to the provisions of the model exploration and production concession contract, which is also published. Among negotiable items normally included are the participation interest applied for (particularly in cases with more than one applicant or when state participation has been indicated), production bonus payments, the production sharing split percentages, cost recovery ceiling, other financial contributions such as payments for the training of government employees and capacity building, and financial support for communities surrounding areas where the petroleum operations are to be carried out. Applicants must also disclose records and details of their company policies on health, safety and environmental protection, and detail their experience with comparable operational environments to those likely to be encountered in the acreage applied for.

(d) Qualification requirements

The government is concerned to ensure that companies participating in the upstream petroleum industry have sufficient technical competence and financial means to conduct petroleum operations effectively – this is a legal requirement. This requirement is designed to ensure that companies can at least fulfil the stipulated obligatory work programme and that they have the capacity and capability to

---

5 All bids are required to be accompanied by the following information relating to the bidder(s):

- legal identity;
- technical capacity, competence and experience in petroleum operations and related activities, and in particular experience in the environment where the operations will take place;
- available markets for the disposal of petroleum;
- economic and financial structure and backing;
- such other details as the bidder considers relevant.

A bidder can provide a technical and commercial evaluation of the blocks for which it is bidding, which shows how the bidder interprets the petroleum potential and economic potential of the area and which demonstrates the technical competence of the bidder.

Bidders can bid for one or more blocks. If a bidder is bidding for more than one block, it is required to indicate an order of preference in its bid.

A bidder can bid on its own or jointly with other bidders. If a joint bid is made, the bid is required to indicate which of the bidders constituting the applicant will act as operator.

In respect of the blocks for which it has bid, a bidder is required to indicate its proposal for work and expenditure obligations to be assumed by the concessionaire, and its proposal for profit sharing between the government and the concessionaire.

develop and produce petroleum in the event of a discovery.[5]

With these requirements in place, Mozambique expects to attract the best international oil companies, whether large multinationals or small and medium sized companies, provided they possess the necessary experience and expertise in the region or the environment where work will have to be performed.

Fig. 5 – Model of second bidding round evaluation criteria table.

			A	B	C	D
Appendix A	**Applicant Details and Financial Information**	5				
	Total Assets					
	Total Investment in E&P Exploration					
	Total turnover of Group					
	Net income after tax					
	Production of Oil and Gas					
	Refinery Capacity					
	Sales of Petroleum					
	Technical Expertise	10				
	Number of E&P wells drilled					
	Technology					
	Number of discoveries					
	Sub- Total	15				
Appendix B / C	**TECHNICAL WORK PROGRAM**	50				
	Technical Database					
	Geotechnical Studies					
	Wells - Depth, Objective					
	3D Seismic					
	2D Seismic					
	Reprocessing					
	Expenditure Commitment					
	Sub- Total	50				
Appendix C / D	**FINANCIAL PROPOSAL**	20				
	Economic Terms					
	Carried Interest					
	Royalty					
	Cost Petroleum					
	Production Bonus					
	Miscellaneous terms	15				
	Training					
	Institutional Support					
	Social Support					
	Health Safety Environment					
	Sub- Total	35				
	TOTAL	100				

Source: INP website

(e) *Minimum work programme*

The minimum obligatory work programme is a negotiable item included in the exploration and production concession contract when it is awarded. In most cases, the content of the obligatory work programme will depend on the maturity of the area concerned, the data available and the expectation of the licensing entity with regard to further work required for the area, as well as the stipulated evaluation criteria. Of course the geology of the area, data available, the technical competence and financial strength of the applicant will play a role in the evaluation by the authorities of the company and its application.

The table above illustrates the qualification terms of Mozambique's second bidding round. It can clearly be seen that the proposed obligatory work programme is given substantial weight in the evaluation process. Despite the fact that the proposed obligatory work programme is highly classified, particularly during the bid evaluation process due to its importance in that process, it is not the only element of the evaluation. Rather, it forms an important component in combination with the other items included in the bid. These other items, normally including the technical data used to make the application, the inclusion of 3D seismic surveys, the commitment to drill wells, the strength of the proposed health, safety and environmental protection systems, and the economic and financial terms offered by the applicant (such as the level of institutional and social support and training), are crucial for the evaluation.

(f) ***Assignment and encumbrance***

Transfer or assignment of all or part of the rights and obligations under a concession contract to a third party may only be made by the holder of such rights with the prior written approval of the Minister of Mineral Resources. The law specifies that the requirements for an application for the award of petroleum rights also apply to cases concerning farming into a concession contract after its award.

Assignments are effected by an instrument in writing executed by the assignee on terms whereby the assignee accepts and agrees to become a person constituting the concessionaire and to be bound by the terms and conditions of the exploration and production concession contract including all associated documents required by an administrative decision or applicable law. With the approval of the assignment, the assignee bears joint and several liabilities under the concession contract.

The model exploration and production concession contract provides that assignment may take place without the need for the minister's consent, by an assignor who is not in material breach of any of the terms and conditions of the contract, in respect of assignment by a defaulting party to a non-defaulting party under the revocation provisions of the exploration and production concession contract, or if it is required to give effect to the default procedures under a joint operating agreement concluded in relation to the petroleum operations.

The concessionaire can finance the cost of all facilities and equipment to be used in petroleum operations and shall have the right to use such facilities and equipment for petroleum operations during the term of the concession contract, in which case the title to the facilities and equipment may, at the option of the government and after cost recovery without additional compensation, be transferred to the government. The facilities whose title can pass to the government does not include facilities or equipment acknowledged by the government as belonging to third parties. Moveable facilities and equipment of such nature owned by foreign third parties may be freely exported.

Third party use of facilities: Third parties may, subject to terms and conditions stipulated by applicable petroleum law, have the right to access and use available spare capacity of facilities and necessary associated equipment on terms and conditions to be agreed between the parties and acceptable to the government. Such terms and conditions shall include a fee representing payment for the concessionaire's cost of additional investments required for facilitating such third party use, as well as operational costs and a profit element reflecting the risk taken by the owner of the facilities. The fee to be paid for third party use of spare capacity in facilities and equipment is subject to approval by the government. When the parties cannot agree on access or a reasonable fee for third party use, the matter may, be settled by:

- an independent commission of three members acting as experts;
- arbitration; or
- the competent judicial authorities.

Access to and use of facilities and equipment can only take place when the third party use does not have a materially negative effect on the concessionaire's petroleum operations and is feasible from a technical, environmental and safety point of view.

Unless otherwise agreed with the government, concessionaires are obliged to arrange all insurance required by applicable Mozambican law in respect of the petroleum operations, and, in the event that the insurance is procured from a jurisdiction other than Mozambique, any other insurance required by the applicable law of that jurisdiction, and such other insurance as MIREM and the concessionaire may agree from time to time.

(g) Local content

Requiring the use of local content in the supply of goods and services to the petroleum industry has to be seen as a new concept for a relatively recent producer country such as Mozambique. Mozambique has not as yet developed a local content policy.

It will be quite some years before the Mozambican manufacturing and service sectors will be able to provide all relevant services to the standard required to supply complex deep-water operations. But even at an earlier stage oil companies and their suppliers will need a lot of land-based logistics and support, some of which will not require advanced skills or infrastructure and which, provided adequate core infrastructure and regulatory systems are put in place, Mozambican suppliers are well placed to provide on competitive terms. In the intermediate and longer term also more advanced goods and services will be provided from the Mozambican private sector.

At same time and taking into consideration its accumulated experience with petroleum activities, the government is considering the approval of a policy focused on corporate social responsibility, which will serve as the guiding principle for the implementation of local content initiatives. In this context MIREM is conducting a study on corporate social responsibility that, in addition to gathering knowledge about the nature and impact of actions that could be taken, analyses the perceptions of different stakeholders on the subject and presents recommendations and principles to be considered in policy making.

(h) National reservation

The existing petroleum regulatory regime does not contain any domestic supply obligations except in situations of national emergency. The five fundamental principles guiding the government's petroleum policy do, however, envisage the use of petroleum to develop Mozambican industrialisation. Currently MIREM is undertaking an analysis of the strategic options available in order to develop a gas master plan that will identify policy options that will maximise the monetary, social and environmental impact of the resources discovered.

According to the published terms of reference for consulting services for development of the gas master plan, the government is aiming, among other outcomes at:

- benchmarking Mozambique's current market conditions with a group of comparable countries with respect to the trajectory followed to develop a domestic gas market;
- reviewing and validating existing plans and studies made available by relevant ministries and agencies (the Ministries of Planning and Development, Industry and Trade, Energy, Transport and Communication, Agriculture, Tourism etc);
- definition of domestic, regional export (neighbouring countries) and global export opportunities to commercialise the country's natural gas production over a period until 2030. Potential domestic markets may include but not be limited to a petrochemical industry, a fertiliser plant, coastal industrial development (metals/heavy industry, light industry/commercial), gas-fired power and compressed natural gas for transport. Consideration will be given to the links between the opportunities identified and sectoral plans, in order to focus on potential directions for growth;
- evaluation of domestic, regional export and global export market opportunities for gas from a current and future demand perspective, including a review of domestic and export markets for products that use gas as a feedstock and/or fuel. In this context the energy mix options will be considered for domestic energy needs (Mozambique has significant coal, hydro and gas potential, but is in many places dependent on biofuels) and for regional power export (eg, to the South African Power Pool). Demand and cost scenarios will be prepared for use in this study.
- identification of investment and operational requirements for new or upgraded facilities and infrastructure to transport gas to different market opportunities;
- consideration of the environmental effects (eg, greenhouse gas emissions and the impact on national parks) and social aspects (eg, access to energy, energy security, health and safety, employment creation, land use, co-existence with tourism, fishing industry and communities, gender dimensions) by the gas market sector; and
- definition of strategic alternatives for the development of the gas sector and evaluation of such alternatives against monetary, social and environmental metrics. Gas allocation profiles will be prepared for each gas market sector.

The government, under the applicable law and the terms of the exploration and production concession contract could, at its discretion, choose to take its petroleum production tax and its profit petroleum share in kind. The government may also under the terms of the exploration and production concession contract purchase the concessionaire's petroleum in order to supply local consumption.

(i) *National participation*

The Petroleum Law provides an option for the state to participate in the petroleum operations undertaken by any concessionaire during any phase of such operations. After the abandonment of the production sharing agreement regime in line with the Petroleum Law in 2001, the state has normally participated in concession contracts through a direct participating interest that is continued throughout the exploration phase up until the approval of the first development plan, or in some cases even until completion of development of production facilities.

There is no legal or mandatory percentage participation interest stipulated for the state. The percentage is a negotiable item in the bidding round documents, and to date agreed shares have ranged from 10% to 20%. These participations are currently managed by the national oil company (ENH) on behalf of the state, and cannot be assigned to any entity that is not totally controlled or held by the state without loss of the right to the interest. All amounts paid under the state's carried interest to the entity holding it are reimbursed to the concessionaires from a percentage of the volume of petroleum available for cost recovery.

The fundamental difference between the previous production sharing agreement regime and the new exploration and production concession contract is that, under the former regime, ENH was awarded a percentage participating interest to be managed on behalf of the state. In the new regime ENH does not negotiate the terms of the exploration and production concession contract, including its carried interest. That is a matter entirely for the government to determine through the National Petroleum Institute (INP).

Where the government decides to increase its interest at a later phase of the petroleum operations, in addition to the existing participation, it will have to pay the commercial market value of that additional participation.

The issue of national participation may also be considered under the recently approved Law on Public and Private Partnership, Megaprojects and Entrepreneurial Concessions. Since the law applies to petroleum concession contracts consideration should be given to an analysis of its effect on state participation in such contracts.

The law appears not to be clear and to conflict with existing laws therefore having serious implications for the stability of existing concession contracts, with the danger of uncertainty, unpredictability, unnecessary bureaucracy and risk to investments, thereby affecting the country's reputation and attractiveness for such investment. As the interpretation is not clear, it must be expected that the government will consider it necessary to act to achieve such clarity. The law and its regulation make reference to a minimum 20% ownership in all public and private partnership projects, including megaprojects and entrepreneurial partnerships, being reserved for individual local investors, with the government facilitating the distribution of that ownership share. The same legislation makes later reference to a free carried interest of up to 5% for the government.

(j) ***Environment***

Environmental considerations during all phases of petroleum operations have always been one of the aspects given particularly consideration by the government. The fundamental principles of environmental protection are established by the Constitution.

Currently, due to lack of regulatory measures, the government relies on studies undertaken by the operators on behalf of concessionaires, and expects that they will comply with legal requirements and undertake the relevant analysis of environmental impacts in the form of environmental impact assessments and environmental management plans, which examine the economic, social and environmental effects of activities to be conducted on surrounding areas. The environmental impact assessment and environmental management plans are subject to government approval. On the operational side, plans for activities required during petroleum operations should also contain protection and mitigation measures to address expected environmental impact to the air, land and sea. Government approvals and consents may also define maximum permissible limits, and include a programme for monitoring and control.

To mitigate the effect of petroleum operations and other economic activities, the government commissioned a strategic environmental assessment of the shallow waters of the entire cost of Mozambique. Among other objectives this assessment is focused on legal, institutional and management concerns with emphasis on:

- creating effective coordination between the different institutions with tasks related to potential intervention directly on the coast, taking in functions currently scattered both at central and regional level and among institutions subordinated to the Ministry of Environment (MICOA) and other ministries, with the aim of defining clearly the roles and responsibilities of the various entities;
- updating the national plan for the management of coastal zones so that it reflects the guidelines and recommendations of the strategic environmental assessment, and implementing it in Mozambique's legal framework;
- providing industry with environmental and social data and information pertaining to the concession contract areas, and the mapping of environmentally sensitive areas and protected species located in such areas, before environmental impact assessments are conducted by concessionaires in relation to specific projects;
- strengthening the monitoring of the implementation of the environmental management plans arising from the environmental impact assessment process, and auditing compliance with those environmental management plans, thereby strengthening the legal enforcement of the management plan obligations;
- ensuring that the awarding of areas for petroleum operations is dealt with at inter-ministerial level, taking into account territorial plans for the region;
- creating territorial plans for environmentally sensitive areas, namely areas where petroleum operations may influence nationally and internationally recognised ecosystems, where there is a need to establish or maintain special

protection status, such as sensitive habitats, conservation areas, artisanal fishing zones, areas with certain tourism activities, or other protected areas that may be particularly adversely affected as a result of petroleum operations;
- promoting corporate social and environmental responsibility, ensuring the internalisation of environmental costs, the principle of compensation for disturbance or destruction of biodiversity and the adoption of relevant and appropriate environmental management systems;
- ensuring access to and public use of coastal resources.

So far the complexity of environmental studies required is determined by how serious the impacts may be, or whether they are expected to bring harmful environmental consequences. The strategic environmental assessment process is considered to be the fundamental tool to map relevant conditions and a prerequisite for dealing with environmental matters along the coast and in sensitive areas. It will help the government to determine the measures that need to be implemented and to decide whether or not to open acreage for petroleum operations.

In the current situation, the establishment of comprehensive policy instruments and high environmental standards is crucial to safeguard the environment and other economic activities against the potential unwanted consequences of petroleum operations. The continuous evaluation of emissions, and the monitoring and control of compliance through all phases of petroleum operations is one of the core activities of the National Petroleum Institute (INP).

Offshore petroleum operations are regulated in part by general legal principles found, for instance, in the 1982 United Nations Convention on the Law of the Sea. There are also a number of other treaties that address prevention of pollution from offshore installations, or identify detailed measures for responding to the emergencies caused by these activities.

(k) Governing law and dispute resolution

Despite the fact that concession contracts are negotiated in English, the Portuguese and English texts are both binding. In the case of a conflict between the two language versions, the Portuguese version shall apply. The applicable law for the concession contracts is Mozambican law as it appears from time to time, meaning that any changes to the regulatory regime, including the relevant laws and regulations, are applicable to previously awarded concession contracts unless specifically exempted.

The concession contracts stipulate that arbitration shall be the final resort for dispute settlement both between the government and concessionaires, and between or among concessionaires. The arbitration procedure is a standard procedure included, in the case of disputes between the government and concessionaires, in the concession contract main document and, in case of disputes between or among concessionaires, in the standard joint operation agreement. Disputes of a technical nature may in all cases be referred to expert determination.

Mozambique is signatory to and has ratified international conventions relevant to dispute resolution, such as the New York Convention on Recognition of Foreign

Arbitral Awards, the Convention on the International Centre for the Settlement of Investment Disputes (ICSID) and the Convention Giving Effect to the Rules Provided by the United Nations Committee on International Trade Law (UNCITRAL).

For this reason the main arbitration rules applied to concession contracts are the UNCITRAL and ICSID rules. These rules are applied as standard terms and, unless an investor's domicile or its principal place of business is in a jurisdiction which is not party to the relevant conventions, these arbitration mechanisms will be applied. In exceptional cases rules from other international institutions, or ad hoc rules, may be applied as long as the parties agree in the concession contract the relevant terms and conditions. But as a general rule the venue of the arbitration is required to be what may be considered as a neutral civil law jurisdiction.

3.2 Government take

There is currently a heated debate in Mozambique about the potential gains that may be derived from the exploration for and exploitation of natural resources. Fiscal, legal and commercial reforms have taken place continuously over the past 10 years in various sectors of the economy, aiming not only to improve tax collection, but also to strengthen the capacities and capabilities of the tax administration and increase its enforcement ability.

The approvals of a new Corporate Tax Income Code, the Value Added Tax Code, the Code of Fiscal Benefit and the Petroleum Production Tax Regulation, just to mention a few legislation packages, are clear examples of the maturing of the fiscal system and Mozambique's adjustment to new world trends. The government has however been very cautious with amendments to the tax regime applicable to petroleum operations.

For a complete picture regarding taxation of the petroleum sector in Mozambique, reference must be made to Decree 19 of June 2 2004, which introduced the petroleum production tax often referred to as a royalty, and the Code of Tax Benefits approved by Decree 16 of June 27 2002, even though both those laws were revoked in 2007. Under Decree 19, to which most concession contracts were subject, the applicable rates of petroleum production tax were 8% for crude oil and 5% for natural gas for all resources located onshore. For petroleum produced offshore, rates were based on a sliding scale according to water depth to the seabed under which the deposit subject to the tax was located.

The corporate income tax rate is 32%. For all upstream projects with investment made in a continuous manner and in relation to a deposit or field where the related investment was commenced before December 31 2010, regardless of whether commercial production commenced at a later date, a 25% reduction in the corporate income tax rate on net income accrued from any such development and production applies for a period of eight years starting from the year of the first production.

Non-resident companies or foreign subcontractors providing services to concessionaires are subject to withholding tax, as a corporate income tax, at a rate of 10%, based on the gross amount of the payments shown on their invoices in respect of work or services performed. The amount is held by the concessionaire which is responsible for payment to the competent tax authority.

Table 1 – Royalty sliding scale using water depth (revoked by Law 12 of June 26 2007). This royalty regime is applicable to the Rovuma Basin exploration and production concession contracts, except for those awarded after the publication of Law 12 of 2007.

Petroleum production tax (royalty) rates		
Location and water depth in meters (m)	**Tax rate for crude oil (%)**	**Tax rate for natural gas (%)**
Onshore	8	5
< 100m	7	4
100m – 500m	5	3
> 500m	3	2

Fiscal regime approved by Law 12 of 2007: With the approval of Laws 12/2007 and 13 of 2007, both dated June 26 2007, which regulate various aspects of Mozambique's tax regime, including fiscal benefits for petroleum and mining operations, the regime was altered considerably. Under the new legislation there are three central elements, namely corporate income tax, petroleum production tax and the profit sharing mechanism, which are of general application and do not have to be included in each exploration and production concession contract. The profit split table and the cost recovery ceiling are negotiable items, and for this reason they are, together with other negotiable economic components, specified in each exploration and production concession contract.

(a) ***Petroleum production tax or royalty***

Tax on petroleum production is:

- 10% for liquid petroleum; and
- 6% for gaseous petroleum.

(b) ***Rental fees***

Rental fees are not applicable. According to terms agreed between the concessionaire and the government, during the exploration period the concessionaire is obliged to relinquish a portion of the acreage awarded, excluding those areas which are deemed to be discovery areas as defined according to the Regulation for Petroleum Operations.

(c) ***Bonus***

Production bonuses are paid on agreed thresholds of production varying between 25,000 barrels of oil equivalent per day (boed) and 50,000 boed for a certain period during which average production must exceed the given level. The level of production bonuses is a negotiable item. The model exploration and production concession contract appears to make bonuses payable multiple times on incremental additional production, as opposed to a one-off payment on achieving a certain production level. Production bonuses are paid in cash to the government, and the amounts paid are by statute directly allocated as earnings to the National Petroleum Institute (INP).

(d) *Other contributions*

Training and institutional support fees are payments made during the various phases of petroleum operations. These fees are negotiable items. Institutional support is a one-off payment, paid 30 days after signature of the concession contract. The other fees are paid on an annual basis and are among the costs that may be recovered.

Social projects fees are another financial obligation that forms part of the competitive bidding items. The fees are dedicated for use in the development of communities surrounding or living inside the concession contract area. These fees are paid on an annual basis and are recoverable costs.

(e) *Corporate tax*

The corporate income tax rate is 32%.

A withholding tax is chargeable on non-resident sub-contractors or those not registered as taxpayers and conducting economic activities in Mozambique. The rate is 20% based on the gross amount of the payments shown on invoices in respect of work or services performed.

(f) *Value added tax (VAT)*

VAT is chargeable on sales of goods and services, and on imports. The rate is 17%. Some activities have lower rates, and for some categories of business enterprises it is refundable.

(g) *Minor taxes*

In the category of minor taxes are included municipality taxes, stamp duties and property transfer taxes.

(h) *Economic and fiscal stability*

The principles of stabilisation and renegotiation of contracts are provided for in the Mozambican Civil Code. Generally speaking, concession contracts do not provide that relevant law will be unchanged or guarantee absolute stability. The 2010 model exploration and production concession contract provides instead for compensatory economic stability, stipulating that:

> *Article 9 – (a) If there is a breach of the warranty set out in this Article or in the event that after the Effective Date there is a change in applicable law the laws of the Republic of Mozambique of the kind referred to in Article 11 and as a result the Parties meet to agree on changes to be made to this EPCC, then during the period starting when the change in the law comes into effect and ending when an agreement between the Parties*

is reached pursuant to Article 11, the portion of Profit Petroleum to which the Concessionaire and the Government would otherwise be entitled shall be adjusted so that the net revenues to be received by the Concessionaire from Petroleum Operations are the same as they would have been if no change in the law had taken place.

(b) Where the Parties have reached agreement on the changes to be made to this EPCC pursuant to Article 11, this EPCC will be deemed to stand amended to the extent necessary to give effect to that agreement in accordance with its terms.

Furthermore it provides for fiscal stability, stipulating that:

Article 11.9 In the event that, after the Effective Date, any other tax is introduced in the Republic of Mozambique which is not of the type set out in Article 11 and, as a result, there is an adverse effect of a material nature on the economic value derived from the Petroleum Operations by the Concessionaire, the Parties will, as soon as possible thereafter, meet to agree on changes to this EPCC which will ensure that the Concessionaire obtains from the Petroleum Operations, following such changes, the same economic benefits as it would have obtained if the change in the law had not been effected.

(i) Exchange regime

The concession contracts usually adopt a special exchange regime approved by the government which is based on the Exchange Law. The foreign exchange regime stipulates the number of bank accounts that the concessionaire is allowed to open in foreign jurisdictions, and imposes an obligation on it to remit the proceeds resulting from petroleum sales to the country, except for the amounts required for making payments.

The concessionaires are obliged to waive banking confidentiality as regards the government in respect of the accounts associated with petroleum operations, and the government is entitled to audit such accounts any time. On a monthly basis the concessionaire has to submit reports regarding operations related to such bank accounts to the Central Bank. The concessionaires have the right freely to declare and pay dividends to their shareholders and to remit such payments to a place outside Mozambique. Foreign exchange rules and formalities are approved by the Central Bank.

Table 2 – Summary of fiscal regime applicable to petroleum operation in Mozambique

Item	Parameters
Fiscal regime	Royalty/tax based with profit sharing mechanism (r-factor)
Royalty	10% for liquid petroleum 6% for gaseous petroleum
Bonuses	Production bonuses according to agreed production threshold No signature bonuses

continued

Item	Parameters
Corporate income tax	32% Ring fence for Income tax around each concession contract area
Withholding tax	20%
Dividend withholding tax	10%
Tax benefits	Carry forward between 4 and 6 years Exemption from custom duties during the first five years after the approval of the development plan for goods and equipment Excise and VAT exempted from custom duties
Depreciation	Depreciation rates of: • 100% for exploration costs • 100% for development costs • 25% for operating costs
Production sharing	According to r-factor mechanism with the following tier: r-factor Share 1.0% (negotiable) 1.5% 2.0% 2.5% >2.5%
Cost recovery ceiling	65–75% average
Acreage fee	Not applicable. Acreage is subject to periodic relinquishment.
Ring fencing	For concession contract area
Other financial bonds	Institutional support – negotiable item (cost recoverable) Training support – negotiable item (cost recoverable) Social support – negotiable item (cost recoverable)

4. Current issues

4.1 Current petroleum exploration and production rights

(In the table on the right, the following abbreviations are used for the contract types: PPA for petroleum production agreement; PSA for production sharing agreement; EPCC for exploration and production concession contract).

4.2 Developments in the Mozambique Basin

The Mozambique Basin is located in the southern part of the country, comprising approximately 500,000 km^2, of which 275,000 km^2 are located onshore and the remaining part on the Mozambican continental shelf. A few smaller onshore basins constitute part of this basin namely the Lower Zambezi Graben, Middle Zambezi Graben and Lake Niassa Basin.

Operator	Blocks	Contract type	Concessionaires (participation interest)	Phase
Sasol Petroleum Temane, Ltd	Onshore Pande and Temane fields	PPA	SPT (70%)/CMH(25%) /IFC(5%)	Production
Sasol Petroleum Mozambique, Ltd	Onshore Pande and Temane Blocks	PSA	Sasol Petroleum Mozambique (100%)	Exploration
Sasol Petroleum Sofala, Ltd	Offshore Blocks 16 and 19	EPCC	Sasol Petroleum Sofala (50%)/ENH (15%)/ Petronas Carigalli Mozambique E&P (35%)	Exploration
Statoil	Area 2 & 5 Offshore Rovuma Basin	EPCC	Hydro Oil & Gas (65%)/ Tullow (25%)/ENH (10%)	Exploration
ENI East Africa SpA	Area 4 Offshore Rovuma Basin	EPCC	ENI (70%)/ENH (10%)/ Galp Energia (10%)/ KOGAS (10%)	Exploration
Anadarko Moçambique Área 1, Ltd	Area 1 Offshore Rovuma Basin	EPCC	Anadarko (36.5%)/ Mitsui (20%)/ENH (15%)/Baharat Petroleum Resources Limited (10%)/ Videocom (10%)/PTT EP(8.5%)	Exploration
Anadarko Moçambique Area 1, Ltd	Area Onshore Rovuma Basin	EPCC	Anadarko (35.7%) + Artumas Petroleos de Mozambique, Ltd (15.3%) + Maurel & Prom, S.A.(24)/ENH (15%)/PTT EP (10%)	Exploration
Sasol Petroleum Sengala, Ltd	Sofala Offshore Block	EPCC	SP Sengala (85%)/ ENH (15%)	Exploration
Sasol Petroleum M-10, Ltd	M10 Offshore Block	EPCC	SP M-10 (42.5%)/ Petronas (42.5%)/ ENH (15%)	Exploration
BUZI Hydrocarbons, Ltd	Buzi Block	EPCC	Buzi Hydrocarbons (75%)/ENH (25%)	Exploration
Petronas Carigalli Mozambique (Rovuma Basin) Ltd	Area 3 and 6 Offshore Rovuma Basin	EPCC	Petronas Carigali Moçambique (Rovuma Basin) (90%)/ENH (10%)	Exploration
Sasol Petroleum Mozambique Exploration, Lda	Area 'A' Onshore	EPCC	Sasol Petroleum Mozambique Exploration, Lda (90%) /ENH (10%)	Exploration

In terms of onshore petroleum operations, several companies, in particular several Sasol affiliates, Petronas and DNO Mozambique AS, have undertaken considerable exploration activities. Currently there are five active exploration and production concession contracts onshore, all of them operated by Sasol affiliates.

Table 3 – Technical information about Mozambican exploration.

Item	Number/quantity
2D seismic	17,020 km
3D seismic	2,150 km^2
Exploration wells	21
Production wells	21
Evaluation wells	14

*Source: INP. *Data acquired from 2000 to the end of October 2012*

For the development and production of the Pande and Temane fields, which were discovered back in the 1960s by Gulf Oil, the government signed a petroleum production agreement with a consortium comprised of Sasol Petroleum Temane Lda and Companhia Mocambicana de Hidrocarbonetos SA, which held 70% and 30% respectively. Later, Companhia Moçambicana de Hidrocarbonetos assigned 5% of its participation interest to the International Finance Corporation, in order to guarantee the financing of the project. A central processing facility unit has been built under an approved development plan and the rights are held on the same participation interest as the upstream fields.

The production project was commissioned in 2004, and the natural gas produced is sold and transported to South Africa through a pipeline of approximately 900km length operated by Republic of South Africa Pipeline Co, an incorporated joint venture in which the governments of both countries hold 25% each and the remaining participation is held by private interests.

From the production of natural gas the government is entitled to receive 5% of the production as a royalty (or tax on petroleum produced), which at the discretion of the government may be paid in cash or taken in kind. In order to be able to take natural gas in kind, the government imposed on the pipeline owners an obligation to instal five off-take points located within Mozambique, enabling the government the possibility of serving the domestic market. Additional agreements related to sales were also approved.

Fig. 6 – Scheme of the Pande and Temane natural gas venture.

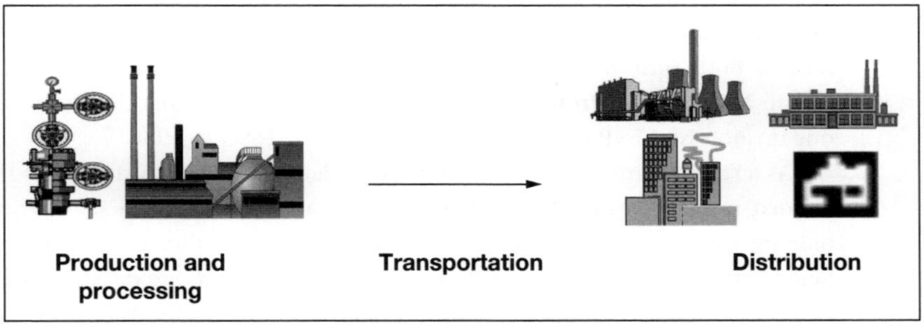

Source: INP

Currently, one of the off-take points is being used by the local Mozambican market for the transportation of natural gas to Maputo, where the major industrial area of the country is concentrated. The 70km pipeline consists of two pressure reduction stations (from 125 to 50 bar and from 50 to 6.2 bar), custody transfer meters, and a pipeline of 219mm with varying wall thickness and connected to a 6.2 bar reduction pressure station that supplies a distribution pipeline network made of steel or PVC.

Fig. 7 – Map of the Pipeline Temane to Secunda in South Africa illustrating the off-take points

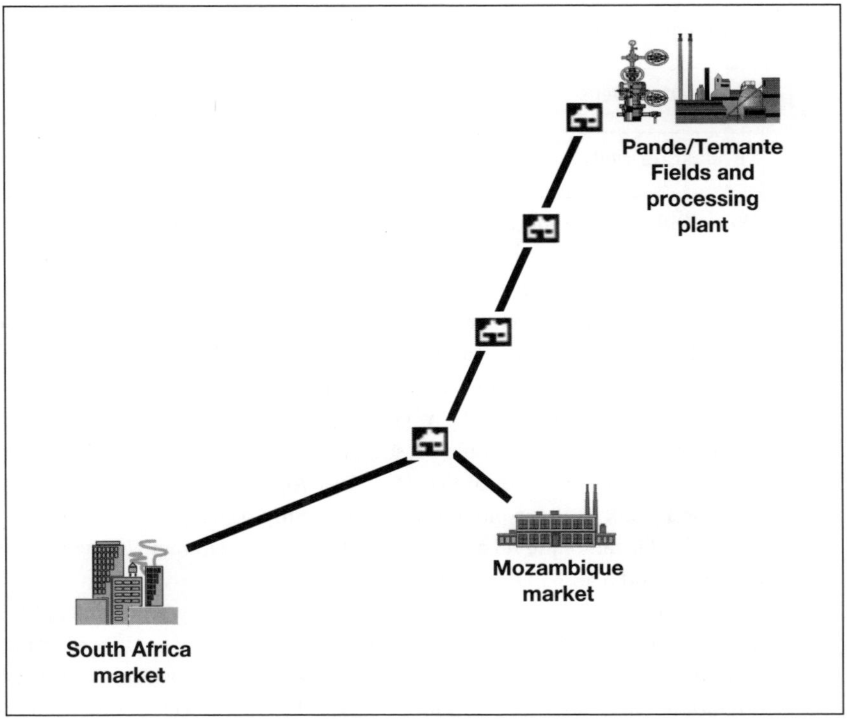

4.3 Developments in the Rovuma Basin

The Rovuma Basin is about 400km long by 160km. The basin is centred on the Rovuma Delta near the border between Mozambique and Tanzania. The basin is located both onshore and offshore. Nearly 30,000km² of the Rovuma Basin lies within Mozambique. In terms of exploration, before the second licence round only one unsuccessful well had been drilled onshore by ESSO in 1986.

As a result of the second licensing round, launched in 2005, the basin has been divided into seven areas, one of which is located onshore and six offshore. The bidding round resulted in four exploration and production concession contracts being awarded. Ambitious work programmes were proposed, and three years afterwards, Anadarko Mozambique Area 1 Lda, as operator of Area 1, and Eni East Africa SpA, as operator of Area 4, declared to the government and announced to the world discoveries which were considered to be world class reserves of natural gas. The data available is given in Table 4.

Table 4 – Technical information about Rovuma Basin.

Item	Number/quantity
2D seismic	29,000km
3D seismic	16,870km²
Exploration wells	18
Production wells	0
Evaluation wells	10

*Source: INP * Data acquired from 2000 to the end of October 2012*

With these announcements the potential of the entire basin for additional petroleum discoveries became substantially increased. As things stand in 2012, after the drilling and appraisal of more than 25 wells, more than 90% of the discoveries made appear to have commercial potential. Based on the results so far, the entire basin is now considered to be very prospective. This, in addition to the recent discoveries in Tanzania, will have a significant positive impact on the perception of the prospectivity of the entire coast of East Africa. Additional discoveries may be made as a result of the exploration work currently being conducted by Statoilhydro Oil & Gas Mozambique AS and Petronas Carigali Mozambique (Rovuma Basin) Ltd in Areas 2 and 5 and 3 and 6, respectively.

With reported reserves in mind, the Rovuma Basin may be considered one of the most promising offshore provinces for natural gas. However the lack of infrastructure services to support either upstream or downstream operations, Mozambique's limitations in power generation and distribution services, low water quality, insufficient distribution and inadequate pressure, poor road quality, limited logistics systems, port services and regulatory and administrative procedures for handling the import and export of goods constitute serious impediments, and raise concern with regard to the ability of the country to support the rapid development of projects.

Exploration reports presented by the concessionaires estimate around 100 trillion cubic feet of recoverable natural gas in place, but with ongoing appraisal and development drilling the figure may raise. The concessionaires are evaluating the possibility of developing large export-oriented liquefied natural gas development projects to commercialise the gas. Ongoing discussions between the companies and the government may lead to the first commercial production by 2019. Since some of the discoveries may be shared between two exploration and production concession contract areas, the issue of unitisation may cause difficulties and delays to jointly developed projects.

4.4 Legal review

Currently, the expressed understanding of the main players is that the legal framework is not sufficiently clear with regard to its scope. The main concerns expressed relate to the regulatory framework's ability to regulate fully the construction and operation of multi-user open access liquefaction facilities. Also the rules relating to third-party use of available capacity in existing or future facilities need to be expanded. The 2001 Petroleum Law does not address the exploration and production of unconventional petroleum such as coalbed methane and shale gas. In order to respond to these concerns, the government is conducting a review of the legal framework with the aims of:

- making the entire legal framework more transparent, predictable, non-discriminatory and applicable in a transparently accountable manner in order to reduce unwanted transaction costs, to open up opportunities for investors and to protect stakeholders' interests;
- allowing the large discoveries made to be developed into production projects serving the international and local markets;
- allowing the government to engage in or allow increased mapping of conventional and unconventional resources (including coalbed methane and shale gas); and
- establishing a standardised platform of model concession contracts in order to enable the industry to assess opportunities in a predictable competitive environment where technical experience, capacity and capability of performance will be the key components in having success in obtaining rights to operate and approvals of projects.

5. Conclusion

5.1 General comments

With recent discoveries, Mozambique has optimal conditions, as far as resources are concerned, to enable the nation to develop a gas-based industry and to play a key role in the regional and international gas markets. In addition to a resource-oriented upstream petroleum policy, a well-conceived industrial policy addressing the use of natural gas in the domestic market and the establishment of petrochemicals, fertiliser and metallurgical industries may assist the development of the country into a diversified economy. Nevertheless, domestic market pricing issues must be carefully considered in order to avoid negative perceptions about the industry.

Mozambique's internal political stability and good relations with countries that share the same basins is another issue to be considered in order to secure long-term investments. Even though Mozambique has a border treaty with Tanzania, it is important to strengthen bilateral relationships with Tanzania and others in terms of exchanges of information and institutional cooperation. Possible trans-boundary unitisation may also have to be considered. This challenge has to be considered not only as a government role and responsibility, but also as presenting a challenge for the concessionaires.

The current oil price forecasts in Asian markets and the conclusion of projects in Australia and Papua New Guinea, whether conventional or unconventional, will also affect the success of future Mozambican projects. No less important for the Atlantic and Asian markets will be the role and development of unconventional gas from the United States.

5.2 Challenges to Mozambique

Legal framework: Legal reform seems to be the most urgent and important issue that the government should look into. Reforms are required in the legislation in order to open the domestic market to other regional markets and to allow improvements in infrastructure such as roads, railways, telecommunications, energy, airports, access to maritime areas and education. This may contribute to the relocation of resources and boost economic growth and the role of Mozambique in terms of regional integration.

Infrastructure and services: Services in the region, with the exception of South Africa, are very limited or even non-existent. The region has no onshore or offshore infrastructure or industry to support upstream operations. An adequate general infrastructure enabling the supply of goods and services is an essential and crucial element for productivity and growth. The participation of the private sector will be vital for the development of an efficient market, will facilitate liberalisation and will reduce supply and operational costs.

Endemic diseases and human resources: Fluctuations in demographics, combined with high child mortality rates and endemic diseases, have direct economic impacts on the labour force's productivity, and consequently affect economic development. Diseases such as malaria, HIV and tuberculosis that strike down the most productive portion of the population may create a high level of uncertainty for investors.

Most Sub-Saharan countries are confronted with mounting social problems, including endemic diseases. These problems are not unique to Mozambique where, in addition, low life expectancy is a critical issue for long-term investments and for estimating whether the labour force required for significant facilities will be available. Well-conceived and implemented labour policies may work as a counter-balance and present part of the solution to these distortions.

Global financial crisis: The effects of the downturn in the global economy may have collateral effects for the economy of Mozambique that could affect the financing of proposed projects.

So far, as an oil and food importer, the effects have already been of a considerable magnitude, with a substantial reduction in aid from donor countries, which has put annual budgets under severe pressure. Apart from this, the reduction of other aid flows, trade flows and the reduction in export commodities completes a relatively gloomy picture.

Security: Petroleum facilities are very expensive and important infrastructure. The increased threat of sabotage, terrorism and piracy on the East Coast of Africa is an issue that needs to be considered in order to guarantee and secure investments. Precautions must be taken with regard to security of infrastructure located both onshore and offshore.

Security concerns must also be considered at a regulatory level in order to support and prepare personnel involved in the operation of emergency and preparedness measures.

References

- Wood Mackenzie, *Asset Analysis, Southern and East Africa – Mozambique,* February 2012.
- D Acemoglu and S Johnson, "Disease and Development: The effect of life expectancy on economic growth", *Journal of Political Economy* (2000).
- Daniel Johnston, *International Petroleum Fiscal Systems and Production Sharing Contracts*, Pennwell Books Publishing Company, Tulsa, Oklahoma, 1994.
- Daniel Johnston, *International Exploration, Economics, Risk, and Contract Analysis*, (first edition), Pennwell, 2003.
- Melissa Cristina Mathias, *Formação da Indústria Global de Gás Natural – Definição, condicionalismos e desafios, Editora Interciência,* Rio de Janeiro, 2012.
- *Natural Gas Master Plan Draft,* draft submitted to the Government of Mozambique Steering Committee by ICF International, 9300 Lee Highway – Fairfax, VA 22031;
- Wood Mackenzie , *LNG supply analysis, Mozambique,* January 2012;
- Norad, *Oil for Development Program,* annual report 2011 – 12.
- Saul Suslick (organizador), *Regulação em Petróleo e Gás Natural,* – Centro de Estudos de Petróleo, CEPETRO, UNICAMP, Agencia Nacional de Petróleo, Editora Komedi.
- *Revista informa/publicação annual publicus,* April 2012 No 2.
- *The Petroleum Geology and Hydrocarbon Prospectivity of Mozambique,* 2000, Volume I Report.
- Terms of Reference for the Selection of Consultants for Development of Gas Sector Master Plan for Mozambique.

Sudan

Mohamed Atabani
Al-Sudan Energia

1. Introduction

Oil has played a central role in the development of the Sudanese economy. Investment in the exploration of the Sudanese oil and gas industry is best understood by three waves of investments.

The first wave of investment was marked by the exploration activity that took place in 1959 when the Italian oil company AGIP started exploration in the Red Sea area, followed by several other oil companies, but without success.

In 1975 the American oil company Chevron was granted concessions in the southern and south-western parts of Sudan, which marked the second wave of investment in Sudan's oil and gas industry. Chevron made its first oil discovery in Sudan in 1979 west of the Muglad area, followed by successful exploration efforts that resulted in the discovery of Unity and Heglig fields. Those discoveries, however, were not commercialised and oil operations were suspended in 1984 because of security concerns. It was not until 1994 that were operations resumed, which marked the beginning of the third wave of investments in the Sudanese oil and gas industry by the entry of such companies as State Petroleum Corporation (Canada), China National Petroleum Company (CNPC-China), Petronas (Malaysia), and ONGC (India). These companies were successful in their quest for oil and gas in Sudan: they managed to commercialise the earlier discoveries made by Chevron and extended those reserves through successful exploration campaigns. Oil was then produced and transported through a 1610 kilometre (km) pipeline and the first shipment of Sudanese oil was exported in 1999 from Port Sudan.

2. Upstream activities

Following the success in the Heglig and Unity fields, several discoveries were made by new operators in Fula, Moga, Falug, Thar Jath, and Mala, among other areas in different concessions in the southern and south-western parts of Sudan. Sudan's estimated total reserves amount to about 6.6 billion barrels. The successful exploration activity which resulted in these discoveries, combined with the construction of upstream and downstream infrastructure, enabled Sudanese production to reach 500,000 barrels per day by 2006.

Sudanese crude oil has different blends with an average American Petroleum Institute (API) gravity of of 32°, is waxy and possesses no sulphur. Internationally recognised blends are Nile Blend, and Dar Blend.

Sudan's crude oil infrastructure consists of processing capacity of about 650,000 barrels per day, pipeline transportation capacity of about 1.1 million barrels per day, and annual refining capacity of about 10 million barrels.

In July 2010, South Sudan separated from Sudan through a referendum mechanism set out in the 2005 Comprehensive Peace Agreement, an agreement that led to the end of Africa's longest civil war. This separation had the result that about 75% of Sudan's reserves and about 80% of its production is now owned by South Sudan. However, all the processing, refining, and transportation infrastructure is owned by Sudan, leaving South Sudan with no capacity to process, refine or export its oil production.

3. Petroleum legal regime

Sudan's oil regime is based on an exploration and production sharing agreement, which is a typical production sharing contract with modified parameters depending on the potentiality and attractiveness of the geological area under consideration.

The prevailing model for conducting oil and gas operations in Sudan is through joint operating companies, each of which is a consortium company formed and owned by the partners to the contract and with the government, with controlling rights proportional to their respective participating shares as defined in a joint operating agreement. Once established, the joint operating company is assigned as the operator of the contract area and is therefore responsible for conducting the oil and gas operations on behalf of the partners.

3.1 Petroleum law and relevant provisions

(a) Regulatory bodies

The Ministry of Petroleum, formerly the Ministry of Energy and Mining, is the main regulator of the oil and gas sector in Sudan and is responsible for presenting changes to the regulatory framework, including laws, regulations, policies and procedures, to the National Assembly for approval.

The main roles and responsibilities of the Ministry of Petroleum are:

- supervision of oil and gas exploitation and production activities in Sudan;
- establishing promotional activities, policies, contracts and licences to attract investors, and regulating the operations of all operating companies;
- monitoring oil and gas companies' activities, although this role is in fact performed by the Oil Exploration and Production Authority, a general directorate within the ministry that supervises and monitors the performance of the operating companies;
- supervision of all government-owned and international service companies working in the oil and gas sector;
- supervision of and coordination with entities involved in research and development activities for the oil and gas sector; and
- representing the government of Sudan in all local and international engagements relating to oil and gas business.

(b) *Types of agreement*

An exploration and production sharing agreement is the model currently used to regulate the relationship between the government of Sudan, represented by the Ministry of Petroleum, and investors in the upstream oil and gas business in Sudan. The agreement follows general international standards, but with modified terms and conditions depending on the exact agreement between the parties involved and according to the geological potential of the area under contract.

In 2012, in an initiative to promote and advance exploration for oil and gas in the frontier areas of Sudan, the Ministry of Petroleum started to sign 'study agreements' with potential inventors for a fixed duration ranging between one and two years, whereby the investor commits to undertake certain data acquisition activities and evaluation studies aimed at getting a better understanding of the geological potential of an area. Following the expiry of the study agreement's term, the investor and the government will decide whether the area should be relinquished, partially or totally, back to the government or whether they should move to an exploration and production sharing agreement.

(c) *Acquisition of acreage*

Access to acreage in Sudan is obtained either through bid rounds or direct negotiation.

In the last decade of the 20th century, when some international companies got interested in the Sudanese oil sector, most of the acquisitions at that time were agreed through direct negotiations with the government, which resulted in big acreages being awarded to potential investors. The government, however, was not comfortable with putting the fate of its oil resources in the hands of a single investor, so a strategy of adopting a joint investment model was followed, and shares in the target asset were divided and awarded to multiple competing investors. However, through the relinquishment mechanism in the exploration and production sharing agreements, a considerable part of those early awarded acreages returned to government custody, and new wave of acquisitions was possible. The most recent international bid round conducted in Sudan was in early 2012, with more than 70 international companies showing interest, ranging from national oil companies to independents. The major international oil companies did not participate as the US embargo on Sudan's oil sector is still in place. The latest bid round was conducted competitively and resulted in licensing of 40% of Sudan's acreage area grouped in seven onshore and offshore blocks, and in awards to seven companies.

Another mechanism for gaining access to acreage in Sudan is by farming into existing exploration and production sharing agreements. Several such opportunities have opened up during the past 15 years, which has also helped in brining new capital and expertise into the industry in Sudan.

(d) *Qualification requirements*

Companies interested in obtaining access to the oil and gas sector in Sudan through either bid rounds or direct negotiation are requested to provide evidence of their technical and financial capabilities. Interest is demonstrated by submitting a letter of interest to the Ministry of Petroleum and filling in a prequalification form provided by the Oil Exploration and Production Authority, which also has to be supplemented by supporting documents. Currently, there is no clear definition of the minimum financial and technical requirements that a company may need to provide in order to be considered. However, all companies interested in getting access to the upstream business in Sudan are requested to demonstrate their capability through their business profiles, which are normally checked and validated by the ministry.

(e) *Duration*

The current duration of the Sudanese exploration and production sharing agreement is 20 years from the effective date of the contract. This period may be extended for a further additional period of five years upon six months prior written notice from the contractor to the Minister of Petroleum, which must be approved by the minister. This approval will only be forthcoming if the contractor has diligently and effectively fulfilled its obligations under the agreement.

The contract duration is divided into two periods, an exploration period and a development period.

Exploration period: The contractor shall be granted a term of six years from the effective date of the contract as the exploration period. This period is divided into three commitment periods, namely, a first commitment period of three years, an optional second commitment period of one and half years and an optional third commitment period of one and half years. The exact layout of the six years is negotiable between the parties and may vary from one area to another. Extensions to any commitment period are possible through a request from the contractor to be approved by the Minister of Petroleum. The general rationale for an extension is to allow the contractor to fulfil its agreed programme of minimum work obligations for the period in the manner stipulated in the contract.

Development and production period: In the event of a successful exploration effort that leads to a discovery, the contractor has to notify the Minister of Petroleum in a written report setting out all relevant information with respect to the discovery within 45 days of completion of drilling and testing of the wildcat well that led to the discovery. This is termed the 'notice of discovery'. In the event that the presence of an oilfield or gas field is established, the contractor has to undertake an economic and technical appraisal of the field. In making the appraisal, the contractor should take into consideration the recoverable reserves, projected production level, transportation tariff, estimated crude oil and/or gas prices, and all other relevant technical and economic factors. The appraisal is to be undertaken by the contractor in full consultation with the Minister of Petroleum, and determines whether in the contractor's opinion the oil or gas field is a commercial discovery worthy of commercial development.

Not later than 90 days following the date of a declaration of commerciality in respect of a field, the contractor must prepare, in consultation with the Minister of Petroleum, a work programme and budget for the development of the discovery, and submit it to the minister for approval. Once approved, it marks the beginning of the development period, which lasts to the end of the contract's term.

(f) *Minimum work programme*

A minimum work programme and budget is specified in the exploration and production sharing agreement, and the contractor is bound to execute it. The minimum work programme is normally specified in terms of activities and minimum expenditure, such as minimum 2D and/or 3D seismic surveys, minimum number of wells to be drilled and so forth. The minimum work programme differs from one area to another, and depends, among other factors, on the availability of geological data for the area, and is normally a competitive item in the bid round, so that interested investors will bid high in order to win the contract.

The minimum work programme is specified and detailed in the contract, and is referenced according to the three minimum commitment periods of the exploration period.

Fulfilment of the work obligations relieves the contractor of the corresponding expenditure obligations. However, fulfilment of the expenditure obligations does not relieve the contractor of the corresponding work obligations.

(g) *Assignment and encumbrance*

The contractor or any funding party may not assign or transfer in whole or in part to any person, firm or corporation any of its rights, privileges, duties or obligations under the exploration and production sharing agreement, nor mortgage, pledge or otherwise encumber its interest, without the prior written consent of the Minister of Petroleum. The minister may grant or refuse to grant his consent to a such request for assignment.

Where more than one company or entity is a party to the exploration and production sharing agreement and included within the definition of the contractor in the agreement, then notwithstanding any other provision in that agreement or in any other agreement between them relating assignments and rights of first refusal thereto, the decision of the minister relating to an assignment shall prevail, be final and binding on the contractor and the parties constituting the contractor.

Where the minister does give his consent to an assignment, the assigning party must submit to the minister a validly executed instrument of assignment. The instrument of assignment shall contain a valid and binding undertaking from the assignee to be bound by all covenants, terms and conditions of the exploration and production sharing agreement including any modifications and additions that have been made to it up to that time.

Where an assignment is made by any party constituting the contractor, the assigning party has to pay an assignment bonus to the government. The exact amount of the bonus varies according to the area where the assignment is to be undertaken.

In the event of withdrawal of any of the funding parties following execution of the agreement, the remaining funding parties assume full responsibility and all obligations regarding the continuation and completion of the work programme, and divide the shares of the withdrawing party in proportion to the percentages of their participating interests under the exploration and production sharing agreement.

The contractor remains liable for any obligations and liabilities which has accrued prior to the effective date of the withdrawal, and petroleum operations should not cease or be suspended during any assignment and/or partial withdrawal.

Where more than one company or entity is a party to the exploration and production sharing agreement and included within the definition of the contractor in the agreement, the liabilities and obligations of such companies and entities are joint and several, and the failure of one such party to perform its share of the obligations in the agreement does not relieve the other parties of their obligations to fully perform all of the contractor's obligations under the terms of the agreement.

(h) Local content

Local content is considered essential and requirements on this issue are normally stated in the exploration and production sharing agreement. It is normally fulfilled by different means and obligations ranging from a so-called Sudanisation plan to gradually replace expatriate employees with local Sudanese, to on-the-job training, annual formal training programmes and attachments.

The contractor must, in consultation with the Minister of Petroleum, prepare and carry out specialised training programmes for its Sudanese employees engaged in petroleum operations with respect to applicable aspects of the petroleum industry. In order to facilitate knowledge transfer, on-the-job training is to be a significant part of the training programme. The contractor has to undertake to replace gradually its expatriate staff with Sudanese nationals, both in technical and managerial posts, provided that capable Sudanese are present with adequate competencies to fill the desired positions.

An annual attachment of a number of Sudanese nationals to the head office of the funding parties constituting the contractor has to be made immediately after announcing the first discovery.

The contractor must, among other measures, provide on a continuous basis for the training and career development of Sudanese nationals in order to qualify them for skilled, technical, administrative and managerial positions. Long-term career development plans must be detailed in yearly programmes, in consultation with the minister and with his ultimate approval. These training programmes should commence in due time upon commencement of the contractor's operations, and may be revised in the light of the progress of operations and, in any event, promptly when directed by the minister.

The contractor also has to undertake on-the-job training of government employees and officers, in numbers and according to a timetable to be mutually agreed upon with the minister. Such training is to include participation in the contractor's and subcontractors' operations.

Another local content element takes the form of a requirement on the contractor to give priority to Sudanese local contractors as long as their terms and conditions are competitive with those of the other contractors tendering for work related to the contractor's operations. The contractor must adopt public tendering as a first priority, although it may adopt closed tendering with the minister's approval.

The contractor must give preference to locally manufactured materials, equipment and consumables that are available on the local market and are comparable in quantity, quality and delivery time to goods to be imported by the contractor.

(i) ***National reservation***

In disposing of petroleum, the contractor must give first priority to local demand on proportional basis with other producers of petroleum in the Sudan. To this end the contractor must comply with any request from the government to sell petroleum for local consumption in Sudan, over such period and in such type, grade, quantity and quality as are determined by the government and the contractor.

The contractor must sell crude oil and gas to all purchasers, including the government and affiliated companies, at prices no lower than the competitive international prices for oil or gas of the same grade, gravity and quality at the time of each sale. The contractor shall furnish the minister with all evidence and information pertaining to such sales, including but not limited to the contract of sale, a statement of the quantities sold including a detailed description of the purchasers, countries of destination and end-users, the per unit price realised free on board at the port of export from Sudan, a statement of prevailing international prices and bank statements.

With respect to any purchase, sale or delivery pertaining to petroleum operations, the agreement provides that no commissions, brokerage fees, allowances or other similar fees will be allowed if internationally efficient operating petroleum companies are capable of undertaking such purchase, sale or delivery by their own means. Brokerage fees, allowances and other considerations or compensation, if allowed, shall in no event be higher than the local or the international rate, as the case may be.

The contractor is not to obtain from any affiliated company, or any other person or entity, any services, assistance, advice or know-how other than those that an efficient petroleum company operating internationally and under normal conditions would provide for itself. The contractor shall pay for any such services, assistance, advice or know-how only on an actual, direct, fair and reasonable cost-reimbursable basis, which shall in no case be higher than competitive international prices and shall be subject to the prior approval of the minister.

(j) ***Environment***

The contractor, its agents and subcontractors must observe, comply with and abide by Sudan's laws and regulations including, but not limited to, regulations for the safe and efficient performance of the petroleum operations required to carry out the agreement, regulations for the protection of the environment, sanitary regulations for the conservation of petroleum and other natural resources of Sudan and the prevention of pollution, and security and employment laws and regulations.

Before commencing any exploration activities the contractor must undertake an environmental and social impact assessment, and must submit all documents required along with an environmental management plan to the minister for review and approval.

Failure to comply with the rules and regulations specified in the exploration and production sharing agreement and in the laws of Sudan with regard to health, safety and the environment may lead to termination of the agreement. If the contractor causes pollution or any damage which is proven to have material adverse consequences for the environment according to applicable Sudanese laws and regulations and/or the rules and practice of the international petroleum industry, the contractor must remedy the situation within a period specified in the contract, following notice being given by the minister, or within any longer period as may be specified in the notice. If the contractor fails to do so, then the minister may by written notice terminate the agreement without resort to any jurisdiction or court, and may also claim damages.

(k) Governing law and dispute resolution

Sudanese exploration and production sharing agreements are governed by and construed in all respects in accordance with Sudan's laws and regulations. The government acknowledges that the contractor has entered into the agreement in reliance on the laws, decrees, rules and regulations of the Republic of the Sudan as they exist on the effective date of the agreement, and the government confirms that all rights granted to the contractor under the agreement are in conformity with those laws, decrees and regulations.

In the event that any change to the laws, decrees, rules or regulations of the Republic of the Sudan occurs after the effective date of the agreement which materially restricts, divests or limits any rights or benefits accruing to the contractor, or which increases the contractor's financial obligations or economic commitment under the agreement or under the Sudanese laws, decrees, rules and regulations in force on the effective date, the contractor may notify the government, and the government and the contractor shall meet to negotiate, in good faith, and agree upon modifications which may need to be made to the terms of the agreement to restore the contractor's economic rights and benefits to a level equivalent to what they would have been, had the change not occurred, or upon such other remedies they may agree to be appropriate.

In the event of any dispute or difference arising between the government and the contractor in connection with the exploration and production sharing agreement, or with respect to its interpretation, application or execution, the parties shall in the first place seek an amicable settlement. If no such such settlement can be reached, the dispute shall finally be settled by arbitration. In such an event the government and the contractor consent to submit the dispute to be finally settled by arbitration in accordance with Arbitration Rules of the International Chamber of Commerce as currently in force.

All Arbitration proceedings under Sudanese exploration and production sharing agreements are to be held in London and shall be conducted in the English language. The number of arbitrators is normally set at three, where the government appoints one, the contractor appoints the second and the two appointed arbitrators appoint the third one.

The government and the contractor undertake to comply with any provisional measures recommended by the arbitration tribunal.

3.2 Government take

The royalties, bonuses and fees described below, including the surface rental fees, cannot either be recovered or amortised by the contractor from cost oil and cost gas.

(a) *Royalties*

While no royalty was provided for in the previous models of the Sudanese exploration and production sharing agreement, one was introduced in 2012.

The government shall be entitled, during the production period, including any renewal periods, to a royalty payable on the total quantity of petroleum produced and saved from the contract area and not used in operations under the agreement. The typical royalty varies according to the contract area in the range of 6% to 12%. It was introduced as a biddable parameter in the 2012 onshore–offshore bid round and became part of the modified model agreement currently in use.

(b) *Bonuses*

There are five types of bonuses in the current model Sudanese exploration and production sharing agreement. These bonuses vary according to the area and are payable to the government.

Signature bonus: A signature bonus is payable on the signature of the exploration and production sharing agreement. It is a one-off payment at the beginning of the agreement.

Production bonus: Production bonuses are specified in the agreement and kick in at various stages in production. The first production bonus is payable with the first commercial production of oil, and is normally the highest. Other production bonuses are payable on the achievement of certain accumulated production thresholds, as measured in barrels of oil equivalent per day. Production bonuses vary in the range of $200,000 to $1 million.

Training bonus: A training bonus is payable at the beginning of each financial year. Training bonuses vary according to the area and the phase of the agreement. The exploration phase has a lower training bonus than the development phase. The training bonus is normally in the range of $100,000 to $200,000.

Social development bonus: Just like the training bonus, the social development bonus varies according to the contract area, and is normally less in the exploration phase than the development phase. The social development bonus is payable at the beginning of the financial year, and is normally in the range of $100,000 to $200,000.

Assignment bonus: An assignment bonus is payable in the event of an assignment of an interest under the agreement, as explained at Section 3.1(g) above.

(c) *Rental fees*

Rental fees are paid by the contractor annually and in advance. The rental fees vary according to the area and the phase of the agreement. The exploration period has lower rental fees than the development period. Each commitment period within the exploration phase has progressively higher rental fees.

During the exploration phase, the rental fees are in the range of $2 to $20 per square metre per year.

During the development phase, the rental fees are in the range of $10 to $50 per square metre per year.

(d) *Special participation*

The only special participation component in the current model Sudanese exploration and production sharing agreement is the carried interest of the national oil company, Sudapet.

Sudapet's interest is carried by the funding parties until commercial production of crude oil or natural gas commences.

All costs and expenditure attributable to Sudapet's share are paid by the funding parties without the accrual of interest, and are recovered as an agreed percentage of Sudapet's share of profit oil or profit gas.

(e) *Corporate taxes*

Currently, there are two types of taxes applied to contractors involved in oil and gas operations in Sudan, namely Sudan income taxes and personal income taxes.

Sudan income taxes include income or profits tax, municipal tax, defence tax and development tax. In respect of these taxes, the government assumes responsibility to pay and discharge them on behalf of the contractor, in other words the contractor is exempted from all these taxes. For practical reasons and to avoid any dispute, Sudanese exploration and production sharing agreements do not state that contractors are exempted from these taxes, instead it is stated that the government will pay these taxes insofar as they are applicable to the contractor's operations out of the sums received as the government share of crude oil and gas. The contractor still has to comply with the requirements of the laws on these taxes with respect to the filling of returns, tax assessments, and keeping relevant books and records for review by authorised persons. The government delivers to the entities constituting the contractor, within six months following the end of each tax year, tax receipts and all other documents certifying that the contractor has fulfilled all of its respective income tax obligations, as well as local tax obligations.

Contractors, however, are not exempted from personal income taxes.

(f) *Customs duties*

With regard to customs duties, the contractor and its subcontractors acting through the contractor are exempt from customs duties with respect to the importation of any machinery, equipment, material, vehicles, supplies and consumable or movable property which is a piece of capital equipment and/or necessary for petroleum operations, and which is to be used solely in carrying out petroleum operations as certified by the minister's representative and as the minister may from time to time approve.

The exemption provided does not apply to imported items when, in the opinion of the minister, items comparable in price, quality and delivery dates are obtainable in Sudan.

Any of the items imported into the Sudan, whether or not exempt from customs duties, may be exported at any time without the payment of any export duty or impost, subject to normal import and export procedures.

Material, equipment and goods belonging to the contractor or its subcontractors, which have been used for petroleum operations but which are still serviceable, may, with the approval of the minister, be sold within the Sudan provided that the applicable custom duties, taxes or imposts are paid.

Material, equipment and goods so damaged or used as to be non-serviceable and which are classified and appraised by the contractor or subcontractors as scrap or junk (with this appraisal being subject to the minister's scrutiny) may be resold as scrap upon payment of customs duties, taxes or imposts at the time of sale.

4. Current issues

The current status of the upstream industry in Sudan is charged with opportunities and challenges.

With about 80% of Sudan's basins still unexplored, there is considerable opportunity for finding more oil and gas resources in those frontiers. However, exploration in Sudan is hampered by lack of serious capital investment and technology necessary to conduct an aggressive exploration campaign, especially in the frontier areas of north Sudan where acreages are large and existing geological data is minimal.

Oil and gas operators in Sudan have historically explored for and produced from conventional hydrocarbon plays. But recent studies conducted by upstream operators and supported by the government suggest the presence of hydrocarbons in uncongenial plays such as in tight sands and fractured basement. These potential plays require competent operators and specialised technical skills, as well as government support and encouragement in terms of incentives and, preferably, more favourable terms in the exploration and production sharing agreement to attract existing and potential investors and to facilitate the foreign direct investment necessary to exploit these opportunities.

Geopolitics play an important role in the global oil and gas business, and Sudan is not an exception. The separation of South Sudan, removing with it 75% of the country's proven reserves left both countries worse-off; with the South holding reserves but unable to produce and export them, and the North with adequate infrastructure and export facilities but less oil to produce and export. With income from oil exports comprising a large share of both countries' income, it is to be hoped that the relationship between the two countries will be maintained at a level of peace and cooperation, which will allow Sudan to extract value from its upstream infrastructure, well trained human resources and well established system by exporting oil and providing upstream services and expertise to South Sudan's oil business, thereby benefiting both countries and further helping to stabilise their relationship through economic ties.

5. Conclusion

The past 20 years have witnessed extensive exploration campaigns mainly focused in the southern part of the country. The Sudanese oil and gas industry has faced several successes, failures, opportunities and challenges. The oil that has been produced and exported has been vital in helping to stabilising the economy, and has provided job opportunities, profits for local businesses and a general growth in the gross national product.

With a well-established oil and gas sector encompassing a settled regulatory framework, a large trained work force, local and foreign service companies, and upstream and downstream infrastructure, Sudan is well positioned to advance its potential to be a leading oil and gas nation offering a good climate for investors.

Geopolitics, however, will remain a major hindrance to those opportunities. With instability having frequently been shown to be a threat to a desirable climate for investment, Sudan faces the challenge of developing and maintaining a more relaxed relationship regionally with neighbouring countries and globally with the international community.

With the separation of South Sudan and the loss of a major part of its proven oil and gas reserves, and with the decision of South Sudan to stop the export of oil through the Sudanese system, Sudan has passed through hard times with a contraction in its economy and devaluation of the Sudanese currency, because of its huge dependence on oil and gas revenue. It is therefore important for Sudan to benefit from its past experience and to use its existing and potential oil wealth to promote other sectors of the economy, in order to establish a well-balanced and diversified economy.

Tunisia

Manel Bondi
Independent Tax Advisor
Mabrouk Maalaoui
PricewaterhouseCoopers

1. Introduction

Real hydrocarbon exploration began in Tunisia in the 1960s, and the first refinery was set up in Bizerta in 1961 to contribute to the processing of Algerian crude oil that passed through Tunisian territory (at Skhira), before being treated in Europe, mainly in France.

It should be noted that despite the granting of numerous exploration permits, Tunisia did not discover oil until 1964. Its production began two years later and grew throughout the 1970s, with the discovery of new oil wells in the south.

Having become a producer, Tunisia created its national oil company in 1972. This is the Tunisian Oil Activities Company (ETAP), which explores for and produces oil in Tunisia.

From 1970 to1986, Tunisia experienced a golden age in terms of oil production.

Tunisia does not offer the important oil and gas reserves of its neighbours, Algeria and Libya; it is rather a minor player in hydrocarbons in comparison with these states.

However, and despite the fact that the country cannot boast billion barrel fields or huge swathes of open acreage, Tunisia does offer a comprehensive and investor-friendly legislative framework, notably a stable fiscal regime, and numerous farm-in opportunities.

Tunisia's proximity to important markets and its close ties with the European Union make it a good place for investment in all fields, including upstream activities.

2. Upstream activities

In 2011, national oil production dropped in comparison with 2010, whereas gas production increased. Oil production fell from 3.7 metric tons to 3.2 metric tons, whereas gas production rose from 2.7 tons of oil equivalent to 3.05 tons of oil equivalent.

At present, there are 51 permits and 39 concessions in operation.

A permit is a hydrocarbon title conferring on its holder the right to undertake prospection and exploration works. In the event of a discovery in the area covered by the permit and proof that reserves exist which are worth developing the permit is converted into a concession. A concession is a hydrocarbon title conferring on its holder the right to undertake exploitation works.

The existing permits are broken down as follows:

- 10 prospection permits; and
- 41 exploration permits.

Among the existing concessions, 25 are held jointly with ETAP.

3. Petroleum legal regime

3.1 Petroleum law and relevant provisions

The legal framework governing companies operating in the exploration and exploitation of hydrocarbons in Tunisia is found in:

- the terms of the specific agreement;
- Decree-Law 85-9 dated September 14 1985, modified by Law 85-93 dated November 22 1985;
- Law 87-9 dated March 6 1987, modifying Decree-Law 85-9 dated September 14 1985;
- Law 90-56 dated June 18 1990 related to the encouragement to the exploration and the production of liquid and gaseous hydrocarbons; and
- the Hydrocarbons Code promulgated by Law 99-93 dated August 17 1999, as modified and completed by Law 99-93 dated August 17 1999, Law 2002-23 dated February 14 2002 and Law 2008-15 dated February 18 2008.

Each time a new law is adopted, all the hydrocarbons titles granted thereafter are governed by the new law. For example, all concessions developed after the promulgation of the Hydrocarbons Code are subject to the provisions of the code, even if they result from permits governed by Decree-Law 85-9.

The hydrocarbons titles existing before the date on which a new law is adopted continue, in general, to be governed by the laws in force at the date the titles were granted.

However, a concession governed by Decree-Law 85-9 may choose to be subject to certain provisions of the Hydrocarbons Code.

(a) Regulatory bodies

The regulatory body in charge of oil and gas exploration and exploitation activities in Tunisia is the Ministry of Industry.

(b) Types of agreement

There are two kinds of agreement that might be concluded by an oil and gas company carrying out exploration and exploitation activities: concession agreements and production sharing contracts.

The holder of a hydrocarbons title is entitled to choose between the two kinds of contracts.

In concession agreements, the oil and gas company is the holder or co-holder of the permit/concession.

Production sharing contracts are concluded between ETAP, the national oil company, which is the holder of the permit and the concession, and a service provider (the contractor).

A production sharing contract is concluded on the basis of the following principles:

- The exploration permit and the exploitation concessions deriving therefrom are granted to ETAP;
- ETAP, acting as the holder, concludes a production sharing contract with a contractor demonstrating possession of the financial resources and the technical experience necessary for the accomplishment of the exploration and the exploitation activities. This contractor may be either a company or a group of companies with one acting as an operator and assuming the related responsibilities.
- The contractor finances at its sole risk all the exploration and exploitation activities for the account of and under the control of ETAP.

(c) ***Acquisition of acreage***

Permits or concessions are acquired through direct negotiations with the competent Tunisian authorities.

(d) ***Qualification requirements***

Activities of prospecting, exploration and exploitation of hydrocarbons may only be undertaken by:

- the state of Tunisia, in accordance with terms to be set for each particular case;
- state-owned or private companies, whether Tunisian or foreign, possessing adequate financial resources and technical competence to conduct such activities under the best conditions.

In this respect, the granting authority may require, at any time, a guarantee for the fulfilment of the expenditure and/or minimum work obligations, to be provided by an entity approved by the granting authority.

(e) ***Duration***

Prospecting work and exploration and exploitation activities may only be undertaken by virtue of a hydrocarbons title granted by the minister in charge of hydrocarbons.

The duration of the exploration and exploitation works under a hydrocarbons title depends on the type of title granted, and the possibility of renewal.

The types of hydrocarbons title that may be granted are:

- prospecting authorisations;
- prospecting permits;
- exploration permits; and
- exploitation concessions.

Prospecting authorisations: A prospecting authorisation confers on its holder the right to undertake works for the detection of the existence of hydrocarbons through the use of geological methods except seismic surveying and drilling.

A prospecting authorisation is granted for a maximum period of one year, whether the permit is governed by the Hydrocarbons Code or Decree-Law 85-9.

Prospecting permits: A prospecting permit confers on its holder the right to undertake works for the detection of signs of existence of hydrocarbons by means of geological and geophysical methods other than drilling.

A prospecting permit is granted for a period of two years.

If the permit is governed by the Hydrocarbons Code, extensions to the period of its validity may be granted upon a reasoned request by the holder of the permit for an additional term not exceeding 12 months.

Exploration permits: An exploration permit confers on its holder the right to undertake studies and works, mainly geological, geophysical and drilling, as well as production tests, which may not exceed seven days each, in order to discover hydrocarbon fields and to assess the importance of the recoverable reserves in place, and, in general, any operations in connection therewith and pursuing the same objectives.

An exploration permit is granted for an initial term with a maximum duration of five years, and is renewable under the terms set out in a special convention and the applicable legislation: which is either the Hydrocarbons Code or Decree-Law 85-9.

Under the Hydrocarbons Code, the holder of an exploration permit is entitled to renew his permit for two consecutive periods, each period having a duration of up to four years. The renewal is subject to certain conditions.

In addition to these two renewals, the holder is entitled to a third renewal for a period not exceeding four years, if upon the expiry of the second renewal period, he has discovered a hydrocarbons field entitling him to obtain an exploitation concession and has filed an application in this regard. The third renewal is also subject to certain conditions.

It is to be noted that the minister in charge of hydrocarbons may, with the agreement of the Consultative Committee of Hydrocarbons, extend the validity of an exploration permit for two years, if certain conditions are met.

In addition, the minister in charge of hydrocarbons may, with the agreement of the Consultative Committee of Hydrocarbons, grant an extension of one year in addition to the extension noted above, where:

- difficulties, duly substantiated by the holder, prevent the normal performance of its exploration activities,
- there is a commitment by the holder to undertake work in addition to its initial obligations.

An extension of a maximum period of two years may also be granted upon the request of the holder, where a hydrocarbons discovery is made during the last period of validity of an exploration permit and the appraisal work in respect of that discovery cannot be carried out during the remaining period of validity. Such an extension only covers the area of the exploration permit where the discovery is located.

Under Decree-Law 85-9, a renewal may be granted upon the request of the holder for a maximum period of two years.

Exploitation concessions: An exploitation concession is granted for a maximum period of 30 years, whether the concession is governed by the Hydrocarbons Code or Decree-Law 85-9.

(f) *Minimum work programme*

A holder of a prospecting permit has to make expenditure commitments and undertake geological and geophysical works as defined by law.

An applicant for an exploration permit must commit to undertake an exploration work programme over the requested area during the period of the permit's validity. The programme has to indicate the nature and the extent of the work to be undertaken, mainly geophysical and drilling work, as well as the minimum amount of expenditure to be incurred for the conduct of the programme.

(g) *Special participation*

Any applicant for a hydrocarbon exploration permit in Tunisia must include in its application an option for the national oil company, ETAP, to participate in any exploitation concession under terms specified by the applicable legislation.

No exploration permit may be granted to any entity except in association with ETAP. The particular agreement concluded between the Tunisian state and the private oil and gas company sets the percentage of ETAP's participation. The contracting company bears all the expenses and risks of the prospecting and the exploration activities. However, in the event of a discovery and before starting the exploitation concession, ETAP may elect to participate in the concession and accordingly bear a proportion of the expenses relating to the prospecting or exploration works, after the approval of the granting authority.

ETAP's participation may take the form of participation in the share capital of a Tunisian joint venture company having its registered office in Tunisia, or any other form.

Agreements as to such a participation and amendments supplementing and/or modifying those agreements have to be approved by decision of the minister in charge of hydrocarbons.

ETAP is entitled to an option of participation in any exploitation concession at a rate decided by and within the limits agrees upon in the particular agreement.

When it chooses to participate in an exploitation concession, ETAP bears its share in the expenditure relating to exploitation activities proportionally to its percentage participation in the concession.

In such cases, ETAP also reimburses its share of expenditure already incurred by the other party or parties that has not been depreciated at the date of ETAP's choosing to participate.

(h) *Assignment and encumbrance*

Prospection and exploration permits as well as exploitation concessions are deemed to be indivisible movable property.

The sale of a prospection or exploration permit or of an exploitation concession is subject to certain conditions.

The total or partial alienation, in any form whatsoever, of the rights held by each co-holder of a prospection or exploration permit or an exploitation concession is prohibited without the prior authorisation of the granting authority.

A prospection or exploration permit or an exploitation concession may only be transferred, in whole or in part, with the authorisation of the minister in charge of hydrocarbons and the agreement of the Consultative Committee for Hydrocarbons.

However, transfers between affiliated companies are exempt from such authorisation requirements. Such transfers must nevertheless be the subject of prior notification to the granting authority.

When a prospection or exploration permit or an exploitation concession is granted jointly to co-holders, the withdrawal of one or several of them does not cause the cancellation of the permit or concession if the other co-holders take over the rights and obligations of those withdrawing, and notify the granting authority accordingly.

However, in event a co-holder's withdrawal from an exploitation concession, the rights to depreciation or reimbursement by ETAP of the share of expenditure incurred by the withdrawing co-holder are not transferred to the remaining co-holders.

In such a case, the withdrawal is treated as a transfer between the co-holders of the exploitation concession.

Where a transfer requires the approval of the granting authority, ETAP has a pre-emption right to acquire the interests that are the subject of the transfer under the same terms and conditions agreed for the transfer, which must be notified to ETAP no later than the date on which request for approval of the transfer is filed.

In the event of a total or partial transfer of a prospection or exploration permit or an exploitation concession, the transferee shall assume the obligations of the transferor and exercise its rights relating to the entirety of the concession/permit or to the share which has been transferred to him.

Subject to authorisation by the granting authority, the transfer shall come into effect as of the date of signature of the deed of transfer drawn up for this purpose by the transferor and the transferee. In all instances, the transfer must be authorised by an order of the minister in charge of hydrocarbons, published in the *Official Gazette of the Republic of Tunisia*.

A transfer is prohibited where the transferee, even if it is affiliated to the transferor, is a company established under the laws of any country not maintaining diplomatic relations with Tunisia.

(i) *Local content*

To the extent compatible with the smooth running of its activities, an operator must give priority to the employment of Tunisian personnel.

Where suitable Tunisian personnel are not available, the operator may be authorised by the granting authority temporarily to employ foreigners. The operator must ensure training for its Tunisian personnel in all disciplines required for its activities under a training programme to be approved by the granting authority.

(j) ***National reservation***

In order to satisfy local Tunisian consumption, the granting authority has a priority right to buy a share of the gaseous and liquid hydrocarbons produced by a concession holder or for its account.

The share of liquid hydrocarbons is prorated at a maximum rate of 20% of the quantities produced by each concession whereas the share of gaseous hydrocarbons is to be specified in a gas supply contract concluded by the granting authority and the holder.

Gaseous hydrocarbons may also be sold to local companies in charge of gas distribution in Tunisia, designated by the granting authority. For this purpose, a supply contract is to be concluded under the aegis of that authority.

(k) ***Environment***

The holder of a prospecting permit, an exploration permit or an exploitation concession is required to carry out its exploration and exploitation activities in compliance with the applicable legislation and regulations regarding technical scope, security, and the protection of the environment, agricultural lands, forests and water in the public domain.

In the absence of applicable legislation, the holder must comply with the rules, criteria and good practices in use in the petroleum industry in similar environments.

The holder shall also:

- carry out, prior to each phase of the exploration and exploitation works, an environmental impact study in accordance with relevant legislation and regulations and obtain approval for the study's conclusions before the commencement of the works;
- take all measures to protect the environment and comply with commitments undertaken in the environmental impact study as approved by the granting authority;
- obtain liability insurance in respect of potential losses or damage suffered by third parties as a result of its activity including, in particular, coverage for damage to the environment.

In addition, in the event of an accident, whether due to a natural phenomenon or to the holder's activities, the holder must take all immediate measures necessary to protect human lives and the environment. If the holder fails to take such measures, the competent authority may take them instead. In such a case, the holder must reimburse all the expenditure incurred for this purpose.

In order to enable such urgent measures to be taken, the holder must:

- have available on location and in sufficient quantities, supplies and equipment to fight against pollution and fire as well as medicines and rescue materials necessary for first aid to be provided to the accident's victims;
- establish specific emergency plans covering all exceptional situations that may occur on its sites and the outbuildings legally pertaining thereto, and provide a copy of these plans to the granting authority and to any other competent authorities;

- establish contingency plans for dealing with limited marine pollution within the port areas of petroleum terminals and in the surroundings of drilling and production platforms, in accordance with the applicable legislation.

Similarly, the holder shall advise the relevant authorities of any serious accident or pollution occurring on its sites.

At the request of the granting authority, the holder shall have its production installation certified by an independent agency recognised by the granting authority.

Upon the expiry of an exploration permit, either upon termination of its last period of validity or in the event of surrender or cancellation or when the holder of an exploitation concession intends to cease its exploitation activities, the holder shall restore to their original condition the areas relinquished and/or production sites abandoned so that no damage is caused, in the short or long term, to the safety of third parties, to the environment or to resources, in accordance with the relevant legislation and regulations.

Abandonment, dismantlement and removal of offshore petroleum installations and restoration of marine sites must comply with the relevant legislation and regulations and with international standards and conventions ratified by Tunisia.

A plan of abandonment, setting the terms of abandonment and site restoration, must be submitted by the concession holder before it starts and production activities. The plan has to be approved jointly by the competent authorities in charge of hydrocarbons and the environment.

(l) *Governing law and dispute resolution*

Under the Hydrocarbons Code, violations of its provisions and of regulations issued for its implementation shall be dealt with by the Tunisian courts.

However, for certain companies governed by particular agreements, disputes arising from their provisions shall be referred to arbitration.

Arbitration is a non-state dispute settlement procedure. It helps resolve a dispute without going through the state courts, by both parties appointing a referee who intervenes to make decisions that are binding on both of them.

3.2. Government take

(a) *Concession agreements*

The main taxes specific to the oil and gas exploitation activities are the proportional royalty and the tax on profits.

Proportional royalty: The royalty is determined in proportion to the value of the hydrocarbons produced and is due whether the company realises profits or losses. It may be paid in cash or in kind.

The proportional royalty rate depends on the R factor, which is determined according to the following formula:

R factor = accrued net earnings/accrued total expenditure

Accrued net earnings: means the sum of all the turnover of all the fiscal years since the start of the concession, including the present one, reduced by the sum of the taxes and levies due or paid for all the previous fiscal years in connection with the concession concerned.

Accrued total expenditure: means the sum of the exploration and evaluation costs incurred on the permit and all the development and exploitation costs incurred on the concession concerned, excluding taxes.

Exploration and evaluation expenditure incurred on a permit and taken into account for the determination of the R factor for a given concession cannot be considered for the purpose of calculating the R factor of other concessions even if they result from the same permit.

The royalty rate varies between 2% (if the R factor is equal to or less than 0.5) and 15% (if the R factor is higher than 2.5) for both liquid and gaseous hydrocarbons (see tables below for further details).

For liquid hydrocarbons:

R factor	Proportional royalty rate (%)
$R \leq 0.5$	2
$0.5 < R \leq 0.8$	5
$0.8 < R \leq 1.1$	7
$1.1 < R \leq 1.5$	10
$1.5 < R \leq 2$	12
$2 < R \leq 2.5$	14
$R > 2.5$	15

For gaseous hydrocarbons:

R factor	Proportional royalty rate (%)
$R \leq 0.5$	2
$0.5 < R \leq 0.8$	4
$0.8 < R \leq 1.1$	6
$1.1 < R \leq 1.5$	8
$1.5 < R \leq 2$	9
$2 < R \leq 2.5$	10
$2.5 < R \leq 3$	11
$3 < R \leq 3.5$	13
$R > 3.5$	15

However, under the Hydrocarbons Code and where ETAP does not participate in the concession, the royalty rate cannot be lower than 10% for oil and 8% for gas.

Proportional royalty rates are the same whether the company is governed by the Hydrocarbons Code or by Decree-Law 85-9.

The proportional royalty is due on a monthly basis whether the paying company is governed by the Hydrocarbons Law or by Decree-Law 85-9.

The amount of the proportional royalty due is calculated by the relevant authorities (the ministry in charge of hydrocarbons) and notified to the company. The company must then pay the royalty due within 15 days starting from the day it receives the notification.

Tax on profits: As a rule, where more than one concession is exploited by the holder, they are ring-fenced, meaning that losses incurred on a given concession cannot be offset against the profits of another concession, regardless of whether the concessions arose from the same permit or not.

However, some exceptions are possible if certain conditions are met.

Tax rate of the tax on profits varies depending on the R factor as follows.

For liquid hydrocarbons:

R factor	Tax on profits rate (%)
R ≤ 1.5	50
1.5 < R ≤ 2	55
2 < R ≤ 2.5	60
2.5 < R ≤ 3	65
3 < R ≤ 3.5	70
R > 3.5	75

For gaseous hydrocarbons:

R factor	Proportional royalty rate (%)
R ≤ 2.5	50
2.5 < R ≤ 3	55
3 < R ≤ 3.5	60
R > 3.5	65

However, for companies subject to the Hydrocarbons Code, the tax on profits rate cannot exceed 50% where ETAP opts to participate in the concession and its participation is at least 40%.

Under the provisions of Article 103.3 of the Hydrocarbons Code, the tax on profits is due annually and is paid through:

- a quarterly payment, at the latest in the end of the civil trimester which follows the trimester concerned; and
- an annual regularisation payment to be made at the latest in the end of six months after the end of the year, that is on June 30 of every year.

Common taxes, duties and levies: The holder, or the co-holder where a permit is granted to several holders, is subject to the following taxes:

- fixed registration taxes (of Td20, the equivalent of about €10 per page and per copy) for agreements, their appendices and associated amendments;
- fixed registration fees for the supply of equipment and services necessary to

the exploration and exploitation works;

- local authority tax, which is due only from companies governed by the Hydrocarbons Code, while companies governed by Decree-Law 85-9 are exempt;
- real estate tax, which is due only from companies governed by the Hydrocarbons Code, while companies governed by Decree-Law 85-9 are exempt;
- tax on customs services and tax on electronic data processing, payable on imports and exports;
- indirect taxes on the purchase of goods and services, other than value added tax (VAT). Companies operating in the hydrocarbons sector, whether governed by the Hydrocarbons Code or Decree-Law 85-9, may acquire VAT-free all the goods and services necessary for their activity subject to the presentation of a certificate issued for this purpose by the relevant tax authorities;
- tax on insurance contracts, which is due only from companies governed by the Hydrocarbons Code, while companies governed by Decree-Law 85-9 are exempt;
- transportation and road taxes, which are due only from companies governed by the Hydrocarbons Code, while companies governed by Decree-Law 85-9 are exempt.

(b) Production sharing contracts

Cost oil: Where hydrocarbons are produced, ETAP transfers to the contractor a portion of that production, up to a percentage limit set by the production sharing contract, which is to cover the expenditure incurred by the contractor under the contract.

Expenditure recoverable in this way includes all costs incurred for the purpose of exploiting the concession, which are mainly those arising from exploration, development and exploitation, including financial charges other than interest on loans contracted in order to finance the prospecting and exploration activities. Interest charges relating to loans contracted in order to finance development activities are tax deductible up to a ceiling of 70% of development expenses.

This deduction is subject to the prior approval of the ministry in charge of hydrocarbons where the concession is governed by Decree-Law 85-9.

Contractors governed by the Hydrocarbons Code are allowed to build up reserves for the restoration of the site. Recovery of these reserves from ETAP is limited to the costs actually incurred.

Profit oil: In addition to the cost oil, ETAP transfers to the contractor, as payment, a percentage of the remaining production as agreed upon in the production sharing contract.

Taxes, duties and levies due from the contractor: Which taxes, duties and levies are due from the contractor in a production sharing contract will depend on whether the concession is governed by Decree-Law 85-9 or the Hydrocarbons Code:

Contractors governed by Decree-Law 85-9 and acting under production sharing contracts are subject to the following taxes, duties and levies:

- indirect taxes on the purchase of goods and services, other than VAT. Companies operating in the hydrocarbons sector and governed by Decree-Law 85-9 may acquire VAT-free all the goods and services necessary for their activities subject to presentation of a certificate issued for this purpose by the relevant tax authorities;
- tax on customs services, payable on imports and exports;
- fixed registration fees for the acquisition of equipment, works and services necessary for exploration, development, production, transport, storage and commercialisation activities;
- tax on profits, which may be paid either by the contractor or by ETAP in the contractor's name and on its behalf, as agreed upon in the production sharing contract.

Contractors governed by the Hydrocarbons Code and acting under production sharing contracts are subject to the following taxes, duties and levies:

- fixed registration fees for the acquisition of equipment and services necessary for exploration and exploitation works;
- local authority tax;
- real estate tax;
- tax on customs services and the tax on electronic data processing, payable on imports and exports. The tax on customs services payable on exports is offset, as an advance payment, against the tax on profits. However, in the particular case of production sharing contracts where the tax on customs services payable on exports by the contractor in its name and on its own behalf is recoverable by ETAP, the latter is also allowed to deduct it from the tax on profits due on its profit oil;
- indirect taxes on the purchase of goods and services, other than VAT. Companies operating in the hydrocarbons sector, and governed by the Hydrocarbons Code may acquire VAT-free all the goods and services necessary for their activities subject to presentation of a certificate issued for this purpose by the relevant tax authorities;
- transportation and road taxes;
- tax on insurance contracts;
- tax on profits, although this tax is paid by ETAP in the contractor's name and on its behalf, and is equal to the contractor's profit oil.

The fixed registration taxes for the agreement, their appendices and associated amendments, the proportional royalty and taxes due on the concession area are payable by ETAP.

4. Current issues

Although exploration began in Tunisia in the 1960s and ETAP was established in 1972, Tunisia has only minor oil and gas resources compared to its neighbours Libya and Algeria, for which reason the biggest oil and gas companies are not motivated to operate in Tunisia.

Therefore, in order to attract the major hydrocarbon companies which are the only ones able to develop fully its potential in the exploitation of oil and gas, Tunisia needs to set up a more favourable tax regime for companies operating in hydrocarbon sector, since the current corporate income tax rate may reach 75% of the profits for liquid hydrocarbons and 65% for gaseous hydrocarbons.

5. Conclusion

This chapter has attempted to show how the Tunisian legal framework for petroleum activities constitutes a distinct regulatory model. The law provides for a licensing regime, with prospection, exploration and production licences.

The state is deeply involved at every stage of relevant activities. In fact, the most appropriate illustration of the Tunisian authorities' interest in hydrocarbons lies in the tax system surrounding this sector. Even if Tunisia is far behind Saudi Arabia, Iraq and Libya in its reserves and production of hydrocarbons, it remains a fact that it is the first Arabic and African country that has developed a, clear, detailed and well-defined set of laws, rules and prerogatives which govern the exploration, exploitation and production of hydrocarbons.

Uganda

Elison Karuhanga
Republic of Uganda

1. Introduction

Uganda is a small country located in East Africa. It is a landlocked country bordered by Kenya in the east, the Democratic Republic of Congo in the west, South Sudan in the north, Tanzania in the south and Rwanda in the southwest. The nearest coastline from Uganda is at the port of Mombasa in Kenya.

Uganda has five sedimentary basins: the Albertine Graben, the Lake Kyoga basin, the Hoima basin, the Lake Wamala basin and the Moroto-Kadam basin.[1] Of these sedimentary basins, the Albertine Graben[2] is the most prospective sedimentary basin.[3] The Lake Kyoga basin, the Hoima basin and the Moroto Kadim basin are said to be under investigation.[4]

Currently all the exploration work in Uganda is being done in the Albertine Graben. The Albertine Graben is located in "the northern most part of the western arm of the East African Rift System."[5] It is close to Uganda's northern border with the Republic of South Sudan and its western border with the Democratic Republic of Congo. The Albertine Graben is divided into 11 exploration areas.[6]

The nearest coastline to the oil fields is almost 1,300 kilometres (km) away in Mombasa, Kenya. The Albertine Graben is also an ecological treasure chest. Over 50% of the birds, 39% of the mammals, 19% of the amphibians and 14% of the reptiles and plants found in mainland Africa are found in this region.[7]

Oil exploration in Uganda occurs in areas that are environmentally sensitive and ecologically rich. This is in addition to the country being landlocked. The legal

1 See *Uganda National Oil and Gas Policy*, p8.

2 A graben is:

> *a relatively low-standing fault block bounded by opposing normal faults. Graben (used as both singular and plural) can form in areas of rifting or extension, where normal faults are the most common type of fault. Between graben are relatively high-standing blocks called horsts. A half-graben is a downdropped block bounded by a normal fault on only one side.*

Definition from the Schulmberger Oilfield Glossary: www.glossary.oilfield.slb.com/Display.cfm?Term=graben.

3 See *Uganda National Oil and Gas Policy*, p 8.

4 See Ernest Rubondo, "Uganda's Petroleum Upstream Sector: Implementation of the National Oil and Gas Policy": www.petroleum.go.ug/uploads/Commissioner%20Jan%202012%20[Compatibility%20Mode].pdf.

5 Ivan Amaniga Ruhanga, Jacob Manyindo and Mark Jordahl, *Maintaining the Conservation and Tourism Value of Protected Areas in Petroleum Development Zones of the Albertine Rift* (2009): wildugandablog.com/wp-content/uploads/2010/02/maintaining-conservation-and-tourism-value-of-pas-in-oil-development-zones.pdf.

6 See FA Kabagambe Kaliisa "Developing Uganda's Oil and Gas Sector and Opportunities for Investment" A Presentation to the UK Uganda Investment Forum 2010.

7 Amaniga Ruhanga, Manyindo and Jordahl above.

regime thus has a significant challenge. On the one hand it should promote investment in the hydrocarbon industry. This is especially so, since Uganda is totally dependent on importing petroleum products through Kenya, mostly by road. On the other hand, the country should promote conservation because of its rich biodiversity. The legal regime also attempts to ensure that international oil companies operating in Uganda are responsible corporate citizens, offering opportunities to the local community, paying taxes and participating in the training of citizens and local business personnel.

This chapter will address all those issues. Uganda is currently in the process of overhauling its Petroleum Law to make the law fit for purpose. This chapter will therefore review the current law and the proposed laws regulating the upstream petroleum sector. It will focus in particular on the legal regime regulating the petroleum industry, the fiscal conditions under which international oil companies and the national government operate and on the current topical issues in Uganda. The chapter starts with a brief description of activities in the upstream petroleum sector in Uganda.

Uganda is, at the time of writing yet to produce any oil. The country is attempting to put in place a new legal regime.

2. Upstream activities

Uganda, like much of East Africa is underexplored. Less than 40% of the Albertine Graben has been licensed or explored. Only 64 exploration wells have been drilled in Uganda. Hydrocarbons have been discovered in 58 of the wells.[8] That represents a 90% success rate. The oil industry average is 35%.[9] Thus, well over 60% of the Albertine Graben remains unexplored but with very good prospects. The 60% is not only unexplored it is currently unlicensed, as at the time of writing.[10]

A significant amount of data has been obtained by the government. Already, 7,500 line km of gravity and magnetic data has been acquired.[11] In addition 9,750km of aeromagnetic data has been acquired, 7,039.55km of 2D seismic data and 1,607.3km of 3D seismic data has been acquired.[12] However, while some exploration work has been undertakena lot to remains be done. There is though, a significant amount of data for any investor interested in considering the prospects in Uganda.

Regarding the current state of the industry in Uganda, the government declared a moratorium on the licensing of new blocks until the Petroleum (Exploration and Production) Act was passed. The act was passed in December 2012. So far, less than 40% of the Albertine Graben has been licensed. Uganda has licensed a consortium of Tullow Oil plc, Total SA and CNOOC (China National Offshore Corporation) in three blocks.[13] The country has discovered 3.5 billion barrels of oil initially in place, with

8 See Rubondo above.
9 See Stanley Reed, "Finding Success on the Oil Frontier" *New York Times*, July 3 2012.
10 A licensing round is expected sometime in 2013. This is discussed later in this chapter.
11 See Rubondo, *op cit*. For a clear understanding of magnetic and gravity methods in mineral exploration see Henry Lyatsky, "Magnetic and Gravity Methods in Mineral Exploration: The Value of Well-Rounded Geophysical Skills": www.cseg.ca/publications/recorder/2010/10oct/oct2010-magnetic-and-gravity-methods.pdf.
12 See Rubondo, above.

1.5 billion barrels estimated to be recoverable. Previously two other independent oil companies had been licensed in Uganda.[14] A licensing round is expected sometime in 2013.

3. Petroleum legal regime

3.1 Petroleum law and relevant provisions

The Ugandan petroleum industry is regulated by a number of laws, including the Constitution, the Petroleum (Production and Development) Act 1985 (revised in 2000), the Petroleum (Exploration and Production) (Conduct of Exploration Operations) Regulations 1993, the Petroleum (Marking and Quality Control) Regulations 2009, the Petroleum Supply Act 2003, the National Environment Act, the Land Act and the Arbitration and Conciliation Act. The government has decided to repeal the Petroleum (Production and Development) Act 1985 and the Petroleum (Exploration and Production) (Conduct of Exploration Operations) Regulations 1993 (which were made under the 1985 act). The Petroleum (Marking and Quality Control) Regulations 2009 and the Petroleum Supply Act 2003 deal with the midstream and downstream petroleum sector and will be considered no further in this chapter. Regarding the upstream sector, Parliament in December 2012 passed the Petroleum (Exploration and Production) Act 2013. This act repeals and replaces the 1985 act. In this chapter, we consider the provisions of the 2013 Act.[15]

The Ugandan Constitution is the supreme law of the land, and any law or act that contravenes or is inconsistent with the Constitution is null and void to the extent of its inconsistency.[16] Article 244 of the Constitution regulates petroleum production in Uganda. It provides that:

Subject to Article 26 of this Constitution [the right to property], the entire property in, and the control of, all minerals and petroleum in, on or under, any land or waters in Uganda are vested in the Government on behalf of the Republic of Uganda.

Subject to this article, Parliament shall make laws regulating–

(a) the exploitation of minerals and petroleum;

(b) the sharing of royalties arising from mineral and petroleum exploitation;

(c) the conditions for payment of indemnities arising out of exploitation of minerals and petroleum; and

(d) the conditions regarding the restoration of derelict lands.

(3) Minerals, mineral ores and petroleum shall be exploited taking into account the interest of the individual landowners, local governments and the Government.

The Constitution also protects fundamental human rights and freedoms. The right to property[17] is constitutionally protected in Uganda. Contracts, licences, judgments and arbitral awards are all considered property under Ugandan

13 See Brian Swint and Fred Ojambo "Tullow Sells Ugandan Stake to CNOOC, Total for $2.9 Action" *Bloomberg Business Week*, August 22 2011.

14 These were Tower Resources and Dominion Petroleum. They did not make any discoveries.

15 As at the time of writing the act is yet to be assented to by the President.

16 See Article 2 of the Constitution of Uganda 1995, as amended in 2005.

17 Article 26 of the Constitution.

jurisprudence and are constitutionally protected. Thus it is unconstitutional to expropriate property unless it is accompanied by fair and adequate compensation. This chapter now considers the detailed aspects governing petroleum law in Uganda.

(a) *Regulatory bodies*

The petroleum industry in Uganda is presently regulated by the Ministry of Energy and Mineral Development. The law empowers the minister to issue licences, sign contracts and revoke licencs. Further, the 1985 Petroleum (Production and Development) Act created the Office of the Commissioner Petroleum Exploration and Development. The commissioner heads a department called the Petroleum Exploration and Production Department that employs various government geologists, geophysicists, petroleum economists and lawyers to mention a few. This department reviews and approves all exploration and development work.

Under the National Environment Act any economic activity that may affect the environment must not be carried out unless there has been an environmental impact assessment and the activity has been approved by the environmental watchdog, the National Environmental Management Authority.

The 2013 act proposes the creation of various institutions. Critics have argued that these institutions have overlapping powers and are likely to lead to regulatory uncertainty.[18] The act creates a Minister for Petroleum whose powers include granting and revoking licences, initiating, implementing and developing oil and gas policy, submitting legislation to Parliament, issuing petroleum regulations, approving field development plans.

The act also establishes the Petroleum Directorate. This directorate will be a directorate within the ministry whose role will be to help co-ordinate policy. The directorate is answerable to the minister and will be concerned not just with upstream but also with midstream and downstream operations in the petroleum sector.

The act then proposes the establishment of the Petroleum Authority of Uganda. The purpose of the authority is to monitor and regulate exploration, development and production of petroleum in Uganda. The authority shall in effect be the regulator approving field development plans and annual expenditure, advising the minister on the grant and revocation of licences and similar tasks.

There will also be a national oil company. This company shall cater for the commercial interests of the government of the Republic of Uganda.

(b) *Types of agreement*

Uganda has a hybrid system using both licensing and production sharing agreements. The law empowers the minister to enter into agreements for the exploitation of the country's hydrocarbon resources. As a matter of practice, the government favoured entering into production sharing agreements. A concession agreement would violate the provisions of Article 244 of the Constitution as it provides that the government owns resources like petroleum in trust. Production

---

18 Presentation of Uganda Chamber of Mines and Petroleum to the Natural Resources Committee of Parliament.

sharing agreements allow for this method of ownership of the natural resources.

The licences in use in Uganda are purely regulatory and should not be confused with licences in concessionary systems. The production sharing agreement envisages both an exploration licence to explore for and find petroleum and a production licence to commence production. A production licence can only be given after the approval of a licensee's field development plans. The holder of an exploration licence has the exclusive right to apply for a production licence.

Uganda uses both these systems (production sharing agreements and licences) for the purposes of flexibility. The law provides for licences and gives the minister the power to enter into contracts. Thus, production sharing agreements are not expressly mentioned in the act. The government can choose in future to use other contractual systems and, depending on the changes in petroleum regulatory regimes around the world, it can adapt and change quickly. The licence therefore, is the basis of the government's regulatory power, while the contract is the basis of its commercial share and its contractual obligations.

(c) Acquisition of acreage

The 1985 act gave the minister unfettered discretion in the award of a petroleum licence.[19] Thus acreage was given solely through direct negotiations with the government.

This is no longer the case. The act now provides for open, transparent and competitive bidding. The minister shall, with the approval of cabinet, announce in local and international media and electronically the areas available for licensing, the period for making an application (three months from the date of the advert or less).[20]

The law, however does provide for direct negotiations in "exceptional circumstances". The law defines exceptional circumstances as instances where "there are non-responsive bids after three attempts, applications in respect of a reservoir within a licensed block which extends to an unlicensed block and promotion of national interest."[21]

When an application for direct negotiations is received, it shall be published in the *Uganda Gazette* and a newspaper with wide circulation in Uganda. The application must, within the limits of commercial confidentiality, be accessible to the public for inspection. Any interested party may on personal, environmental grounds lodge an objection with the minister within 30 days from the date of the publication. The minister shall then exercise his quasi-judicial role and make a decision within 14 days.[22]

(d) Qualification requirements

While the law does not expressly state detailed qualification requirements, it provides that any person applying for a petroleum exploration licence must show his technical and financial capacity. The applicant must also provide details of its work programme and minimum expenditure commitments.

---

19 Section 3 of the Petroleum (Exploration and Production) Act 1985.

20 Clause 58 of the Petroleum (Exploration, Development and Production) Bill 2011.

21 *Ibid*, Clause 59.

22 *Ibid*, Clause 60 and 61.

It is clear that the applicant must have strong technical expertise and proper financial ability in order for their bid even to be considered.[23]

(e) *Duration*

An investor is granted two distinct rights. He is granted an exploration licence and a production licence. However, the production sharing agreement deals with both exploration and production because the holder of an exploration licence is the only person who can apply for a production licence. Therefore, there is no need to have separate contractual terms. Further, the existence of a long-term contract guarantees the holder of a licence who has complied with all the requirements of the law and the licence security of tenure. The dual licences therefore operate as regulatory oversight for the government. While the contract operates as security of tenure and protection of the investor.

The exploration period is for a maximum of six years. This is divided into three periods of two years each. The first two years are for initial exploration. Thereafter, a party can apply for two extensions.

A petroleum production licence runs for a period of 20 years.[24] The production licence can be only be renewed once for a period of five years.[25] Altogether, exploration, development and production can run for a maximum of 31 years.

(f) *Minimum work programme*

The minimum work programme is matter that is usually determined in the production sharing contract. Existing contracts are currently confidential, however, the campaign group Platform leaked copies of previous production sharing agreements between the government of Uganda and certain licensees.[26] in addition, the government has commented quite extensively on the terms of the production sharing agreements as have the international oil companies. While the terms of the production sharing agreements have since changed tremendously[27] the work obligations in the leaked production sharing contracts can provide some guidance as to the work obligations generally required in Uganda.

Under the production sharing agreement[28] the exploration period is six years divided into three two-year periods. During the first exploration period the investor must drill two firm wells at the cost of US$6 million. The investor must further acquire process and interpret 200 line km of 2D or 3D contingent seismic data. During the second exploration period, a similar amount of work must be done and in addition a minimum of $1.5 million must be spent on acquisition of data together

---

23 *Ibid*, Clause 62.

24 *Ibid*, Clause 82.

25 *Ibid*, Clause 85.

26 Taimour Lay and Mika Minio-Paluello, *Contracts Curse – Uganda's oil agreements place profit before people* (2010) and Taimour Lay and Mika Minio-Paluello, *Uganda's contracts – a bad deal made worse. Preliminary analysis of Uganda's Production Sharing Agreements* by PLATFORM (2010), both available on www.carbonweb.org/uganda.

27 The government subsequently signed a new production sharing agreement with the Tullow Oil led consortium as detailed on the Tullow website: www.tullowoil.com/index.asp?pageid=137&newsid=727.

28 The leaked copy of one of the agreements can be found at: www.platformlondon.org/carbonweb/documents/uganda/leaked_Uganda_PSA_Block3A_Heritage_part1.pdf.

with $6 million on drilling a minimum of two exploration wells. Similar conditions exist for the third exploration period: a minimum of $6 million on drilling and $1.5 million on the acquisition of data.

The exploration wells are to be drilled on a location determined by the licensee and the government and to a depth necessary for the evaluation of the sedimentary section established by the available data and cognisant of good oil field practice.

(g) Assignment and encumbrance

A petroleum licence is property under Ugandan law. It can be sold, mortgaged or assigned.

An exploration licence has even been held to be immovable property (like land) by the Ugandan courts.[29]

Under the new Petroleum Act, however, a licence may not be transferred without the express approval of the minister.[30] The minister must first satisfy himself of the technical capacity, competence and the financial strength of the person to whom the licence is being transferred.[31] The minister's consent shall not however be unreasonably withheld.

The new act also allows for a petroleum licence to be used as security for a loan. However, it provides that the minister "may" in consultation with the Petroleum Authority, consent to the use of the licence as security for a credit facility. The licence can only be used in "exceptional circumstances" to finance activities not related to the licence. These exceptional circumstances must be approved by the minister.[32]

(h) Local content

One of the biggest issues in new petroleum provinces is the issue of local content. This implies opportunities for nationals to get employed and to supply goods and services.

In order for a licensee to be able to obtain a petroleum exploration licence, in a competitive process, he must give his plan for local content beforehand. The same is true for a petroleum production licence. The onus, therefore, is on the investor to create a plan that uses local labour and as much as possible employs local services. Local content provisions are also contained in the production sharing agreements themselves. As much as is practicably possible oil companies should employ citizens of Uganda and use the services of Ugandan businesses.

The law provides that the licensee shall give "preference to goods which are produced or available in Uganda and services which are rendered by Ugandan citizens."[33] A controversial provision was added to the new law providing that where the services are not available in Uganda, the foreign supplier must enter into a joint venture agreement with a Ugandan company and the Ugandan company shall have a 48% stake in the venture.

---

29 This was decided in the case of *Heritage Oil and Gas Limited v Uganda Revenue Authority*, Tax Appeals Tribunal Application 26 of 2010.

30 Clause 89(1) of the Petroleum (Exploration, Development and Production) Bill 2011.

31 *Ibid.* Clause 89(3).

32 *Ibid.* Clause 130(1) and (2).

33 *Ibid.* Clause 127.

The law further provides that 60 days before the end of the year a licensee must submit to the Petroleum Authority a report of the licensee's achievements and the achievements of his subcontractors in utilising Ugandan goods and services.[34]

It is also incumbent upon a licensee to ensure that 12 months after the grant of a licence and on each subsequent anniversary of the grant, he submits to the Petroleum Authority for approval a detailed programme for the recruitment and training of Ugandans in all phases of petroleum operations.[35] A licensee must also have a clearly defined training programme for local employees,[36] whether through scholarships or training within or outside Uganda.

(i) National reservation

There is no reservation for local companies in the petroleum sector who wish to undertake exploration and production work. There is no restriction on supplying to the local market. However, the new act does provide the minister with power to require deliveries to cover the needs of the local market. In such a case, the minister must give the licensee 45 days clear notice.[37]

(j) Environment

As pointed out earlier, the Albertine Graben is an ecological treasure chest. It is by far one of the most environmentally sensitive places in Africa and the world in terms of its rich wild life, both flora and fauna.[38] The Petroleum legal regime therefore takes due cognisance of this fact.

Under the Constitution, every Ugandan has a right to a clean and healthy environment.[39] Ugandan law provides for 12 principles of environment management. These include but are not limited to the following:

- to use and conserve the environment and natural resources of Uganda equitably and for the benefit of both present and future generations, taking into account the rate of population growth and the productivity of the available resources;
- to conserve the cultural heritage and use the environment and natural resources of Uganda for the benefit of both present and future generations;
- to maintain stable functioning relations between the living and non-living parts of the environment through preserving biological diversity and respecting the principle of optimum sustainable yield in the use of natural resources;
- to reclaim lost ecosystems where possible and reverse the degradation of natural resources;
- to establish adequate environmental protection standards and to monitor changes in environmental quality;
- to publish relevant data on environmental quality and resource use;

---

34 ibid, Clause 127(4).
35 ibid, Clause 128.
36 ibid, Clause 129.
37 ibid, Clause 118.
38 See Amaniga Ruhanga, Manyindo and Jordahl *op cit.*
39 Article 39 of the 1995 Constitution.

- to require prior environmental assessments of proposed projects which may significantly affect the environment or use of natural resources;
- to ensure that environmental awareness is treated as an integral part of education at all levels; and
- to ensure that the true and total costs of environmental pollution are borne by the polluter.[40]

The 2013 Petroleum Act provides that every licensee shall take into account and give effect to these principles.[41]

Accordingly, environmental law in Uganda is concerned with sustainable development and the principle of the 'polluter pays'.

In the case of petroleum production, the licensee is liable for pollution without regard to fault.[42] Where, an unavoidable event outside the licensee's control has contributed significantly to the damage, the liability may be reduced to the extent that it is reasonable.

(k) Governing law and dispute resolution

The Constitution mandates Parliament to make laws for the good governance of Uganda.[43] The Constitution further provides specifically that Parliament shall make laws regulating the "exploitation of minerals and petroleum".[44] Thus the governing law regulating Petroleum activities in Uganda is Ugandan law.

Regarding dispute resolution, the High Court of Uganda has unlimited original jurisdiction regarding any dispute that arises under Ugandan law.[45]

Notwithstanding the above, Ugandan law does recognise international and national arbitration. Parties are permitted to agree a venue for arbitration.[46] Therefore parties can choose between local or international dispute resolution tribunals. The decisions of either would be applicable and enforceable in Uganda.

Uganda is also a signatory to the New York Convention on the Enforcement of Arbitral Awards and has domesticated the convention in Ugandan law.[47] The country is also a signatory to the International Centre for the Settlement of Investment Disputes (ICSID) Convention. This convention allows for investors from member states to take states to the ICSID tribunal when their assets have been expropriated. Uganda has also signed 15 bilateral investment treaties with various states giving investors from those states investment treaty protection.

The leaked production sharing agreements also contained international arbitration clauses and clauses for expert determination. The international arbitration was to be conducted in London under the rules of the United Nations Commission on International Trade. Uganda, therefore recognises, participates in

---

40 National Environment Act (Cap 153), Section 2.
41 Clause 3 of the Petroleum (Exploration, Development and Production) Bill 2011.
42 *Ibid*, Clause 132(1).
43 Article 79 of the 1995 Constitution.
44 *Ibid*, Article 244(2)(a).
45 *Ibid*, Article 139.
46 Section 20 of the Arbitration and Conciliation Act (Cap 4).
47 *Ibid*, Section 43.

and upholds international arbitration as a method of dispute resolution. Ugandan courts, however, do have jurisdiction notwithstanding any arbitration clauses or investment treaties. Joint venture parties are free to agree on their own mechanism of dispute resolution.

3.2 Government take

This part of the chapter focuses on the government's share of the proceeds from a petroleum project. Uganda does offer fairly competitive terms. Some have argued that the terms are too friendly to oil companies,[48] while others have argued that the terms are reasonable when compared to countries in a similar position.[49] This part reviews the new Petroleum Act and the leaked production sharing agreements to give an indication of current fiscal terms in Uganda. It is worth noting that the government has promised to tighten the fiscal terms in subsequent licensing rounds.

(a) Royalties

For purposes of this chapter, the term 'royalty' includes the government take from production sharing agreements.

The law provides that a royalty shall be paid by the licensee to the government as stipulated in the petroleum agreement.[50] Under the leaked production sharing agreements the royalty rate increases progressively according to the quantities of oil produced. It varies from 5% when oil production is less than 5,000 barrels of oil per day (boed) to 12.5% when oil production is more than 7,500 boed.

After the royalty has been removed and paid to the government, then the cost oil[51] is capped at 60%. The remaining oil is then divided between the investor and the government.[52] This is called profit oil. This too is divided on a sliding scale dependent on the level of production. It varies from a 46% profit share for the government when production is below 5,000 boed to 67% when above 40,000 boed. The overall government take, at peak production, including all taxes and royalty will be 76%.[53]

Presently there is no windfall tax. It is worth noting that the government take is not oil-price-sensitive. It is fair to suggest that in subsequent licensing rounds, the profit share and the royalty will indeed be oil-price-sensitive.

(b) Bonus

The 2013 Petroleum Act provides that a bonus shall be paid by the licensee. The bonus payment will be determined by regulations.[54] Currently though bonus payments are determined by the production sharing agreements themselves. The first production sharing agreements did not contain provision for a signature bonus. However, in 2004 a production sharing agreement was signed with Dominion Petroleum that had a signature bonus of US$2 million.

---

48 Platform, in its reports cited above, makes this case rather strongly.
49 Speech by HE President Yoweri Museveni to Parliament on February 10 2012.
50 Clause 156 of the Petroleum (Exploration, Development and Production) Bill 2011.
51 This is a reimbursement in kind for the expenses already incurred in petroleum exploration.
52 For a proper understanding of the workings of production sharing agreements, read Bindeman, *Production Sharing Agreements: An Economic Analysis*, Oxford Institute for Energy Studies (1999).
53 Speech by HE President Yoweri Museveni to Parliament on February 10 2012.

(c) *Rental fees*

The law provides that the holder of a petroleum Licence shall pay surface rental fees. This payment shall be made annually.[55]

(d) *Special participation*

The law allows the government to participate in petroleum activities through a share of the licence, contract or joint operating agreement. The minister shall, with the approval of cabinet specify the government share in any project.[56]

Under the leaked production sharing agreements the state is given a 15% equity stake in the projects.

(e) *Corporate tax*

The rate of taxation on corporate profits in Uganda is 30%.[57]

Disposal of assets in Uganda is subject to a capital gains tax. The tax rates are set by statute and the minister has no authority to offer relief from corporate taxes in petroleum contracts.[58]

4. Current issues

Owing to the fact that Uganda is a landlocked country that is totally energy-dependent, various issues have arisen. While the international oil companies reportedly want a pipeline built to export crude, the government wants a refinery to refine petroleum products for domestic consumption. This debate has partly slowed down development. The government has, however, resolved to have a refinery first and then a pipeline if the reserves allow.

Another big issue is the contest between civil society and political actors on the one hand and the government on the other hand. Civil society groups are advocating harsher fiscal terms and greater transparency. They want the government to join and comply with the Extractive Industry Transparency Initiative. These groups contend that anything short of joining this initiative makes the resource curse "inevitable". For its part, the government contends that keeping some information like available data and fiscal terms confidential is standard commercial practice and gives the country a better bargaining position. A number of cases have already been filed in the courts by different political and civil society actors. The government has in each case mounted a fairly robust defence of its position.[59] The right to access information in the custody of the state is guaranteed by Article 41 of the Constitution subject to certain limitations. At issue in the various courts is whether the petroleum agreements fit within the clearly defined limitations.

---

54 Clause 158 of the Petroleum (Exploration, Development and Production) Bill 2011.

55 *Ibid*, Clause 157.

56 *Ibid*, Clause 126.

57 Part X of the Income Tax Act.

58 This was held in the case of *Heritage Oil and Gas Limited v Uganda Revenue Authority,* above.

59 In *Angello Izama vs Attorney General*, the government won the right to keep the documents private. However, the case has been appealed. Another case, *Hon Abdu Katuntu v Attorney General* (in which the author has been counsel) is pending.

5. Conclusion

Uganda is yet to produce a single barrel of oil. It hopes to avoid the experiences of other African petroleum producers and, furthermore, not to become another footnote in the long and tragic story of Africa and its oil. It is also a difficult place in which to invest because of the current infrastructure challenges. The law therefore seeks to ensure proper regulation, an attractive investment climate and strong environmental laws. To date the law has been able to attract investment and build partnerships. But a lot remains to be done. However, the country has embarked on the journey of petroleum exploration, development and production. The learning curve is steep. The challenges are plenty. The 2013 Petroleum Act seeks to meet all these challenges. It remains to be seen whether this law will be translated from paper into meaningful action.

Argentina

Dario Arias
Qatar Petroleum
Dario Gerardo Lamanna
CNP

1. Introduction

Argentina benefits from rich natural resources, a highly literate population, an export-oriented agricultural sector and a diversified industrial base. Historically, however, economic performance has been very uneven, with high economic growth alternating with severe recessions, particularly during the late 20th century, when inequality of income distribution and poverty increased substantially. Early in the last century, Argentina was the southern hemisphere's richest country, and one of the wealthiest in the world. It is currently rated as an emerging market on the FTSE Global Equity Index, and one of the G-20 major economies.

2. Upstream activities

There were reports of oil discoveries in Argentina by the late 18th century in the provinces of Jujuy and Salta. The first hydrocarbon concession was granted in 1865, and a deposit was commercially exploited from 1887 until 1891, before the famous 1907 discovery in Comodoro Rivadavia, Chubut Province. The Comodoro Rivadavia discovery is considered the official starting date of the oil business in Argentina.

The country was also one of the world's first to create a national oil company: Yacimientos Petrolíferos Fiscales (YPF); an example later followed by other countries in the region (YPFB in Bolivia, PDVSA in Venezuela, Petroecuador and Petrobras in Brazil).

Argentina has oil and gas production, but cannot be called a hydrocarbon country because of the limited relative importance that hydrocarbons have had in its economy. In the mid-1990s, Argentina not only became self-sufficient in hydrocarbons, but briefly exported gas to Chile and Uruguay. The country has pioneered natural gas use in various activities such as domestic cooking and heating, generating electricity, and recently as a vehicular fuel.

3. Petroleum legal regime

3.1 Petroleum law and relevant provisions

(a) Regulatory bodies

The Argentine legal framework for the oil sector is governed both by federal and provincial legislation. It is substantially composed of the Federal Constitution and, particularly, the Hydrocarbons Law (Law 17,319, enacted on June 23 1967). This remains in force, with a number of amendments, including Law 24,145, Law 24,474 and Law 26,197. Several provincial constitutions also contain provisions governing oil and gas exploration and production. A number of provincial hydrocarbons laws have also been enacted. In addition, there are resolutions, laws and national and provincial decrees regulating the sector.

An amendment to the Constitution in 1994 contained a significant change, transferring the ownership of natural resources from the federal to the provincial authorities. However, this did not mean the complete transfer of oversight and control powers; federal authorities retained general policy and lawmaking power. This constitutional amendment is consistent with the provisions of Article 1 of Law 24,145/92 on the Federalisation of Hydrocarbons, which gives the provinces the right to grant exploration permits and exploitation concessions, and to regulate storage and transport of hydrocarbons in their jurisdictions, in those areas that were transferred to the provinces; and with Decree 1955/1994 which approved a transitional regime for awarding areas for exploration – and further hydrocarbon exploitation – called 'transfer areas', although its application was restricted as it was not supported by all the provinces. Following the constitutional amendment, a legally ambiguous situation had to be resolved. This was created by the fact that the provinces (the resource owners) lacked the legal instruments properly and effectively to exercise the rights deriving from that ownership. The provinces received the authority to grant exploration permits and exploitation concessions in certain areas under Decree 546/2003, and to grant permits for storage and transport under Decree 1955/94, although such permits and concessions have to meet the requirements and conditions of the Hydrocarbons Law and the regulations and standards made thereunder.

Law 24076/92 created the regulatory authority for the gas sector, ENARGAS, with nationwide powers.[1] Among the powers of ENARGAS, however, the law listed that of progressively delegating to provincial governments the execution of those functions that they consider compatible with their authority.[2]

In November 2004, Energía Argentina SA (ENARSA) was created by National Law 25,943,[3] as a multipurpose company in the energy sector.[4]

The company received some initial advantages, such as ownership of exploration permits and exploitation concessions on all national maritime areas not subject to a concession at the date of enactment of the law that created it (Section 2). In total, ENARSA's activities to date have been purchasing liquid hydrocarbons from PDVSA, installing a few gasoline stations, and purchasing natural gas from Bolivia.

---

1 Ley 24076, Gas Natural, *Boletín Oficial* (June 12 1992).

2 L Barrera-Hernandez, "South America Energy Future", in D Zilman *et al*, *Beyond the Carbon Economy, Energy Law in Transition* (Oxford University Press, 2008), p 138.

3 Promulgated by Decree of the Executive 1529/2004.

4 Its purpose is (Article 1):

the exploration and exploitation of hydrocarbons, solid, liquid and gas, transportation, storage, distribution, commercialisation and industrialisation of these products and their derivatives, as well as the provision of public transportation and distribution of natural gas, to which effect it may develop them, process them, refine them, buy them. It may also generate, transport, distribute and sell electricity and engage in trading activities related to energy goods. These activities may be carried out by itself or through third parties or by association with third parties both at home or in foreign countries.

Reforms intended to increase reserves and refining capacity included Law 26,154 of October 2006. This was a promotional plan for hydrocarbons exploration and exploitation, the so-called 'Long Law', created in furtherance of the Hydrocarbons Law, applicable in all provinces and the Argentine continental shelf, and granting tax incentives for exploration and exploitation.

At the end of 2006, the so called 'Short Law', Law 26,197,[5] was enacted. This allows the nation's final transfer, to the provinces, of the ownership and management of hydrocarbon deposits within their territory.[6] It therefore repealed Article 1 of the Hydrocarbons Law, which stated that hydrocarbon deposits inalienably belonged to the nation state, and finished off the reforms required under the 1994 Constitution. It is clear that responsibility for setting energy policy at the federal level is reserved for the executive branch.

The new regulations permit provinces directly to develop their own hydrocarbon investment programmes, and allow oil companies to discuss directly with the provinces their investment programmes and exploitation agreements following the expiry of the contracts awarded by the national authorities (most of which expire around the year 2017).

At the beginning of 2007, Law 26,217 was enacted, extending for five years the rules on the export of hydrocarbons created by Article 6 of Law 25,561 on Public Emergency and Exchange System Reform. This law, enacted in January 2002, created a structural crisis and a public emergency in social, economic, administrative, financial and exchange matters which plagued Argentina following a currency devaluation. There was an economic recession and mass unemployment, especially in the poorer sectors.

On May 2 2012 parliament passed Law 26,741, which expropriated 51% of the oil company YPF SA, in the context of a move by the government to enforce sovereignty over hydrocarbons. The YPF shares were at that date held by the Spanish company Repsol.[7]

The new YPF Corporation has 51% of its shares held by the federal government and the provinces constituting the Federal Organisation of United Oil Products (OFHEPI). The remaining 49% is primarily held by the Petersen Group (which is in turn held by the Ezkenazi family) and the Spanish company Repsol, with some shares being listed on the Buenos Aires and New York Stock Exchanges.

By Decree 660, dated May 4 2012, the President brought into force Law 26,741 calling for national self-sufficiency in hydrocarbons in the public interest. It also created the Federal Hydrocarbons Council, composed of the Ministry of Economy and Public Finance, the Ministry of Planning, the Ministry of Labour, the Ministry of

5 Law promulgated on January 3 2007.

6 With the exception of those areas under federal domain such as any offshore deposits beyond the 12-mile limit of provincial jurisdiction.

7 As background information it is worth mentioning that YPF produces a third of the country's 570,000 barrels of oil per day, almost a quarter of its 125 million cubic meters per day of natural gas and is responsible for approximately 55% of fuel sales on a national basis. Oil and gas reserves in Argentina have dropped sharply in recent years causing the country to start importing energy, having reached self-sufficiency in the 1990s. Energy imports amounted to more than $9 billion in 2011. The president indicated that YPF will focus on boosting exploration and production of both conventional and unconventional hydrocarbons. See www.allendebrea.com.ar/newsletter.php.

Industry, the provinces and the government of the autonomous city of Buenos Aires. The intent was to promote coordinated action by the involved stakeholders regarding matters related to the law. At the same time it aimed to guarantee compliance with the law's purposes and to set out national hydrocarbon policy. It established the principles of that hydrocarbon policy, including: promotion of employment in the industry, increasing reserves and production, maximisation of investment in oil and gas, incorporation of new technologies and the protection of consumer interests.

Meanwhile, Decree 1277/2012 approved the regulations to implement Law 26,741. Among other things, this creates a national hydrocarbon investment plan, the Committee on Strategic Planning and Coordination (discussed below) and the National Hydrocarbon Investment Register.

(b) *Regulatory authorities*

The Hydrocarbons Law establishes the office of the Secretary of Energy as the supervisory authority, based on Section 2 of Law 26,197. Decree 27/2003 enumerates its powers, among which it is authorised to prepare a national energy policy following federal criteria; to supervise and coordinate negotiations relating to international and inter-jurisdictional cooperation and integration agreements to which the nation is party; to supervise compliance with the regulatory framework; and to intervene in the oversight of the bodies responsible for services that have been privatised or the subject of concessions when these are in a functional relationship with the office of the Secretary of Energy.

Since the enactment of Law 26,197, energy policy design at the federal level is the responsibility of the executive branch, and the provinces assume control over hydrocarbons located within their boundaries. Under this law, the provinces are designated as the enforcement authority, and they grant exploration permits and exploitation concessions, regulate the transport of hydrocarbons, and monitor and control permits, concessions and any other type of contract for exploration and/or exploitation granted or approved by the national government. The provinces oversee compliance with legal and contractual requirements relating to investment, rational exploitation of resources, information supply, payment of fees and royalties, they decide on contract extensions, and apply sanctions under the Hydrocarbons Law.

Another highlight of Decree 1277/2012 is the creation of the Commission on Planning and Coordination under the Secretariat of Economic Policy and Planning of the Ministry of Economy and Finance, the Secretary of Energy of the Ministry of Federal Planning and the Secretary of Domestic Trade of the of the Ministry of Economy and Finance.

The Commission's task is to establish a plan of minimum budgets and investment goals, to arrange for the investments necessary to ensure self-sufficiency, to establish a specific sanctions regime, and to oversee hydrocarbon planning and fuels marketing.

(c) *Types of agreement*

Concession contracts granted under the Hydrocarbons Law remain in force in

Argentina. However, since the enactment of the Short Law, Law 26,197 of 2007, ownership and management of hydrocarbon reservoirs located within their territories is transferred to the provinces.

The contracts are made by means of administrative decrees, complemented by the legal and regulatory framework applicable to the industry. A decree granting a concession to a particular company authorises that company – in its capacity as the concession holder for hydrocarbon exploration and exploitation – to conduct the activities involved, and in return the company pays an annual fee for each square kilometre covered by the concession.

Hydrocarbon concessions are subject to public law. A concession involves the action or effect of granting a right, whereby the natural resource leaves the domain of the state and enters the domain of a private company. Grantors keep the ownership of hydrocarbon deposits and the hydrocarbons contained therein. Concession holders, in turn, are granted the right to exploit the hydrocarbons, and ultimately to acquire the ownership of the hydrocarbons they produce at the wellhead.

The exploitation concession confers the exclusive right to exploit hydrocarbon deposits existing in the area covered by the concession for a period specified by law.

The overall strategy and energy policy are set by the state, in its capacity as regulator, and the planning and execution of these are driven by the company, which also provides the financing and technology, and assumes the risks.

Other types of arrangements have also been used by the federal state, the provinces and by national and provincial state-owned companies, based on the flexible contractual framework allowed under the Hydrocarbons Law and provincial statutes. One examples of this is the use of service contracts. In this type of arrangement, private companies undertake exploitation and exploration activities, utilising their own resources, typically on behalf of and for the benefit of national and provincial state-owned companies. In the event of the discovery of a commercially exploitable deposit, the state or the state-owned company reimburses the contractor's costs and investments, and the contractor then receives a fee per barrel produced. The main features of this type of contract are:

- the contractor receives a full refund of investments, costs and expenses;
- the contractor also receives a fee per barrel produced;
- royalties are paid by the state-owned company;
- the private contractor is subject to income tax on its earnings; and
- the public company or state owns the oil produced.

Joint venture arrangements in the form of UTEs[8] have also been widely used.

(d) Acquisition of acreage

According to the Hydrocarbons Law, activities relating to hydrocarbon exploration, exploitation, processing, transportation and marketing may be in the charge of private companies, state-owned companies or mixed ownership companies. Permits

8 The formation of a UTE, an acronym deriving from the Spanish for a transitory union of undertakings, is regulated by Law 19,550.

and concessions covered by this law are awarded through bids, in which individuals or companies legally domiciled in the country with sufficient financial strength and technical capabilities compete for the right to undertake the relevant activities.

Concessionaries have ownership of the hydrocarbons they extract and are allowed to transport, industrialise and commercialise derivatives in accordance with applicable regulations, which are issued for technical and economic reasons, taking into account domestic market needs and the objective of enhancing exploration and exploitation. The executive branch determines the areas for which the enforcement authority may solicit bids for the granting of permits and concessions.

ENARSA, however, holds all offshore exploration permits. Private companies may partner with this state-owned company to undertake offshore projects.

(e) Qualification requirements

The Hydrocarbons Law requires prospective concession holders to prove their financial and technical capabilities and be registered with the National Registry of Oil Companies. Some provinces have separate equivalent registries. However, in general these have identical requirements to those established in the national Hydrocarbons Law.

Article 5 of that law regulates bids using methods typical of public administration. The executive branch decides that there will be a call for bids (which it may do on its own initiative or as a result of a private proposal). The applicable enforcement authority prepares the bid sheet, which sets out the necessary information, conditions, guarantees and the criteria on which the bids will be evaluated. Once the offers have been presented, the authority will study them, and may require improvements in bids it considers suitable, the selection of these being explained in a reasoned opinion. All bids may be rejected or, on the other hand, even if there is only a sole bidder the contract may be awarded if it is justified. Whatever the result, there is no right to indemnification or compensation for presenting an unsuccessful bid.

(f) Duration

The concession system awards mining rights on a temporary basis.[9] The time frame of the exploration phase (under an exploration permit) can be up to nine years (divided into three successive exploration periods) with a possible extension for a further five years, and that of the production phase (under an exploitation concession) is 25 years, with an option for an additional 10 years. Offshore permits and concessions may entail longer periods of time.

(g) Minimum work programme

In addition to the obligations for payment of rent, royalties and taxes, the law imposes the following obligations on the concessionaires:

- Investment within a reasonable time frame of amounts that allow the

---

9 Vasena, Krieger *et al*, "*Mensaje de elevación de la Ley 17319/67*", see mepriv.mecon.gov.ar/Normas/17319.htm.

maximum production reasonably possible using modern techniques (Article 31 of the Hydrocarbons Law).

- Presentation of a development programme for any field discovered within 90 days after the find has been declared commercial. The programme shall detail the investment commitments to be met. The programme must be periodically updated (Article 32).

Decree 1277/12 established a strategic hydrocarbon planning commission (Article 2) to "increase and maximise investments" in order to guarantee self-sufficiency in hydrocarbons, and to create the National Registry of Oil Companies (Article 7).

(h) Assignment and encumbrance

If a company wishes to transfer its rights in respect of an area, it must present a request to the Secretary of Energy. The request is passed to executive branch of the province in which it the area concerned located, and undergoes the following steps:

- approval by the Secretary of Environment and Sustainable Development;
- approval by the Legal and Technical Secretary;
- finally, the issuing of a provincial decree (see Law 26,197).

Transfers are governed by Articles 72 of the Hydrocarbons Law, which provides that permits and concessions can be transferred, after authorisation by the executive branch, to another party who meets and complies with the conditions and requirements established for licensees or concessionaires, as applicable.

Likewise, a holder of an exploitation concession may (Article 73) use the concession as collateral for a loan where non-fulfillment of the loan contract will result in legal transfer of the concession to the creditor. Such contracts are subject to the prior approval of the executive branch, which will only be assured if compliance with the conditions set out in Article 72 is satisfactorily guaranteed.

(i) Local content

There are no nationwide requirements to give preference to local content in the purchase of goods or services that are applicable to the hydrocarbons industry in particular. However, some provincial governments have included local content provisions in the terms of bidding rounds organised by them.

Law 25,551[10] establishes that the national public administration, state-owned companies, other public entities and public services concession holders[11] and their respective subcontractors shall give preference to the purchase or leasing of goods of national origin – which are those where the cost of the imported raw materials does not exceed 40% of the gross production cost – provided that the cost of the national goods is no more than 5% higher than the equivalent imported goods (7% when the Argentine supplier is a small or medium sized undertaking).

10 Buy Argentine Law; enacted in 2001.

11 Distribution of natural gas and gasoline falls under the category of public services.

(j) ***National reservation***

In addition to the reservation by Law 25,943 of all offshore exploration permits and exploitation concessions for ENARSA, some provinces have created their own provincial mining and energy companies[12] and have reserved for them all free areas, as a way of forcing private companies to join the provincial state-owned companies in oil and gas activities in their territories.

(k) ***Environment***

Argentina's National Constitution, amended in 1994, includes protection of the environment as an inalienable right of all inhabitants. Article 41 states that all citizens have the right to enjoy a healthy and balanced environment, suitable for development and productive activities that meet current needs without compromising those of future generations. The authorities are required by the Constitution to provide protection of this right, the rational use of natural resources, the preservation of natural and cultural heritage and biodiversity, and environmental education and information. It is a duty to preserve the environment. To this end, the nation is responsible for establishing the rules containing the minimum standard of protection, while the provinces are responsible for what is necessary to reinforce them, without altering their local jurisdictions.

Further, the Constitution prohibits entry into the country of waste that is actually or potentially dangerous, or radioactive.

Due to delay on the part of Congress in enacting the minimum standards mandated by the Constitution, the provincial legislatures took the initiative to enact laws to regulate environmental protection.

Eventually, on November 6 2002, the Senate and House of Representatives enacted Law 25,675, the General Environmental Law, which sets minimum standards for sustainable and appropriate management of the environment, protection and preservation of biodiversity and the implementation of sustainable development. One of the objectives of the national environmental policy is to establish procedures and mechanisms to minimise risks, prevent and mitigate emergencies and restore damage caused by pollution. It also requires that any work or activity likely to degrade the environment or harm the population's quality of life must be subject to an environmental impact assessment prior to its execution.

There are also a number of environmental regulations relating specifically to oil and gas activities: Resolution 105/92 regulates protection of the environment during exploration for and exploitation of hydrocarbons, requiring a mandatory environmental impact assessment prior to initiating activities; Resolution 340/93 requires annual environmental audits; Resolution 341/93 approves the regulation approved by Decree 20481/73 to prevent marine pollution by oil; Law 20,284 regulates pollutant emission sources; Resolution 252/93 approves guidelines and recommendations for implementing the environmental assessments and monitoring

---

12 These include Recursos Energéticos y Mineros SA (REM SA) in Neuquén province; Empresa Mendocina de Energía SA (EME SA) in Mendoza; Jujuy Energía y Minería Sociedad del Estado (JEMSE) and Recursos Mineros y Energeticos Salta SA (REMSA SA), see D Arias, "What REMSA (Salta's Mining and Oil state-owned company) should be and do", *El Tribuno*, April 8 2010.

the work and tasks required by Resolution 105/92; and Decree 3395/96 addresses the generation of gaseous emissions, among other things.

Moreover, Argentina has signed the following international conventions relating to environmental issues and hydrocarbons:

- International Convention for the Prevention of Pollution (1973), amended by the 1978 Protocol (MARPOL73/78).
- Bilateral Agreement between Argentina and the Republic of Chile on the Environment (1992), regarding environmental management, environmental protection and rational use of natural resources.
- Bilateral Agreement on Environmental Cooperation between Argentina and the Federative Republic of Brazil (1998).
- Bilateral Cooperation between Argentina and the Republic of Tunisia (2001), to protect the environment (approved by Law 25,388).
- Mercosur Multilateral Agreement on Environment (2004), an environment framework agreement signed in Asunción whose goal is the environmental protection and rational use of natural resources.
- International Maritime Organisation (IMO) Convention on the Prevention of Marine Pollution by Dumping of Wastes and Other Matter (1972) and the so-called 'London Protocol' (1997).
- Multilateral Agreement on Civil Liability for Oil Damages (1969), including the Protocol of 1992 to amend the International Convention on Civil Liability for Oil Damages (1969) and the Protocol of 1992 to amend the International Convention on Compensation for Damage from Oil Pollution (1971).
- Multilateral Agreement on the United Nations Framework Convention on Climate Change (2001) in the Kyoto Protocol to the UN Framework Convention on Climate Change, adopted in Kyoto, Japan, on December 11 1997.

(l) Governing law and dispute resolution

Hydrocarbon exploration permits and exploitation concessions are governed by Argentine law.

Article 86 of the Hydrocarbons Law allows arbitration as a method of dispute resolution under the concession agreement for certain technical matters.

Arbitration has been the method commonly employed to resolve conflict without referring disputes to ordinary courts. It is also the most widely used means of alternative dispute resolution among companies. Disputes over provincial concessions are, however, often subject to the jurisdiction of provincial courts of law.

The most used centre for arbitration has been the International Centre for Settlement of Investment Disputes (ICSID or CIADI in Spanish), a World Bank internal institution, based in Washington DC, and created by the Washington Convention of 1966. ICSID was set up to facilitate resolution of conflicts between governments and nationals of other states. Its main goal is to provide legal certainty in international investment under international treaties for the protection of investments.

3.2 Government take

There are various forms of taxation on hydrocarbon contracts with the state. These include:

- signature bonuses;
- production bonuses;
- royalties;
- income tax;
- windfall taxes; and
- other indirect taxes.

(a) *Royalty*

The payment of a royalty is the state's principle reward under concession contracts (Hydrocarbons Law, Article 59). The licensee must pay monthly to the state, by way of royalties, 12% on the proceeds of liquid hydrocarbons extracted at the wellhead; paid in cash or in kind. The executive branch may reduce this percentage to 5%, taking into account productivity, the conditions and the location of the wells. The royalty is received in cash unless, 90 days prior to the payment date, the state communicates its preference to receive payment in kind (Article 60). In that event, the licensee is required to store at no charge, for a maximum of 30 days, and to deliver liquid hydrocarbons as royalties. The royalty cash payment is calculated on the wellhead value of crude, discounting freight to the location taken as a basis for setting its commercial value. This value is determined monthly by the enforcement authority. Natural gas production is taxed monthly on 12% of the value of the volumes extracted and effectively used (Article 62). This percentage can also be reduced to 5% by the executive branch by reference to the same factors as apply to the royalty on oil. For this royalty payment, the gas value is set using the same procedure as for crude. Hydrocarbons used by the licensee or permit holder in their field operations are exempt from royalties.

(b) *Bonuses*

There is no obligation to pay signature bonuses for exploration blocks. Signature bonuses have, however, become common as consideration for the granting of the optional 10-year extension to production concessions.

(c) *Rental fees*

Following precedents in Spanish law, Argentina has established the obligation to pay one fee in respect of exploration, and another in respect of exploitation. Article 57 of the Hydrocarbons Law provides that, in order to maintain its right to exploration a permit holder must make annual payments in advance. The amount of the fee is based on the number of square kilometres covered by the permit at issue.

(d) *Special participation*

The terms applying to bidding rounds may provide that national or provincial state-owned companies are to be granted carried interests.

In addition, the Oil Plus and Refining Plus programmes, created by Decree

2014/2008 and regulated by the Secretary of Energy's Resolution 1312/08, provide that companies that increase reserves and production will be guaranteed an additional tax credit against the payment of export duties applicable to the export of hydrocarbons.

(e) Corporate tax

In early May 2005, the government announced a special regime for hydrocarbon exploration, aimed at encouraging investment in exploration and exploitation, improving the outlook for reserves, turning 19 unexploited basins into productive ones and strengthening ENARSA's position in the hydrocarbons market. Accordingly, in October 2006, Law 26,154 was enacted, creating, under the Hydrocarbons Law, promotional schemes for hydrocarbon exploration and exploitation applicable in all Argentine provinces and to the continental shelf.

Among the tax benefits, the law provides for refund of value added tax (VAT) on investments made during both the exploration and exploitation phases, and for the amortisation of expenses and investments in the exploration stage and investment in the operating period.

Regarding income tax, there is a special term regarding treatment of certain unencumbered assets with respect to the tax on minimum presumed income, and there is also an exemption from import duties for certain capital goods or parts necessary for the activities covered by the scheme.

The benefits under this law are valid for 15 years in areas on the continental shelf, 12 years in non-producing sedimentary basins and 10 years in productive ones.

Since the enactment of Law 26,217, the application of export taxes on crude oil, gas and derivatives has been extended until January 2012. From March 5 2002 all such exports have been taxed, including crude oil which is taxed at 25%. In addition, from August 2004 there has been an additional levy on West Texas Intermediate when its price is above $32 per barrel, the amount being based on a preset price range.[13]

In addition, foreign sales of diesel, gasoline and fuel oil are taxed at 5%, liquefied petroleum gas at 20% and natural gas at 45%, and these rates are expected to remain in effect for several years.

Meanwhile, Law 25,154 enacted in October 2006 created tax incentives for hydrocarbons exploration and exploitation, but there have never been any implementing regulations.

In October 2011, Decree 1722 forced oil companies to maintain funds in the country. Oil companies must repatriate 100% of their export revenue to Argentina, where the funds must be exchanged for Argentine currency on the local markets.

4. Current issues

4.1 The current position of resources

Currently Argentina is going through an energy crisis. Its production reserves have fallen to the lowest levels for a decade, and the country has changed from being a

13 Darío Lamanna and Darío Arias, "Argentina's Hydrocarbons Export Regime", *Oil, Gas & Energy Law Intelligence*, Volume 6, Issue 2, April 2008 (UK), (www.ogel.org).

net energy exporter to importing natural gas at high prices from Bolivia and liquefied natural gas from overseas.

In recent years Argentina has suffered energy shortages and a number of black-outs, affecting mainly the industrial sector (including hydrocarbons producing regions).

The country imported 2,412 gigawatt hours (GWh) of power from neighbouring countries in 2011, slightly more than the 2,351GWh imported in 2010. Argentina's power exports have significantly declined in recent years; dropping from 1,292 GWh in 2009 to 359 GWh in 2010 and 265 GWh in 2011, as domestic demand for electricity has increased.

Currently, the contribution of alternative energy sources in Argentina (excluding hydro) remains relatively low (around 1.5%). Recently, a number of new laws and regulations have been enacted in an attempt to encourage the development of these non-traditional sources of energy and incentivising investments in this field (for example Law 25,019 on the Solar and Aeolic Legal Regime, which declared the generation of electricity using these sources to be in the national interest, and Law 26,190 which enacted a "national incentive for the use of renewable sources for electricity generation").

The Ministry of Federal Planning, Public Investments and Services launched a "Renewable Energy Generation Programme" (GENREN) with the intention of reaching the target of having 8% of total electricity originate from renewable sources by 2016, as set out in Law 26,190.

A further manifestation of this project also is the creation of the Fiduciary Fund for Renewable Energy, administered by the National Council for Electricity (CFEE).

Biodiesel Production & Exports from Argentina. 2007–2011

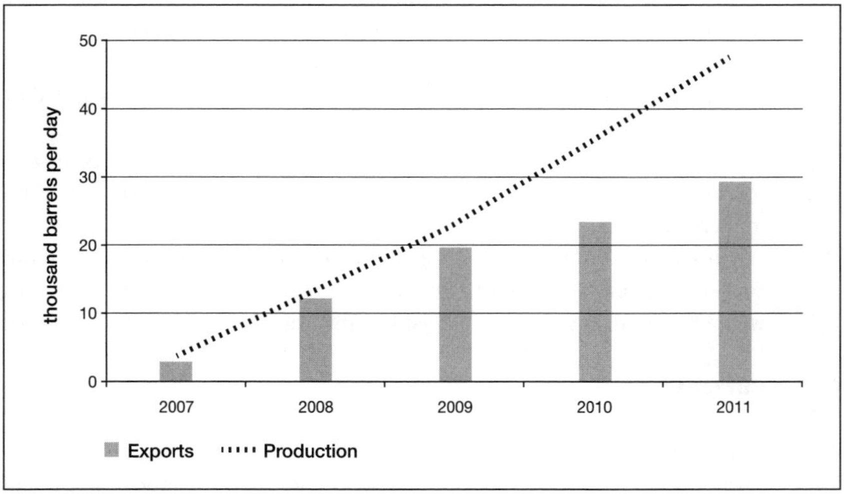

Source: US Energy Information Administration[14]

14 See US Energy Information Administration, *Country Analysis Briefs, Argentina*, at www.eia.gov/emeu/cabs/argentina/pdf.

Shale gas basins in southern South America

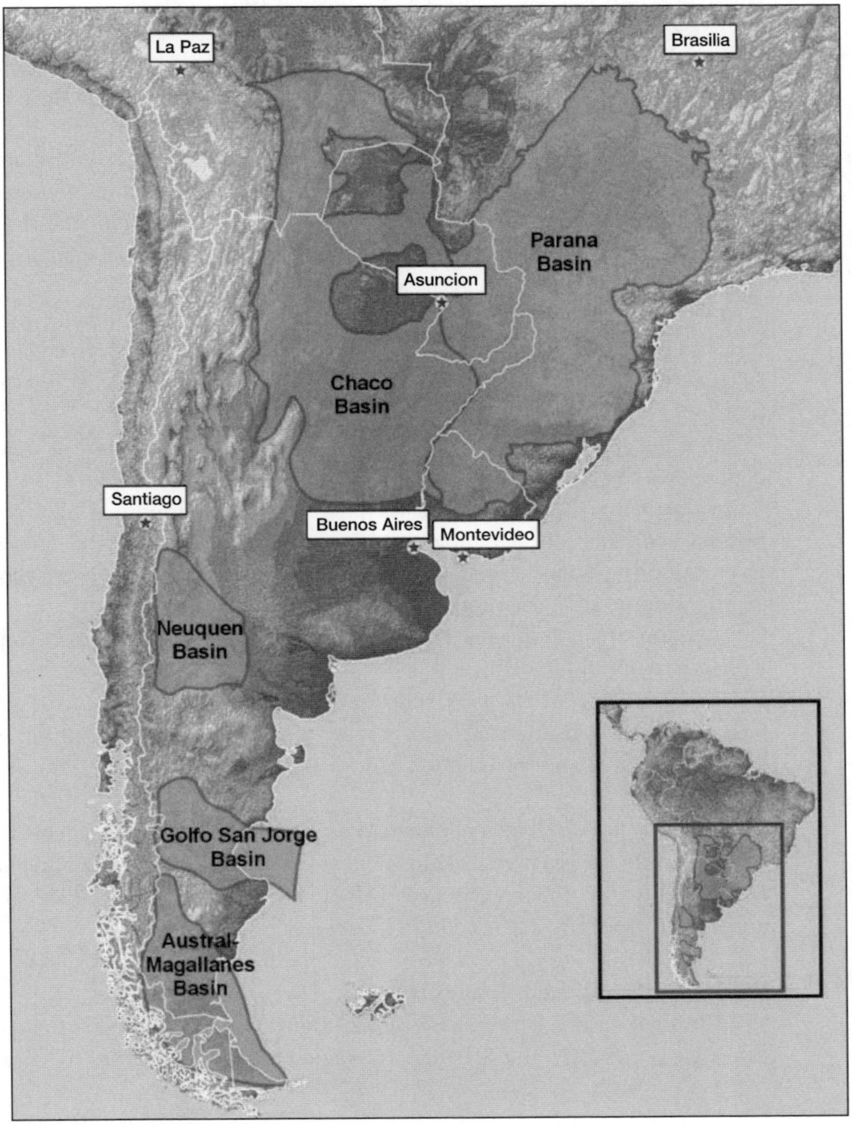

Source: US Energy Information Administration, World Shale Gas Resources: An Initial Assessment of 14 Regions Outside the United States, March 2011.

The *Oil & Gas Journal* estimates that Argentina had proven natural gas reserves of 13.4 trillion cubic feet (tcf) as of January 1 2012 – a decline of approximately 50% from a decade ago. Almost three-quarters of proven reserves are in the Neuquén and Austral basins (42% and 30% respectively), with the remainder in the Noroeste (northwest), Golfo San Jorge and Cuyana basins.

Argentina is among the world's largest producers of biodiesel, and the largest exporter. Its soybean-based biodiesel production reached almost 47,500 barrels per day in 2011, according to the Argentine government. Biodiesel production has dramatically increased over the past five years, including an increase of over 25% from 2010 to 2011. Exports increased by almost 20% to nearly 30,000 barrels per day in 2011.[15]

According to recent analysis by the US Energy Information Administration and Advanced Resources International, Argentina has 774 tcf of technically recoverable shale gas resources – the world's third largest, behind only China and the United States. The Neuquén Basin in western Argentina contains more than half of the country's technically recoverable shale gas resources.[16]

Last year, YPF announced discovery of a large, commercially promising formation of tight gas and shale gas – thought to total 4.5 tcf – near Neuquén's Loma La Lata field, which for decades has been a leading source of conventional production.

After the expropriation of 51% of YPF and its return to the stage as Argentina's national oil company, several issues need to be addressed by Congress, such as the future distribution of shares among the provinces, the decision-making process, the possible content of shareholders' agreements, relations with the Federal Hydrocarbons Council (created by the same decree that brought about the expropriation) and with other existing organisations such as the Federal Organisation of Oil-Producing Provinces, the constitution of the board, and other matters that are still undefined.[17]

Similarly, ENARSA's role is still unclear – so far it has been limited to only trading fuels – as is YPF's relationship with respect to the various provincial mining and energy companies and the question of how they will avoid competition with each other.[18]

Argentina has unveiled a new system of export taxes on oil shipments that will cut levies as the government seeks to lure investment to revive stagnant production.[19] Analysts have said this regulation is part of a series of measures aimed at luring investment, especially in the country's vast shale resources.[20]

4.2 The Malvinas (Falkland) Islands issue

Since its 1994 reform, Argentina's National Constitution has asserted the country's sovereign power over the Malvinas (Falkland) Islands.[21] Argentina is engaged in

---

17 Dario Arias, "*El problema no es el qué sino el cómo*", article regarding the YPF's expropriation, in *Reporte Energía* magazine, Bolivia, April 2012.

18 *Ibid.*

19 Resolution 1/2013 of the Secretary of Energy (Repealed Resolution 438/2012 and item 4 of Section A), Production, Annex I of Resolution 1312/2008.

20 See www.upstreamonline.com/live/article1303708.ece.

21 The First Transitory Provision provides that:
Argentina reaffirms its legitimate and permanent sovereignty over the Malvinas, South Georgias and South Sandwich Islands and the relevant maritime and insular areas, as they are an integral part of the Argentine territory. The regaining of those territories and the full exercise of sovereignty, with respect for the lifestyle of their inhabitants and in accordance with the principles of International Law, are a permanent and unrelinquished objective of the Argentine people.

efforts to garner regional and international support on the Malvinas issue, meanwhile imposing limited sanctions on the territory, in order to maintain pressure on the British government to engage with Argentine concerns. The United Kingdom has affirmed its commitment to the Falklands, maintaining that it is not open to sovereignty negotiations with Argentina unless the Falkland Islanders themselves request them.

Further, from the UK standpoint, the Malvinas (Falkland) Islands have the autonomy to regulate local energy exploration and production; with the ultimate authority to issue licences held by the governor of the islands under an 'open door' licensing system. Significantly, all companies operating in the Falkland Islands are UK-based, with Falkland Oil and Gas Ltd currently holding the highest percentage of acreage.[22]

The dispute over the archipelago, and ongoing oil exploration by UK companies in the islands' waters, has led to increasingly hostile rhetoric between Argentina and the United Kingdom, and the two have traded allegations of colonialism.

The energy situation provides a highly significant economic dimension to the dispute. Exploratory drilling in the basins surrounding the Malvinas (Falkland) Islands has revealed petroleum systems with a yet to be confirmed value. The most significant exploration event so far has been the announcement of an oil discovery on Rockhopper Exploration's Sea Lion prospect. Estimates indicate a potential 350 million barrels to date, with further finds possible as the exploration process continues. Based on conservative estimates, IHS Herold's valuation of the Sea Lion oilfield presently stands at US$3.1 billion, and Rockhopper is seeking a large international partner to fund further development.[23]

Given its own claims to sovereignty of the Falkland (Malvinas) Islands, Argentina maintains that all hydrocarbon exploration without a permit from its own government is illegal; issuing threats of legal action and enacting sanctions against all companies involved with that exploration, and barring them from operating in Argentina. If enforced, such sanctions could affect companies currently involved in exploration around the islands.

5. Conclusion

In the 1990s, with legislative reforms, institutional empowerment of regulators and clear rules towards the opening of the industry to foreign direct investment, Argentina enjoyed a bonanza period that allowed the country to be well positioned amongst Latin American players. However, nowadays the heavily regulated energy sector labours under policies that limit the industry's attractiveness to private investors while shielding consumers from rising prices. Consequently, demand for energy in Argentina's growing economy continues to rise, while production of both oil and gas are in decline – leading Argentina to depend increasingly upon energy imports.[24]

---

22 See *The Falkland (Malvinas) Islands*, IHS networked report, April 2012, at www.ihs.com.
23 *Ibid.*
24 US Energy Information Administration, see *supra* note 14, p 11.

Currently, energy prices in Argentina are very low, compared with neighbouring countries, due to heavy subsidies paid by the national government (around US$7 billion a year). This scheme has deterred genuine investment in exploration, has caused increases in consumption and put off concerns regarding energy efficiency and saving. It is foreseeable that this scheme will change shortly (in two to three years) as the current status is unsustainable. The new scenario will very likely raise energy tariffs dramatically, and will also cause a larger demand for alternative sources.

Bolivia

Dario Arias
Qatar Petroleum
Raul A Baldivia
Baldivia Unzaga & Asociados

---

1. Introduction

During the first years of the 21st century Bolivia was considered South America's energy hub as its hydrocarbons reserves grew at exponential rates. The sector turned out to be critical to Bolivia's economy due to its contribution to the country's gross domestic product, exports, investments and government take.

The hydrocarbons boom, mainly in natural gas, started back in 1996 when the then Bolivian government privatised 50% of shares in the country's national oil company, Yacimientos Petrolíferos Fiscales Bolivianos (YPFB). YPFB was split into three corporate vehicles, two operating in the upstream sector (Empresa Petrolera Chaco SA and Empresa Petrolera Andina SA and one operating in the downstream sector (Transportadora de Hidrocarburos – Transredes SA), plus a participation in Gas Transboliviano, the gas export pipeline from Bolivia to Brazil (which is around 4,500km long).

The new Hydrocarbons Law was issued in April 1996 aimed at attracting fresh capital, and several regulations reflecting international industry standards followed in 1996 and 1997 creating a friendly legal framework to attract substantial investments. World-renowned international oil companies like Petrobras, Repsol, BG, BP Amoco (through PAE) and Total acquired participating interests in several fields through shared risk contracts. Royalties were in the order of 18% and companies acquired ownership rights over the hydrocarbons produced at the wellhead. Bolivia's certified reserves grew steadily from less than 5 trillion cubic feet in 1995 to almost 27 trillion cubic feet of proven reserves (52 trillion cubic feet proven and probable reserves) by 2004.

In October 2003, then Bolivian President Sánchez de Lozada was ousted from government by a popular uprising against his project to export Bolivia's natural gas to Mexico and California by constructing an liquefied natural gas terminal in Chile (Bolivia's neighbour to whom Bolivia lost territory and access to the Pacific Ocean in a war back in the late 1800s).

In 2004 a national referendum ordered the recovery of state ownership of all hydrocarbons and control of the entire value chain, including production, commercialisation, transportation, storage, industrialisation and retail sale. Private international oil companies could no longer dispose freely of their own production and were forced to migrate to new types of contract as provided in the new Hydrocarbons Law (3058) which was enacted in March 2005. Such changes went even further to increase the government stake from 18% to 50% in terms of royalties and a new direct hydrocarbons tax. Previously state-owned companies that had been capitalised were nationalised again.

In January 2006 Evo Morales was sworn in as the new president, and in May of that year he issued Supreme Decree 28701 implementing certain provisions of the new Hydrocarbons Law. It provided for the recovery of state ownership and absolute control over all hydrocarbons. Companies were given six months to migrate to a new type of petroleum contract, the so-called 'operations' agreement'. Under this agreement, the international oil companies were basically turned into service providers and YPFB took control of the entire industry, including the commercialisation of hydrocarbons nationally and abroad.[1]

It has been six years since that nationalisation, and the government has started sending signals that it will enact a new hydrocarbons law adjusted to current industry needs and also a new investments law.

2. Upstream activities

Upstream production has started to recover since 2010, although only slightly. From 2006 to 2010 investments in exploration and production were at best sluggish and at worst stopped altogether. Producers had no incentive to invest in either exploration or production primarily due to the nationalisation process having such a great impact, not only on the international oil companies already based in Bolivia but also on potential investments from abroad. The process lasted about three years. Needless to say the international financial crisis played its part as well, because of its effect on demand and international prices.

The share of gas in Bolivia's production increased from 71% in 1998 to 86% in 2010, while the share of liquids fell from 29% to 14% in the same period. This prompted the government to import liquids, especially diesel oil and gasoline from abroad, particularly from Venezuela. Hydrocarbon exports represented 42% of all Bolivia's exports in 2010.

Only 11 wells were drilled from 2006 to 2010, a low number in comparison to the 61 wells drilled in the period from 2001 to 2005, and the 102 wells drilled previously to that from 1998 to 2000.[2] There have been certain signs of recovery in the last couple of years, but YPFB has still had some difficulties in conducting international bidding rounds for exploration areas.

In 2011, average natural gas production reached 45.07 million cubic metres per day, and production of oil and condensate reached an average of 44.60 million barrels per day. In February 2011 gas production reached 48 million cubic metres per day. Approximately 80% of the natural gas is intended for the export markets.[3]

---

1 The new agreements could perhaps be more accurately construed as 'service with risk' contracts that provide for the companies to assume full responsibility for all exploration, development, and production operations at their own risk and expense in exchange for an agreed amount of compensation from YPFB, see CA Lopez, "A Fragile Compromise: Bolivia's New E&P Contracts", *CERA Insight newsletter*, December 2006.

2 Data from the Bolivian Hydrocarbons Chamber, document: *2010 Figures*.

3 Source: YPFB 2012 exploration bidding round: *Bolivia Today* – country profile.

Oil and natural gas production 2010–2011

Year	Natural gas (million cubic metres per day)	Oil and condensate (million barrels per day)
2010	41.71	42.91
2011	45.07	44.6
2012 (at May 1)	53	49

Prospective resources and reserves

	Natural gas (trillion cubic feet)	Oil and condesate (million barrels)
Proven reserves	9.94	209.81
Probable reserves	3.71	98.22
Possible reserves	6.27	4.34
Prospective resources	60.00	2500.00

Bolivia's largest gas purchasers are Brazil and Argentina, which have entered into long-term gas supply agreements with YPFB, terminating at the end of 2019 and in 2026 respectively.

International oil companies still operating in Bolivia that have been there since 1997 are Petrobras, Repsol, Total, BG, Pluspetrol, and newcomers from 2007 are Gazprom, PDVSA, Petrovietnam, NIOC (Iran), and YPF.

3. Petroleum legal regime

3.1 Petroleum law and relevant provisions

(a) Laws

Constitution: Bolivia's new Political Constitution was approved by a national referendum and entered into effect in February 2009. The Constitution provides for a strong state presence in all activities related to exploration and production of natural resources, particularly hydrocarbons. The Constitution sets out the principles, rules and procedures governing the hydrocarbon sector.

Paragraph I of Article 359 of the Constitution states that hydrocarbons, regardless of the state in which they are found or how they are extracted, are the inalienable[4] and imprescriptible[5] property of the Bolivian people. The state, on behalf of the Bolivian people, holds ownership of all hydrocarbon production in the country, and as such only the state is authorised to undertake its commercialisation. All proceeds received from the sale of hydrocarbons are considered the property of the state and are within the ownership of state. Put another way, the resources belong to the Bolivian people,[6] and it is the duty of the state to administer the resources and their proceeds in the collective interest.

Article 351 of the Constitution establishes that the state will take control of and direct the exploration, exploitation, processing, transportation and commercialisation of strategic natural resources through public, cooperative or communitarian entities, which may in turn hire private companies and form joint ventures, through association contracts with legal entities, whether Bolivian or foreign.

YPFB is the sole entity empowered to carry out all activities throughout the hydrocarbon value chain including commercialisation. Article 362 authorises YPFB to enter into contracts for the provision of services with public, private or mixed capital companies, whether Bolivian or foreign, in exchange for a fee or payment for their services.

Hydrocarbons Law: The current Hydrocarbons Law (3058) was enacted on May 17 2005. It is broad in scope, covering all entities, individually and collectively, whether national or foreign, public, semi-public or private, that conduct activities in the hydrocarbon sector.

Article 5 of the Constitution states that, under the sovereign mandate of the Bolivian people, ownership of all hydrocarbons at the wellhead is recovered on behalf of the Bolivian state. It is for this reason that Article 16 states that no contract shall grant ownership of hydrocarbon deposits or hydrocarbons at the wellhead. Contractors under production sharing,[7] operation or association agreements are obligated to deliver to the state, all hydrocarbons produced in accordance with the terms of their contracts.

Article 8 of the Hydrocarbons Law provides that the state shall retain 50% of the total value of oil and gas produced.

Exploration, production, commercialisation, transportation, storage, refining and industrialisation of hydrocarbons and byproducts is the preserve of the state, and its rights in this respect may be exercised by itself, through autonomous entities, or through concessions or contracts with mixed capital companies or with private entities, for a limited period of time.

---

4 Rights that cannot be surrendered or transferred to another or others.

5 Not subject to being taken away by prescription or by lapse of time.

6 It is worth noting that the views of the current Bolivian government are predominantly oriented to state capitalism and thus interventionism in all aspects of the economy. The Constitution reflects such ideas.

7 Despite the fact that the Hydrocarbons Law expressly allows contractors to be paid in kind, this right was taken away by the government, by removing this option from the model contracts. Consequently, a contractor neither acquires ownership rights over hydrocarbons produced nor is it paid in kind.

Specific decrees and sectoral regulations: The following is a list of the most important decrees and regulations affecting the upstream industry in Bolivia:

- Supreme Decree 28223 of June 27 2005, Implementation of the Direct Tax on Hydrocarbons;
- Supreme Decree 28224 of June 27 2005, Assignment of Specific Responsibilities to State Institutions in the Processing, Control of Production, Transportation, Refining and Marketing of Hydrocarbons;
- Supreme Decree 28310 of August 26 2005, Exploration and Production: Traditional and non-Traditional Areas;
- Supreme Decree 28312 of August 30 2005, Regulation of Natural Gas Flaring;
- Supreme Decree 28324 of September 9 2005, Statutes of YPFB;
- Supreme Decree 28393 of October 6 2005, Regulation of Working Units for Hydrocarbon Exploration;
- Supreme Decree 28397 of October 6 2005, Regulation of Technical Standards and Safety for Exploration and Exploitation of Hydrocarbons;
- Supreme Decree 28398 of October 6 2005, Regulations on Bidding for Areas in the Exploration and Exploitation of Hydrocarbons;
- Supreme Decree 28701 of May 1 2006, Nationalization of Hydrocarbons and Transfer of Shares of Capitalised Companies to YPFB; and
- Supreme Decree 28420 of October 25 2010, Regulations for Area Relinquishment, Selection and Retention.

(b) Regulatory bodies

The institutions in charge of the hydrocarbons sector in Bolivia are the Ministry of Hydrocarbons and Energy, the National Hydrocarbons Agency, as regulator, and YPFB as the state company.

Ministry of Hydrocarbons and Energy: The Ministry of Hydrocarbons and Energy develops, promotes and monitors government policies relating to hydrocarbons, and includes four deputy ministers:

- vice minister of exploration and exploitation of hydrocarbons;
- vice minister of industrialisation, marketing, transportation and storage of oil;
- vice minister of energy development; and
- vice minister of electricity and alternative energy.

According to Supreme Decree 29894 dated February 7 2009, the main responsibilities of the Ministry of Hydrocarbons and Energy are to:

- propose and direct the country's energy policy and promote integral development;
- ensure sustainable and equitable energy sovereignty;
- assess and monitor compliance with the country's energy policy;
- plan the development of the energy sector and develop strategies for meeting the country's energy policy;
- establish pricing policies for domestic supply and for export of surplus oil and electricity;
- monitor, control and supervise the exploration, production, transportation,

storage, marketing, refining, manufacturing, distribution, use and disposal of hydrocarbons and their derivatives;
- define and implement policies to promote oil exploration areas; and
- monitor, control and supervise the companies and institutions under its jurisdiction.

In addition, Article 21 of the Hydrocarbons Law gives the ministry the power to determine the price of hydrocarbons at the control point, for the payment of royalties and other forms of remuneration.

National Hydrocarbons Agency: The National Hydrocarbons Agency is the body responsible for the regulation, control, monitoring and supervision of hydrocarbon activities along the value chain. Its main duties under the Hydrocarbons Law are to:
- regulate, control, supervise and monitor the natural and legal entities, public or private, Bolivian or foreign, that are active in hydrocarbon production;
- control, monitor and supervise the implementation of oil contracts signed by YPFB;
- control and monitor YPFB's controlling activities;
- organise and update the country's hydrocarbon map and additional studies to expand the country's hydrocarbon potential;
- monitor and supervise compliance with environmental regulations of activities in the hydrocarbon chain;
- approve rates and prices for regulated activities;
- approve the cost structure of all activities along the entire production chain; and
- check the process of quantification and certification of hydrocarbons reserves.

Yacimientos Petrolíferos Fiscales Bolivianos (YPFB): YPFB is an autonomous state-owned company, whose rights and obligations are not transferable, under the supervision of the Ministry of Hydrocarbons and Energy. Since ownership rights over all hydrocarbons are constitutionally vested in the people of Bolivia, YPFB manages those resources on their behalf, and represents the state in carrying out activities in the entire production and commercialisation value chain, in signing petroleum contracts, and in the operation and enforcement of ownership rights abroad. It is also the sole importer and wholesale distributor in the country. YPFB controlling bodies are:
- the company board;
- the executive chairman and legal representative;
- the vice president of operations; and
- the vice president of contract administration and supervision.

Supreme Decree 29507 of April 9 2008 establishes the legal framework for YPFB to become a corporate body and to incorporate subsidiaries in order to operate at different stages of the hydrocarbon value chain.

Activities in the hydrocarbon sector are deemed of public interest and enjoy the state's protection and are divided into upstream and downstream activities. Upstream activities include exploration and the exploitation of deposits by way of drilling and production.

The export of natural gas, crude oil, condensate, natural gasoline, liquefied petroleum gas, oil byproducts and natural gas byproducts are performed exclusively by YPFB.

In accordance with the provisions of Article 35 of the Hydrocarbons Law, YPFB is in charge of inviting national and international oil companies to participate in the international competitive bidding process, to select the companies and to award available plots within certain areas of interest, and to enter into service agreements for the exploration and exploitation of hydrocarbons in Bolivia. Procedures that contravene the bidding process and award areas directly are expressly prohibited under the Hydrocarbons Law.

Prior to a tender being issued certain provisions of the Hydrocarbons Law must be complied with.[8] The Hydrocarbons Law, in accordance with Convention 169 of the International Labour Organisation[9] which was ratified by Act 1257, of July 11 1991, provides that communities and organisations of peasants, indigenous and native, regardless of the type of organisation should be consulted beforehand, in a mandatory and timely manner. Decisions resulting from the consultation process must be respected. In all cases consultation will be performed in two stages: first prior to the bidding, licensing, procurement, invitation and approval of actions, works or hydrocarbon projects, and second prior to the approval of the environmental impact assessment studies.

In relation to hydrocarbon activities in protected areas, Article 32 of the Hydrocarbons Law states that the Ministry of Hydrocarbons and Energy, the Ministry of Sustainable Development and the Service of National Protected Areas, shall coordinate activities within their respective jurisdictions.

Hydrocarbon activities, whatever their nature, may be undertaken in protected areas, forest reserves, permanent forest production lands or natural private equity reserves, only when an approved strategic environmental assessment has been completed prior to the authorisation or concession, and the activity does not jeopardise conservation objectives, environmental services, genetic resources, archaeological and cultural spaces or sustainable development.

Supreme Decree 28398 of October 6 2005, establishes an expedited and non-discriminatory bidding process, divided into two stages:

- nomination of areas; and
- tendering for the nominated areas.

Article 34 of the Hydrocarbons Law, Article 3 of Supreme Decree 28398 and Supreme Decree 28310 provide that for the purpose of entering into petroleum contracts, the country is divided into two areas: traditional and non-traditional.

---

8 Title VII, Chapter I of the Hydrocarbons Law.

9 Articles 4, 5, 6, 15 and 18.

The executive branch of the government, by supreme decree, divides the country into parcels that make up the contract areas both for traditional and non-traditional areas. Traditional areas are those areas in which there is production of hydrocarbons on a commercial basis and existing infrastructure, and areas categorised as non-traditional are those areas where there is no production on a commercial basis.

Periodically and by supreme decree, the executive branch can determine the incorporation of new traditional areas based on criteria relating to geological knowledge, commercial production of hydrocarbons and the existence of infrastructure.

For exploration, a contract area will consist of a maximum of 40 parcels[10] in traditional areas and 400 parcels in non-traditional areas.[11]

With regards to exploitation, there will be from one to 10 parcels in each designated field, both in traditional and in non-traditional areas. If an extent of 10 parcels is not enough to cover an entire field, it may be increased by as many parcels as are necessary to cover the full extent of the field.

In addition, some traditional and non-traditional areas of hydrocarbon interest are reserved on behalf of YPFB, for it to undertake exploration and exploitation activities on its own or in partnership, and these are preferentially and directly awarded to it.

Nomination proceedings start each year when YPFB generates for the Ministry of Hydrocarbons and Energy an updated version of the official map of available areas with hydrocarbon potential. This map indicates areas with existing contracts, areas granted to YPFB, relinquishments and nominations made for tender areas.

Any individual or legal entity, domestic or foreign, may request the ministry to nominate one or more available areas. There is no limit on the number of areas that an entity can propose. According to Article 16 of Supreme Decree 28398 making a request that an area be made available does not exclude the requesting entity from participating in the bidding for any other nominated area.

Under Article 35 of the Hydrocarbons Law, the executive branch, by decree, decides the frequency of nominations and bid rounds, and officially nominates or supports applications for the nomination of areas. Any company that is awarded an area must sign the relevant contract with YPFB as specified in the tender's terms of reference.

Paragraph II of Article 262 of the Constitution provides that contracts relating to exploration and production activities must have the express prior approval of the Legislative Assembly. Failure to obtain this authorisation would render the contract null and void. Contracts must be concluded within 30 calendar days from the date of approval of the contract by the assembly. The awardee must be legally domiciled in Bolivia and, for each area awarded, must submit the guarantees stipulated in the specifications.

---

10 A 'parcel' is a square 5,000m wide and having a total area of 2,500 hectares.

11 Article 34 of the Hydrocarbons Law.

(c) *Types of agreement*

As mentioned above, according to Article 5 of the Hydrocarbons Law and consistent with Article 139 of the Constitution, the state, through YPFB, exercises ownership rights over all hydrocarbons.

The Hydrocarbons Law provides for three types of petroleum agreement.

Production sharing agreements: Under a production sharing agreement a corporate entity, domestic or foreign, performs at its own expense and risk, exploration and exploitation activities on behalf of YPFB. The contractor in a production sharing agreement has a stake in the production, at the control point, after royalties, taxes and participations are deducted.

According to Article 73 of the Hydrocarbons Law, YPFB has a stake in the production once the contractor's costs for its investments in development, hydrocarbon production and abandonment of the field and the payment of royalties have been deducted.

A board is appointed for each production sharing agreement, to monitor and control all operations and actions carried out during the term of the contract. Their powers and form of representation are established by regulations approved by the Ministry of Hydrocarbons and Energy.

YPFB and the holder of a production sharing agreement pay royalties, taxes and other participations based in proportion to their respective share in the commercialised production.

Operation agreements: This is the contract model that up to now has been used by YPFB with all companies. In this type of contract, the private operator takes all the risk on behalf of YPFB, and conducts exploration and production operations within the contract area in exchange for a fee.[12]

YPFB neither pledges any investment whatsoever, nor does it assume any risk or responsibility for investment results.

Under Articles 78 and 79 of the Hydrocarbons Law, YPFB repays the operator for the operating services, with a percentage of production, in cash or in kind.[13] This fee covers all operating costs and profits. YPFB for its part pays royalties and taxes on the production.

Basically, companies become service providers. Once produced, hydrocarbons are measured at the control point and delivered to YPFB for commercialisation. As owner and marketer of all hydrocarbons YPFB makes payments for transport services and compression, royalties, and the direct tax on hydrocarbons.[14] The distribution of profits is based on a number of factors, such as levels of production, investment, depreciation, taxes and profits earned.

Association agreements: An association agreement can be entered into between YPFB and the holder of an operating agreement that has made a commercial

12 Although for the last bidding rounds YPFB did produce a service agreement.
13 Currently there is no payment in kind, see footnote 5 above.
14 This tax is described below.

discovery. The association agreement establishes the participation in production that each of the parties will have. The administration and operation of this contract is the responsibility of an operator jointly designated by the associates.

Under Articles 82 and 84 of the Hydrocarbons Law, in order to exercise its option to enter into an association agreement, YPFB has to reimburse the operator a percentage of the direct exploration costs of the wells that have become producing wells.

This share of the direct exploration costs is reimbursed to the associate by YPFB either in money or in the form of part of the production belonging to YPFB. YPFB assumes the benefits and risks of operations performed by the association in proportion to its ownership rights arising out of the association agreement.

Similarly, the operator distributes to the parties to the contract their net participation after payment of royalties. The operator is obligated to pay royalties, rental fees and taxes.

(d) *Acquisition of acreage*

Paragraph I of Article 359 of the Constitution states that hydrocarbons, regardless of the state in which they are found or how they are extracted, are the inalienable and imprescriptible property of the Bolivian people. The state, on behalf of the Bolivian people, holds ownership of all hydrocarbon production in the country and is the only entity authorised to undertake its commercialisation.

Consequently, there are no constitutional, legal nor contractual ways to acquire surface or subsurface rights for hydrocarbon exploitation in Bolivia.

Instead, oil companies may bid to enter into service contracts as outlined above in the description of YPFB's role and responsibilities.

(e) *Qualification requirements*

There are no specific qualification requirements except those that YPFB may require on a case-by-case basis for each bid round. Mainly, the potential bidders' creditworthiness, exploration and production expertise are reviewed.

(f) *Duration*

Generally, any company may enter into one (or more) contract for a period not exceeding 40 years.

Specifically, Article 36 of the Hydrocarbons Law states that the initial exploration period shall not exceed seven years in a traditional area and 10 years in a non-traditional area, divided thereafter into three phases:

Traditional zone	Non-traditional zone	
Years 1 to 3	Years 1 to 5	Phase 1
Years 4 and 5	Years 6 to 8	Phase 2
Years 6 and 7	Years 9 and 10	Phase 3

Exploration of areas with an original extent exceeding 10 parcels have a number of areas which should be returned:

- At the end of Phase 1, return of no less than 20% of the original exploration area in excess of 10 parcels;
- At the end of Phase 2, return of no less than 30% of the original exploration area in excess of 10 parcels;
- At the end of Phase 3, return of 100% of the remaining exploration area is required, if the titleholder has not declared a commercial discovery, or is not making use of the retention period.

Article 37 of the Hydrocarbons Law also states that if one or more commercial discoveries are made during any phase of the initial exploration period, or if the retention period is being used in any of the above phases, the contractor may opt for an additional exploration period that will last up to seven years, starting from the end of the third phase. In such circumstances, the contractor may retain up to 30% of the original exploration area, which is called the 'remaining area', to continue exploratory tasks.

The additional exploration period includes the following phases:

Traditional zone	Non-traditional zone	
Years 8 to 10	Years 11 to 13	Phase 4
Years 11 and 12	Years 14 and 15	Phase 5
Years 13 and 14	Years 16 and 17	Phase 6

At the end of Phase 4, no less than 20% of the remaining area in excess of 10 parcels must be returned.

At the end of Phase 5, no less than 30% of the remaining area in excess of 10 parcels must be returned.

At the end of Phase 6, 100% of the remaining exploration area shall be returned.

The effective date of the contract period is the date the contract is notarised before the Government Notary.

(g) ***Minimum work programme***

As noted, for each contract area, the initial exploration period is divided into phases that will have a specific duration according to each particular contract. YPFB may also determine an additional exploration period, its length and the phases in which it will be subdivided.

The contractor shall, at its sole discretion, select and determine the nature and location of the work units to be undertaken within the contract area, to carry out its minimum working obligations.

Article 7 of Supreme Decree 28393 provides that the minimum required work units will depend on the size of the original exploration area.

The minimum number of work units for the parcels and for the phases into which the exploration period is divided are to be defined in the relevant contract, according to the terms of the bid round and the obligations offered by the contractor.

In no case shall the minimum numbers of work units committed for each phase be less than those established in the regulations. These minimum work unit obligations apply to the whole of the contract area.

No change in the classification of traditional and non-traditional areas during the life of a contract will affect the obligations of the contractor in relation to the agreed number of work units.

Under Article 4 of Supreme Decree 28393, each work unit is assigned a value to establish the required performance bond. This valuation is $5,000.00 per work unit.

During the exploration period, the contractor shall submit for YPFB's approval a work programme and budget, which should include obligations relating to the work units to be undertaken. This programme must be submitted within 90 days after the effective date of the signing of the contract before the Government Notary.

As a result of advances in exploration work, the contractor may make changes to the approved work programme and budget, provided that it obtains YPFB's prior approval.

The duration of each phase of the exploration period, the minimum amount that the operator shall invest and the work units applicable to each phase depend and vary according to each specific contract. The agreed investment should be spent undertaking the work and activities previously approved by YPFB in the relevant work programme and budget.

The amount of work units to be performed in each phase is to be established in the work programme and may include, among other activities, drilling exploratory wells, and undertaking seismic surveys. The amount of work to be undertaken is approved by YPFB and its completion is a condition of evaluating and certifying compliance with work unit obligations.

At least 30 days before the expiry of the term of each phase the contractor must notify YPFB of its decision to enter into the next phase. The contractor's right to enter the next phase is subject to the timely performance of its obligations to perform the work units agreed for the relevant phase.

Guarantees provided for each phase will be reduced or cancelled at the request of the contractor, and YPFB issues a certificate of compliance to this effect.

(h) Assignment and encumbrance

Those who enter into operation contracts, production sharing or association agreements with YPFB cannot assign, transfer or subrogate, in whole or in part, directly or indirectly, their rights and obligations arising from such contracts, except with prior approval and authorisation from the Ministry of Hydrocarbons and Energy and YPFB. YPFB will accept the assignment, transfer or subrogation when the beneficiary of the transaction has the technical and financial capacity to comply with the obligations established in the agreement.

A party to a contract cannot undergo, directly or indirectly, a voluntary change of control (that is a change in control of its parent company) during the term of the contract without the written consent of YPFB. Failure to obtain this allows YPFB to terminate the contract immediately.

If a contractor undergoes an involuntary or hostile change of control, it must notify YPFB of the circumstances, indicating the person who exercises control. YPFB may object to the change of control on grounds of state policy or where the new controlling entity has sued YPFB or the state before an international tribunal.

If this is the case, YPFB may request that the interest in the contract belonging to the affected party be transferred to a third party within a maximum time of one year. Non-compliance permits YPFB to take over the participation of the affected party without any compensation.

(i) Local content

Article 67 of the Hydrocarbons Law establishes mandatory clauses for all petroleum agreements, one of them being the obligation to give preference to hiring local personnel. Contracts reflect this obligation in detail, especially with regard to providing internships to students or graduates of higher level education courses relating to the oil and gas industry. The number, time and dates are usually agreed with YPFB. There is also an additional legal obligation to train YPFB's personnel.

Also there is an obligation to contract local goods and services whenever such goods or services offer the same conditions in terms of quality, quantity, price and time availability.

(j) National reservation

Certain areas of hydrocarbon interest may be reserved to YPFB both in traditional and non-traditional areas, in order for it to undertake exploration activities whether alone or in partnership. These areas are to be granted to YPFB with priority and will be directly awarded.

There is also an obligation to supply domestic market needs first.

(k) Environment

With regard to environmental issues and the preservation of natural resources, hydrocarbon activities are subject to the provisions established in the Constitution, the Environment Law and its regulations, the Forest Law, the Special Legal Regime for Protected Areas and international environmental agreements ratified by Bolivia.

In accordance with Article 130 of the Hydrocarbons Law, prior to the beginning of each new exploratory activity, work or project, entities that will be carrying out such activities must deposit an amount equivalent to 0.5% of the total investment in the account of the Ministry of Sustainable Development (MDS), which will finance activities of state control and supervision.

The Environmental Regulation for the Hydrocarbon Sector provides, in Article 7, that all companies active in the hydrocarbon sector must submit to the competent agency each year, or within the period stipulated in each contract, an environmental plan and budget for the following year. They must also submit by March 31 of each year, a report on environmental activities carried out in the previous year, which must describe the activities undertaken, to be compared with those that were budgeted in its annual programme.

Each area under a petroleum contract has a committee for the monitoring of the socio-environmental impact on the area, comprised of one representative from each section covered by the area municipality, two representatives of indigenous communities and a representative of the contractor. The committee's role is to assess the potential socioeconomic impacts produced locally and on community lands, and to implement actions that enhance the positive and mitigate the negative impacts of oil and gas activity in that area.

Under Article 131 of the Hydrocarbons Law, when the committee cannot reach agreement, either party may appeal to the Appellate Committee of the National Socio-Environmental Monitoring Agency, which will assess and rule on the socioeconomic impact on the indigenous population caused by the hydrocarbon activity, and also determine the mitigation measures to be applied. This committee is comprised of the Ministry of Hydrocarbons and Energy, the Ministry of Sustainable Development, the Ministry of Popular Participation, YPFB and a representative of the indigenous people.

The giving of information to, and the consultation and participation of affected indigenous people and communities are required for the preparation of environmental impact assessments, as provided for in Law 1257 of July 11 1991 approving International Labour Organisation Convention 169 on Indigenous and Tribal Peoples in Independent Countries.

Similarly, the Hydrocarbons Law refers to sacred sites and areas of natural and cultural value, providing in Article 132 that they may not be tendered, granted, authorised or opened by concession to activities, works or hydrocarbon projects. Such protected areas, included sites of archaeological and paleontological interest, sacred places which might have a spiritual heritage of historical value, or other areas known for their biodiversity, as established by a competent authority.

Article 133 exceptionally allows hydrocarbon activities in protected areas, when a strategic environmental impact assessment has established the viability of the activity in the framework of national integrated sustainable development, a management plan is in place, and following a public consultation.

Article 33 of the Hydrocarbons Law, states that it is possible, with the authorisation of the Ministry of Hydrocarbons and Energy, to conduct surface reconnaissance work, consisting of topographical, geological, geophysical, geochemical and seismic surveys and drilling for geophysical purposes, in contract or available areas. Those conducting surface reconnaissance activities must execute their work without interfering or causing any damage to operations under the contract, and shall be required to indemnify the contractor, the state or third parties for any environmental damage they produce.

Undertaking surface reconnaissance work does not confer any right or priority as regards the award of hydrocarbon contracts.

If any activity produces environmental harm, the company is obliged to inform the competent environmental authority and immediately to start mitigation and environmental restoration efforts.

Article 137 of the Hydrocarbons Law determines that the costs of environmental remediation work required as a result of accidents directly attributable to petroleum companies may not be considered as operating costs.

(l) *Governing law and dispute resolution*

Under Article 366 of the Constitution, all foreign companies operating in the hydrocarbon sector on behalf of the state are subject to the state's sovereignty, its laws and authorities. No court or foreign jurisdiction shall be recognised in any way, no exceptional situation of international arbitration may be invoked, and there may be no resort to diplomatic claims.

Although this language appears to be a disincentive to foreign direct investment, the language provided in current operation agreements foresees international arbitration as a means of dispute resolution. The existing Constitution was approved after the current model operation agreements entered into effect, so it is difficult to predict whether they will be affected in the future. They might have to adapt to a new contractual scheme.

Applicable law: Any petroleum contract is governed and interpreted according to Bolivian laws.

Technical experts: In the event of disputes over technical matters, the parties may agree to rely upon a ruling prepared by independent experts to resolve the dispute.

Arbitration: In accordance with Article 69 of the Hydrocarbons Law any dispute in relation to the contract is to be resolved by arbitration. The seat of arbitration is La Paz, Bolivia. The applicable laws are those of Bolivia. Arbitration is to be conducted under the Arbitration Regulations of the International Chamber of Commerce. Proceedings are in the Spanish language.

There is a waiver to ensure that the contractor does not make claims through diplomatic channels.

Bolivia denounced the Convention on the Settlement of Investment Disputes Between States and Nationals of Other States on May 2007, thereby avoiding the risk of being taken to arbitration under that forum. However, several bilateral investment treaties remain valid and enforceable, so investors should take a careful look at those international treaties to which Bolivia is still a party.[15]

(m) *Contract termination*

Upon expiry of the term of any contract or its termination for any reason, the area will be returned by the contractor to the state through YPFB. The area will then be subsequently nominated, tendered for and awarded again as provided by the Hydrocarbons Law.

---

15 For instance, the bilateral investment treaty with the United States that was terminated on June 10 2012 ceases to have effect, except that it will continue to apply for another 10 years to covered investments existing at the time of termination. According to the website of the United Nations Conference on Trade and Development (www.unctadxi.org) Bolivia has concluded 23 bilateral investment treaties.

Under Article 41 of the Hydrocarbons Law, a contractor that fulfils its contractual obligations in any exploration phase, may unilaterally terminate the contract without further liability, except the obligations established by law.

At the end of a contract term, whether arising from expiry or for any other reason, the contractor must leave the premises to YPFB in such condition that operations can be continued. The contractor bears all environmental liabilities incurred up to the time of the transfer.

If the fields within a contract area are in production at the time of the contract's termination, YPFB may operate them directly or under an association agreement.

Termination by YPFB: YPFB has the right to terminate a contract immediately:

- if the contractor fails to present the bank guarantees stipulated in the contract;
- for substantial non-compliance with the obligation to undertake certain exploration work units;
- if the contractor fails to present the development plan, or if the contractor does not initiate the development plan, or fails to remedy non-compliance with the development plan;
- if the contractor refuses to supply the domestic market;
- if the contractor fails to obtain or fails to maintain the bank guarantees or the insurance policies required in the contract;
- if the contractor fails to refund YPFB for rental fees;
- if production in an exploitation area is interrupted other than for justified technical causes;
- if the contractor or any guarantor becomes insolvent;
- if the contractor defaults on the agreement for the delivery of hydrocarbons.

3.2 Government take

(a) Royalties

'Royalties' are defined as mandatory financial compensation payable to the state for the exploitation of non-renewable natural resources. Royalties are calculated on the supervised production of all hydrocarbons. There is a royalty rate of 12% which is divided into:

- departmental royalties of 11% on all hydrocarbons produced, payable to the department where the well is situated; and
- the national compensatory royalty of 1% of production, payable to the non-hydrocarbon-producing departments of Beni and Pando.

(b) Direct tax on hydrocarbons

Article 53 of the Hydrocarbons Law creates a direct tax on hydrocarbons, which applies to the production of hydrocarbons at the wellhead, and is measured and paid as a royalty by all hydrocarbon producers.

The tax is applied to the total volume of hydrocarbons produced at a rate of 32% at the control point.

(c) ***Bonus***

No bonuses are payable.

(d) ***Rental fees***

YPFB pays a form of rental fee based on the number of hectares that comprise a determined contract area.

They are paid in advance by YPFB on an annual basis. The operator must reimburse YPFB all amounts paid within 30 days from receipt of evidence of payment by YPFB.

(e) ***Special participation***

Under Article 52(3) of the Hydrocarbons Law, there is a 6% participation in favour of the National Treasury, which is calculated at the control point in the same way as the royalties.

(f) ***Corporate tax***

The income tax rate is 25%, and a withholding tax on remittances abroad is in the order of 12.5%.

Contractors are subject to all other tax laws including the Tax Code and Law 843 as amended.

4. Current issues

The recent laws that have granted consultation rights to native people together with a broad interpretation of International Labour Organisation Convention 169 have often led to excessive interference from neighbouring communities. Several times it has turned into a veto right, impeding the development of projects even from the state company YPFB; and sometimes these communities have used force, disregarding all applicable laws. Hence stakeholders need to work together to build up the necessary consensus in furtherance of a correct balance between social and economic rights.

In September 2012, YPFB called for a second bidding round for the exploration and exploitation of hydrocarbons in areas reserved for YPFB. One of the innovations in these rounds was the use of service agreements. At the time of writing this chapter it still remains to be seen whether the bidding round was successful.

An amendment to the Hydrocarbons Law, or even the enactment of a much needed new Hydrocarbons Law, aimed at attracting foreign direct investment, securing investment rights and reinforcing the primacy of the rule of law, has been on the table for several years now to no avail. 2013 might be the year that will see these changes.

5. Conclusion

In the 1990s, because of legislative reforms, institutional empowerment of regulators and clear rules about the opening of the industry to foreign direct investments, Bolivia enjoyed a drilling boom and a substantial increase in reserves and production that allowed the country to be well positioned among Latin American players.

Now, however, the industry is at a crossroads. Either the government makes a substantial change in terms of a more friendly and stable legal framework, or it will be very difficult for the current situation to improve in the short term.

Furthermore, industry players have lately been attracted to unconventional hydrocarbon sources which may in the end impact on the plans of investors to maintain focus on the traditional arena.[16]

16 See, Dario Arias, "Echoes of the World Petroleum Congress", *Reporte Energía* magazine, Bolivia, February 2012, p 6.

Brazil

Ludmilla Franklin Corkey
Marcelo Viveiros de Moura
Pinheiro Neto Advogados

---

1. Introduction

In 1953, with the enactment of Law 2004, oil exploration, production and refinement became a federal government monopoly. After that, Petróleo Brasileiro SA – Petrobras, a government-controlled corporation, was for decades the only relevant player in the Brazilian oil and gas market. The state monopoly would only end in 1995, through the enactment of Constitutional Amendment 9, which mitigated governmental control over oil and natural gas resources. This constitutional amendment represented a significant change for the Brazilian oil sector, as the activities of exploration, development, production, refining, export, import and transportation, which in the past had only been performed by Petrobras, could finally be carried out by other companies, either state-owned or private.

The opening of the Brazilian oil industry initiated by Constitutional Amendment 9 required considerable modifications in the legal and regulatory framework, in order to allow the new market structure to progress. To this end, two years after Constitutional Amendment 9, the Petroleum Law was enacted with the purpose of providing flexibility to the former federal government monopoly over oil and gas.

The Petroleum Law introduced significant changes in the Brazilian oil industry through the creation of a competitive environment in which companies must participate in a bidding procedure in order to be legally authorised to explore and produce hydrocarbons. Besides representing the definitive opening of the market, the Petroleum Law also chose the concession model as the legal regime for the exploration and production of hydrocarbons in Brazil.

Since the enactment of Law 12,351 of 2010 in 2010, which created the production sharing regime for the pre-salt layer, Brazil has experienced the existence of a mixed regime – with the coexistence of concession and production sharing agreements. The pre-salt areas, which were not subject to bid rounds under the concession regime, will be subject to a bid round under the production sharing regime and its exploitation will be governed by production sharing agreements. Nevertheless, under Article 8(I) of Law 12,351 of 2010, the federal government can opt to enter directly into a production sharing agreement with Petrobras, without the need for a prior bid round. It is worth mentioning that Law 12,351 of 2010 does not define the cases in which the federal government might opt for direct contracting with Petrobras, which means that this prerogative can be exercised by the federal government at its sole discretion. On the other hand, in the event that a bidding procedure occurs, Petrobras will necessarily be part of the successful consortium, holding a minimum stake of 30%. However, if Petrobras wants to have a larger ownership interest, it will have to take part in the bidding under the same conditions as those enjoyed by the other bidders.

In addition to Law 12,351 of 2010, two other legal instruments have been enacted as part of the regulatory effort triggered by the discovery of the pre-salt layer, namely Law 12,276 of 2010 and Law 12,304. Law 12,276 of 2010 authorised the federal government to enter into an onerous assignment of rights agreement with Petrobras under which the government transferred to Petrobras an area with estimated reserves of five billion barrels of oil equivalent. As a compensation for this transfer of rights, the federal government increased its ownership interest in Petrobras – taking into account the stakes held by the federal government itself, BNDESPar, BNDES, the Social Interest Fund and the Sovereignty Fund – from approximately 40% to 47.1% of the total stockholders' equity, according to information made available on the company's website.

Finally, Law 12,304 created Pré-Sal Petróleo SA (PPSA), a state-owned company, which will be party to all the production sharing agreements in the pre-salt area. It is important to highlight though that the pre-salt area accounts for only 2% of the total of Brazilian sedimentary basins. Therefore, the concession regime is still applicable to areas representing 98% of Brazilian sedimentary basins.

2. Upstream activities

The Petroleum Law, in line with the Constitution, expressly states that all rights to oil and natural gas exploration and production in the national territory[1] are federal property and shall be regulated by the National Petroleum, Natural Gas and Biofuel Agency (ANP). It is worth mentioning that when a private company is granted a concession to conduct upstream activities, the scope of this authorisation encompasses only the right to explore and produce oil and gas, while the ownership of the resources until they are produced and received at the production measurement points, continue to belong to the state.

It should be noted that, under Article 22 of the Petroleum Law, technical assets, consisting of data and information on the Brazilian sedimentary basins are also considered an integral part of national petroleum resources, to be collected, maintained, and managed by the ANP.

3. Petroleum legal regime

3.1 Petroleum law and relevant provisions

The Petroleum Law restated the state's ownership of oil reservoirs, natural gas and other fluid hydrocarbons existing in the national territory, which encompasses the terrestrial part, the territorial sea, the continental shelf and the exclusive economic zone. The relevant change has been the granting of rights to explore and produce hydrocarbons to companies distinct from Petrobras, and conceding the ensuing ownership of the oil produced to these companies.

The Petroleum Law also established the new organisation of the public entities

1 This includes the onshore part, the territorial sea, the continental shelf and the exclusive economic zone.

responsible for the regulation and inspection of the oil industry and provided that exploration, development and production activities in respect of petroleum and natural gas are to be undertaken under concession contracts preceded by public bidding. In addition, the Petroleum Law specifies some goals that are to be pursued by domestic policies for the utilisation of energy sources:

- defending Brazilian interests;
- protecting consumers' interests as to price, quality and availability of products;
- preserving the environment and furthering energy conservation;
- ensuring the supply of oil products throughout Brazil;
- increasing, on an economic basis, the utilisation of natural gas;
- promoting free competition; and
- attracting investment in the area of energy production.

Furthermore, the Petroleum Law also provides in Item V of Article 44, that the concessionaire is liable for the acts of its agents, notwithstanding its duty to provide indemnity against any damage arising out of the exploration and production activities contracted. In this situation, the concessionaire has to reimburse the ANP or the federal government in respect of any expenses they might incur deriving from possible lawsuits arising from the concessionaire's acts.

Pre-salt regime: Following the discovery of huge reservoirs of oil in the pre-salt layer, the government enacted three laws:

- Law 12,304 of 2010, which provides for the Incorporation of the Brazilian company Pré Sal Petróleo SA (PPSA);
- Law 12,276 of 2010, which assigned to Petrobras certain areas of the pre-salt layer; and
- Law 12,351 of 2010 which set out the production sharing regime for the pre-salt area.

Under Article 3 of Law 12,351 of 2010, exploration and production in the pre-salt layer and strategic areas may only be performed under the production sharing regime. This regime provides for the sharing of profit oil among the members of a consortium formed by Petrobras, PPSA and the contractor (the auction winner). In this consortium, Petrobras will be the operating company, responsible for conducting and executing all activities of exploration, evaluation, development, production and decommissioning of the exploration and production facilities. On the other hand, PPSA is responsible mainly for defending and representing the state's interests under the agreement, monitoring and auditing the exploration and production plans, in accordance with Law 12,304 of 2010.

It is important to highlight that PPSA will not take on any risk or be responsible for costs related to oil and gas exploration activities. In addition, PPSA will nominate half of the members of the operating committee of each consortium, including its president, and will have voting rights and a power of veto over all decisions in connection with the activities conducted under the production sharing agreement.

(a) Regulatory bodies

National Energy Policy Council: The National Energy Policy Council (CNPE) is an advisory governmental body linked to the Presidency of the Republic and chaired by the Minister of Mines and Energy. Its overriding role is to recommend to the President national policies and specific measures regarding the energy sector. In accordance with the principles established by the Petroleum Law, the CNPE promotes the rational use of Brazilian energy resources as well as setting guidelines for import and export, in order to satisfy internal demand for oil and its byproducts and natural and condensed gas. Furthermore, CNPE is responsible for ensuring the proper functioning of the National System of Fuel Stocks and implementation of the Annual Plan of Strategic Fuel Stocks, which is provided for in Article 4 of Law 8,176.

Ministry of Mines and Energy: The Ministry of Mines and Energy is a ministry created in 1960 with authority to develop public policies and to monitor the implementation of such policies in the following areas:

- geology;
- mineral and energy resources;
- efficient use of hydraulic energy;
- mining and metallurgy;
- petroleum, fuels, electric energy and nuclear energy.

Furthermore, Law 12,351 of 2010 conferred on the ministry new prerogatives specifically in relation to the pre-salt layer. The widening of the ministry's scope here represents a considerable change in comparison with the prerogatives that it has in relation to the post-salt areas. In regard to the pre-salt layer, the ministry shall define, through normative rulings, several conditions to be applied in exploration and production agreements.

Another relevant change in the ministry's role refers to the fact that contracts for exploration and production in the pre-salt areas will be entered into between the members of the consortium and the ministry itself, whereas in the concession regime the contracts are executed between the concessionaires and the ANP.

In this regard, Article 10 of Law 12,351 of 2010 establishes, among other things, the following new powers for the Ministry of Mines and Energy:

- to plan the use of oil and natural gas;
- to propose to the National Energy Policy Council, after consulting with the ANP, the definition of the blocks that are to be the object of concession or production sharing agreements;
- to propose to the National Energy Policy Council the following technical and economic parameters in respect of production sharing agreements:
  - criteria for the definition of profit oil;
  - minimum percentage of profit oil to accrue to the state;
  - minimum interest that Petrobras should hold in a consortium as provided for in Article 20, which shall not be less than 30%;
  - restrictions, terms and conditions for the calculation and appropriation,

    by the contractor, of the cost oil and the production volume corresponding to royalties due;
  - minimum local content and other criteria related to the development of the national industry; and
  - value of the signing bonus, as well as the portion to be allocated to the public enterprise dealt with in Paragraph 1 of Article 8.
- to establish guidelines to be observed by the ANP when the it promotes a bidding process; and
- to approve initial tender protocols and draft production sharing contracts prepared by the ANP.

ANP: The ANP, is an entity indirectly controlled by the federal administration and is the regulatory agency for the oil industry. It is a relatively recent agency, created in 1997 due to the need for an independent technical agency to regulate oil and gas activities after the end of the legal monopoly.

Under the Petroleum Law, the ANP's main goals are regulation, retention and inspection of economic activities within the oil industry. In order to implement these goals, the ANP is provided with the following main responsibilities:

- publishing public notices and opening bidding procedures for concessions in respect of hydrocarbons exploration, development and production, executing the resulting agreements and supervising their implementation;
- authorising the pursuit of refining, processing, transportation, import and export activities, in accordance with the Petroleum Law and its regulations;
- establishing criteria for the calculation of pipeline transportation taxes and determining their amounts, in accordance with the rules set out in the Petroleum Law;
- inspecting, directly or through the offices of the states or federal district agencies, oil industry activities, and applying the administrative and pecuniary penalties established by law, regulation or agreement;
- filing supporting documents explaining the public need in expropriation cases, and arranging the required easements in areas needed for the exploration, development and production of oil and natural gas, or the construction of refineries, pipelines and terminals; and
- inspecting the proper working status of the Brazilian System of Fuel Stocks and implementing the Annual Plan of Strategic Fuel Stocks provided for in Article 4 of Law 8,176.

The ANP's organisational structure is set out in Article 11 of Law 9,478, which establishes that the agency shall be directed by a collegiate board composed of one general director and four directors, who shall be appointed by the President after having their names approved by the Federal Senate. With a view to maintaining the independence of the members of the board and to guarantee their impartiality, they shall serve a mandate of four years which does not coincide with the years of Brazilian presidential elections. Moreover, the ANP has total financial autonomy which is achieved through appropriations from the federal government budget and a portion of the amounts paid as signature bonuses, special participation and fees for the occupation or retention of contract areas, among others sources.

(b) *Types of agreement*

So far, the Brazilian legal framework has provided for three possible types of agreement:

- a concession agreement;
- a production sharing agreement, and
- an onerous transfer of rights agreement, which has only been used once, in respect of Petrobras, as provided in Law 12,276 of 2010.

Concession agreements: Under Article 43 of the Petroleum Law, a concession agreement must reflect the terms of the public bidding process and of the winning proposal. In addition, a concession agreement must contain the following essential clauses:

- a definition of the block that is the object of the concession;
- the duration of the exploration phase and the conditions for its extension;
- the work programme and the volume of investment foreseen;
- the obligations of the concessionaire regarding participations;
- an indication, if applicable, of the guarantee to be provided by the concessionaire in respect of compliance with the contract, including the investments committed to each phase;
- rules on handing back and relinquishment of areas, including the removal of equipment and facilities, and the reversion of goods;
- procedures for the follow-up and inspection of exploration, development and production operations and auditing of the contract;
- an obligation on the concessionaire to present to the ANP reports, data and information regarding the activities undertaken;
- procedures relating to the transfer of the contract;
- rules for the settlement of disputes relating to the contract and its execution, including by conciliation and international arbitration; and
- penalties applicable in the event of non-fulfilment of the contractual commitments by the concessionaire.

Besides setting out these essential clauses, a concession agreement also establishes some other obligations that must be fulfilled by the concessionaire. Among these are obligations to report immediately the discovery of any reservoirs of oil, natural gas, other hydrocarbons or minerals to the ANP and to evaluate such a discovery and present a report on its commercial viability. Apart from these obligations, the concessionaire must also submit to the ANP a development plan for any field that is declared commercially viable, including a timetable and the estimated investment.

Production sharing agreements: Production sharing agreements are used in respect of either the pre-salt layer or other strategic areas, according to Article 3 of Law

12,351 of 2010. Under this arrangement, the company with the winning bid at auction forms a consortium with Petrobras and Pré Sal Petróleo SA, both government-controlled corporations, in order to explore a certain block located in the pre-salt layer or another strategic area.

The production sharing regime is based around sharing the profit oil[2] among the members of the consortium, in which Petrobras shall necessarily be the operating company, in line with Article 4 of Law 12,351 of 2010, with the responsibility of conducting and executing, either directly or indirectly, all activities of exploration, evaluation, development, production and decommissioning of the exploration and production facilities. The ownership of the facilities goes to the federal government and the contracting procedure may occur through bidding in a public auction or, in some cases where Petrobras is the contractor, through direct negotiation.

It should be noted that production sharing agreements are significantly different from concession agreements with respect to the ownership of production and facilities, which belong to the concessionaire in the latter.

Onerous transfer of rights agreement: The last type of agreement is the onerous transfer of rights, which has been used once (as provided in Law 12,276 of 2010), when Petrobras announced that the company had entered into an agreement with the Brazilian federal government. The agreement's subject matter was the onerous assignment by the state of the right for Petrobras to undertake exploration for and production of oil and natural gas in areas of the pre-salt open acreage, without the need for a bidding procedure. As a result of the agreement, Petrobras is authorised to carry out exploration activities in certain blocks which have not been granted to other companies.

The agreement provides that Petrobras shall undertake, always and exclusively, all investments, costs and risks relating to the implementation of operations and their consequences. On the other hand, Petrobras shall have the ownership of all the oil and natural gas produced in the fields.

One tax issue that has emerged from Law 12,276 of 2010 concerns the omission of any provision regarding the payment of the special participation, which is a government levy due as a compensation for the potential environmental and social damage caused by oil-related activities. Because of this, the oil-producing states filed a claim of unconstitutionality before the Brazilian Supreme Court, which has not yet come to judgment. On the other hand, royalties are normally levied on the oil produced in the areas covered by the onerous assignment agreement. Furthermore, the ANP has the prerogative, at its sole discretion, to authorise other private entities to perform, within the contract area, geological, geochemical, geophysical and other works of the same nature used for oil exploration, with a view to the collection of technical data to be marketed on a non-exclusive basis, in accordance with Article 8, Section III, of Law 9,478.

---

2 The oil is divided in 'cost oil', which belongs to the contractor as reimbursement for its operational costs, and 'profit oil', which refers to the total amount of oil that has been produced minus the cost oil.

(c) *Acquisition of acreage*

Under Article 23 of the Petroleum Law, the acquisition of acreage for the development and production of oil and natural gas shall be carried out through concession contracts assigned in ANP auctions (bidding rounds).

However, although the general rule is that the acquisition of acreage must be preceded by bidding rounds, there is one specific exception under which Petrobras can be granted exploration and production rights without a proper auction. This exception is provided in Article 8 of Law 12,357 of 2010, which states that Petrobras may enter into production sharing contracts directly with the Ministry of Mines and Energy without a bidding process.

(d) *Qualification requirements*

The requirements set by the ANP might differ from one bidding round to another. However, as from the ninth bidding round, in order to participate in the bidding procedure, a company must fulfil a list of requirements which can be divided based on the type of document that the ANP demands, as follows:

- statement of interest;
- technical qualifications;
- financial qualifications and
- legal qualifications.

Once the entire procedure of presenting documents and information has been completed, the company is considered to be qualified, being able to bid for the sector(s) of the basin for which it has paid the necessary participation fees.

A company which has dully submitted a statement of interest, containing all the documents and required information, must pay a participation fee before submitting its technical, legal and financial qualifications and, therefore, having access to the information and data package.

Moreover, with respect to the technical qualifications, it should be noted that the applicant companies may request that it be considered either as an operator or as a non-operator. If the company has requested qualification as a non-operator, it must submit an overview of its primary activities, as well as its relationship to the main office or parent company, as applicable. As a rule, a company qualified as a non-operator may only participate in the bidding procedure through a consortium that has a company qualified to operate the block.

On the other hand, if the company seeks to be qualified as an operator, which is necessary in order to submit an individual bid, it must deliver a technical summary with all information relevant to the evaluation of its technical capability. This technical summary should include information regarding areas where current exploration and/or production activities are carried out, along with the investment levels, separated into exploration and production investment, and the volume of production achieved in the most recent five years. The ANP will ascribe different weights to the items of information provided in the technical summary based on the extent to which they verify the applicant's previous experience regarding oil production.

Furthermore, with respect to proof of financial qualification, the applicant company must deliver a number of financial documents to the agency. Notwithstanding the delivery of such documents, the ANP can at its sole discretion request additional information that might further substantiate the company's financial capacity. In addition, the tender protocol also requires that the company have a minimum equity which varies depending on its technical qualifications.

Finally, with respect to legal requirements, the list of documents that the applicant company must deliver to the ANP varies depending on where the company is headquartered.

(e) ***Duration***

The duration of a concession agreement might differ from one bidding round to another, however, as from the ninth bidding round, the total term for each section of the concession area is equal to the sum of the term starting at the effective date until a declaration of commerciality for that area, plus a period of 27 years. It is worth mentioning that the duration of the exploration phase will vary depending on the bid round rules.

(f) ***Minimum work programme***

Since the sixth bidding round, the ANP has required that companies submit a proposed minimum exploratory programme, which has become one of the main criteria for evaluating the offers in the bidding process. The importance given to the minimum exploratory programme reflects the agency's policy of increasing the longevity of wells and the knowledge about national reservoirs. Therefore, in executing its minimum exploratory programme, during the exploration period, the concessionaire is responsible for carrying out the minimum work programme included in its offer.

Under the concession agreement used in the ninth bidding round, in order to comply with the minimum exploratory programme required, the wells had to be drilled at least to a minimum target depth specified in lithostratigraphic units. Setting a required minimum depth aimed to ensure the full investigation of the target area, and it was set according to the stratigraphic-structural features of each individual prospect. However, the ANP may, at its own discretion, accept another target with proven prospects.

With a view to ensuring the effectiveness and enforceability of the provisions set out in the minimum exploratory programme, the concessionaire must give a guarantee in the form of irrevocable letters of credit, insurance-guarantee, mortgage agreement and oil pledge agreement. Such guarantees will be enforced by the ANP if the concessionaire fails to carry out the tasks specified in the minimum exploratory programme.

(g) ***Assignment and encumbrance***

With the prior agreement of the ANP, in accordance with Article 29 of the Petroleum Law, blocks within a concession area may be assigned. It is worth mentioning that the concession agreement used in the ninth bidding round establishes that all and any transfer of ownership under the contract, even in the event of merger, spin-off or incorporation of a company belonging to the concessionaire, is considered an assignment. The concession agreement also provides that companies which do not meet the applicable economic, legal and technical requirements may not be assignees of rights under the concession agreement.

At its sole discretion, the ANP may require as a condition for the assignment, the execution and delivery of a performance guarantee by the appropriate affiliate, which shall be kept in force throughout the term of the agreement or until the effective date of an assignment of all interests acquired.

As from the date of receipt of the assignment request, the ANP has 90 days to approve it or not, under Article 29 of the Petroleum Law, or to request additional documents that the agency deems necessary. If the agency requests amendments or additional documents, the parties must comply with such requirements and re-submit the assignment request within a maximum of 30 days from the agency's request. Any assignment shall only become effective on the date of its formal approval by the Board of Directors of the ANP.

(h) National reservation

Brazilian laws and regulations do not expressly set aside a proportion of oil production for the local economy. Nevertheless, Article 1 of the Petroleum Law establishes that national policies shall guarantee the supply of oil products throughout the country. In addition, Article 2 of that law provides that the National Council of Energy Policy shall guarantee the proper functioning of the National System of Fuel Stocks, and its compliance with the Annual Plan of Strategic Fuel Stocks. Given such provisions, in the event that Brazil does face a period of oil shortage, in which export might compromise domestic oil supply, national reservation could be imposed. Apart from that possibility, it should be emphasised that there is no law or regulation that establishes a national reservation at the present moment.

(i) Environment

Exploration for and production of oil are subject to general rules of environmental licensing which are set at Article 10 of Law 6,938. This law specifies that certain economic activities, due to their nature, require prior approval through an environmental licensing procedure.

In furtherance of the objectives of Law 6,938, Article 2 of Resolution 1 of 1986, enacted by the Environmental National Council, provides that the operations for the production of and exploration for oil shall only be considered lawful if they are preceded by the preparation of an environmental impact assessment and a consequent report on environmental impact. Moreover, in 1994 the Environmental National Council established, through Resolution 23, some specific criteria on the licensing of activities relating to drilling for and production of oil and natural gas.

(j) Governing law and dispute resolution

Both the Petroleum Law and Law 12,351 of 2010, provide that concession agreements and production sharing agreements must contain rules for resolving disputes, which may include recourse to conciliation and arbitration. In fact, all concession agreements have favoured arbitration for resolving disputes involving disposable rights. The Brazilian courts are therefore given jurisdiction to settle disputes with regard to non-disposable rights and precautionary measures, when they cannot be granted by an arbitration tribunal. Regarding the merits of a dispute, the arbitrators shall decide based on substantive Brazilian law, which is the governing law in all concession agreements executed so far.

3.2 Government take

The government take is legally treated as financial compensation for the right to explore for and produce oil, given the potential environmental impacts associated with these activities and the nature of oil as a non-renewable resource. It was first introduced by the Brazilian Constitution in Article 20, Paragraph 1, and has since been regulated by the Petroleum Law (which defines the types of government participation) and by Presidential Decree 2,705 of 1998 (which sets the calculation and collection guidelines). Under the Petroleum Law there are four types of government take:

- royalties;
- bonuses;
- rental fees; and
- special participation.

The rules regarding these aspects of the government take can only be changed through a change in the decree if it touches on the mechanics of the take, or else a change to the Petroleum Law if it touches on the applicability of the various charges, their extinction or the substitution of a new type of take.

(a) Royalties

Royalties are a mandatory government take, payable on a monthly basis, in domestic currency, as of the production start-up, calculated on the total actual production of oil at each field. The amount due to the state is set at 10%, but taking into account geological risks, the expected production and other factors, the ANP may reduce that rate to, at a minimum, 5% of production. The value of the total production subject to the assessment to royalties is calculated by the application of reference prices announced by the ANP on a monthly basis. The reference prices are equal to the weighted average of the concessionaire's crude oil sale prices, a fair market price or a minimum price established by the ANP, whichever is greater.

(b) Signature bonus

A signature bonus is an optional government take, which can be set by the ANP at each auction. The bonus consists on the amount offered by the concessionaire for the block for which it is bidding and is only payable at the time of the concession agreement's signature.

(c) ***Rental fees***

The "rental payment for withholding or occupation of the area", or more simply the rental fee, is the third type of government take. It must be stipulated in the invitation to bid and in the concession agreement. Liability for payment of this fee arises as from the effective date of the concession agreement. It is payable on a yearly basis.

(d) ***Special participation***

The special participation is an optional government take payable on a quarterly basis once production has started, in respect of each block where the field is distinguished by a high volume of production or high profitability, exceeding thresholds established in Presidential Decree 2,705.

(e) ***Corporate taxes***

Companies operating in Brazil are subject to several corporate taxes, besides the specific types of government take mentioned above. In this regard, the most relevant taxes that have to be paid by oil producing companies are:

- corporate income tax;
- withholding income tax; and
- social contributions.

Corporate income tax: Generally speaking, corporate income tax is levied at 15% on book taxable income assessed at the end of each tax period. A surtax will apply at 10% on any portion of annual book taxable income above R240,000.00. 'Book taxable income' is the company's net book income adjusted by statutory additions, exclusions and deductions. In practice, book taxable income is determined by deducting a company's costs and expenses from its gross income. Not all costs and expenses are allowed as deductible, because of their nature or the amount involved. In addition, some items are treated as tax-exempt when ascertaining a company's book taxable income.

Withholding income tax: With respect to withholding income tax, it should be noted that, as a rule, income, capital gains and other earnings paid, credited, delivered or remitted by a Brazilian source to a foreign-based individual or legal entity are subject to withholding income tax as follows:

- at a generic rate of 15%;
- at a rate of 25% for income reported by employees or service providers;
- at a rate of 25% for income paid to a person residing at a place offering favourable tax laws for foreign businesses and individuals (ie, without taxing income or imposing a maximum tax rate below 20%).

Social contributions: With respect to social contributions, it is worth noting that Brazilian companies are subject to a social contribution on net profits, which is figured on net income adjusted by the additions, exclusions and offsetting events prescribed by the tax laws. The tax base may be lowered (by up to 30%) by carrying over the negative tax bases reported in past periods. Since September 28 1999, the tax base for the social contribution on net profits has been subject to the worldwide income taxation principle, so that as a result, profits, income and capital gains earned abroad by Brazilian companies are subject to the contribution. The contribution is currently assessed at 9% for legal entities in general.

Other social contributions that have to be paid are the profit participation programme and civil servants' investment programme contributions and the social security financing contribution. As a general rule, these two social contributions are levied on a company's gross income (ie, the overall income earned by the legal entity, whatever the activity or accounting classification adopted).

It is important to highlight that the corporate tax rules outlined here are valid for companies subject to both the Petroleum Law and to the Pre-Salt Law.

4. Current issues

There are many challenges faced by the oil industry and by the governmental bodies in the country. The prospect of Brazil becoming one of the biggest producers of oil and gas in the world, owing to the huge pre-salt reserves, is more than a 'gift of god', as stated by former President Luiz Inácio Lula da Silva. It is also a source of several legal issues that must be taken into account and analysed on the basis of constitutional and contractual principles.

4.1 Unitisation agreements

One of the subjects that has been widely discussed since the enactment of Law 12,351 in 2010 and that remains unsettled, concerns production unitisation between two different parties producing oil in a pre-salt area, one of which is operating under the rules applicable to a production sharing agreement and the other under the rules applicable to a concession agreement.

First, it is important to emphasise that production unitisation itself is not a problem, given that several unitisation agreements have already been executed in Brazil between two concessionaires. On this point, Article 27 of the Petroleum Law provides that whenever a field extends over adjoining blocks, each one operated by a different concessionaire, the parties shall agree on the splitting of production.

However, the problem arises when the two different parties operate pre-salt blocks that are not subject to the same legal regime, but, on the contrary, one is subject to the production sharing regime and the other to the concession agreement regime. The reason why a production segregation arrangement is considerably more complicated in such a situation is because of the differences in the financial and regulatory structures applying to the two blocks. It should be stressed that Law 12,351 is silent on unitisation between blocks subject to different legal regimes, as it merely provides a general rule for mandatory unitisation in the pre-salt areas, without going into specifics.

Accordingly, the main dilemma is how the ANP will manage to harmonise the two different regimes, since each one has its own rules regarding the minimum works programme, government take, procedures related to the assignment of obligations, inspection mechanisms and ownership of production. In practice, it is fairly likely that certain pre-salt areas may involve overlapping multiple blocks assigned under different bid rounds, making this problem even worse.

Another additional issue concerns a potential conflict of interests that might arise for Petrobras. Article 3 of Law 12,351 of 2010 establishes that the winning company in an auction shall form a consortium with Petrobras and Pré Sal Petróleo SA. Therefore, it is possible to have a scenario in which Petrobras appears as a consortium member of one block, together with a private company and, at the same time, is the sole concessionaire of an adjoining block which extends over the same field.

This hypothetical situation, which might plausibly arise within a short period of time, creates a problem in terms of a conflict of interests, both in terms of the assessment of production volumes, which is a key aspect of unitisation and in terms of financial aspects, given the different regimes applying to the blocks.

Moreover, Law 12,351 of 2010 specifies dangerous consequences if the parties do not enter into an agreement regarding unitisation, which has to be agreed within the time limit set by the ANP which starts running as from the discovery of overlapping reserves. In the event that the parties cannot reach an agreement within the time frame set by the agency, it must determine, within 120 days and based on a technical opinion, the conditions of the unitisation agreement. Nevertheless, Article 40 of Law 12,351 of 2010 establishes that a refusal of any of the parties to sign the production unitisation agreement, following a decision of the ANP, shall be taken as repudiation of the production concession or production sharing contract.

In this regard, another question that arises is if only one member of a consortium refuses to sign, will the whole production sharing agreement be terminated, or will the agreement survive with the remaining parties becoming responsible for the rights of the non-signing party? The ANP has not faced such an issue so far, but with the development of the pre-salt blocks this sort of scenario is likely to arise.

4.2. Expansion of Brazil's offshore territorial limits

Brazil has a great interest in expanding the limits of its continental shelf, in particular due to the discovery of the huge oil and gas reservoirs in the pre-salt layer.

The United Nations Convention on the Law of the Sea, which was ratified by Brazil in 1987, sets out the rights and obligations of nations in their use of the world's oceans, defining guidelines for businesses, the environment and the management of subsea natural resources. Furthermore, Paragraphs 1 and 4 of Article 77 establish that coastal states exercise sovereignty over the continental shelf for the purpose of exploitation of its natural resources, which comprise mineral and other non-living resources of the seabed and subsoil. It is worth mentioning that in 1993 Brazil enacted Law 8617 that defined Brazil's maritime territorial limits according to the convention.

On May 17 2004, Brazil submitted to the United Nation Commission on the Limits of the Continental Shelf a request for expansion of the limits of its continental shelf, in accordance with Paragraph 8 of Article 76 of the convention. Three years later, the commission partially approved Brazil's request, so the country was only able to expand its continental shelf in some regions. The areas not accepted are situated in the northern and Amazonas fan region, the northern Brazilian and Fernando de Noronha ridge, the Vitória-Trindade ridge and the São Paulo plateau and southern regions. Together, such areas represent approximately 19% of the initial submission, as the rest was accepted.

Nevertheless, in August 2010, the Brazilian authorities issued an inter-ministerial resolution which provides that any state or company must request governmental authorisation to explore the outer limits of the continental shelf.

4.3 Shale oil production

Brazilian production of shale oil looks set to increase dramatically within the new few years, as the federal government has already publicly announced its intention of opening bidding for areas which have substantial reservoirs of bituminous shale. For this reason, debates on this subject have gained much importance.

Nevertheless, there is one specific issue related to the production of shale oil that is being discussed by the Brazilian authorities: which governmental body shall have jurisdiction to regulate the production of shale oil: the ANP or the National Department for Mineral Production?

In relation to this issue of jurisdiction, it should be stressed that shale is an organic-rich sedimentary rock which might contain hydrocarbons such as tar, asphalt, petroleum and natural gas. Therefore, the activity of mining shale does not have the purpose of extracting the rock itself, which has no relevant economic value, but rather to extract the hydrocarbons.

In view of the above, it should be noted that Article 61 of Law 9,478 defines 'oil' as a category of which "oil obtained from wells", "oil obtained from shale" and "oil obtained from other rocks" are samples. In this sense, there is no legal reason to differentiate oil obtained from shale from oil obtained from wells, and, thus, both should be under the authority of the ANP.

4.4 Dispute over distribution of royalties

On November 30 2012, the Brazilian Congress enacted Law 12,734, which provides new rules applicable to royalties. The law introduced new rules regarding the distribution of royalties between the political entities that make up Brazil (the union, states and municipalities).

The rules regarding the distribution of royalties have engendered a considerable amount of debate because under the new law the royalties must be distributed among all states and municipalities of the country, instead of being directed mostly to the oil-producing states, resulting in considerable loss of revenue for the oil-producing regions – mainly Rio de Janeiro and Espírito Santo.

The most controversial issue refers to the constitutionality of the new provisions. While the oil-producing states claim that the new rules may only be applicable to blocks that have not yet been auctioned, as they violate the agreements that have already been executed, the non-producing states want the immediate application of the new rules to the distribution of royalties from existing blocks.

President Rousseff has accepted the claim of the oil-producing states and exercised a veto over some provisions of the bill, in order to maintain the distribution of royalties on existing fields unchanged. Nevertheless, under the Brazilian Constitution, Congress still has the prerogative of overriding the presidential veto through a vote that is scheduled to occur in February 2013. It should be noted that if the presidential veto is overridden the oil-producing states can appeal to the Supreme Court.

5. Conclusion

The legal and regulatory challenges faced by the oil industry are likely to be enhanced within the next few years with the significant increase in Brazil's oil production from the pre-salt reserves. Therefore, companies engaging in such activities should closely monitor the enactment of new rules as well as the ANP's and other governmental bodies' interpretation of those which already exist, in order to avoid non-compliance issues.

Canada

Nigel Bankes
University of Calgary

1. Introduction

Canada is a federal state comprised of 10 provinces and three territories.[1] Oil and gas resources are owned either by the state or by private parties. In general, the earlier the land was first titled the greater the chance that the grant included oil and gas rights. In the main producing province of Alberta 80% of the oil and gas rights are owned by the province.[2] Within each province, state or publicly owned oil and gas rights are owned by the province and not the federal government (with some minor exceptions such as the lands underlying national parks).[3] Offshore oil and gas resources are all owned by the federal government, although on the east coast management of oil and gas resources is shared between Canada and the provinces of Nova Scotia and Newfoundland Labrador.[4] There is a long-standing moratorium on oil and gas activity on the west coast of Canada.[5] Oil and gas resources in the large northern territories of Nunavut and the Northwest Territories continue to be owned and administered by the federal government, although in case of Yukon Canada transferred oil and gas rights to the territorial government in 1998.

2. Upstream activities

Canada has seven large sedimentary basins: the Western Canada Sedimentary Basin, the Atlantic Margin, the Arctic Cratonic, the Pacific Margin, the Intermontane and the Eastern Cratonic. Of these seven basins, the Western Canada Sedimentary Basin is by far the most significant and includes parts of the four western provinces of British Columbia, Alberta, Saskatchewan and Manitoba as well as the Northwest Territories and Yukon. Important discoveries in the Western Canada Sedimentary Basin include Turner Valley (Alberta) (1914, 1924 and 1936), Norman Wells (Northwest Territories) (1920) and Leduc (Alberta) (1947). The first major discovery

---

1 For a general survey see Peter Hogg, *Constitutional Law of Canada*, Carswell, Toronto.

2 Alberta, *Alberta's Oil and Gas Tenure*, 2009 available on line at www.energy.gov.ab.ca/Tenure/pdfs/tenure_brochure.pdf.

3 Constitution Act 1867, Section 109.

4 This conclusion is based on a series of decisions of the Supreme Court of Canada: *Offshore Minerals Reference*, [1967] SCR 792, *Re Strait of Georgia*, [1984] 1 SCR 388, *Re Newfoundland Continental Shelf* [1984] 1 SCR 86. Following these decisions the federal government negotiated agreements providing for shared management and revenue sharing with respect to offshore resources. See Atlantic Accord (Newfoundland), 1985 (www.servicenl.gov.nl.ca/printer/publications/aa_mou.pdf), Nova Scotia Accord, 1986 (www.gov.ns.ca/energy/resources/RA/offshore/1986-Canada-NS-Offshore-Petroleum-Resource-Accord.pdf).

5 www.nrcan.gc.ca/energy/sources/offshore-oil-gas/1265.

on the Atlantic coast was the Hibernia discovery off Newfoundland and Labrador in 1979.

The first production in Canada was obtained in southern Ontario in 1858 – the first producing well in North America. Southern Ontario still produces small amounts of oil and natural gas and depleted fields provide important sites for natural gas storage.[6]

Canada has total proven reserves of 174.2 billion barrels of oil of which 169.9 billion barrels represents the oil sands resource (mainly located in Alberta). This affords Canada the third largest oil reserves in the world behind Saudi Arabia and Venezuela. Canada produced an average of 2.72 million barrels per day in 2009 of which 1.34 million barrels was from the oil sands. Conventional production is expected to grow marginally over the next five years (principally due to tight oil developments mirroring those in the United States) while oil sands production is expected to grow significantly to reach over three million barrels per day by 2020.[7]

3.3 Petroleum legal regime

As noted in the introduction, with the exception of some limited private oil and gas rights, each province owns the oil and gas rights within the boundaries of that province. As a result there is no uniform oil and gas leasing legislation in Canada, since each province has developed its own petroleum laws. In addition, the federal government has adopted its own oil and gas legislation, the Canada Petroleum Resources Act, for the two territories of Nunavut and the Northwest Territories.[8] This federal legislation also forms the basis of the leasing scheme that applies to the areas offshore of Nova Scotia and Newfoundland and Labrador although there is separate legislation for each offshore area which provides for the shared management of the resource.[9]

The following sections describe and analyse the petroleum leasing regime for Alberta and for the federal lands. Since Alberta has adopted a distinctive legal regime for oil sands dispositions the discussion of Alberta covers each of those regimes. The most important petroleum statutes in Alberta are the Mines and Minerals Act,[10] the Oil and Gas Conservation Act[11] and the Oil Sands Conservation Act.[12] All three are supplemented by extensive regulations. The most important petroleum statutes that apply to the federal lands are the Canada Petroleum Resources Act and the Canada Oil and Gas Operations Act.[13]

---

6 These two paragraphs draw on a number of sources including Canadian Centre for Energy Information, *Evolution of Canada's Oil and Gas Industry*, 2004.

7 This paragraph draws on Natural Resources Canada, *Canadian Crude Oil, Natural Gas and Petroleum Products: Review of 2009 and Outlook to 2030*, May 2011, and Canadian Association of Petroleum Producers, *Crude Oil, Forecast, Markets and Pipelines*, June 2012.

8 Canada Petroleum Resources Act, RSC 1985, c 36 (2nd Supp).

9 The Accords referred to in note 4, above, are implemented through mirror legislation of federal government and the provincial governments. For the relevant legislation for Newfoundland see the website of the Canada\Newfoundland Offshore Petroleum Board (www.cnlopb.nl.ca/leg_statutes.shtml).

10 RSA 2000, c. M-17.

11 RSA 2000, c. O-6.

12 RSA 2000, c. O-7.

13 RSC 1985, c. O-7.

3.1 Petroleum law and relevant provisions

(a) *Regulatory bodies*

Canadian petroleum laws generally draw a clear distinction between the government as owner and the government as regulator. In Alberta, for example, the Department of Energy makes all of the decisions that the government makes as owner of the resource under the terms of the Mines and Minerals Act. The key regulator responsible for well licensing and all other aspects of oil and gas conservation is the Energy Resources Conservation Board.[14] The Energy Resources Conservation Board is modelled on state oil and gas conservation commissions in the United States. It administers the Oil and Gas Conservation Act and the Oil Sands Conservation Act.[15]

The federal government follows a similar model. Thus, leasing decisions are made by a federal minister (ordinarily the Minister of Aboriginal Affairs and Northern Development) while the technical regulatory decisions (including well licensing decisions and important decisions in relation to the scope of a discovery) are made by the National Energy Board operating under the terms of Canada Oil and Gas Operations Act and the National Energy Board Act.[16]

(b) *Types of agreements*

Alberta's Petroleum and Natural Gas Tenure Regulation[17] (promulgated under the authority of the Mines and Minerals Act) describes two forms of tenure: a petroleum and natural gas licence and a petroleum and natural gas lease. Most lands are offered by way of licence. Both the licence and the lease offer the same rights and are subject to the same continuation rules. The principal difference between the two is the duration of the exploration phase: the period within which the licensee or lessee must establish production. Both confer the exclusive right to drill and recover petroleum and natural gas within the area of the agreement.[18]

Alberta's Oil Sands Tenure Regulation 2010[19] describes two principal forms of agreement, a permit, and a primary lease.[20] Both the permit and the lease grant the same rights which are:[21] "the exclusive right to drill for, win, work, recover and remove oil sands that are the property of the Crown within the location of the agreement".

The Canada Petroleum Resources Act adopts a three-stage tenure scheme consisting of an exploration licence, a significant discovery licence and a production licence. While the Act does not require a tenure holder to progress from one form of

---

14 For the homepage of the Energy Resources Conservation Board see www.ercb.ca/. This page provides links to all of the legislation administered by the board, its decisions and its technical guidelines (known as Directives).

15 Bill 2, Responsible Energy Development Act (passed November 2012) will, when it enters into force, transfer the Energy Resources Conservation Board's responsibilities to a new 'single window' Provincial Energy Regulator.

16 RSC 1985, c. N-7.

17 Alta. Reg. 263/1997.

18 Petroleum and Natural Gas Tenure Regulation, Section 4. The standard forms are available here (www.energy.gov.ab.ca/Tenure/875.asp).

19 Alta. Reg. 196/2010.

20 There are various other forms of rights based on older tenures some of which are referred to in the current regulations.

21 Oil Sands Tenure Regulation, Section 4.

tenure to another, this has been the general practice. An exploration licence grants:[22]

- the right to explore for, and the exclusive right to drill and test for, petroleum;
- the exclusive right to develop those lands in order to produce petroleum; and
- the exclusive right to obtain a production licence.

A significant discovery licence is effectively a holding licence which allows a licensee to hold a property for which it has made a significant discovery until it has established the commercial nature of the discovery. A production licence permits the licensee to produce from the lands.

(c) Acquisition of acreage

Alberta's Mines and Minerals Act contemplates that the Crown may dispose of oil and gas rights in one of three ways: (1) direct issuance on application, (2) sale by public tender, (3) any other procedure determined by the minister.[23] In practice, the vast majority of all conventional and non-conventional rights are disposed of by way of by public tender (ie a bonus bidding scheme). The province holds sales every two weeks. The industry nominates the blocks it would like to see included in subsequent rounds. The bidding system does not allow for any direct negotiation. In very rare circumstances (such as the early developments in the oil sands), the province has negotiated what are referred to as "Crown agreements".[24] These agreements were one-of-a-kind negotiated agreements which, among other things, prescribed the royalty regime for the individual project. They stand in stark contrast to standard practice which favours bidding and standard form agreements.

Under the federal Canada Petroleum Resources Act (Section 14) rights are disposed of by a public call for bids. As a matter of practice the call for bids is preceded by a call for nominations in which industry identifies areas of interest.[25] The call for bids must stipulate the "sole criterion that the Minister will apply in assessing bids."[26] The bidding variable could be a cash bonus payment but in practice the most common bidding variable is a work bid (ie, the minimum amount of money that the bidder proposes to spend on exploration including seismic survey and the drilling of wells).

(d) Qualification requirements

There are very few formal qualification requirements under either the Mines and Minerals Act or the Canada Petroleum Resources Act. For example, Section 23 of the Mines and Minerals Act merely requires that a corporation be registered or incorporated under provincial corporations law. There are no qualification requirements for acquiring federal lands. Both the federal and provincial schemes

---

22 Canada Petroleum Resources Act, Section 22.

23 Mines and Minerals Act, Section 16.

24 For example, for the Syncrude Project. The Crown Agreement for the Syncrude Project, February 4 1975 is available here: www.google.ca/url?q=http://www.sedarpush.com/extractfile.aspx%3Ffn%3D/pdfdocs/00002709 _Mar242008_02.pdf&sa=U&ei=eYCQUIj9BoagiQLu8YC4Bg&ved=0CB8QFjAE&usg=AFQjCNHfdWJptSONW96S1P1-_HhDntj1hw.

25 For details of the practice including the bidding documents see the website of Aboriginal Affairs and Northern Development Canada:, www.aadnc-aandc.gc.ca/eng/1100100036371/1100100036372.

26 Canada Petroleum Resources Act, Section 14.

defer any scrutiny of an applicant until the stage where the party has already acquired its property interest and is applying for a well licence or other form of authorisation under the terms of the Oil and Gas Conservation Act (Alberta) or the Canada Oil and Gas Operations Act (federal).

(e) Duration

Alberta, conventional: Three concepts govern the duration of a petroleum and natural gas licence in Alberta: the initial term, the intermediate term, and continuation at the end of the intermediate term. The petroleum and natural gas licence is issued in the first instance for an initial term of two years, four years or five years depending on the area of the province for which it is issued (plains, northern or foothills region).[27] Maximum sizes of licences are prescribed in the regulations. In order to carry the licence from its initial term into the intermediate term, the licensee must drill a 'validating' well. A validating well need not identify hydrocarbons in paying or any other quantities. The depth of the well determines the amount of the licence area that can be carried into the intermediate term. The intermediate term is a five-year period (for all three regions).[28] Subject to some exceptions a licence only continues at the end of the intermediate term for those areas of the licence that are shown to be productive. Lands below the deepest productive horizon are relinquished (and may therefore be posted by the government in a subsequent bidding round). Once extended, a licence continues indefinitely until the lands cease to produce.

A petroleum and natural gas lease has a five-year term[29] subject to continuation. The continuation rules for leases are exactly the same as for licences[30] and are described in the previous paragraphs.

Alberta, oil sands: An oil sands permit is issued for a term of five years during the term of which the permit-holder must apply for one or more primary leases within the area covered by the permit.[31] The application must be supported by a statement of the 'minimum level of evaluation' to be applied to the application and the necessary technical reports.[32] A primary lease may be acquired either through a permit or directly through a Crown sale. A primary lease is issued for a term of 15 years.[33] The lessee must apply for continuation by the last year of the lease, and must support that application with appropriate technical assessment reports or through production. A lessee can hold a non-producing lease indefinitely but will be subject to a steadily escalating rent.[34]

---

27 The rationale is that exploration in the plains region is cheaper (oil and gas formations closer to the surface, infrastructure already in place, simpler geology, surface access easier) than in the north or foothills (deep wells, significant faulting, complex geology).

28 Petroleum and Natural Gas Tenure Regulation, Section 5(1).

29 Mines and Minerals Act, Section 81(1), for leases issued after 1976.

30 Petroleum and Natural Gas Tenure Regulation, Part 2, Sections 14 and following.

31 Petroleum and Natural Gas Tenure Regulation, Section 8. The number of leases applied for will largely be determined by the configuration of the areas of the permit that are proposed for inclusion within the lease.

32 Petroleum and Natural Gas Tenure Regulation, Section 3(5).

33 Petroleum and Natural Gas Tenure Regulation, Section 12.

34 Principles and Procedures, Section 6(1).

Canada Petroleum Resources Act: An exploration licence may be issued for up to a maximum of nine years.[35] As a matter of practice an exploration licence is typically issued for two periods. As part of this practice the licence will stipulate a work commitment that must be fulfilled during the first period (eg, the drilling of a well). Completion of the well is a condition precedent to proceeding to the second period of the exploration licence. At the expiry of the term of the exploration licence the lands revert to the Crown[36] except to the extent that they have been converted to a significant discovery licence or a production licence. A significant discovery licence may be issued in relation to lands for which there is in force a declaration of significant discovery.[37] Where the lands subject to the declaration of significant discovery fall within the area of an exploration licence the minister shall, on application, issue a significant discovery licence to the holder of the exploration licence. A significant discovery licence has an indefinite term. The holder of a significant discovery licence has the right to obtain a production licence once it has established that its discovery is commercial and it has obtained a declaration of commercial discovery. A production licence is issued for a term of 25 years (Section 41) and can be extended thereafter "for such period ... during which commercial production of petroleum continues."

(f) Minimum work programme

There are no prescribed minimum work programmes for conventional oil and gas operations in Alberta. However, as noted above, a licensee must drill a validating well in order to proceed from the initial term to the intermediate term. The holder of an oil sands permit or lease must attain a minimum level of evaluation of the lands (to prove the deposit) in order to proceed from the permit to the lease, or to extend the lease beyond its primary term.

Under the federal scheme, a minimum work programme is based on the work bid of the applicant licensee. The licensee must provide a security deposit to cover 25% of the work bid. In addition, and as noted above, the exploration licence is typically divided into two periods, and in order to proceed to the second period the holder of the exploration licence must have drilled an evaluation well on the lands.[38]

(g) Assignment and encumbrance

Neither the federal scheme nor the Alberta scheme requires prior approval of any assignment or encumbrance. Thus companies are free to farm out or assign their lands on commercial terms as they see fit. However, Section 85 of the Canada Petroleum Resources Act requires the holder of an interest in any licence to provide the minister with notice of any agreement that results, or may result, in the transfer

---

35 Canada Petroleum Resources Act, Section 26(2).

36 Canada Petroleum Resources Act, Section 26(6), ie, the lands become Crown reserve lands.

37 A significant discovery is a discovery of an accumulation of hydrocarbons which suggests the potential for sustained production. The threshold is low. For a important case on the definition see *Petro-Canada v Canada-Newfoundland Offshore Petroleum Board* (1995), 127 DLR (4th) 483.

38 *Polaris Resources v Canada-Newfoundland Offshore Petroleum Board*, 2006 NLTD 143.

of an interest in the licence. There are no such requirements under the Alberta legislation. In sum, licences and interests in licences in both schemes are freely assignable. Both schemes provide registration systems which permit the registration of transfers of interests and security interests.[39]

(h) *Local content*

There are no local content provisions in Alberta's petroleum legislation. A licensee under the federal scheme is required to commit to a statement of Northern benefits requirements associated with new exploration programmes[40] and must develop a more comprehensive benefits plan as part of proceeding to production.[41] The Newfoundland Offshore Board has developed more detailed requirements implementing these benefit requirements, and in particular the requirements for research and development expenditures within the province. These requirements have been the subject of litigation both domestically and internationally. The domestic courts have accepted that the requirements are lawful[42] but a recent arbitral award has ruled that certain of the requirements breach Canada's obligation under Article 1106 of the North American Free Trade Agreement (NAFTA) not to impose domestic performance requirements.[43]

(i) *National reservation*

There is no provision in either the federal regime or Alberta's regime that reserves to the state (either federal or provincial) a share of any of the forms of tenure described above. The predecessor legislation of the Canada Petroleum Resources Act, the Canada Oil and Gas Act, did reserve a 25% 'Crown share' but that disappeared when the Canada Petroleum Resources Act entered into force in 1986.

(j) *Environment*

Oil and gas operations are subject to both federal and provincial environmental laws since the environment is an area of shared constitutional competence. The key federal laws include the Canadian Environmental Assessment Act 2012,[44] the Canadian Environmental Protection Act,[45] the Species at Risk Act[46] and the Fisheries Act.[47] Oil and gas operations in northern Canada may also be subject to the additional environmental and other requirements of land claim agreements between Canada and its indigenous peoples (Inuit, Metis and First Nations).[48]

---

39 Canada Petroleum Resources Act, Part VIII and Mines and Minerals Act, Part 6.

40 See www.aadnc-aandc.gc.ca/eng/1100100036393/1100100036394.

41 See Canada Petroleum Resources Act, Section 21 and Canada Oil and Gas Operations Act, Section 5.1.

42 *Hibernia Management and Development Company Ltd v Canada-Newfoundland and Labrador Offshore Petroleum Board*, 2008 NLCA 46.

43 *Mobil Investments Canada Inc Oil v Canada*, May 22 2012, text available at www.italaw.com/sites/default/files/case-documents/italaw1145.pdf.

44 SC 2012, c 19.

45 SC 1999, c 33.

46 SC 2002, c 29.

47 RSC 1985, c F-14.

48 For example, the Nunavut Final Agreement, 1993 between Canada and the Inuit people of Nunavut. Such agreements have the force of law. Copies of the agreements are available on line at www.aadnc-aandc.gc.ca/eng/1100100030598/1100100030599.

Oil and gas operations in Alberta are subject to federal environmental laws (as above) and also applicable provincial environmental laws of which the most important is the Environmental Protection and Enhancement Act.[49] Landscape level planning (designed to deal with the challenge of cumulative impacts) occurs under the terms of the Alberta Land Stewardship Act.[50] Greenhouse gas emissions in Alberta are regulated under the Specified Gas Emitters Regulation, which establishes a baseline and credit form of trading system based upon emissions intensity targets rather than hard caps.[51]

(k) Governing law and dispute resolution

The governing law for all petroleum operations is the law of the jurisdiction where the operations occur (eg, Alberta law including applicable federal laws). Dispute resolution principally occurs in the ordinary courts (although working interest owners increasingly agree to resolve their disputes through arbitration). Actions against the state are typically presented as administrative law claims in which the courts show a high level of deference to government decision-makers.[52] Foreign investors may be able to take advantage of an international arbitral forum to the extent that their investment is covered by an international investment agreement to which Canada is a party. Canada is a party to a number of such agreements including the North American Free Trade Agreement. A recent case in point is the arbitral award in *Mobil Investments Canada Inc Oil v Canada*, discussed above.

3.2 Government take

(a) Royalties

The federal scheme provides for a small gross royalty until 'payout' is achieved (1%, rising incrementally to 5%) at which point the licensee pays the greater of a 5% gross royalty or 30% of net revenues.[53] The regulations adopt a ring fence approach to determining payout and project net revenues. The Alberta royalty rules are much more complex and comprise separate royalty rules for petroleum, natural gas and oil sands.[54] Royalties are sensitive to both price and volume.

(b) Bonus

The bonus bid is an important element of the government take in Alberta. For example Alberta took in C$3.2 billion in bonus bids for conventional oil and gas sales in the fiscal year 2011/12 and C$78 million for oil sands rights in the same period. While the federal regime allows for bonus bids, in practice (and as noted

---

49 RSA 2000, c E-12.

50 SA 2009, c 26.8. The most important plan adopted to date is the Lower Athabasca Regional Plan which covers the oil sands region of the province.

51 Specified Gas Emitters Regulation, Alta. Reg. 139/207. For the most recent report on emissions see environment.gov.ab.ca/info/library/8616.pdf.

52 And the reality is that there is very little litigation, especially in Alberta, but see for example *R v Industrial Coal and Minerals Ltd*, [1977] 4 WWR 35, [1979] 5 WWR 103 (Alberta Court of Appeal).

53 Frontier Lands Petroleum Royalty Regulations, SOR/92 – 26.

54 For a summary see *Oil and Gas Fiscal Regimes, Western Canadian Provinces and Territories*, June 2011: www.energy.alberta.ca/Tenure/pdfs/FISREG.pdf.

above) the federal government has preferred to dispose of oil and gas rights on the basis of work bids rather than bonus bids.

(c) ***Rental fees***

Under the Alberta regime a rental of C$3.50 per hectare per year is payable for all lands held under an agreement.[55] Under the federal scheme, rentals are fixed by the terms of the relevant bidding documents. The most recent bidding rounds for blocks in the Mackenzie Valley waived rental for the first period of the exploration licence; during the second period rentals were fixed at C$3.00 per hectare for year 1, C$5.50 per hectare for year 2 and C$8.00 per hectare for years 3 and 4 (all in the second period); rental payments may be refundable against a schedule of allowed expenditures.[56]

(d) ***Special participation***

As noted above, neither the federal nor the provincial leasing schemes allow for direct state participation and thus, in general, there is no government equity share. There are some isolated exceptions. For example, the early Crown oil sands agreements provided for some degree of participation by the government of Alberta, as did the Norman Wells project in the Northwest Territories in which the federal Crown had an equity share. Norman Wells commenced production during the Second World War and is still producing today. But these are isolated examples.

(e) ***Corporate tax***

The basic provincial corporate tax rate (Alberta) is 10% of taxable income. The general federal corporate tax rate is 15% (as at 2012). Allowable deductions include operating expenses, capital cost allowance, interest expenses, resource expenses, and general and administrative expenses. Provincial Crown royalties have been generally deductible against income since 2007. Provincial taxes are not deductible. Capital cost allowance provides a deduction for tangible capital investment. Many classes of depreciable property exist, the most frequent being Class 41 for oil and gas equipment, which provides a 25% write-off rate on a declining balance basis. Resource expenses are grouped into one of three pools: (1) Canadian Exploration Expense, which covers 100% of the costs incurred to determine the "existence, location, extent or quality" of a crude oil or natural gas reservoir not previously known to exist; (2) Canadian Development Expense, which covers 30% of the costs of drilling, converting or completing a well, building a temporary access road or preparing a site (to the extent such costs are not covered as Canadian Exploration Expense), and (3) Canadian Oil and Gas Property Expense, which covers 10% of the cost of acquiring rights to explore for, drill or extract oil or natural gas, or to acquire an oil or natural gas well or other resource property.[57]

---

55 Mines and Minerals Administration Regulation, Alta. Reg, 262/1997, Section 20.

56 The bidding documents are available at www.aadnc-aandc.gc.ca/DAM/DAM-INTER-HQ/STAGING/texte-text/nog_rm_ri_cmv_cmv12_bid_1328893415146_eng.pdf.

57 See *Oil and Gas Fiscal Regimes*, cited above in footnote 54, at p 54.

4. Current issues

The three most important current issues are:

- infrastructure and market access issues;
- the management of carbon emissions; and
- foreign investment.

All three issues are particularly salient in the oil sands sector. As to the first, the increased production of oil sands (current 1.34 million barrels a day projected to increase to 3.16 million barrels a day by 2020) requires additional pipeline capacity to move product to market. Furthermore, increased production in Canada's traditional market, the United States (principally tight oil), has led to Canadian crude trading at significant discounts against the standard benchmarks. This in turn has led to an increased interest in expanding pipeline capacity to the west coast of Canada so as to be able to access Asian markets including China, India, Korea and Japan. Currently there is one pipeline to the west coast, the Kinder Morgan Trans Mountain pipeline, but proposals to expand the capacity of that line and to construct a new greenfield pipeline (the Enbridge Northern Gateway pipeline) face strong opposition from environmental organisations and indigenous peoples both along the proposed pipeline route and on the coast.

The oil and gas sector in Alberta (and in particular the oil sands portion of that sector) is a significant source of greenhouse gas emissions. Total provincial emissions for 2010 were 233 megatonnes of which 41% is attributed to the oil sands and oil and gas sectors. Managing these emissions presents a significant challenge given the projected growth in production. This has led both the federal and provincial governments to invest heavily in carbon capture and storage projects, including the recently approved Quest Project which will capture emissions from an oil sands upgrader for injection into a saline aquifer.[58] One concern is that if governments and operators are unable to manage the carbon footprint of these projects then imports of oil sands products will face border-based carbon measures such as those proposed under certain implementing measures for the EU's Fuel Quality Directive.[59]

As to the third issue, oils sands developments are very capital intensive and it is apparent that Canada will need significant international investments to realise the projections of increased production described above. In addition to the majors, state oil companies, and in particular Chinese state oil companies, have increased their investments significantly, both by acquiring land positions and through takeovers. For example, in 2012, CNOOC offered C$15.1 billion to acquire the Canadian company Nexen. The proposed takeover requires the approval of Investment Canada which must certify that the takeover is in the public interest. The proposal is still under review at the time of writing. This growing investment by state oil companies

---

58 For the details see the Energy Resources Conservation Board decision, *Shell Canada Limited, Application for the Quest Carbon Capture and Storage Project, Radway Field*, July 10 2012, (www.ercb.ca/decisions/2012/2012-ABERCB-008.pdf).

59 See Matthew Ducharme, "The European Fuel Quality Directive: will it stay or will it go?" on the University of Calgary Faculty of Law Blog on Developments in Alberta Law (ablawg.ca/wp-content/uploads/2012/03/blog_md_eufuelquality_march2012.pdf).

leads to concerns as to the role of such companies in this sector and the lack of transparency in the governance of such entities.

5. Conclusion

The oil and gas leasing regimes developed by Canadian provinces and the federal government favour standard form leases and cash bonus bidding schemes. Such schemes have the virtue of transparency and leave little, if any, room to governments to favour one company over another beyond the objective bidding criterion. Similarly, none of the current regimes provide for state participation in the upstream petroleum sector. Canada has seen some increased production of oil and natural gas in recent years due to the application hydraulic fracturing techniques to shale oil and gas and tight oil and gas, but future increases in production will depend upon the continued development of Alberta's massive oil sands resources. Such projects are very capital intensive and pose significant environmental challenges.

Colombia

Dario Gerardo Lamanna
CNP

1. Introduction

The Colombian economy has been showing major recovery since 2003. The country has increased exports and has reduced public debt levels, while increasing foreign investment. Colombia's gross domestic product in 2011 reached more than $566 billion.[1] Proven reserves of oil at December 31 2011 were 2.549 million barrels of oil equivalent.[2] Average oil production in the country in 2012 was 950,000 barrels per day. As for exports, the total value at the end of 2011 was $56.954 million, including crude oil and coal.[3] According to Proexport,[4] Colombia shows remarkable export growth. For the last 10 years Colombia has had decreasing inflation and constant growth in its gross domestic product. The country is currently at its highest level of international reserves ($28,400 million). According to the projected scenarios, Colombia has economic and political stability and investor confidence is evident.

Regarding hydrocarbons, it is estimated that the country has great geological potential. Oil is the country's main export product and the major contributor to the state's finances. The government has set as a priority the discovery of new oil reserves, with the aim of maintaining energy independence. Thus, beginning in 1999 there have been a series of oil policy reforms, concerning both contractual aspects, tax and royalties. According to the agency Invest in Bogotá,[5] Colombia has a dynamic economy, political stability and good quality of life, and is beginning to be on the radar for international businesses, and Bogota has the conditions to become an important oil and gas services hub.

The country is recognised for having one of the best business environments in the region. According to the International Finance Corporation and the World Bank's *Doing Business Report 2012*, Colombia is one of the easiest places to do business in Latin America (42nd in the global rankings). According to the *Global Competitiveness Report 2011–2012* from the World Economic Forum, Colombia displays competitive strengths in macroeconomic environment quality, large market

---

1 Source: International Monetary Fund, *World Economic Outlook Database*; Economist Intelligence Unit, 2012.

2 Source: National Hydrocarbons Agency, Ministry of Mines and Energy.

3 Source: National Administrative Department of Statistics of Colombia.

4 Proexport is Colombia's entity in charge of the promotion of foreign direct investment, and non-traditional exports, with 28 offices around the world and eight offices in Colombia (www.proexport.com.co).

5 Invest in Bogota (www.investinbogota.org) is the city's promotion agency, attracting and supporting foreign investment in Bogotá.

size, fairly sophisticated business, successfully adopting technology and enhancing innovation. Is the fifth most competitive country in Latin America, according to the International Institute for Management Development's *World Competitiveness Yearbook 2011*. Colombia's credit rating has been boosted to "investment grade" by main international agencies such as Moody's, Standard & Poor's and Fitch.

With the support of the armed forces and the national police, the Colombian government has made significant security improvements in hydrocarbon industry. According to the International Institute for Management Development, the country ranks second in Latin America in terms of personal security and adequate protection of private property.

Colombia has recently signed free trade agreements with the United States, Canada, the United Kingdom, Norway, Japan and South Korea, and is a member of the Andean Community of Nations, the Union of South American Nations and an associate member of Mercosur. By the end of 2012, Colombia will have signed 21 international investment agreements, including bilateral investment treaties and free trade agreements, with investment sections.

2. Upstream activities

Several exploration and production companies have large bases in Colombia. The main oil companies operating in the country are Ecopetrol, Pacific Rubiales, CEPSA, Chevron, Total, Shell, Equion (former BP), Mansarovar Energy, ExxonMobil, Hocol-Maurel et Prom, Lukoil, Sinopec, Sinochem, CNPC, Oxy, Conoco-Phillips, Petrobras, Perenco, Repsol, ONGC-Videsh, ENAP-Sipetrol, Interoil, OGX, BHP Billiton, Lewis Energy, Pluspetrol, Tecpetrol, YPF, Statoil, Petrominerales, Gran Tierra, C&C, Nexen, Talismán and Canacol, among others.

Although it is no longer available as contractual form there still are some concession contracts in force, there is one field that is private property, and more than 60 association contracts are nearing termination. Currently the oil companies conduct business, both onshore and offshore, mostly under the type of agreement called an exploration and production contract, which is executed between the National Hydrocarbons Agency and the operating companies both private and state-owned, where Ecopetrol or a partner is the operator company. Most of them include joint operating agreement provisions. Upstream activity is regulated as to technical matters, available property, extension of blocks, contracts, economics, the rights and obligations of operators and so on, mainly in the Petroleum Code[6] and the National Renewable Natural Resources Code.[7] Since the adoption of those Codes, several rules have been enacted, legal or regulatory in nature, including changes to the regulation of hydrocarbons, rules on exploration for and exploitation of oil and gas to prevent physical and economic waste of reserves and ensure maximum ultimate recovery,[8] and rules that specify the measures for prevention and control of environmental pollution.[9] In 2003[10] the Colombian government implemented some important

6 Law-Decree 1056 of 1953 (Oil Code).
7 Law 23 of 1973; Decree 2811 of 1974.
8 Resolution 181495 of 2009 of the Ministry of Mines and Energy.

changes in the upstream sector:

- a new role for the national oil company Ecopetrol as a competitive player,
- incorporation of the National Hydrocarbons Agency to administer oil and gas resources; and
- introduction of the new exploration and production contract model, and changes to the tax/royalty system with inclusion of a percentage of oil and gas production for the National Hydrocarbons Agency and other economic rights.

3. Petroleum legal regime

3.1 Petroleum law and relevant provisions

The Constitution establishes that the state is the owner of the subsurface and non-renewable natural resources.[11] Property in public use, the communal lands of ethnic groups, security zones, parks and archaeological resources are also declared to be inalienable and indefeasible.

The Petroleum Code[12] also regulates various aspects of hydrocarbon activities. In addition to this code there are several laws, decrees and resolutions governing various fields of this activity.[13] Among these, there are rules regarding ownership of hydrocarbon deposits reiterating that they belong to the nation, with the exception of charges made to third parties.[14]

(a) Regulatory bodies

Ministry of Mines and Energy: The Ministry of Mines and Energy[15] is the public body responsible for managing non-renewable natural resources to ensure that they are used appropriately, and for formulating policies and plans for the hydrocarbons sector.[16] It is also responsible for regulation, ensuring supply and ensuring its protection. It adopts national policies related to these activities, makes regulations and operates a register of mineral deposits and hydrocarbons.

On the other hand, the National Hydrocarbons Agency (see further below), which is an administrative entity affiliated to the Ministry of Mines and Energy with legal personality, equity capital and administrative and financial autonomy, actually manages the country's hydrocarbon reserves, assesses their potential, promotes exploration and exploitation, and negotiates and implements new oil contracts.

---

9 Decree 1895 of 1973; Decree 2811 of 1974; Law 99 of 1993; Law 1333 of 2009; Decree 3678 of 2010; and Decree 2820 of 2010.

10 Law-Decree 1760 of 2003.

11 Article 332 of the Political Constitution of Colombia of 1991; Article 42 of Decree 2811 of 1974.

12 Decree 1056 of 1953 (Oil Code).

13 *Legal Regime of Exploration and Exploitation of Hydrocarbons and Social and Environmental Standards Applicable*, compiled by Ecopetrol, LEGIS Editors SA, First Version 2011, Legisnet, Colombia: www.legis.com.co.

14 Decree 1994 of 1989, regulating Article 1 of Law 20 of 1969.

15 Decree 70 of 2001 establishes the functions of the Ministry of Mines and Energy.

16 Decree 1056 of 1953; Decree 381 of 2012.

Empresa Colombiana de Petróleos SA: Empresa Colombiana de Petróleos SA (Ecopetrol) is Colombia's national oil company, which is responsible for the exploration, development, administration and management of oilfields, pipelines, refineries and the distribution and sale of products and derivatives. Ecopetrol is a mixed capital company,[17] under the Ministry of Mines and Energy, which is subject to the exceptional contractual regime applying to the public administration. Since 2007 it has been listed on the Bogota and New York stock exchanges.

Until 2003, it devoted itself to exploration, production, transportation, refining, marketing and general management of Colombia's hydrocarbon resources. In that year, however, the sector was restructured with the creation of the National Hydrocarbons Agency, which now deals with the administration and regulation of the sector. These changes were implemented, according to the government, because of the critical situation that had arisen as a result of declining oil reserves (with the risk that the country would have to start importing oil). Since the restructuring, Ecopetrol has specialised in finding business opportunities and in the operation of its oilfields, working in all phases of the petroleum chain, in order to compete on equal terms with other companies. Ecopetrol has extraction operations in oilfields in several areas of the country, two refineries, export and import terminals both on the Atlantic and Pacific, and a transport network of over 8,000km of pipeline.

Under the 2003 law, Ecopetrol was empowered to explore and exploit hydrocarbons directly, or it can enter into agreements for financial and technical cooperation in exploration and production, expansion of transport networks, installation of infrastructure and refinery upgrades.

Empresa Colombiana de Gas: Empresa Colombiana de Gas (Ecogas) came into existence in 1997.[18] It is an industrial and commercial entity, linked to the Ministry of Mines and Energy, with legal, administrative and financial autonomy, subject to regulation by the Regulatory Commission for Energy and Gas and the Superintendence of Public Services. It operates Colombia's gas pipelines.

National Hydrocarbons Agency: The National Hydrocarbons Agency (ANH) was created in 2003,[19] as a special administrative unit within the Ministry of Mines and Energy, to manage the country's hydrocarbon reserves, and be in charge of managing the new hydrocarbons exploration and production contracts and technical evaluation agreements.

The main objective of the ANH is to administer Colombia's oil reserves, promote the signing of contracts by granting licences for exploration and development in areas of interest, and achieve a balance of the interests of all parties involved in the oil industry. It also manages the technical information regarding the geological potential of the country. For this purpose, the ANH also enters into contracts with national and international services companies for seismic surveys, aerogravimetry, interpretation and

17 Law 154 of 1948; Law 165 of 1948; Decree 30 of 1951; Decree 2310 of 1974; Decree 1760 of 2003; and Law 1118 of 2006. Its website is www.ecopetrol.com.co.

18 Law 401 of 1996.

19 Law-Decree 1760 of 2003; Decree 2288 of 2004; and Decree 4137 of 2011. Its website is www.anh.gov.co.

re-interpretation of seismic data, stratigraphic drilling, environmental studies, design of new types of contract, and other services, in order to acquire better information on the country's geological basins and to maximise its hydrocarbon potential. The ANH has its own procurement regulations[20] which establish criteria for licensing exploration for and exploitation of hydrocarbons on state property, and set the rules for the selection of contractors and the award, execution, performance and supervision of oil contracts, as well as comprehensive management of the country's hydrocarbon reserves.[21]

Other bodies: Other regulatory authorities involved in hydrocarbons sector are:

- the Ministry of Environment and Sustainable Development created in 1993, which is the authority in charge of the protection of the natural resources and environment;
- the Ministry of Internal Affairs, the authority in charge of the protection of the indigenous communities and ethnic minorities; and
- the Mining and Energy Planning Unit,[22] a special administrative unit associated to the Ministry of Mines and Energy, which is in charge of the planning policies for the industry.

(b) Types of agreement

Until 2003 the contract being used was an association agreement with Ecopetrol (concession contracts had been dropped in 1975).[23] The association agreement was a joint venture between Ecopetrol and a partner, where the partner carried 100% of the exploration costs and once the field was declared commercially viable Ecopetrol entered into a joint operating agreement that was part of the association contract with a 30% participation in past exploratory and all future costs. Reforms made in recent years give greater incentives for the private contractor, who can currently enter into two types of contract:[24] an exploration and production contract or a technical evaluation agreement.[25] The new scheme replaces the previous one and allows extra time for each stage (exploration, appraisal and production). Also, the production period is now calculated for each particular discovery, so one contract may cover to several fields, each one with its own period.

The ANH can approve an extension to the term of an association agreement[26] provided it will result in a higher economic benefit for the state. An extension of the term shall include, to the extent possible, new exploration projects, the development of existing fields, the use of new technologies or a reduction in the state's exposure to risk. Currently, oil and gas areas can be assigned through exploration and production contracts, technical evaluation agreements or any other form of agreement established by the ANH.

---

20 ANH Accord 04 of 2012.
21 Source: ANH and Ministry of Mines and Energy.
22 Decree 255 of 2004
23 Legislative Decree 2310 of 1974; and Decree 743 of 1975.
24 *60 years of ECOPETROL, Chapter 11, 2011*: www.ecopetrol.com.co/especiales/Libro60anios/esp/presentacion.htm.
25 ANH Accord 04 of 2012.
26 Decree 2288 of 2004.

Exploration and production contract:[27] This is a long-term contract model, which uses a royalty/tax system and includes a participation in the oil and gas production and other economic rights for the ANH. The main terms and conditions of the exploration and production contract are:

- There is an exploration period, which lasts six years with a possible extension of up to two additional years conditional on the subsequent completion of an exploration programme. The six years period can be divided into phases. At the end of each phase the private operator can back out of the contract, or continue to the next phase.
- Next there is an evaluation period of up to two years, with a possible extension of up to one year. The operator has up to two years to carry out an evaluation programme, and three additional months to determine whether the field can be declared commercially viable. Once commerciality has been declared, a production programme has to be submitted to the ANH for approval.
- There is then a production period, which can begin once the ANH has reviewed and approved the results of the evaluation and the production programme. The duration of the production period is 24 years, which can also be extended provided that, among other requirements, the contractor demonstrates that during the four years preceding the date of the application it has developed a drilling programme with at least one well per year and/or a project that involved active pressure maintenance or secondary, tertiary or enhanced recovery.

In this scheme private investors can operate, explore for and exploit hydrocarbons independently, at their own risk and cost. The contractor owns the hydrocarbons produced, after applying a series of tiered royalties, the ANH's participation in the production and other taxes. The exclusive rights granted make reference to hydrocarbons that are discovered within the contracted area and cannot apply to any other natural resource. All the risks and costs are assumed by the private contractor. A declaration of commerciality must include technical support and a reservoir delimitation. The ANH requires the implementation of best industry practices at the private contractor's cost and risk.

The ANH has economic rights arising from subsurface use, and high price participation (when a minimum cumulative level of production or a trigger price are reached). The ANH collects the royalties, which are a percentage of the total daily production, based on monthly averages. Royalties are calculated for each field.[28]

The private contractor has the option of total or partial relinquishment of the area after each exploration phase. Relinquishment is generally 50% of the area at the end of the six-year exploration period if the contractor continues exploring.

---

27 ANH Accord 0010 of 2004 ; ANH Accord 04 of 2012.
28 Articles 360 and 361 of the Political Constitution of Colombia; and Legislative Act 5 of 2011.

Exploration and production contract stages
(royalty/tax system/% production)[29]

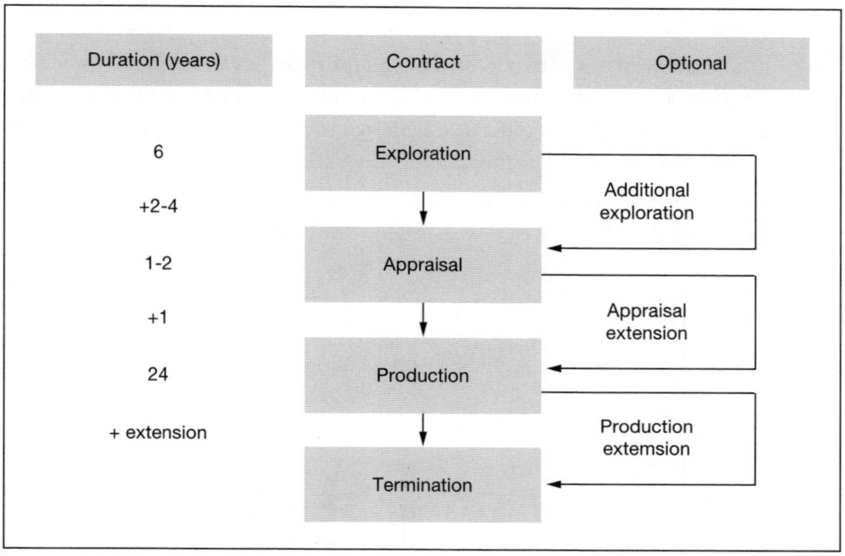

Technical evaluation agreement:[30] This is a short-term contract and is used to assess areas of exploration that might be economically viable in order to determine their prospectivity. Under this arrangement, the contractor undertakes to perform a technical evaluation at its cost and risk, such as seismic reinterpretation of information, drilling of exploration wells, and so forth. The technical evaluation agreement runs for up to one and a half years (two years for marine areas), with the possibility of an extension.

If the result of the evaluation is positive, the contractor can invoke its right to conclude an exploration and production contract. It gives the evaluator a right of first refusal within the area covered by the technical evaluation agreement. The contractors are entitled to meet or exceed any proposal that a third party has made in respect of the same area.

At the commencement of this type of contract, the contractor must pay a fee to the ANH per hectare per year in respect of the evaluated area. This fee is denominated in dollars.

The main terms and conditions of the technical evaluation contract model are:

- The objective is to analyse existing data and to acquire new information to evaluate and update the knowledge regarding the prospectivity of a given area.
- The duration depends on the proposed work programme. It can have a maximum duration of 18 months in continental areas, and 24 months in offshore areas.

29 Source: *ANH, Ministry of Mines and Energy and Ecopetrol.*
30 ANH Accord 0030 of 2004; ANH Accord 04 of 2012.

- At any time a technical evaluation contract can be converted into an exploration and production contract subject to the limit on maximum areas allowed for exploration and production contracts.

A technical evaluation contract can end at any given moment, provided that the contractor has met at least 50% of its minimum commitment. The balance of the committed investment must be transferred to the ANH (or it can be used for another technical evaluation agreement with the ANH's consent).[31]

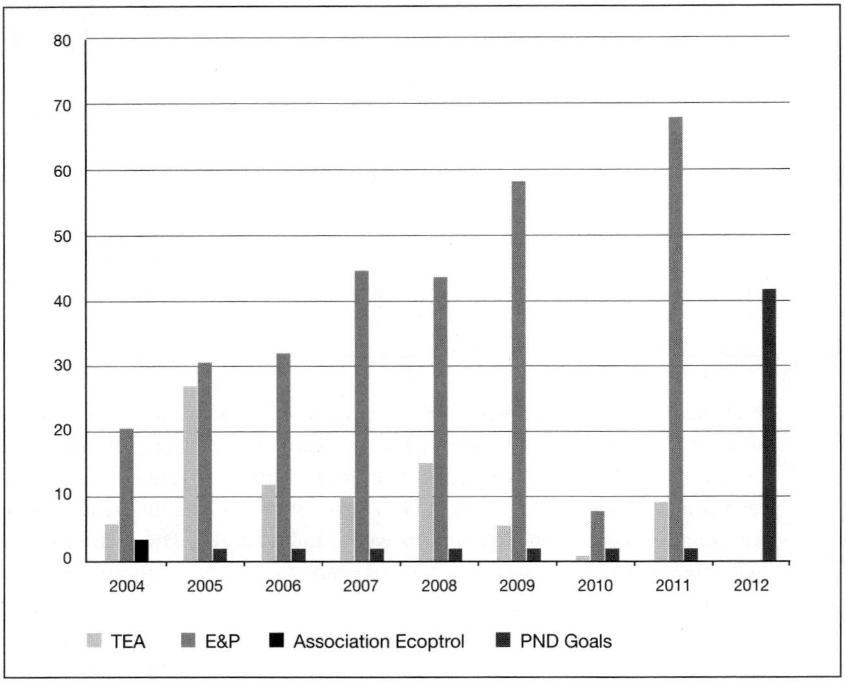

(c) ***Acquisition of acreage***

The Petroleum Code[32] and subsequent resolutions of the ANH set the requirements for the allocation of areas for exploration and production of oil and gas in Colombia. The allocation process of areas may be through different ways.

Competitive bidding processes: Open public processes are organised by the ANH every two years. To this end, the ANH opens a bidding process and invites national and international oil companies to participate and submit proposals. Companies must undergo a qualification process (the parameters of which vary depending on the area) after which those that meet the qualification requirements can submit proposals that are evaluated based on competitiveness. Investments above the

31 Source: ANH, Ministry of Mines and Energy and Ecopetrol.
32 Law-Decree 1056 of 1953 (Oil Code).

minimum commitment and the ANH's participation in the production are the main criteria. The successful bidders proceed to signature of a contract. All the applicable requirements are contained in the terms of reference for the bidding round.

Direct contracting: The ANH may enter directly into agreements in favour of a company or group of companies, provided they meet the technical, legal and financial requirements applying to contractors, and recognise the payment of royalties and other economic rights in favour of the ANH. Other criteria include experience in certain areas – particularly in conditions similar to those of the area being offered – financial capabilities and additional benefits to the government (ie, a higher percentage of production).

Invitation to bid: A number of companies selected by the ANH are invited to bid, and the most favourable offer is selected.

Area nomination: Under this arrangement, a company (the nominator) proposes an exploration and production contract with regard to an area that has been contracted out under a technical evaluation agreement. Whereas direct negotiation is initiated by the government, area nomination comes from the company approaching the government when it is interested in a specific area.

In the case of available areas (free areas) that have never been subject to exploration, the winner is the first direct investor who requests them. The allocation of areas under the direct contracting method usually involves individual bidders new to the industry and companies with limited capacity acting jointly or in associations. The direct allocation procedure was suspended for a time,[33] but has been reinstated.[34]

In pursuit of its function of assigning areas for exploration and/or exploitation, the ANH has opened the nomination process for available areas,[35] through which interested companies can acquire data packages which allow the acquiring company to submit a formal proposal for one or more areas.

Private arrangements: Investors can also purchase interests in oil and gas assets in Colombia through agreements between private parties. The purchaser must request prior authorisation from the ANH and comply with technical, legal, financial and environmental requirements.

(d) Qualification requirements

National or international companies interested in submitting proposals, whether individually or as part of a consortium, for the allocation of blocks for exploration and/or exploitation of oil and gas, whether onshore or offshore, and whether through competitive processes or by direct allocation, must prove the relevant legal, financial, technical, operational, environmental and corporate social responsibility

33 ANH Accord 02 of 2010; and ANH Accord 04 of 2011.
34 Article 37 of ANH Accord 04 of 2012.
35 Resolution ANH 331 of August 2 2012.

capacities to meet the requirements and conditions for carrying out activities under the contract to be signed.[36]

To substantiate the company's legal capacity it must produce a certificate proving its existence and legal representation, its bylaws, certificates of good standing, corporate minutes and resolutions, proof of appointment of a legal representative and powers of attorney. In the case of consortium or joint venture, the parties must also produce the joint venture agreement with a description of the parties, the duration of the agreement, the participation percentage of each member, appointment of the operating partner and a promise of incorporation of a future corporate entity under Colombian law. Any energy investor who wants to enter into an agreement for exploration and production activities must register a local legal entity in Colombia, either through a Colombian subsidiary or a branch office of the foreign corporation.

Evidence of economic and financial capacity can be by any means that show the company has the economic and financial capacity to meet its obligations under the contract. Companies must submit audited financial statements and other accounting information prepared under international financial reporting standards or US generally accepted accounting principles and credit ratings issued by an international agency. They must also submit bank guarantees.

To show their technical operational capacity, companies must show that they have experience operating the type of field that they intend to participate in by presenting copies of relevant contracts, production reports and reserves reports. To show their environmental capacity, companies must certify that the company has established and implemented environmental management systems. They must also provide ISO 14001 certification or the equivalent, if applicable.

Finally, interested companies must demonstrate that they have implemented and executed rules and practices demonstrating corporate social responsibility. Where appropriate, they may submit ISO 26000 certification or similar.

(e) *Duration*

The duration of an exploration and production contract is made up as follows:

- the exploration period lasts six years and can be extended under certain conditions for up to four additional years. The six year period is divided into phases, at the end of each of which the private operator can back out of the contract, or continue to the next phase;
- the evaluation period gives the operator up to two years to carry out an evaluation programme, and three additional months to determine whether the commerciality of the field can be declared;
- the production period begins once commerciality has been declared and a production programme has been submitted to the ANH for approval, and runs for up to 24 years, with a possible extension under certain conditions if approved by the ANH.

---

36 Articles 11 to 19 of ANH Accord 04 of 2012; and Terms of Reference of Bidding Process.

The duration of a technical evaluation agreement depends on the proposed work programme. It can have a maximum duration of 18 months in onshore areas, and 24 months in offshore areas. At any time a technical evaluation contract can be converted into an exploration and production contract subject to the limits on maximum areas allowed under exploration and production agreements, which depend on the financial and technical capabilities of the interested company.

(f) ***Minimum work programme***

An initial minimum work programme for the exploration phase is agreed when the contract is entered into. It can be adjusted before each exploration phase. Requirements for the minimum work programme are set out in the terms of reference of each bidding process conducted by the ANH. The minimum programme is then incorporated by the companies into their respective contracts, and backed by a bank guarantee in favour of the ANH in case of breach of the related minimum investment commitments. During the exploration period, the contractor must carry out each phase of the exploration programme committed to, which will involve the drilling of exploratory wells, seismic surveys and so on. The contractor must submit the exploration plan for each phase to the ANH for approval. Companies can make changes to the mandatory minimum programme, under certain circumstances and on the fulfilment of various obligations. The contractor may perform additional exploration at its own cost and risk. At the end of the last phase of the exploration programme, the contractor should opt to continue to the next phase of the contract or relinquish the area.

(g) ***Assignment and encumbrance***

The transfer of an interest or participation in oil and gas assets in Colombia is legally permitted through agreement, sale or the transfer of rights between private companies. The purchaser must request prior authorisation from the ANH and must comply with technical capacity, legal and financial requirements. Once the agreement between private companies is agreed, it has to be approved by the ANH after ensuring that the buyer meets the operational, technical, legal, economic, financial, environmental and social requirements.

An agreement to acquire or participate in an exploration and production agreements involving private parties must comply with a procedure including the following documents:

- confidentiality agreement;
- data room;
- letter of intent or memorandum of understanding;
- due diligence;
- farm-out agreement, stock purchase agreement or participation agreement;
- request for official approval from the ANH;
- closing and formal assignment; and
- joint operating agreement, if applicable.

Under the Colombian model contract, the contractor has the right to assign or transfer all or part of its interests, rights and obligations under the contract, with the prior written permission of the ANH, to another company or consortium that has the required skills in the process of bidding round selection for the respective block.

In terms of procedure, the contractor must make a written request to the ANH, indicating the essential elements of the negotiations, such as the name of the transferee, information on their legal, financial, technical, operational, environmental and corporate social responsibility capabilities, the value of the rights and obligations to be assigned, the scope of the operation, and so forth.

Within 60 working days after receipt the request, the ANH will exercise its discretion to analyse the information provided by the contractor and adopt its determination, without being obliged to give reasons.

(h) *Local content*

Colombian law does not provide specific rules or requirements or minimum percentages for the procurement of goods or services provided by domestic companies. However, in the exploration and production contracts and the technical evaluation agreements there is a section that stipulates that the contractor shall give preference to suppliers of local goods and services.

(i) *National reservation*

The ANH has reserved certain areas of national strategic interest that are called 'reserved areas', which are not offered in competitive processes or direct assignments. Reserved areas are defined as such by the ANH for reasons of energy policy, national security or public order, for geological, environmental or social reasons, or because it has studied them and has valuable geological information or has considered undertaking such studies directly.[37] Amazonas is one the largest reserved areas.

'Released areas' are contracted areas returned by private companies to the ANH or Ecopetrol, either as a result of termination of the relevant contract or following partial relinquishment of the area.

(j) *Environment and social responsibility*

The National Renewable Natural Resources Code[38] aims to modernise all environmental legislation in the country. The code was published in 1974 and was the first of its kind in Latin America. It details the activities permitted and prohibited within the national park system. Among its provisions it states that the right to use renewable natural resources can be acquired by law, permit, concession or association, and that individuals may request the granting of the right to use any renewable natural resource in the public domain, unless the resource is reserved for a special purpose or under a legal exception.

The socio-environmental scheme applicable to the exploration and exploitation of hydrocarbons is intended to prevent pollution and improve the environment to protect the health and welfare of the population.[39] Colombian environmental policy

---

37 Article 4.9 of the ANH Accord 04 of 2012.
38 Law 23 of 1973; Decree 2811 of 1974.
39 Law 23 of 1973; Decree 2811 of 1974; Law 99 of 1993; Political Constitution of Colombia of 1991.

is based on the universal principles of sustainable development and preservation of natural resources offset out in the Rio Declaration on Environment and Social Development.[40] To this end, the Ministry of Environment and Sustainable Development, created in 1993,[41] is responsible for promoting and monitoring the implementation of national environmental policies, coordinating the National Environmental System[42] to ensure compliance with and respect of the Colombian law. The National Environmental System includes:

- the national environmental authority (the Ministry of the Environment and Sustainable Development);
- the regional authorities; and
- the National Environmental Licensing Agency.

The Ministry of the Environment and Sustainable Development has issued many decrees to regulate the prevention and control of pollution. Activities relating to exploration for and exploitation of hydrocarbons requires the prior completion of an environmental impact study, an environmental licence and other environmental permits issued under Colombian law.[43] The environmental licence and other environmental permits are granted by the respective National Environmental Licensing Agency to authorise and regulate any project or activity that may have a negative impact on natural resources, land or water.[44] Moreover, the Colombian state recognises and protects the ethnic and cultural diversity of the nation and the integration of its population.[45] There are also specific laws for the protection of indigenous and tribal peoples and Afro-Colombian communities.[46] According to the Constitution[47] the state has a duty to protect the diversity and integrity of the environment, to conserve ecologically important areas, to promote education in this respect and to ensure sustainable development, conservation, restoration or replacement, by planning the management and use of natural resources. As for factors that may lead to environmental degradation, is also the state's duty to prevent and control them, and to impose legal sanctions and demand reparation for damage caused.[48]

Consultation and participation of communities: When a project will affect an indigenous reservation or an Afro-Colombian collective territory, a process of prior consultation and participation of minorities in the areas affected by the project has to take place.[49] This requires organised public hearings in order to publicise the project to the community and to receive opinions, advice and suggestions.[50] Colombian law

---

40 Declaration of Rio de Janeiro of June 1992.

41 Law 99 of 1993.

42 Law 99 of 1993; Decree 2372 of 2010.

43 Law 99 of 1993; Decree 1753 of 1994; Decree 1728 of 2002; Decree 1180 of 2003; Decree 1220 of 2005; Resolution 1023 of 2005 of the Ministry of the Environment and Sustainable Development); Decree 2820 of 2010; Law 1450 of 2011.

44 Decree 2820 of 2010.

45 Article 7 of the Political Constitution of Colombia of 1991; International Labour Organisation Convention 107/57.

46 Law 21 of 1991 (International Labour Organisation Convention 169); and Law 70 of 1993.

47 Political Constitution of Colombia of 1991.

48 Law 1333 of 2009 and the Criminal Code.

49 Decree 2811 of 1974; Law 99 of 1993; Decree 1320 of 1998; Regulatory Decree 2820 of 2010.

is one of the most advanced in the world when it comes to protection of indigenous rights. The Constitution recognises the multiethnic nature of the country and claims to land rights of indigenous peoples. Criminal law is also applied to environmental matters[51] providing for a system under which the following are offences:

- any act or omission which constitutes a violation of environmental regulations;
- any violation of administrative orders issued by the environmental authority; and
- the commission of environmental damage.

The ANH also sets policy for community relations and social investment.[52]

International treaties: Colombia has signed various international conventions relating to the environment, including the Basel Convention on the Control of Transboundary Movements of Hazardous Wastes and their Disposal (1989);[53] Convention 169 on Indigenous and Tribal Peoples in Independent Countries adopted by the General Conference of the International Labour Organisation in Geneva (1989);[54] the United Nations Framework Convention on Climate Change to promote the sustainable management and conservation support and reinforcement of sinks and reservoirs of all greenhouse gases not controlled by the Montreal Protocol (1992); and the Kyoto Protocol to the United Nations Framework Convention on Climate Change (1997), among many others.

Easements and expropriation: The hydrocarbon industry in Colombia in the exploration, production, transportation, refining and distribution phases is declared to be a matter of public interest.[55] When a company needs to use land owned by a private party for hydrocarbon activities of any kind, it can negotiate with the private party the compensation for its use, or it can go to a government authority to authorise the use and set the level of indemnification. Public or private properties must have the necessary legal easements to carry out the relevant activities, including the right to build any required infrastructure on the lands needed for occupation. The appropriate authority can also enact the expropriations necessary for the exercise and development of the industry, with prior payment of compensation for the damage incurred.

(k) Governing law and dispute resolution

All oil and gas contracts are governed entirely by Colombian law. Colombian law allows companies to use the arbitration procedure as an alternative means of conflict resolution. Companies must abstain from resorting to diplomatic channels in all matters relating to their contractual rights and obligations. Both the law and the

50 Regulatory Decree 330 of 1997.
51 Law 1333 of 2009 and its implementing regulations.
52 ANH Accord 05 of 2011.
53 Law 253 of 1996.
54 Law 21 of 1991.
55 Decree 1056 of 1953, Law 1274 of 2009.

contract terms allow contractors to resort to arbitration to resolve their disputes. Meanwhile, there is a law that regulates conciliation,[56] as an alternative dispute resolution mechanism. Arbitration may be agreed in the terms of the contract, in which case it is understood that there is an arbitration clause, or it could be brought into play with an agreement to use arbitration after the conflict has arisen, if the parties are able to compromise. The parties are free to appoint the arbitrators. The choice can be made by agreement between them, choosing from a list of specialists, or appointing a third party to appoint the arbitrators.

In most cases, if the parties are to use arbitration, it will have been previously specified in the contract or agreement with an arbitration clause stating that in the event of any conflict the parties undertake to submit to an arbitral tribunal, and specifying the jurisdiction and applicable law. There are several dispute management centres in Colombia. The most important and prestigious and most used by foreign investing companies is the Arbitration and Conciliation Centre of the Chamber of Commerce of Bogota (CACCCB),[57] which is established by regulation and lists arbitrators by specialty. For the CACCCB to have jurisdiction the parties must refer to arbitration by the CACCCB in its contracts and insert a model clause. Contracts with state agencies also may be submitted to arbitration, in which case the settlement is by arbitration in law (in other cases it is arbitration in equity), and there shall be a minimum of three arbitrators except in the case of minor contracts, in which case only one arbitrator is required. Additionally the parties may agree that the settlement of any dispute will be submitted to international arbitration, provided that at least one of the following conditions is met:

- the parties are domiciled in different countries;
- the place of performance of the obligations in dispute is located in a country other than that in which the parties are domiciled;
- the matter subject to arbitration links interests of more than one country and the parties expressly agreed so;
- the dispute directly affects the interests of international trade;
- it is agreed in a bilateral investment promotion and protection treaty, signed by Colombia and the other party's country of nationality.

The parties may agree on the use of substantive rules and procedures applicable internationally. The international dispute management centre most used by companies doing business in Colombia is the International Centre for Settlement of Investment Disputes, which is an institution of the World Bank, based in Washington, United States of America.

International arbitration is governed by international treaties signed and ratified by Colombia,[58] without prejudice to any other economic law agreed upon by the parties.

---

56 Law 640 of 2001.

57 www.cacccb.org.co.

58 New York Convention of 1958; Hague Convention of 1889; Convention of Panama – Inter-American Convention on International Commercial Arbitration of 1975; Washington Convention of 1966; and the Convention on the Settlement of Investment Disputes between States and Nationals of Other States of 1965.

3.2 Government take

There is the participation by or compensation for the Colombian state in the division of the benefits from the production of petroleum. Different forms of taxation exist in Colombian oil and gas contracts in favour of the state:

- revenue bonuses;
- production bonuses;
- royalties;
- income tax;
- windfall taxes; and
- other indirect taxes.

All of them represent what is in total the government take. In Colombia oil revenue from each barrel is split into the government take (bonds, production bonuses, royalties, taxes, etc) and the contractor's take, both composed of reimbursement of operational costs, development costs and exploration costs and a normal profit.

(a) Royalties

Royalties are calculated as a fixed or variable percentage of the amount of oil and gas produced, payable in cash or in kind, according to the decision of the government. The exploration and production contracts specify that the contractor must make available to the ANH the percentage of hydrocarbon production established in the law relating to royalties,[59] without prejudice to any other agreed economic right. The payment of this percentage is made in cash or in kind, as determined by the competent authority and the National Royalties Fund. With regard to exploration areas, the contract states that the contractor must pay to the ANH a rental fee based on the number of hectares licensed under the contract. In the event of the discovery of associated natural gas, the contractor must submit to the ANH a plan for its use in the three years following the discovery. In 2002 new royalty scheme variables were adopted.[60] Since the implementation of this new law a new schedule of payments has been introduced, setting a percentage based on average daily production, which is calculated monthly, and varies between a minimum of 8% and a maximum of 20%.

(b) Bonus

In the international oil and gas industry, it is quite common for contractors to have to pay bonuses, which are one-off payments made upon the signature of a contract, the start of production at a project, or the achievement of certain goals laid down by law or in contract. In Colombia, there are no such bonuses applicable to the oil and gas industry. However, a bid bonus is required in the bidding process organised by the ANH, in order to guarantee the good faith of the bidder's proposal. It takes the form of a bond in favour of the ANH, effective from the date of submission of the proposal to the date on which the contract is going to be signed, plus three months.

---

59 Articles 360 and 361 of the Political Constitution of Colombia; and Legislative Act 5 of 2011.
60 Law 141 of 1994, amended by Law 756 of 2002; and Decree 4923 of 2011.

It is a guarantee that the offer being made is genuine. The ANH must ensure that the bidder will actually fulfil its proposal and payments under it. The bond ensures the good faith and firmness of each proposal submitted A further guarantee is also required in the bidding process. This guarantee consists of an insurance policy or a bank guarantee issued in favour of the ANH and covering the performance of the proposed contract.

(c) ***Rental fees***

Use of the subsurface by the contractor requires the payment of certain fees to the ANH. For each phase of the contract, the contractor must pay to the ANH a fee per unit area, denominated in US dollars, as set out in a table annexed to the agreement. This payment must be made within one month of the start of each phase, and thereafter annually. The average fee is around $0.75 per hectare, depending of the phase, size and location of the block. With regard to use of privately owned land, when a company wants to use part or all of a particular property for hydrocarbon activities of any kind, it can negotiate with the private party to agree the necessary rights and set the level of compensation, or it can go to a government authority to authorise the use and set the correct compensation.

(d) ***Windfall tax***

When oil produced on state land fetches prices above a certain threshold, the contractor has to pay the ANH an extra royalty, in kind or in cash at the ANH's option. The ANH specifies that where the cumulative production of light crude from an area exceeds five million barrels and when the international oil price for West Texas Intermediate exceeds a variable value (calculated using an specific formula), in addition to the usual royalties, companies must make a payment of an additional percentage of surplus earnings. There is a formula to compute the payment to ANH included in the exploration and production contracts. There are similar provisions for natural gas.

(e) ***Corporate taxes***

The Colombian tax regime establishes taxes at national and regional (departmental and municipal council) level. Taxes in Colombia are declared under the provisions of the Corporate and Individual Tax Regime,[61] which is divided into national and regional systems. The national tax system is regulated by the Tax Code, and the applicable regional tax system is regulated by each department and municipality. The Colombian tax authority is the National Tax and Customs Administration.[62]

The main national taxes are:

- income tax, which for all corporations is currently payable at a rate of 33%;[63]
- value added tax, which applies to sales, services and imports and for which the general rate is 16%;

---

61 Tax Code: Decree 624 of 1989 as modified; Law 223 of 1993; Law 633 of 2000; Law 788 of 2002; Law 1430 of 2010.

62 www.dian.gov.co.

63 Law 1429 of 2010, created a progressive income tax rate regime.

- property tax, which is payable by individuals who exceed a certain level of wealth at a rate of 1.2%;
- financial transactions tax, which applies to all transactions for the disposal and/or transfer of funds in current bank accounts, savings or deposits of any kind at a rate of 0.4%; and
- stamp duty, which attaches to public or private documents executed in Colombia, in which there is recorded the existence, modification or completion of obligations.

The main regional taxes are:[64]

- industry and commerce tax, which is payable on the gross income of all corporations that carry on business, at a rate that varies between 0.414% and 1.104%;
- predial tax, which relates to land or farming; and
- registry tax.

Colombian tax law[65] provides for amortisation and depreciation of assets through a system of production units, over a period of five fiscal years or more. In addition, costs and charges incurred in acquiring goods or providing services are deductible for income tax purposes. International standards on transfer pricing are applied in Colombia based on the terms and rules established by the Organization for Economic Cooperation and Development.

The foreign investment and exchange regime[66] treats as foreign investment all foreign capital held in Colombia by individuals or corporations not resident in the country. All foreign investments must be registered with the Bank of the Republic of Colombia to receive the legal benefits. For its part, the bank[67] operates a special exchange rate regime for domestic companies with foreign capital in the country where they are engaged in exploration for and exploitation of oil and gas.

It is possible for a Colombian contract to provide for legal stability, whereby, in agreements between an investor and the Colombian government, the government guarantees the stability of rules and regulations that were in effect when the investor decided to make the investment. Legal stability clauses can be included in contracts for new investment or where existing investment is being expanded throughout Colombian territory.

(f) *Double taxation treaties*

These treaties are signed to avoid double taxation and to prevent fiscal evasion with respect to taxes on income. At present, Colombia has signed double taxation treaties with Spain, Mexico, Canada, India, Chile and Switzerland, among others. Treaties with Germany, France, Portugal, the Netherlands and Japan are under negotiation. As at the end of 2012, Colombia had signed 16 double taxation treaties.

---

64 Law 84 of 1915 regulates the powers granted to municipal councils and departmental assemblies.
65 Law 488 of 1998.
66 Law 9 of 1991; Decree 2080 of 2000; Resolution 8 of 2000; and Regulatory Circular DCIN-83.
67 Resolution 8 of 2000.

4. Current issues

Usually, the ANH organises bidding processes to offer areas to interested national and international companies every two years.

During 2012 the ANH organised the Colombian Round 2012[68] in order to offer blocks located in different Colombian basins, and invited all national and international petroleum companies (private, public or mixed-capital) interested in participating in the bidding process under the bid's terms of reference. As with previous rounds, companies interested in participating in the bidding round had to show they were qualified as an operator or investor, by reference to legal, technical, financial, operational, environmental and corporate-social criteria, and to buy a data package. Companies could apply to be approved as a qualified company by the ANH, in the following categories:

- Type 1: exploration and production mini-round – exploration and production contracts in respect of blocks located in mature basins.
- Type 2: exploration and production (newly prospective basin) – exploration and production contracts in respect of blocks located in newly prospective basins in both onshore and offshore areas.
- Type 3: special technical evaluation agreement – special technical evaluation agreements in respect of blocks in frontier areas in both onshore and offshore areas.

The main change from previous rounds was that the ANH offered blocks located in basins with potential for unconventional hydrocarbons.[69]

In October 2012 the ANH organised Fifth Colombia Oil and Gas Investment Conference, in Cartagena de Indias. The main objective of this conference was to consolidate investor interest, strengthen the business environment and promote investments in the oil and gas industry, and to announce the final results of the Colombia Round 2012 bidding process.

Additionally, the ANH has opened the nomination process for open areas. During 2012 it opened four separate processes for areas of the Caguan-Putumayo basin called Achapo, Apple, Walnut and Cardon.[70]

In addition, the Colombian Chamber of Petroleum Goods and Services (Campetrol) organised the largest petroleum exhibition in the country, Expo Oil and Gas Colombia 2012[71] in the International Business and Exhibition Centre in Bogotá, from October 30 to November 2 2012. The event was aimed at international petroleum goods and services companies, operators, capital providers and experts in the oil sector, and sought to contribute to the economic development of the country. The next one will take place in Bogotá at the end of 2013.

5. Conclusion

Colombia has a great business environment for investment in the hydocarbons

68 www.rondacolombia2012.com
69 Resolution 18 0742 of May 16 2012 Ministry of Mines and Energy.
70 ANH Resolutions 331 and 286 of 2012.
71 www.expooilandgascolombia.com and www.campetrol.org.

industry. Colombia has a dynamic economy, political stability and a good quality of life, and is beginning to catch the attention of international oil and gas companies. The country is recognised for having one of the best business environments in the region. It has the third best business environment in Latin America, according to the World Bank's Doing Business 2012 report. It is a country with investment grade status and excellent legal and economic performance. In terms of oil production, the government objective is to reach close to 2 million barrels within 10 years.

There are several reasons to invest in Colombia. First, legal certainty: the country has an adequate legal framework, a solid and proven system of conflict resolution, and an extensive background of respect for the law and for contracts. The new model of exploration and production contract royalties and taxes are among the most attractive in the region, providing security with flexibility and profitability to domestic and foreign investors, as it is the one country in the region where royalties and participation in the production are based on production up to a certain level. Another aspect to consider is its economic stability: the financial environment, exchange rate and taxation are stable, providing guarantees to investors and a free inflow and outflow of foreign capital.

From a geological point of view, the country has great potential for hydrocarbon exploration, with potential to increase the proven oil reserves through new discoveries in unexplored basins both onshore and offshore. Infrastructure is another aspect to be highlighted as is the excellent geographical location, with access to both the Pacific Ocean and the Atlantic Ocean, offering access to the most attractive markets. The pipeline network for oil and products is booming, both domestically and internationally.

It is also important to highlight the development of human resources and a highly skilled workforce, as required by the oil industry, as a valuable strategic asset. There are already highly skilled Colombian workers currently involved in many operations. Finally, Colombia offers foreign investors legal stability of contracts to guarantee upstream investment projects.

Mexico

Miriam Grunstein
Center for Advanced Economic Research and Learning

I seem to lean on old, familiar ways
– Paul Simon

1. Introduction

The Mexican upstream sector has stood out as being closed to private investment for over half a century, since the word 'contracts' was preceded by an explicit prohibition in Article 27 of the Mexican Constitution.[1] Contrary to popular belief, however, Lazaro Cárdenas, the renowned general who in 1938 nationalised the Mexican petroleum industry, did not forbid production sharing or service contracts. At the time of the nationalisation, the prohibited forms of agreement were the early concessions, which allegedly awarded ample rights to title holders while leaving the Mexican state with no control over or substantial benefit from its natural resources.[2]

Thus, the peculiarity of the Mexican hydrocarbon industry does not lie in that resources are national property, as this is the case in most countries of the globe. What makes this industry different is the rather limited variety of exploration and production agreements that can be entered into with Petróleos Mexicanos (Pemex), the national oil company. Since the constitutional reform of 1960, only a restricted range of service contracts may be used to hire companies in Mexico. While certain types of service contracts allow contractors to be paid in kind or in cash, the Mexican type only allows cash payments that may not be representative of the value of hydrocarbon production.

Albeit timidly, fairly recent legislative developments have broadened the scope of Mexican exploration and production contracts. Before the reform, the contracts which served the hydrocarbon industry had the same legal and regulatory basis as those entered into for generic construction and service activities. For instance, a drilling contract was based on the same laws and regulations as a state-owned highway or a public hospital. Drilling activities were regulated and compensated in a way that was incoherent with the nature of the business. The contracts that were allowed in Mexico until the 2008 reform, instead of protecting its wealth, were costly

1 The reform which prohibited contracts was the initiative of President Adolfo Ruiz Cortines, and was enacted on January 20 1960.

2 As of the constitutional reform of 1939, the federal government was barred from awarding any concesions for the exploration, extraction, refining, transport, storage or distribution of crude oil, its byproducts and natural gas; see José Ovalle Favela, *"La Nacionalización de la Industria Petrolera y Eléctrica"* in Boletín Mexicano de Derecho Comparado, available at www.juridicas.unam.mx/publica/rev/boletin/cont/118/art/art6.htm.

and inefficient as they provided a powerful incentive for service companies to drill as many wells as possible without being accountatable for the output in terms of barrels. This situation may have benefited the companies, but also accounted for a decline in Mexican production and reserves. Ironically, the constitutional and legal provisions which mandate Mexico and Pemex to maintain a staunch hold of the control and ownership of the resources by only hiring service contractors were diminishing the returns of a strategic industry. As Pemex carried the entire risk of operations, service companies were content enough to drill without producing. This situation has undergone important changes which show in the current model exploration and production contract which will be described later in this chapter.

2. Upstream activites

The reform of the exploration and production contracts was strongly influenced by the decline in Mexico's main oil reservoirs, which had been developed by Pemex using conventional low-cost technology. Easily available oil allowed Pemex to perform well in combination with service contractors, which faced neither financial nor geological risk. This explains why, while today's international hydrocarbon recovery rates are approximately 100%, Pemex's reach a mere 77.1%, although they have improved since 2004.[3] Falling production aside, upstream operations have faced other hinderances of a managerial, operational and regulatory nature. The natural and expected decline in the production of a non-renewable resource has been intensified by a tight regulatory framework, poor project management and insufficient technology transfer.

In light of the above, it is not surprising that Mexico's crude oil production collapsed from approximately 3.4 million barrels per day in the third quarter of 2004, the period in which production reached its peak, to a level of approximately 2.6 million barrels per day in 2011; a reduction of roughly 22%. Official sources predict that production will continue to decline, but were hoping for a return to from 2.6 to 2.8 million barrels per day by 2013.[4] Clearly, however, the golden age of Mexican easy oil is over, and the country's fiscal dependency on oil revenues has stirred doubts in policy makers about the appropriateness of the contracts entered into by Pemex in an effort to increase production. Is Mexico's constitutional and legal regime so protective that it actually endangers this country's energy security? Could Mexico's restrictive contractual regime force the country into become an importer, leaving behind a legacy of oil richness? Is history keeping Mexico away from crossing the new frontiers of deep water and unconvential drilling for which new forms of agreement, with a different sort of company, may be indispensable?

Pemex has reported that, as of January 1 2010, total proven hydrocarbon reserves amounted to 14.0 billion barrels of crude oil equivalent (boe), out of which approximately 74% consisted of crude oil (10.4 billion). Further, Mexico's hydrocarbon potential may be deemed substantially higher if we consider 3P (proven

3 See Goodrich, Riquelme & Asociados, *The New Mexican Upstream Legal Regime. A Change of Paradigm Towards Private Venture*, 2nd ed, 2011.

4 *Ibid.*

+ probable + possible) crude oil reserves which Pemex estimates in about 43.1 billion boe, located in both onshore and offshore fields.[5] Hence, Pemex has come to terms with the fact that Mexico's future as an oil exporter cannot rely on expectations of discovering other giant oilfields. Rather, Mexico's promise must be based on the conception of a mixed portfolio, including deep-water projects, unconventional fields (such as Chicontepec)[6], reserves in medium/shallow waters and mature fields.[7]

The great challenges involved in developing such potential have led Pemex to the understanding that, if success is to be achieved, the following measures must be undertaken:

- Innovative and optimal technologies must be made available;
- Activities and risk reduction in the deep waters of the Gulf of Mexico must be accelerated;
- The success rates of exploratory wells must be improved by focusing on specific hydrocarbon-producing areas; and
- The demarcation of wells must be accelerated to minimise risk of their development.[8]

Due to the great geological complexity of the location of much of the country's hydrocarbon deposits, it is believed that the prospects for Mexico's development of its reserves largely depend of the types of associations Pemex can enter into with other companies. If this is true, the overarching question then is whether service contracts will attract the proper partners. As will be explained below, even following the 2008 reform, which brought about a more flexible type of service contract, it is questionable whether these aims are attainable even under such contracts. So far, after two bid rounds, the market has rendered a sobering judgement concerning their commercial attractiveness.[9]

3. Petroleum legal regime

Mexico's legal framework concerning exploration and production contracts is based on the Constitution, which lays the ground for principles to be contained in the main secondary laws,[10] which will be described in further detail in this section. After

---

5 According to Goodrich, Riquelme & Asociados, *op cit.*:

> *The total 1P reserves are geographically distributed as follows: 29% in onshore fields and the rest in offshore fields. With respect to 3P reserves PEMEX estimates that 51% are located in onshore fields while the remaining 49% are found in offshore fields.*

6 Chicontec has complex geological features and low permeability, which accounts for a substantial gas release during extraction which blocks oil flow towards the well. Further, exploiting Chicontepec involves high production costs and is technologically challenging. Chicontepec is considered as one of the largest fields in the Americas, and the official estimates consider that it holds approximately 39% of the 3P hydrocarbons reserves in Mexico. However, and despite the Mexican government spending US$4.5 billion since 2006, production has only reached about 70,000 barrels per day at the end of 2012, which is significantly less than forecasted by Pemex; see Alejandra López, "*Da poco la Mejora de Extracción de Crudo*" in *Reforma*, October 8 2012.

7 Goodrich, Riquelme & Asociados, *op cit.*

8 *Ibid.*

9 See Laurence Whitehead, *Coping with Adversity in the Mexican Oil Industry: Como Pemex No Hay Dos*, p 14, James A Baker III Institute for Public Policy, Rice University, (2011), available at bakerinstitute.org/publications/EF-pub-WhiteheadAdversity-04292011.pdf.

10 Principally the Pemex Law, *Diario Oficial de la Federación*, November 28 2008 and the Petroleum Law, as amended, *Diario Oficial de la Federación*, November 29 1958.

half a century of being frozen, the legal framework underwent a reform in 2008 which brough about some significant changes in Mexican exploration and production contracts. It is important to note that, before this reform, these contracts were of a strictly administrative kind with inflexible terms pre-established by laws and regulations.[11] However, as will be explained below, the new Mexican contracts are still restricted to being service contracts in which cash compensation prevails, as this is the only form permitted by the Constitution and applicable laws.

3.1 Petroleum law and relevant provisions

Article 27 of the Mexican Constitution is hailed by some for guaranteeing national sovereignty, while others regard it as the primary obstacle for modernising the industry. Beyond such judgements, it is necessary to address the contents of this provision in order to point out the practical limitations it poses on exploration and production agreements.

It is important to understand that Article 27 is the product of the Mexican revolution of 1917. As regards hydrocarbon matters, it was drafted in order to assert national ownership of natural resources in the subsoil, thus eliminating any possibility of a private claim on them. The article states that all hydrocarbons in the national subsoil, be they in solid, gaseous or liquid form are in the "direct ownership" of the Mexican nation. As mentioned previously, this form of public ownership is no different from that of many countries in the world. Further, when this article was enacted, private companies operated widely in Mexico under concessionary agreements.

The first strong contraction of the Mexican industry to private investment occured when Lázaro Cárdenas nationalised the industry. It was in 1938 when the Constitution was amended and concessions were outlawed. Still, it was not Cardenas' intent to impede all private participation in exploration and production so, while concessions were prohibited, some contracts were left as a possibility for engaging private companies. The Petroleum Law established which types of contracts were permitted. Under Article 6 of that law, the permitted contracts were of a hybrid kind between production sharing agreements and risk service contracts, as compensation was paid in kind or in cash depending on specific circumstances established in the law.[12]

The final push towards the current legal regime ocurred under the presidency of Adolfo Ruiz Cortínez in the 1950s, who, for reasons which remain unclear,[13] placed contracts under the same prohibition as concessions. From that moment on, the Constitutional text has stated that the exploitation of all hydrocarbons shall be performed directly by the nation and that, for such purpose, neither concessions nor contracts may be executed. The wording of the Constitution remains unchanged to

---

11 The Procurement Law, *Diario Oficial de la Federación*, January 4 2000; The Public Works Law, as amended, *Diario Oficial de la Federación*, January 4 2000.

12 See José Ovalle Favela, *op cit.*

13 The reasons given in the preamble of the reforms to the Petroleum Law explained that as the contracts were commercially unsuccesful, it made sense that the state should take over the entirety of such activities; *Ibid.*

this day. And, while all contracts could be construed as prohibited in Mexico by the Constitution, the latter delegates the legislative branch with legal power to define which contracts are actually forbidden. Historically, the Mexican legislature has interpreted this prohibition in the sense that contracts which commit production, or its revenues, as compensation to the contractor are forbidden by the Constitution. This means that contractors may be compensated with cash, but not with barrels of oil or with cash compensation directly based on sales of oil and thus related to its market value.

Other provisions of the Constitution impose significant restrictions on the scope of private participation in Mexican upstream contracts. Articles 25 and 28 of the Constitution, although frequently glossed over by international and domestic analysts, are of significant consequence to the industry and hence to contractual models, as they establish a state monopoly in hydrocarbon exploration and production activities. Article 25 states that the Mexican economic model rests upon the participation of the public, private and social[14] sectors, with the exception of certain activities, which are deemed 'strategic' by the Constitution, which may be performed solely by state-owned and controlled entities. In effect, Article 25 provides the constitutional basis for the exclusivity of Pemex, as a state-owned and controlled entity, in the vast majority of hydrocarbon activities.

Article 28, which sets out the principles of domestic antitrust law, states that the exclusivity of state entities in hydrocarbon activities may not be considered a monopoly punishable by law. This provision, not only entitles Pemex to act as the sole operator in the Mexican subsoil, but it prohibits it from entering into contracts which would minimise its control of the 'strategic activity'. Article 28 greatly limits the scope of exploration and production contracts, as does Article 27, in that it forbids the execution of a vast variety of contracts which may reduce the constitutionally mandated state monopoly of hydrocarbon exploitation.

Above it was explained that the Constitution prohibits Mexico from entering into 'contracts' for the exploitation of oil and gast, while providing only a general view of which specific contracts may be deemed unconstitutional. Also, it was noted that the Constitution delegates to the legislature the power to specify which contracts are proscribed. In this regard, Article 6 of the Petroleum Law[15] has been the marker that sets the principles and characteristics governing such contracts.

The original text of Article 6[16] provided a tight framework for service and works contracts. It specified that Pemex could enter into the works and service contracts it required for the better performance of its activities, as long as the compensation stipulated in them did not entitle the contractor to a percentage of the production or of the results of its exploitation. This provision was congruent with interpretations

14 By the 'social sector' is meant the participation of labour unions, cooperatives and other civil organistions.

15 Petroleum Law of 1958, Article 6.

16 The original text of 1958 said:

> *Petróleos Mexicanos may enter into the works and services agreements, with individuals or legal entities, required for the better execution of its activities. The compensation provided in such agreements shall always be in cash and under no circumstances will entail a percentage of the production, nor of the results of hydrocarbon exploitation.*

of the Constitution, and reduced Mexican contracts to the pure service type in which flat fees could be paid for works and services performed. This was the rule for over 50 years until the reform of 2008, at which time it became clear that the flat fee scheme provided a perverse incentive to drill inefficiently, in exchange for greater compensation, without guaranteeing production. Further, exploration and production contracts had to comply with the generic works and services laws and regulations which were incompatible the nature of hydrocarbon activities.

The legislative debate that took place during the 2008 reform acknowledged that the legal scheme for works and service contracts had not benefited Mexico as expected. A sharp decline in production[17] could account for that. Further, it was recognised that the prohibition, in Article 6 of the Petroleum Law, on tying works and services to results was a barrier towards achieving better efficiency from works and services providers. Still, and even when the different political factions realised that the current scheme was inappropriate, there were sharply contrasting views about which scheme could better serve the interests of Mexico and Pemex. Should contracts be more flexible? Or should Pemex contract at all?[18]

Following an intense phase of legislative debate and political negotiations, the text of Article 6 of the Petroleum Law was finally amended, in that the language which prohibited the tie between compensation to results was eliminated.[19] However, as a result of rough political bargaining between the proponents of an opening and its attackers, the deletion of that limitation was counterbalanced by the introduction into the text of an explicit prohibition of 'production sharing agreements' or any other similar agreement which entitles the contractor to a percentage of the production, the proceeds of the sale of the hydrocarbons or of their byproducts.

Until the 2008 reform, Article 6 of the Petroleum Law was the only hydrocarbon-specific legal provision to govern exploration and production contracts. Other mandatory provisions were based on the generic procurement laws, which set forth specific contents such as duration, guarantees, pricing, termination and other important aspects. Hence, the reform created a wholly new contractual regime just for Pemex. In order to get its contracts out of this the generic box the Pemex Law was enacted to provide new mandatory guidelines for them. Chapter IV of the Pemex

---

17 As one article put it:

In recent years, Mexico has lost almost a quarter of its production capacity, dropping from 3.9 million barrels per day in 2004 to 2.98 million in 2010. Production at most of Mexico's most important fields is falling.

See Tim R Samples and José Luis Vittor, "Energy Reform and the Future of Mexico's Oil Industry: The PEMEX Bidding Rounds and the Integrated Services Contracts" *Texas Journal of Oil, Gas and Energy Law*, Volume 7, 2012.

18 See Ioan Grillo, "Opening Up Mexico's Oil to Foreigners: A First Step", *Time*, October 31 2008, (www.time.com/time/world/article/0,8599,1855621,00.html), describing opposition to the energy reforms and citing an expert opinion that the reforms did not adequately address the problems behind declining production.

19 It now reads:

Petróleos Mexicanos and its affiliates may enter into the works and services agreements, with individuals or legal entities, required for the better execution of its activities. The compensation provided in such agreements shall always be in cash and under no circumstances may ownership over the hydrocarbons be granted for the services rendered and works executed, nor may it enter into production sharing agreements or any other agreements which commit a percentage of the production or the proceeds of the sale of the hydrocarbons or its by-products, or the profits of the contracting entity.

Law, concerning its contractual regime, sets out the basic rights and obligations of the parties to Pemex's most recent model exploration and production agreement.

The crux of the reform consisted in creating and providing a constitutionally permissible and effective incentive which would encourage different types and sizes of companies to increase production, while neutralising the temptation to drill intensively for a fee. Thus, the first and foremost challenge in designing the legislation was determining the nature of that incentive within the boundaries of the Constitution and of Article 6 of the Petroleum Law, which explicitly ruled out production sharing and other similar agreements. Approval of such a scheme required intense political negotiation between the players who pushed for an opening and those who resisted it adamantly. If there could not be production or revenue sharing agreements, how and what type of incentive could Mexico offer companies in order to reverse the decline in production?

Articles 60 and 61 of the Pemex Law are the basis of such an incentive. While Article 60 reiterates the elements that are not permitted in Pemex's contracts,[20] Article 61 establishes the possible bonuses to be obtained by contractors. In sum, pursuant to this provision:[21]

- Contracts may provide compensation for benefits derived from technological developments.
- The compensation shall be determined by a previously established formula, in accordance with civil legislation.
- Contracts may include bonus schemes whenever, as a result of the performance of the contractor, Pemex receives better profits, reduces costs, or acquires better technology.

From the mere text of the law, it was difficult to ascertain what kind of incentive would be included in the contracts. Tensions and opposing views during the legislative process of the reform caused prohibitions to be stated more clearly than possibilities. Accordingly, the type of incentive permitted in contracts under the Pemex Law was a vague one within a restricted realm of service contracts. The specifics of contractual compensation were left to be developed in legal instruments to be designed and issued within the executive branch, away from the legislature, in a politically safer environment. Thus, the scope of the price formulae to be used was left to be determined by a regulation, which could be issued by the president. The hard and controversial decision as to contractual compensation was to be made within the confines of the federal public administration.

Following the enactment of the Pemex Law, months went by until further detail was unveiled about the awaited price formulae to be used in the contracts. Companies, although already discretely disappointed by the prohibitive language of the legislation, nonetheless expectantly waited further detail about the economics of

20 Compensation cannot be paid in kind, or in the cash equivalent thereof. For the first time in Mexican legislative history, production sharing, risk sharing and other similar agreements are expressly prohibited.

21 As translated and summarised by Luis Cuervo in "The New Law of Petroleos Mexicanos and the Basis of the Service Contract" at frvf-law.com/news.php?id=2843.

the contracts. Much mystery surrounded the office of the Energy Ministry of the Calderon administration which, in conjunction with Pemex, was in charge of the drafting of the regulations for implementing the Pemex and the Petroleum Laws. Their delay raised much speculation. Was the Calderon administration unsatisfied and hence sabotaging the reform, which had been diluted in political negotiation? Finally, the political opposition, which had participated actively in the reform, pressed hard on the Calderón administration until Pemex released the regulations.[22]

The regulations were less forthcoming than expected as to the terms of the contracts. After months of anticipation, industry participants and followers were expecting more than just hints about the compensation scheme. The most telling provision was Article 62 of the Pemex Regulation, which finally disclosed the nature of the incentive in the contracts. Article 62 states that:

> *compensation may be agreed to on the basis of the success rate of the projects or on explicit and quantifiable indicators, expressed in units commonly applied in the hydrocarbon industry, which may account for productivity, capacity, incorporated reserves, reserve recovery, execution time, costs, savings, among others.*

In other words, the compensation could effectively entail a fee per barrel, which, by Mexican standards, was a considerable step forward in securing productivity in service activities. As contractors would be paid depending on barrels produced, and not wells drilled, this regulatory change was consistent with the original aim of the reform to link compensation to results, rather than just works and services provided, productive or not. Still, political pressures made the language of the regulation somewhat obscure and coy. Although implied, the fee per barrel was not explicitly stipulated. It was only later on, when the Pemex Model Contract was made public, that it became clear that a fee per barrel was the new compensation scheme to be adopted in the newest agreements.

Another applicable law is the administrative provisions ssued by the Pemex Board of Managers as will be explained further on in this chapter. The scope of these provisions is to provide the basis for drawing up the contracts and bidding procedures, payment and other administrative requirements for the valid execution of the contracts.

(a) Regulatory bodies

As a state-owned monopoly, the overpowering presence of Pemex in Mexico's oil and gas industry has hindered the possibility of regulating its activities. Not until recently have efforts been made to coax Pemex to become a compliant, regulated entity rather than act as an authority. The 2008 reform also came to terms with the fact that Pemex behaves more as a regulator rather than as a subject of regulatory enforcement. Since its creation, and although it has been governed by the legal framework described above, the Mexican national oil company has called its own bid rounds, has chosen its contractors, has issued its own safety rules, and is still

---

22 Carlos Elizondo Mayer-Serra, *Stuck in the Mud: The Politics of Constitutional Reform in the Oil Sector in Mexico*, p 35, James A Baker III Institute for Public Policy, Rice University (2011), available at bakerinstitute.org/publications/stuck-in-the-mud-the-politics-of-constitutional-reform-in-the-oil-sector-in-mexico/view.

bestowed with many of the legal powers commonly held by regulators. In many ways, Pemex is conceived, not as a company, but as a law-enforcing government entity.

This empowerment may strengthen Pemex in some ways, but it is deemed by some experts to affect Mexico negatively, as it reinforces the argument that Pemex is an end in itself and not a instrument of value creation for Mexico. The recent steps towards regulating Pemex have responded to a need to clarify that it is the only authorised licensed operator in Mexico, but that it is equally only an operator licensed by the Mexican government. As such, it should not be conceived as a branch of government, empowered to enforce the law, but as a regulated government entity. The 2008 energy reform took steps towards widening the scope of external regulated activities undertaken by Pemex.

Secretariat of Energy: As head of the head of the energy sector, the Secretariat of Energy plays a dual role as a regulator and as a policy maker. Not only is it in charge of aiding the executive in issuing crucial regulations concerning the hydrocarbon industry, but it also holds legal power to issue plans and other strategic documents which should serve as guidelines for Pemex's business plan. Hence, several of the relevant regulatory codes are crafted within the Secretariat of Energy and are binding on Pemex. As explained, the Pemex Regulation established important aspects that must be present in the exploration and production contract models, which may not be freely negotiated between Pemex and its contractors. Thus, the regulation issued by the secretariat is of crucial importance to the contracts' contents.

One of the main powers exercised by the Secretariat of Energy is awarding Pemex the individual licences[23] for each specific projects. Under the Petroleum Law and its implementing regulation, the secretariat is empowered to authorise the petroleum operations in a particular area. The singularity of this process is that, because of its monopolistic status, the single entity that may be authorised by this agency is Pemex. Therefore, to this day, not a single authorisation has been denied.

Another important role of the Secretariat of Energy is the participation of many of its primary officers in the Pemex Board of Managers. By law, the Secretary of Energy is chairperson to the board. Thus, the Secretary of Energy is key in making many of the commercial, technical and legal decisions within Pemex. The participation of the Secretariat of Energy as chairperson, although intended to strengthen state control over Pemex, has been criticised by experts as it creates a conflict of interest in the person playing this dual role. It creates great confusion between the regulatory agency and the regulated entity, and it accounts for many of the difficulties in making Pemex comply with the rules issued by the secretariat.

---

23 Rogelio López Velarde, "Mexico" in *Getting the Deal Through. Gas Regulation 2012,* available at www.lvhsmexico.com/attachments/2012/GR2012_Mexico.pdf:

> *PEP's exploration and production activities are subject to the previous granting of an 'assignment' of land by Sener. These 'assignments' are authorisations granted by Sener to PEP, upon request of the Mexican president or with his consent, to explore and exploit the subsoil of certain lands. Pemex may be granted an unlimited number of assignments, each of which shall refer to a continuous surface of at least 100,000 hectares. Assignments have an initial term of 30 years, renewable upon request by PEP. Preliminary exploration activities, however, are only subject to a permit, granted also by Sener.*

National Hydrocarbons Commission: Conceived as a hybrid between the Norwegian Petroleum Directorate and the Brazilian Hydrocabons Commission, the National Hydrocarbons Commission is entrusted with the role of being the first regulatory authority to challenge Pemex's power in exploration and production activities. The singularity of the interaction between the commission and Pemex is that, in this particular case, the agency regulates the sole licensee in Mexican territory. Thus, market forces present in industries in which there is a competitive demand for acreage, and which might diminish Pemex's rersistance to being regulated, are absent in Mexico.

The National Hydrocarbons Commission, on the other hand, provides the technical elements for the design and definition of national policy on hydrocarbons, participates with the Secretariat of Energy in the determination of policies for the restitution of hydrocarbons reservoirs, and establishes technical and safety guidelines and standards for the exploration and production of domestic hydrocarbons.

Pemex Board of Managers: As mentioned above, Pemex is headed by a Board of Managers which is composed of representatives of several secretariats, among which the Secretariat of Energy and the Secretariat of the Treasury have outstanding influence in the company's decision-making process. As a result of the 2008 energy reform, four additional board members were added with the purpose of balancing that influence by introducing more technical and commercial criteria into the process.[24]

Under the Pemex Law, the Pemex Regulation, and the administrative contractual provisions, the Board of Managers comprises four committees out of which the Acquisitions, Leases, Goods and Services Committee is of particular importance in the drafting and approval of contracts. In the specific case of the exploration and production model contracts, while Pemex drafts them, they have to be discussed, first, within the aforementioned committee, and then in a plenary session of the board.

The most recent contractual models were the first to undergo discussion by the board. As will be explained below in greater detail, it was the first time that a model contract had undergone a review and discussion that was publicly accessible. This increased transparency and public scrutiny over the contractual models but it also delayed their approval. In any case, it allowed companies and other stakeholders to witness the approval process, and to have access to contractual information which was otherwise unavailable before the 2008 energy reform.

Other agencies: As exploration and production of hydrocarbons involve a wide range of activities, other regulatory authorities have competence to enforce specific

---

24 This purpose was in part defeated as the original bill, submitted by President Calderón, was not approved as such. The bill proposed that four private citizens be board members to lessen the political influence on Pemex's decisions. However, during the legislative process, the bill was amended by congressional members who redrafted the applicable provisions so that the new board members had to be public servants, appointed by the President and ratified by the Senate. Therefore, it was predictable that their outlook would be politicised.

matters. To mention the most important: environmental matters are subject to the regulation of the Environmental Secretariat; imports and exports fall under the Secretariat of the Economy; while fiscal matters are regulated and enforced by the Secretariat of the Treasury. These agencies can enforce rules and regulations on both Pemex and their contractors.

(b) *Types of agreement*

As explained above, the Mexican Constitution, as interpreted by secondary legislation, does not allow the majority of agreements that are common in much of the global hydrocarbon industry. The Constitution forbids both concessions and contracts. While concessions are forbidden in any shape or form, the legislators have interpreted the Consitution to mean that, insofar as contracts do not commit percentages of the production, cash equivalents thereof, or parts of the revenues received from oil sales, service contracts may be entered into between Pemex and contractors.

It should be noted that Pemex enters into a very large amount and variety of service contracts.[25] Discussing the whole variety of them, even in limited detail, would go beyond the purpose and scope of this chapter. Therefore, this chapter refers only to the most recent contractual arrangements deriving from the 2008 energy reform, which in popular jargon are called 'performance contracts' or 'incentive contracts' but are officially named by Pemex as integrated service contracts. According to Tim Samples and Jose Luis Vittor:

> *Fundamentally, the PEP Model Contract is a service contract with the possibility of performance-related bonus payments. Compensation to the contractor is paid according to a volume-based fee for delivered production with certain bonus rewards available for volumes above base production. Under the Pemex Law, such bonus payments are permitted only in certain situations.*[26]

Following lenghty discussions and controversy, the first model for the integrated service contract was approved by the Pemex board on November 24 2010. The model contract was the product of international and domestic consultants, who were hired and collaborated with Pemex. Once a first draft was produced, it also was submitted for feedback from industry players, potential bidders and legal experts in roadshows and private meetings. The great challenge was to align the expectations of the industry with the constitutional and legal restrictions which framed the contract.

The feedback received on the first model contract, both from industry players and from Pemex board members defined the types of project for which it could be used. It should be noted that the model contract was initially conceived for the deep-water projects in the Gulf of Mexico, but the risk involved in such projects made its economic model unattractive to capable players. Then came discussions as to its applicability to Chicontepec, a complex field of lesser geologic risk than ultra-deep waters, but technologically rather challenging. As before, in the face of such

---

25 Pemex enters to seismic data acquisition contracts, drilling contracts, engineering procurement and construction contracts, multiple service contracts and many others.

26 See Samples and Vittor, *op cit.*

challenges, the model contract did not appear economically apt for such complex or high risk projects. In the end, it was decided that the model contract could apply to projects in the mature fields of the Mexican south east, and in March 2011, Pemex officially opened the first bidding round with the publication of an inaugural call for bids. At stake were service contracts for the mature oil fields of Carrizo, Santuario and Magallanes in the southern region of Mexico. Subsequently, in January 2012, Pemex released the bidding terms for the second bidding round for fields in the northern region of Mexico. Further, most recently, in late October 2012, the preliminary draft of the model contract for Chicontepec was released for industry review and is currently being discussed by the Pemex board. Since it first was released, the model contract has undergone some changes in its three versions, which will be noted in the following sections of this chapter, while the salient provisions of the model contracts will be analysed below.

(c) Acquisition of acreage

In Mexico, the general rule is that any contract to be executed with a Mexican public entity, such as Pemex, should be awarded by way of a competitive procedure, such as a public tender. This is mandated by Article 134 of the Mexican Constitution, which requires the Mexican state to contract for works, services and leases under the best conditions available by way of competitive bid processes. Further, this provision establishes that any exception for the obligation on the state to award contracts by way of tender procedures must be established by law.

It should be noted that, since 2008, Pemex has its own legal regime for public tenders which is intended to be suitable for the specific needs of a dymamic industry. Before that, Pemex's bid rounds were subject to the same rules as other government entities. The Pemex Law, which is the main framework now in force, contains a more flexible, less cumbersome legal framework applicable to works and service contracts. With this new framework, Pemex has been able to justify and implement certain exceptions to the bidding rounds in the form of restricted calls for tenders (in which only certain companies may participate), and, in certain limited cases, contracts may be directly awarded and negotiated. Generally speaking, the exceptions in the law refer to hydrocarbon accidents and spills, the hiring of experts and other specialised professionals and patented technologies. The Pemex Regulation empowers the Pemex Board of Managers to review specific cases in which restricted calls for tenders or direct contractual negotiation may be undertaken.[27]

The first rounds of procurement and contracting under this regime presented challenges, being the first ones using the new model contract. In the first bid round, Pemex was bombarded with questions "and struggled to provide substantive feedback to all the comments within the time frames originally contemplated." However, the process has improved "with experience as issues in the contracts are resolved and as bidders become more familiar with the Mexican bidding and contracting process."[28]

---

27 *Ibid.*
28 *Ibid.*

(d) *Qualification requirements*

Specific qualification requirements are established in the bidding rules[29] for each round of tenders rather than in the Pemex Law or the Pemex Regulation. Under the bid rules, companies undergo a preliminary qualification review prior to the presentation and opening of the bid proposals. In general terms, the review takes into account the experience and the technical, financial and legal soundness of each company, as specified by the bid rules. Companies that do not fulfil these requirements are not able to submit a bid and continue with the process. The model contract states that the suitability of the companies shall be determined by Pemex in accordance with best industry practices. Notwithstanding this element of discretion, there are certain specific requirements to be fulfilled by companies participating in bid processes.

Legal: Companies must be able to prove their legal existence by submitting current articles of incorporation, a 'certificate of good standing' and other relevant corporate documents. In the case of consortia, each company must present its own, separate corporate documents.

Technical: Companies must prove that they have undertaken integrated production services in similar oil fields during any of the previous four years before the bid round according to the detailed technical annex of the model contract. For this purpose, companies may submit copies of contracts or concessions entered into which may prove that the company has operated in such fields in accordance to the technical annex, or a certified report issued by an independent engineering certifying company in the field of exploration and production. Other technical requierements concern capabilities in respect of operating quality, safety and environmental systems.

Financial: Should the company be publicly traded, and authorised and regulated by a securities authority in the United States or Canada, it must submit its final financial report. If not publicly traded, companies must submit audited and certified financial statements.

Companies must also submit a credit rating document issued by Fitch México SA de CV, Standard & Poor's SA de CV, Moody's de México SA de CV or HR Ratings de México SA de CV. This document should contain all relevant comments by the rating agency concerning the acreage.[30]

(e) *Duration*

Unless otherwise stipulated in the model contract,[31] its duration is 30 years for all services. Notwithstanding this, some of its provisions may remain in force as they

---

29 The bid rules referred to in this chapter were published on January 19 2011.

30 Likewise, bidders must submit to the rating agency their evaluation of the project based on : (i) a crude price of $70 dollars per barrel; (ii) the bidder's cash flow for each period, equivalent to 90% of the available contractual cash flow; (iii) an investment which equals the sum of all work obligations; and (iv) an accumulated production volume equivalent to the proven and probable reserves in the contract area.

31 See Provision 3.1 of model contract.

may have to be executed after the expiry of the contractual term. These provisions concern demobilisation, clean up, and other environmental and safety obligations. It should be noted that the term of the contract may be prolonged as a result of an extension of the contract area,[32] or should Pemex deem it appropriate.

(f) Minimum work programme

Minimum work requirements[33] must take place during the first phase of the contractual term, this being the exploratoratory period.[34] The minimum financial obligations vary according to the contract area in which services are performed. For example, for the second bidding round, which included onshore and offshore fields, the largest minimum investment required was $75 million dollars (for the offshore Arenque and Atún fields), while the onshore fields each had a minimum obligation of $10 million. The broad range of minimum work commitments may suggest Pemex's intent to attract a wider variety of companies.[35]

Under the model contract, the investment committed may comprise technological tests, operational practices, acquisition and interpretation of seismic information, well drilling, construction of surface facilities, or other activities agreed with Pemex. Once approved, the contractor may add, remove or modify activities in the minimum work programme, with the prior approval of Pemex.

Breach of the obligation to complete the minimum work program is penalised with a requirement to pay 100% of the value of the work not executed.

(g) Assignment and encumbrance

The contractor's freedom to assign or encumber its interest under the model contrtact is limited.[36] Neither the contractor as a consortium, if applicable, nor any of its separate participating companies, may assign, encumber or in any way transfer any contractual rights and obligations, without the prior written consent of Pemex, which may refuse to approve the assignment or transfer if, in its judgement, the assignee lacks the proper financial or technical qualifications for performance of the contract. However, the model contract does provide that Pemex may not delay or refuse to approve an assignment without due justification if the assignment is to take place between the contractor's affiliated companies, or between or among the companies which are part of the contractor's consortium, or if it involves collection rights.

---

32 Under Provision 1.1 of the model contract, the contract area is the surface described in Annex 1 of the contract, divided into sectors, as well as the geographical formations beneath the surface, regardless of their depth.

33 As stipulated in Provision 10.2 of the model contract.

34 At the latest one month after the contract is entered into and in force, the contractor must submit a work programme for the initial period, which shall include the services to be performed during thta period and must comply with the minimum work programme, stipulated in Provision 10.1 of the model contract.

35 As the model contract is for operations in mature fields, Pemex intended to attract medium to small sized companies, specialised in these areas, with which Pemex had ample communication during the design and promotion of the contract.

36 Under Provision 23.1 of the model contract.

(h) *Local content*

Explicit local content obligations were first introduced in the Pemex Law, following the 2008 reform. In the course of the political negotiations, the nationalist wing of Congress[37] pressed for the inclusion of legal obligations to enforce local content obligation in exploration and production contracts. Accordingly, Article 50 of the Pemex Law establishes that Pemex must take the necessary measures to increase local participation in the supply of goods and services for the national petroleum industry. Such local content must however comply with Mexico's obligations under international free trade agreements to which it is party, while maintaining the commercial competitiveness and sustainability of contracts.[38]

The main challenge for Pemex in the implementation of a succesful local content policy is accommodating the demands of Mexican suppliers of goods and services, who claim a right to greater participation in the industry, with the pressing demands of hydrocarbon production.[39] However, it is likely that Pemex will not sacrifice the restitution of reserves for the sake of keeping domestic suppliers content by enforcing substantial local industry obligations. In this vein, Pemex's model contract includes a broad definition of local content which facilitates a more flexible implementation of the policy.

The contractual provision[40] regarding local content is rather brief, and states that local content shall be calculated on the basis of national value added; this being the value added, or created in Mexico, which shall not be below 40% of the total of the goods and services used in fulfilment of the contract.[41] The origin of the labour force, goods and capital are used as criteria for determining the fulfillment of this obligation. However, the origin of the capital of the companies providing those goods and services is not taken into account when calculating local content. Therefore, acquiring goods and services from foreign-owned companies may actually comply with such a requirement, as long as they have a Mexican subsidiary.

---

37 Mainly composed of Senate members of the Party of the Institutional Revolution (PRI); see Carlos Elizondo Mayer-Serra, *op cit.*

38 Pemex has established that it will invest between $18 and 20 billion per year, for the next 10 years. In that same 10 year period, Pemex will increase its local content in materials contracts by an average of 1% per year. This past year Pemex, published its study on prospective demand for goods and services, as the basis for determining the allotment of local content in its investment. Pemex's investment strategy for suppliers is available at www.pemex.com/desarrollodeproveedores.

39 Industry organisations, such as the Mexican Association of Oil Services Providers, have been pressing for the publication of a study such as the one Pemex has now produced, and will be paying close attention to Pemex's signals concerning areas of opportunity for local goods and services in Pemex's materials procurement.

40 Provision 19.7 of the model contract.

41 Samples and Vittor, *op cit:*

> *Mexican law requires that a minimum percentage for national content be set in the PEP Model Contract. The national content requirements are provided in Clause 19.7 and are calculated according to formulas provided under Annex 17. The required minimum for national content is 40% and is based on value added or created in Mexico. This requirement might pose practical problems for bidders at the beginning of the contract term, as suggested by some bidders during the commenting and clarification phase. The goal of value creation in Mexico might be better served with a graduated scale that starts with a lower degree of national content at the beginning of the term that increases gradually to a level higher than the 40% mark. This provision might also benefit from more specific language regarding the timing of the requirement and the consequences for noncompliance.*

(i) National reservation

There is no national reservation provision as such, in Pemex's model contracts, as all hydrocarbon reserves belong to Mexico, and the contractor is not entitled to the hydrocaborns produced in any way.

(j) Environment

Pemex's contracts have tended to place heavy environmental liabilities upon contractors. Leading consultants have noted that not only the initial drafts of the model contract, but Pemex's service contracts in general, have placed a burden of unlimited liability upon its contractors. Not only does this hinder the contracts' competitiveness, but it has also been seen as creating an incentive for contractors to inflate their service fee in order to cover potential liabilities.

The first version of the model contract maintained this trend of liability, despite the critical feedback from industry stakeholders. However, and even though the current model contract[42] still provides for substantial liability on the part of contractors, its provisions do draw new limits to their contractual liabilities which did not feature in previous Pemex contracts:

> *The contractor's environmental, abandonment, and archeological liabilities ... are far-reaching and, as previously drafted, could even include damages not caused by the contractor ... However, during the First Bidding Round, Pemex improved Clause 14.3 by adding language that intended to clarify liability for pre-existing damage.*[43]

Other improvements were also implemented by way of revisions made to the model contract as a result of the feedback from the oil companies during the second bidding round. As a result, the model contract:

> *now provides a mechanism for an environmental study by a third party during the transition period to determine a baseline for liabilities. Although the three-month transition period might be a relatively short period in which to assess environmental conditions in a large area, these revisions represent a major improvement for bidders. At the same time, the environmental liability provisions remain a cause for concern and a source of uncertainty to many bidders.*[44]

For example, the environmental provisions in the model contract are drafted in broad language whose interpretation favours Pemex. They state that the contractor is the sole party responsible for all environmental obligations, commitments and conditions as established in applicable laws, experience and prudent industry practices. As a result of this, the contractor is responsible for providing all necessary remedies and compensation arising from environmental claims, and it is also obligated to undertake all necessary measures mandated by the environmental authorities. Further, Pemex's environmental liability is explicitly limited, notwithstanding its character as chief operator and owner of the hydrocarbons.[45] "These provisions have been the subject of frequent questions and comments from bidders during the clarification periods of both bidding rounds."[46]

---

42 Under Provisions 14.2 and 14.3 of the model contract.

43 See Samples and Vittor, *op cit.*

44 *Ibid.*

45 The provision entitles Pemex to sue the contractor for tort liability.

The environmental provisions also obligate the contractor to implement a programme of community and environmental support for the benefit of persons who live near the contract area. These obligations include the following, among others:

- to target investments towards actions that may contribute to obtaining a 'social licence' to operate, which is to be interpreted as the promotion of conditions which make the contractor's activities favourable to local communities;
- to undertake actions for the benefit of education, health and sustainability;
- to take action aimed at the conservation, restoration and sustainable management of hydrologic and forestry resources and of biodiversity, and towards mitigation and adaptation to climate change, education and environmental culture.

(k) Governing law and dispute resolution

Article 72 of the Pemex Law establishes that Pemex's legal acts entered into on Mexican territory shall be governed by Mexican law and shall fall under the jurisdiction of the Mexican federal courts, unless arbritration is agreed to between or among the parties.

As required by the Pemex Law, the model contract[47] establishes the applicability of Mexican law to the performance and interpretation of the contract. Further, the contractor waives all recourse to diplomatic protection from any foreign government or authority, under penalty of losing its rights to the Mexican state.

On this basis of Article 72 of the Pemex Law, the model contract:

provides for a three-stage dispute resolution process through an independent expert if the parties fail to agree on technical issues, operational matters, accounting, or calculations related to taxation and payments. This is a useful and efficient tool for dispute resolution that is widely used in similar agreements.[48]

This three-stage dispute resolution process consists of the following: the parties agree that any dispute resolution mechanism shall begin with a direct approach between the parties, so that a negotiated solution may be reached. Should this agreement not be reached, the parties may request the opinion or subject themselves to the decision of an independent expert. Such an expert may be called on to resolve technical, operational, accounting, tax and payment calculation matters.

Should an agreement not be reached by way of either of these two mechanisms, the parties agree that the dispute shall be resolved by arbitration in accordance with the rules of the International Chamber of Commerce.

It is worth noting that, in the model contract, both parties waive their rights to place liens on each other's property prior to an award being issued. That is, neither party may take legal action to place a lien as guarantee for compliance with the award or the enforcement or payment of damages.

---

46 See Samples and Vittor, *op cit.*
47 As established in Provisions 25.1 to 25.7.
48 See Samples and Vittor, *op cit.*

3.2 Government take and contractor compensation

As this is a service contract, in which Pemex does not compensate the contractor in kind, or with the cash equivalent, there are no royalties or bonuses to be paid by the contractor to Pemex or to the Mexican state. On the other hand, the model contract does establish a fee per barrel plus cost recovery,[49] subject to the available cash flow from the contract area or block. This provision reiterates that Pemex shall at all times have title over the hydrocarbons and the exclusive right to their sale. Further, the contract establishes that, from the moment of delivery of the hydrocarbons to the measuring point, and subject to the available cash flow, Pemex will pay the contractor the corresponding compensation on a monthly basis.

In addition to the above, the model contract[50] stipulates the following:

- Cash payment is the only compensation the contractor has a right to under the contract;
- The contractor will only have right to compensation inasmuch as extracted hydrocarbons in the contract area are delivered to the metering point;
- It is also expressly agreed that contractor shall not have at any moment title to partake in production, nor any claim to any economic benefit deriving from the exploitation, marketing or sales of the hydrocarbons; and
- Pemex does not guarantee in any form that contractor will recover all expenses incurred in the fulfilment of its obligations, nor does Pemex guarantee the profitability of the contract itself.

4. Current issues

Compared to its rigid predecessors the new exploration and production contract has taken steps forward as a more flexible and modern contractual arrangement. However, the two bid rounds undertaken by Pemex have shown that the market has responded tepidly to its efforts to bring newer, bigger and more varied players into Mexican fields.

One of the major and persistent issues is the still-prevailing resistance to a decisive constitutional reform that would permit, if not concessions, whose historic resonance might still be negative, at least the types of contract that have proven to be commercially attractive in the international arena. Minor legal reforms, such as the one undertaken in 2008, have proven to be insufficient to draw the companies that could help Mexico bring its production back to its previous level. Without constitutional reform, agreements that are standard in the international petroleum industry, such as concessions, production sharing agreements and risk-service contracts, will still be out of reach.[51]

Mexican politicians have long resisted proposing constitutional reform which

---

49 One key difference between the first and second rounds is that recoverable costs for exploration will be 100% instead of 75%. Among other adjustments, changes to the pre-qualification procedure and credit rating requirements have been implemented. Revisions to certain provisions in the model contract offer key improvements since the first bidding round. Also, with fields in northern Mexico, security considerations for the second bidding round were more significant than in the first bidding round, which was exclusively located in southern Mexico.

50 As provided for in Provisions 16.1 to 16.4.

51 See Samples and Vittor, *op cit.*

might allow these agreements to be available in Mexico. In this regard, however, the most recent presidential campaigns and elections have shown an interesting change. With the exception of the left-leaning candidate, Andrés Manuel López Obrador, the three market-friendly candidates[52] finally spoke of the need for constitutional reform as an unavoidable step to reaching Mexico's hydrocarbon potential. For the first time, politicians spoke of altering the terms of the Constitution, which until that moment had seemed to be carved in stone. Following the elections, however, the discourse of the winning candidate, Enrique Peña Nieto, seems to have lost momentum. It is likely that political pressures are accumulating and that the incoming government may act all too cautiously once again, thereby reducing the possibilities of a profound contractual change.

Notwithstanding its great importance, and even if it is undertaken, a reform of Article 27 of the Constitution will not be enough to ensure efficient exploitation and production of hydrocarbons in Mexico. For that purpose, it is crucial to reform, not only Mexico's contractual framework, but also the almighty status of Pemex in the Mexican industry. A contractual reform, in which Pemex remains a staunchly self-regulated, state-owned entity, may not have all the positive effects of a more thorough reform in which Pemex is compelled to act more competitively and efficiently.

One of the major fallacies that has prevailed in the shaping of the Mexican hydrocarbon industry is that the interests of Pemex and the nation are invariably aligned. As Pemex is a state-owned company, it is believed that it is directed to serve the public good. It is not so, at least not consistently. There are many interests at play within Pemex which, even following a liberalisation of contracts, could prevent it from being truly effective.

One main concern is whether contracts should remain being drafted, negotiated, awarded and administered by Pemex. This scheme, which has allowed Pemex significant power, also confuses its purpose and nature. In contractual matters, Pemex behaves as much as a policy maker and a regulatory agency rather than as a party to those contracts. This scheme has been abandoned successfully in Colombia and Brazil, where a clear separation between regulatory authorities and regulated companies has been drawn. In these countries, it is the hydrocarbon regulatory agency which, as the trustee of the natural resources, leads contractual decisions concerning drafting, bidding and award. This has created a healthy distance between the regulatory agencies, the state company and its competitors. Being treated as one company among many has made the state companies more competitive, not only in their native countries, but also internationally. Petrobras and, to a lesser extent Ecopetrol, have become players in the international field and partner with peer companies.

Another issue which must be addressed in conjunction with contractual reform, is Mexico's reliance on oil as a secure source of fiscal revenues. If Pemex remains the main source of those revenues, it is possible that exploration and production projects

52 Enrique Peña Nieto, of the Party of the Institutional Revolution, Josefina Vázquez Mota, of the National Action Party and Gabriel Quadri of the New Alliance Party.

will be decided on the basis of fiscal urgencies rather than on commercial convenience, as happens today. Contractual reform that does not address and remedy Mexico's fiscal over-dependence on oil revenues will increase production while aggravating other economic and social ills.

A final issue, which may not be solved even with thorough constitutional, legal and institutional reform, concerns what has been called the social rather than the legal contract. Should the new government succeed in making these changes, does that necessarily imply that they have the necessary social backing for it to last? Many countries in Latin America, during the past few years, have undergone a backlash against the liberalisation and opening of their hydrocarbon sectors. Experiences like those of Ecuador, Bolivia, Venezuela and Argentina show that a lack of social legitimacy, together with political circumstances, may undermine and reverse what seemed like robust contractual reforms. If it is to last, it is therefore of crucial importance that any contractual reform be made under conditions of transparency and open public debate, however socially and politically complex this may be. Surrepticious reform will not be socially sustainable in the long run. The backlash of false 'resource nationalism' and the concurrent reneging of contracts is there to prove that.

5. Conclusion

From its inception in 2008, it was believed that the model contract discussed in this chapter, if not the best imaginable, was at least the best of those available to serve Mexico's dire needs in respect of hydrocabon exploration and production. If it is true that the reform left a wider space for contractual transactions, but it is still too narrow for many companies which are not drawn to low risk, low profit mature fields. The model contract, although initially conceived for all types of fields, has proven to be useful for only a restricted group of them. Initially it was discussed as a model for deep-water projects. However, when it was determined that it was unsuitable for such projects, efforts were made to adapt the model to the complexities of the Chicontepec field. But, once again, following internal discussion and exposure within the industry, the model contract was deemed inappropriate to attract the necessary companies, whose expectations went beyond a compensation scheme based on a fee per barrel plus cost recovery. In the end, the model contract has been moderately succesful in the bid rounds for onshore mature fields of the south and northeast regions. Only time will tell if the individual contracts entered into with the companies are succesful, as operations commence and evolve.

In light of the above, for some it was surprising that very recently Pemex announced the launch of the model contract for Chicontepec, when a few years ago it had been determined that the giant field held too many complexities for a service contract. Nonetheless, the Calderon administration, now ready to leave office, sensed the urgency of calling for this third bid round.[53] The question here is what

---

53 Pemex has selected six areas for bids under the integrated exploration and production contracts. These areas should yield two billion barrels of crude oil equivalent, approximately 15% of Chicontepec's reserves; see contratos.pemex.com/portal/index.cfm?action=home&language=2.

changes were made to the model contract to make its launch plausible, after the idea of using it for that purpose had been abandoned? What makes this version of the model contract a better suited one, compared to the one discussed in recent years?

A perplexing sensation surfaces following a review of the Chicontepec preliminary model, as no major differences come to mind, when it is compared to the contract used for other fields. As Chicontepec is a very complex, unconventional field, specialised companies would be required to operate the blocks. If experience with the model contract has shown that it has been only moderately appealing with low risk onshore mature fields, what makes the Mexican government think that it will draw more sophisticated players into the rough areas of Chicontepec? Or is this a political gesture of victory, after all?

The message was fairly clear when Mexico's energy reform began. The Mexican equation composed of state monopoly plus service contracts would not serve the purpose of accessing riskier hydrocarbon areas. The works and service contracts previously entered into by Pemex were inappropriate for the high risks and rewards of the hydrocarbons industry, as they had been conceived for the purpose of building schools and hospitals. The step towards the alignment of incentives had to be taken, but the Constitution and its barriers stood in the way.

Pemex invested significant efforts in designing a model contract that bore a greater resemblance to industry practice. It circled the globe promoting an agreement that had been crafted within the narrow boundaries of Mexican legislation. For this reason, it was quietly understood that the model contract, while not the best imaginable, was the best possible under Mexico's political circumstances. At that point, the model contract was seen as a stepping stone rather than as an end in itself. For this reason, even in between bid rounds, President Calderón announced that a second generation of reforms was needed. This could be interpreted as meaning that the model contract was not fit to play an important part in the solution to the problem of reversing Mexico's declining production and reserves.

However, as the end of the administration approaches, events have occured which send confusing signals to the international industry. First came the statements from Pemex's director, through which he made clear that the state company can fend for itself and Mexico, if given the liberty to set and dispose of its budget. In other words, there is no need for better-knit associations through contracts, as Pemex can do it solo if it were to be given the money to invest without external controls. This announcement was consistent with the deep-water drilling operations in the Perdido area, close to the maritime boundary with the United States, that Pemex undertook accompanied by a small, local service company. A few months later came the triumphant presidential announcements that, by having drilled two wildcat wells, Mexico's production had been doubled and secured for future generations.

The latest steps taken by the Calderon administration trace a path of uncertainty for the incoming one. Do these announcements mean that great wealth is yet to be discovered and that, for that purpose, Pemex needs partnerships? Or is it a message that Pemex must remain the dominant and indeed sole player, which makes it unnecessary to enter into bigger and better negotiations with peer companies.

A sage oil man of a global company once said that countries often resist change until they 'feel the pain'. So far, Mexicans have not. When long queues of cars line up in service stations and electricity is rationed, Mexicans may scream for the constitutional reform that we now resist. No pain, no constitutional reform, no contracts.

The author would like to thank Omar Salamanca for his assistance in drafting this chapter.

United States

Andrew B Derman
Debra J Villarreal
Thompson & Knight LLP

---

1. Introduction

The United States and, to a limited extent, Canada are the only two countries that allow individual ownership of minerals. Unlike in other countries where oil and gas companies contract with the government to explore for and produce oil and gas, in the United States, companies typically enter into oil and gas leases with individuals to obtain mineral interests.

In the United States, interests in oil and gas may be owned by individuals, trusts, local, state, or federal governments, Indian tribes, corporations, partnerships, limited liability companies, or other forms of business entities. Unless expressly separated from the surface by a reservation, conveyance or other transfer, the surface owner owns the mineral rights. Once the mineral rights are severed from the surface, they can be bought, sold or transferred separately from the surface.

The exploration, development and operation of oil and gas interests owned by the federal government are governed by federal regulations. In addition, each state has its own laws (both statutory and common) regarding the development of privately owned minerals. The states that have experienced ongoing exploration, development and production of oil and gas over the years, such as Texas and Oklahoma, have well-developed bodies of law. Other states that have experienced sporadic drilling activity, such as Pennsylvania, lack a well-developed common law and are now in the process of adopting statutes to address burgeoning oil and gas production from shale plays.

Given the complexity of various laws in the United States that govern oil and gas rights, it is impossible to summarise all of the relevant laws in one chapter. This chapter, therefore, is limited to a summary of some of the more important regulations and common law that govern oil and gas interests in the United States. The chapter first summarises the laws governing oil and gas ownership and the transfer of privately owned mineral interests in some of the most productive states, namely Texas, Pennsylvania, Louisiana, Oklahoma and North Dakota. The chapter then summarises a few of the issues most commonly faced by energy companies, such as the retention of a lease past its primary term and the interaction between a leasehold owner and a surface owner.

1.1 Private ownership of minerals

As noted above, the private ownership of minerals is fairly unique to the United States. Each state has developed common law principles and enacted statutory schemes which govern privately owned minerals and the leasing and assignment thereof.

(a) *Texas*

In Texas (as in most states), interests in minerals constitute real property interests. A mineral estate consists of five rights:

- the right to explore for and develop the minerals;
- the executive right, which is the right to execute an oil and gas lease;
- the right to receive a bonus;
- the right to receive a royalty; and
- the right to receive delay rentals.[1]

These rights can be owned or conveyed separately and each constitutes a real property interest.

A person who obtains an oil and gas lease from a mineral owner holds a 'leasehold interest' by virtue of the lease. A 'working interest' refers to the interests held by a leasehold owner when it is participating in the drilling and operation of a well. Typically a leasehold owner's working interest in a well is less than its leasehold interest because of the proportionate reduction resulting from the pooling of leases in the drilling of the well. An 'overriding royalty interest' is a real property interest created out of a leasehold. Overriding royalties do not bear expenses and, in Texas, terminate upon the termination of the applicable lease unless the overriding royalty explicitly applies to renewals and extensions of the lease.[2] The mineral interest owners who have executed an oil and gas lease are royalty owners.

An oil and gas lease is a conveyance of real property. An oil and gas lease or conveyance of a mineral interest that is not recorded in the real property records of the county where the minerals are located is void as to a creditor or subsequent purchaser who pays consideration for the same interest and takes without notice of the prior lease or conveyance (a '*bona fide* purchaser'). An unrecorded instrument remains binding upon the parties thereto.

In a quitclaim, the grantor does not represent ownership of any interest in the property being conveyed, but rather he is conveying whatever (if any) interest he owns. In Texas, a quitclaim prevents any subsequent owner from being a *bona fide* purchaser and, therefore, all subsequent owners are subject to any equitable interests. Quitclaim language is typically characterised as granting conveyance of "all of the assignor's right, title and interest." The Texas Supreme Court has held, however, that a conveyance of "all our undivided interest" in the minerals in a described tract of land was not a quitclaim because it was a conveyance of the land itself.[3]

(b) *Pennsylvania*

The first productive oil and gas well was drilled in Pennsylvania in 1859. By 1901,

---

1 *Altman v Blake*, 712 SW 2d 117, 118 (Tex 1986).
2 *MacDonald v Follett*, 180 SW 2d 334 (Tex 1944).
3 *Bryan v Thomas*, 365 SW 2d 628 (Tex 1963).

Spindletop had been discovered in Texas, and oil and gas production moved West. Pennsylvania oil and gas law, therefore, did not evolve much until the recent development of the Marcellus shale. The Commonwealth of Pennsylvania has relatively modern legislation and regulation that was adopted as a result of the shale play, but is also saddled with longstanding common law that is at odds with the laws of many other producing states.

Pennsylvania common law has not clearly defined the elements of a mineral estate, but it most probably has attributes similar to those outlined for Texas, including the right to drill and produce, the right to execute an oil and gas lease, and the right to receive bonuses, royalties and other payments. Pennsylvania has a statutory minimum royalty of one-eighth of the oil or gas produced from a lease.[4] Failure of a lease form to provide for a royalty of at least one-eighth may result in an invalid lease. In an important recent case, *Kilmer v Elexco Land Services*, Incorporated,[5] the Pennsylvania Supreme Court held that leases deducting post-production costs from the one-eighth royalty did not violate the Guaranteed Minimum Royalty Act.

Longstanding common law in Pennsylvania has held that a general grant or reservation of "minerals" in an instrument, does not include the oil and gas unless the parties can clearly show an intent to include oil and gas. This is typically known as the Dunham rule because it was first articulated in *Dunham v Kirkpatrick*.[6] The Dunham rule has resulted in cases in Pennsylvania in which the courts have held that a grant or reservation of rights in "gas" cannot be assumed to be a grant of "oil" and vice versa. In Dunham, the court held that the word "minerals" when used in a deed or lease should be narrowly construed and does not include oil and gas. In 1906, the Dunham Rule was expanded to exclude natural gas from the meaning of the term of "minerals".[7]

There is a case currently pending in Pennsylvania that raises the question of whether unconventional Marcellus shale gas is included with the term "minerals".[8] While there is a rebuttable presumption in Pennsylvania that the term "minerals" does not include oil and natural gas, there is also Pennsylvania case law that supports the idea that coalbed methane belongs to the owner of the coal, not the owner of the natural gas.[9]

In *US Steel Corporation v Hoge* the Supreme Court of Pennsylvania decided in favour of the coal owner because at the time of a deed reserving "oil and gas", methane gas was considered a lethal byproduct of coal mining, so the original grantor and grantee could not have intended to convey the coalbed methane when the rest of the gas was conveyed. An argument can be made, therefore, that under *Hoge* the rebuttable presumption of the Dunham rule would not apply to unconventional shale gas rock in the pending *Butler* case because at the time the

4 58 Pa Cons Stat § 33.

5 990 A 2d 1147 (Pa 2010).

6 101 Pa 36 (Pa 1882).

7 *Silver v Bush*, 62 A 832 (Pa 1906).

8 *Butler v Charles Power Estate*, 29 A 3d 35 (Pa Super Ct 2011), remanded so that the parties could obtain experts on whether Marcellus shale constitutes a type of mineral such that the gas falls within the deed's reservation.

9 468 A 2d 1380, 1383 (Pa 1983).

reservation was made in *Butler* (1881), the grantor and grantee would have been unaware of the gas contained in the shale; therefore, "minerals" would include unconventional shale gas rock.

In Pennsylvania, each element of a mineral estate can be owned or conveyed separately. Pennsylvania courts have classified oil and gas leases in a variety of ways, from mere leases to estates in fee. A recent appellate decision articulated the classification of an oil and gas lease as follows:

> *A lease of minerals in the ground is a sale of an estate in fee simple until all of the available minerals are removed; this leaves the lessor with only an interest in the royalties to be paid under the lease, which are personal property. Specifically, the interest granted to the leasee is a fee simple determinable, the lessor retains a reversionary interest. The interest reverts to the grantor upon the occurrence of a specified event.*[10]

The court's decision was based upon the commonwealth's longstanding coal analysis. Pennsylvania has not classified overriding royalty interests, but it is likely that they would be considered real property interests.

To be effective under Pennsylvania law, a conveyance must contain a description sufficient to enable the lands to be identified. However, full metes and bounds descriptions are not required. It is important to note that Pennsylvania tax assessment numbers are not appropriate identifiers for land descriptions. Assessment numbers change as parcels are combined or subdivided. Descriptions based on assessment numbers may not adequately describe a parcel of land over time.

Pennsylvania tax sales may cause title issues. In certain counties, the county tax assessment authority overlapped township assessing responsibilities resulting in dual assessment systems for occupied and non-developed, non-occupied lands. Non-occupied lands (also known as 'unseated lands') were subject to abbreviated tax sale standards. Some authority exists for the proposition that a tax sale of unseated lands made after a recorded severance of the underlying oil and gas will reunite the surface and the oil and gas in the purchaser at the tax sale. The danger is that the occurrence of such a sale cannot be determined by a search of the oil and gas title chain; therefore, special grantee searches of all surface parcels must be constructed to avoid missing a reuniting of the oil and gas and the surface.

It is important for oil and gas operators with operations in those parts of Pennsylvania with coal deposits to be aware that the law governing interaction between coal and oil and gas operations remains unsettled. The Coal and Gas Resource Coordination Act,[11] gives coal operators a right to object to the issuance of well permits that are over, or that will pass through, coal deposits, whether or not they are currently being mined. The act further provides a special spacing for all wells drilled in such areas. Pennsylvania case law has established that owners of oil and gas estates that are severed or operated after a coal severance or lease owe damages to the coal operator in some form.[12]

---

10 *Hetrick v Apollo Gas Co*, 608 A2d 1074 (Pa Super Ct 1992).
11 58 Pa Cons Stat Sections 501 and following.
12 *Chartiers Block Coal Co v Mellon*, 25 A 597 (Pa 1893).

(c) *Louisiana*

Basic mineral rights under Louisiana law include the right to create a mineral servitude, the right to a mineral royalty and the right to execute a mineral lease. These rights are real property rights and are subject to prescription in the event of non-use for 10 years or to special rules of law governing the terms of their existence.[13] Prescription is a means of acquiring the ownership of property by:

- the effect of time, the time period for oil and gas being 10 years; and
- conditions regulated by law, which for oil and gas is the failure to develop and produce.

Ownership of land does not include ownership of oil, gas and other liquid or gaseous minerals; however, the landowner has the exclusive right to explore and develop his land for the production of such minerals.[14]

Under the Louisiana Mineral Code, if a mineral servitude is created without a specific term, prescription for non-use commences running from the date of creation and accrues 10 years later unless interrupted by good faith drilling operations or by production being obtained from the servitude tract or the acreage pooled.[15] Prescription for non-use running against a royalty is interrupted by production from or attributable to the royalty tract.[16] The production does not have to be in paying quantities for the prescription to be interrupted.[17] A mineral lease is not subject to prescription but cannot be maintained in effect for more than 10 years without drilling operations or production.[18]

A mineral lease is defined in the Louisiana Mineral Code as being a contract by which the lessee is granted the right to explore for and produce minerals. A mineral lease is considered to be a real right and an incorporeal immovable (a legal right to real property) which is alienable.[19]

Louisiana law requires that the former owner of a mineral right which has terminated or expired shall, within 30 days after a written demand, execute a recordable act of release.[20] If a mineral lease is extinguished prior to expiry of its primary term, Louisiana law requires the former lessee to file a release within 90 days after the expiry of the lease, even if no written demand for release is received.[21] If a lessee fails to comply with the release requirements, the defaulting lessee may be liable for damages plus attorney's fees.[22]

Louisiana is a pure 'race' jurisdiction.[23] The first party to record its interest of record prevails over a party holding under a subsequently recorded instrument, even

13 La Rev Stat Section 31(16).
14 La Rev Stat Section 31(6).
15 La Rev Stat Sections 31(29) and (36).
16 La Rev Stat Section 31(87).
17 La Rev Stat Sections 31(38) and (88).
18 La Rev Stat Section 31(115).
19 La Rev Stat Sections 31(16) and (18).
20 La Rev Stat Section 31(206(A)).
21 La Rev Stat Section 31(206(B)).
22 La Rev Stat Section 31(207).
23 In resolving conflicts in title claims, the traditional rule, which is the 'race' rule as in effect in Louisiana, is that the person whose interest is first recorded prevails over anyone who later records an interest. Louisiana does not, unlike most other jurisdictions, recognise an exception for a *bona fide* purchaser.

if it was executed before the first recorded instrument. An instrument affecting real (immovable) property in Louisiana is binding on third parties only from the time the instrument is recorded in the parish records.[24]

(d) Oklahoma

In Oklahoma, the mineral estate consists of the right to drill, the right to execute an oil and gas lease, the right to receive a bonus and the right to receive a royalty.[25] Each element of the mineral estate can be owned, conveyed or reserved separately from the other elements. The right to lease has been held in Oklahoma to be a personal right and is not, therefore, inheritable when reserved by a grantor. However, the executive right is inheritable under Oklahoma law when it is reserved by the "grantor, his heirs, executors, administrators and assigns."[26]

Overriding royalty interests are real property interests created out of the leasehold estate and burden the leasehold owner. An overriding royalty interest terminates upon the expiry of the oil and gas lease it burdens unless the instrument creating the overriding royalty provides that the overriding royalty applies to renewals and extensions.[27]

(e) North Dakota

Under North Dakota law, a mineral interest is a real property interest created in oil and gas in place. Royalty interests and overriding royalty interests are also real property interests.[28] The North Dakota Supreme Court has not addressed such issues as extensions and renewals of leases in the context of overriding royalties.

North Dakota's Dormant Mineral Act is perhaps the state's greatest difference in oil and gas law when compared with many of the other major oil producing states. Caution must be exercised by any energy company where a potential dormant mineral estate is involved. Under the Dormant Mineral Act, a mineral interest is deemed to be abandoned if the interest is unused for a period of 20 years before the first publication of a statutorily required notice. Title to the abandoned mineral interest vests in the owner of the surface estate in the land under which the mineral interest is located.[29] If a person intends to succeed to the ownership of a mineral interest, the person must give notice of the lapse of the mineral interest by publication. The publication must be made once a week for three weeks in the newspaper of the county in which the mineral interest is leased, and if the address of the mineral interest owner is shown on record, notice must be given by mail to the owner of the mineral interest within 10 days after the last publication is made. A copy of the notice and an affidavit of service of the notice must be recorded in the Office of the County Recorder of the county in which the mineral interest is located and constitutes *prima facie* evidence in any legal proceedings that such notice has been given.

---

24 La Rev Stat Section 9:2721.
25 *Jolly v Wilson*, 478 P 2d 886 (Okla 1970).
26 *Stone v Texoma Prod Co*, 336 P 2d 1099 (Okla 1949).
27 *O'Neill v American Quasar Petroleum Co*, 617 P2d 181 (Okla 1980).
28 *GeoStar Corp v Parkway Petroleum, Inc*, 495 NW 2d 61, 67 (ND 1993); *ANR Western Coal Development Co v Basin Electric Coop*, 276 F 3d 957 (8th Cir 2002).
29 ND Cent Code Section 38-18.1-02.

The Dormant Mineral Act provides dormant mineral owners a means to preserve their interest by filing a statement of claim within 60 days after first publication of the notice described above.[30] A mineral interest is deemed not to be dormant if:

- any minerals are produced;
- operations are being conducted for injections, withdrawal, storage or disposal of water, gas or other fluid substances;
- the mineral interest on any tract is subject to a lease, mortgage or conveyance of the mineral interest recorded in the recorder's office in the county in which the mineral interest is located;[31]
- the mineral interest is subject to a recorded order or an agreement to pool or unitise;
- taxes are paid on the mineral interest by the owner; or
- a statement of claim containing the name and address of the mineral interest owner and a legal description of the mineral interest is recorded.

2. Upstream activities

In the United States, exploration and production of oil and natural gas has expanded into shale formations over the last several years. Shale formations that are currently being developed include, but are not limited to: the Barnett and Eagle Ford shales in Texas, the Marcellus shale in Pennsylvania, the Haynesville shale in Louisiana, the Woodford shale in Oklahoma and the Bakken shale in North Dakota. The development of shale formations has led to increased exploration and production activities in these regions.

3. Petroleum legal regime

3.1 Petroleum law and relevant provisions

(a) *Regulatory bodies*

Onshore oil and gas interests owned by the federal government of the United States are under the control of the United States Department of the Interior, Bureau of Land Management (BLM). The BLM has offices in 13 states plus its national office in the District of Columbia. The primary regulations that govern leasing and operation of federal minerals are in Title 43 of the Code of Federal Regulations, Parts 3100 to 3180.

Where onshore oil and gas interests are owned by private parties, each state has its own regulatory body which oversees development and production. In Texas, the regulatory body is the Railroad Commission. In Pennsylvania, development is overseen by the Office of Oil and Gas Management. Louisiana's regulatory body is called the Department of Natural Resources. In Oklahoma, the development of oil

30 ND Cent Code Section 38-18.1-05.

31 If the landowner leases, conveys or mortgages the mineral interest, the 20 year period is stopped. For example, if a mineral owner executes an oil and gas lease one year before the expiry of the 20 year period, the minerals will not be considered dormant even if production has not been obtained from the property.

and gas resources is regulated by the Corporation Commission, and in North Dakota, oil and gas development is regulated by the Department of Mineral Resources.

(b) Types of agreement

Whether located beneath privately owned lands or lands owned by the United States, the basic agreement under which oil and gas are developed is the oil and gas lease. The oil and gas lease is an agreement between the mineral owner and the mineral developer which allows the developer to explore, develop and produce the oil and gas situated beneath a particular property. In exchange for these development rights, the mineral owner typically receives, among other things, the right to receive royalty payments on production. There are countless other types of oil and gas agreements, but given the broad use of the oil and gas lease in developing oil and gas in the United States, it is the primary type of agreement addressed in this chapter.

(c) Acquisition of acreage

If minerals are owned by the United States, development rights are acquired from the BLM through a competitive bidding process. When lands are available for leasing, the BLM's state offices conduct oral auctions for oil and gas leases at least quarterly.[32] Bids for parcels of land are placed on a dollar per-acre basis. All lands that are not sold at a competitive lease sale become available for non-competitive leasing for two years from the date of the auction.[33] Any interested party may submit an offer for a non-competitive lease on a BLM-approved offer form.

If minerals are privately owned, development rights are acquired by approaching the mineral owner to obtain an oil and gas lease. There is no formal process for the acquisition of privately owned oil and gas development rights, and the terms of such acquisitions are negotiated by the mineral owner and the developer.

(d) Qualification requirements

Lessees of federal mineral leases must be US citizens, associations of US citizens, domestic corporations or municipalities. Associations include partnerships, trusts, joint ventures and joint tenants. All members of an association must be US citizens. Foreign-born residents and entities formed under the laws of a foreign country may not directly own an interest in a federal lease. An alien may indirectly own an interest through its ownership in a US corporation so long as the home county of the alien affords US citizens the same rights.

Before submitting a bid for a lease with the BLM or filing an assignment of an existing lease with the BLM, a potential lessee must file the required forms with the bureau and obtain approval to be a lessee.[34] Interests in federal leases can be transferred to qualified lessees, subject to filing and approval requirements.

Lessees of privately owned minerals are typically not subject to qualification

---

32 43 CFR Section 3120.1-2.

33 *Ibid:* Section 3120.6.

34 To submit a bid on a new lease, the current version of BLM Form 3000-2 is required. To assign record title to an existing lease, the current version of BLM Form 3000-3 is required. To assign operating rights to an existing lease, the current version of BLM From 3000-3a is required.

requirements. Mineral owners in the United States can typically lease their minerals to any individual or entity they choose. However, before beginning operations a lessee generally must be qualified and registered with the regulatory body of the state in which the property is located.

(e) Duration

Federal leases: The primary term of a federal oil and gas lease is 10 years. A federal lease may be extended beyond its primary term by:

- the payment of rentals or minimum royalties;
- the production of oil or gas in paying quantities;[35] or
- the completion of a well physically capable of production in paying quantities.

For a well to be physically capable of production in paying quantities, it does not have to be actually producing, but the well casing must be perforated and physically capable of production. If a lessee fails to place the lease in production within 60 days after notice from the BLM to do so, the lease will expire.[36] In addition, actual drilling operations conducted diligently through to the end of the primary term will extend a lease for two years. The determination of whether or not the operations are being conducted diligently is made by the BLM. If the lease is perpetuated beyond its primary term by virtue of drilling operations, the lessee must pay rentals for the first year of the extended term prior to the expiry date of the lease. Failure to do so will result in the termination of the lease even if operations are being diligently conducted.

A federal lease will terminate for:

- a lessee's failure to make timely and proper rental payment;
- a lessee's failure to discover or develop a well physically capable of producing in paying quantities;
- the cessation of production; or
- cancellation of a lease due to violations.

A cancellation of a lease requires administrative or judicial action whereas terminations occur automatically by operation of law. There are two general grounds for cancellation of a lease: for cause, or for error or mistake. Cancellation for cause arises when the lessee has violated regulations, orders or lease provisions. Cancellation for error or mistake occurs when a lease was issued by an administrative error or mutual mistake of the BLM and the lessee.

A recorded title holder may elect to relinquish a lease. Upon relinquishment, the lease terminates. When a lessee relinquishes a lease, the lessee remains liable for any accrued rentals and royalties. Upon relinquishment, the lessee must plug and abandon any well, and comply with all reclamation obligations.

---

35 'Paying quantities' for federal leases is typically defined as an amount sufficient for a reasonable profit over costs of operating.

36 43 CFR Section 3107.2-3.

Texas: In Texas, oil and gas is owned in fee simple. The form of oil and gas lease typically contains an 'unless' clause providing that the lease will terminate unless production is obtained.[37] The lease constitutes a fee simple determinable in the oil and gas. The term of the lease is divided into two terms: the primary term and the secondary term. The primary term is for a fixed term of years during which the lessee has the option, but not the obligation, to explore for and produce oil and gas. If no production is obtained during the primary term, the lease automatically terminates at the end of the primary term. The secondary term commences when there is actual production, or a contractual substitute for production, such as the payment of shut-in gas royalty.[38]

A well that is producing in paying quantities on the land covered by a lease, or lands pooled with the lease, will continue the lease on all the lands described therein. Texas has no statutory requirement as to termination of part of a lease for non-production from such lands. The lessor must protect itself by including partial termination language in the lease itself. It is not uncommon for leases to contain a 'Pugh clause' that terminates the lease as to lands from which production is not being obtained at the end of the primary term. Leases may also contain provisions that allow partial termination either vertically or horizontally. Vertical termination applies to lands outside a producing proration unit. Horizontal termination allows termination of the lease as to non-producing formations, typically providing for termination as to all depths below the producing formations but sometimes terminating more broadly as to all non-producing formations.

Once production is obtained, a lease will continue so long as the well produces in "paying quantities". The test of whether a well is producing in paying quantities is whether or not a prudent operator would, for the purpose of making a profit, continue to operate the well in the manner being operated.[39] Relevant factors in making such a determination in Texas include:

- the price for which the lessee can sell the production;
- the relevant profitability of other wells in the area;
- the lessee's net profit;
- the lease provisions;
- the operating and marketing costs of the lease; and
- whether the lessee is holding the lease solely for speculation.

A lessee's net profit takes into account all income received by the lessee less only the royalty paid.[40] Operating and marketing costs exclude all drilling expenses, depreciation for equipment used in drilling and productions and administrative expenses attributable to the well.

One of the contractual substitutes for actual production in the secondary term is the payment of a shut-in gas royalty. A shut-in gas royalty must be provided for in the lease and is paid to the royalty owners. The payment is typically due within 60

37 *Stephens County v Mid-Kansas Oil & Gas Co*, 254 SW 290 (Tex 1923).
38 *Skelly Oil Co v Harris* 352 SW 2d 950 (Tex 1962).
39 *Clifton v Koontz* 325 SW 2d 684 (Tex 1959).
40 *Ibid.*

to 90 days from well completion. Some leases provide that shut-in royalty payments can continue a lease only for a certain period of time, such as two years, after which production in paying quantities must be obtained to continue the lease. If a shut-in royalty payment is not paid to the correct party in a timely manner, or the incorrect amount is paid, and the lease is not continued by some other means, the lease terminates as a matter of law.[41]

Some lessees are changing the traditional delay rental provisions to include a savings clause. Such savings clauses provide that if a lessee attempts to pay a delay rental but fails to pay the rental correctly, the lessor must provide written notice of such failure, and the lessee has 30 days to make the payment correctly.[42] The lease terminates only if the lessor has given written notice of the lessee's failure, and the lessee fails to cure its default in a timely manner. To avoid termination for an incorrectly paid delay rental, the practice in Texas is to pay the delay rental at the time of the execution of the lease, along with the bonus, so that the lease is fully paid up, and the lessee has no further delay rental obligation.

The duty to pay a royalty is a covenant, not a condition. Failure to pay royalty in Texas does not cause a lease to terminate unless the lease expressly so states.[43] In Texas, by statute, the operator is required to distribute funds to the interest owners within 120 days after the end of the first month in which production is sold, and then 60 days after the end of each calendar month thereafter where oil is produced or 90 days where gas is produced. Failure to pay royalties in time results in interest being due on the amount owed. A royalty owner can file suit if he does not receive royalty payments, and can recover the royalty plus interest, costs and attorney fees. An operator can suspend payment without interest until a royalty owner signs a division order, so long as the division order conforms to the statutory provisions.[44]

Pennsylvania: The clause of a Pennsylvania oil and gas lease setting out the rights conferred under the lease also establishes the period for which the lease rights will extend. The term is typically divided between the primary term and the secondary term. The primary term is for a fixed number of years during which the lessee has the right, but not the obligation, to pay delay rentals and to explore for and produce oil and gas. Unless there is production, or a contractual substitution for producing such a drilling operation or shut-in payments, at the end of the primary term, the lease automatically terminates. The secondary term continues so long as there is production of oil and gas, or its contractual substitution. Pennsylvania imposes an implied covenant of continuous development as a condition of the continued validity of a lease; however this implied covenant does not apply when a lease provides that the lessee can make non-royalty payments to continue the lease in the absence of production.

In Pennsylvania, the term 'production' in the secondary term means "production

41 *Gulf Oil Corp v Reid*, 337 SW 2d 267 (Tex. 1960).
42 *Kincaid v Gulf Oil Corp*, 675 SW 2d 250 (Tex App – San Antonio 1984).
43 *Hitzelberger v Samedan Oil Corp*, 948 SW 2d 497 (Tex Civ App – Waco 1997).
44 Tex Nat Res Code Sections 91.401, and following.

in paying quantities".[45] The determination of whether oil and gas is being produced in paying quantities is a question of fact. The lessee has the burden of proof. Pennsylvania has generally recognised the principle that temporary cessation of production will not terminate an oil and gas lease.[46] There is not, however, sufficient case law to determine how long a lease may be maintained under the principle of temporary cessation.

If a well consistently pays a profit, however small, over operating expenses, it will be deemed to have produced "in paying quantities" within the terms of the lease. In Pennsylvania, where production from a well is marginal or sporadic and the well fails to pay a profit over operating expenses over time, a determination of whether the well has produced in paying quantities requires consideration of the operator's good faith judgment in continuing the operations of the well.

Louisiana: In Louisiana, an oil and gas lease is considered to be producing in paying quantities under Louisiana law when production is sufficient to induce a reasonably prudent operator to continue production in an effort to secure a return on its investment or to minimise any loss. The royalties paid may be considered only insofar as they show the reasonableness of the lessee's expectations in continuing production. A court generally requires that production be sufficient to enable the lessee to recover its operating costs over some period of time at a minimum. Expenses attributable to drilling, equipping, reworking and recompleting a well are generally excluded from the determination of paying quantities. Properly included expenses include normal monthly operating expenses, such as the expenses of pumps, gauges, electricity and fuel costs.[47]

The characterisation of shut-in payments as either rentals or royalties depends upon the language in the lease agreement itself. Generally, in South Louisiana lease agreements, shut-in payments are treated as rentals and must be paid on time in order to maintain the lease. In some lease agreements used in North Louisiana, shut-in payments may be characterised as royalties. If treated as a royalty, a lessee's failure to pay a shut-in royalty properly would not result in automatic termination of the lease, but instead would require the lessor to make a written demand for payment.

Oklahoma: In Oklahoma, oil and gas is owned in fee simple, and an oil and gas lease is a conveyance of a fee simple determinable in the oil and gas. The term of a lease is divided between the primary term and the secondary term. The primary term is for a certain number of years during which the lessee has the right to explore for oil and gas. At the end of the primary term, a lease terminates as a matter of law unless there is capability of commercial production.[48] In Oklahoma, the discovery of hydrocarbons capable of production in paying quantities will satisfy the requirement that there be production at the end of the primary term, so long as the lessee is making a diligent effort to market the gas.[49] The need for a shut-in clause in

45 See *Babb v Clemensen*, 687 A 2d 1120 (Pa Super Ct 1996).
46 See *Cole v Philadelphia Co*, 26 A 2d 920 (Pa 1942).
47 *Noel Estate, Inc v. Murray*, 65 So 2d 886 (La 1953); *Lege v Lea Exploration Co*, 631 So 2d 716 (La App3d Cir 1994); CCH, *Inc v Heard*, 410 So 2d 1283 (La App 3d Cir 1982).
48 *Shields v Moffitt*, 683 P 2d 530 (Okla 1984); *Mason v Ladd Petroleum Corp*, 630 P 2d 1283 (Okla 1981).

Oklahoma to prolong a lease is not, therefore, as important as in Texas.

The term 'production in paying quantities' means that the lessee must produce in quantities sufficient to yield a return in excess of lifting expenses even if the drilling and completion costs may never be recovered.[50] The following have been held to be directly related to lifting expenses: royalties, pumper salaries, electricity costs, repair costs, pump operation costs, and other incidental operating expenses.

Oklahoma has a statutory provision that provides that a lease executed after May 25 1977 will expire as a matter of law 90 days after the expiry of the primary term to the extent that the land covered by the lease exceeds a drilling and spacing unit of 160 acres or more in size.[51] A lessee is statutorily required to release a lease within 30 days after a written demand by the lessor.[52]

Even if a lease does not contain a provision addressing temporary cessation of production, if the temporary cessation results from mechanical problems in the secondary term, the lease will not terminate for a reasonable time if the lessee is making reasonable good faith efforts to restore production. Whether a cessation of production is temporary is a question of fact. To avoid this uncertainty, most lease agreements used in Oklahoma contain a cessation of production clause that defines the length of time the lease will continue after cessation of production without additional reworking or drilling operations. The clauses are strictly construed against the lessee, but generally provide for a 60 to 90 day period.

North Dakota: In North Dakota, actual production in paying quantities must be established on the lands covered by or pooled with the leased lands to extend a lease beyond its initial term. A temporary cessation of production will not automatically terminate a lease. To determine whether a cessation is temporary or permanent, the North Dakota Supreme Court has held that the following factors must be considered:

- the period of time of the cessation;
- the operator's interest; and
- the cause of the cessation.[53]

North Dakota is unique in providing by statute that failure to pay royalties may void a lease, if a court determines that equity so requires.[54] The North Dakota legislature has deemed payment of royalties to be of essence to the lease and, as such, traditional damage remedies are inadequate to protect the interests of the royalty owner.[55] The legislature decided that because forfeiture would be within a court's discretion, the rule would not inequitably cancel a lease when an operator has a good reason for failing to pay royalties.

At the expiry of the primary term of a lease, the lease will automatically

49 *McVicker v Horn*, 322 P 2d 410 (Okla 1958).
50 *Stewart v Amerada Hess Corp*, 604 P 2d 854 (Okla 1980).
51 Okla Stat tit 52, Section 87.1(b).
52 Okla Stat tit 41, Section 40.
53 *Greenfield v Thill*, 521 NW 2d 87 (ND 1994).
54 ND Cent Code Section 47-16-39.1 (it also provides for an 18% interest payment once payments are 150 days past due without the royalty owner having to request it).
55 *Imperial Oil of ND, Inc v Consolidated Crude Oil Co*, 851 F 2d 206 (8th Cir 1988).

terminate unless there is actual production or the lease is perpetuated by virtue of a savings clause in the lease. Production must be in paying quantities to extend a lease beyond the primary term. The North Dakota Supreme Court has not offered specific guidance as to the calculation by which it should be determined whether this criterion is satisfied. The Supreme Court did hold that a lease was extended into the secondary term where the production of a well was marginal but still sufficient to cover the costs of production and royalties payable to the mineral owners.[56]

North Dakota has two statutory provisions addressing termination, or partial termination, of an oil and gas lease. The first statute applies to oil and gas leases submitted to compulsory unitisation. Two years after the effective date of the order that approved the unit or the expiry of the primary term of the lease, whichever is later, the lands covered by the lease that are outside the unit can be maintained only by the terms of the lease.[57]

The second statute applies to leases that appear to have expired by their own terms and provisions but in respect of which the lessee has failed to file a release. The lessor may serve upon the lessee a notice in writing demanding that the lessee release the lease. If the lessee contends the lease is valid, the lessee must file a notice in the county records stating that the lease has not been forfeited.[58] The North Dakota Supreme Court has clarified the statute by holding that the statute cannot be used by a mineral owner to obtain a release of a lease if the alleged breach is for a breach of the implied covenant to develop.[59]

North Dakota has a statutory provision that allows the owner of an oil and gas lease to record an affidavit of production with the county recorder. The affidavit, together with the record of the lease, is notice to the public of the existence and continuing validity of the applicable lease.[60] The North Dakota Supreme Court has not yet had to address the possible consequences of a failure to comply with this provision.

(f) *Assignment*

Federal leases: Federal regulations recognise assignments of recorded title, operating rights (subleases), overriding royalties and production payments. An assignment of record title differs from an assignment of operating rights.

A recorded title holder bears the obligation to pay rent and can assign or relinquish the lease. Recorded title cannot be transferred partially by reference to particular depths or separately as to either oil or gas. Any assignment of recorded title requires the BLM's approval. Once the BLM approves an assignment of recorded title, the assignee is treated as if it were the original lessee, and the assignor's obligations terminate.

Operating rights are interests carved out of the recorded title and include the

56 *Olson v Schwartz*, 345 NW 2d 33 (ND 1984).
57 ND Cent Code Section 38-08-09.8.
58 ND Cent Code Section 47-16-36.
59 *Ridl v EP Operating Ltd Partnership*, 553 NW 2d 784 (ND 1996).
60 ND Cent Code Section 47-16-40.

right to conduct drilling and production operations. An assignment of operating rights may be limited to certain depths or zones. An assignment is effective only upon the BLM's approval. Under an assignment of operating rights, the recorded title remains with the existing holder of the recorded title and that holder remains responsible for all lease obligations.

A request for approval of an assignment must be filed with the BLM within 90 days after execution of the assignment. If the request is filed after that 90 day period, the BLM may require verification that the assignment is still in effect. Transfers of production payments and overriding royalties must be filed with the BLM but do not require approval. The effective date for approval of an assignment is the first day of the month following the month in which all required documentation is provided to the BLM.

Assignments of either record title or operating rights must be prepared on BLM-approved forms and accompanied by a filing fee. A mass transfer form of assignment may be used if rights in numerous leases are being assigned. If the assignor was required to post a bond to support its obligations under a lease, then the assignee must either file a new bond or obtain the surety's consent to an assignment of the bond.

The recording of an assignment with the BLM is for administrative purposes, and does not constitute constructive notice of the assignment to third parties. An original assignment still needs to be recorded in the appropriate county real property records to provide constructive notice. Double filings are, therefore, necessary for assignments of interests in federal leases. The form of assignment filed in the appropriate county does not have to comply with the BLM's form requirements. The assignments filed with the BLM and the county should cross-reference each other so that it is clear that there is only one assignment of interest.

Leases of privately owned minerals: Whether an assignment of a lease covering privately owned minerals can be assigned is determined by the language of the oil and gas lease as negotiated by the parties. In the absence of an agreement to the contrary, leases are generally freely assignable. When an oil and gas lease is assigned, the assignment should be recorded in the county in which the lease is located in order to provide constructive notice of the assignment to third parties.

(g) Surface use

Federal: For federal lands, the operator must obtain BLM approval before conducting any drilling activities that disturb the surface.[61] The operator must submit an application for a permit to drill and attach a plan of operations for surface use describing the location and construction of the well and the plans for restoring the surface.[62] Additionally, the BLM requires the operator or lessee to post a bond of at least $10,000 to ensure compliance with plugging, reclamation and restoration

61 43 CFR Section 3162.3-1(c).
62 43 CFR Section 3162.3-1(f).

requirements.[63] The BLM may require a higher bond amount, up to the total estimated costs of plugging and reclamation, if it determines that the present bond amount is insufficient to ensure the operator's compliance with the lease obligations.[64]

Texas: If the mineral estate has been severed from the surface estate, the mineral estate is deemed the dominant estate in Texas. There is no common law or statutory duty to pay damages to the surface owner for drilling operations. A surface owner that seeks to recover damages must either prove specific acts of negligence or that more of the land was used than was reasonably necessary in the drilling operations.[65] There is no common law duty in Texas to restore the surface after drilling operations have terminated.[66] Nevertheless, lessees typically pay surface owners damages or reach agreement as to the amount of reimbursement for damages prior to the commencement of operations. If the surface owner uses force to prevent the lessee from entering the property, the lessee can obtain a temporary restraining order and commence operations prior to a scheduled hearing before the court. The surface use by an oil and gas lessee must accommodate, if reasonably possible, the prior use of the surface owner.[67]

Pennsylvania: There is no common law or statutory duty to pay damages to the surface owner for drilling operations. Pennsylvania law imposes a burden of reasonable accommodation upon the use of the surface by mineral estate owners.

Louisiana: Louisiana does not recognise a separate and discrete accommodation doctrine. The prior use of the property by the surface owner will be considered by a court in allowing both the surface owner and the mineral lessee each to exercise their rights. In the absence of a breach of contract, the mineral lessee is held to the standard of a reasonably prudent operator who must exercise his rights with due regard to the rights of others, including the surface owner. The lessee may have liability if it is using more of the surface than is reasonably required for its operations. Substantial authority exists for the proposition that an implied obligation to restore the leased premises exists in Louisiana.[68] In 2005, a Louisiana court restricted the lessee's implied restoration obligation to those instances in which the use of the surface was either excessive or unreasonable.[69] If a lease contains an express restoration obligation, a court applying Louisiana law may require the lessee to incur costs or pay damages in excess of the market value of the leased premises to accomplish restoration.[70]

---

63 43 CFR 3104.1(a).
64 43 CFR Sections 3104.1 to 3104.5.
65 *Humble Oil & Refining Co v Williams*, 420 SW 2d 133 (Tex 1967).
66 *Warren Petroleum Corp v Monzingo*, 304 SW 2d 362 (Tex 1954).
67 *Getty Oil Co v Jones*, 470 SW 2d 618 (Tex 1971).
68 La Rev Stat Section 31:122; *Wemple v Pasadena Petroleum Co*, 85 So 230 (La 1920); *Smith v Schuster*, 66 So 2d 430 (La App 2d Cir 1953).
69 *Terrebonne Parish School Board v Castex Energy, Inc*, 893 So 2d 789 (La 2005).
70 See, for example, *Corbello v Iowa Production*, 850 So 2d 686 (La 2003).

Oklahoma: The Oklahoma Surface Damage Act requires a lessee to pay a surface owner for damages. Under the act, the lessee must notify the surface owner in writing of its intention to commence operations and institute good faith negotiations as to damages. If the parties enter into a written agreement regarding damages, the lessee can immediately commence operations. If the parties fail to reach an agreement, then the lessee must file a petition for the appointment of appraisers in the district court before it can enter the property. The appraisers determine the damages. The determination is binding unless one of the parties requests a jury trial.[71] A lessee's failure to comply with the Surface Damage Act can result in treble damages being awarded to the surface owner.

North Dakota: North Dakota has adopted a surface owner protection provision. Section 38-11.1-04 of the North Dakota Century Code requires the mineral developer to pay the surface owner a sum of money equal to the amount of damages sustained by the surface owner for loss of agricultural production and income, lost land value, lost use of and access to the surface owner's land and lost value of improvements caused by drilling operations.

The surface protection provision requires the mineral developer to give the surface owner written notice of the contemplated drilling at least 20 days prior to commencement, unless waived by both parties. If a developer fails to provide the notice, the surface owner may seek appropriate relief and may receive punitive as well as actual damages.[72] At the time of the notice, the developer must also make a written offer of settlement. If the surface owner rejects the offer, he may bring an action for compensation in the court. If the amount awarded is greater than the developer's original offer, the court will award the surface owner reasonable attorney's fees and costs.[73]

As in most states, the operator's implied grant of surface use is limited by the doctrine of reasonable necessity and by common law concepts such as nuisance and trespass. In North Dakota, if there is only one reasonable means by which to develop minerals, the operator is entitled to use it, regardless of damage to the surface or interference with the usage made by the surface owner. However, if an alternative means of production exists that is reasonable given the time, place and current surface use, that alternative means should be utilised. A North Dakota federal district court applied this doctrine as recently as 2012, holding that the use of reserve pits for storing water, drilling fluid and well cuttings was reasonable notwithstanding the fact that a closed-loop system could also be used to accomplish the same goal.[74]

(h) Governing law and dispute resolution

Federal law and regulations, including the Mineral Leasing Act of 1920,[75] as amended, the Mineral Leasing Act for Acquired Lands of 1947,[76] and the Federal Oil

71 Okla Stat tit 52, Sections 318.1 and following.
72 ND Cent Code Section 38-11.1-04.1.
73 ND Cent Code Section 38-11.1-09.
74 *Kartch v EOG Resources, Inc*, 845 F Supp 2d 995 (D ND 2012).
75 30 USC Section 181 and following.
76 30 USC Section 351 and following.

and Gas Royalty Management Act of 1982,[77] govern the development of oil and gas on federal lands. In addition, the BLM promulgates regulations, codified in the Code of Federal Regulations in Title 43, Part 3100, and issues administrative orders related to oil and gas development. If a dispute arises, any party who suffers a legal wrong or who is adversely affected by federal agency action may seek judicial review in accordance with the Administrative Procedure Act.[78]

Where disputes arise over privately owned minerals, the law of the state in which the minerals are located typically governs. However, the parties to an oil and gas agreement may select the laws of a specific state to control in the event of a dispute. The agreement may also provide for mediation or arbitration.

3.2 Government take

(a) *Royalties*

If an oil and gas lease covers federal lands, the United States is entitled to a royalty of one-eighth of all oil and gas produced. If a private mineral owner leases his minerals, he will be entitled to the royalty that is negotiated in the oil and gas lease. The amount of royalty typically ranges from one-eighth to one-quarter.

(b) *Bonus*

For federal lands, the bonus payment is determined at the competitive lease auction, where bids for leases are placed on a dollar per-acre basis. The current minimum bonus bid is $2 per acre, and the winning bidder must make a one-time bonus payment calculated using his bid price per acre multiplied by the number of acres in a particular parcel of land.[79] As with royalties, the bonus payable for a lease covering privately owned minerals is subject to the negotiation of the lessor and the lessee. Bonus prices can be highly volatile depending upon the location of the minerals and the nearby mineral development.

(c) *Rental fees*

The rental fees for federal leases, both competitive and non-competitive, are $1.50 per acre for the first five years, and $2 per acre for each following year.[80] The lessee must pay the first year's rental fees in advance at the time they make the lease offer to the BLM, and must pay subsequent rentals on or before the lease anniversary date.[81] As with bonus and royalty payments, rental fees are subject to the negotiation of the lessor and the lessee. However, many leases have done away with the typical delay rental provisions and replaced them with so called 'paid-up' oil and gas leases in which no delay rental is required during the primary term of the lease. In theory, lessors are compensated for the lack of delay rentals through higher bonus payments.

---

77 30 USC Section 1701 and following.
78 5 USC Section 702.
79 43 CFR Section 3120.5-2.
80 43 CFR Section 3103.2-2
81 *Ibid.*

4. Other issues

Pooling is an important concept in US oil, and gas law and the laws applicable to pooling differ from state to state. This section contains an overview of the pooling laws in some of the more productive states.

4.1 Texas

Pooling occurs when two or more oil and gas leases covering separate tracts of land are brought together to enable the lessees to have sufficient surface acres to create a large enough proration unit so that the Railroad Commission of Texas will grant a full allowable amount for the unit production of oil and gas. In Texas, there are at least six types of units: voluntary units, force pooled units, field wide units, drilling units, spacing units and proration units.

A voluntary pooled unit is created by designation of a unit. The unit is designated to the Railroad Commission with the drilling application and completion papers by a form P-12 that lists the interests that are pooled and those tracts that contain non-pooled interests. All leasehold owners of record are required to execute a designation of unit and, if required by the lease, the designation should be recorded in the appropriate county prior to the expiry of the primary term of the first non-drill-site lease to expire.[82] Once pooled, production from one lease will be considered as production upon all pooled leases. A voluntarily pooled unit will terminate when all unit wells stop producing in paying quantities.

A non-participating royalty interest is a royalty interest carved out of the mineral estate.[83] The owner of a non-participating royalty interest is not bound by the pooling provisions of a lease executed by the owner of the executive right. To have its interests pooled into a unit, the owner of the non-participating royalty interest must either ratify the lease or ratify the designation of unit.[84] If the owner of such an interest does not ratify either the lease or the designation of unit and a well is drilled on his land, the owner of the non-participating royalty interest is entitled to a royalty that is not reduced based on his proportionate ownership in the unit. If the drill site is not on his land, he can then ratify the unit and be entitled to receive his proportionate part of the royalty from the unit. Otherwise he will not be entitled to royalty payments.

The Texas Natural Resources Code includes a forced pooling statute. The Texas forced pooling statute has limited application because it covers only "reservoirs discovered and produced" after March 8 1961 and reservoirs for which the Railroad Commission has established temporary or permanent field rules.[85] Therefore, the statute does not apply to areas that are subject to state-wide spacing rules. A forced pooled unit in Texas is formed only after notice and hearing and corresponds to an individual proration unit.

Field-wide units are generally formed to conduct enhanced recovery operations. The units can cover an entire field or a portion of a field. There is no forced field-wide unitisation in Texas.

---

82 *Sauder v Frye*, 613 SW 2d 63 (Tex Civ App – Fort Worth 1981).
83 *Plainsman Trading Co v Crews*, 898 SW 2d 786 (Tex 1995).
84 *Montgomery v Rittersbacher*, 424 SW 2d 210 (Tex 1968).
85 Tex Nat Res Code Sections 102.001 and following.

A drilling unit is the area that is required by the applicable spacing regulations for the granting of a drilling permit from the Railroad Commission. It is designated by completing a form W-1, application for a drilling permit, with a plan attached. A drilling unit has no title significance.

A spacing unit is not a geographic area, but rather refers to the requirement that a well be a certain distance away from lease lines and other wells. Rule 37 is the statewide spacing rule, and provides that a well will not be closer than 467 feet to a lease line and no closer than 1,200 feet to any other well completed or drilling to the same reservoir. Parties often apply for exceptions to the spacing rules.

The proration unit is determined after completion of a well to designate the acreage assigned to the well to obtain the volume of hydrocarbons that the well is authorised to produce. A proration unit is designated by a form P-15 filed with the Railroad Commission. The well does not need to be in the centre of the proration unit. Proration units can be amended at any time. Proration units arise only when there are special field rules and the allocation formula includes acreage as a factor (acreage is typically a factor in allocation). If there is no specific language in the oil and gas lease, prorations units do not determine the manner in which production is allocated among the mineral interest owners.

4.2 Pennsylvania

Pennsylvania is a 'rule of capture' state.[86] The only statutory pooling requirements or alternatives are:

- potential statutory pooling for wells drilling in or below the Onondaga formation under the Oil and Gas Conservation Act;
- possible actions under the 2006 Dormant Oil and Gas Act which has adapted 'correlative rights' as a term in defining potential targets of actions; and
- voluntary pooling or unitisation under the express terms of property-specific leases.

The Oil and Gas Conservation Act has not been widely used and the Onondaga formation, which is its jurisdictional trigger, is below the Marcellus, so activities in the Marcellus are excluded from the benefit of its compulsory pooling. However, parts of the Utica shale lie below the Onondaga formation, subjecting it to the act. The 2006 Dormant Oil and Gas Act has never been used in any reported case. Voluntary pooling and unitisation are more common in Pennsylvania than statutory pooling, but there are few judicial decisions in Pennsylvania on issues related to pooling and unitisation.

4.3 Louisiana

Units generally fall into three categories in Louisiana: compulsory units created by the Commissioner of Conservation; declared units created by declaration under the terms of mineral leases that give the lessee pooling power; and voluntary units created by agreement among all parties having an interest in the mineral rights and

86 The 'rule of capture' means that the first person to 'capture' a resource owns that resource.

land included in the unit. Voluntary units can be created by agreement of all mineral, royalty, overriding royalty and working interest owners. A voluntary unit can be made any size or shape.

4.4. Oklahoma

'Pooling' is defined as bringing together two or more oil and gas leases covering two or more separately owned tracts of land for the purpose of accumulating sufficient surface acreage to enable the drilling parties to create a sufficiently large unit. The voluntary pooling clause is seldom used in Oklahoma because the Oklahoma Corporation Commission can establish drilling and spacing units that supersede voluntary units. To avoid the possibility of future changes in the unit, lessees generally apply to the Corporation Commission to establish drilling and spacing units.

A forced pooling order is normally obtained when the owners of unleased minerals and working interest co-tenants cannot agree on a development plan. The forced pooling order establishes the operator, the dry hole costs, the completed well costs and the elections in which the lessee or minerals owner must either lease its interest at a stated value or participate in the drilling and development of the initial well and unit. A drilling and spacing unit established by the Corporation Commission essentially pools the royalty owners so that they share in the revenue from any well in the unit.[87]

4.5 North Dakota

When two or more separately owned tracts are within a spacing unit, or when there are separately owned interests in all or a part of the spacing unit, then the owners and royalty owners may either voluntarily or forcibly pool their interests.[88] A spacing unit in which there is production may be voluntarily pooled by the lessee filing a declaration of pooling if all of the leases contain broad pooling clauses. A spacing unit may also be voluntarily pooled by obtaining a voluntary pooling agreement from all mineral owners and lessees.

Section 38-08-08 of the North Dakota Century Code provides for forced pooling. Any interested owner may file an application before the Industrial Commission, Oil and Gas Division, seeking forced pooling of a spacing unit before or after production is established. The Commission must grant the pooling order if it is established that there are two or more separately owned tracts or separately owned interests in a spacing unit. Because forced pooling orders are easy to obtain, operators often prefer to seek compulsory pooling rather than voluntary pooling.

Owners of unleased minerals may be the subject of forced pooling. Without pooling, an owner of unleased minerals is entitled to his proportionate share of eight-eighths of production after payout, less his proportionate share of operating costs. If the spacing unit is forcibly pooled, the owner of unleased minerals is entitled to a cost-free royalty interest equal to the average royalty interest of the leased tracts

---

87 *Shell Oil Co v Corporation Commission*, 389 P 2d 951 (Okla 1963).

88 ND Cent Code Section 38-08-08.

within the spacing unit, weighted by acreage, or 16%, at the operator's election, but in no event may the royalty interest of an unleased tract be less than a one-eighth interest. The lessee may recover a 50% non-consent penalty against an owner of unleased minerals for that owner's proportionate share of the reasonable actual costs of drilling and completing the well.

5. Conclusion

The laws governing the development of oil and gas in the United States vary from state to state. However, they all share one underlying concept: the individual ownership of minerals. Grasping this concept is essential to understanding oil and gas laws in the United States.

On privately owned lands in the United States, oil and gas development usually begins with a lease agreement between a mineral owner and a lessee. The terms of the lease are negotiated between the parties, and the government's involvement is typically limited to regulating development and production. As a result, unlike most other countries, the economic benefits from oil and gas development will generally flow to the mineral owner.

This chapter has provided a summary of some of the laws governing oil and gas production in the United States as such laws exist in 2012. New technology has resulted in tremendous changes in the methods of drilling and production. Current oil and gas laws do not always adequately address the issues now faced by oil and gas companies in the United States. As these issues are addressed by the courts and legislatures, the oil and gas laws of the United States will continue to evolve.

Venezuela

Julian Cardenas Garcia
Law Center University of Houston
CREDIMI – Université de Bourgogne

1. Introduction

Venezuela is currently the country with the biggest proven oil reserves in the world with an amount of 297.5 billion barrels of recoverable crude oil,[1] of which two-thirds are heavy-crude oil reserves located in the Orinoco belt, the richest oil region in the country.[2] In order to illustrate this, Francisco Monaldi, director of the IESA International Centre for Energy and the Environment,[3] has pointed out that Venezuelan reserves represent 92% of the oil reserves in South America, 90% of Latin American oil reserves, 75% of the oil reserves in the western hemisphere, 26% of all Organisation of Petroleum Exporting Countries (OPEC) reserves and 20% of the oil reserves in the world.[4] With these figures in mind we might assume that Venezuela should be the most attractive country for foreign investment in the oil industry, since it has a minimum exploration risk, given the existence of proven reserves, and because all these reserves are located onshore, so there are none of the worries associated with deep water projects. However, despite the astonishing figures, during the last decade this South American giant has seen declining oil production with a current average of 2.8 million barrels per day, down from 3.142 million barrels a day in the early 2000s,[5] and has an extraction rate of only 0.4%, the lowest among OPEC members.[6] As a result, the country is going through a crucial time when it needs to take advantage of this significant potential or face delays and high opportunity costs.

---

1 BP, *Statistical Review of World Energy 2012*, on proven oil reserves.

2 Petróleos de Venezuela SA (PDVSA), the Venezuelan national oil company and the consulting firm Ryder Scott have quantified the reserves in the Orinoco belt in a process based on seismic studies involving international oil companies such as Petrobras, CNPC, ONGC, Petropars. This process has certified 227.5 billion barrels of original oil in place with an API from 8º to 9º, using a 20% oil recovery factor, despite the fact that the current recovery factor has only reached 10%. The amount of heavy oil reserves should be added to the already confirmed 70 billion barrels of conventional oil. Moreover, in October 2009, the US Geological Survey estimated a mean volume of 513 billion barrels of technically recoverable heavy oil in the Orinoco oil belt, using a 45% recovery factor taking into account the evolution of extractive technologies.

3 IESA (Instituto de Estudios Superiores de Administración) is the leading business school in Venezuela. More information about the Centre for Energy and the Environment can be found at: www.iesa.edu.ve/profesores-e-investigacion/centros-academicos/energia-y-ambiente.

4 Francisco Monaldi, *"La Industria Petrolera Venezolana: Una nueva oportunidad historica"*, *Debates IESA*, Volume XVII Issue 2, April–June 2012, p 13.

5 BP, *Statistical Review of World Energy 2012*, on oil production.

6 The extraction rate is the percentage of oil reserves extracted in one year with respect to the current amount of oil reserves: (3 million × 365 days) ÷ 297.5 billion = 0.0037. This extraction rate was reduced after the certification of new reserves. However, this points out the need to take advantage of the huge potential while fossil fuels remain the main source of energy in the world. Even to reach a extraction rate of 1% like most oil producing countries in the Middle East, requires Venezuela to double production.

The government's decisions so far indicate that it is searching for international investment in capital and technology in order to increase investment and production. This is moving the country into a period of high expectations, after the agreement of seven multibillion-dollar projects for the production of heavy oil in the Orinoco belt signed between 2009 and 2012.[7] Each of these projects requires up-front investment of between $12 billion and $20 billion within the next six years. The investment is needed for the construction of a number of upgrading facilities to reduce the gravity of the heavy oil before it can be commercialised from 8º API to 20º and 31º API. This amounts to a figure over $120 billion investment that is expected to happen in the country in the coming years.

The success of these projects relies in some measure on investor's confidence in Venezuela's legal framework and government's respect for the rule of law, and it is here where foreign investors' major apprehensions arise.[8] *The Global Petroleum Survey* published by the Fraser Institute in 2012, in its discussion of barriers to oil and gas investment, placed Venezuela as the second worst jurisdiction in the world in term of risk for petroleum investment.[9] The level of risk is based on recent government policies which have revealed three main threats. First, property rights have been affected through a wave of expropriations in different sectors of the economy that have included oil exploration and production projects[10] and oil service companies.[11] Second, the intervention of the tax regime has been recurrent, having an impact on the value of investment and the profit take for foreign investors.[12] Finally, Venezuela has taken a hostile (though sometimes pragmatic) approach to international arbitration, reducing ways to access international settlement of disputes.[13]

---

7 Julian Cardenas, "Rebalancing Oil Contracts in Venezuela", *Houston Journal of International Law* Volume 33:2, 2011, p 235. See also,"Rosneft President Igor Sechin Takes Part in First Oil Ceremony at Junin-6 Block in Venezuela", September 28 2012, available at www.rosneft.com/news/news_in_press/28092012.html

8 F Monaldi, presentation: "Perspectivas Conindustria 2012", November 21 2011, available at: www.youtube.com/watch?v=wyZgzf4BgoQ. Monaldi interestingly pointed out that foreign investor's concerns in the oil sector in Venezuela are more focused on matters above ground than under the ground given the economic, politic and legal conditions.

9 Fraser Institute, *Global Petroleum Survey 2012* (June 2012), p 14. Available at: www.fraserinstitute.org.

10 Decree 5.200 "with Rank, Value and Force of Law on the Migration to Mixed Companies of the Association Agreements of the Orinoco Oil Belt, as well as the Shared-Risk-and-Profit Exploration Agreements", *Gaceta Oficial* 38.632, February 26 2007. Also relevant on this point is the Decree with the Rank, Value and Force of an Organic Law on Public Properties, *Gaceta Oficial* 39.945, June 15 2012, which sets the rules of control and supervision of state-owned companies or companies where the state has a minority participation, in particular Articles 4 and 36.

11 Organic Law that Reserves to the State the Assets and Services Related to Hydrocarbon Primary Activities *Gaceta Oficial* 39.173, May 7 2009. Also relevant is the Public Contracting Law originally published in *Gaceta Oficial* 5.877, March 14 2008, and reformed in *Gaceta Oficial* 39.165, April 24 2009.

12 In particular the introduction of a Windfall Profit Tax Law in 2008 which was reformed in 2011, amended in 2012 and once again reformed in February 20 2013: Law on Special Contributions over Extraordinary Prices in the International Market of Hydrocarbons *Gaceta Oficial* 38.910, April 15 2008, reformed by the Decree Law that Creates a Special Contribution on Extraordinary and Exorbitant Hydrocarbon Prices in the International Markets *Gaceta Oficial* 8.163 GO Ext 6.022, April 18 2011, amended by Decree 8.807, *Gaceta Oficial* 39.871, February 2 2012 and reformed *Gaceta Oficial* 40.114, February 20 2013.

13 Agreement of the National Assembly to Support the Decision of the Presidency to Withdraw from the International Centre for Settlement of Investment Disputes (ICSID), *Gaceta Oficial* 39.972, July 26 2012. But see also, on the pragmatic approach of the government, Cardenas, above note 7, at 272, and Alfredo De Jesús O, "Venezuela: Supreme Court adeopts transnational approach to arbitration agreement. GAR, Vol. 5 ISS. 6, November 25 2010..

While this is happening in Venezuela, in the international context factors such as current oil prices, the evolution of extractive technologies and the abundance of shale oil and gas are creating emerging oil producing countries in Latin America, Africa and Asia, and are improving local developments in Europe and the United States. Accordingly, these new trends may introduce some changes in oil companies' strategies that might see them prioritising projects in investor-friendly jurisdictions or the development of local reserves, as appears to be the case with Brazilian, US and Russian investors.[14] It is therefore important for the Venezuelan authorities to have a close look at these events and to assess their relationship with foreign investors in order to promote enduring relations for the development of the Orinoco belt projects.

On October 7 2012, President Hugo Chavez was re-elected for a period of six more years, until 2019, which would complete 20 years in office. However, just two months after his re-election, Chavez found himself unable to continue in office due to adverse health conditions and appointed Vice President Nicolas Maduro as president in charge – a decision that has been ratified by the legislative and judicial branch.[15] This complex situation may lead to a political transition, with the departure of Chavez from the political scene and potentially new presidential elections in the near future,[16] which could trigger drastic changes after more than a decade of the so-called Bolivarian Revolution. Although continuity of the current governing party may provide stability for foreign national oil companies from politically aligned countries, international oil companies remain uncertain of the future direction of the government and of the authorities' respect for the rule of law.

2. Upstream activities

The 2001 Organic Law on Hydrocarbons (amended in 2006) defines upstream petroleum activities as primary activities such as exploration, production, gathering, and initial transportation and storage of petroleum and associated natural gas.[17] Under the regime established by this law, primary activities must be carried out directly by the state through the Venezuelan national oil company, Petróleos de Venezuela SA (PDVSA), or an affiliated company, or by a mixed company (a form of joint venture company) with participation of private investors, in which more than 50% of the shares are held by a state company.[18] Despite private participation in these mixed companies, the ownership of the hydrocarbons reservoirs remains in the hands of the state and the title to hydrocarbons passes at the wellhead to the shareholders of the mixed company.

---

14 Press releases have announced that two of the five Russian companies from a Russian consortium which owns 40% the mixed company PetroMiranda, are leaving and selling their share to the partner Rosneft. TNK-BP and Surgut have decided to concentrate their activity in Russia (see uk.reuters.com/article/2012/11/07/surgut-venezuela-idUKL5E8M734Q20121107). Also it has been reported that the US company Harvest Resources has requested the authorisation of the Venezuelan authorities to sell its 32% stake in Petrodelta to PT Pertamina, Indonesia's national oil company, however, the initial deal for $725 million purchase was rejected by the Indonesian government. See www.ogj.com/articles/2013/02/pertamina-harvest-venezuelan-deal-rejected.html)

15 Decision of the Constitutional Chamber of the Venezuelan Supreme Court, January 9 2013.

16 Article 233 of the Venezuelan Constitution of 1999.

17 Article 9 of the Organic Law on Hydrocarbons.

18 Articles 22, 33, 34 and 55 of the Organic Law on Hydrocarbons.

3. Petroleum legal regime

The general conditions for foreign investment in the upstream oil sector in Venezuela are articulated in a network of rules involving contractual conditions, national law and international sources of law. This means that international petroleum transactions in Venezuela involving PDVSA, or one of its affiliates, and a foreign investor are required to respect national law and international commitments. The case of Venezuela involves an interesting interaction between petroleum agreements, specific national petroleum regulation and international treaties, such as bilateral investment treaties (BITs) and energy cooperation agreements, which have important consequences for the conditions under which upstream activities in the country are performed. Also, despite the rejection of international arbitration, arbitration still remains the main dispute resolution method for settling international claims, either under institutional or *ad hoc* arbitration rules.[19]

3.1 Petroleum law and relevant provisions

(a) Regulatory bodies

The National Assembly of Venezuela is the legislative body of the Venezuelan state and is in charge of the creation and approval of national legislation. The National Assembly, under special circumstances, can delegate this function to the executive branch, which will legislate by decree in the sectors or subjects authorised by an enabling law, which could involve the petroleum sector.[20] Oil and gas regulation in Venezuela is reserved to the federal government, and neither state nor municipal governments have the power to regulate or tax oil or gas activities.

The Ministry of Popular Power for Energy and Petroleum is the branch of the executive in charge of the design and execution of hydrocarbons policy. The ministry has, among other responsibilities, the function of assigning exploration and production rights to mixed companies, or revoking them, and has a discretionary power on issues such as the authorisation tax or royalty incentives established by law or by energy cooperation agreements.[21] Since 2002 the minister has been Rafael Ramirez, who has also been the president of PDVSA since 2005. PDVSA is the company responsible for the execution of the country's hydrocarbons developments plans, both domestically and internationally, through its companies and affiliates. One of the main affiliates is the Corporación Venezolana de Petroleo (CVP), which

19 Venezuelan bilateral investment treaties include dispute resolution clauses referring to the arbitration rules of the International Centre for the Settlement of Investment Disputes (ICSID), the International Chamber of Commerce (ICC), the Stockholm Chamber of Commerce (SCC), and the United Nations Commission on International Trade Law (UNCITRAL). These rules comprise articles that give arbitrators discretionary power to apply the substantive rules that they consider most appropriate in cases where the parties failed to make such designation. Also, the ICC and UNCRITRAL rules provide that arbitral tribunals shall take account of the usages of trade applicable to the transaction. See Article 42 of the ICSID Convention, Article 22 of the SCC Arbitration Rules 2010, Article 35 of the UNCITRAL Rules 2010 and Article21 of the ICC Arbitration Rules 2012.

20 Article 203 of the Venezuelan Constitution.

21 See Article 44 of the Organic Law on Hydrocarbons; Article 12.1 of the Windfall Profit Taw Law, *Gaceta Oficial* 40.114, February 20 2013; Article 4 of Annex 1 to the Venezuela-Russia Cooperation Agreement for the Development of Specific Projects, *Gaceta Oficial* 39.312, November 23 2009.

is 100% owned by PDVSA and is its vehicle for entering into all joint ventures with foreign investors in Venezuela.[22]

Other relevant institutions that can enact regulations applicable to the petroleum sector are the National Integrated Customs and Tax Administration Service, which is in charge of the collection of taxes and can approve resolutions on the interpretation of tax law. Also the Ministry of Finance, the Ministry of the Environment, the Special People's Fund, which is the beneficiary of the special contribution under the Windfall Profit Tax Law, and the Currency Administration Commission are all relevant institutions for the distribution of the government take, regulatory procedures regarding protection of the environment and the administration of the foreign exchange control rules currently in force in the country.

(b) Types of agreement

The participation of private and foreign investors in upstream activities in the petroleum sector in Venezuela is only allowed through a model mixed company (joint venture) contract approved by the National Assembly in 2006 and amended in 2009, which is structured in accordance with Articles 33 and 34 of the Organic Law on Hydrocarbons.[23] This model contract was introduced when existing operating service contracts for conventional oil and strategic association agreements for the production of heavy crude oil were renegotiated in a process called 'migration' in which PDVSA acquired operational control of all the projects, taking more than 50% of the shares in all the joint ventures.[24] According to George Kahale, the new model grants the state power over three significant aspects:

- economic, by increasing the government's profit share;
- corporate governance, giving government control over the mixed companies' operations, and
- legal, by eliminating stabilisation clauses and eliminating contractual access to arbitration.[25]

The model contracts have evolved over the years and we can identify four types of mixed companies that have been set up under them:

---

22 It is interesting to inquire why the Venezuelan government uses CVP as a vehicle for joint ventures with foreign investors in Venezuela. One answer could be that CVP has no assets abroad since PDVSA is the owner of all such assets as a result of the internationalisation strategy implemented in the 1980s, when PDVSA transferred money and assets overseas by buying refineries in Germany and Curacao, and CITGO in the United States, which could be seized in the execution of an arbitral award by creditors. Since contractual disputes are submitted to Venezuelan tribunals it seems that the government and PDVSA have made efforts to reduce creditors' options in the search for assets (ie, in the execution of international arbitration awards).

23 Resolution Approving the Terms and Conditions of the Creation and Operation of Mixed Companies and Mixed Company Bylaws, *Gaceta Oficial* 38.410, March 26 2006, as amended by *Gaceta Oficial* 39.273, September 28 2009. See also Articles 33 and 34 of the Organic Law on Hydrocarbons.

24 President Chavez issued a decree in late February 2007 requiring the four strategic associations to convert to joint ventures in which PDVSA would hold a 60% stake. The decree established an April 30 2007 deadline for completing the conversion. Most of the companies reached agreement and stayed, but ConocoPhillips and ExxonMobil refused to transfer their investment stakes in three of the four associations. As a result, the government took control of their investments. Both companies treated the government's actions as expropriations and filed international arbitration claims against Venezuela.

25 G Kahale, conference paper, *"Tendencias en Contratos Aguas Arriba en la Industria Petrolera Internacional"* July 2–10 2009.

- Mixed companies for the development of conventional oil: This model was the first one implemented after the migration, and it provides for a 60% stake to be held by CVP, and 40% by foreign investors, a ratio that has been retained in all the projects so far. It includes an obligation to sell the oil produced to PDVSA through a sales contract agreed by the parties. This model contract was implemented over ongoing production projects.
- Mixed companies for the development of heavy crude oil from public bid assignment: This model was used during the Carabobo Bid Round for the mixed companies PetroIndependencia and PetroCarabobo. These projects have provision for accelerated depreciation and carry-forward of losses whereby the mixed company's investments in assets for the development of hydrocarbon primary activities will be entirely deducted in the fiscal year that they are incurred; investments made in connection to hydrocarbons upgrading will be deducted during a 10-year period using the straight-line method; and net operating losses incurred by the mixed company in any fiscal year can be carried forward to be deducted over the subsequent 10 fiscal years from the fiscal year in which they were incurred.[26] These companies must sell early production of heavy oil to PDVSA, but retain the right to sell upgraded oil directly on the international markets once the upgrader is in operation.
- Mixed companies benefiting from an energy cooperation agreement: These are the cases of mixed companies formed with foreign national oil companies which benefit from energy cooperation agreements such as PetroUrica (formed by CVP and China National Petroleum Corp) and PetroMiranda (formed by CVP and a Russian consortium). These agreements provide that the company's activities will reach an internal rate of return of 18% and 19%, respectively, allowing for a seven-year investment payback period counted from the first commercial production of upgraded crude oil.[27] These companies must also sell their early production of heavy crude oil to PDVSA but have the right to sell upgraded oil directly on the international markets once the upgrader is operative.
- Mixed companies for integrated projects: This model was agreed between CVP and ENI, and required the creation of two different legal entities for tax purposes, with PetroJunin subject to income tax of 50% on production and PetroBicentenario paying 34% on its refining activities, but project operations are in practice integrated.

(c) Acquisition of acreage

Article 37 of the Organic Law on Hydrocarbons establishes two methods of awarding contracts for the constitution of a mixed company in association with CVP. The first

---

26 C Bellorin, "Venezuela's Petroleum Fiscal and Contractual Regime Flexibility Provisions" *IAEE Energy Forum*, Third Quarter 2011, p 41 (International Association for Energy Economics).

27 The Venezuela-Russia Energy Cooperation Agreement, *Gaceta Oficial* 39.312, November 23 2009 and the Venezuela-Russia Cooperation Agreement for the Development of Specific Projects, *Gaceta Oficial* 39.312, November 23 2009. Law Approving the Agreement between the Bolivarian Republic of Venezuela and the People's Republic of China Concerning Cooperation in the Development of Junin Block 4 in the Orinoco oil belt, *Gaceta Oficial* 38.527, October 8 2010.

method is in the form of licensing rounds, with the first part of the Article 37 setting out that: "[t]he competent public body shall promote the existence of various offers for the selection of the operators." This method was used, for instance, in February 2010, when the Carabobo auction for blocks in the Orinoco belt awarded two projects to international consortia to work in association with CVP.

Second, Article 37 establishes that "[f]or reasons of public interest or for special circumstances related to the activities, the operators may be directly selected, with the prior approval of the Council of Ministers." This method has been the more widely used by the Venezuelan government, with four out of six projects in the Orinoco belt being assigned by direct negotiations between the government and national oil companies from politically aligned countries and international oil companies with a long-standing relationship with the government. They are granted by the state through the Ministry of Energy and Petroleum and must be approved by the National Assembly.

(d) *Qualification requirements*

Qualification requirements may vary between direct assignment to public bids, since the first process is carried out with greater confidentiality. However, current conditions applying to both cases require a formula combining the amount of the signing bonus normally to be paid in cash, upfront, upon the contract signature; a participation bonus, to be paid in instalments through the life of the project; a marketing proposal for the heavy crude oil produced; and a funding proposal to reduce the financial burden of PDVSA.[28]

(e) *Duration*

The duration of a mixed company contract in Venezuela can reach a total length of 40 years. Under the Organic Law on Hydrocarbons a mixed company contract shall not exceed 25 years, but it is renewable for a term to be agreed on, which shall not exceed 15 years and must be approved by the Ministry of Energy and Petroleum as long as the project has complied with all the requirements of the contract.[29] For instance, the decree transferring rights of exploration and production of oil to the mixed company PetroCarabobo SA provided in Article 2, that the renewal must be approved after PetroCarabobo has proved two obligations: that the upgrader has been put into operation and is operating; and that the project has reached a production of 40 millions of barrels of heavy crude oil. The renewal does not require the payment of an additional participation bonus.[30]

---

28 Bellorin above, note 26. For instance, as oil prices recovered in 2009, PDVSA took an aggressive position, seeking a minimum of $500 million to $1 billion as a signing bonus and $1 billion per project of loan guarantees for the PDVSA investment, Cardenas above, note 7 at 287.

29 Article 34.1 of the Organic Law on Hydrocarbons.

30 Article 3, PetroCarabobo Transfer Decree, *Gaceta Oficial*, July 29 2010. In case of bilateral investment treaty protection, the question of renewal may be relevant to the discussion of compliance with treaty standards on fair and equitable treatment, good faith and the legitimate expectations of the investors. See Daujotas, Rimantas and Audzevi ius, Ram nas, *The Concept of Legitimate Expectation in Investor-State Arbitration and the European Court of Human Rights* (January 5 2013), in a comment on a case of renewal of a lease and the discussion on legitimate expectations in the case *Stretch v United Kingdom*, 44277/98, 35, June 24 2003, at the European Court of Human Rights.

(f) ***Minimum work programme***

The minimum work programme may vary depending on the characteristics of the project concerned. Also, although many forms, clauses and conditions of the mixed company contracts have been made public, the minimum work programmes have remained confidential, as documents under the annual expenditure programme of the project. The projects for heavy crude oil in the Orinoco belt have minimum work requirements that involve:

- an amount of early production of heavy oil as a source of cash flow for the investment in upgraders;
- the construction of upgraders (or a refinery in the case of PetroJunin); and
- a minimum level of production.

Minimum work programmes are based on the annual development plan and are adjusted every year with the approval of a qualified majority of the shareholders, which – in the case of minority shareholders holding the standard 40% applicable in petroleum contracts in Venezuela – is a right for the foreign investors to exercise control over this decision. Failure to comply with minimum work programmes incurs sanctions as set out in the mixed company contract. For instance, in case of failure to comply with agreed contributions or loans, these sanctions involve a reduction in capital or a distribution of paid-in surplus that corresponds to the shares of the debtor party by the end of the year; where the debtor is the foreign investor, CVP may even request the transfer of shares to cover the amount due.[31]

(g) ***Assignment and encumbrance***

Rules for assignment have been included in the mixed company model contract approved by the National Assembly.[32] The rules are severe, and limit the possibility of transferring or assigning of the contract, or rights and obligations under it. Under the mixed company contract neither party may assign or transfer the contract, in whole or in part, or any of its rights or obligations, without the prior written consent of the other parties and the consent of the Minister of Energy and Petroleum, except for cases of corporate transformations or transfers to associated undertakings:

- CVP may assign or transfer the mixed contract to any other entity that is, directly or indirectly, exclusively owned by the state, in which case CVP only has to notify the foreign investor; and
- the investor may assign or transfer the contract to any other company that is, directly or indirectly, exclusively owned by the investor's ultimate parent

31 See Terms and Conditions of the Creation and Operation of Mixed Companies and Mixed Company Bylaws, *Gaceta Oficial* 38.410, March 26 2006, as amended by *Gaceta Oficial* 39.273, September 28 2009. Sanctions for breach of contracts or municipal law by a foreign investor with the protection of a bilateral investment treaty shall be conducted in good faith, in a non-discriminatory manner and respecting the principle of proportionality. In the ICSID case *Occidental v Ecuador*, the tribunal found that a *caducidad* 'termination' decree violated the proportionality principle in the sanction to Occidental for the execution of a unauthorised farmout agreement. Award, October 05 2012.

32 Resolution Approving the Terms and Conditions of the Creation and Operation of Mixed Companies and Mixed Company Bylaws, *Gaceta Oficial* 38.410, March 26 2006, as amended by *Gaceta Oficial* 39.273, September 28 2009.

entity, as the case may be, provided it jointly and severally guarantees the performance of the obligations assumed by the assignee.

Also neither party may, without the prior written consent of the minister, transfer, assign or pledge in any way its shares in the mixed company, or permit the transfer, assignment or pledge of such shares or any shareholder rights or interests.[33] Finally, the investor shall ensure that there shall be no direct or indirect change of control of its company[34] during the term of the mixed company, without the prior written consent of the minister. This last scenario has led to the inclusion in the contracts of a clause that penalises a change of control to "an entity that is involved in any judicial, arbitral or administrative proceeding of a significant nature, with the Republic, PDVSA, CVP or any of its affiliates."[35] This specific clause has been included as a consequence of an increase in international ligation in the petroleum sector in Venezuela. Violation of this clause can lead to termination of the mixed company contract and the transfer of all the investor's shares in the mixed company to CVP, without CVP having to pay any amount for the transferred shares. In addition to the foregoing, in the event that a change of control of the foreign corporation occurs (irrespective of whether the acquiring party is involved in any proceedings of the sort mentioned above) and that change of control is not approved by the minister, CVP shall acquire, within a period of 12 months from the date of the notice of that change in control, all of the Class B shares of the mixed company owned by the foreign investor at a price equal to the average of the valuations of those shares made by two internationally recognised independent experts.[36]

These provisions set forth an important element of control for the Minister of Energy and Petroleum over companies that may sell shares or seek to farm out their rights under agreements. It is important to note that in this kind of case, where the discretionary power of the state is invoked because an oil company is seeking to transfer its shares either to raise capital or because it is seeking to leave the country, the decision of the minister is to be made in good faith and respecting international obligations such as the duty to ensure fair and equitable treatment, and the principle of proportionality and non-discrimination where the protection of a BIT is relevant to the case.[37]

(h) *Local content*

The Venezuelan Labour Law of 2012[38] is the most important piece of labour legislation, and its provisions are considered to be a matter of public policy, giving the greatest possible protection to the worker. Article 27 of the law sets out quantitative and total wage cost restrictions on the employment decisions made by

---

33 *Ibid.*

34 *Ibid.* In this context, 'control' of a corporation is to be understood as the power to appoint a majority of directors of its board of directors, or the ability to direct in any other manner its management or policies.

35 Harvest Natural Resources, Inc, Quarterly Report (Form 10-Q), Contract for Conversion of a Mixed Company – Petrodelta SA, Article 6, 2007.

36 *Ibid.*

37 Although the case has been challenged for annulment, the award made by the International Commission on the Settlement of Investment Disputes in *Occidental Petroleum Corp v Republic of Ecuador* (ICSID Case ARB/06/11), October 5 2012, explores the interaction of a farm-out operation with the applicable standards of a bilateral investment treaty.

38 Decree 8938, Labour Law, *Gaceta Oficial* 6076 Extraordinary, May 7 2012.

foreign investors. Under that article at least 90% of workers must be Venezuelan in firms that have 10 or more workers, and payments to foreign employees may not exceed 20% of the total company payroll. Article 32 of the Organic Law on Hydrocarbons is more specific, establishing that "the workers of state-owned oil companies shall enjoy labour stability and may only be dismissed for the reasons expressly set out in the labour legislation". However, Article 28 allows the Ministry of Labour to authorise temporary exceptions for activities that require special technical knowledge, and for which no Venezuelan personnel are available.

(i) *Environment*

The Venezuelan Constitution makes special reference to environmental rights that must be respected in regard to the exploitation of natural resources. In this regard, Article 129 expressly says:

> *In contracts into which the Republic enters with natural or juridical persons of Venezuelan or foreign nationality, or in any permits granted which involve natural resources, the obligation to preserve the ecological balance, to permit access to, and the transfer of technology on mutually agreed terms and to restore the environment to its natural state if the latter is altered, shall be deemed included even if not expressed, on such terms as may be established by law.*

The general Venezuelan environmental regime is applicable to oil and gas companies, and there are also special regulations issued by the Ministry of Energy and Petroleum that are specific to the oil and gas sectors.[39] Furthermore, Venezuelan criminal environmental law is generally considered as more stringent than that of other countries in the region, but less stringent than in the United States or western Europe.[40]

In all cases, the policies and procedures of the mixed company must have as their objective that it will carry out its operations in an efficient and transparent manner, in accordance with prudent petroleum industry practices and applicable laws, but according to the mixed company contract provisions "it being understood that, in the event of conflict, the applicable laws shall prevail over petroleum industry practices."[41] The mixed company must prepare and carry out an endogenous development policy based on the principles of preservation of cultural and biological diversity, minimisation of adverse environmental impacts and social responsibility as expressed in the National Development Plan.[42] Moreover, the mixed company must prepare, or commission from an internationally renowned environmental consulting company, an environmental audit in accordance with applicable regulations and standard petroleum industry practices.

It is also important to note that while foreign investors must fully respect and comply with national legislation, since their activity is directly related to the

---

39 Specifically, there are measures that include monetary allotments for atmospheric emissions control, treatment and disposal of solid and toxic waste, treatment of industrial wastewater, treatment of oil-tainted residues, contingency plans for oil spills and other emergencies, and for environmental impact studies.

40 According to Omaña and Troconis, "Oil & Gas – Venezuela", LatinLawyer.com, 2012.

41 Article 1.9 of the Mixed Company Contract Terms and Conditions.

42 National Assembly Agreement for the Constitution of the Mixed Company Petroindependencia, Article 10, *Gaceta Oficial* 39404, April 15 2010.

development of an economic sector in the country, the government authorities must also be aware that BITs contain clauses on "fair and equitable treatment" and "national treatment" which may be relevant with regard to enforcing compliance with environmental regulation. It is important to consider whether the national oil company and international oil companies are being treated differently as regards compliance in a particular territory. Privileged treatment of a national oil company with regard to environmental compliance may amount to discriminatory treatment in violation of international commitments if the foreign investor is the only one required to comply with higher standards. Accordingly, decisions not requiring same standards from both national oil companies and international oil companies, in similar circumstances, but giving privileged treatment to the national oil company, might end up actually lowering environmental standards in the country.

(j) Governing law and dispute resolution

Large oil-producing countries like Venezuela insist on the exclusive application of their national law as the governing law to international petroleum agreements, trying in this way to nationalise the petroleum venture to some degree.[43] In this sense, the Venezuelan government has argued that oil contracts are matters of public utility and social interest and they must be governed by Venezuelan law, excluding any reference to international law, insisting in the hierarchy of national over international law and also, despite their being permitted by the Venezuelan Investment Law,[44] excluding the practice of including stabilisation clauses in long-term agreements. Furthermore, any dispute arising from a mixed company contract must be submitted to the jurisdiction of Venezuelan tribunals, leaving the settlement of disputes to national judges.[45] This approach is in the line with the conception of petroleum contracts as administrative contracts where the state can wield its exorbitant powers unilaterally to modify the agreement. The current framework allows the government contractually and legally to maintain more control over the investment, and to lead the petroleum industry in accordance with its national policy priorities. This is perfectly legitimate and has been recognised as such by the actors in the international petroleum community, as long as the state also respects the rule of law and recognises the contractual equilibrium and legitimate expectations of investors, which are essential for long-term investments.[46] However, recent experiences have shown that there is a significant legal risk of unilateral intervention in Venezuela.

---

43 It is widely accepted that the law of the host country applies to petroleum agreements given the close connection with the country where the upstream activities are taking place. However, other sources of law might also apply which neutralise to some extent the degree to which the state can change of the legal conditions affecting petroleum agreements.

44 Articles 17 and 18 of the Venezuelan Investment Law, *Gaceta Oficial* 5390, October 22 1999.

45 The mixed company contract has the following dispute resolution clause:

> *This Contract shall be governed by and interpreted in accordance with the laws of the Republic. Any dispute or controversy that may arise from or in connection with this Contract shall be submitted exclusively to the courts of the Republic having jurisdiction. Before initiating any litigation, the Parties shall in good faith and within the framework of the Organic Hydrocarbons Law, explore the possibility of utilising mechanisms to amicably resolve controversies of any nature that my arise, including, for technical matters, the possible request of opinions of independent experts appointed by mutual agreement. Where it is decided to use such mechanisms, there shall be a written record of the contents of such agreement.*

The threats and acts of state intervention have motivated oil companies to rely more and more on BITs, since they contradict the two key tenets of the Venezuelan government approach: the exclusive application of the state's law, and the exclusive jurisdiction of the state's courts.[47] The integration of BITs into petroleum transactions has created a network of sources of law that increases the complexity of the legal framework since they represent international commitments on the part of the state. Unlike commitments under national provisions, international commitments, once subscribed to, are out of the hands of national regulators. In addition, settlement of disputes is delocalised, giving an enormous responsibility to international arbitrators with regard to interpreting the interaction of national law and international sources of law and the possible formulation of real transnational petroleum law applicable to petroleum transactions. The Venezuelan network of BITs has so far allowed foreign investors to access remedies in cases of expropriation, but they also include other standards such as fair and equitable treatment and national treatment. In this regard, we cannot ignore the consequences of the decision on jurisdiction in the case of *Mobil Corp v Venezuela* (ICSID Case ARB/07/27), which stated that the aim of restructuring an investment to ensure the protection of a BIT was "perfectly legitimate as far as it concerned future disputes". This decision has created an increase in cases where foreign investors have implemented corporate planning strategies to get access to international arbitration through BITs, making Venezuela the country with the second highest number of claims before the International Commission on the Settlement of Investment Disputes after Argentina.

3.2 Government take

The government take in Venezuela is in the form of a combination of royalty and taxes which was set up under the 2001 Organic Law on Hydrocarbons in order to grant the state the most effective form to capture revenue. According to Bernnard Mommer, one of the designers of the Venezuelan petroleum tax model, the royalty is the most effective method to capture revenue by the owners of the resources, since it is collected based on two variables – volumes and price – and unlike in the case of income tax, the royalty system is immune to the manipulation of production costs by venture partners. As Mommer points out, the problem with a system based on income taxes is that their effective collection is more difficult to achieve, especially for a state like Venezuela, whose bureaucratic capabilities might not ensure effective collection.[48]

(a) Royalty

Under the Organic Law on Hydrocarbons a royalty is collected at a rate of 30% for oil, with a lower 20% rate for production from mature reservoirs or extra-heavy crude

---

46 International oil companies have accepted tax increases in Venezuela when they are granted a profit margin. However, the companies may be reluctant to accept any fiscal increase that would upset the economic balance of their investment and that may not be considered a mere amendment, but rather a breach of the investment contract by the state.

47 O Garibaldi, "Calvo Redivivus: The Rediscovery of the Calvo Doctrine In the Era of Investment Treaties", *The Proceedings of the 57th Annual Institute on Oil and Gas Law Procedures* (2006).

48 Bernard Mommer, "Subversive Oil", Chapter 7 in Steve Ellner and Daniel Hellinger (editors) *Venezuelan Politics in the Chávez Era: Polarization and Social Conflict*, Lynne Rienner, November 2002.

oil reservoirs, but only where the reservoir cannot be commercially developed without the reduced rate which can later on be raised to the standard rate of 30% if the government considers it appropriate.[49] Currently, the calculation of royalties is capped at a price of $70 per barrel under the Windfall Profit Tax Law of 2011. Over this price, the windfall profit tax applies three tiers of rates in the form of a special contribution. A royalty reduction from 30% to 20% has been approved for all current projects in the Orinoco belt.[50]

(b) Extraction tax

Oil and gas operating companies must pay to the state one third of the value of all liquid hydrocarbons extracted from any reservoir, calculated on the same basis as that applied to the payment of royalties in cash. This tax therefore functions as an additional royalty of 3.33% since the royalty (30%) can be deducted. For practical reasons, if the royalty is reduced the extraction tax must be reduced in the same proportion. The Organic Law on Hydrocarbons establishes that the extraction tax can only be reduced to 20%.[51] From this total, 2.22% will be distributed to the Special People's Fund dedicated to the financing of endogenous development projects, and 1.11% directly to the municipalities where oil activities are conducted in the country.[52]

(c) Surface tax

This tax is based on the extent of the contract area not subject to exploitation, consisting of 100 tax units for every unused square kilometre, increased by 2% annually over the first five years and 5% annually after the sixth year.[53]

(d) Fuel consumption tax

This tax is levied at 10% of the value of each cubic metre of hydrocarbon byproducts produced and used as fuel by the mixed company to run their operation, calculated on the price at which the product is sold to the end-user.[54]

(e) Exports tax

Exporting oil and gas operating companies must pay to the state 0.1% of the value of all hydrocarbons exported from any Venezuelan port, calculated on the price at which they are sold to the purchaser.[55]

---

49 The state may request that the royalty be paid in kind or in cash, fully or partially. When the state has chosen to receive the royalty in kind, it may use the transportation and storage services of the producing company, up to the location indicated by the state, which shall pay the price agreed upon for such services. On the other hand, when the state decides to receive the royalty in cash, the producer shall pay the royalty for the corresponding volumes of hydrocarbons measured at the production field at market value, or at the agreed value set by the tax authority.

50 Article 44 of the Organic Law on Hydrocarbons.

51 *Ibid.*, Article 48.

52 *Ibid.*

53 *Ibid.*

54 *Ibid.*

55 *Ibid.*

(f) ***Special advantage or shadow tax***

The shadow tax is triggered where the fiscal take does not reach at least 50% of gross profits after applying royalties, taxes and other levies. In such a situation, the mixed company must pay the difference between this threshold and the fiscal take. The amount of this 'special advantage' will be zero if the sum of all previous components is higher or equal to 50% of the value of the hydrocarbons extracted.

(g) ***Social investment***

Mixed companies must pay 1% of their earnings before taxes arising from the previous calendar year, in order to create and implement a plan of local development based on the principles of cultural and biological diversity and social responsibility. The plan must be approved by the national government and must be designed to reduce any negative impact on the environment and to reflect the principle of social responsibility contained in the Plan for National Development.

(h) ***Windfall tax***

In February 2013 the government modified the tax tier applicable to the Windfall Profit Tax Law, first enacted in 2008, for the second time in five years.[56] Four tiers of a special contribution on oil prices emerged as a result:

- the lowest tier is 20%, applicable to 'extraordinary' oil prices between the price fixed by the Venezuelan budget for the relevant fiscal year ($55 per barrel for 2013) and $70 per barrel;
- next, the tax reaches 80% on 'exorbitant' oil prices of more than $80 but less than $100 per barrel;
- it expands to 90% when prices are equal or over than $100 but less than $110 per barrel; and
- it peaks at 95% when oil prices equal or over $110 per barrel.

Article 14 of the reform caps the royalty and export tax set out in the Organic Law on Hydrocarbons at $80 per barrel. The reform directly affects all the projects exporting oil or selling oil to PDVSA. However, Articles 12 and 13 set out a number of exceptions, which have to be considered on case-by-case basis by the Ministry of Energy and Petroleum, for projects which increase oil production, or which have not recovered their investment, or projects in the framework of cooperation agreements as in the case of those undertaken with Chinese and Russian companies.

(i) ***Anti-drug Law***

Article 98 of the Anti-drug Law provides that any entity with 50 or more workers must allocate 1% of its annual net profits to drug use prevention programmes for its workers and their close relatives; 0.5% must be used for programmes involving the

---

56 The Windfall Profit Tax Law, first enacted on April 15 2008, has had three partial reforms: February 27 2011, February 27 2012 and February 20 2013, *Gaceta Oficial* 40.114, February 20 2013. The 2011 and 2013 reforms on 2011 modified the tax tier applicable for the law.

57 Article 98 of the Organic Law Against the Illegal Trafficking and Consumption of Narcotic and Psychotropic Substances, *Gaceta Oficial* 38.337, December 16 2005.

protection of children and teenagers. This tax is payable on a yearly basis at the beginning of each year.[57]

(j) ***Science, technology and innovation contribution:***

Under Article 26 of the Law on Science, Technology and Innovation of 2010, mixed companies must contribute or invest on a yearly basis 2% of their gross annual income generated in Venezuela towards activities listed in Article 42 of the Law on Science, Technology and Innovation.[58]

(k) ***Income tax***

According to the Law on Income Tax, Venezuelan companies that are engaged in hydrocarbon exploration and production activities are subject to the payment of income tax, at a tax rate of 50%. However, mixed companies engaged in integrated projects such as PetroBicentenario, working exclusively in oil refining or upgrading of extra-heavy crude are subject to regular corporate rates (maximum 34%) since refining activities are not considered as primary activities.

(l) ***Value added tax***

Value added tax (VAT) is also applicable to petroleum activities and the rate may vary from 8% to 16.5%. Article 27 of the VAT Law provides that VAT credits related to exports are subject to a 0% rate, which means that the exporter must request a refund of credits related to its exports sales from the tax administration. This zero rate regime also applies to the sale to PDVSA by a mixed company of conventional oil. This is a very important feature of the VAT system applicable to these companies, because it implies that mixed companies will most likely have to apply for a refund of their input VAT through a special procedure.[59]

(m) ***Bonuses***

New mixed company contracts have provided for payment of two kinds of bonus, a signing bonus and a participation bonus. The participation bonus is a payment that the foreign investors must pay to the state for the right to participate in the project and is calculated at $1 per recoverable barrel up to the amount of the non-state partner's participation. The participation bonus payments are divided into several instalments that are payable throughout the life of the project. On the other hand, the signing bonuses must be paid up-front upon signature of the contract. For instance, Venezuela asked for signing bonuses from $500 million to $1 billion from each company that was assigned a contract during the direct negotiations in the Carabobo auction. Signature bonuses are usually paid in cash, up-front, upon the signature of the contract.[60]

---

58 Article 26 of the Organic Law on Science, Technology and Innovation, *Gaceta Oficial* 39.575, December 16 2010.

59 Eljuri and Clamens, "Navigating through the regulatory framework of the Venezuelan oil industry", in *International Oil and Gas Transactions in Latin America*, edited by Colmenter and Enriquez, ITAM, 2011.

60 Bellorin, above.

(n) Overall tax take

In conclusion, according to an economic study on the Venezuelan hydrocarbons fiscal regime by Tozzini Freire Advogados and Bain & Co, the combined fiscal burden of a 50% tax rate on profits, 33.33% on royalties, 1% tax for social programmes, the 'shadow tax' and the Law on Special Contributions could mean the government's overall take reaches 90%.[61] This percentage may be reduced in the case of projects that benefit from a royalty reduction and exemption from the application of the Windfall Profit Tax Law.

3.3 Foreign currency exchange controls

Since February 5 2003, Venezuela has applied foreign currency exchange controls, under a set of regulations that limit the purchase, sale, offer, transfer, acceptance, export and import of foreign currency.[62] The legislation seeks to avoid capital flight in response to the levels of inflation and eventual devaluation of the national currency, in order to protect the level of international reserves in foreign currency. The agency monitoring the exchange control is the Currency Administration Commission, which is empowered to establish regulations and requirements for the purchase of currency, to admit or deny currency purchase petitions, and to verify and control the use of currency, among other tasks. Under this framework the commission approved special Exchange Covenant 9,[63] which allows PDVSA and the mixed companies to have bank accounts abroad in foreign currency in order to receive and make payments outside Venezuela.[64] Accordingly, mixed companies selling production to PDVSA, or foreign providers of services or goods contracting with PDVSA or with mixed companies may receive payments abroad under these provisions.[65] This special regulation also embraces the repatriation of investments and returns clauses included in many of Venezuela's BITs which give investors the rights to repatriate their profits from capital investment.[66]

Furthermore, there have been two important developments. First, a decision of the Constitutional Chamber of the Venezuela Supreme Tribunal, of November 2 2011, has elaborated the standards by which payments of debts in foreign currency, in Venezuela or abroad, can comply with the exchange control system, illustrating the procedure for acquiring foreign currency legally through the System of Transactions with Securities in Foreign Currency.[67] The second development is the

---

61 See Tozzini Freire Advogados and Bain & Co, *Relatório I – Regimes Jurídico-Regulatórios E Contratuais de E&P de petróleo* (2009).

62 *See* the Currency Exchange Covenant 1, *Gaceta Oficial* 37.625, February 5 2003, re-published in *Gaceta Oficial* 37.653 of March 19 2003; and the Law Against Exchange Crimes, *Gaceta Oficial* 38.282, September 14 2009, amended in *Gaceta Oficial* (Extra), May 17 2010.

63 Exchange Covenant 9, September 15 2005, amended, *Gaceta Oficial* 39.239, August 11 2009.

64 The regulation was imported into contracts, that is, Article 4 of the National Assembly Agreement for the Creation of the Mixed Company PetroCarabobo, *Gaceta Oficial* 39.419, May 5 2010.

65 However, PDVSA's accumulated debt has caused renegotiations with these service providers which have sometimes been forced to accept payments in bolivars.

66 See, for example, Article 6 of the Venezuelan – Barbados bilateral investment treaty:

> *Each Contracting Party shall in respect of investments guarantee to nationals or companies of the other Contracting Party the unrestricted transfer of their investments and returns. Transfers shall be effected without delay in the convertible currency in which the capital was originally invested or in any other convertible currency agreed by the investor and the Contracting Party concerned. Unless otherwise agreed by the investor transfer shall be made at the rate of exchange applicable on the date of transfer pursuant to the exchange regulations in force.*

approval of Currency Exchange Covenant 20, which allows legal entities domiciled in Venezuela to hold deposit accounts denominated in foreign currency in universal banks in Venezuela from which transfers may be made to banks abroad.[68]

4. Current Issues

4.1 Venezuela denounces the ICSID Convention

On July 25 2012, Venezuela officially withdrew from the International Centre for the Settlement of Investment Disputes (ICSID) at the end of the six month cooling-off period required by Article 71 the Washington Convention.[69] Venezuela's departure was no surprise to the foreign investment community in Venezuela since many threats had been made before the decision was actually taken. Also it arrived only a month after Venezuela was ordered to pay $908 million dollars to ExxonMobil in arbitration at the International Chamber of Commerce, the first decision on the merits in an arbitration arising from the migration process of 2007. Furthermore, during the last few years clauses referring to the ICSID had been deliberately excluded from newly negotiated BITs, following the government's public position criticising the ICSID as being partial and favouring corporations. The reasons for the withdrawal are political in nature and seek to reduce the opportunities for international claims against the state after the wave of expropriations in the country.[70]

Venezuela's departure raises a number of issues that investors need to address, including the need to review their existing corporate structure and determine to what extent they can protect their investment, since the exclusion of recourse to the ICSID narrows the arbitration sources included in the Venezuelan network of BITs.

---

67 Ruling of the Constitutional Chamber of the Venezuelan Supreme Tribunal, of November 2 2011, in Case 09-1380.

68 Exchange Covenant 20, *Gaceta Oficial* 40.002, September 6 2012.

69 On January 25 2012, after many years of threats, a press release from the Ministry of Foreign Affairs of Venezuela announced that on January 24 2012, Venezuela had officially denounced the Convention on the Settlement of Investment Disputes between States and Nationals of Other States of 1965 (the ICSID Convention).

70 The denunciation of the ICSID Convention follows the nationalistic policies that the Venezuelan government has been pursuing in recent years. It was reflected diplomatic pacts in the framework of the Bolivarian Alliance for the Peoples of Our America (ALBA) whereby the other two members, Bolivia (in 2007) and Ecuador (in 2009) had taken the same step in rejecting arbitration in international forums in disputes involving the extractive industries. Although Article 71 of the convention does not require a statement of reasons for a denunciation, a press release from the Ministry of Foreign Affairs stated some reasons which are shameless. The press release misinterpreted basic notions such as "foreign claims" and "international claims" and presented figures asserting that the International Centre for the Settlement of Investment Disputes had favoured transnational interests in 232 of 234 cases, arguing the bias of the system. Although, we could share criticisms and ideas for reform to the ICSID system, the figures presented by the Venezuelan government are just inaccurate and a clear misrepresentation of the reality. The results of investor–state international litigation may vary every year, but reports from the United Nations Conference on Trade and Development and ICSID statistical reports show that the final award has favored states in a majority of cases. These reports have also included in their statistics cases resolved by settlement, and claims dismissed at the stage of establishing jurisdiction. Furthermore, as has been noted by Professor Sebastien Manciaux, Venezuela is well placed to know that decisions by ICSID arbitrators are far from what the ministry asserted. Recently there have also been decisions favourable to Venezuela, as for example, the rejection of claims and cases based on declining jurisdiction (ie, *Brandes Investment partner LP v Venezuela* (ARB/08/03); see S Manciaux, "*Le Venezuela se retire du CIRDI*", *Revue de l'Arbitrage*, Issue 1 2012, pp 215–221). Venezuela has also claimed as victories the International Chamber of Commerce award in *Mobil v Cerro Negro*; the ICSID decision on jurisdiction in *Mobil v Venezuela*, and the rejection of interim measures requested by CEMEX at the ICSID.

Although clauses on recourse to the ICSID were included as a first option for international arbitration in most of Venezuela's BITs they also contain reference to arbitration under the rules of the United Nations Commission on International Trade Law or the ICSID Additional Facility Rules,[71] giving to investors other options for the international settlement of any dispute.

Nonetheless, there is an extensive debate on the proper interpretation of Articles 71 and 72 of the ICSID Convention, and three interpretations have been proposed about the effects of a denunciation of the convention with regard to offers of ICSID arbitration in the network of Venezuelan BITs.[72] Many authors believe that denunciation does not preclude suing before the ICSID when the parties agreed to this jurisdiction through the BITs signed previously and containing an offer of ICSID arbitration.[73] Other authors believe that the denunciation must have effect immediately and only investors who consented to ICSID jurisdiction prior to the termination may still use that arbitration as a method of dispute resolution.[74] Finally, there is an intermediate position that the denunciation of the Washington Convention does not take effect – under Article 71 – until six months after its receipt, thus giving investors time to accept offers of ICSID arbitration issued by a state which has made its decision to denounce the convention.[75]

Previous denunciations of the Washington Convention in the case of Bolivia and Ecuador have not yet provided a decision in this regard.[76] Only *Pan and American Energy LLC v Bolivia* (ARB/10/8) was filed after the denunciation took effect. The arbitral tribunal in that case was constituted on August 12 2012 but no decisions have yet been taken. As for Venezuela, nine claims have been filed and registered by the ICSID between January 25 2012 and November 2012.[77]

4.2 Recent final arbitration awards in the petroleum sector

ICC Arbitration Case 16848 *ConocoPhillips v PDVSA*:[78] The case involved a shareholders' dispute over the parties' former petroleum joint ventures, Petrozuata

71 With the exception of the Venezuelan-French bilateral investment treaty, which only provides access to ICSID.

72 S Manciaux, above.

73 See, E Gaillard, "The Denunciation of the ICSID Convention", *New York Journal*, Volume 237, Issue 122, June 26 2007; F Mantilla-Serrano, "The effect of Bolivia's Withdrawal From the Washington Convention: Is BIT-Based ICSID Jurisdiction Foreclosed?", *Mealey's International Arbitration Report*, Volume 22, Issue 8, 2007, pp 39–44 ; N Blackaby, "ICSID Withdrawal, a Storm in a Teacup?", *Cahiers De l'arbitrage*, 2010, 45.

74 C Schreuer, *The ICSID Convention, a Commentary*, Cambridge University Press, 2009, pp 1279–1282; J Fouret, "Denunciation of the Washington Convention and Non-Contractual Investment Arbitration: 'Manufacturing Consent' to ICSID Arbitration", *Journal of International Arbitration*, 2008, 71.

75 S Manciaux, *"La Bolivie se retire du Cirdi"* *Revue de ''Arbitrage*, 2007, 351.; W. Ben Hamida, *"La dénonciation de la Convention de Washington: un adieu ou un simple au revoir?"*, in F Horchani (ed), *Cirdi, 45 ans après: bilan d'un système*, Pedone, 2011, p 109.

76 A request for arbitration was registered against Bolivia on October 31 2007, in *Euro Telecom International NV v Bolivia* (ARB/07/28), a few days before the expiry of the period set out in Article 71, and another was filed on April 12 2010, in *Pan and American Energy LLC v Bolivia* (ARB/10/8), after the expiry of the time limit. But the tribunal in the first of these cases did not have to decide because of the agreement of both parties to terminate the proceedings before the ICSID in order to continue with an *ad hoc* arbitral tribunal composed of the same referees, but acting in application of the arbitration rules of the United Nations Commission on International Trade Law. Regarding Ecuador, ICSID recorded a request for arbitration against it on December 30 2009, in *Corporación Quiport SA v Ecuador* (ARB/09/23), a week before the expiry of six months set out in Article 71, but the case has been discontinued.

and Hamaca. The dispute occurred as a result of PDVSA's failure to compensate Conoco for production curtailments imposed by the Organisation of Petroleum Exporting Countries (OPEC), affecting Hamaca and Petrozuata's output during late 2006 and early 2007. The tribunal rejected the claim in respect of the Hamaca project for $102.9 million on the grounds that the claimant had failed to establish a sufficient causal link between the failure of mitigation measures within the framework of OPEC curtailments and breach of the Hamaca Association Agreement. However, the tribunal awarded $66.8 million payment to ConocoPhillips for the Petrozuata project. The tribunal concluded that PDVSA was liable under a PDVSA–Petrozuata guarantee for any damage or loss resulting from the failure of Maraven (a PDVSA affiliate) to comply with its obligations under a Petrozuata side letter, in particular the obligation to absorb the relevant OPEC curtailments of oil production.[79] The aim of the side letter was to ensure at all times a minimum level of production in order to ensure the financial viability of the project and the good functioning of the upgrader. The main idea was therefore that if production cuts were imposed by the government in implementation of its OPEC commitments that affected the level of production required by the project, those cuts would be absorbed by the state-owned party to the project, Maraven, out of its own production. The arbitral tribunal stated that the respondent had failed to meet the burden of proof that compliance with OPEC commitments justified the application of the principle of 'external non-imputable cause' to excuse Maraven from its obligations under the Petrozuata side letter. Therefore the side letter granted indemnification against a curtailment imposed by the government of such a nature as to affect the financial viability of the project and/or the good functioning of the upgrader. The main point was that ensuring a minimum production level at all times notwithstanding possible OPEC curtailments was essential to the viability of the project from a financial and operational perspective.[80] The logic underlying this point was that claimant, as a provider of funds to Petrozuata, would have received a return commensurate to the opportunity cost of providing the capital in the absence of the breach of contract, and that otherwise, the principle of full compensation would not be satisfied. After the award was rendered, Venezuela complied voluntarily with its enforcement.

ICC Arbitration Case 15415 *ExxonMobil v PDVSA*:[81] The award in this case declared the enforceability of an economic equilibrium clause that obliged PDVSA to compensate Mobil for acts of the government. In this case, increases in the rates of

---

77 *Saint-Gobain Performance Plastics Europe v Bolivarian Republic of Venezuela* (ICSID Case ARB/12/13); *Valle Verde Sociedad Financiera SL v Bolivarian Republic of Venezuela* (ICSID Case ARB/12/18); *Rusoro Mining Ltd v Bolivarian Republic of Venezuela* (ICSID Case ARB(AF)/12/5); *Ternium SA v Bolivarian Republic of Venezuela* (ICSID Case ARB/12/19); *Blue Bank International & Trust (Barbados) Ltd v Bolivarian Republic of Venezuela* (ICSID Case ARB/12/20); *Fábrica de Vidrios Los Andes, CA v Bolivarian Republic of Venezuela* (ICSID Case ARB/12/21); *Venoklim Holding BV v Bolivarian Republic of Venezuela* (ICSID Case ARB/12/22); *Tenaris SA v Bolivarian Republic of Venezuela* (ICSID Case ARB/12/23); *Transban Investments Corp v Bolivarian Republic of Venezuela* (ICSID Case ARB/12/24).

78 *Phillips Petroleum Company Venezuela Ltd and Conocophillips Petrozuata BV v Petroleos de Venezuela, SA (PDVSA)*, International Court of Arbitration Case 16848/JRF/CA (C-16849/JRF/CA) – final award, September 17 2012.

79 *Ibid* at paragraphs 282, 235, 212–217, 229 and 234.

80 *Ibid* at paragraph 210.

the royalty, extraction tax and income tax by the Venezuelan government diminished the investor's profit returns. The tribunal stated that increases in royalty and extraction tax did not meet the discriminatory test in the contract and thus rejected the claims. However, it found that the increase in income tax from 34% to 50% was discriminatory and justified compensation under the liability clause that required PDVSA to provide compensation. In this case, a starting claim for $12 billion was reduced to $908 million through the rejection of claims on royalty and extraction tax increase, but also through a cap in the liability clause for the calculation of damages that limited PDVSA's liability to a specific price per barrel of the oil. Venezuela celebrated the result as a victory as it was found liable for less than 10% of the initial claim. ExxonMobil has also referred to the result as a victory[82] since this was only the claim concerning tax issues; an expropriation claim is also still pending a decision on the merits at the ICSID.[83] Again, Venezuela complied voluntarily with enforcement of the award.[84]

4.3 Article 22 of the Venezuelan Investment Law: not a unilateral offer of arbitration

So far, four ICSID decisions have confirmed the interpretation that Article 22 of the Investment Law cannot be interpreted as a unilateral offer to have access to ICSID arbitration.[85] There are a few decisions pending where Venezuela is also challenging jurisdiction on this ground, such as *Opic v Venezuela*.[86]

4.4 ICSID claims pending from the migration of exploration and production projects

So far the ExxonMobil case[87] is proceeding to a decision on the merits after a decision which affirmed the jurisdiction of the ICSID, while the *ConocoPhillips Case*[88] will have

---

81 Final award in *Mobil Cerro Negro, Ltd v Petróleos de Venezuela, SA* (ICC Case 15415/JRF, December 11 2011).

82 Statement made by Jack Balagia, general counsel for ExxonMobil Corp, during an October 12 2012 presentation to the Energy Environment and Natural Resources Centre of the University of Houston.

83 *Mobil Corp v Venezuela*, ICSID Case ARB/07/27.

84 Many people might be surprised that a country that has promoted an international campaign against international arbitration has complied voluntarily with the execution of the two latest ICC awards ordering Venezuela to pay compensation to foreign investors. It would appear that the country has complied for the following reasons:

- The government has viewed the awards as a positive result, since in *ExxonMobil v PDVSA* final compensation represented less than 10% of the initial claim and in *ConocoPhillips v PDVSA* the final award was around 40% of the initial claim.
- Non-compliance with arbitral awards might increase insurance and interest rates for credits and loans for the development of new projects in the Orinoco belt affecting the PDVSA and foreign investors.
- Non-compliance might have an negative impact on Venezuelan bonds in international debt capital markets. And
- Legal strategies on *res judicata* in case of similar claims in the ICSID arbitration on the same projects may have influenced its decision.

It may be concluded that a country's transnational connections may incentivise compliance with international arbitration awards, since non-compliance may have adverse effects on the international markets or the oil and gas financial sector.

85 *Brandes v Venezuela* (ICSID Case ARB/08/3), decision on jurisdiction, August 2 2011; *CEMEX v Venezuela* (ICSID Case ARB/08/15), decision on jurisdiction, December 30 2010; *Mobil Corp v Venezuela* (ICSID Case ARB/07/27), decision on jurisdiction, June 10 2010, and *Tidewater v Venezuela* (ICSID Case ARB/10/5), decision on jurisdiction, February 8, 2013.

86 *Opic Karimun Corporation v Venezuela* (ICSID Case ARB/10/14).

87 *Mobil Corp v Venezuela* (ICSID Case ARB/07/27).

88 *ConocoPhillips v Venezuela* (ICSID Case ARB/07/30).

a joint decision on jurisdiction and on the merits before moving to the quantum phase of the arbitration, if any. Therefore, decisions may be delayed until the end of 2013 or even until 2014, given the complexity of the cases.

4.5 Oil service company expropriation decision

On February 8 2012, in *Tidewater v Venezuela* (ICSID Case ARB/10/5), the arbitral tribunal rejected jurisdiction on the basis of Article 22 of the Investment Law, after interpreting the Venezuelan rule in light of Article 25 of the ICSID Convention. It concluded that this does not require the written consent of Venezuela to submit all investment disputes with nationals of other ICSID contracting states to ICSID jurisdiction.[89] However, jurisdiction was confirmed on expropriation claims, since the Reserve Law that initiated the expropriation measures was introduced without warning and enacted within just three days, from May 4 to 7 2009, with the seizure of Tidewater's assets taking effect on May 8 2009. The tribunal concluded that the acts of expropriation were not reasonably foreseeable by the claimants either in December 2008, when they began restructuring, or in March 2009, when the restructuring took effect. As a result, and following the standard on treaty shopping used in *Mobil Corp v Venezuela* (ICSID Case ARB/07/27),[90] the ICSID had jurisdiction over the claims of Tidewater Barbados insofar as they related to causes of action that arose after its acquisition of the shares of Tidewater Caribe, given that Venezuela had given its consent by virtue of Article 8 of the Barbados BIT and there had been no abuse of that treaty by the claimants of a kind that might render inadmissible their invocation of such jurisdiction.[91]

5. Conclusion

Venezuelan legislation applying to upstream investment in the oil sector has turned into a sophisticated legal regime in which the state has concentrated its control over such investment. The country offers great potential for production and access to the biggest oil reserves in the world, but investors should assess their leeway for exposure to risk given the current legal framework and the attitude to respect for the rule of law.

The legal framework for upstream activities in the petroleum sector in Venezuela comprises a network of rules arising from contractual agreements, national petroleum law and international commitments under bilateral investment treaties and energy cooperation agreements, and increasingly an arbitral jurisprudence available for the oil sector which provides standards for the performance of

---

89 In *Tidewater* Venezuela proposed an interpretation of Article 22 of the Investment Law by reference to the ILC Unilateral Declaration Principles. This shows how non-state law can also be seen as beneficial to the arguments of state parties in international arbitration. This also adds to the discussion of non-state sources of law, such as the UNIDROIT Principles, as was demonstrated by Walid Ben Amida in "*Les principes d'UNIDROIT et l'arbitrage transnational: L'expansion des principes d'UNIDROIT aux arbitrages opposant des États ou des organisations internationales à des personnes privées*", *Journal du Droit International* ("Clunet") (Vol 139, no 4, Oct/Nov/Dec 2012)

90 *Mobil Corp v Venezuela* (ICSID Case ARB/07/27). Decision on Jurisdiction, June 10 2010 ¶ 206 .The arbitral tribunal stated that the aim of restructuring the investment to secure the protection of a BIT was "perfectly legitimate as far as it concerned future disputes".

91 In reference to *Phoenix Action v Czech Rep* ICSID Case ARB/06/5, Decision of Jurisdiction 2009.

operations and for the placement of investments and ways to protect investments against unilateral actions of the government. Accordingly, foreign investors and the government authorities, in making their decisions, should consider all the elements of applicable law in order to ensure the best possible performance and development of new projects in the country.

Denmark

Bent Ole Gram Mortensen
Department of Law, University of Southern Denmark

1. Introduction

Denmark has been pumping oil since 1972 and natural gas since 1984.[1] The existence of oil was first discovered in 1966. Denmark's supply of energy in 2011 was calculated as being 110% of its gross consumption. Denmark is therefore one of the few western European countries that is self-sufficient in energy. However, this level of self-sufficiency is declining, and it is expected that by 2018 the country's consumption of oil and natural gas will exceed its domestic supply.[2] Denmark has a population of about 5.6 million and an area of about 43,000 square kilometres (km^2).

The first exploration licence was granted in 1935, covering oil and gas, salt and other raw materials.[3] On July 8 1962 a 50-year exclusive licence was given to AP Møller (of the Maersk Group),[4] which entered into a collaboration in the form of the Dansk Undergrunds Consortium (DUC), which now consists of AP Møller-Mærsk A/S, Shell Olie- og Gasudvinding Danmark BV (Holland) and Chevron Denmark Inc. The exclusive licence originally only applied on land, but with Denmark's ratification of the Convention on the Continental Shelf in 1963,[5] offshore areas were covered by the exclusive licence, including the subsoil of the Danish sector of the North Sea. This agreement has been renegotiated several times, whereby several areas have been given up.[6] For the remaining areas, where commercial finds have been made, the licence has been extended to July 8 2042.[7]

1 See the Danish Ministry of the Environment, *Danmarks energifortider*, 2001.

2 This information is based on an estimate from the Danish Energy Agency (www.ens.dk). The predictions are somewhat uncertain and depend, among other things, on the development of the degree of extraction from the oil and gas fields, the exploitation of newly discovered fields, and the transition to renewable energy sources.

3 The licence was granted to an American, FF Ravlin, who formed DAPCO (the Danish American Prospecting Company). The licence was renewed several times, and first Gulf Oil and then Esso took over DAPCO and continued exploration activities until 1959; see the Danish Ministry of the Environment: *Danmarks energifortider*, 2001. The earliest exploration (drilling) for hydrocarbons seems to have been on-land drilling for natural gas in 1905. However, this was not found to be commercially viable, even though there was some local exploitation; see Bo Sandroos, *Undergrundsloven med kommentarer* [The Danish Subsoil Act – with Comments], DJØF Publishing, 2012, p 37 and following.

4 Executive Order 372 of November 7 1963 on the Grant of an Exclusive Licence for the Exploration and Exploitation of Hydrocarbons etc in Denmark's Subsoil.

5 Royal Decree 259 of June 7 1963 on the Exercise of Danish Sovereignty Over the Continental Shelf. This was later replaced by the Law on the Continental Shelf, most recently Law 1101 of November 18 2005 on the Continental Shelf.

6 Starting in 1981, the Danish government entered into an agreement with the licensee AP Møller on the gradual handing back of some areas.

7 See www.ens.dk/sw13621.asp.

2. Upstream activities

In Denmark oil and/or natural gas is produced from 19 fields with about 400 wells, of which 278 are in active production. There is currently extraction in the Danish sector of the North Sea in five production areas: Dan/Halfdan, Gorm, Tyra, Siri and Syd Arne. So far, no commercial resources have been found elsewhere, including on land. Extraction is supported by about 55 platforms. Extraction rights in the Danish oil and gas fields are held by a number of national and international operators. However, actual operational activities are mostly carried out by Danish undertakings. Thus, Mærsk Olie og Gas A/S operates in 15 fields (in the Dan/Halfdan, Gorm and Tyra production areas), while DONG E&P A/S operates in three fields (in the Siri production area). Hess Denmark ApS (part of a US group) is the only non-Danish operator (in the Syd Arne production area). Currently there is no extraction onshore in Denmark.

In 2011, total oil production in Denmark was 12.8 million cubic metres (m^3). This was a reduction of 9.8% compared with 2010. In 2011, natural gas production was 6.5 million m^3, of which 5.6 million m^3 was landed with a view to sale, a reduction of 21% compared with the previous year.[8] This reduction was not unexpected. Many of the extraction installations are old, and it must be anticipated that there will be more frequent closures, among other reasons on safety grounds. In addition there is the general reduction in production from older wells.

3. Petroleum legal regime

Denmark is signatory to a number of international conventions which establish certain frameworks for the regulation of the extraction and use of hydrocarbons. The most important of these is the United Nations Convention on the Law of the Sea (UNCLOS), which Denmark ratified in 2004. The Convention on the Continental Shelf was ratified in 1963. The Convention on Environmental Impact Assessment in a Transboundary Context (the Espoo Convention) was signed by Denmark on the February 26 1991. Denmark has also ratified the OSPAR Convention (the Convention for the Protection of the Marine Environment of the North-East Atlantic) against pollution from sources on land or by dumping by ships or aircraft.

Denmark is also a Member State of the European Union, joining the then European Communities on January 1 1973.[9] This means that various EU legislative acts, such as the Hydrocarbons Licensing Directive, also establish the framework for Danish legislation.

3.1 Petroleum law and relevant provisions

The exploitation of oil and natural gas in Denmark is regulated under several legislative acts. Thus, there are the general laws that are relevant to commercial

---

8 The Danish Energy Agency, *Danmarks Olie- og gasproduktion* 2011, p 20.

9 The legislation is described by Bo Sandroos, *Undergrundsloven med kommentarer* (The Danish Subsoil Act – with comments), DJØF Publishing, 2012; Bent Ole Gram Mortensen & Anita Rønne, "Olie- og naturgasindvinding" (Oil and natural gas exploitation), in EM Basse (ed), *Miljøretten (Environmental Law)*, Volume 6, *Energi og klima (Energy and Climate)*, DJØF Publishing, 2008, pp 189-254; Martha Roggenkamp *et al*, Energy Law in Europe, Oxford University Press, 2007, pp 454–476; and Danish Energy Agency, *A Guide to Hydrocarbon Licences in Denmark – Exploration and Drilling Activities*, September 2011.

undertakings as well as the more specific laws aimed at the exploitation of particular resources. Only the latter are discussed here. The main legislation regulating the exploitation of oil and natural gas in Denmark is the Consolidated Act on the Use of the Danish Subsoil (the 'Subsoil Act').[10] In addition to oil and natural gas, the act also governs salt production and geothermal energy. The act also regulates the installation and operation of pipelines from the Danish fields, with the exception of transit pipelines and pipelines from the North Sea to Fredericia, which are subject to separate legislation.[11] The act implements the most important EU requirements in Danish law.[12]

In addition, there is the Continental Shelf Act,[13] a special Offshore Safety Act,[14] a Hydrocarbon Tax Act[15] as well as a number of other legislative acts of more peripheral importance. These in turn are supplemented by rules that are, in form, of a more advisory nature but which can, in practice, be applied in the administration of the Danish licensing system. These advisory rules can be found in model licences and guidelines.[16]

The starting point is that Danish law applies on Danish territory and in Danish territorial waters, unless otherwise provided for in legislation. According to its Article 1(3), the Subsoil Act also applies in the Danish exclusive economic zone and in the Danish continental shelf area. The act covers preliminary investigations, the exploration for and extraction of raw materials in the Danish subsoil that were not subject to private commercial exploitation in this country prior to February 23 1932, which is the date of the entry into force of the first Danish law on the subsoil. Raw materials that were not subject to private commercial exploitation prior to that date belong to the Danish state; see Article 2, first sentence, of the Subsoil Act.[17]

Generally, the Danish law on the extraction of raw materials is based on internationally known principles. There is thus legislation on licensing based on a set of permits, environmental impact assessments and standards. Denmark has chosen to apply the licensing system that is characteristic for the countries surrounding the North Sea. Danish legislation in this area has also been influenced by British and Norwegian law.

The Subsoil Act requires all exploration for and extraction of raw materials to be

---

10 In its most recent form in Consolidated Act 960 of September 13 2011.

11 The Pipelines Act, in its most recent form in Consolidated Act 957 of September 9 2011 on the establishment and use of a pipeline for the transport of crude oil and condensate.

12 Thus it implements Directive 94/22/EC of the European Parliament and of the Council; parts of Council Directive 92/43/EEC; parts of Directive 2011/92/EU of the European Parliament and of the Council; parts of Directive 2009/28/EC of the European Parliament and of the Council; parts of Directive 2009/31/EC of the European Parliament and of the Council; and parts of Directive 2009/147/EC of the European Parliament and of the Council.

13 Consolidated Act 1101 of November 18 2005.

14 Law 1424 of December 21 2005 on Safety etc for Offshore Installations for Exploration, Extraction and Transport of Hydrocarbons.

15 Consolidated Act 971 of September 20 2011 on the Taxation of Income in Connection with the Extraction of Hydrocarbons in Denmark, and Consolidated Act 966 of September 20 2011 on the Calculation and Collection etc of Tax on the Extraction of Hydrocarbons.

16 There is a comprehensive overview, in English, of the relevant rules in Danish Energy Agency, *A Guide to Hydrocarbon Licences in Denmark – Exploration and Drilling Activities*, 2011, p 10 and following.

17 Corresponding provisions apply under Article 1(1) of the Continental Shelf Act. In contrast to this, rights to raw materials that have been subject to private economic exploitation in Denmark prior to this date go with the ownership of the land, though they are subject to comprehensive requirements for permits.

subject to public regulation. The act states that its purpose is to ensure the appropriate use and exploitation of the Danish subsoil and its natural resources. With a view to achieving this, a special system has been built up based on a requirement for separate permits and approvals for virtually every phase of exploration and/or extraction. In general the act has resulted in a concession system in which the concessionaire is given a sole right over a defined area for a defined period. The concessionaire obtains ownership rights in the extracted hydrocarbons, but is subject to certain taxation requirements as well as a number of conditions concerning the exploration and extraction itself.

Article 10 of the Subsoil Act requires exploration and production to be carried on in a safe and appropriate manner that prevents any waste of raw materials. This includes regard for safety, and technical and financial resources. A plan for production activities, including the organisation of production and the layout of production installations must be approved by the Minister for Climate, Energy and Building.

(a) *Regulatory bodies*

In Denmark the energy sector now falls under the remit of the Ministry of Climate, Energy and Building. The energy sector is the particular responsibility of the Danish Energy Agency which is responsible both for the granting of concessions and for public supervision. The Agency dates from 1976 and during its existence it has come under the wing of a number of different ministries. The Energy Agency is regarded as being very independent in its area of operation and to a large extent it undertakes tasks which, in Danish practice, would normally be a matter for the ministry. The ministerial powers under the Subsoil Act, the Continental Shelf Act, the Pipelines Act and the Offshore Safety Act, are in principle delegated to the Energy Agency.[18] Under the Subsoil Act there is the notable exception that the grant of an exclusive licence for exploration and extraction of oil and natural gas must be granted by the minister.[19]

In addition to upstream oil and natural gas, the Energy Agency also has responsibility for the downstream side, for renewable energy and to a certain extent for building policy.

A kind of one-stop-shop principle is followed in the area of hydrocarbons, so that in the offshore area the Energy Agency acts as the access portal in relation to the official requirements, including permits, even where these fall under the authority of other public bodies. However, decision-making powers still rest with those other public bodies.[20]

Central government bodies that are of particular relevance include the Danish Maritime Authority, which has powers over approvals of offshore installations,

---

18 See Article 3(1)(1) to (4) of Executive Order 436 of May 11 2012 on the Tasks and Powers of the Energy Agency.

19 See Article 11 (for the Subsoil Act) and Article 12 (for the Pipelines Act) of Executive Order 436 of May 11 2012 on the Energy Agency's Tasks and Powers.

20 Onshore, if there were to be production of hydrocarbons – which there is not – the administration would be a matter for the individual municipal authorities and the Ministry of the Environment.

including their operation.[21] In addition the Danish Nature Agency and the Danish Environmental Protection Agency have powers with regard to the marine environment.[22] Moreover, drilling operations often require permits from a number of other authorities such as the Danish Working Environment Authority, the Danish Safety Technology Authority, the Directorate of Fisheries, the Ministry of Defence and the Danish Health and Medicines Authority.[23] Thus, several different ministries have decision-making powers in connection with exploiting oil and gas.

(b) *Types of agreement*

There are basically two types of agreement: prospecting licences and exploration and exploitation licences.

Preliminary investigations are governed by Part 2 of the Subsoil Act. This gives the Minister authority to grant non-exclusive licences for specific kinds of preliminary investigations with a view to subsequent exploration and extraction of the raw materials covered by the act. The power to grant licences for preliminary investigations has been delegated to the Energy Agency. The aim of a preliminary investigation is to map out the potential for finding hydrocarbons in a given area. The licence covers a defined geographical area; it can be for up to three years, with the possibility of renewal. Among other things, preliminary investigations can include seismic, geological and geochemical research. The licensee of a prospecting licence does not obtain a preferential position for a possible exploration or exploitation licence for the specific area. The Energy Agency can require the licensee to pay for a licence and to share the information gathered.

All exploration for and extraction of raw materials requires permission from the Minister; see Part 3 of the Subsoil Act. Permission will normally be given as an exclusive right within a defined geographical area (a block). It is also possible to define an area vertically, limited to certain geological layers.

The requirements for a licence will appear from the model licence attached to the licensing round. The requirements have varied in the licensing rounds held hitherto.

Pursuant to Article 6 of the Subsoil Act, an exclusive right is only granted after an application has been approved by the Danish Parliament's Climate, Energy and Building Committee.[24] If approval is refused, the Committee must, upon the request of the applicant, give a reason for its decision to refuse permission. This is a requirement under the Hydrocarbons Licensing Directive.

The grant of a licence does not give an automatic right to start work. Every job

---

21 Executive Order 673 of June 21 2006 on the Delegation of Certain Powers to the Danish Maritime Authority. In contrast to the Energy Agency, the Maritime Authority is organised under the Ministry of Business and Growth.

22 Executive Order 1411 of December 8 2010 on the Delegation of Powers to the Nature Agency; and Executive Order 1391 of December 8 2010 on the Delegation of the Powers of the Minister for the Environment in Environmental Protection Act and other Acts to the Environmental Protection Agency. Both the Nature Agency and the Environmental Protection Agency are under the Minister of the Environment.

23 See Bo Sandroos, *Undergrundsloven med kommentarer* (The Danish Subsoil Act – with comments), DJØF Publishing, 2012, p 233, for a more comprehensive list of the relevant authorities.

24 Until October 2011, the Climate, Energy and Building Committee was called the Energy Policy Committee; it is one of the standing committees of the Danish Parliament.

requires permission from the minister (delegated to the Energy Agency). Under Article 28 of the Subsoil Act, the minister must approve the equipment, working programme and working methods in each individual case.

(c) *Acquisition of acreage*

Both licensing rounds and an open door procedure are used in Denmark. Hitherto, areas west of 6°15′ east (situated in the North Sea) have been subject to a bidding procedure. The three most recent licensing rounds have only covered areas west of 6° 15′ east.

Acreage is acquired either by licensing rounds or by an open door procedure. So far there have been six licensing rounds, the first being held in 1984. Licensing rounds are published in the Danish *Law Gazette* and the *Official Journal of the European Union.*

The open door procedure was introduced in Denmark in 1997 and is used in the area east of 6°15′ east. Applications must be made from January 2 to September 30. If the Energy Agency receives an application it must be published in the Danish *Law Gazette* and in the *Official Journal of the European Union,* thereby enabling other parties to make applications within the deadline.

(d) *Qualification requirements*

Licensees must be registered with the taxation authorities in Denmark and provide necessary information for that purpose. For example, companies can register a business address in Denmark or establish a Danish subsidiary. Article 5(3) of the Subsoil Act states that licences for exploration and exploitation may only be granted to applicants that are deemed to have the necessary expertise and financial resources, and who can be expected to carry on the activities in a manner that benefits society as a whole. Article 12a of the Subsoil Act provides that additional criteria can be used for selecting applicants. Such criteria will appear in the model licence accompanying the tender documents.

The criteria in Article 12a of the Subsoil Act concern the applicant's expertise and financial capacity, the way in which the applicant intends to carry out production in the area in question and the extent of the intended exploration activities (the applicant's willingness and capacity to explore whether there are hydrocarbons in the area applied for). The work programme can be considered part of the licensee's payment for the licence. Where any part of a work programme is not performed, the licensee can be required to pay an amount equal to the cost of performing the obligations not carried out; see Section 36 of the model licence. If an applicant has shown any lack of efficiency or non-compliance with obligations under previous licences, this can also be taken into account. Applicants who do not already have rights for the exploration and extraction of hydrocarbons in Danish territory must give evidence of their goals and organisation for environmental protection, as well as their organisation and plans for dealing with environmental problems and any experience they have for combating accidents. These provisions primarily implement the requirements in the Hydrocarbons Licensing Directive.

(e) *Duration*

Under Article 3 of the Subsoil Act a licence for preliminary investigations is given for a period of up to three years. It is possible to obtain an extension.

A licence for exploration and extraction is given for a period of up to six years; see Article 13(1) of the Subsoil Act. This can be extended by up to two years at a time. In principle the total period for research may not extend beyond 10 years. The most recent Danish model licence (the sixth licensing round) uses a six-year period with the possibility of extensions up to 10 years. However, there can be extensions beyond 10 years if, for example, the commercial exploitation of marginal finds depends on developments in other fields. An extension may be granted for part of the area, and it may also be made conditional on carrying out new explorations.[25]

For those parts of an area where finds have been made and where extraction is intended, the licence can be extended by up to 30 years; see Article 13(2) and (3). It is possible for the 30-year period to be extended, but only up to a total period of 50 years; see Article 7 which contains a general upper limit for licences under the Subsoil Act. However, particularly in the area of hydrocarbons, the legislator has allowed the possibility of an extension even beyond 50 years. Such an extension is intended for concessions where production can be maintained longer than expected. Specifically, this provision has been applied to the Dansk Undergrunds Consortium (DUC) concession which has now been extended up to mid-2042. This brings the total period of the concession up to no less than 80 years.

(f) *Minimum work programme*

The model licence sets out a minimum work programme which a licensee for an exploration and extraction licence must carry out. This varies with each licence, but it will typically include a requirement for seismic research and at least one exploration well to enable logging of the relevant formation. The licensee must submit a report on findings of hydrocarbons, and must state in an assessment programme what further exploration steps should be taken to assess whether what has been found is commercially viable.

(g) *Assignment and encumbrance*

Under Article 29 of the Subsoil Act, a licence can only be assigned with the approval of the minister. The minister must also approve the terms of the assignment. A licence granted under the Subsoil Act is not available to the recourse of creditors.

(h) *Local content*

Danish legislation does not contain any special provisions on the use of Danish labour, products made in Denmark or Danish subcontractors. To some extent Denmark is prevented from imposing such terms by its membership of the European Union. However, the general provisions of legislation on foreign nationals apply to work and residence permits for non-Danish workers.

---

25 Bo Sandroos, *Undergrundsloven med kommentarer* (The Danish Subsoil Act – with comments), DJØF Publishing, 2012, p 144.

Section 15 of the model licence also contains a provision whereby, in order to comply with the Utilities Directive, the Energy Agency can require the licensee to comply with the principles of non-discrimination and competitive procurement when awarding supplies, works and service contracts, and can be required to give information to the European Commission relating to the award of contracts.

(i) National reservation

Article 8 of the Subsoil Act states that licences may stipulate that the state shall be entitled to take part in the activity covered by the licence. State participation in licences has been the established practice in Denmark since the first licensing round in 1984. The previously granted concession with the DUC was renegotiated so that as from 2012 the state has a 20% share of ownership. This share of state ownership was also part of the conditions for the latest sixth licensing round, and it must be expected to be the norm for the foreseeable future.[26] In principle the state participates on the same terms as the other participants. State participation only takes the form of an ownership share. The state does not acquire special rights over part of the hydrocarbons produced, and is not required to market these.

From 1984 to 2005 the state's ownership shares were administered by the state-owned DONG concern. Since 2005 they have been administered by the state-owned Danish North Sea Fund.[27] The North Sea Fund does not act like a normal oil company. It cannot act as an operational undertaking, and in principle it cannot acquire (further) shares of licences on commercial terms.[28] In its administration, the North Sea Fund is limited to taking care of the interests referred to in the Subsoil Act, and it may not try to prevent other rights holders from acting on commercial terms. Moreover, Article 8 of the Subsoil Act contains restrictions on the North Sea Fund's exercise of its voting rights as co-owner of a company, as Article 6 of the Hydrocarbons Licensing Directive requires that any vote by the state must be based exclusively on transparent, objective and non-discriminatory principles.

(j) Environment

As a member of the European Union, Denmark is bound by the Environmental Impact Assessment Directive. According to points 14 and 16 of Annex I, the directive covers extraction of more than 500 tonnes per day in the case of crude oil and 500,000m^3 per day in the case of gas, as well as pipelines with a diameter of more than 800mm and a length of more than 40km for the transport of gas, oil or chemicals. In accordance with this Directive, Article 28a(1) of the Subsoil Act states that licences and approvals pursuant to the act that are assumed to have a major

---

26 In the fourth and fifth licensing rounds and in the open door areas the Danish state (through DONG E&P A/S) was also a fully paying participant with a 20% share. DONG also purchased additional shares on commercial terms.

27 The Danish North Sea Fund was established by Law 587 of June 24 2005 on a Public Fund for Custodianship of the State's Ownership Shares in Hydrocarbon Licences and a State Entity to Administer the Fund. The fund's articles of association are set out in Executive Order 710 of June 21 2007 on Articles of Association for the Public Fund for Custodianship of the State's Ownership Shares in Hydrocarbon Licences.

28 This is in contrast to the situation in the period 1984 to 2005, when state participation was administered by the DONG concern.

impact on the environment may only be granted following an assessment of the effects on the environment and after the public, authorities and organisations that are affected have been given an opportunity to express their opinions. If the project is assumed to have a major impact on protected nature conservation sites, the licence or approval may only be granted following an assessment of the impact of the project on the site, with due consideration for the objectives of conservation of the site.[29]

The more detailed requirements are set out in the Executive Order on Environmental Impact Assessments for Offshore Areas.[30] In line with the Environmental Impact Assessment Directive, Article 4 of the executive order requires environmental impact assessments to be made for projects for extractions for more than 500 tons of crude oil or 500,000m^3 of natural gas per day, pipeline projects[31] for the transport of gas, oil or chemicals with pipe diameters of more than 800mm and a length of more than 40km, as well as storage projects for oil products, petrochemicals or chemicals with a capacity of more than 200,000 tons. Such projects are subject to a requirement for an environmental impact assessment, since it is always assumed that they can have a major impact on the environment.

If it must be assumed that a project can have a major impact on the environment, then projects in addition to those referred to above, as well as changes to or expansions of existing projects that were required to have an environmental impact assessment will be required to have a separate environmental impact assessment. On the basis of the project's specific characteristics, its location and the nature of the potential environmental impact, the Energy Agency decides whether it may be assumed that it could have a major impact on the environment, and that an environmental impact report must therefore be drawn up. If the Energy Agency decides that an environmental impact report is not required, the decision must be made public when the approval or licence is granted to the applicants. The same requirement follows from Article 4 of the Continental Shelf Act. If such an activity may be assumed to have a significant affect on the environment, a licence to lay down pipelines for the transport of hydrocarbons in the area of the Danish continental shelf can only be granted on the basis of an assessment of the environmental impact. The public, public authorities and other organisations concerned must have an opportunity to submit their views before a licence is granted.

Pursuant to Articles 10, 17 and 28 of the Subsoil Act, before permission can be given for any plan for extraction measures, establishment and operation of pipeline facilities, or actual drilling activities to be carried out, the applicant must draw up an environmental impact report at their own expense and submit it to the Energy Agency. The Energy Agency will then publish information about the application and

29 These requirements are in line with Article 6(3) and (4) of the Habitats Directive.

30 Executive Order 632 of June 11 2012 on Environmental Impact Assessments, Assessment of the Impacts on Internationally Protected Nature Conservation Areas and the Protection of Certain Species in Connection with Offshore Exploration for and Extraction of Hydrocarbons, Underground Storage, Pipelines etc.

31 Transit pipelines that are not connected with hydrocarbon extraction in the Danish continental shelf area are regulated separately.

the environmental impact report in national newspapers, and send the information to the organisations concerned. The published notice must include information about the nature of possible decisions, where the application and the environmental impact report are available for inspection, and the deadline for the submission of opinions (minimum period, eight weeks). Public authorities concerned must be sent the application and the environmental impact report for their opinions.

Annex 2 of the executive order contains a list of the topics which must, as a minimum, be dealt with in the environmental impact report. The report must contain a description of the project, including the physical characteristics of the project and the area that needs to be used during the construction and operational phases, the most important characteristics of the production processes and an estimate of the kinds and quantities of expected waste materials and emissions associated with the operation of the proposed project. In addition, the report must contain an overview of the most relevant alternatives which the developer/applicant has examined, information about the most significant reasons for their choice, having regard to the impact on the environment, including a description of the consequences of the project not being carried out (the zero option), as well as a description of the subsequent construction phases, links with other fields and any coordination of extraction activities. The report must also contain a description of the area and its surroundings which can be significantly affected by the project, including the population, the seabed, the water, fauna, flora, air, landscape and physical properties (raw materials and archaeological status).

For the benefit of the public there must also be a non-technical summary, as well as an overview of any gaps in the information and the assessment of the effects on the environment. The Energy Agency can demand further information to illustrate the impact on the environment; see Article 5(3) of the executive order. There are no special requirements as to the experts who draw up an environmental impact report, but the report must contain a description of those who have been involved in drawing it up.

The purpose of drawing up the environmental impact report is primarily to give the relevant authorities and the general public an acceptable basis for having a view on the project. The environmental impact report and the responses received to the consultation must be included as part of the basis for the authority's decision. The decision on the application for a licence must be published in the same newspapers in which the application and the environmental impact report have been announced.

In line with the Aarhus Convention, under Article 37a of the Subsoil Act, any party having a substantial and individual interest may file an appeal to an administrative body (the Energy Board of Appeal) against decisions concerning an undertaking's plan for production activities and production measures (Article 10), the establishment and operation of pipeline facilities (Article 17) and works that are carried out in connection with activities covered by the Subsoil Act. However, it is a condition of a right to appeal that, in addition to being covered by Articles 10, 17 and 28 of the Subsoil Act, the activities are also covered by the Executive Order on Environmental Impact Assessments. Both local and national associations or organisations whose main purposes are the protection of nature and the environment have the same right to appeal. If a decision affects important recreational interests, both local and national associations or organisations whose main purposes are the care of those interests also have a right to appeal. The deadline for submitting an appeal is four weeks. Under Article 37a of the Subsoil Act, a licence granted under the provisions referred to above may not be put to use before the four-week period for appeals has expired. An appeal does not have suspensive effect unless the Energy Board of Appeal decides otherwise. The board's decision cannot be brought before any higher administrative body, but may be referred to the courts.

As for transit pipelines and pipelines for the transport of hydrocarbons to Denmark from offshore, under Article 6a of the Continental Shelf Act, any party having a substantial and individual interest in a licence for the installation of such may submit an appeal to the Energy Board of Appeal on the environmental circumstances of the licence.

Under Article 30(1) of the Maritime Environment Act[32] the Minister for the Environment may lay down rules on emissions into the sea and other disposal of waste and materials derived from exploration and exploitation of undersea mineral deposits, including hydrocarbons. The minister has issued an executive order on this.[33] The executive order covers platforms and other installations (including drilling rigs) for use in connection with exploration, production drilling and the extraction of undersea mineral deposits, as well as pipelines and other installations to transport such materials, and it contains more detailed provisions on emissions into the sea in connection with exploration and extraction of hydrocarbons. Article 11 of the executive order contains a prohibition of throwing away tools, materials and waste from exploration, production drilling and extraction activities into the sea. Such materials must be collected and sent to land. Article 5 of the executive order states that waste and materials may only be emitted under a permit.[34] The requirement for a permit includes drilling mud and cuttings. The executive order is therefore an exception to the general prohibition of dumping in Article 25(1). In connection with permits for emissions, the environmental interests may be balanced against other interests, including technical and financial considerations and the safety of employees.

(k) Governing law and dispute resolution

Under the licences granted so far, disputes are generally to be resolved in the Danish courts. In Section 40 of the model licence, Copenhagen is given as the forum for litigation. If both parties agree, a dispute can be settled by arbitration. A licence can also incorporate a provision that any disputes between licensor and licensee must be resolved by arbitration.

3.2 Government take

Article 9 of the Subsoil Act contains a general statement that licences granted under

32 Consolidated Act 929 of September 24 2009 on the Protection of the Offshore Environment.

33 Executive Order 394 of July 17 1984 on Emissions into the Sea of Waste and Materials from Certain Offshore Installations.

34 The term 'waste' probably does not include food waste; see Article 23(1) which prohibits the depositing of waste, other than food waste, in the Baltic and the North Sea.

the act shall stipulate the consideration to be paid by the licensee to the state. As non-exhaustive examples it is stated that the consideration may take the form of area rental, royalties on production volumes, or profit-sharing.

Tax laws also contain a number of provisions which generate public revenues from hydrocarbon extraction.

According to estimates for 2011, oil production accounted for a production value of about Dkr48.3 billion and gas production for about Dkr9.9 billion. The Danish state derives direct revenue from North Sea oil and gas production from various taxes and fees. In 2011 the estimated state revenue was about Dkr30.6 billion. The state revenue in 2011 was made up of: corporation tax 32%; hydrocarbon tax 32%; profit sharing 29%; oil pipeline tariff (including a compensatory fee) 7%; and royalty 0%. Shared profit is only derived from the DUC concession.

(a) *Royalties*

There is no provision for the payment of royalties in recent licence agreements. However, Article 9 of the Subsoil Act contains authority to impose a requirement for royalties, and Article 18 contains authority to require any royalty to be paid in the form of extracted hydrocarbons. However, licences issued before January 1 2004 included a demand for the payment of a production tax. Only licences from the second licensing round are subject to a production tax.

A special provision on profit-sharing applies to the DUC concession. From January 1 2004 to July 8 2012, 20% of the taxable income, before tax and net interest payments, was paid to the state. The provision has been replaced by the state taking a 20% share of the ownership.

(b) *Corporation tax*

In 2007 the rate of corporation tax was reduced from 28% to 25%. The revenue from corporation tax is the most important source of revenue from oil and gas.[35] The corporation tax paid is deductible from the hydrocarbon tax base.

(c) *Hydrocarbon tax*

Hydrocarbon tax was introduced in 1982 with the aim of taxing windfall profits, following the rapid increase in oil prices. For licences granted after January 1 2004 the tax is 52% with an allowance of 5% for six years (a total of 30%) for investments. For licences granted before January 1 2004, the hydrocarbon tax was 70% with an allowance of 25% over 10 years (a total of 250%) for investments.

(d) *Oil pipeline tariff /compensatory fee*

There is an oil pipeline between the Gorm field and Fredericia on the eastern coast of Jutland; it is owned by DONG Olierør A/S and is therefore state-owned. Payments to the state included a tariff of 5% of the value of the transported oil. However, this tariff has been abolished with effect from July 8 2012.

---

35 See www.ens.dk/en-US/OilAndGas/Licences/fiscal_regime/Sider/Forside.aspx.

(e) ***Special participation***

All grants of new licences, whether in licensing rounds or by the open door procedure, are conditional on state participation in the form of a 20% share of the ownership. The Danish North Sea Fund and the Danish North Sea Partner were established by Law 587 of June 24 2005. The Danish North Sea Partner is an entity established to administer the Danish North Sea Fund. The fund represents the state's participation in future licences. The fund also holds the state's 20% stake in the DUC.[36]

4. Current issues

The primary Danish extraction area, west of 6°15′ east, must be considered mature. However, there are still parts of the area that have not been intensively explored, and there is currently a debate about the possibilities of finding reserves in Jurassic, Paleogene and Neogene strata. In several locations there has been a fall in production from existing wells. If the Danish installations are to be retained, it is assumed that there must either be increased efficiency of extraction or new sources must be found.

As part of the development and maintenance of Danish hydrocarbon production a new licensing round is planned for areas west of 6°15′ east in 2013, with a view to exploration and extraction of oil and gas, as well as a possible separate licensing round for licences to inject CO2 in existing oil fields west of 6°15′ east, in order to increase extraction. A strategic environmental assessment is currently under public consultation.[37]

In Denmark, onshore licences have been issued for a six-year exploration period for shale gas in North Jutland and Northeast Zealand. In both areas Total E&P Denmark BV is the licensee (80%) together with the North Sea Fund (20%). There is an alum shale formation at a depth of about 4km.

Some of the installations in the Danish sector of the North Sea are now so old that their decommissioning must be considered. A disused offshore installation can be dealt with in three ways: it can be left standing, it can be dumped, or it can be taken back to land. All three solutions, or combinations of these solutions, involve a number of risks, among other things in relation to maritime traffic, the maritime environment and the working environment. Offshore installations are often so big that scrapping them on land can be quite expensive.[38]

In both the Danish state's model licence for the open door procedure and the model licence for the sixth licensing round, Section 37(6) contains a provision on the removal of disused installations. According to this, the Energy Agency can require the licensee to remove, in whole or in part, all installations whether they belong to the licensee or to others, in accordance with a winding-up plan drawn up by the Energy Agency. There have typically been conditions requiring the removal of

---

36 See www.ens.dk/en-US/OilAndGas/Licences/state_participation/Sider/Forside.aspx

37 Denmark is obliged to carry out a strategic environmental assessment under EU Directive 2001/42/EC of June 27 2001 on the Assessment of the Effects of Certain Plans and Programmes on the Environment.

38 In the Danish sector of the North Sea, offshore installations are typically made of steel. The sub-sea structure (the jacket) can weigh up to 4,000 tons. See Bent Ole Gram Mortensen and Anita Rønne, "Olie- og naturgasindvinding", in EM Basse (ed), *Miljøretten*, Volume 6, *Energi og klima*, Jurist- og Økonomforbundets Forlag, 2008, p 194.

offshore installations in previous licences and permits. Given the size and positioning of the Danish offshore installations, they must all be assumed to be covered by the International Maritime Organisation (IMO) guidelines and standards for the removal of offshore installations. However, these rules do not cover pipelines. The law is unclear with regard to the removal of pipelines.

Under the Executive Order on Environmental Impact Assessments of Projects for Extracting Hydrocarbons and the Establishment of Pipelines in Danish Territorial Waters and the Continental Shelf Area, environmental impact reports for projects for which such reports are obligatory must include a description of how the installation can be removed.

Neither the model licence nor the legislation contains precise provisions on methods of disposal. This means that they do not contain prohibitions of dumping disused installations. However, the dumping of an installation requires the permission of the Energy Agency. So far such permission has not been given. Alternatively, when a licence comes to an end by expiry, lapse, surrender or revocation, the state can choose to take over, without payment, either the whole of the area in question or part of it, the installations and equipment that are intended for longer-term use, as well as necessary equipment and materials such as logbooks and manuals.

The Danish rules largely reflect Denmark's obligations under Annex III, Article 5, to the OSPAR Convention, under which disused offshore installations or pipelines may only be left in offshore areas with the specific permission of the competent national authority. Such permission may not be given if the disused offshore installation or offshore pipeline contains substances which result or are likely to result in hazards to human health, harm to living resources and marine ecosystems, damage to amenities or interference with other legitimate uses of the sea. The Convention does not actually prohibit dumping, but its Annex III, Article 2, requires the application of the principles of the best available techniques (BAT), best environmental practice (BEP) and where appropriate, clean technology. Moreover, Denmark is bound by the Convention on the Continental Shelf, Article 5(5) of which requires any installations that are abandoned or disused to be entirely removed. Likewise, Article 60(3) of the UN Convention on the Law of the Sea requires any installations or structures which are abandoned or disused to be removed to ensure safety of navigation, taking into account any generally accepted international standards. The IMO guidelines and standards for the removal of offshore installations leave it to the individual member country to make the concrete evaluation, but it does list a number of considerations that should be taken into account in the assessment. These include the risk of pollution and the potential danger to the maritime environment in general. However, installations with a jacket weight of less than 4,000 tons standing in less than 75m of water (installed prior to January 1 1998) or 100m of water (installed after January 1 1998) must be completely removed.

5. Conclusion

In general, the Danish legislation on the exploitation of oil and natural gas resources is based on four pillars. The state is an owner of the resources, the administrator of licensing, the taxing authority and a part-owner of concessions.

Over the years, Danish regulation and exploitation of hydrocarbons has been affected by the fact that back in 1962 a 50-year sole concession was granted for the whole of Denmark's undersea area. Danish regulation is also influenced by the frameworks laid down by EU law and international conventions.

If Danish production is to be maintained, this will require investments in new fields and increased exploitation of existing fields.

Greenland

Bent Ole Gram Mortensen
Department of Law, University of Southern Denmark

1. Introduction

In recent years there has been a growing interest in exploration for hydrocarbons (oil and natural gas) in the waters around Greenland.[1] Exploration for Greenland's offshore oil and natural gas resources began in the 1970s, though this came to an end relatively soon (in 1978). Exploration was renewed in the 1990s with seismic research, and licences were granted in the course of the 2000s.[2] So far the current exploration has not made any major finds, but there are great expectations. It is assumed, but not yet confirmed, that there are significant oil and natural gas resources offshore from both northeast and northwest Greenland. The United States Geological Survey (USGS) estimates that there are reserves of about 7.3 billion barrels of oil and 52 billion cubic feet of natural gas offshore between northwest Greenland and northeast Canada.[3] The USGS estimates that there is oil and natural gas equivalent to 31.4 billion barrels of oil offshore from northeast Greenland.[4]

Greenland is a former Danish colony which is now part of the Danish Realm, together with Denmark and the Faeroe Islands. Greenland obtained a measure of self-government in 1979,[5] and since June 21 2009 it has had a more extensive degree of self-government in relation to the Danish Realm. Under the Act on Greenland Self-Government,[6] Greenland has a classic separation of powers, with courts which have judicial powers, a Parliament with legislative powers, and a government with executive powers.

A number of policy areas have now been transferred to the Greenland government authorities. The Act on Greenland Self-Government determines which matters fall within the jurisdiction of the self-government authorities and which fall within the jurisdiction of the Danish Realm (effectively Denmark). The act also lays down which matters can and shall be taken over by the self-government authorities. This includes the mineral resources sector; see List II, Point 26, of the Schedule to the Act on Greenland Self-Government. The mineral resources sector was taken over by

1 In Greenland there is offshore exploration for hydrocarbons. There is no current expectation of finding hydrocarbon resources on land, and there is no current exploration for hydrocarbons on land.

2 See Martha M Roggenkamp, Cathrine Redgwell, Iñigo del Guayo and Anita Rønne, *Energy Law in Europe*, Second Edition, 2007, p 447.

3 See USGS, *Assessment of Undiscovered Oil and Gas Resources of the West Greenland–East Canada Province*, 2008: pubs.usgs.gov/fs/2008/3014/pdf/FS08-3014_508.pdf.

4 See USGS, *Assessment of Undiscovered Oil and Gas Resources of the East Greenland Rift Basins Province:* pubs.usgs.gov/fs/2007/3077/pdf/FS07-3077_508.pdf.

5 Self-government was introduced by Act 577 of November 29 1978 on Greenland Self-Government.

6 Act 473 of June 12 2009 on Greenland Self-Government.

the self-government authorities from January 1 2010.[7] The act also determines the amount of economic support given by Denmark to Greenland. In connection with Greenland's revenues from the mineral resources sector, if the revenue accruing to the self-government authorities from mineral resource activities in Greenland exceeds a given amount, the Danish government's subsidy to Greenland will be reduced and there will be negotiations on the distribution of revenue from mineral resource activities in Greenland; see Articles 8 and 10 of the Act on Greenland Self-Government.

Greenland has about 57,000 inhabitants and a land area of 2,180,000 square kilometres (km^2). This gives a population density of 0.025 persons per km^2. Greenland lies in the North American continent, northeast of Canada. The territory is in the polar zone and about 80% of it is covered by an ice sheet. Sea ice also characterises the coastal areas.

The economic potential of oil and other mineral resources has major political implications for Greenland society. It can contribute the necessary basis for Greenland's further independence from the Danish Realm. Revenues from oil and other mineral resources could make the aid which Greenland currently receives from the Realm superfluous. This is clearly apparent in the legislative history of the current legislation on Greenland's self-government, and Article 21 of the Act on Greenland Self-Government concerns Greenland's access to full independence.[8]

> *The development of the mineral resource area in Greenland constitutes a potentially significant element in the future industrial development in Greenland and in the creation of revenue capable of replacing in whole or in part the Danish Government's subsidy, thus helping to make Greenland more economically self-sustaining.*[9]

2. Upstream activities

For the time being, there is no extraction of oil or natural gas in Greenland. It is expected that the commercial exploitation of oil and natural gas still lies some years in the future. Meanwhile, a number of exploration licences have been issued for the offshore areas west and south of Greenland. As of October 1 2012 there were 20 current (exclusive) exploration and exploitation licences and 27 (non-exclusive) prospecting licences.[10] These licences cover more than 200,000 km^2. The licences have mostly been granted to a number of international operators.

---

7 There is a list of the areas taken over at: www.stm.dk/multimedia/GR_oversigt_sagsomr_270110.pdf.

8 In connection with its ratification of the International Labour Organisation (ILO) Convention 169 of June 28 1989 Concerning Indigenous and Tribal Peoples in Independent Countries, the Danish government declared the indigenous people of Greenland (Inuit) to be an indigenous people within the meaning of the convention: see Danish Executive Order 97 of October 9 1997 on ILO Convention 169 of June 28 1989 Concerning Indigenous and Tribal Peoples in Independent Countries. In a decision of November 28 2003 (Cases 489/1999 and 490/1999) the Danish Supreme Court ruled that the Thule people in northwest Greenland were not an indigenous people pursuant ILO Convention 169 distinct from or separate from the Greenlandic people as a whole, and thus did not have independent rights under the convention. Only the Greenlandic people as a whole have such rights. This view is problematic and has been criticised; see, for example, the Inuit Circumpolar Council (ICC): *Universal Periodic Review – Denmark 2011*. Joint Submission – Greenland NGOs, November 6 2010.

9 The explanatory notes on the Act on Greenland Self-Government, Section 5.3.3 of the general notes.

10 According to a list on the Bureau of Minerals and Petroleum (BMP) website; see www.bmp.gl/images/stories/minerals/list_of_licences/list_of_licences.pdf.

Bidding rounds for licences have been held in 2002, 2004, 2006 and 2010. There will be a new bidding round in 2012/2013 for the Kanumas Project. The project involves an area of 50,000 km^2 offshore from northeast Greenland (the Greenland Sea). What is special about this project is that a prospecting licence for the area was previously given to a group called the Kanumas Group, consisting of Exxon, Statoil, BP, Japan National Oil Corporation, Texaco, Shell and NUNAOIL. The bidding round consists of two phases, a pre-licensing round and an ordinary round. Only members of the Kanumas Group could take part in the first round, with a bidding deadline of December 15 2012. Any party may take part in the second round. The deadline for pre-qualification applications for the second round is July 1 2013 and that for licence applications is October 15 2013.

A number of exploration wells were sunk in 2011, and these found signs of both oil and natural gas. However, these findings have not resulted in specific plans for extraction.[11] Seismic research has been undertaken in several locations in the course of 2012.

3. Petroleum legal regime

Greenland is covered by a number of international conventions. These establish certain frameworks for regulating the exploitation of hydrocarbons. The most significant of these are briefly discussed below.

Denmark has ratified the United Nations Convention on the Law of the Sea (UNCLOS) on behalf of the Danish Realm. Greenland is thus also covered. What is of particular interest is that coastal states exercise sovereign rights over the continental shelf for the purpose of exploiting its natural resources; see Article 77 of the convention. If the continental shelf extends beyond 200 nautical miles, a coastal state's rights also cover the area up to a maximum of 350 nautical miles from the baseline. In the case of Greenland, three areas are of interest with regard to rights extending beyond 200 nautical miles. These are the areas south, north and northeast of Greenland. Altogether, these three areas cover about 328,000 km^2. Under Annex II, Article 4, of UNCLOS, a claim extending rights beyond 200 nautical miles must be submitted within 10 years of ratification of the convention. Denmark ratified the Convention on behalf of the Realm on November 16 2004, so that claims must be made by 2014. On June 14 2012, the Danish government and the Greenland government authorities submitted scientific documentation for the area south of Greenland to the UN Commission on the Limits of the Continental Shelf (CLCS). The processing of the claim can take up to two years, and the final determination of the extension is complicated by the fact that the claim overlaps possible claims by Iceland and Canada. It should be noted that it is not the job of the CLCS to determine where the boundary lies when two or more countries have overlapping claims.

The Convention on Environmental Impact Assessment in a Transboundary Context (the 'Espoo Convention') was signed by Denmark on the February 26 1991. Upon signature, the Danish government made a reservation concerning the

11 See BMP, *Report to Inatsisartut on mineral resource activities in Greenland*, 2012, p 18.

application of the convention to the Faeroe Islands and Greenland. However, Greenland is now part of the convention, as the secretary-general received a communication from the Danish government on December 12 2001 declaring that the convention applied to Greenland as from March 14 1997. The Protocol to the Espoo Convention on Strategic Environmental Assessment (the 'SEA Protocol') was signed by Denmark on May 21 2003.[12] Upon signature, Denmark made a reservation regarding the Faroe Islands and Greenland, as their environmental affairs were governed by the right of self-determination. This declaration implies a territorial exclusion, and until further notice the SEA Protocol does not apply to Greenland.[13] This may change in the near future as the Prime Minister of Greenland, Kuupik Kleist, is reported to have said in June 2010 that Greenland would now consent to the SEA Protocol.[14]

On behalf of the Danish Realm, Denmark has also ratified the OSPAR Convention (the Convention for the Protection of the Marine Environment of the North-East Atlantic) against pollution from sources on land or by dumping by ships or aircraft. The OSPAR Convention is relevant to the eastern part of Greenland.

The members of the Danish Realm are members of the Arctic Council.[15] In this connection the Protection of the Arctic Marine Environment Working Group (PAME) has developed a set of minimum requirements for the protection of the marine environment in connection with oil extraction,[16] and these apply in Greenland.

Denmark has ratified the Climate Change Convention and later the Kyoto Protocol on behalf of the Realm, thus including Greenland. In particular the Kyoto Protocol's quota system has been criticised. The quotas are based on a reference year (1990) when Greenland did not have much industry. The quota system has thus been seen as distorting competition and being a possible barrier to the building up of Greenland's industries, in particular in the mineral extraction sector.[17] In 2012, Denmark and Greenland entered into an agreement giving Greenland a greater degree of autonomy in determining its climate policies. The agreement was entered into pursuant to Article 13 of the Act on Greenland Self-Government, which deals with the involvement of the Greenland government authorities in negotiations regarding agreements under international law which are of particular importance to Greenland. In effect, this means that for future international climate agreements, including extensions of the Kyoto Protocol, Denmark will presumably make a reservation excluding Greenland from an agreement, unless Greenland itself agrees to be party to it.

Greenland is not a member of the European Union. Denmark became a member of the then European Communities from January 1 1973. As part of the Danish

---

12 Since Greenland forms a part of the Danish Realm, relevant conventions and protocols must be endorsed by Denmark with a remark on the inclusion or exclusion of Greenland.

13 The declaration can be found at: treaties.un.org/Pages/ViewDetails.aspx?src=TREATY&mtdsg_no=XXVII-4-b&chapter=27&lang=en#EndDec.

14 Anne Merrild Hansen, *SEA effectiveness and power in decision-making – A case study of aluminum production in Greenland*, Doctoral Thesis, November 2010, pp 29–30.

15 www.arctic-council.org.

16 Arctic Offshore Oil and Gas Guidelines (2009). These are available on the BMP website: www.bmp.gl/petroleum/environment/international-reference-docs.

17 On Greenland and climate change and the relationship to the Kyoto Protocol, see Per Vestergaard Pedersen, "Regulating of Climate Matters in Greenland", *Carbon & Climate Law Review* 2012, pp 47–62.

Realm, Greenland also became a member of the EC. After the introduction of Greenland's self-government in 1979 and a consultative referendum, Greenland decided to leave the European Communities with effect from February 1 1985. Greenland is therefore not bound to follow EU legislation.[18] However, Greenland has a special fisheries agreement with the EU, and has entered into a special association agreement with the EU pursuant to Article 204 of the Treaty on the Functioning of the European Union.[19]

3.1 Petroleum law and relevant provisions

The exploitation of hydrocarbons in Greenland is governed by the Mineral Resources Act.[20] Under Article 2(1) of this act, the government of Greenland has the right to use and to exploit hydrocarbons (and other mineral resources) in the subsoil in Greenland (and offshore).

Under its Article 9(1), the act extends to the territory and territorial waters and the continental shelf area and the exclusive economic zone off Greenland. Thus the act governs the extraction of raw materials wherever Greenland exercises sovereignty or administers sovereignty on behalf of the Danish Realm.

In general, Greenland's legislation on the exploitation of raw materials is based on internationally recognised principles. There is thus legislation on licensing based on a set of licences, environmental impact assessments and standards. Among others things, Greenland looks to the Norwegian NORSOK (*Norsk Sokkels Konkuranseposisjon*) standards,[21] which are in turn based on international standards.

(a) Regulatory bodies

The Greenland Bureau of Minerals and Petroleum (BMP) is the responsible and competent authority with regard to raw materials and the subsoil in Greenland, including all matters relating to mineral raw materials, the exploitation of the subsoil and related energy activities. The BMP is an agency under the Greenland Ministry for Industry and Mineral Resources. It was established in 1998.

The BMP applies the one-stop-shop principle; applicants only need go to one agency (the BMP), which applies a single, integrated regulatory process, involving other authorities to the extent necessary. The one-stop-shop principle was introduced in 1991 on the recommendation of a politically appointed strategy group, which considered that the overall advantages of the principle outweighed the potential disadvantages.[22] The same solutions are seen in other parts of the world. Investors (oil companies) generally favour this principle, expecting it to reduce the time and uncertainty connected with obtaining the necessary permits.

---

18 Greenland is thus not bound by Directive 94/22/EC of the European Parliament and of the Council of 30 May 1994 on the conditions for granting and using authorisations for the prospection, exploration and production of hydrocarbons (the Hydrocarbons Licensing Directive).

19 Formerly Article 188 of the Treaty on the Establishment of the European Community.

20 Greenland Parliament Act 7 of December 7 2009, on mineral resources and mineral resource activities came into force on January 1 2010.

21 On NORSOK, see www.standard.no/petroleum.

22 Hans Ølgaard, *Strategigruppen vedrørende Mineralske Råstoffer i Greenland* (the Strategy Group regarding Mineral Resources in Greenland), Report of May 23 1990.

However, the BMP is expected to involve the general administrative authorities in consultations and coordinated supervision so that the overriding policies in the area are respected. On this front, general environmental and technical approvals and the authorities' handling of raw material activities must be carried out by personnel that have experience and knowledge of such matters, including the Danish Centre for Environment and Energy (DCE)[23] and the Geological Survey of Denmark and Greenland (GEUS).

The Mineral Resources Act was recently revised,[24] giving the Environmental Agency increased influence over environmental issues in connection with mineral extraction. Further, administrative complaints are now possible.

(b) Types of agreement

Rights connected with the exploration for and extraction of minerals in Greenland are based on a licence system which in turn is based on a number of specific licences with associated conditions. The Mineral Resources Act has separate rules for hydrocarbon licences[25] and for other mineral licences.[26]

Under Article 2(2)(1) of the Mineral Resources Act, prospecting, exploration and exploitation of mineral resources in Greenland may be performed only under a licence granted by the Greenland government.[27] This takes the initial form of a prospecting licence (Article 15 of the Mineral Resources Act) and subsequently a licence for exploration and exploitation (Articles 16 to 21 of the Mineral Resources Act). There can also be a special subsoil licence pursuant to Articles 39 to 41 of the Mineral Resources Act.

Prospecting licence: A prospecting licence typically covers initial exploration of a limited area. The aim of prospecting will typically be to obtain sufficient knowledge as to whether full exploration should be carried out. The licence is granted by the Greenland government. A prospecting licence does not give an exclusive right, and prospecting licences can be granted to others in respect of the same area.

Exploration and exploitation licence: The Greenland government can grant exclusive rights for exploration and exploitation of a defined area. Separate licences can also be given for exploration or exploitation. Exploration activities are typically more detailed, for example including geological, geochemical and geophysical investigations, as well as drilling.[28] A licence can lay down conditions concerning the licensee's obligation to carry out certain work, as well as a gradual reduction of the area covered by the licence. A licence for exploitation can only be granted to a company that is not jointly taxed with another company. The company may not have thinner capitalisation than the corporate group of which it is part, and the ratio

23 DCE is part of Aarhus University. Formerly Danmarks Miljøundersøgelser.
24 Act 26/2012.
25 Chapter 6, Articles 22–28, of the Mineral Resources Act.
26 Chapter 7, Articles 29–31, of the Mineral Resources Act.
27 However, a licence is not required if the activity is covered by Articles 45–48 on non-commercial extraction by a person who is a permanent resident of and fully liable to pay tax in Greenland.
28 Article 16(1) in the explanatory notes of November 1 2009 on the Mineral Resources Act.

loan capital to equity capital may not exceed 2:1. During the term of a licence the licensee may not be subject to financial difficulties such as entering into a reconstruction, insolvency or a similar situation. In principle the company must be based in Greenland and trade at arms length prices and on arms length terms. Moreover, licensees must have the necessary professional skills and financial basis for exploitation activities, which will vary according to the extent, complexity and risks of the activities.[29]

Subsoil licence: When granting a licence for prospecting, exploration or exploitation of hydrocarbons the Greenland government may also grant a subsoil licence. A subsoil licence applies to the injection of materials in the subsoil in connection with the exploration for and extraction of hydrocarbons.[30] A subsoil licence applies for a defined area on fixed conditions for a period of up to 50 years. However, the licence can be extended in special circumstances. Finally, under Article 41 of the act, the Greenland government may lay down specific provisions on subsoil licences. In principle it is expected that the individual activity will be exhaustively regulated by the licence which the licensee must have prior to starting activities. However, it can be appropriate to lay down general provisions for the sector.[31]

(c) Acquisition of acreage

Under Article 23 of the Mineral Resources Act, there are two procedures for granting licences in connection with hydrocarbons: a licensing round and an open door procedure.

Bidding in a licensing round is used for areas in which it is reckoned that there is a good probability of finding hydrocarbon deposits, while the open door procedure is intended for areas where there is greater uncertainty about the existence of hydrocarbons and thus less competition for licences. Bidding can take place in licensing rounds which must follow a public invitation to apply for licences. There is a distinction between bidding for areas where the Kanumas Group[32] has priority and 'normal' areas. For example, in licensing rounds for certain areas northeast of Greenland in 2012 – 2013,[33] a preliminary bidding round was held exclusively for Kanumas companies.

With the open door procedure, the Greenland government may determine that for a specified period a specified area must be open for the granting of licences. Applications for licences for a given area under the open door procedure can be submitted 90 days after the publication of the notice at the earliest.

For hydrocarbon licences, under Article 23(5) of the Mineral Resources Act, if

---

29 Article 16(3) in the explanatory notes of November 1 2009 on the Mineral Resources Act.

30 A subsoil licence need not relate to the exploitation of minerals but could, for example, be connected with storing something underground.

31 Article 41 in the explanatory notes of November 1 2009 on the Mineral Resources Act.

32 The Kanumas Project is a consortium of Exxon, Statoil, BP, Japan National Oil Corporation (JNOC), Texaco, Shell and NUNAOIL. The project was set up in 1989 as a long-term investment in promoting oil activities in Greenland. The participants had an obligation to carry out exploration activities and were therefore given priority in licensing rounds.

33 www.bmp.gl/petroleum/exploration-a-exploitation/licensing-round-2012-13.

warranted by geological or exploitation-related considerations the Greenland government may grant a licence under a neighbouring block procedure. Thus the Greenland government can dispense with licensing rounds or the open door procedure and instead grant a licence to the holder of the rights for a neighbouring area. The Greenland government sends all licensees with licences for neighbouring areas a notice of the neighbouring block procedure with information on the application procedure and the possibility of applying.

(d) Qualification requirements

With regard to hydrocarbon licences, Article 24(2) to (5) of the Mineral Resources Act stipulates four criteria by which an application is assessed. If two or more applicants fulfil the criteria equally, the Greenland government may stipulate further qualification criteria. The first criterion is the applicant's previous experience in exploration or exploitation of hydrocarbons, particularly in areas with similar climatic conditions. The second criterion is the applicant's financial background, where the ability to bear the major costs associated with the exploration and exploitation of hydrocarbons is important. The third criterion is the applicant's systems and procedures for safety, health and the environment, as well as their willingness and ability to perform a thorough exploration for hydrocarbons in the area covered by the application. As the last criterion, any non-efficiency or non-performance of obligations in connection with the applicant's previous licences in Greenland can have a negative influence on an application; see Article 24(5) of the Act.[34] Invitations to tender must set out these criteria and their relative weighting.[35]

(e) Duration

A prospecting licence is granted for a period of five years, with the possibility of an extension.

For hydrocarbons, combined licences for both exploration and exploitation are granted for a period of 10 years; see Article 22(1) of the Mineral Resources Act. In special circumstances a licence can be extended up to 16 years without there being exploitation. Such special circumstances can be climatic or other challenges of nature. A licence can be extended for three years at a time, which can be especially relevant for ensuring that ongoing exploration can be continued with a view to assessing whether finds of hydrocarbons or minerals are commercially viable. If finds of hydrocarbons or minerals are commercially viable, a licence can be extended up to a period of 30 years; see Article 22(2) of the Act, which gives the licensee a right to extend a licence for exploitation as long as the conditions in Article 22(1) are fulfilled. If justified by special circumstances, the Greenland government may extend a licence for up to no more than a total of 50 years; see Article 16(5). A licence may be granted on condition that the licensee submits a plan of their activities; see Article 19.

---

34 Nothing is said about whether previous positive experience with an applicant has any influence.

35 With the licensing round in April 2008 (invitation to apply for licences for hydrocarbon exploration and exploitation under the open door procedure), the primary selection criteria were professional capacities, financial basis, and the applicant's willingness and ability to undertake a thorough exploration, whereas the applicant's contribution to environmental impact assessments was a secondary consideration.

(f) ***Minimum work programme***

An exploration and exploitation licence stipulates which specific exploration measures the licensee must carry out. The model licences under both open door procedures and bidding for the Kanumas Project (2012–2013) state that the licensee must carry out the following:

- In the first phase there must be an appropriate seismic survey of the whole of the licensed area, corresponding to a stated number of kilometre lines.
- In the second phase the licensee must sink a predetermined number of exploration wells of a given depth. The date by which spudding of wells must begin is stipulated.
- In the third phase the licensee must take core samples, mineral samples and carry out test production, and otherwise act in accordance with the guidelines laid down by the BMP for the approval of each drilling programme. A thorough analysis and interpretation of the data gathered must be carried out.

(g) ***Assignment and encumbrance***

Under Article 88 of the Mineral Resources Act, any direct or indirect transfer to a third party of a licence granted under the act requires approval by the Greenland government. Licences granted under the Mineral Resources Act are exempt from legal proceedings by creditors.

(h) ***Local content***

Article 18 of the Mineral Resources Act provides that a licence for exploration and/or exploitation may lay down the extent to which the licensee must use labour from Greenland, must use Greenlandic enterprises for contracts, supplies and services, and must be socially sustainable. The provision is a key part of the strategy for the mineral extraction industry to contribute to Greenlandic society, as is made clear in a report to the Greenland government in 2011:

> *The development of the mineral extractions sector must be undertaken in such a way as to be of the greatest possible benefit to Greenlandic society. Society must be ensured the highest possible competitive share of the profits from extractions, and it must likewise be ensured that there is local insight into and knowledge about these activities, among other things to ensure that local labour and local undertakings are used to the greatest possible extent.*[36] (Unofficial translation)

Article 21 of the model licence for hydrocarbons contains a special provision requiring the licensee, as a point of departure, to employ manpower from Greenland or Denmark in carrying out activities under a licence. However, this does not apply if qualified manpower does not exist or is not available in Greenland or Denmark. The licensee must also, as a point of departure, use Greenlandic contractors and subcontractors, suppliers and service providers, unless Greenlandic enterprises are

36 BMP, *Report to Inatsisartut on mineral resource activities in Greenland*, February 2011, p 8 dk.nanoq.gl/Emner/Landsstyre/Departementer/R%C3%A5stofdirektoratet/Udgivelser/~/media/0A9A0A70B30340228462742C07E06758.ashx.

not technically or commercially competitive.[37]

In connection with an actual licence, an impact benefit agreement has been entered into between the government of Greenland, local municipalities and the licensee.[38] In this case a benefit and impact plan, a monitoring plan and an evaluation plan have been adopted. Thus an impact benefit agreement for a drilling programme for the summer of 2010 covered four oil exploration wells.[39] The agreement was entered into between the government authorities, three Greenlandic municipalities and the licensee, Cairn Energy. The agreement contained measures such as the involvement of Greenlandic undertakings as direct subcontractors, the holding of seminars for potential new suppliers, and the appointment of Greenlandic labour through Arctic Base Supply and Cairn. The licensee's obligations appear to be vague, and there is a question about how far they can be enforced. There are no penalties attached to these provisions.

The impact benefit agreement model is not referred to in the explanatory notes to the Mineral Resources Act for the oil and gas sector. The model has some connection with Article 76 of the Mineral Resources Act, according to which if an activity covered by the act must be assumed to have significant impact on social conditions, a licence for the activity can be granted only when a social sustainability assessment (effectively a social impact assessment) has been made of the performance of the activity. The Greenland government may decide whether an social sustainability assessment is to be undertaken, can lay down the criteria to be used for the decision, and can approve the assessment report as a whole. The social sustainability assessment is drawn up by the applicant, involving public authorities and the BMP in the process. The underlying purpose of the social sustainability assessment report is not stated in the act or in the explanatory notes to the act. However, there are guidelines for the mining sector.[40] These guidelines state the underlying purposes, including recruiting Greenlandic labour and engaging Greenlandic enterprises. These aims apply to oil and natural gas extraction.

(i) *National reservation*

Since the introduction of self-government, the Greenland government has been the sole owner of the company NUNAOIL A/S, which was set up in 1984.[41] Today, the company is a non-operating oil company which is custodian of the Greenland government's ownership shares of licences.

Article 17(2) of the Mineral Resources Act allows a licence to prescribe that a company owned or controlled by the Greenland government will be entitled to participate in the licence. It is established practice that there is a requirement for NUNAOIL to have a share of exploration and exploitation licences. In the model licence, both for the latest Kanumas Project (the 2012/13 licensing round)[42] and for

---

37 Greenlandic undertakings are understood as meaning undertakings which have their registered office in Greenland and which, through their commercial activities in Greenland, have a genuine connection with Greenlandic society.

38 There is a model impact benefit agreement available at bmp.gl/minerals/terms-rules-laws-guidelines.

39 BMP, *Report to Inatsisartut on mineral resource activities in Greenland, Spring 2011*, p 25.

40 BMP, *Guidelines for Social Impact Assessments for mining projects in Greenland,* November 2009.

41 Set up under Danish Act 595 of December 12 1984.

open door licences,[43] NUNAOIL is to participate in the licence with a share determined in advance. Hitherto, this share has been between 8% and 12.5%.[44] This practice is expected to continue.[45]

NUNAOIL has a kind of risk-free option, during the exploration period. Article 12.02 of the model licence provides that:

NUNAOIL shall have the rights and obligations attaching to the exploration licence in proportion to its percentage share, but NUNAOIL's share of costs, expenses, obligations and liability in damages regarding activities performed under the exploration licence, including expenses for the fulfilment of obligations and terms stipulated in the exploration licence or pursuant to the exploration licence, shall be borne solely by the other parties participating in the exploration licence ('a carried interest') unless NUNAOIL is not carried under the joint operating agreement.

There are expectations that, over time, NUNAOIL will develop into an active operator on the Norwegian model (Statoil).[46]

The model licence also states that, at the request of NUNAOIL, the other companies holding shares in an exploitation licence must buy all or part of NUNAOIL's share of the hydrocarbons produced. Such a request must be made with at least six months' notice. The hydrocarbons must be bought 'at a fair market price and on usual terms of delivery'.

(j) Environment

The Arctic environment may make the environmental consequences of certain activities much more severe than they would be in more temperate climates. The Arctic environment is vulnerable and must be treated with special care. The different stages of the operation will affect their surroundings. The environmental effects of exploration and extraction thus justify a requirement for carrying out environmental impact assessments, and there are restrictions for special sensitive areas of nature conservation.

Article 83 of the Mineral Resources Act states that: "Activities covered by licences granted under the Greenland Parliament Act must be performed in accordance with acknowledged best international practices in the area under similar conditions." It further states that: "Activities must be performed appropriately as well as in a sound manner as regards safety, health, the environment, resource utilisation and social sustainability". Article 83 repeats what is already stated in Article 1(2) of the Mineral Resources Act. "Best international practices" must be considered a dynamic standard. As well as the explanatory notes to the Mineral Resources Act,[47] the Guidelines for

---

42 See the model licence for the Kanumas Project at www.bmp.gl/petroleum/exploration-a-exploitation/licensing-round-2012-13.

43 See Article 12 of the model licence. (bmp.gl/images/stories/petroleum/exploration_exploitation/opendoor/model_licence_open_door_2010_uk.pdf).

44 See Per Vestergaard Pedersen, Minerals and Mining, Globe Business Publishing Ltd, 2012, p 109. See also www.transportkommissionen.gl/LinkClick.aspx?fileticket=iyjHfpdL2Ws%3D&tabid=61&language=da-DK.

45 See Article 17(2) in the explanatory notes of November 1 2009 on the Mineral Resources Act.

46 BMP, *Report to Inatsisartut on mineral resource activities in Greenland*, 2012, pp 23–24.

47 In the legal tradition followed in Greenland, explanatory notes are not legally binding but are generally an important element in the interpretation of legislation.

Environmental Impact Assessment refer to generally acknowledged principles such as "as low as reasonably practicable",[48] "best available techniques" and "best environmental practice". The use of such standards means it is always possible to adjust the standards to the latest techniques, but it also leaves a lot of discretion in the hands of the BMP in applying such standards.

Environmental impact assessments (EIAs) are regulated in Articles 73 to 75 of the Mineral Resources Act. An EIA is mandatory for exploitation. The approval of an activity subject to an EIA and a licence for exploitation will not be issued until an EIA has been made and approved. Since 2007 the Greenland government has had the authority to lay down rules, pursuant to an executive order, for EIAs for large facilities.[49] The EIA Executive Order is inspired by EU Council Directive 85/337/EEC of 27 June 1985 on the assessment of the effects of certain public and private projects on the environment, which includes mining operations. The purpose of an EIA is to make the BMP and the mining company aware of specific environmental concerns at an early stage of a project. However, the EIA is not in itself binding, and the BMP may decide contrary to the conclusions in the EIA. Further, an EIA is required before the grant of an exploitation licence but not before the grant of an exploration licence, even though an exploration licence may be the first step towards exploitation.

Article 74 of the Mineral Resources Act requires the EIA to be made by the applicant. The EIA must be based on the BMP's Guidelines for Preparing an Environmental Impact Assessment.[50] According to the guidelines, a detailed plan for the EIA process, "including plans for environmental studies (baseline studies and project related studies as described below), must be forwarded to and approved by the BMP prior to the start of the EIA process." The findings are included in an EIA report.

Among other things, the EIA report must include:

- an extended, non-technical summary;
- an introduction, which describes the project, its background and objectives;
- a thorough description of the state of the environment before mine start;
- a description of the mine project with all phases from exploration to closure and beyond;
- an assessment of environmental impacts of the project with an evaluation of alternatives compared to the preferred option;
- an environmental management plan, which describes how the identified impacts are dealt with;
- an environmental monitoring plan with a description of, for instance, species, stations and parameters to be monitored.

The executive order leaves a lot to the discretion of the BMP. However, certain issues are mandatory in an EIA. These include:

48 Meaning that the residual risk must be as low as reasonably practicable.
49 See Executive Order 8 of November 15 2007.
50 The latest, second, edition is from January 2011.

- habitat disturbance (most critical in areas important to wildlife);
- pollution;
- CO^2 emissions;
- existing area use (fishing, hunting, tourism and so on);
- archaeology.

Further, the guidelines state that the:

public should be involved throughout the EIA process and informed about the activities when the mine is in production. A public consultation meeting at an early stage of the process for input to the EIA report is recommended as a minimum.

The Aarhus Convention does not apply in Greenland. Under Article 75 of the Mineral Resources Act, information about the submission of an EIA report must be published on the Greenland government's website or in some other suitable manner. In general it does not seem that much public involvement is ensured, and it is not possible to appeal to any administrative authority against a decision following an EIA report. It is therefore necessary to rely on the courts, which may not be easy for all affected parties in Greenlandic society. If the aim is public involvement, the implementation of the Aarhus Convention could help, but the Aarhus Convention is not even mentioned in the explanatory notes to the act.

According to Article 74(2) of the Mineral Resources Act, the Greenland government (through the BMP) may decide that additional material must be provided for an EIA, or that the party responsible for the EIA must make additional studies or assessments of specific conditions that are important to the EIA.

Because of the one-stop-shop principle mentioned above, environmental issues connected with oil and gas operations are not dealt with by the Ministry of Domestic Affairs, Nature and Environment, which otherwise normally deals with environmental protection and nature conservation. The Mineral Resources Act has its own regulations on environmental issues, including environmental protection, climate protection, nature conservation, liability and environmental impact assessments. Environmental protection may rely on the environmental powers vested in the BMP and its decisions, which is not regulated.

There is no formal legislation on strategic environmental impact assessments in Greenland. The Danish legislation on such assessments[51] does not apply in Greenland as explicitly stated in its Article 18. However a strategic environmental impact assessment is prepared prior to the opening up of new areas for exploitation.[52] Such assessments and related research on hydrocarbon exploration are carried out in cooperation between the Greenland Institute of Natural Resources, the BMP and the Danish Centre for Environment and Energy (DCE).[53] In the absence of Greenlandic legislation on strategic environmental impact assessments, these reports are mainly

51 Executive Order 936 of September 24 2009 on the Law on Environmental Assessments of Plans and Programmes.

52 www.bmp.gl/petroleum/environment/environmental-regulation.

53 Until July 1 2011 DCE was known as the National Environmental Research Institute (NERI). DCE is (and NERI was) part of Aarhus University. See www.dmu.dk/en/. When the government of Greenland took control of mineral resource administration in 2009, it was agreed with Denmark that Greenland should use the DCE as an adviser on the minerals sector for a number of years.

based on Danish principles. Several such reports have been issued so far,[54] and many are characterised as 'preliminary'. These preliminary reports contain recommendations as to which studies should be carried out as soon as possible or at least before extensive activities are initiated.[55] Other reports, of more a final nature, are issued after such studies have taken place, though they may state that some studies still are in progress or have to be carried out.[56]

The maritime environment generally falls under the jurisdiction of the Danish Realm and it is the Danish Ministry of Defence, in cooperation with other authorities, which deals with oil pollution in the sea and parts of sea areas close to the coast. However, Greenland has taken over responsibility for protection of the environment up to a limit of three nautical miles.

(k) Governing law and dispute resolution

Licences granted under the Mineral Resources Act are subject to the law of Greenland, and to the jurisdiction of the Greenlandic courts. According to the model licence, licence agreements are drawn up solely in the Danish language.

Article 29 of the model licence contains provisions on arbitration, according to which disputes (other than about decisions made at the discretion or on the order of the government of Greenland or the BMP) can be submitted to arbitration. The arbitration tribunal consists of three members, sits in Copenhagen and applies Danish law.

In the impact benefit agreement referred to above, the law of Greenland is chosen in the choice-of-law provision, and the jurisdiction chosen is that of the court in Nuuk, Greenland. There is no arbitration clause. The agreement is drawn up in both Greenlandic and English, and the English version takes priority.

3.2 Government take

According to Article 17 of the Mineral Resources Act, an exploration and exploitation licence determines the consideration to be paid by the licensee to the Greenland government. Non-exhaustive examples are given of consideration in the form of an annual fee calculated on the basis of the size of the area covered by the licence (area fee), a fee calculated on the basis of the mineral resources extracted (royalty), or a share of the profits from the activities under the licence (profits fee). The provision also gives authority to grant the licensee:

> *exemption from taxation of the activities covered by the licence if the activities are subject to fees at least as onerous as the taxation would have been, and the fees are fully covered by Section 7 of the Act on Greenland Self-Government.*

---

54 A list of environmental reports on hydrocarbon exploration can be found at www.bmp.gl/petroleum/environment/environmental-reports.

55 For example, NERI Technical Report 652/2008, *A preliminary strategic environmental impact assessment of mineral and hydrocarbon activities on the Nuussuaq peninsula, West Greenland*; NERI Technical Report 719/2009, *The Western Greenland Sea – A preliminary strategic environmental impact assessment of hydrocarbon activities in the KANUMAS East area*; and DCE Scientific Report 26/2012 (only available in Danish), *En foreløbig, strategisk miljøvurdering af aktiviteter forbundet med olieefterforskning og -udvinding i den østlige del af Davis Stræde*.

56 For example, NERI Technical Report 618/2007, *Strategic Environmental Impact Assessment of hydrocarbon activities in the Disko West area*; and DCE Scientific Report 9/2011, *Eastern Baffin Bay – A strategic environmental impact assessment of hydrocarbon activities*.

The reference to Article 7 in the Act on Greenland Self-Government means that, for a tax exemption under this provision, the taxes should be payable to the self-government authorities.

The amount of the royalty or other payment demanded is to a large extent a matter for the Greenland government and is thus a matter for negotiation. This in line with the 2009 hydrocarbon strategy,[57] in which the BMP stated:

> *When exploration is in a preliminary phase (as is the case in Greenland) the prospectivity of the area, all else being equal, will be considered extremely uncertain. With this background, it is important that private companies are given an incentive to explore in the new areas and they must be able to see a chance of reasonable financial returns if they discover anything, to compensate for the significant financial risk they are accepting in the exploration.*

In this connection a benchmark analysis has been carried out of the financial terms for exploration and exploitation of oil and gas in 16 selected countries and on a number of different models, and it is on the basis of these that the existing model was chosen.

Article 16(3) of the Mineral Resources Act contains a number of tax and technical rules whereby an exploitation licence can, in principle, only be granted to a limited company, the company must have its registered office in Greenland, the company may not be more thinly capitalised than the group of which the company forms part, and the company's loan capital may not exceed the shareholders' equity by more than a ratio of 2:1. The company must generally trade at arm's length prices and on arm's length terms.

In total the government take generally involves the following:

- corporation tax and withholding taxes on dividends, together 37%;
- no royalty on turnover but a royalty on profits;
- 12.5% of the costs of NUNAOIL A/S in the exploration phase;
- various costs and fees to cover the expenses of the administrative authorities (Article 19 of the model licence).

The above model was laid down for licensing rounds in 2010, 2012 and 2013.[58] However, percentage rates are not given, and it is stated that corporation tax and withholding taxes on dividends are payable, as well as a progressive royalty on profits, which is in line with the model. The model means that public authorities collect about 59% of the profits of oil activities.[59] It must be assumed that the percentage rates will be re-evaluated if there is a breakthrough in oil and gas finds.[60]

(a) *Royalties*

No royalty on turnover is payable. A royalty is placed on profits of 7.5% if the internal profit before tax is above 21.75% plus the official discount rate, rising to 17.5% and 30% if the internal profit before tax is above 29.25% plus the official discount rate and 36.75% plus the official discount rate, respectively.

---

57 *Exploration and Exploitation of Hydrocarbons in Greenland Strategy for Licence Policy 2009*, December 2009.
58 BMP, *Report to Inatsisartut on mineral resource activities in Greenland*, Spring 2011, p 28.
59 BMP, *Report to Inatsisartut on mineral resource activities in Greenland*, Spring 2011, p 29.
60 *Exploration and Exploitation of Hydrocarbons in Greenland Strategy for Licence Policy 2009, December 2009*, p 45.

(b) ***Special participation***

NUNAOIL A/S is to participate in the licence with a share determined in advance. Hitherto, this share has been between 8% and 12.5%.

(c) ***Corporation tax***

Corporation tax is at a flat rate of 30% for undertakings with licences under the Mineral Resources Act. This does not include withholding taxes on dividends.

4. Current issues

On July 30 2012 a proposal for an amendment of the Mineral Resources Act was published for consultation. The amendment would mean that in future environmental matters will be dealt with by an entity of the normal environmental authorities, in order to strike a better balance between mineral exploitation and considerations for the environment. However, the one-stop-shop principle will be retained. Moreover, a procedure for administrative appeal to the Greenland government is introduced in the Mineral Resources Act. It is not yet certain what effect this legislative proposal will have.

Draft law on large projects: It will not be possible to supply all labour necessary for the extraction of minerals exclusively from Greenland. The import of labour has therefore been a matter of political debate in Greenland. In August 2012 a draft law on large-scale building and construction projects was put forward and passed by the Greenland Parliament in December 2012.[61] The act regulates certain matters connected with the import of labour to Greenland in the establishment phase, when there is expected to be a large demand for foreign labour. The draft law is not intended to deal with the hydrocarbons sector in the first instance, but rather mining projects and energy intensive industries that may be based on cheap hydropower.[62] However, according to its wording the draft law could be applicable to all projects for the exploitation of minerals in respect of which licences are granted under the Mineral Resources Act. As hydrocarbons (oil and natural gas) are defined as mineral resources in Article 5 of the Mineral Resources Act, and as under Chapters 5 and 6 of that Act licences must be given for their exploration and exploitation, the hydrocarbons sector will also be covered by the draft law.

The new law covers projects whose construction costs exceed Dkr5 billion, where the need for labour for a project exceeds the suitable, available and accessible labour in Greenland, or if the demands in respect of the technical and financial capacities of undertakings that carry out construction works exceeds the technical and financial capacities of Greenlandic undertakings. The main points of the law are that imported labour need not be paid in accordance with Greenlandic agreements on

---

61 The draft law, with comments, is available in Danish at the consultation portal: dk.nanoq.gl/Service/Hoeringsportal/Inatsisartutlov/2012/Storskalalov.aspx. Now Act 25 of 2012 on building and civil engineering work on large-scale projects.

62 Specifically, in the first instance the law is aimed at iron ore mining and an aluminium smelter.

63 There is no general legislation on minimum wages in Greenland. As in other parts of the Danish Realm, wages and salaries are primarily regulated by collective agreements entered into between employees' and employers' organisations.

pay and conditions.[63] This means that it is expected that some of the imported labour may be paid at lower rates than normal in Greenland. It must merely be ensured that foreign workers have pay and conditions that are acceptable and objectively and properly justified. The law does not specify exactly what is meant by this. Greenlandic legislation on holidays will not apply to workers covered by the law.

Foreign workers must hold residence permits. Jurisdiction over immigration has not been transferred to the Greenland government and remains a matter for the Danish Realm.[64] The conditions for obtaining a residence permit for Greenland are laid down in the Danish Immigration Act, which entered into force in Greenland by Decree 150/2001 on the application of the Immigration Act in Greenland. As a consequence, the implementation of the law on large-scale building and construction projects depends on the Danish Parliament amending the Danish Immigration Act.

Moreover, the special rules on carriage of goods by sea to and from Greenland will not apply in full.[65] This means that the special exclusive right to carry goods by sea between 16 specified destinations in Greenland, and between these destinations in Greenland and Reykjavik (Iceland), Aalborg (Denmark) and various ports in Sweden, Norway, the United Kingdom, Germany, the United States, Canada and Newfoundland, or in transit via Iceland and/or Denmark will not apply to the large-scale projects covered by the draft law.

Termination of activities: Articles 42 to 44 of the Mineral Resources Act contain provisions on the termination of activities. According to Article 42, licences under the act must include specific provisions on the licensee's obligations on the termination of activities. According to Article 43, when applying for approval of exploitation measures, the licensee must also submit a plan for the steps to be taken on termination of activities. The closure plan must set out what is to happen upon termination of activities and state how to ensure that the plan can be financially implemented. The provision focuses in particular on environmental and safety concerns upon closure and termination of exploitation activities. According to the model licence, the closure plan must be sent to and approved by the BMP before construction may begin.

Generally, a complete clean-up will be required, but in some cases where facilities can be used for other purposes, it may be decided that such facilities are not to be removed.[66]

The Greenland government may lay down terms to ensure that the licensee complies with its obligations upon termination of activities. This can take the form of the provision of security by making a deposit in a credit institution, giving a bank guarantee, a guarantee by a parent company or similar. The provision of security will be determined in discussions with the licensee and will be in proportion to the

---

64 However, immigration is one of the policy areas could be taken over by the Government of Greenland; see List II, No 6, of the Schedule to the Act on Greenland Self-Government; see Section 2 of the act.

65 Greenland Parliament Order 16 of October 30 1992 on Carriage of Goods by Sea to, from and within Greenland.

66 Article 42(1) in the explanatory notes of November 1 2009 on the Mineral Resources Act.

extent of the licence. The more detailed provisions will be contained in the licence. The aim of the provision of security is to strike a balance between the performance of the obligations arising on termination of activities and regard for the carrying on of the licensee's activities. If changes occur which go beyond the original scope of the provision of security, the Greenland government may lay down new terms, including with regard to the provision of security.

If a licensee does not comply with an order or enforcement notice to implement the measures connected with the termination of activities, the Greenland government may implement them at the licensee's account and risk.

If the licensee wants to suspend activities, the Greenland government must also approve this. Such approval requires it still to be possible to implement the closure plan at any time and that plans for safety, health, the environment and so on are adapted to the temporary suspension of exploitation activities. Approval may be granted for up to two years at a time. Renewed approval may be granted on modified terms. If temporary suspension has lasted six years, or if the terms for suspension are not met, the Greenland government may order the licensee to implement the closure plan.

5. Conclusion

Greenland's legislation on mineral resources is in many ways fully on a level with that of other western countries. However, so far Greenland has not experienced proper commercial exploitation of hydrocarbon resources. It appears that considerable discretion has been left to the government. Given the limited size of Greenlandic society and the special nature of the Greenlandic natural environment, it must be expected that certain changes will be made to the legal basis.

Netherlands

Harm Kerstholt
Paul JH Verkleij
NautaDutilh NV

1. Introduction

This chapter gives a general overview of the legal environment of the Dutch oil and gas upstream regime. The Dutch upstream sector started in the middle of the last century and nowadays consists of various oil majors, such as NAM (a joint venture between Shell and ExxonMobil), Chevron, Total and various other large, medium and smaller companies.

2. Upstream activities[1]

2.1 Oil

In 1943, the Schoonebeek oilfield was discovered in the Netherlands and was the start of oil production in the country. Some 250 million barrels of oil were pumped up to the year 1996 when extraction became too expensive. Due to the introduction of more cost effective extraction technology, the Schoonebeek field returned to production in 2010, but production now mainly takes place at sea.

Proven oil resources as at January 1 2012 add up to 40.4 million cubic metres (m^3). 28.6 million m^3 of which reside in onshore oilfields and 11.8 million m^3 in fields on the continental shelf. In 2011, a total of 1.27 million m^3 of oil was produced in the Netherlands. Average oil production during 2011 ran at about 3,500m^3 per day. Companies are still investing in new fields.

2.2 Gas

The first gas discovery in the Netherlands dates from 1948, but more important is the 1959 discovery by NAM of gas in the village of Slochteren. The so-called Groningen field covered a surface of some 900 square kilometres (km^3) and estimates suggested the original field contained 2,700 billion m^3 of accessible gas – the then largest gas field in the world. In 1961, drilling for North Sea gas started. Following the 1973 oil crisis, the decision was taken to reduce gas production from the Groningen field, and the government began to encourage the development of smaller fields, the so-called 'small fields policy'. This policy entailed preference being given to the exploitation of small fields in order to reduce the load on the Groningen field and retain its value

1 *Natural resources and geothermal energy in the Netherlands: Annual review 2011.* A review of exploration and production activities and underground storage by the Ministry of Economic Affairs, Agriculture and Innovation.

as a balancing field. The preferential treatment sought by the policy was implemented through various measures, including tax incentives, statutory responsibilities on the gas transmission system operator in respect of producers of small fields[2] and an obligation for GasTerra (which is 50% state-owned) to apply a production ceiling for the Groningen field and to purchase gas from small fields on reasonable terms and in line with market prices.

Dozens of small fields have been discovered since. Current expectations suggest that the Groningen field will continue to produce for some 50 years, but the balancing function of the field will decrease significantly as from 2020. Production from the smaller fields will decline, but will still make a significant contribution to national needs for the coming 10 to 20 years.

Proven natural gas resources as at January 1 2012 are estimated to be 1,230 billion m^3. Of that, 900 billion m^3 reside in the Groningen gas field, 168 billion m^3 in the other onshore fields and 162 billion m^3 in the fields on the continental shelf. In 2011, total production from Dutch gas fields was 78.6 billion m^3.

3. Petroleum legal regime

3.1 Petroleum law and relevant provisions

Under international law, the Netherlands exercises sovereign rights over the Netherlands continental shelf for the purpose of exploring it and exploiting its natural resources. Those sovereign rights are exclusive in the sense that without the permission of the coastal state no exploration or exploitation activities may be conducted.[3] This implies the power to regulate third party exploration or exploitation on the continental shelf. The Mining Act[4] stipulates that a licence is required for exploration activities (exploration licence) and production activities (production licence). Reconnaissance activities (eg, seismic surveying) do not require a licence under the Mining Act but may be regulated under other laws. The Mining Act furthermore determines that all unproduced hydrocarbons[5] in the continental shelf are owned by the state of the Netherlands. In the area for which a production licence is granted, title to the hydrocarbons passes at the wellhead upon production. The same regime applies onshore.[6]

The continental shelf does not generally form part of the Kingdom's territory, which – among other things – means that Dutch law does not apply beyond the territorial zone (12 nautical miles from the coast), unless specifically (and on a case-by-case basis) provided otherwise. The current trend is that legislation regulating onshore activities has increasingly been made applicable to exploration and exploitation on the continental shelf as well.

---

2 Laid down in Articles 54–55 of the Gas Act.

3 Article 2 of the Convention on the Continental Shelf and Article 77 of the UN Convention on the Law of the Sea.

4 An English unofficial translation of the Mining Act and other relevant legislation can be found at www.nlog.nl/en/legal/legislation.html.

5 In this chapter, reference is specifically made to hydrocarbons, but the Mining Act covers all minerals.

6 Under onshore production licences, the holders still own the unproduced hydrocarbon if their production licence was granted before the new Mining Act came into effect in 2003.

(a) ***Regulatory bodies***

The main regulatory bodies involved in Dutch upstream activities are the Ministry of Economic Affairs and the State Supervision of Mines.

The ministry is the competent authority for the application of the Mining Act. The ministry is the primary authority that issues, approves transfers of, or cancels licences, which are mandatory for conducting mining activities. In addition, the ministry has legislative powers conferred by the Mining Act to issue specific rules, or guidelines and policy rules to clarify the ministry's interpretation of the legislative framework within which it exercises its statutory duties and powers.

The State Supervision of Mines advises the ministry with regard to the technical capacities of a licence applicant, and assists the ministry to enforce the applicable legislation by using preventive monitoring, supporting administrative (and sometimes civil) enforcement and collecting, distributing and providing information for criminal enforcement purposes. The State Supervision of Mines is answerable to the ministry.

In addition, several other regulatory bodies have defined advisory roles in relation to mining activities, such as the Mining Council, the technical committee on soil movement and the Netherlands Organisation for Applied Scientific Research (TNO; a semi-public body). Several non-sector-specific regulators may also be relevant (the provinces, municipalities, competition authorities, labour inspectorates, etc).

(b) ***Types of agreement***

Typically, licence holders conclude a joint operating agreement between themselves. The state participant, EBN, is entitled to a 40% working interest (covering costs and benefits) under the Mining Act, but does not become a licence holder. Therefore, EBN is not a party to any joint operating agreement, but concludes a so-called 'agreement of cooperation' with the license holder(s). The agreement of cooperation is very similar to a joint operating agreement and must be approved by the ministry. EBN is also allowed to participate in exploration, but unlike its mandatory participation in production, it only participates in exploration activities at the request of exploration licence holders.

Where a reservoir straddles the border of another licence area with one or more different licence holders, it is mandatory for the relevant licence holders to conclude a unitisation agreement. Production may not start from a reservoir "that can reasonably be assumed to straddle the border of the licence area", as long as there is no unitisation agreement in place. The ministry may grant an exemption with respect to the obligation to conclude a unitisation agreement. If, during or after the production of hydrocarbons, it appears that the reservoir concerned straddles the border of the licence area, the licence holder concerned is obliged to notify the party authorised to undertake the production of hydrocarbons in the adjacent area and to cooperate in the conclusion of a unitisation agreement.

Under the Gas Act, GasTerra is obligated to take natural gas from small fields on reasonable terms and at market prices. The Gas Act also obliges the national gas transmission manager, Gas Transport Services (which is 100% state-owned), to facilitate the entry into the transmission grid of natural gas produced from small fields. It is, however, not an obligation for licence holders to sell and deliver their gas to GasTerra or to use Gas Transport Services' transmission network. The parties are free to determine the contents of gas sales agreements, although GasTerra uses a standard from which only limited deviations are possible.

Other agreements between licence holders that are regularly concluded include condensate sales agreements, processing agreements, joint facilities agreements and transportation agreements. EBN is also a party to licence-specific agreements, such as gas sales agreements, processing agreements and so on.

(c) Acquisition of acreage

The Mining Act determines that production and exploration licences are to be granted through a system of competitive applications. When an application for a licence is submitted, other persons are invited to submit a competing application by means of a publication in the *Official Gazette*. If the application is for an exploration or production licence for hydrocarbons, the invitation will also be published in the *Official Journal of the European Union*. The timeframe for submission of competing applications is 13 weeks.

Certain exceptions to the competitive application procedure exist. First, the holder of an exploration licence who under that licence has demonstrated the presence of hydrocarbons in (part of) the area, will be granted a production licence for that area without competition. Second, when a party applies for a licence in respect of an area for which a licence has already been issued, the licence application is refused. Last, if an application is submitted in respect of a reservoir which plausibly extends beyond the border of an area for which the applicant already holds a licence, only the licence holders of the areas adjacent to the area for which the application has been made will get the opportunity to submit a competing application for a production licence.

(d) Qualification requirements

A production license will be granted only if it is feasible that production of hydrocarbons within the area to which the licence will apply is commercially viable. An application for an exploration or a production licence must specify the time frame and the area in respect of which the licence is sought and the substances to which the application relates. An application for an exploration licence for an offshore area must specify for which area, consisting of one or more blocks, the licence is sought. The applicant must also provide information about its financial capacity and technical abilities.

Applications for licences must be submitted to the Ministry in duplicate and need to be accompanied by several documents, such as geological reports, a programme indicating which exploratory surveys and exploration activities the applicant intends to perform, the associated time schedule and which techniques will be used.

No licence will be granted insofar as it would apply:

- to an area for which at that moment in time a licence is already held by another person for the same hydrocarbons; or

- in respect of a reservoir for which at that moment in time a storage licence, held by another person, would already apply.

In addition, the licence can be refused on the basis of the financial and technical capabilities of the applicant, the manner in which the applicant intends to carry out the activities, or a lack of efficiency and sense of responsibility based on the applicant's behaviour under previous licences. When two applications are adjudged equal on an evaluation of the above grounds, the licence will be granted to the applicant that in the ministry's view will undertake exploration or production in the most energetic and efficient manner. In the end only one licence can be granted.

Operatorship: If a licence is awarded to, or held by, more than one person, those persons are regarded as the joint applicants or holders of the licence. When a licence is held by two or more persons, one of the licence holders must be designated as the operator responsible for carrying out the actual operations or commissioning them. Only the operator is permitted actually to carry out operations or to commission them. The designation of the operator will be noted in the licence, and the joint licence holders can designate another person as operator subject to prior written consent from the ministry. The qualification requirements for operators are those mentioned above: financial and technical capabilities, evidence of the manner in which the operator intends to carry out its activities and good conduct under other licences granted previously.

(e) ***Duration***

Until 1988 it was possible to grant production licences with a perpetual duration. Very few such perpetual licences are still valid however. The Mining Act does not specify a specific duration for which licences are to be granted. The criterion used for determining the term of a licence is that it should be no longer than is necessary for carrying out the activities for which the licence is granted. Usually production licences are therefore awarded for a period of 30 to 40 years, but prolongation may be requested from the ministry. No compulsory relinquishment obligations exist, other than the so-called 'fallow fields policy' (see section 4.1 below).

The duration of an exploration licence is much shorter. Normally, the initial duration is around four years with the possibility for renewal/extension.

(f) ***Minimum work obligations***

An exploration licence will state minimum work obligations by specifying within which periods after the licence has become irrevocable the exploration activities indicated in the licence must be carried out. Other conditions may not be attached to the licence.

A production licence will not specify work obligations in the licence itself. If a production licence has been granted, the holder of the production licence needs to file a production plan with the ministry. Only after the production plan has been approved by the ministry, is the holder of the licence allowed to start producing hydrocarbons in accordance with that plan. The ministry may only withhold its approval in the interest of systemic reservoir management or in connection with a risk of soil movement. The ministry is allowed to impose conditions on the approval of a production plan.

The production plan needs to describe, among other things, the anticipated volume of hydrocarbons to be produced (in total and annually), the composition of the hydrocarbons, the duration of production, the method of production and the activities related thereto, the expected cost of production and, if the production takes place on or near land, any soil movement expected as a result of the production and the measures to be taken to prevent damage as a result of soil movement.

In addition, there is an annual obligation to file with the State Supervision of Mines a work plan, on the basis of which the production activities will take place. This work plan must contain an overview of the main mining activities within the licence area that are foreseen for the next five years. The work plan mainly contains a technical description of the activities, such as the number of new wells and the construction activities linked to production under the licence.

The licence holder has to produce hydrocarbons in accordance with the approved production and work plan. If the licence holder wishes to deviate from the production plan, an amendment to it should be filed with the ministry for consent. If the licence holder wishes to deviate from the work plan, these deviations should be notified to State Supervision of Mines at least four weeks beforehand.

If the holder of an exploration licence does not comply with the minimum work obligations in the licence, the ministry may withdraw the licence after issuing a formal warning specifying a period in which the defects may be remedied. There is some debate whether the ministry may also withdraw a production licence when production activities are not carried out in accordance with the production plan.[7] A violation of the production plan is in any event an economic offence and a breach of Article 34(1) of the Mining Act.

(g) Assignment and encumbrance

Assignment: Dutch law allows the transfer of shares or interests in a licence holder (ie, a change of control) without requiring the consent of the ministry.

Transfer of an exploration licence or production licence itself is subject to prior written consent from the ministry. The consent will at least be withheld:

- if, at the date of the transfer, the exploration or production licence would apply to a reservoir for which at that moment in time a storage licence, held by another person, would already apply;
- if the applicant lacks the necessary technical or financial capabilities;
- if the manner in which the applicant intends to carry out the activities is not appropriate; or
- if the applicant's behaviour under previous licences has demonstrated a lack of efficiency and sense of responsibility.

---

7 MM Roggenkamp and I Brinkman, *"Evaluatie van de mijnbouwwet: is het veld halfvol of halfleeg?"*, TVE 2008-4/5 p 256.

If licence holders wish to transfer part of the licence to another party, they must also submit an application for the division of the licence.

Transfer of a licence is effected by execution of an authentic deed or private deed, signed by the assignor and the assignee, which must comply with the requirements of Dutch law.

Encumbrance: There is no legislation regarding whether an exploration or production licence can be encumbered with a right of pledge or usufruct. We are of the view that such licences can be encumbered subject to the same terms and restrictions that apply to an assignment of a licence. This implies that in principle an exploration or production licence can be encumbered, but only subject to the ministry's consent. It is still debated whether the ministry's consent is required to create the encumbrance on the licence, or for enforcement of the encumbrance, or for both.

(h) ***Local content***

There are no regulations in the Netherlands which impose a duty on licence holders to obtain certain services or goods from the government or from Dutch persons or companies.

(i) ***National reservation***

The Petroleum Products (Stockpiling) Act 2012 (not yet in force) implements EU Regulation 1099/2008. The act obliges certain market participants to stock a specific amount of crude (mineral) oil and/or petroleum products, as further defined in the regulation. Market participants that must meet this obligation are licence holders for excise warehouses in respect of mineral oils (as further defined in the Excise Duty Act), including producers and non-producers such as dealers. The explanatory memorandum to the act refers to 'producers' as "oil companies with refinery capacity in the Netherlands", so mere upstream activities thus do not fall under the scope of this act.

(j) ***Environment***

Upstream oil and gas activities in the Netherlands are subject to a range of national and international regulations. The most important regulations are outlined below, but this list is not exhaustive.

International environmental regulation concerning offshore activities: Based on the United Nations Convention on the law of the sea (UNCLOS), the Netherlands has established its territorial waters (12 nautical miles), a contiguous zone (24 nautical miles) and the boundaries of the Netherlands continental shelf and exclusive economic zone.

The Convention for the Protection of the Marine Environment of the North-East Atlantic (OSPAR) constitutes a coordinating legal framework for the protection of the marine environment of the north-eastern part of the Atlantic Ocean, which includes the North Sea and Wadden Sea. The Bonn Agreement of 1983 arranges mutual cooperation by the coastal states of the North Sea for the avoidance and combating of environmental pollution.

Relevant Dutch legislation: Both in the exploration phase and in the production phase an integrated environmental permit will have to be applied for on the basis of the Permitting (General Provisions) Act. Because the Permitting (General Provisions) Act does not apply to the exclusive economic zone, the Mining Act provides for a mining environmental permit for mining installations in that zone.

If activities are planned in or near a Natura 2000 protected area (or a protected nature reserve) that might have a harmful impact on protected natural assets, a permit under the Nature Conservation Act is required. When undertaking oil or gas activities an exemption under the Flora and Fauna Act might also be necessary. Such a permit or exemption can be part of the integrated environmental permit. A legislative proposal to extend the scope of the Nature Conservation Act and the Flora and Fauna Act to the exclusive economic zone is being debated in the House of Representatives.

The Environmental Management Act and the Environmental Impact Assessment Decree – based on the EU Environmental Impact Assessment Directive (2011/92/EU) – determine those activities and decisions in respect of which it is mandatory to undertake an environmental impact assessment and those activities in respect of which the competent authorities will decide whether an environmental impact assessment is required. The Environmental Impact Assessment Decree and the chapter on environmental impact assessments in the Environmental Management Act also apply to the exclusive economic zone.

Specific environmental rules applicable to mining activities are given in the General Environmental Rules (Mining Industry) Decree.

Under the Spatial Planning Act municipalities adopt zoning plans, in which the designated use of their territory is laid down. The onshore production of oil and gas has to be in accordance with these zoning plans, and an integrated environmental permit for the necessary construction works is withheld if the relevant zoning plan does not allow for it. The municipal authorities have to agree to changes to a zoning plan. The national government is exploring the possibility of adopting a state zoning plan for the North Sea.

The Dutch government intends to integrate and simplify all environmental and planning law into one Environmental and Planning Act and all nature conservation laws into one Nature Conservation Act.

(k) Governing law and dispute resolution

The Netherlands has a system of freedom of contract, and therefore does not impose Dutch law on any contractual relationship in the upstream sector, other than in respect of the agreement of cooperation with EBN which, under mandatory law provisions, must be governed by Dutch law.

3.2 Government take

As mentioned, the central principle of the Mining Act is that the state is the legal owner of all existing hydrocarbons in the subsoil, and that the hydrocarbons become owned by production licence holder upon production.

(a) Royalties

The state imposes a fee calculated as a percentage of the turnover of the holder of the production licence during the calendar year for which the fee is determined. The tariff for production at sea has been set at zero, the fee for production at land for 2013 is between 0% and 7%. The relevant turnover is calculated as the number of units of mineral oil or natural gas produced in the licence area during the calendar year and accruing to the holder, multiplied by the price per unit at which these units have been sold. Where units have been disposed of by other means than sales, it will be presumed they were sold.

The fee is increased by 25% if, for the relevant year, the weighted average price of crude oil imported into the Netherlands exceeds €25 per barrel. The fee will be increased by 100% if the licence holder has not concluded an agreement of cooperation in relation to the production licence.

(b) Bonus

There is no legislation in the Netherlands regarding bonuses in connection with the exploration or production of hydrocarbons.

(c) Rental fees

Surface rental fees are imposed for offshore exploration licences and for onshore and offshore production licences. The basis for determination of the fee is the surface of the area for which an exploration or production licence is effective as at January 1 each year.

In 2013, the tariff for a production licence was €713 per square kilometre. The tariff for an exploration licence depends on the number of years for which the licence is held, with a maximum equal to the amount of the production licence.

(d) Special participation

EBN is a 100% state-owned company whose role under the Mining Act is to:

- participate in exploration activities;
- participate in mining activities;
- carry out agreements of cooperation; and
- provide the ministry with data.

As mentioned, EBN is allowed to participate in exploration but whereas it is mandatory that it participate in production, it will only participate in exploration activities at the request of exploration licence holders.

(e) Corporate tax

Corporate income tax: Dutch resident companies are subject to corporate income tax on their worldwide income. The current statutory rate is 20% to 25%. Non-resident companies are only subject to corporate income tax with respect to income derived from certain specific Dutch sources, like Dutch permanent establishments, Dutch real property and substantial Dutch shareholdings.

Corporate income tax can be credited against the state profit share, meaning that any change in the corporate income tax rate does not affect the total tax take.

State profit share: The state profit share is a special tax levied on income from Dutch oil and gas production. The tax is levied on holders of an onshore or offshore Dutch production licence. The tax rate is 50%, with a tax credit for the deemed allocable corporate income tax. Most allocable expenses, including exploration expenses, may be deducted at 110% instead of 100% of the cost. The state profit share is a deductible expense for corporate income tax purposes.

Without going into detail on the state profit share, a financial incentive for the small fields policy is contained in the Decree on Investment Deduction for Marginal Gas Accumulations on the Continental Shelf. Licensees and co-licensees may charge 25% of the investments made to designated small fields or prospects against the resulting revenue, subject to payment of the state profit share. Applications for investment deductions are reviewed against the following three parameters:

- the volume of gas that it is technically feasible to produce;
- well productivity; and
- transport distance to a platform.

Dividend withholding tax: Profit distributions made by Dutch companies are generally subject to dividend withholding tax at the statutory rate of 15%. The tax must be withheld by the Dutch distributing company. The EU Parent/Subsidiary Directive or relevant tax treaties can reduce this rate, potentially, to zero.

Value added tax: The value added tax rate is 21%.

Miscellaneous: In the Netherlands, as in all other member states of the European Union, customs duties have to be paid when goods originating from outside the Union are brought into free circulation within its customs territory. These duties will be due at the time of importation of the goods into the European Union (ie, when they gain customs clearance for free circulation). As a result, if goods are imported into the Netherlands, customs duties have to be paid in the Netherlands. The rates of the import duties vary considerably, depending on the type of the goods imported and/or their further processing. The tariff in the Netherlands (and the rest of the European Union) in respect of petroleum (crude oil) is 0%.

There is no Dutch withholding tax on interest and royalties paid by companies that are resident in the Netherlands. Additionally, no capital contributions tax and stamp duties are levied in the Netherlands.

Other taxes such as payroll tax, real property transfer tax and local taxes may apply.

4. Current issues

4.1 Licence area reduction and fallow fields

To stimulate production activities in areas for which a production licence has been issued, the Mining Act authorises the Ministry to reduce a licence area. The Ministry, before April 1 of each year, makes an inventory of those parts of an area for which a production licence applies, where:

- in the previous two calendar years no significant activities have taken place with respect to the exploration for, or production of, hydrocarbons; and/or
- production activities ceased.

These areas are called 'fallow fields'.

However, with regard to the continental shelf, the ministry in 2010 agreed with mining companies active there a Covenant for the Stimulation of Exploration and Development of Hydrocarbon Reserves and the Storage of Substances on the Dutch Continental Shelf. Under this covenant, the ministry agreed not to reduce fallow fields during the term of the covenant while instead using alternative methods to stimulate exploration and production activities.

The covenant is initially valid for five years, and is to be evaluated two years after entering into effect. If the agreement is not terminated before five years have passed, it will be extended every five years for another five years.

4.2 Role of EBN

EBN is considering its role in the upstream sector. It is exploring the possibility that instead of just being a party to agreements of cooperation, it will become a holder of exploration and production licences. It would then actively participate in upstream activities and would not need to wait for companies to start upstream activities in order to become a party to their contracts.

In addition, EBN is considering an amendment to their standard agreement of cooperation.

4.3 Mining versus wind farms

Since December 13 2006, the Mining Act and associated regulations have been amended to provide the ministry with the explicit authority to refuse its approval for the erection of a mining installation "in connection with the generation of electricity". According to the ministry, this addition was necessary to prevent mining installations having a restrictive effect on the construction of wind farms in the North Sea. The government has issued licenses for 15 wind farms at sea so far, but a moratorium on new licences has been in place since 2009 pending new regulations.

Future government policy[8] with regard to the continental shelf is aimed at parallel use of space, while the wind farms policy is aimed at erecting wind farms only in designated areas. Applications for licences to erect wind farms outside these

---

8 As set out in the National Water Plan, the Policy Document on the North Sea and the Integrated Management Plan for the North Sea 2015.

designated areas will be refused. In these designated areas, the principle of first come, first served applies. The government aims at cooperation and consultation between parties that wish to make use of the same area for different purposes, while the underlying principle is that the party taking the initiative is only allowed to undertake activities in that designated area if it does not cause disproportionate damage to the interests of other parties. It is, however, the government that makes the final call on whether to issue a licence and on its conditions.

4.4 Carbon capture and storage

A recent amendment to the Mining Act introduced a chapter relating to carbon storage. There are no plans for carbon storage onshore, and the government does not permit onshore carbon capture and storage demonstration projects. There is, however, a large offshore demonstration project, the Rotterdam Storage and Capture Demonstration Project, which captures carbon from a coal-fired power plant to be stored in an empty gas field 20km off the coast.

5. Conclusion

The Dutch upstream sector is a mature market with declining reserves and a solid regulatory framework. The government will keep encouraging the small fields policy which offers small parties with new techniques, focus and efficiency enough opportunities to make a profit.

Norway

Ivar Alvik
Scandinavian Institute of Maritime Law

1. Introduction

When oil in commercial quantities was first discovered in the Norwegian part of the North Sea in December 1969, it was the beginning of an economic adventure. The field that was discovered was the gigantic Ekofisk field, which turned out to be one of the world's largest offshore oilfields and is still producing. For Norway as a country, and for the Norwegian economy, the discovery of oil had a transformative effect. It has not only made Norway into one of the world's most prosperous countries, but also created a whole new industry, which today is the most important contributor to the Norwegian economy and to government income.[1] While oil was most important in the early years, production of gas is now equally important. The major share of the oil and gas produced in the North Sea is exported. In 2011 Norway was the world's seventh largest oil exporter and second largest gas exporter.[2] Most of the government's revenues from petroleum production are funnelled into a separate wealth fund owned by the Norwegian state and managed by the central bank.[3] However, the importance of the petroleum industry for the wider Norwegian economy consists today not only of the direct revenues from oil and gas production. As important is the large offshore supply industry that has been developed on the basis of the oil and gas in the North Sea. This industry is rooted in a long Norwegian tradition in the shipping and maritime industries. Today the supply of highly specialised services to the global oil industry, especially offshore, has become an important export industry for Norway in its own right.[4]

The development of the oil and gas industry in Norway is the result of regulatory policies and a distinct regulatory model.[5] A main aim of the early regulatory policies was to develop a truly national petroleum industry based on a transfer of technology

1 The direct revenues to the government from oil and gas production amounted in 2010 to Nkr276 billion, approximately 25% of the total government income. The petroleum sector overall represents approximately 20% of the Norwegian gross national product and 50% of Norwegian export, see *Facts 2012 – the Norwegian Petroleum Sector* (official publication of the Norwegian Ministry of Petroleum and Energy and the Norwegian Petroleum Directorate), p 21

2 Norway averaged oil exports of 1.7 million barrels per day, and had gas exports in total of 100.6 standard cubic metres in 2011, see *Facts 2012 – the Norwegian Petroleum Sector*, p 20.

3 The first deposit to the Norwegian Government Pension Fund – Global was made in 1995. Today it is the largest sovereign wealth fund in the world, currently (October 2012) valued at approximately Nkr 3700 billion, equivalent to approximately US$650 billion.

4 Total exports from Norwegian companies involved in petroleum sector related services and supply equalled Nkr118 billion (approximately US$20 billion) in 2011, as compared to Nkr15 billion in 1995.

5 Early on, the parliament formulated the so-called '10 oil commandments' which underpinned Norwegian regulatory policy, see *St meld* 76 (1970–71).

and know-how from the international oil companies. A main instrument to facilitate this was the establishment and development of the Norwegian state oil company Statoil, which was given a participating interest in all major oil fields and trained by the international companies to become an independent operator. In addition, a regulatory policy of preferential treatment of Norwegian suppliers was put in place, in order to facilitate the development of an independent Norwegian supply and service industry. These regulatory policies have today essentially been abandoned, and have left few direct imprints on the current regulatory framework governing petroleum activities in Norway.[6] They nevertheless deserve mention in a chapter on Norwegian petroleum regulation, given their essential importance for the development of a national petroleum industry.

Underneath the current regulatory framework in place in Norway still lies a consistent policy of extensive government participation in and control of the petroleum industry. The regulatory framework has undergone significant development during the last 40 years, but one of its consistent features is a concessionary system where the government retains extensive powers at each stage of the petroleum activities. The most distinctive feature of the Norwegian concessionary system may be the concept of a step-by-step progression, meaning that in addition to the actual production licence, a number of successive approvals from the government are required before and after a field is set in production.[7] The most important is the plan for development and operation (PDO) that needs to be approved before a discovery is developed for production.[8] Before the plan is approved, a licensee has no definitive right to develop any discoveries it has made. Another distinctive feature of the Norwegian system is the practice of assigning licences to groups of companies, each of which are customarily given a licence share and required under the licence to enter into a joint operating agreement based on standard terms and conditions set by the government. Although framed in terms of an agreement, the joint operating agreement represents in reality mandatory public regulation of the relationship within the licence, since it cannot be derogated from by agreement between the licensees. A third distinctive feature is the model of state participation, where a certain share of each new licence bloc is usually retained by the state, which participates with the other licence partners on equal terms according to its share. The state's direct interests are managed through the separate state-owned company Petoro. This is a purely managerial company. It may only incur commitments and make profit on behalf of the state, and has no substantial ownership interests of its own.[9]

---

6 Statoil was privatised in 2001, and is now a publicly traded company, listed on the Oslo and New York stock exchanges. Although the Norwegian continental shelf is still a core focus, Statoil also has extensive international operations. The Norwegian state retains a 62% ownership share in the company. Moreover, Norway's affiliation to the European Union through the European Economic Area Agreement since 1994, which essentially makes Norway a full member of the EU internal market, now prohibits any preferential treatment being given to Norwegian suppliers and service providers.

7 See Erling Selvig, *Petroleumsrett til studiebruk* (1988), p 78.

8 See the Petroleum Act, Section 4(2).

9 See the Petroleum Act Sections 11(2) and 11(3).

2. Upstream activities

Petroleum activities in Norway are entirely offshore based. Most of the fields in production are located in the North Sea, south of 62° latitude, and most of this area is today considered a mature area where it is expected that the major part of exploitable reserves have already been discovered. However, the discovery of the so-called 'Johan Sverdrup' field, as recently as in 2011, shows that there is still potential for major new discoveries also in the mature areas.[10] The area north of 62°, the sea areas known as the Norse Sea and the Barents Sea, have so far not been explored to the same extent as the southern part. Only a minor part of these areas have been subject to significant exploration, and the major parts are therefore still immature and have great potential for future exploration activity.

The Norwegian continental shelf is divided into defined areas which again are divided into blocks.[11] Each of these blocks may be subject to individual licences for exploration and production. Before blocks may be licensed, the larger area must however be opened for petroleum activity. The decision to open new areas is made by the Norwegian parliament according to a process meant to ensure that all consequences for the environment and other interests are taken into account before the area is opened for petroleum activity.[12] Large areas of the Norwegian continental shelf with significant potential have not yet been opened for petroleum activity. In particular, there is a political controversy in Norway about exploration activity in the area around the Lofoten islands, where the proximity to land creates additional environmental risks, and the wildlife and environment is particularly vulnerable. Furthermore, petroleum activity in the eastern part of the Barents Sea has so far been prevented by an unresolved border issue with Russia. However, a final treaty between Norway and Russia resolving this issue was ratified in 2011, and it is likely that this area will be opened for activity in the near future together with the area around the Jan Mayen island. The sea areas around Svalbard/Spitsbergen in the north of the Barents Sea, and in Skagerrak towards Denmark, have not yet been opened for petroleum exploration. Due to political and environmental concerns it is unlikely that they will be in the near future, although there may be undiscovered petroleum reserves in these areas.

A new government policy to enhance exploration and facilitate new discoveries on the Norwegian continental shelf was implemented in 2003. This new policy has two main aspects: a simplified procedure for awarding licences in mature areas, and a tax incentive scheme whereby companies with no taxable income are allowed to claim a refund of exploration costs that they would otherwise have been entitled to deduct from taxable income. The latter in particular has provided an incentive to

---

10 According to current estimates, total exploitable reserves at the two related Avaldsnes and Aldous Major fields, which together make up the field that has been named Johan Sverdrup, are between 1.7 and 3.3 billion barrels, which makes it the largest discovery made on the Norwegian continental shelf since the 1980s.

11 See the Petroleum Act Section 3(2):

> *Offshore areas inside the outer boundary of the continental shelf are divided into blocks of 15 latitude minutes and 20 longitude minutes in size, unless adjacent land areas, common boundaries with the continental shelf of other states, or other circumstances warrant otherwise.*

12 See the Petroleum Act Section 3(1).

smaller and more specialised companies to apply for new licences and undertake exploration programmes, often with the aim of selling out to more established oil companies if petroleum is found. This new policy has so far been a spectacular success, new discoveries on the Norwegian continental shelf having increased significantly in recent years. Another activity with increasing significance is extended production from existing fields, where one may also see a surge of new companies specialising in so called tail-end production moving in to exploit fields nearing depletion in their end-life.

3. Petroleum legal regime

3.1 Petroleum law and relevant provisions

The main legislative basis of the Norwegian petroleum legal regime is the Petroleum Act (72 of November 29 1996).[13] This provides the basis of a number of more detailed regulations, the most significant of which is the Petroleum Regulation of June 27 1997.[14] In addition there are a number of regulations concerning different issues such as third party use of facilities,[15] safety,[16] the licence register[17] and so on. In significant respects, the Norwegian licensing and regulatory system is also subject to the European Economic Area (EEA) Agreement. While upstream activities on the continental shelf as such are generally not deemed subject to the EEA Agreement,[18] the awarding of licences has been deemed part of the EEA and subject to both the main provisions of the EEA Agreement and the Licensing Directive.[19] Moreover, sale and distribution of gas, including access to upstream gas pipelines, is heavily subject to EU regulations. This falls outside the scope of the present work however. In the following, the more specific aspects of the Norwegian regulatory regime shall be further described.

(a) Regulatory bodies

The main regulatory body and licensing authority is the Ministry of Petroleum and Energy, but some issues, such as major developments of new fields and opening of new areas, are also regularly subject to parliamentary treatment. The Norwegian

---

13 Most relevant legislation and regulations concerning petroleum activities are available in English translations on the webpages of the Norwegian Petroleum Directorate, see www.npd.no/en/Regulations. For an English translation of the Petroleum Act, see www.npd.no/en/Regulations/Acts/Petroleum-activities-act.

14 For an English translation of the Regulation, see www.npd.no/en/Regulations/Regulations/Petroleum-activities.

15 Regulation of December 20 2005 relating to the use of facilities by others, see www.npd.no/en/Regulations/Regulations/Facilities—-use-by-others.

16 The safety regulations fall under the authority of the Petroleum Safety Authority and can be found in English translation on their webpage, see www.ptil.no/regulations/category216.html. The main regulation here is the so called Framework Regulation, see www.ptil.no/framework-hse/category 403.html, and see further below.

17 Regulation of June 19 1997 relating to the Petroleum Register, see www.npd.no/en/Regulations/Regulations/Petroleum-register.

18 See generally Finn Arnesen, Simply, Marlus 400 (2010).

19 EC Directive 94/22/EC of May 30 1994 on the conditions for granting and using authorisations for the prospection, exploration and production of hydrocarbons. See also generally Finn Arnesen, *Statlig styring og EØS-rettslige skranker* (Universitetsforlaget, Oslo, 1996), p 83 and following.

Petroleum Directorate is a separate government body which is subordinate to the Ministry of Petroleum and Energy. It exercises delegated powers from the ministry, and has significant functions especially in relation to the management of petroleum resources. It is also serves as an important knowledge resource and advisory organ for the ministry. All issues relating to safety are subject to another government body, the Petroleum Safety Authority. This organ is the main decision-making authority under the health, safety and environment regulations. Although different aspects of these regulations may be subject to the authority of other government organs, the Petroleum Safety Authority has coordinating authority and handles the internal relationship between the other organs. Thus, where a certain approval necessitates the involvement of other government organs, such as the Labour Inspection Authority or the Climate and Pollution Agency, the Petroleum Safety Authority is responsible for coordinating contact with the proper bodies in their areas of authority.

(b) Types of agreement

Under Norwegian law, all offshore petroleum resources are owned by the state, and the state has exclusive rights of resource management.[20] This important principle is stated in Section 1 of the Petroleum Act. In practice, the state depends on private companies for exploration and production, and grants concessions to groups of companies for this purpose, as already mentioned. The main concession is the so-called 'production licence' awarded by the King in Council in accordance with the Petroleum Act, Section 3(3).[21]

The production licence gives an exclusive right to explore for and produce petroleum in the area covered by the licence. As already mentioned, it does not give an unconditional right to develop and produce any discoveries made, however. Field development is subject in particular to the government's approval of the plan for development and operation under Section 4(2). In addition, the ministry may also grant exploration licences in areas which have been opened for petroleum activity, in accordance with Section 2(1) of the act. An exploration licence does not give an exclusive right, however, and mainly envisages seismic exploration.

Under Norwegian law, there is no formal agreement between the state and the concessionaires. The concession system is at least formally based on a mere licence whereby the concessionaires acquire ownership to the petroleum being produced.[22] It was the subject of some discussion whether the early petroleum concessions in reality represented contractual commitments on the part of the state, although this

---

20 As mentioned, only offshore petroleum resources have been found in Norway. However, a separate statute has been enacted in respect of any petroleum resources in the ground under Norwegian land territory and the part of the seabed subject to private ownership, which also makes such resources subject to state ownership, see Act 21 of May 4 1973 on Exploration for and Production of Petroleum in the Ground Beneath Norwegian Land Territory.

21 The King in Council is the highest executive authority in Norway meaning that decisions are taken by the cabinet, but formally presided over and signed by the King.

22 This follows from the Petroleum Act, §Section 3(3) third part:

> *A production licence entails an exclusive right to exploration, exploration drilling and production of petroleum deposits in areas covered by the licence. The licensee becomes the owner of the petroleum which is produced.*

is now mostly a historical issue. In a contemporary setting, it is relatively clear that the underlying intention of the government at least is that the state does not undertake any contractual obligations by awarding a concession. Notwithstanding this, the relationship being formed between the state and individual licence groups undoubtedly has certain contractual elements. This may at least in theory have some significance in relation to the government's power to change the individual terms and conditions under a licence. When a licence is awarded, the individual terms and conditions are to some extent subject to negotiation. This is so in particular in respect of the work commitment undertaken by the licensees.[23] Moreover, for this reason, the licence is also required to be signed by the licensees. A contractual element on a different level lies in the terms and conditions of state participation. The state participates directly in most licences through the state-owned administration company Petoro, and commits in this respect to the joint operating agreement on equal terms with the other licence partners.

The joint operating agreement governing the relationship within the licence is a standard instrument drafted by the ministry and in principle updated for each licence round. As already mentioned, the licensees are required to enter into the agreement as a specific condition under the licence. As such, the agreement is perhaps best described as a kind of mandatory regulation replacing ordinary principles of company law within the licence groups. Each joint operating agreement contains a special part and a general part. The former is specific to the individual licence and typically contains rules on the parties, voting rights, the operator and so on. The latter on the other hand contains the general rules which are similar to all licences. It covers aspects such as management principles, cost sharing and liability, field development and sole risk, lifting of petroleum and assignment. Any changes in the agreement require the approval of the Ministry of Petroleum and Energy.

(c) Acquisition of acreage

As mentioned, the key licence in the Norwegian system is the production licence awarded on the basis of the Petroleum Act, Section 3(3). Production licences are awarded in licence rounds, where a distinction may be made between the ordinary licence rounds and a simplified procedure for awarding of licences in mature areas, instigated in 2003 (awards in pre-defined areas or APA).[24] As mentioned, the awarding of licences on the Norwegian continental shelf is subject to the Licensing Directive, EC Directive 94/22. The directive is mainly implemented in Norwegian law through the Petroleum Act, Section 3(5), which sets down certain main requirements and provides objective criteria for awarding licences. The main procedural requirement is that before licences are awarded, the relevant licensing area must be subject to announcement in both the Norwegian official publication *Norsk Lysningsblad* and the *Official Journal of the European Union*, with a specified time limit

23 See Ulf Hammer *et al*, *Petroleumsloven* (Universitetsforlaget, Oslo, 2009), p 181.

24 As of October 2012 there had been 22 ordinary licence rounds (usually biannually the last 10 years), and an annual APA licensing round since 2003; see generally on licensing policy the cabinet report (white paper) to the Storting: *An Industry for the Future – Norway's Petroleum Activity* (Meld St 28 (2010–2011)), p 85 and following.

for application that cannot be less than 90 days.[25] The subsequent awarding of licences must be based on the requirements and conditions announced in the invitation, and generally in accordance with "rational and objective criteria".[26] According to the Petroleum Regulation Section 10, the award of licences shall as a rule be based on two main criteria; the applicant's technical capability and financial strength, and its plan for exploration and development of the area applied for.[27]

(d) *Qualification requirements*

The main rule is that production licences can only be awarded to companies incorporated and registered in Norway, and to individuals domiciled in Norway or another EEA country.[28] In practice, licences are only awarded to companies. Therefore, foreign oil companies applying for and holding licences must as a rule act through a Norwegian subsidiary. Moreover, the criterion in the Petroleum Regulation, Section 10 relating to technical capability and financial strength constitutes essentially an additional minimum qualification requirement for applicants.[29] In order to facilitate the entry of new actors, the ministry has however, since 2000, operated a pre-qualification procedure, where potential applicants may apply for and achieve pre-qualification as licensees. This nevertheless does not give any legal right as such to be awarded a licence, nor does it ensure that the applicant will always be deemed to qualify for any licence.[30] Its main significance is that it gives potential applicants a good indication that they will be deemed to be qualified. In addition, it simplifies the award process for the government.

(e) *Duration*

The Petroleum Act, Section 3(9) stipulates that production licences shall have an initial duration of up to 10 years. The initial period is the time intended for the performance of the work commitment undertaken by the licensee. Subsequent to having performed the work commitment, the licensee is legally entitled to an extension of the licence beyond the initial 10 years. The extension period is stipulated in advance in the individual licence, but as a rule it is 30 years and may in special circumstances be up to 50 years. It follows from this that the ministry may not award a licence for more than 60 years from the time of the initial award of the licence. Extension of the licence beyond the stipulated licence period may nevertheless be given upon application at the end of the licence period.[31] Such an application must be submitted at the latest five years before the expiry of the licence period.

---

25 See Petroleum Act Section 3(5) (1) and (2).

26 See Petroleum Act Section 3(5), and see further Finn Arnesen (et al), "Energy Law in Norway" in *Energy Law in Europe*, edited by Martha M. Roggenkamp et al, (Oxford University Press, Oxford, 2007) p 897.

27 See generally Hammer *et al, op cit*, pp153-157.

28 This includes all EU member states in addition to Iceland and Liechtenstein.

29 Hammer *et al, op cit*, p155.

30 *Ibid* p 158.

31 See the Petroleum Act Section 3(9), fifth part.

(f) *Minimum work programme*

Under the Petroleum Act, Section 3(8), the award of a licence may, and usually will, be combined with a work commitment undertaken by the licensee. The work commitment will usually be based on the plans for exploration submitted in the licence application. It is however also subject to specific negotiation between the authorities and the licensee prior to the award of the licence. An important policy underlying the work commitment is the government's interest in exploration of the continental shelf, where it is also significant to have confirmation that a certain area does not contain significant petroleum deposits. The work commitment can therefore be seen as a part of the consideration for the rights obtained under a licence.[32]

Usually the work commitment will consist in the drilling of one or more exploration wells in the relevant area, and often in addition the collection of further seismic data in the area. The wells to be drilled will always be specified through criteria defined in the licence. Whether the criteria have been satisfied can however sometimes be ascertained only after the well has been drilled. Since the cost of drilling a well on the Norwegian continental shelf may be very high, the licensees will usually apply in advance to have a planned well approved as an 'exploration well'.[33]

In accordance with the Petroleum Regulation Section 13, the time limit for performance of the work commitment may not exceed the initial licence period of 10 years, but the individual licence may also stipulate a shorter time limit. A quite common practice in more recent years has been to introduce a 'drill or drop' obligation, which sets a short time limit for performing drilling obligations and obliges the licensee to relinquish the licence if this is not done. As already mentioned, satisfactory performance of the work commitment is a condition of the right to get an extension of the initial licence period.

(g) *Assignment and encumbrance*

In accordance with the Petroleum Act, Section 10(12), assignment of licences and shares in licences requires the consent of the Ministry of Petroleum and Energy. Moreover, other transactions involving a direct or indirect transfer of interests in the licence, such as a change of control in a company holding a licence share, also require government consent. The purpose is to secure government control over the composition of the licence groups. The ministry will of course be particularly concerned to ensure that a new licensee satisfies the minimum requirements as to financial strength and technical capability.

Previously, the joint operating agreement governing the relationship within the licence group contained pre-emption rights both for the state and the other licensees. It also contained a separate requirement of consent from the other licensees, although a refusal of consent could only be based on a limited number of grounds such as financial strength and capability. Under the current joint operating

---

32 Hammer *et al, op cit,* p181.
33 *Ibid* p183.

agreement, only the state, through Petoro, is given a pre-emption right, and the consent of the other licensees is no longer required after the work commitment has been performed.[34] The purpose of this change is to facilitate the transfer of licence shares and encourage new actors on the Norwegian continental shelf. The concerns of the remaining licensees are considered sufficiently accounted for by the requirement that the ministry must consent to the transfer. A particular issue relating to assignments that has caused some concern in Norway is the continuing liability of the assignor for abandonment costs, under the Petroleum Act, Section 5(3). In practice this means that the assignor always requires a guarantee from the assignee in respect of the abandonment costs.

Subject to the same requirements as assignment, a licence share may also be mortgaged as collateral for a loan or other financing of the activity under a licence, or in special circumstances also activity under other licences. Mortgaging of licences or licence shares is governed by the Petroleum Act, Chapter 6. The main requirement is that the Ministry of Petroleum and Energy must give its consent to the mortgage, under the Petroleum Act, Section 6(2). Moreover, further transfer of the rights of the mortgagee also requires the ministry's consent.[35] The mortgage encompasses all assets connected to the licence as well as all other rights related to the activity under the licence, or in the case of a licence share, an ideal share of the total assets and rights.[36] The mortgage is registered in the petroleum register, and otherwise follows the rules on priority and security in ordinary property law.[37]

(h) *Local content*

In the early days of petroleum activities in Norway, an underlying policy of the regulatory framework was to facilitate the use of Norwegian contractors and suppliers. To this end, the concessionary system put certain formal and informal incentives in place for the oil companies to use Norwegian suppliers. Documented previous use of Norwegian suppliers would, for instance, be taken into account by the ministry in awarding new licences, and the oil companies were to a certain extent required to favour Norwegian suppliers to the extent that they could be deemed competitive with international actors.[38] As already mentioned, this policy may be deemed to have been very important in developing a truly competitive Norwegian petroleum industry, where Norwegian players today are world leaders in a number of fields such as specialised vessel services, subsea construction and offshore drilling and well services.

Under the current system, the EEA Agreement prohibits discrimination based on nationality, and the Norwegian petroleum sector is today subject to a detailed regulatory framework on public procurement.[39] This is not only applicable to the government and public entities, but also applies to all activities of private actors

34 See Article 23 of the standard joint operating agreement from the 20th licence round.
35 See the Petroleum Act, Section 6(4).
36 See the Petroleum Act, Section 6(3).
37 See the Petroleum Act, Section 6(1), final part.
38 Skirbekk, *"Norske varer og tjenester"* in Selvig (ed), *Petroleumsrett til studiebruk* (1988), p 495 and following.
39 The main statutory basis is Act 69 of July 16 1999 on Public Procurement.

based on a concession or licence to explore for or produce oil and gas.[40] The main obligation this entails for the oil companies is that all supplies exceeding a certain threshold value must be subject to a competitive process where the award of contracts must be based on objective criteria. In particular, favouring suppliers based on nationality or local connection is not allowed.

(i) ***National reservation***

Previously, the concessionary system was based on an arrangement where the Norwegian state oil company Statoil received a carried interest in most licences awarded to foreign oil companies, with options to increase its share in the licence after the exploration programme had been performed.[41] Essentially this meant that the foreign oil companies had to carry the exploration risk, while the government reserved a certain share in case the exploration was successful and a discovery was made.

It is still current policy to reserve a certain share in most licences to the government, which is administered by the state-owned management company Petoro. The government no longer retains a carried interest however. Petoro now as a rule participates in the licences on equal terms with the other licensees, and has to carry its share of the exploration costs. It still has certain special privileges however, such as having a pre-emption right in the event of assignment of licence shares, that do not apply to the other licensees.[42]

(j) ***Health, safety and the environment***

Health, safety and environmental concerns are significant in the Norwegian regulation of petroleum activities. Due to the harsh weather, a vulnerable environment, and the inherent challenges of offshore activity, a strong focus on environment and safety issues has always been necessary. With increasing activities in the Barents Sea, which poses new challenges connected with operating under arctic conditions, this is likely to become even more important. The main government approach in this regard is a policy of zero tolerance with regard to any kinds of accidents or hazards. This is implemented through an independent regulatory framework governing all aspects of petroleum activities with regard to health, safety and environmental issues. To secure independence, the authority supervising, controlling and making decisions under the relevant regulations is not under the Ministry of Petroleum and Energy and the Norwegian Petroleum Directorate, but is the province of a separate government organ known as the Petroleum Safety Authority, which is subordinate to the Ministry of Labour and Inclusion.

The most striking feature of the Norwegian regulatory approach to these issues is perhaps the extensive use of so-called 'function requirements', which for most

---

40 The main regulation applicable to procurement in the energy and petroleum sector is the Regulation on Procurement in the Supply Sectors (Water and Energy Supply, Transport and Postal Services) of April 7 2006.

41 See further Arnesen *et al*, *op cit*, p 892.

42 See Section 3.1(g) above.

purposes do not require minimum technical solutions but instead impose detailed standards of diligence, set out in the regulations, in respect of all essential functions. The main requirement is set out in the Petroleum Act, Section 10(1), which states that petroleum activity shall be conducted in a prudent manner, which takes due account of safety concerns and the economic value represented by facilities and vessels involved in the activity, including their operational availability. The purpose of this regulatory technique is to leave the design and engineering of appropriate technical solutions to the companies, and to facilitate the continuing improvement of such solutions over time, while retaining government supervision and control. An important element of this is the use of extensive documentation, reporting and approval requirements. Thus, the licensees are required to develop extensive internal control and management systems to verify and document compliance. For mobile installations, the owners are required to apply for a so-called 'approval of compliance' before the installation is used for petroleum activity on the Norwegian continental shelf, in which compliance with the regulations must be documented and verified.[43] Moreover, as a rule, distinct approval from the government is required in respect of all significant new activities, where again compliance with the relevant regulations must be documented in detail.[44] The general responsibility of the licensees and the operator for compliance with the regulations also extends further than their own activities and encompasses all suppliers and contractors performing activities connected to the licence. According to Norwegian law, the operator and the licensees have what is known as a 'see to it responsibility', in other words, they must see to it that everyone performing work under the licence complies with relevant regulations.[45]

(k) Governing law and dispute resolution

All licences awarded on the Norwegian continental shelf are subject to Norwegian law and the Norwegian courts. A common licence requirement is that "all activity conducted on the basis of the licence" shall be subject to Norwegian law and grounded on the "Norwegian contractual tradition".

This provision extends far beyond the relationship between the licensees and the government. For practical purposes, it means that all contracts entered into by the operator in respect of the licence must be based on Norwegian law and the Norwegian contract tradition. This encompasses for instance all seismic and drilling contracts entered into during the exploration phase, and all construction and supply contracts entered into in the field development phase. It may be questioned whether this does not indirectly favour Norwegian companies, which may have been part of its purpose when the requirement was introduced, but the requirement has been maintained as a part of the terms and conditions of individual licences and has been included also in the latest licence rounds.

---

43 See the Framework Regulation, Section 25, available in English at www.ptil.no/rammeforskriften/category381.html.

44 See the Management Regulation, Section 25, available in English at www.ptil.no/management/category401. html?lang=en_US#_Toc280619416.

45 See the Petroleum Act, Section 10(6).

As regards the relationship between the licensees (including Petoro), the mandatory joint operating agreement contains a separate provision on disputes, which provides that disputes in connection with the agreement shall be subject to arbitration in Norway and subject to Norwegian law.[46]

3.2 Government take

The total government take under the Norwegian system has four elements, only two of which are essential however. The four distinct elements are the royalty (or production fee), the area fee, the state direct participation and the petroleum tax, with the latter two being the essential elements.

(a) Production fee

Royalties, which in the Norwegian legislation are called a 'production fee', shall in accordance with the Petroleum Act, Section 4(10) not apply to licences where the plan for development and operation was approved before January 1 1986. In practice, the government has also granted an exemption from the production fee to the remaining licences where it still applied.[47] Accordingly, royalties no longer have any practical significance in the Norwegian system.

(b) Area fee

In accordance with Section 4(10), the licensees are obligated to pay an area fee per square kilometre (km^2) of the licensed area, but only after the expiry of the initial licence period. The area fee does not primarily have a fiscal purpose, but is meant to provide an incentive for the licensees to relinquish parts of the licensed area where no substantial activity is taking place. This also means that the area fee does not apply to areas covered by a plan for development and operation, under the Petroleum Regulation, Section 39. Because of its purpose as an incentive to relinquish parts of the licensed area, the area fee increases exponentially in each of the first three years. Currently, the fee is Nkr30,000 per km? the first year, while it increases to Nkr60,000 NOK in the second year and Nkr120,000 in the third year, after which it remains stable.[48]

(c) State participation

The state's direct participation in petroleum activities on the Norwegian continental shelf has two components: its direct financial interest and its part ownership of Statoil.

State's direct financial interest: As already mentioned, an important part of the Norwegian concessionary system is that the state participates directly in most licences with a certain share administered by the state-owned management company Petoro.[49] This entitles the state to receive a proportional share of the production under each licence, on equal terms with the other licence partners. In practice, this

---

46 See Article 29 of the standard joint operating agreement (20th licence round).
47 Hammer *et al, op cit,* p 390.
48 Hammer *et al, op cit,* p 362.
49 The role of Petoro is regulated in the Petroleum Act, Chapter 11.

constitutes a significant part of the state's income from the petroleum resources on the Norwegian continental shelf. While the state in principle is entitled to petroleum as it is extracted on the same terms as the other licence partners, neither the state nor Petoro in practice lifts and markets its own petroleum. Under a special arrangement known as the 'marketing instruction', put in place in connection with the reorganisation and privatisation of Statoil in 2001, Statoil maintains responsibility for the sale and distribution of the state's direct share of petroleum where it participates as a licence partner.

State ownership of Statoil: As mentioned, Statoil was reorganised and privatised in 2001, but the state retains a majority shareholding in the company and still receives a substantial share of its income from petroleum activities in the form of an annual dividend from Statoil.[50] Statoil also has activities in many other areas than the Norwegian continental shelf, however, and the state's interest in Statoil should strictly speaking be considered as a mere financial placement and not as an element of the total government take from petroleum activities on the Norwegian continental shelf. Beyond its majority shareholding, the state does not have any special privileges in the company, and is legally treated as any other shareholder. The state's ownership position in Statoil is handled by the Ministry of Trade and Industry, and is therefore separated from the Ministry of Petroleum and Eenergy's authority in respect of the management of petroleum resources.

(d) *Petroleum tax*

The most significant element of the government's revenues from the petroleum resources on the Norwegian continental shelf is the petroleum tax system.[51] In broad terms, the state taxes the net income from petroleum activities at a general tax rate of 78%. This consists essentially of the ordinary corporate tax of 28%, and a special petroleum tax of 50% on the net income from petroleum production and pipeline transportation activities.[52] The special petroleum tax is justified on the basis of the state's ownership of the petroleum resources, and constitutes what is commonly termed the 'resource rent'.

Valuation of the production for the purpose of the special tax is generally based on a system of normal prices pitched to reflect arm's length transactions in a functioning market.[53] While aiming to give the state its just share, a significant objective of the tax system is also to provide incentives to the oil companies to make the investments that are necessary and desirable for optimal exploitation of the resources. Accordingly, the other significant element of the system is its rules on depreciation and deductions. As a rule all costs incurred in relation to taxable income are deductible. A crucial issue, however, is whether costs are deductible against the special petroleum tax of 50% (78% in total) or only against the 28% ordinary

---

50 As of October 2012, the state owns 67% of the shares.

51 For an overview of the petroleum tax system, see Jan B Jansen and Joachim Bjerke, *Norwegian Petroleum Taxation – An Introduction*, MarIus 404 (2011), p 314.

52 *Ibid*, p 315.

53 See the Petroleum Tax Act (35 of June 13 1975), Section 4.

corporate tax. The general rule deriving from the principle of net taxation is that all investments and costs connected with the activities subject to the special tax are also deductible against the special tax. This is however in practice a difficult issue.

Another significant issue is whether investments are deductible when they are incurred, or subject to depreciation. As a rule, exploration costs are deductible when they are incurred irrespective of whether a discovery is made, while investments in production facilities are depreciated over six years. Since the facilities usually have a much longer lifespan than six years, this constitutes a substantial tax credit during the initial production period. The same can of course be said for the immediate deductibility of exploration costs. However, as mentioned, even stronger tax incentives have been put in place in respect of exploration costs. From 2003 onwards, licensees with no or insufficient taxable income are also entitled to an annual refund from the government of their deductible share of exploration costs.

4. Current issues

Apart from ordinary day-to-day issues shaped by individual cases and circumstances, some main legal currents connected with structural developments in the petroleum sector can also be discerned, although singling out particular issues in this regard will fail to provide justice to the larger picture.

In general, the legal landscape is increasingly shaped by large parts of the Norwegian continental shelf now being mature areas, meaning that the areas are well charted and developed with existing infrastructure. One consequence of this is that the joint use of infrastructure has gained increasing significance. It is very common on the Norwegian continental shelf that new fields are tied in to existing fields to share existing production facilities. The Petroleum Act has special provisions on joint development and third party access to existing facilities, with extensive powers for the government to impose convenient arrangements in this regard. The underlying government policy at work here goes far beyond that of ensuring unitisation of connected fields however. It also extends more generally to facilitating joint infrastructure wherever this is deemed cost-efficient and rational from a socio-economic perspective. Where this is a current concern on the mature part of the Norwegian continental shelf, is that the policy has the effect that production facilities on older fields which are nearing, or have already reached, depletion nevertheless remain significant as a common infrastructure used by surrounding licences. This again raises a number of complex licensing issues, for instance regarding the continuing ownership and operation of such facilities.

Another trend is the involvement of new and more specialised actors in activities on the Norwegian continental shelf, for instance small specialised exploration companies and companies specialising in tail-end production. This has the consequence that assignment of licences and issues relating to financing and securities are becoming increasingly significant. Moreover, this development together with a shift of focus to smaller fields and technological developments has also created a need for new operational solutions and new organisational models. This development is likely to be even more accentuated in the future.

An overview of current issues would not be complete without a mention of environmental concerns and policy. In particular, climate policy is likely to have an increasing impact on the regulatory framework for petroleum activities. One current issue concerns the government's ambition to connect the offshore petroleum installations to the land-based electricity grid, in order to reduce greenhouse gas emissions. This raises a number of licensing and regulatory issues that have not yet been resolved.

A number of other issues could also have deserved mention in this section. We have not covered the regulation of downstream aspects of the petroleum activities in this chapter. However, it should be mentioned that an important issue, relating both to the increasing significance of gas and the increased activities in the Barents Sea, concerns how to transport the gas raised to the markets. This is of course also an issue of extraordinary importance for upstream developments in these areas. Developments within the European Union could also have been mentioned, since the European Union may be moving more into upstream regulation. A legal issue with particular significance for Norway in this regard is the extent to which increasing EU regulation of upstream activities will be EEA-relevant, and therefore subject to implementation in Norway.

5. Conclusion

The Norwegian legal framework for petroleum activities constitutes a distinct regulatory model. Its main characteristic is a concessionary system where the state is deeply involved at every stage of the relevant activities. The state's involvement has two main elements: on the one hand as the licensing and regulatory authority, and on the other hand as a direct licence partner in most fields. Regulatory policies have developed in accordance with the general development of the Norwegian petroleum industry, and how those regulatory policies implemented through the legal framework have in themselves been significant in shaping a distinct national petroleum industry in Norway from a starting point back in the 1960s when the country had little or no practical experience of this industry.

Poland

Piotr Pszczel
Kawalko & Godlewski

---

1. Introduction

Poland is rarely associated with the role of petroleum producer. There are several reasons for this.

First, being a main route for the transport of oil and natural gas from east to west (between Russia and the European Union), Poland's domestic production of hydrocarbons is often overlooked. Second, as in many other European countries, the dominant role of the state or state-owned companies has been seen as a major disadvantage from the point of view of potential competitors.

Obviously the Poland's oil and natural gas resources cannot be compared with those of the largest producing countries. However, with genuine expectations as regards shale and tight gas there is potential for a significant change in the status quo.

2. Upstream activities

In recent months, Poland has become one of the most interesting countries for companies involved globally in exploration for and exploitation of shale and tight gas. Nearly all the major players have announced their interest in engaging in exploration for unconventional gas, and have consequently applied for the licences for exploration of shale gas and tight gas in Poland.

Currently, the most significant number of licences for exploration and exploitation is held by the Polish incumbent, Polish Oil and Gas Company (PGNiG). Other Polish companies like Lotos, PKN Orlen and Petrobaltic are also active, but their role is less significant. Nevertheless, some licences for exploration for natural gas are also held by independent and international companies that believe there are opportunities relating to production of shale and tight gas in Poland.

However, there is currently no reliable and published data as to what quantities of shale or tight gas exist or can be produced. There are several reports which have been published and the quantities shown in these reports vary significantly. The US Energy Information Administration published a report in April 2011 saying that shale gas sources in Poland amount to the 180 trillion cubic feet. However, the report has been followed by several other sources giving a different assessments in that respect. A general conclusion would be that a more precise assessment of amounts of shale gas in Poland will be available in the year 2013, as the new assessments will be based on the latest drilling results and not, as in the case of the Energy Information Administration report, on comparisons and historical data. Nevertheless the steps taken by the Polish government clearly suggest that in the not-so-distant future, Poland might join to the group of hydrocarbon-exporting countries. Currently nearly all consumption of oil in Poland is satisfied by imports, mainly from the Russian Federation, and domestic production of natural gas amounts to only one third of consumption of natural gas in Poland.

3. Petroleum legal regime

As a consequence of Poland's accession to the European Union in 2004, all national laws, including the legal regime governing the exploitation of hydrocarbons have to comply with relevant EU laws. The most significant element of EU law, which was due to be implemented into Polish national law, is Directive 94/22/EC on the conditions for granting and using authorisations for the prospection, exploration and production of hydrocarbons.[1]

3.1 Petroleum law and relevant provisions

Principally, for the upstream oil and gas sector in Poland the most relevant laws are:

- the Geological and Mining Law,[2] which regulates most of the matters concerning prospection, exploration and exploitation of hydrocarbons in Poland; and
- the Polish Civil Code;[3]

However, as the legal background in Poland is currently undergoing substantial change, this chapter also gives a brief summary of:

- the draft of the new Gas Law[4] and the Energy Law;[5]
- principles for a new law on hydrocarbons.[6]

The main act which regulates matters relating to upstream oil and gas activities is the Geological and Mining Law. According to the provisions of this act activities relating to production of hydrocarbons are prospection, exploration and exploitation.

It ought to be pointed out that at present the rules for these activities are the same for all hydrocarbons, without any particular differences in relation to shale and tight gas. Additionally the same provisions of the act are applied for exploration for methane. The act expressly names three main activities related to the production of hydrocarbons in Poland namely prospection exploration and exploitation. It is worth of noting, however, that only prospection, and exploration for hydrocarbons are actually defined by the provisions of the Geological and Mining Law.

Each of these activities is subject to a licensing regime. In fact there are two separate types of licence and associated procedures: first a licence for prospection and

1 Directive 94/22/EC of the European Parliament and of the Council of May 30 1994 on the conditions for granting and using authorisations for the prospection, exploration and production of hydrocarbons.
2 Geological and Mining Law of June 9 2011, *Journal of Laws* of 2011, Issue 163, Item 981.
3 Civil Code of April 23 1964, *Journal of Laws* of 1964, Issue 16, Item 93.
4 Draft of the new Gas Law available at legislacja.rcl.gov.pl/lista/2/projekt/19302.
5 Energy Law of April 10 1997, *Journal of Laws* of 2012, Item 1059.
6 Principles published by the Ministry of Environment, available at www.mos.gov.pl.

exploration, and second a licence for exploitation of hydrocarbons. These are discussed in further detail below.

Currently, all the major legislative acts relating to energy are undergoing significant change. A part of this substantial change consists in separation of all matters relating to natural gas from the general scheme of regulation under the Energy Law.

The recently published draft of the new Gas Law is of direct and significant importance for upstream activities. Although the provisions of the draft expressly stipulates that the provisions of the Gas Law should be not applicable to matters relating to exploration for natural gas, because of the system adopted in the draft Gas Law some obligations will seriously affect the situation of entities that undertake exploration for natural gas in Poland.

As a consequence of the relevant provisions of the Energy Law, activities consisting in transporting, distributing and storing natural gas can only be carried out after obtaining the relevant licence. The competent authority for granting this licence is the president of the Energy Regulatory Office (ERO).

The president of the ERO is also competent in matters relating to approval of tariffs for transmission and distribution or storage services. Furthermore, as a consequence of the existing regime of natural gas pricing, the president of ERO has an obligation to supervise the process of natural gas pricing. The supervision consists of approving tariffs both on the wholesale market and tariffs for households.

Under the draft new Gas Law the entire licensing scheme in the gas sector will be amended. Part of the change consists in replacing the existing licence to trade in natural gas with licences to sell natural gas. As a consequence of this change all entities involved in the sale of natural gas in the territory of Poland will be obliged to hold a licence. The amendment seems to be crucial for upstream companies as the obligation will cover also natural gas produced domestically, and consequently they will soon be obliged to apply for such licences and this way come under the supervision of the president of the ERO.

Moreover it should be also mentioned that as a consequence of the new Gas Law export of natural gas will also require an export licence, regardless of whether it is conventional or unconventional gas such as shale or tight gas.

A substantial part of the rules regarding exploration for hydrocarbons will be replaced by a new law which was due to be passed by the end of 2012. The parts of this chapter referring to the matters covered by the anticipated new legislation are based on the principles for a new law on hydrocarbons, published by the Ministry of Environment.

The principles cover the main elements likely to be relevant to exploration for hydrocarbons in the coming years. Principally, the document covers matters relating to oil and natural gas, including shale and tight gas, with regard to issues including licensing, royalties, taxes and, importantly, rules in the scope of states supervision over hydrocarbons in Poland.

(a) Regulatory bodies

Ministry of Environment: The discretionary power regarding granting licences for prospection exploration and exploitation of hydrocarbons is entrusted mainly to the Ministry of Environment. Nevertheless a minor role is also played by the Mining Authority.

Mining Authority: The Mining Authority is relevant with regard to matters relating to mining rights, particularly those concerning technical issues, safety conditions, geological works and supervision of geological works, which are discussed in more detail below.

Energy Regulatory Office: The ERO is the main administrative body supervising the activities of energy entities in Poland. Both the Energy Law and the draft Gas Law give the President of the ERO broad powers over the gas market in Poland, as the transmission, distribution, storage and final sale of natural gas must be performed under his supervision. The ERO is also set to become important for upstream matters in Poland.

(b) Types of agreement

At first sight, the polish model is based on a simple licensing scheme: the entire cycle of production of hydrocarbons – prospection, exploration and exploitation – is subject to special licences. There are separate licences for prospection and exploration of hydrocarbons and for exploitation of hydrocarbons.

However, it ought to be pointed out that the licensing process is only a part of the entire procedure that has to be followed by an interested party. The overall procedure, despite the terminology used, should not be identified with a typical licensing procedure used in other countries.

The Polish state acts on two levels here. First, it can grant the relevant licence as an act of public law in exercise of its public power. Second, after such an act the state acts on the basis of private law as party to a mining rights agreement, where the licence holder is the second party to the agreement. The dual nature of this process is often criticised, especially by private sector players, but it nevertheless still remains in force and governs the conditions for exploration for hydrocarbons in Poland.

Licences: Both types of licence, that for prospection or exploration and that for exploitation, are issued in the form of an administrative decision by the Ministry of Environment. The provisions of the Geological and Mining Law provide a list of the necessary steps to be taken by any interested party.

As a first stage of the process is the application for a licence for prospection for hydrocarbons. Consequently all geological works intended to identify or map oil or gas fields require a licence for prospection and exploration.

The basic starting point is that under the Polish law all hydrocarbons belong to the State Treasury. A licence for prospection for hydrocarbons does not transfer the ownership of the hydrocarbons. Instead it merely entitles an interested party to conduct prospecting activities on a relevant territory. Ownership is only transferred after the fulfilment of several conditions established by the relevant provisions of the Geological and Mining law and the Civil Code. One of the main preconditions is concluding of a mining rights agreement.

Mining rights agreement: The second element of the entire procedure is regulated by the provisions of the Geological and Mining Law with a number of references to provisions of the Polish Civil Code.

The provisions of the Geological and Mining Law are treated as a law governing specific subject matter for the purposes of the Civil Code. In particular, the provisions of the Geological and Mining law stipulate that a mining rights agreement should be subject to the provisions on lease agreements set out in the Civil Code.

Nevertheless, it would be wrong to draw the conclusion that the mining rights agreement is a simple example of the lease agreement regulated by the Civil Code. The provisions of the Geological and Mining Law provide for several differences when compared to the provisions of the Civil Code. The differences lie particularly in the maximum term of a mining rights agreement and in some peculiarities with regard to fees and other details.

It also important to note that, despite the fact that the mining rights agreement has a totally different character and role, it is still to be concluded by the same parties as in the licensing procedure: the interested party (at this stage of the procedure, the licence holder) and the state, which is again represented here by the Ministry of the Environment.

(c) Acquisition of acreage

It is important to note that as it currently stands the Geological and Mining Law stipulates that issuing of licences for prospection for hydrocarbons should be, with some minor exceptions, initiated by a tender procedure.

The relevant authority, the Ministry of the Environment, is obliged to publish in the *Official Journal* of the European Union a formal notice on the state's intention of granting a licence, specifying a given territory, the planned start date, the relevant activity, the essential conditions of the mining rights agreement and the period for which the licence will be granted. Assessment of the submitted bids is carried out in the light of the following criteria:

- technical and financial capabilities of the interested party;
- the proposed technology to be used in geological works;
- proposed fees for the award of mining rights.

The second possible way of granting a licence, the so-called 'open door' procedure, is usually initiated by a company showing interest in a particular territory. The Ministry of Environment is obliged to publish the expression of interest, attaching some essential data like minimum fees for the award of mining rights and also an invitation for other participants to submit bids.

Assessment of the submitted bids is carried out in the light of the same criteria as in the case of the tender procedure. The Ministry of Environment is obliged to conclude an agreement on mining rights with the successful bidder. Under the provisions of the Geological and Mining Law, the agreement must provide a description of the relevant territory covered by the licence, the duration of the licence and a list of the parties' rights and obligations. Obviously the main right which is granted for the licence holder is the exclusive right to undertake prospection or exploring activities within the territory. The agreement should be concluded in writing and should also define its term.

Exploitation of hydrocarbons is subject to a separate licence, which is also issued by the Ministry of Environment. Thus all interested parties should also apply for exploration licences and subsequently for mining rights.

It is worth of nothing that the procedure for the award of an exploitation licence is not subject to a tendering procedure, and the general rules provide some advantages for the party who engaged in prospecting and explored the well. The main advantage consists in having access to relevant geological information and also priority in the application procedure. However it should be noted that the European Commission has sent a formal letter to Poland, and it might be expected that a new law will adjust the exiting scheme.

(d) Qualification requirements

The existing laws set out strict and formal qualification requirements.

The requirements for entities involved in exploration for hydrocarbons covers a number of aspects. First, their technical ability to cope with exploration matters is assessed during the licensing procedure. In some particular cases it might be that the companies that do not offer the relevant level of experience cannot be successful in their application for a licence for prospection for hydrocarbons. As mentioned above, an applicant's financial capabilities and their proposal for the level of fees for the award of mining rights are also assessed.

Furthermore, the Geological and Mining Law provides several formal requirements for the personnel involved in exploration for hydrocarbons. The fourth chapter of that law stipulates that personnel involved in geological works, particularly those supervising or directing such geological works should have certain defined skills and necessary qualifications. The geological activities must be performed by certified personnel. Such certification is the responsibility of the Ministry of the Environment. The procedure is initiated by an interested party and the relevant provisions of the Geological and Mining Law provide for several essential skills and requirements that have to be demonstrated by the candidates for such certificates.

In addition, for all miners and drillers who are to be involved in the process of prospection or exploration for hydrocarbons, the Geological and Mining Law provides for an entire scheme of required qualifications or proof of necessary experience.

(e) Duration

Under the provisions of the Geological and Mining Law priority rights over discovered fields last no longer than five years from the decision of the relevant authority confirming the geological information. However as established by the provisions of the law, the maximum term for any licence is 50 years. The minimum term is three years. In practice the duration of a licence is established in the licence itself, together with a list of conditions related to particular periods of the licence, which have to be met by the licence holder. The Ministry of Environment is entitled to cancel a licence if the licence holder does not undertake the relevant activity for which the licence has been granted. The maximum term for which a mining rights agreement can be concluded is also set at 50 years.

(f) ***Minimum work programme***

When applying for a licence for prospection and or for the exploitation of hydrocarbons, an applicant should specify the range and types of geological and other works which will be performed in order to achieve the given goal.

Additionally, confirmation that a licence will be issued should be followed by a draft of the planned geological works. The final version of the work programme is included in the licence and reaffirmed in the agreement establishing mining rights.

Although the process of establishing of the work programme is a part of the licensing procedure, supervision of compliance with the work programme is mainly the responsibility of the Mining Authority or its branches. Nevertheless the Ministry of Environment also has the right to withdraw a licence if the licence holder does not undertake the activity for which the licence has been granted in a timely manner.

(g) ***Assignment and encumbrance***

Assignment of a licence is possible in two ways. First, the provisions of the Geological and Mining Law stipulate that a licence can be transferred by a licence holder to an entity which accepts all the conditions of the licence, can prove it has rights to the necessary geological information, and also is able to prove its legal title to mining rights. Nevertheless, the Geological and Mining Law also provides that a change of licence holder cannot be made if it would be contrary to the public interest or detrimental to environmental protection.

Second, the provisions of the Geological Mining Law allow for assignment on the basis of other terms, especially those leading to legal succession. Therefore a merger or acquisition of a company to which a licence has been granted should not lead to cancellation of the licence, although the legal successor is obliged to inform the relevant authorities within 30 days of the succession, attaching proof thereof.

(h) ***Local content***

Polish laws set out several obligations as regards work permits for foreign workers. Principally, the validity of work permit is limited to three years, though there are some special rules in the case of particular professions. Exceptions from the scheme can be justified in cases where the worker's profession is unusual due to the special character of the planned work.

(i) ***National reservation***

The system of tendering for licences and the open door procedure gives the state significant discretionary powers as to where and under what conditions exploration for hydrocarbons should be allowed.

Given the history of exploration in Poland, where exploration for hydrocarbons was mainly done by state-owned companies, there was no need for detailed regulation of the issue of national reservation. The new scheme will be worked out on the basis of the principles mentioned above. The core measure in that respect will be establishment of a national hydrocarbons operator, which will be responsible for relevant matters. The draft of the new law on hydrocarbons was due to be presented at the end of 2012.

(j) Environment

The environmental matters relating to exploration for hydrocarbons are very broad. Exploration for hydrocarbons poses a potential threat to the environment, and environmental protection provisions relating to such projects are to be found in several Polish acts. As an example, in the case of exploration for shale and tight gas, when significant amounts of water are used the most important questions relate to water permits. Detailed regulation on these is to be found in the Water Law, which also regulates matters relating to water extraction equipment, which will be of importance in the exploration for hydrocarbons.

Nevertheless, the main issue arising in respect of prospection, exploration and exploitation of hydrocarbons is the need for an environmental impact assessment. This specific procedure, which entered Polish national law as an consequence of EU directives, is the core element which needs to be taken into account when planning any project relating to the production of hydrocarbons in Poland.

The procedure is regulated by the provisions of the Law of October 3 2008 on the Provision of Information on the Environment and its Protection, Public Participation in Environmental Protection and Environmental Impact Assessments.[7] Essentially the provisions of this law divide all potential projects into two groups: those for which an environmental impact assessment is always required, and those where the proposed project may require an environmental impact assessment. The decision whether an environmental impact assessment is required in the second case is dependent on the discretionary power of the relevant authority.

It is important to note that as well as an obligation to prepare an environmental impact assessment there is a related right for interested parties to participate in the assessment, which might be costly and time-consuming for a hydrocarbons project. As a general rule, it might be pointed out that in practice all projects relating to exploitation of hydrocarbons in Poland require an environmental impact assessment. Projects relating to prospection and exploration may need an environmental impact assessment depending on the decision of the relevant authorities.

Last but not least, it is important to note that for the projects planned on the territory of Natura 2000 sites the environmental impact assessment regime is even more strict due to the special protection areas and special areas of conservation

---

7 *Journal of Laws* of 2008, Issue 199, Item 1227, as amended.

which have been created in relation to the Natura 2000 programme. More than 20% of the territory of Poland is covered by Natura 2000.

(k) Governing law and dispute resolution

Given the dominant role of the state or state-owned companies in the production of hydrocarbons in Poland all potential disputes are mainly dealt with under national law.

3.2 Government take

(a) Royalties and fees

Currently, the royalties, fees and taxes relating to the production of hydrocarbons in Poland are believed to be the lowest among hydrocarbon-producing countries. The fee for issuing licences for prospection is €25 per square kilometre of the territory covered by the licences. For a licence which is issued for prospection and exploration for hydrocarbons the fee is €50 per km^2.

The royalty for exploitation of natural gas is set at €1.50 per 100 cubic metres of natural gas. The royalty for exploitation of crude oil is €9 per ton.

Additionally all entities to which mining rights have been granted are obliged to pay relevant remuneration on an annual basis. The remuneration is a combination of fixed and variable fees. The fixed fee is calculated in relation to the value of a well. The variable fee is 50% of the exploitation fee in a given year. Remuneration for each year shall be paid no later than in February of the subsequent year.

The scheme of the fees will be subject to substantial change in the coming months, with the fees noted above being significantly increased, and additional levies and taxes being imposed on exploring companies. The principles for a new law on hydrocarbons provide that new types of taxes relating to exploitation of hydrocarbons should be introduced (probably including a windfall tax). The document specifies that a type of cash flow tax with a rate of 25% will be imposed on producer companies.

In the document there is also a general goal that cumulated levies from all relevant taxes combined, including corporate income tax, real estate tax and specific sectoral taxes, should aim at taking 40% of the income of producer companies.

(b) Corporate income tax

Companies in Poland are required to pay corporate income tax. The Polish system of corporate income tax does not display any significant differences in comparison to similar taxes other European countries, although it does offer some particular schemes of deductions and incentives for companies. The rate of corporate income tax in Poland is 19%.

(c) Special participation

Currently the state does not participate in the licences it awards in the way that many other countries do, with the rather obvious exception of companies which are owned fully or partially owned by the state. This, though, is a traditional participation, and as such it does not have the aim nor the function of stimulating or supervising the exploitation of hydrocarbons in Poland.

However as a consequence of the dramatic change in the opportunities for exploitation of hydrocarbons domestically and also as a result of pressure from the European Union, the Polish government has decided to establish a new scheme for exploration of hydrocarbons. While there is currently no draft available, the basic contents of the future modifications are known and the impact of the future legislative changes for ongoing as well as future projects for exploration of hydrocarbons cannot be overlooked. Generally the published principles aim at both increasing flexibility in exploration for hydrocarbons in Poland and at the same time securing the country's interests.

The main change, which should be implemented in the coming months, consists in the establishment of a national hydrocarbons operator. The planned state-owned company is expected to engage in all main activities relating to exploration for hydrocarbons in Poland. Details are not known at this stage, but it seems that its main task will consist in participating in exploring consortiums with the role of overseeing the state's interests and having a direct impact on petroleum activities. Regardless of the details of the future law, the main goal of the national hydrocarbons operator will be securing the state's interest in the domestic production of hydrocarbons.

It is expected that the new law will provide a dual model for interested parties, allowing for certain activities without the participation of national operator, but simultaneously imposing a more stringent licensing regime, or offering some incentives as regards applicable royalties for agreeing to participation by the national operator. The underlying goal is no doubt the development of national capabilities.

The possibility of participation by the national operator should be seen as an advantage for interested parties, especially for those to whom prospection licences have been already granted, as these licences holders will enjoy freedom of choice as to whether to create a consortium with the national operator or to explore for hydrocarbons on their own.

4. Current issues

The most important issue currently is the planned new model for the licensing scheme with participation of the national hydrocarbons operator. Introducing this new party into the scheme will seriously impact the framework of ongoing projects and obviously changes the conditions for any new projects.

Introduction of the national operator should give the state better control over its natural resources at all stages of the process of production of hydrocarbons. The holder of a licence for prospection or exploration will still enjoy priority in the procedure for obtaining a licence for exploitation of hydrocarbons, but after the lapse of a three-year period the national operator will be entitled to participate as a shareholder within any consortium that is created for exploration for hydrocarbons. For new projects further participation by the national operator will be legally required at the stage of the licence for prospection.

Another milestone for upstream companies will be the planned change in the scope of the natural gas price regime. Importantly, under provisions currently in force, the natural gas costs (and consequently the price of gas) is taken to consist of two elements: first, the cost of importing natural gas under long-term contracts from third country suppliers (mainly Russia and Germany), and second the cost of producing natural gas domestically in Poland.

Such a pricing scheme implies a fiction, namely that production of natural gas in Poland is not a part of the value chain of natural gas but merely an element of the costs which are taken into consideration when setting the final price of gas. Change to the current pricing scheme is a vital condition for creation of a properly functioning gas market in Poland, and should subsequently lead to better use of domestically produced natural gas.

Furthermore, the most crucial decisions as regards the scope of exploration for hydrocarbons are to be taken by the Polish government and legislature. Some of the matters has been outlined briefly above, especially with regard to the principles underlying the proposed new law on hydrocarbons, but the future shape of the scheme still remains partly unknown.

5. Conclusion

The obvious conclusion is that the entire legal framework in Poland is undergoing substantial change. All stages in the value chain will be affected by the draft legislation, the main of aim of which is to create a new scheme for the exploitation of hydrocarbons which should provide fair conditions for new investment. The new rules regarding exploitation of hydrocarbons are expected to be fully enacted in 2013, and will be followed by tax measures including the new cash flow tax.

From the point of view of potential investors, the most important issue will be to what extent should unconventional gas and oil be taken into account. All rights to information about potential finds belongs to the licence holder who has mapped an area and the state. Consequently, any potential investors need constantly to analyse all information from active parties. As of the date of writing a number of test wells had been drilled. In the case of several of them their results were positive, however in order to asses potential quantities of shale gas, much more test drilling must be undertaken.

The environmental aspects of Polish regulation of hydrocarbon production seem to be fairly stable, but, as mentioned in this chapter, the stricter environmental regulation and percentage of the Polish territory covered by the Natura 2000 system should be borne in mind, and potential investments should be carefully planned.

Russia

Anna Ovcharova
TNK-BP Management

1. Introduction

The aim of this chapter is to provide an overview of the Russian legal framework pertaining to the exploration for and production of natural resources, especially oil and gas. The most important federal laws dealing with the oil and gas sector have been enacted since 1995. Almost all laws pertaining to the oil and gas sector have been subject to continuous amendments. Despite this there are still plenty provisions that need to be improved in order to provide users of the subsoil with more flexibility and to increase investors' interest in the sector.

Given Russia's status as one of the world's biggest oil and gas countries, both by production and reserves, the significance of these laws is difficult to overestimate as is the importance of stability in the legal regulation of the upstream sector.

2. Upstream activity

Russia's proven oil reserves are estimated by different sources at 60 billion to 69 billion barrels.[1] Currently production primarily takes place in the Volga-Urals/Precaspian, Timan-Pechora, East Siberian and Far Eastern regions. Presently West Siberia is undergoing immense development in its production, while East Siberia's share of oil and gas exploration and development activity is expected to grow significantly.

The Russian Federation is extremely rich in natural gas reserves, and according to various estimates might amount to 47 trillion cubic metres (km^3). Geographically most of the gas reserves are located in the Nadim-Pur-Taz, East Siberian and Far Eastern regions and offshore. Exploration and development of the East Siberia, Far East and Yamal deposits is the priority for the coming years.

Russian oil production has been growing during recent years, and in 2007 it was claimed to have reached its highest peak since the collapse of the Soviet Union.

It is not a secret that oil and gas production and export is a major sector in the Russian economy, providing a positive balance to the state budget.

Only recently, the oil and gas sector was owed by state-owned companies, but following the privatisation process of the 1990s most of the state-owned companies undertaking exploration, development and production activities in the oil sector were privatised. This could not be said about gas sector, where Gazprom (the state-owned company) still dominates gas exploration, development and production activities.

1 See www.theoildrum.com/story/2006/2/9/211031/3684.

The corporate structure of the oil market was changed drastically during the first ten years of the 21st century. Such companies as Yukos, controlled by Mikhail Khodorkovskiy, and Sibneft, controlled by Roman Abramovich, were eliminated from the oil market scene. The head of Yukos, Mikhail Khodorkovskiy, was imprisoned and his company's assets were sold off at auctions to interested parties. As a result, most of the assets were directly and indirectly bought by Rosneft. Sibneft's assets were bought by Gazpromneft in the course of a normal acquisition transaction.

Currently the oil sector in the Russian Federation mainly comprises seven vertically integrated oil companies which produce about 90% of Russian crude oil. There are also a number of foreign project operators (Exxon Mobil, Shell, BP, KNOC, Statoil, Total) working under production sharing agreements. There are in addition a number of minor oil producers, whose share of production is insignificant.

Major Russian oil producers[2]

Company name	Revenue in 2011 (million US$)	Profit in 2011 (million US$)	Hydrocarbon reserves in 2010 (billion barrels)	Production of hydrocarbons in 2010 (million barrels daily)
Lukoil	123,108	12,822	17.3	2.2
Rosneft	83,388	12,680	15.2	2.5
TNK-BP Holding	54,170	9,047	9.6	1.9
Gazpromneft	44,021	5,048	6.2	1.1
Surgutneftegas	43,185	8,386	N/A	1.4
Tatneft	20,941	2,331	5.96	0.51
Bashneft	17	2	2.1	0.28

There is a state monopoly over gas production, where the state-owned company Gazprom ultimately dominates the Russian gas production sphere. There are certain privately owned gas companies, such as Novatek and Itera, however their share in production is insignificant in comparison to Gazprom's volumes and these minor gas producers' strategy is always to seek a strategic alliance with state-owned companies. Such alliances often ensure sharing of investment risks between the private and state

2 Source: expert.ru/ratings/krupnejshie-neftyanyie-kompanii-rossii/.

companies and access for the private companies to the transportation system, which is state-owned. The state-owned companies are interested in these alliances because of the possibility to expand their reserves base and in order to use the private companies' advanced technologies. The most recent example of such a strategic alliance is the establishing of joint venture between Rosneft (a state-owned company) and Itera (formerly a major private gas producer).

3. Petroleum legal regime

3.1 Petroleum law and relevant provisions

Oil and gas development, exploration and production activity in Russia are based on the legal framework resulting from the following major legal acts:

- the Constitution of the Russian Federation;[3]
- the Civil Code of the Russian Federation;[4]
- the Federal Law on Subsoil;[5]
- the Federal Law on the Continental Shelf of the Russian Federation;[6] and
- the Federal Law on Production Sharing Agreements.[7]

There are some other federal laws and sub-laws regulating activities in the oil and gas sector which will be considered later in this chapter.

(a) Regulatory authorities

Russia has a multiple layered system of federal authorities, overseeing activities in the oil and gas sector. The two executive bodies occupying the key positions in the system are the Ministry of Natural Resources and Ecology of the Russian Federation and the Federal Agency for Subsoil Use (Rosnedra), which is hierarchically subordinate to the Ministry of Natural Resources. The current structure of the executive bodies acting in the oil and gas sector was established by Presidential Decree 724 on Questions of the System and Structure of the Federal Executive Bodies.[8]

The Ministry of Natural Resources is a federal executive authority performing functions of public policy making and statutory regulation concerning the study, use, renewal and conservation of natural resources, including the subsoil, bodies of water, forests located in designated conservation areas, fauna and their habitat, as well as in the field of hunting, hydrometeorology and related areas, environmental monitoring and pollution control, including radiation monitoring and control, and functions of public environmental policy making, implementation and statutory regulation, encompassing issues relating to production and consumption, waste management, conservation areas and state environmental assessments.

Rosnedra is a federal executive authority performing functions relating to the

3 *Legislation bulletin of the Russian Federation*, January 26 2009, Number 4, Article 445.
4 *Legislation bulletin of the Russian Federation*, December 5 1994, Number 32, Article 3301.
5 *Legislation bulletin of the Russian Federation*, March 6 1995, Number 10, Article 823.
6 *Legislation bulletin of the Russian Federation*, December 4 1995, Number 49, Article 4694.
7 *Legislation bulletin of the Russian Federation*, January 1 1996, Number 1, Article 18.
8 *Legislation bulletin of the Russian Federation*, May 19 2008, Number 20, Article 2290.

provision of state services and, most importantly, federal property management in the sphere of subsoil use. Rosnedra's sphere of responsibility includes acting as the owner of the federal property required for performing the functions of the state, organising geological studies of the subsoil, appraisal of geological study projects, and undertaking economic and geological evaluations of mineral deposits and subsoil sites.

Rosnedra organises most of the tenders and auctions for the right to use the subsoil, either by issuing licenses or taking decisions on production sharing agreements in accordance with the procedure laid down by law, makes decisions on the approval of tenders and auction results with regard to the right to use subsoil sites in accordance with the procedure laid down by law, and reviews and approves project and technical documentation for the development of mineral deposits.

While Rosnedra's major functions are conducting auctions, reviewing tenders and issuing licenses, the major functions of another state authority in the oil and gas sector, the Federal Supervisory Natural Resources Management Service (Rosprirodnadzor) are controlling and overseeing the licensees' compliance with the terms of their subsoil licence, and their compliance with the requirements of environmental law. It has the power to examine the licensee's activities and to impose fines and other negative legal consequences, if necessary. Rosprirodnadzor is responsible to the Ministry of Natural Resources.

(b) Types of agreement

There are two main scenarios under which subsoil rights could be provided to an interested party: by way of a licence or by the conclusion of a production sharing agreement. In the latter case, to complete the formalities regarding the right of subsoil use, within the 30 days after the execution of the production sharing agreement Rosnedra also issues a subsoil licence. In this case the licence agreement reflects the general terms and conditions of the production sharing agreement.

License: The Federal Law on Subsoil provides for the following types of subsoil licences: exploration, production or a combined licence.

An exploration licence is awarded in relation to the area where a geological survey is required. In most cases the exploration licence is provided to the applicant by the decision of a special commission within Rosnedra. In the event that a licence is sought in relation to an area on the continental shelf, the decision on the licence is taken by the federal government.

A production licence is awarded where proven deposits have already been discovered and have been recorded in the state register of natural reserves. As a rule the production licence is usually issued as a result of a tender submitted in response to an auction. However, where the applicant has itself undertaken the geological exploration and made a discovery, the production licence is granted to that applicant in accordance with a simplified procedure, by the decision of the special commission within Rosnedra. Where the area for which a production licence is sought is designated as an area of federal importance, the licence has to be awarded by a resolution of the federal government.

A combined licence is given where deposits have already been discovered but they require further substantial geological surveying and exploration. Combined licences are awarded by tendering or through auctions.

The agreement on the terms and conditions of subsoil usage (the licence agreement) is concluded at the same time as the licence is issued. The licence agreement usually sets out the conditions for the issue the licence, and provisions on minimum work obligations to be fulfilled by the licensee, production sharing, regular payments, information usage, conditions for extension of the licence, subcontracting policy, and oversight of the licensee to ensure compliance with the licence's conditions.

Production sharing agreements: Unlike the licensing regime, where the arrangements between the parties are based on administrative relations and governed primarily by administrative law, a production sharing agreement is based on the flexible grounds involving a combination of administrative and civil law relations.

Under the Federal Law on Production Sharing Agreements, a production sharing agreement is a contract entered into between the Russian Federation and an investor which primarily stipulates the terms and conditions for production sharing. Under the agreement the Russian Federation, for consideration, provides the investor with the exclusive rights of exploration, development and production in relation to a certain deposit, designated in the agreement, for a certain term, and the investor is obliged to undertake all necessary exploration, development and production activities at its own risk and expense.

A production sharing agreement should detail:

- the development costs incurred by the investor which will be compensated out of revenue arising from production under the agreement. In general the cap on such compensation is 75% of that revenue. If the agreement concerns a deposit on the continental shelf, the cap on development costs compensation is 95% of the revenue;
- the proportion of the profit division after the recovery of the exploration costs from revenue;
- the legal regime covering the particular deposit's exploration and development. It is important to understand that the individual production sharing agreement is the exclusive legal framework, establishing the legal regime for the particular field. Where the production sharing agreement is concluded in relation to a particular field, the terms and conditions of that agreement prevail over the general legislative regulations applicable in the upstream sector. This is quite a unique situation, in which the provisions of the contract could override the provisions of otherwise mandatory laws; and
- confirmation that the investors enjoying the terms of the production sharing agreement are subject to a stabilisation mechanism, which protects them from significant negative changes in the applicable Russian legislation.

Within 30 days after conclusion of a production sharing agreement the relevant licence is given. The licence conditions mainly reiterate the terms and conditions of the production sharing agreement.

In accordance with the Federal Law on Production Sharing Agreements the geographic area and the deposits over which usage rights are being granted to the investor on the basis of a production sharing agreement must appear on a list established by federal law. Sixteen such federal laws have been enacted so far, providing lists of the fields in respect of which production sharing agreements may potentially be concluded. The last of these laws was passed in 2003. Ironically, almost all the production sharing agreements currently in force were concluded before the Federal Law on Production Sharing Agreements was passed (eg, those in respect of the Sakhalin – 1, Sakhalin – 2 and Kharyaginskoye fields). The only exception is the agreement in relation to the Samotlor field, which was concluded after the enactment of the federal law, and which specifies a simplified production sharing structure.

The lack of production sharing agreements concluded after the enactment of the Federal Law of Production Sharing Agreements suggests that the regime put in place by that law does not look attractive to potential investors. Investors' main concerns still relate to Russia's economic instability, and its lack of a good level of investment protection and a reliable court system and arbitration institutions.

(c) Acquisition of acreage

The procedures for the acquisition of rights of subsoil usage are mainly governed by the Federal Law on Subsoil and the Regulation on Subsoil Usage Licensing.[9] The rights for exploration, development and production over known oil and gas fields might be acquired through the following procedures:

- by application by the potential licensee, the decision being taken by a special commission within Rosnedra;
- through a tender procedure, where the bidders should offer not only monetary compensation for the licence, but also submit a working plan and the conditions under which the bidder is willing to obtain rights over the deposit in question;
- through an auction procedure, where the winner is decided on the criterion of the highest price offered alone.

The procedure by which a licence can be granted by the special commission within Rosendra is usually only used for insignificant fields, having merely local importance.

As a rule, almost all licences are rendered as a result of tenders. Even auctions have become less frequent due to the fact that Russia is trying to avoid accusations of corrupt procedures in the issuing of licences.

Decisions on tenders, and auctions, conduct are rendered by the Russian government in relation to deposits of federal importance, and by Rosnedra in relation to the other most significant deposits. They define the tender/auction

9 *Bulletin of the Counsel of deputies*, August 20 1992, Number 33, Article 1917.

procedure and members of the tender/auction commission. It is important to note that where the tender/auction commission is taking a decision on a deposit located in a particular geographic region, representatives of the executive bodies of that region will be included in the members of the commission.

The winner of the auction is the bidder which offers the highest payment for subsoil use.

There are certain criteria which the tender commission takes into consideration when considering the contents of the applicant's documents and determining the winner of the tender:

- Russia's national security interests;
- the scientific and technological level of the exploration and development programmes proposed and the timeline for these programmes' performance;
- the efficiency and volume of hydrocarbons, withdrawal the bidder is going to achieve in developing the deposit;
- the efficacy of the bidder's proposed subsoil and environmental protection measures;
- the applicant's proposed input into the socio-economic development of the region where the deposit is located.

(d) Qualification requirements

Looking at the provisions of the Federal Law on Subsoil, one might come to a conclusion that a foreign legal entity might obtain an exploration and production licence for deposits in Russia. However, for a foreign entity to undertake oil exploration, development and production activities in Russia, it ought to establish a subsidiary company in Russia. Only in this event will it be able to meet the legal, tax and other legislative requirements of the Russian Federation.

There are certain specific requirements relating to obtaining rights of subsoil use in respect of the continental shelf. In this case the legal entity has to meet the following requirements:

- It should be incorporated in accordance with the laws of the Russian Federation.
- It should have at least five years' experience in the exploration and development of offshore deposits.
- The Russian Federation should have a participation interest of greater than 50% in the charter capital of the legal entity.

As can be seen from the above, under the current Russian legislation, only joint ventures in which the Russian Federation or companies controlled by the Russian Federation have more than 50% of the participating shares can work on the continental shelf. The logical conclusion is that this requirement significantly restricts the rights of Russian-based private companies as well as the rights of foreign investors to participate in oil and gas activity on the continental shelf. Evidence of this effect can be seen from the fact that there are only a few examples of joint ventures working on the Russian shelf: the Shtokman project (Gazprom, Statoil, Total), the successful Sakhalin – 2 project (Gazprom, Royal Dutch Shell, Mitsui and

Mitsubishi), the geological exploration project on the Kamchatka shelf (KNOC and Rosneft) and a few others.

To be able to participate in an auction or tender procedure, or to have the opportunity to obtain a licence through an application to Rosnedra, the legal entity should provide the Russian authorities with the following:

- proof of its good and plausible relations with its financial and production partners;
- proof of the financial stability necessary for smooth operations under the anticipated licence;
- proof of its technical and technological capacity, and if the applicant itself lacks sufficient capacity, proof that its subcontractors have the technical and technological capacity to run the project;
- information on its experience and activity in the oil and gas field during the past five years; and
- information as to the proposed investment and technical details of the project, illustrating the terms and conditions of how the activity on the particular field will be undertaken.

In order to qualify to participate in a production sharing agreement, the legal party or parties should agree to bear sole responsibility for the entirety of the proposed activity.

(e) *Duration*

The term for an exploration licence is usually five years. Where the exploration is to be undertaken on the continental shelf, in shallow waters and in certain other specific geographical areas, the standard licence term is 10 years. It is worth noting that the licence term can be prolonged at the request of the licensee, which must provide supporting arguments explaining why the longer term is required. Such arguments could relate to the complexity of the exploration of the deposit, the large area concerned, and so on.

Short-term licences are given for the term of one year and are usually not subject to prolongation.

The Federal Law on Subsoil does not provide for a specific term for production licences, however the Regulation on Subsoil Usage Licensing provides that the term for production licences should be 20 years, which can be prolonged for whatever term is required for comprehensive and reasonable usage of the deposit.

Combined licences contain two terms: one, for the exploration period, which is regulated by the law (five to 10 years); and the other one, for the production period, which is at the discretion of the governmental bodies, but with an initial combined term of 25 years, which can be prolonged by the licensee as required.

(f) *Minimum work programme*

There are no specific requirements in relation to minimum required actions of the investor under the Federal Law on Production Sharing Agreements. However all such agreements and licences contain certain minimum obligations on the subsoil user.

These are usually:

- that the investor/licensee meet certain annual exploration and production targets;
- that the investor/licensee keep the level of environmental contamination within prescribed limits, and arrange for the necessary procedures to minimise the negative consequences of environmental contamination; and
- in certain cases, that the investor/licensee meet certain social obligations, such as provision of support to local communities.

Failure by the licensee/investor to comply with these minimum obligations will lead to (depending on the significance of the non-performance) penalties, suspension of production, or. in the event of a significant failure to comply with the minimum obligations, revocation of the licence, and if a production sharing agreement has been concluded termination of that agreement together with simultaneous revocation of the licence.

(g) *Assignment*

As a general rule the rights provided to the licensee under the licence have an individual character and cannot be transferred to other entities. However, in certain limited cases, designated in Article 17.1 of the Federal Law on Subsoil, the transfer of subsoil use rights is possible. These cases are where the rights holder:

- undergoes changes in its organisational form and legal status;
- merges with another entity;
- divides, or part of the company is spun off; or
- goes into insolvency.

The rights of subsoil use may also be transferred to a subsidiary of the licensee's established specifically for the purposes of conducting exploration and production activity on a particular deposit and in the charter capital of which at the time of the licence transfer the participation of the original licensee should be not less than 50%, provided, however, that certain conditions are fulfilled:

- The new subsidiary should be incorporated in Russia;
- The necessary facilities, technical equipment and so on should be transferred to the newly established entity; and
- The subsidiary should obtain the licences required for its operations.

The Federal Law on Subsoil also permits the transfer of subsoil rights within the group of companies:

- from a parent company to its subsidiary;
- from a subsidiary to a parent company; or
- between subsidiaries, as directed by the parent company.

The Federal Law on Production Sharing Agreements provides that the rights and obligations under a production sharing agreement can be assigned to any legal entity or natural person subject to the prior consent of the Russian Federation. The potential assignee should qualify as a new investor and should possess the required financial and managerial capacity to operate under the production sharing agreement.

There is a special document – an assignment act – which formalises the assignment. The procedure for executing such an act should be prescribed in each production sharing agreement. The act of assignment must be a written document, which will constitute an inherent part of the production sharing agreement. In the event of an assignment, the licence is re-issued in the name of the assignee within 30 days after the execution of the act of assignment.

(h) Local content

There are no specific requirements as to local content under the licensing regulations. However there are requirements on local content in production sharing agreements:

- Russian legal entities should have pre-emption rights to participate in the operations under the agreement in the capacities of suppliers, sub-contractors, suppliers of transportation and other services.
- At least 80% of the employees on the project should be the citizens of the Russian Federation.
- Foreign workers can only be employed on the project for the purpose of undertaking certain labour functions on the initial stage of the project, or alternatively only in the event that there are no employees with the required qualifications and experience among Russian candidates for the position.
- Not less than 70% of expenditure that will be compensated from the revenues from the field's production, incurred in each calendar year, in the acquisition of equipment necessary for exploration, development and production activity on the field, or for transportation and refining, should be spent on agreements with local Russian suppliers.
- Not less than 70% of the equipment acquired for undertaking operations under the agreement should be of Russian origin.

(i) National reservation

Russian legislation does not provide for any specific regime for access by foreign oil companies to the local Russian oil and gas sales market. There are, though, certain specific provisions relating to the transportation of oil and gas and export regulations.

Transportation and export of crude oil: The state-owned company Transneft has a monopoly over oil transportation and export. Oil producers have access to the Transneft pipeline systems. Transneft's pipeline capacity is allocated among oil producers in proportion to the amount of crude oil each oil producer is allowed to pump into the Transneft's pipeline for export.

Transneft submits quarterly schedules of crude oil transportation for the approval of the Ministry of Natural Resources.

Transnefterproduct, a subsidiary of Transneft, is another Russian state monopoly, responsible for the transportation of oil products through the territory of the Russian Federation and to export destinations. Seventeen Russian refineries pump their oil products into its pipeline system.

Since both Transneft and Transnefteproduct are state monopolies, their tariffs are subject to regulation by Federal Tariff Agency.

Sales, transportation and export of gas: Where gas producers sell natural gas on the local market there are certain circumstances where pre-emption rights to buy the gas arise:

- The consumers use the gas for state purposes;
- The consumers are public utility companies; or
- The consumers have gas supply agreements containing pre-emption rights.

Gazprom has a monopoly over the transportation of natural gas (both in gaseous and liquefied form) either on Russian territory or for export abroad. Gazprom's activity is mainly regulated by three federal laws: the Federal Law on Gas Supply in the Russian Federation, the Federal Law on Natural Monopolies and the Federal Law on the Export of Gas.

The unified gas supply system is the centralised system for transportation of the natural gas. Gazprom owns this system.

Under the Federal Law on Gas Supply Gazprom is obliged to provide gas producers with the access to the unified gas supply system on non-discriminatory grounds, but subject to certain conditions:

- There must be spare capacity available in the system;
- Independent producers' gas must meet certain quality requirements; and
- Connecting and branch pipelines to consumers must be be available.

Since Gazprom holds a monopoly, prices for transportation of natural gas are regulated under the General Provisions on Formation and State Regulation of Gas Prices and Tariffs, and the Federal Tariff Agency is the authority responsible for price regulation.

Under the Federal Law on the Export of Gas, Gazprom as the owner of the unified gas supply system, and its wholly owned subsidiary Gazpromexport, hold the exclusive right to export gas abroad.

(j) Environment

Russian environmental regulation is based on two general principles. In accordance with the Federal Law on Environmental Protection:[10]

- the users of natural resources should make compensatory payments in the event of damage being caused by environmental contamination;
- Rosprirodnadzor establishes limits for polluting emissions and contaminants and in relation to other types of negative impact on the environment.

---

10 *Legislation bulletin of the Russian Federation*, January 14 2002, Number 2, Article 133.

Subsoil licenses are awarded under the conditions that the licensee will comply with the environmental requirements provided in Russian legislation (norms on air, water and soil pollution, waste management requirements, etc).

When it awards a subsoil license to a particular licensee Rosnedra consults with Rosprirodnadzor in relation to possible specific environmental requirements appropriate for the specific area in which deposit at issue is situated. Should the licensee fail to comply with the environmental requirements, it may result in penalties, suspension of the license or even its termination (depending on the significance of the particular failure).

(k) Governing law and dispute resolution

Production sharing agreements: There are no special legislative requirements in relation to the law applicable to production sharing agreements.

However, the provisions on the responsibility of the parties under the agreement should be governed by the laws of the Russian Federation, as the agreement, in its execution and performance, will be closely connected with the territory of the Russian Federation, and there are strictly speaking no foreign elements in the agreement. This being so, the only logical conclusion in this situation would be that the Russian law should be the law applicable to the agreement. Additional support for this position comes for the fact that the government authorities negotiate production sharing agreements on behalf of the Russian Federation and the government of the Russian Federation approves and confirms each such agreement. It is very unlikely that the government of the Russian Federation would be likely to accept any agreement, containing a clause making a foreign law applicable.

Under the Federal Law on Production Sharing Agreements, all disputes arising out of, or in connection with, the performance, termination or invalidity of production sharing agreements are to be resolved by reference to the provisions of the particular agreement in court, in a court of arbitration, or in arbitration proceedings (including international commercial arbitration). The law provides the parties to the agreement with the discretion to decide which forum they will choose as competent.

When considering the dispute resolution conditions for production sharing agreements, it is worth taking into consideration that most of such agreements are concluded in relation to an area of the continental shelf of the Russian Federation, and therefore the provisions of the Federal Law on the Continental shelf dealing with dispute resolution will also apply. In addition, the provisions on dispute resolution of the Federal Law on Subsoil will be also applicable as the general rules for the dispute resolution.

The general rule of the Federal Law on the Continental shelf provides that all disputes related to rights and obligations linked to the continental shelf should be resolved in the course of administrative procedures or in the courts of the Russian Federation. The same rules are contained in the Federal Law on Subsoil.

However the legislator made an attempt to avoid contradictions among the three federals laws: the Federal Law on Production Sharing Agreements, the Federal law on the Continental Shelf and the Federal Law on Subsoil. The latter two laws therefore provide that disputes arising out of the relations between investor and the state under a production sharing agreement concluded in relation to an area either on the continental shelf or onshore are to be resolved in accordance with the dispute resolution provisions contained in the particular production sharing agreement. In view of this, it is important that the state and the investor define in the production sharing agreement the competent forum to which they are agreeing to refer possible disputes between them.

If the investor is a foreign entity or has foreign participation, it is clear that this investor would consider international arbitration as a more appropriate forum to decide any disputes arising out of the agreement, and any such investor should therefore insist on the inclusion of provisions designating that forum in the agreement.

Licensing: If the rights to use the subsoil are obtained through the issuing of a licence, the relations in between the state and the licensee are mainly governed by the regulations and administrative procedures specified by Russian law. In this context, the Federal law on Subsoil provides that disputes arising out of subsoil usage shall be resolved by the competent state bodies, courts or courts of arbitration in accordance with their respective competence.

The following disputes are to be resolved in courts or courts of arbitration:

- financial or other proprietary disputes relating to subsoil usage;
- appeals against the decisions of state bodies;
- appeals against the actions of government officers acting contrary to the law; and
- appeals against standards and regulations.

If agreed between the parties in the relevant license agreement, or separately, proprietary disputes can be referred to the resolution of a competent arbitration forum.

3.2 Government take

(a) Licensing

Under the Federal Law on Subsoil the following payment obligations are imposed on licensees:

- a one-off payment upon the occurrence of events designated in the particular licence, such as the occurrence of a discovery;
- payments in the event of modifications of the deposit boundaries in the licence;
- regular payments for subsoil use, the amounts and frequency of which are regulated by specific provisions, usually in production sharing agreements; and
- fees for participation in tendering procedures and auctions.

Besides these payments, licensees are obliged to pay normal and special taxes in accordance with the Russian legislation on fees and taxes.

As regards corporate profit tax, there are certain specific rules on the amortisation of assets and deductions applying to companies engaged in the oil and gas operations.

The basic tax a licensee is obliged to pay is the mineral extraction tax. This tax is imposed on legal entities and entrepreneurs engaged in the extraction of natural resources, including oil and gas. The amount of this tax is determined either on the basis of the physical quantity extracted, or on the basis of physical quantity and value.

(b) Production sharing agreements

The government take and tax regime applying to production sharing agreements differs from that applying to the normal licensing regime. Thus an investor under the Federal Law on Production Sharing Agreements is released, wholly or partially, from paying certain taxes and other mandatory payments.

Under the Federal law on Production Sharing Agreements the payment obligations imposed on investors are:

- one-off payments upon the occurrence of events designated in the particular agreement (bonuses);
- annual payments for use of the area of water and portion of the sea bottom specified in the contract;
- fees for participation in tendering procedures and auctions;
- a fee for the issuing of the licence;
- regular payments for subsoil usage (rent);
- compensation to the state for its expenditure incurred as a result of exploration and development of the deposit concerned;
- compensation for any damage incurred by local native small ethnic groups as a result of the exploration, development and production activity in the deposit area.

The main principle of the tax regime applicable to production sharing agreements is that the investor is released from payment of several taxes and fees under the Russian legislation, such as customs duties, property and transport taxes. At the same time the investor shares part of its revenues from the field with the state.

4. Regulation of foreign investments in strategic sectors

There are certain regulatory restrictions on the ability of foreign companies and Russian companies with foreign participation to acquire licensing rights in respect of oil and gas deposits in Russia. First of all the holder of the deposit having federal significance can only be a purely Russian company.

Russian national defence and security bodies might refuse to allow foreign companies to participate in tender procedures and auctions for the rights to use deposits of federal significance.

The Federal Law on the Procedure of Foreign Investment in Business Entities

Having Strategic Significance for Securing the Defence of the Country and Safety of the State[11] provides that the prior approval of the Governmental Strategic Commission is required:

- where the investor wishes to acquire 25% or more of the voting rights in a strategic entity having the right to use a crude oil deposit of federal significance;
- where, as a result of the transaction, the investor will acquire the right to appoint the sole executive body, or more than 25% of the collegiate executive body; and
- where the investor already has 25 % or more of the voting rights of the strategic entity and wishes to increase its level of participation.

5. Current issues

Recently the president of the Russian Federation proposed draft legislation to the Russian Parliament that would totally replace the tendering procedure for the licences with an auction procedure. The draft of the relevant amendment to the Federal Law on Subsoil has been submitted to parliament. From the point of view of the most Russian players this initiative would create additional opportunities for corruption, and therefore cannot be considered as positive.

6. Conclusion

Russia is currently one of the largest gas and oil producers and exporters: it is the largest gas exporter and second largest oil exporter. The current levels of supply are backed by still enormous reserves.

The potential for future production, especially on the continental shelf is significant. However, new exploration and production will require huge investments, including foreign investments, which raises the need to stabilise the business climate, and to make the Russian legal framework more friendly for subsoil users and investors. All this could stimulate current Russian producers to increase their levels of production as well as attracting new foreign investment. To realise all this, it will be important to ensure that the legislative framework is modified accordingly.

11 *Legislation Bulletin of the Russian Federation*, May 5 2008, Number 18, Article 1940.

United Kingdom

Justyna Bremen
Peter Roberts
Ashurst LLP

1. Introduction

The North Sea contains Western Europe's largest oil and natural gas reserves. The commercial production of oil and gas in the UK continental shelf dates back to the late 1960s and 1970s. Since 1970, approximately 39.5 billion barrels of oil equivalent have been extracted from the UK continental shelf. The volume of production of oil and gas reached a peak in 1999 and 2000 respectively, and has seen a decline in the last decade. Production of oil and natural gas liquids stood at 52 million tons in 2011, compared to 116.7 million tons in 2001. For gas, in 2011 the level of production was 43 billion cubic metres, well under half the level produced in 2000.

Despite being a province in decline, the United Kingdom is still a significant producer. It is the third-largest producer of natural gas in Europe, after Norway and the Netherlands, and the second-largest producer of oil, after Norway. On a global scale, the United Kingdom is the world's 19th largest oil and gas producer. According to figures published by Oil & Gas UK (the UK oil and gas industry association), in 2011 production from the UK continental shelf satisfied 68% of UK oil demand and 58% of gas demand. Despite declining reserves, it is also estimated that the UK continental shelf has the potential to satisfy close to 50% of the United Kingdom's oil and gas demand in 2020 if the current rate of investment is sustained.

The UK oil and gas industry has faced some challenges in recent years. As in some other jurisdictions, the Deepwater Horizon oil spill of April 2010 triggered a review of the health and safety regime by both the government and industry. While there was no suspension of operations, with the need for a moratorium on deepwater drilling rejected by a parliamentary select committee, there has been an increased level of regulatory oversight, particularly in the form of an increased number of inspections of the ageing infrastructure, and a certain level of uncertainty about possible future changes to the health and safety regime. In addition, 2011 saw a steep rise in the level of taxation of profits from oil and gas production. However, the UK government is anxious to ensure that the oil and gas industry continues to thrive – not just because it is an important source of government revenue, but also because it is vital to maintain energy security and is an important generator of employment along the supply chain. For this reason the government has been undertaking various initiatives to support the UK oil and gas industry. As discussed below, one example of regulatory reform has been the introduction of a streamlined third-party access regime. In terms of the fiscal regime, while the current rate of taxation is high, the government has been rolling out a series of field allowances to provide tax incentives for certain categories of field.

A major trend in the last decade has been an increased number of small and medium-sized companies investing in UK continental shelf assets, as some of the major companies exit the UK continental shelf to focus on new developments.

2. Upstream activities and infrastructure

The United Kingdom is now a net importer of gas, although at times of low demand it is also an exporter. Gas is imported via pipelines and as liquefied natural gas (LNG).

The major pipelines linking the United Kingdom to the rest of Europe are as follows:

- the Bacton-Zeebrugge interconnector linking the IBT terminal in the United Kingdom and the IZT terminal in Belgium;
- the BBL pipeline between Balgzand in the Netherlands and Bacton in the United Kingdom;
- the Vesterled pipeline between the Heimdal Riser platform in the North Sea off the west coast of Norway and St Fergus in the United Kingdom;
- the Tampen link between Statfjord in the North Sea off the west coast of Norway and the Far North Liquids and Associated Gas (FLAGS) pipeline (terminating at St Fergus in the United Kingdom);
- the Gjøa pipeline, which links Gjøa/Vega off the coast of Norway with the FLAGS pipeline in the United Kingdom; and
- the Langeled pipeline between Nyhamna in Norway and Easington in the United Kingdom.

There are also four existing LNG receiving terminals, with a number of other facilities planned for the future.

Gas which is delivered to the United Kingdom either by pipeline or as LNG is processed at one of nine gas reception terminals, and then enters the high-pressure National Transmission System, for transportation throughout the country.

The United Kingdom is also a net importer of crude oil, although as discussed above, production levels from the UK continental shelf remain significant. There are eight refineries in the United Kingdom, which process a significant proportion of UK oil into petroleum products. The refineries are supported by a network of petroleum product pipelines, as well as inland and coastal oil storage terminals. Oil is transported by pipeline, rail and sea.

3. Petroleum legal regime

3.1 Petroleum law and relevant provisions

(a) Regulatory bodies

The principal legislation governing the development of natural oil and gas reserves in the United Kingdom is the Petroleum Act 1998. The Petroleum Act establishes a licensing regime, which applies onshore and offshore in the whole United Kingdom. The only exception is Northern Ireland, which has a separate regime for its onshore oil and gas resources. Offshore, the Petroleum Act applies to the territorial sea and the UK continental shelf. The act consolidates and replaces all previous legislation dealing with petroleum licensing – for example, the Petroleum (Production) Act 1934.

Under the Petroleum Act, all rights to petroleum – including the rights to "search for, bore for and get" petroleum – are vested in the Crown. The Department of Energy and Climate Change (DECC) is the government department primarily responsible for regulating the development of UK oil and gas resources. The secretary of state for energy and climate change is the minister in charge of the DECC, and is responsible for discharging many of the rights and duties of the state under the Petroleum Act.

In addition to administering the Petroleum Act regime, DECC is responsible for administering and enforcing environmental legislation applying to offshore oil and gas activities.

The Health and Safety Executive (HSE) is responsible for overseeing and enforcing the health and safety legal regime applying to upstream oil and gas development. The Maritime and Coastguard Agency (MCA) also performs a more limited but important function, particularly in the context of emergency response to any offshore accidents.

(b) Types of agreement

As mentioned earlier, a petroleum licensing regime applies in the United Kingdom. Under the Petroleum Act, the secretary of state "may grant to such persons as he thinks fit licences to search and bore for and get petroleum".

There are three main types of licence:

- Seaward production licences, which are granted in relation to offshore fields. These cover the full life of a field, from exploration to production. As explained below, there are some different sub-categories of seaward production licence.
- Petroleum exploration and development licences, which are granted in relation to onshore fields. These also cover the full life of a field.
- Seaward exploration licences, which cover offshore exploration activities only. This type of licence is particularly aimed at seismic contractors that wish to gather data to sell rather than exploit geological resources themselves. The cost is a flat rate of £2,000 a year and the licence covers non-intrusive exploration. The rights granted under an exploration licence are non-exclusive.

In recent years DECC has recognised that a standard seaward production licence, often referred to as a 'traditional licence', may not be appropriate in all cases. For this reason, DECC also issues the following special types of seaward production licence:

- Promote licences, aimed at smaller companies which may be new entrants to the UK continental shelf. The distinguishing feature of this licence is that the licensee is given two years to attract funding or investment from other parties to ensure it has the technical and financial capacity to complete the agreed work programme.
- Frontier licences – these licences are intended for more technically

challenging areas of the North Sea. The initial term, which is the exploration period, is longer than standard.

- West of Shetland frontier licence – these are a variation of the frontier licence, specifically targeted at blocks located west of Shetland, with an even longer exploration period. And
- Licences specifically tailored to cover the redevelopment of a decommissioned field.

(c) Acquisition of acreage through bid rounds or direct negotiation

The DECC issues licences through competitive licensing rounds. Seaward licensing rounds take place on an annual basis, while landward licensing rounds are less frequent.

A party can apply for a licence over a particular area (either by itself or as part of a joint venture) during a declared licensing round. The EU Hydrocarbons Licensing Directive (94/22/EC) sets out rules that EU member states must follow when issuing petroleum licences, including the factors that may (and may not) be taken into account when deciding whether to issue a licence and the minimum amount of public consultation required. The directive is implemented in the United Kingdom by the Hydrocarbons Licensing Directive Regulations 1995. The regulations require an invitation for applications to be published in the European *Official Journal* at least 90 days in advance, together with the criteria on which applications are to be determined.

Details of the most recent licensing round – the 27th Seaward Licensing Round – were published on February 1 2012, resulting in a record-breaking number of applications. The results of that licensing round were announced on October 25 2012, with an initial tranche of offers of 167 production licences, covering 330 blocks. The last landward licensing round took place in 2007.

It is also possible for a licence to be issued outside a licensing round, but a company seeking to apply for a licence outside of a round would need to present compelling reasons to the DECC for it to invite out-of-round applications.

Where a party wishes to acquire another party's interest in a licence or sell its existing licence interest, it may do so at any time, although such transfers are subject to prior approval from the DECC (see below).

(d) Qualification requirements

Before awarding licences or approving the transfer of a licence, the DECC must be satisfied that the applicant meets certain criteria. The DECC issues guidance on these requirements with each licensing round. The areas that the DECC focuses on are financial capacity and technical expertise.

Financial capacity: Each licence applicant must demonstrate to the DECC's satisfaction that:

- it is financially viable and it is likely to continue business for the foreseeable future; and
- it has sufficient financial capacity to fund its share of the anticipated work,

meeting costs within a reasonable timeframe and decommissioning costs (except in applications for promote licences).

The DECC will always consider a company's track record and, if the company is a new entrant to the UK continental shelf, will look at its track record outside the UK continental shelf. Where the proposed licensee is a subsidiary of a foreign parent, the DECC will generally require an undertaking from the parent to support the licensee in its licence operations.

Applicants which are new to the United Kingdom must also provide evidence such as constitutional documents demonstrating details of their place of incorporation and/or principal place of business, and the location from which activities related to the licence will be managed or controlled. Licensees must have a place of business within the United Kingdom.

Technical expertise: The DECC distinguishes between applicants for licences according to whether they are operators or non-operators.

The key requirement for non-operator applicants is that the joint venture parties as a whole can demonstrate technical expertise sufficient to exercise responsible oversight of the project. In practice, this would mean that the DECC would not permit a significant vote to be exercised by a licensee under the joint operating agreement without the necessary technical expertise.

The DECC is mainly concerned with the technical capabilities of the operator. Under the terms of the licence, the appointment of an operator by a joint venture group must be approved by the DECC. There are two types of operator approval:

- exploration operator approval (typically granted at licence award); and
- production operator approval (typically granted at field development approval stage).

The degree of scrutiny that the DECC exercises over a prospective field operator will depend on that company's existing track record of technical, management and financial capacity both in the UK continental shelf and elsewhere.

(e) Duration

Some of the earliest seaward production licences, issued from 1964 onwards, were granted for a period of 46 years. The seaward production licences issued now have a much shorter duration. Under the existing regime, petroleum exploration and development licences (onshore) and seaward production licences (offshore) are valid for a sequence of terms. These are designed to comprise the typical lifecycle of a field: exploration, appraisal and production. Each licence will expire automatically at the end of each term, unless the licensee has sufficiently progressed to warrant a chance to move into the next term.

The initial term is usually an exploration period. For seaward production licences this is usually set at four years, but it is longer for frontier licences. For petroleum exploration and development licences the exploration period is six years. The licence will expire at the end of the initial term unless the licensee has completed the work programme. At this time, the licensee must also relinquish a fixed amount of acreage (usually 50%).

The second term is for appraisal and development. It is four years for seaward production licences and five years for petroleum exploration and development licences. The licence will expire at the end of the second term unless the secretary of state has approved a development plan.

The third term is intended for production. It is set at 18 years for seaward production licences and 20 years for petroleum exploration and development licences.

At the end of the production period the acreage is returned to the DECC's competitive licensing system so that the secretary of state can decide who, if anyone, should have the next opportunity to exploit it. However, in some circumstances, the secretary of state may grant an extension of the licence term. The DECCs policy is that a licence extension is justified only by continuing production, so a licence should continue for as long as production lasts and no longer. The DECC's approach is to extend the licence until the end of a set period (currently one year) with no production. From that moment onwards, unless and until production restarts, the secretary of state is empowered to terminate the licence to the extent that it relates to the producing area.

There may be cases where a discovery is so close to becoming a producing field when the licence expires that the DECC will already have issued a production consent over it. The DECC considers that in such a case it would generally be reasonable for it to grant a short extension to allow the discovery to start production. Such short-term extensions are typically for two to three years. The DECC will generally terminate the acreage if it has not reached production in that time.

There may also be some discoveries (and even prospects) that have not even reached the production consent stage, but are actively being brought to development. The DECC will also consider such cases for an extension, but only where there is already an ongoing work programme. The DECC recognises that there may be cases where factors beyond the licensee's control keep it from starting a development until near the end of the licence term. Such factors might include late technical advances and availability of infrastructure.

(f) *Licence conditions*

Most licences follow a standard format and incorporate specified conditions called 'model clauses', which govern the relationship between the licensee and the government. The model clauses are published in statutory instruments made pursuant to the Petroleum Act.

The model clauses applicable to a particular licence are those which are in force at the time it was granted. The model clauses applicable to older licences are set out in the Petroleum (Current Model Clauses) Order 1999, while the Petroleum Licensing (Exploration and Production) (Seaward and Landward Areas) Regulations 2004 include the full text of the four major sets of model clauses applying to more recent licences. Licences issued after April 6 2008 will have model clauses as set out in the schedule to the Petroleum Licensing (Production) (Seaward Areas) Regulations 2008.

The model clauses deal with various matters, including:

- the term of the licence – that is, the first, second and third term, as discussed above;
- the rental payable;
- the requirement that the operator be approved by the secretary of state;
- approval of work programme and development and production programme;
- the requirement to obtain consent from the DECC before drilling or abandonment of any well;
- the requirement to conduct operations in accordance with the methods customarily used in good oilfield practice and to take all steps practicable in order to prevent the escape or waste of petroleum, and to prevent the escape of petroleum into any waters in or in the vicinity of the licensed area;
- an indemnity by the licensee in favour of the DECC against all actions, proceedings, costs, charges and claims by any third party in relation to the licence and the operations conducted under it;
- restriction on assignment and change in control; and
- revocation of the licence.

(g) *Minimal work programme*

The DECC closely monitors the work progress of licensees during each term of the licence, by requiring them to seek approval of their work programmes and then to carry out the agreed programmes.

During the initial term of the licence – the exploration period – the licensee is required to carry out exploration work. The minimum amount of exploration that the licensee must carry out to ensure that the licence does not expire is referred to as the 'work programme'.

The licensee is also required to submit for approval a development programme for the second term, and then a production programme for the third term.

(h) *Field development plan*

Before development of the field can start, the operator must apply to the DECC for development consent. This process is initiated by the submission of a field development plan, together with an environmental statement discussing the environmental impact of the proposed development.

The Offshore Petroleum Production and Pipelines (Assessment of Environmental Effects) Regulations 1999 (as amended by the Offshore Petroleum Production and Pipelines (Assessment of Environmental Effects) (Amendment) Regulations 2007) require that any operator which wishes to carry out certain activities must first carry out an environmental impact assessment and then summarise and present the conclusions of this in an environmental statement. This environmental impact assessment process applies to the granting and renewal of production consents for field developments, the drilling of wells (deep boring) and the construction and installation of production facilities and pipelines.

(i) *Joint operating agreement*

In the United Kingdom, as in other jurisdictions, the majority of licences are held by two or more co-licensees. Those co-licensees enter into a joint operating agreement to govern their joint venture and appoint an operator. A joint operating agreement entered into by co-licensees will apportion liability and profits between the parties. For this reason, every joint operating agreement entered into must be approved by the secretary of state. The secretary of state must also approve the operator appointed under the joint operating agreement.

(j) *Assignment and encumbrance*

The model clauses prohibit the assignment of a licence, except with the prior consent of the secretary of state. If a licence assignment is made without obtaining prior consent, this constitutes grounds for revocation of the licence. The prohibition applies equally to assignments to third parties and to affiliates, as well as situations where a licensee exits the licence and transfers its interest to the other co-licensees. There are a number of considerations that the DECC will take into account when deciding whether to give its approval.

In cases involving inter-group assignments, if the assignment is being made specifically for the purpose of the future disposal of the licence interest by way of a share sale, the DECC will want to be given details of any such future sale before consenting to the assignment.

The secretary of state's prior consent is also required to any assignments of interests under a joint operating agreement. The only exception to the need to obtain the secretary of state's consent is where there is simply an adjustment of the respective interests held by existing co-licensees, but this does not apply to all licences. An 'open permission' to adjust licence interests, without obtaining prior consent, used to apply to all licences, but recently the DECC introduced new systems for processing licence assignments, and as at November 2012 the open permission applies only to landward licences.

The model clauses also provide that a change in control of a licensee is grounds for revocation of the licence, but there is no provision allowing for the secretary of state's prior consent to be obtained. The DECC acknowledges that this creates a practical difficulty for licensee companies. It has therefore developed a practice whereby parties can apply to the DECC for an assurance that the power of revocation will be not exercised. This assurance operates as a comfort letter rather than as statutory approval.

Similarly to an assignment, the creation of a charge on a licence requires the consent of the secretary of state. In practice, in most cases prior consent is not required before a charge is created because an open permission, which is a form of automatic consent, applies to any fixed or floating charge or debenture. It is a condition of the open permission that the licensee give notice to the DECC within 10 days of creation of the charge, providing information about the date of the charge, the size of the loan secured by it, the licences affected and the identity of the charge.

(k) *Local content*

The UK oil and gas regime imposes no local content obligations.

(l) *National reservation*

In the United Kingdom, there is no system of reservation of petroleum for local use. However, certain special emergency powers may be used in the event of an energy security emergency to ensure that fuel is available for local use. Under the Energy Act 1976 the secretary of state may make an order to regulate or prohibit the production, supply, acquisition or use of substances used as fuel, including oil and natural gas, in the event of an actual or threatened emergency in the United Kingdom that will affect fuel supplies.

(m) *Environment*

The DECC's Offshore Environment Unit is responsible for all environmental issues relating to offshore oil and gas operations. In particular, the environmental management team within the unit is responsible for the environmental assessment of offshore oil and gas activities, and for the administration of environmental legislation including:

- the Offshore Petroleum Production and Pipelines (Assessment of Environmental Effects) Regulations 1999;
- the Offshore Petroleum Activities (Conservation of Habitats) Regulations 2001;
- the Offshore Combustion Installations (Prevention and Control of Pollution) Regulations 2001;
- the Offshore Chemicals Regulations 2002; and
- the Greenhouse Gas Emissions Trading Scheme Regulations 2005.

Separate controls apply to onshore oil and gas operations. Local authorities and other government departments (eg, the Environment Agency) play a role in overseeing and enforcing planning and environmental consents relating to onshore exploration and production.

There is a well-developed regime for preventing and dealing with environmental pollution. The Merchant Shipping (Oil Pollution Preparedness, Response and Cooperation Convention) Regulations 1998 and the Offshore Installations (Emergency Pollution Control) Regulations 2002 are the main components of the legal framework under which the UK government regulates potential environmental incidents involving offshore installations, with a view to ensuring that preventive measures are in place to limit pollution. In particular, obligations are imposed on operators to implement robust emergency planning arrangements, and powers are reserved to the UK government to step in and take measures to enforce any necessary remedial actions.

The Offshore Petroleum Activities (Oil Pollution Prevention and Control) Regulations 2005 supplement the emergency planning requirements under the Merchant Shipping (Oil Pollution Preparedness, Response and Cooperation Convention) Regulations and the Offshore Installations (Emergency Pollution Control) Regulations by imposing a permitting system for oil discharges from an offshore installation, with enforcement powers available to the UK government to require remediation of pollution in the event of an unauthorised discharge and to recover costs if it has to intervene should the operator fail to do so.

A number of other environmental regimes may be relevant in the event of an oil pollution incident, depending on the extent of its impact. In particular, where there is damage to biodiversity, the various remediation measures envisaged under the Environmental Damage (Prevention and Remediation) Regulations 2009, which transposed the EU Environmental Liability Directive (2004/35/EC) in the United Kingdom, may be applicable. Otherwise, the directive regime applies only onshore and in territorial waters (up to 12 miles from the coast). Moreover, an incident arising onshore or having onshore impact may be caught by established UK pollution liability controls (eg, the Environmental Protection Act 1990).

(n) *Health and safety*

A stringent and well-established health and safety regime applies to the UK upstream sector. The Piper Alpha disaster, which occurred in 1988, triggered a major review of the regime. Piper Alpha was a large North Sea oil and gas platform that started production in 1976. In July 1988 there was a leak of gas condensate which caused a massive explosion, leading to the death of 167 people. The subsequent public inquiry[1] recommended a large number of changes to the regulatory regime, which were subsequently implemented. One of the most significant changes was the transfer of responsibility for health and safety regulation of offshore installations from what was then the Department for Energy (now the DECC) to the HSE, the organisation already responsible for the regulation of hazardous installations and other workplaces onshore. A safety case regime was developed, set out under the Offshore Installations (Safety Case) Regulations 2005 and other associated legislation. One of the main requirements is that written safety cases and risk assessments be prepared by the operator and then approved by the HSE for all fixed and mobile offshore installations before such installations are brought into use on the UK continental shelf.

The HSE Offshore Safety Division employs a team of inspectors who are responsible for enforcing both the offshore specific regulations (notably, in addition to the main safety case regulations referred to above, the Offshore Installations (Prevention of Fire and Explosion and Emergency Response) Regulations 1995 and general safety legislation common to all industries, including the overarching Health and Safety at Work etc Act 1974.

Decommissioning: The decommissioning of offshore installations and pipelines is regulated under Part IV of the Petroleum Act 1998. Responsibility for ensuring compliance rests with the DECC. The main objective of the decommissioning regime under the Petroleum Act is to ensure that the cost of decommissioning is not borne by the DECC, and therefore by taxpayers.

Decommissioning obligations arise when the secretary of state serves a Section 29 notice to the operator of the field and each of the licensees, requiring them to submit a decommissioning programme. Once the decommissioning programme is approved, following the DECC's review of the details, including the cost estimates,

---

1 The Cullen Inquiry, chaired by Lord Cullen.

the Section 29 notice holders are legally obliged to carry it out on a joint and several liability basis. If a programme is not carried out or its conditions are not complied with, the secretary of state may, by written notice, require remedial action to be taken. Failure to comply with any such notice is an offence and the secretary of state may carry out the remedial action and recover the costs from the party to which the notice was given.

The DECC will usually request the submission of a decommissioning programme three or more years before cessation of production, although for smaller fields the DECC may require a programme at the time of approval of the final field development plan. If the DECC is not satisfied that the licensees will be capable of carrying out their decommissioning obligations, it may require them to provide security, (eg, a letter of credit) in order to reduce the risk to the UK taxpayer (who would otherwise bear this liability). The DECC also obliges companies to provide adequate financial information (including management accounts and revenue predictions) in order to enable the secretary of state to assess whether decommissioning security ought to be provided at an earlier stage. Any funds set aside in a secure manner (eg, a trust or other arrangement which was established on or after December 1 2007) to meet decommissioning obligations will not be accessible to creditors under insolvency legislation.

Because the objective of the regime is to shield the government from decommissioning costs, the DECC may also serve a Section 29 notice on a wider group of parties, not just the current licensees, including:

- anyone with an ownership interest in the installation or pipeline;
- a parent or associated company of a licensee;
- any person intending to carry on specified activities in relation to the installation or pipeline in the future;
- any transferor of an interest in an offshore installation or pipeline, where such transferor has failed to obtain the consent of the secretary of state to the transfer; and
- any licensee or party to joint operating or similar agreements in relation to a petroleum exploration or extraction licence, regardless of whether such party benefited or had the potential to benefit from the particular installation.

Typically, the DECC will send a Section 29 notice to this wider class of parties if it is of the view that the decommissioning arrangements proposed by the operator and licensees are unsatisfactory. In addition, and crucially, Section 34 of the Petroleum Act extends the right to issue a Section 29 notice to anyone who, at any time since the first Section 29 notice for the installation is issued, was liable to have a Section 29 notice served on it (ie, former licensees).

Until such time as the Section 29 notice has been withdrawn, the licensee remains liable for decommissioning obligations. When an asset changes hands, the secretary of state may release a former licensee from its Section 29 obligations. In most cases the Section 29 notice will be withdrawn, provided that the DECC is satisfied that adequate financial security arrangements are in place in relation to the decommissioning liabilities. Such security arrangements are usually in the form of a decommissioning security deed to which the secretary of state may be a party, which ensures that the new incoming licensees can discharge the decommissioning liabilities. However, even if a former licensee is discharged from its Section 29 obligations, in some circumstances the secretary of state may use its claw-back power under Section 34 to impose liability on that party.

(o) *Revocation*

The model clauses set out the circumstances in which the licence may be revoked. Where a licence is revoked, the licensee will lose its rights under the licence, but will remain subject to any obligations or liabilities already incurred under the licence. The main circumstances in which the licence may be revoked are:

- insolvency of the licensee;
- an assignment of the licence without the prior consent of the secretary of state;
- a change in control of the licensee;
- an assignment of the joint operating agreement without consent;
- any rental being outstanding for two months after it is due;
- breach of any condition subject to which the DECC provides an approval; and
- other breach or non-observance of the licence terms.

While DECC's revocation powers are quite broad, it is not in the DECC's interest to revoke licences if this can be avoided. The revocation power is an effective enforcement tool, but to date DECC has never revoked a licence.

(p) *Governing law and dispute resolution*

As discussed above, the Petroleum Act applies to all upstream oil and gas exploration and production in the United Kingdom, other than onshore in Northern Ireland. However, the fact that the United Kingdom is made up of four separate jurisdictions – England, Wales, Scotland and Northern Ireland – means that there can be some differences in the regulatory regime that applies to upstream oil and gas operations, depending on where the oil or gas field is located. This is particularly true for onshore fields, because of the application of jurisdiction-specific legislation dealing with such matters as environmental and planning consents, which are the responsibility of the devolved governments (ie, the National Assembly for Wales, the Scottish Parliament and the Northern Ireland Assembly).

In addition, some differences arise depending on whether the applicable governing law is the law of England and Wales, Scotland or Northern Ireland. For example, Scots law has a different system of security interests from English law, so if a security interest were to be granted in relation to a licence off the coast of Scotland, this would need to be considered in the context of Scots law.

The United Kingdom has a well-functioning court system for the resolution of disputes. In some cases, other modes of dispute resolution may be applicable. In particular, if a dispute arises between a licensee and the secretary of state in relation to any matter arising in relation to the licence, the dispute must be referred to arbitration, unless the model clauses specify that a different method of dispute resolution is to apply to any particular issue.

Third-party access to upstream infrastructure: It has been recognised in the United Kingdom that in the interests of efficiency, and to encourage investment in the UK continental shelf, a well-functioning regime of third-party access to infrastructure is a crucial element of the regulatory structure for upstream oil and gas. Until recently, provisions dealing with third-party access to upstream oil and gas infrastructure were set out in a number of different acts:

- the Pipelines Act 1962, for onshore petroleum pipelines;
- the Gas Act 1995, for onshore gas processing facilities;
- the Petroleum Act 1998, for offshore 'controlled' petroleum pipelines; and
- the Energy Act 2008, for oil-processing facilities.

As a result, there were some gaps and inconsistencies in the various provisions. For this reason, the Energy Act 2011 introduced a new consolidated third-party access regime to replace the earlier provisions.

The starting position is that a party seeking access to upstream infrastructure is expected first to approach the owner of the relevant infrastructure to apply for access. The UK oil and gas industry has developed the Infrastructure Code of Practice, which is a voluntary code of practice on access to upstream oil and gas infrastructure on the UK continental shelf. The code sets out the principles and procedures to be followed in negotiating third-party access to oil and gas infrastructure, and obliges parties to comply with the more general obligations under the oil and gas industry's Commercial Code of Practice. Although both codes are voluntary and non-statutory, the DECC encourages all parties to follow them.

Pursuant to the Energy Act 2011, where a party that seeks access to upstream oil and gas infrastructure cannot agree rights of access with the owner, it has the right to apply to the secretary of state for a determination of the issue and a grant of third-party rights where appropriate. The secretary of state may consider such an application only if he or she believes that the parties have had reasonable time in which to reach an agreement, and that the granting of such rights will not prejudice the transportation or processing of quantities of petroleum which the infrastructure owner may reasonably be expected to require, or the rights of other third parties with respect to such infrastructure.

If the secretary of state decides to accept the application and issues a third-party access notice, such notice may be subject to various provisions, including such provisions as the secretary of state considers necessary to secure the right of access and necessary ancillary rights, including the charges that may be made for the exercise of such rights. When considering an application, the secretary of state will assess whether the pipeline or facility needs to be modified so as to increase its capacity or to install a junction or other apparatus through which an applicant's pipeline can be connected. If such modifications are necessary, the secretary of state will also determine the financial contribution that the applicant must make to the owner to cover the cost of such modifications.

Significantly, the secretary of state can also intervene under his own initiative where the parties have had reasonable time in which to reach agreement and there is no realistic prospect of agreement being reached.

3.2 Government take

(a) *Royalties*

No royalties are payable in the United Kingdom. Previously, a royalty regime applied, but this was abolished from January 1 2003.

(b) *Bonus*

No bonuses are payable in the United Kingdom.

(c) *Rental fees*

An annual charge (a 'rental') is payable under each licence. Rentals are charged at an escalating rate on each square kilometre that the licence covers at that date. This method of calculating the rental provides an incentive to licensees to surrender acreage that they do not want to exploit. The amount of the rental is relatively small. Taxation is the main means by which the government derives revenue from oil and gas resources.

(d) *Special participation*

There is no system of special participation in the United Kingdom.

(e) *Corporate tax*

Corporate tax is the principal means by which the government derives revenue from upstream oil and gas production.

A uniform taxation system applies to all fields in the United Kingdom and the UK continental shelf, although, as discussed below, some special tax deductions are available for fields which would not otherwise be commercially attractive.

Ring fence corporation tax: Ring fence corporation tax applies to profits from oil and gas extraction activities and rights in the United Kingdom and the UK continental shelf, instead of normal corporation tax. It applies regardless of when development consent was given and aims to prevent profits from these activities being reduced for tax purposes by the set-off of losses from other trading activities. The profits from oil and gas extraction activities and rights are 'ring fenced' and treated for tax purposes as a separate trade, so that only losses derived from these activities can be offset against profits from these activities. The current rate of ring fence corporation tax is 30% (as opposed to the 24% rate of normal corporation tax, falling to 23% from April 1 2013 and 21% from April 1 2014). Ring fence corporation tax liabilities are based on the book profits of the company, which are then adjusted to arrive at the taxable profits. Deductions are available for items such as capital expenditure, plant and machinery allowances, research and development, expenditure on mineral exploration and access, and decommissioning.

Supplementary charge: A supplementary charge is also imposed on profits arising from any ring-fenced activities. The charge was first introduced in 2002 at a rate of 10%. In 2011 the government raised the rate of the supplementary charge from 20%

to 32%. The government justified this increase on the basis that the rise in oil prices had provided unexpected profits for oil and gas companies. The government has undertaken to reduce the supplementary charge back towards 20% if the oil price falls, on a sustained basis, below a set trigger price of £45 a barrel.

Petroleum revenue tax: Petroleum revenue tax applies to net income from oil and gas extraction. Petroleum revenue tax was abolished on March 16 1993 for all fields that were given development consent on or after that date. However, it still applies in respect of those fields for which development consent was given before March 16 1993. Ring fence corporation tax and the supplementary charge are also payable in respect of profits from these fields, but petroleum revenue tax is deducted when calculating these charges. Petroleum revenue tax is currently levied at a rate of 50%.

In 2009 the government introduced a tax incentive regime in the form of field allowances to apply to small or new technically challenging fields. A field allowance reduces the amount of adjusted ring-fence profits for the licensee's accounting period on which the company's supplementary charge is charged. In July 2012 the government introduced a new field allowance for large shallow-water gas fields. Most recently, in September 2012 the government announced a new brownfield allowance to support investment in older oil and gas fields. The brownfield allowance will shield up to £250 million of income in qualifying brownfield projects, or £500 million for projects in fields paying petroleum revenue tax, from the 32% supplementary charge rate (providing tax relief of up to £80 million or £160 million, respectively). The level of relief available to an individual project will depend on its size and unit costs.

4. Current issues

4.1 Decommissioning tax relief

As indicated above, the UK government has been introducing a range of tax measures to incentivise continued investment in the UK continental shelf.

One significant measure announced as part of the UK Budget 2012 was the introduction of legislation in 2013 giving the government statutory authority to sign contracts with companies operating in the United Kingdom and the UK continental shelf to provide assurance on the tax relief they will receive when decommissioning assets. According to Her Majesty's (HM) Treasury's figures, profits from UK oil and gas production are currently taxed at a total of 62% (or 81% in the case of older fields). Therefore, the prospect of greater certainty on decommissioning tax relief is very much welcomed by the industry. The issue is that at present, oil and gas companies are entitled to receive tax relief on the costs of decommissioning (at a rate of at least 50%), but there is some uncertainty because the level of relief could be changed in the future. Therefore, the signing of long-term contracts, which specify the level of relief that will be available, is designed to deliver greater certainty.

4.2 Regulatory review post-Deepwater Horizon

Following the Deepwater Horizon disaster of April 2010, the UK government and the oil and gas industry responded with various reviews to ensure that the UK regulatory regime, and the policies and practices implemented pursuant to that regime, are fit for purposes both to prevent a similar disaster from occurring in the UK continental shelf and to respond appropriately if such an incident did take place. A parliamentary select committee sought evidence on the safety of offshore oil and gas operations, with a particular focus on deepwater drilling. The committee's report, published in January 2011, concluded that the existing regime is generally sound and rejected proposals for a moratorium on deepwater drilling, but it did recommend greater scrutiny of the industry's ability to respond to a catastrophic event such as Deepwater Horizon.

At industry level, the Oil Spill Prevention and Response Advisory Group (OSPRAG) was established in May 2010, consisting of representatives from the government and industry, to examine the UK offshore oil and gas regime and arrangements for oil spill prevention and response, and to assess the adequacy of financial provisions for a response to a catastrophic event. It published its final report in September 2011. Some of OSPRAG's recommendations have already been implemented – for example, there have been some changes to the United Kingdom's voluntary oil pollution compensation agreement, known as the Offshore Pollution Liability Agreement. Under that agreement, operators are subject to strict liability (where proof of fault is not necessary) for pollution damage and the cost of remedial measures up to a maximum of $250 million per incident. The limit was originally $120 million per incident, but in response to concerns over its adequacy following the Deepwater Horizon incident, in August 2010 the Offshore Pollution Liability Agreement membership voted in favour of an increase in the Offshore Pollution Liability Agreement limit from $120 million to $250 million per incident.

Perhaps most significantly, the UK government commissioned the independent Maitland Report to review the regulatory regime for the UK offshore oil and gas sector from a safety perspective. The report, published in December 2011, concluded that overall the existing regime was effective, but that there was scope for some improvement. The Maitland Report made a number of recommendations aimed at strengthening the existing regime. In particular, the report recommended that the three regulators – the DECC, the HSE and the MCA – carry out their functions in a more integrated and coordinated manner. One option tabled is the creation of a single competent authority to take responsibility for regulating offshore operations, to be supported by the DECC and the HSE, and perhaps also by the MCA. At the end of 2012 the government published a full response to the Maitland Report and appointed a new senior oversight group, comprising the DECC, the HSE and the MCA, to supervise the successful implementation of the recommendations that are still being delivered. For the time being a new and enhanced memorandum of understanding has been agreed between the various regulators, but at the time of writing it is unclear what concrete changes, if any, will be made to the regulatory regime, because to some extent this will depend on developments at the EU level.

There may also be future changes flowing from developments at the EU level. In 2011 the European Commission published a proposal for a regulation on safety of offshore oil and gas exploration and production activities,[2] which purports to improve safety standards across the European Union. The proposed law deals with various issues, such as a requirement for all member states where offshore oil and gas activities take place to appoint a 'competent authority' to be responsible for the duties laid down by the regulation. Significantly, it is intended that the competent authority be independent of any body responsible for licensing and economic regulation of oil and gas. This is to ensure that there is no conflict of interest between the regulation of safety and environmental protection and the economic development of the member state. The law also seeks to amend the Environmental Liability Directive to extend the scope of water damage under the directive to apply within all EU marine waters, not just territorial waters. When the proposed law was first tabled, the UK government and industry were vocal in their concern that the law could potentially require unnecessary changes to the existing UK regime, particularly if the law took the form of a regulation, which would have direct application to member states. It now appears that these concerns are being heeded: in October 2012 the European Parliament's Committee on Industry, Research and Energy voted for the law to take the form of a directive. However, the full impact of the proposed law on the UK regulatory regime cannot be determined until it makes further progress through the EU legislative process.

4.3 Shale gas

Reflecting global trends, there has been considerable interest in the United Kingdom in exploiting unconventional hydrocarbons. There have been shale gas discoveries, but at this stage it is difficult to predict the extent to which shale gas will meet the United Kingdom's future energy needs.

A 2010 British Geological Survey study estimated that shale gas potentially recoverable resources in the United Kingdom could be 150 billion cubic metres of gas (5.3 trillion cubic feet). Exploratory drilling conducted in 2011 indicated that shale gas reserves could far exceed that earlier estimate. However, up to December 2012 all exploratory drilling operations were suspended on environmental and safety grounds following two small earthquakes which took place in April/May 2011 near Blackpool in Lancashire. These earthquakes were suspected to be linked to hydraulic fracturing ('fracking') treatments at the Preese Hall well operated by Cuadrilla Resources Ltd. The DECC commissioned an independent assessment of the risks, which suggested that it was safe for fracking to proceed, provided that appropriate monitoring and mitigation measures are in place.

A public consultation on the safety and environmental issues was also carried out. The moratorium was finally lifted in December 2012, subject to new controls to mitigate the risks of seismic activity. The lifting of the moratorium closely followed the publication of the government's Gas Generation Strategy, in which the government confirmed its commitment to gas for the foreseeable future. The strategy clearly indicates that the government considers that gas and gas infrastructure will play a pivotal role, in the short to medium term at least, in ensuring energy securing and boosting the economy. In particular, the strategy announced that the DECC will

---

2 Proposal for a Regulation of the European Parliament and of the Council on Safety of Offshore Oil and Gas Prospection, Exploration and Production Activities 2011/0309.

establish an Office for Unconventional Gas and Oil, which will join up responsibilities across government and provide a single point of contact for investors and streamline the regulatory process. In October 2012 HM Treasury announced that it would be consulting on tax incentives for any future shale gas industry. These developments demonstrate an appetite by the government to support further work to explore the potential that may be offered by shale gas in the United Kingdom.

5. Conclusion

While it is an undisputed fact that the United Kingdom's petroleum reserves are declining and the peak of the industry has passed, the UK oil and gas industry is still a very significant component of the UK economy and continues to offer investment opportunities. New greenfield discoveries are still being made and, with new technological advances and rising hydrocarbon prices, brownfields offer new prospects for reserves which were previously impossible or uneconomic to recover. The growth of interest in unconventional hydrocarbons will also be of interest.

Notwithstanding significant increases in the tax levied on production, the UK regime is still regarded as offering a stable investment environment. It is to be hoped that the UK government and industry will continue to collaborate to ensure that the regime continues to be fit for purpose and evolves to cater for future opportunities, such as onshore shale gas or offshore carbon capture and storage in depleted fields.

Azerbaijan

Samir Hadjiyev
Grata Law Firm

1. Introduction

Azerbaijan is one of the birthplaces of the oil industry; its history is linked to the fortunes of petroleum. A turning point in the country's oil industry was reached on September 20 1994, when one of the most significant documents in Azerbaijan's oil history – the joint development and production sharing agreement for the Azeri, Chirag and Gunashli (deepwater) field – was signed. Later this agreement came to be known as the 'contract of the century' because of its importance. This contract boosted other countries' confidence Azerbaijan and encouraged oil companies to go there. This was how Azerbaijan opened its doors to foreign investment. However, there was still the problem of how to deliver the oil to European markets. This problem was solved by the 1998 agreement between Azerbaijan, Georgia and Turkey for the construction of the Baku-Tbilisi-Ceyhan pipeline.

In order to encourage their participation in the development of the oil sector in Azerbaijan, investors can enter into either production sharing contracts, or traditional joint ventures, which constitute the main types of agreement allowed by Azerbaijan's oil legislation. Azerbaijan originally preferred production sharing agreements because, as a young state, especially one lacking financial capital, it was unable to utilise other types of contract that would be beneficial to it as a host country. Moreover, at that time Azerbaijan's low credit rating meant that it was unable to get long-term loans from foreign credit institutions to fund its oil and gas projects.

The legal framework for the regulation of oil and gas contracts is based on the Law on the Subsurface of February 13 1998, the Energy Act of November 24 1998 and the Law on Energy Resources Consumption of May 30 1996. Although these acts provide a general framework for exploiting energy resources, in many instances their provisions clash with each other. It is also unclear whether the Energy Act has priority over the Subsurface Act. In order to improve the preparation and implementation of state policy on oil and gas production, the president of Azerbaijan signed a decree on May 15 2006 for the founding of the Ministry of Industry and Energy. Since then, the State Oil Company of the Azerbaijan Republic (SOCAR) has been charged with conducting commercial functions, while the ministry is responsible for non-commercial functions such as preparing, negotiating and implementing production sharing agreements and other types of contract on behalf of the government. There is currently no legislation in Azerbaijan specifically governing the oil and gas sector. Azerbaijan still lacks independent regulatory institutions, rules on the rehabilitation of petroleum refinery plants, resolution of the legal status of the Caspian Sea, laws and regulations such as oil legislation, pipeline legislation, and environmental legislation for the administering of oil and gas operations. These issues remain the main challenges facing Azerbaijan in developing its oil and gas industry in the future.

2. Upstream activities

2.1 History

The history of the development of Azeri oil industry can be divided into several stages, each with its own peculiarities.

(a) 1847–1920

The first stage started with the mechanical production of oil in 1847 and continued to 1920. The years 1847 and 1848 saw the first industrial production of oil from the wells that had been made by digging in the Bibieybat field and later the Balakhany field. This started the development of the Azerbaijan oil industry.

The first oil refinery was constructed in Baku in 1859. The development of well drilling technologies led to the discovery of a number of oil wells, an increase in the production of oil, the development of oil infrastructure and oil refining and the creation of hundreds of companies engaged in oil production, refining and sales. The national bourgeoisie formed in Azerbaijan and Baku turned it into one of the industrial centres of the world.

At that period unused state lands were commissioned for 24 years for the exploration of oil and the development of new oil fields. The leaseholders had a right to export the oil that they produced and to fix its price. Their production made up 14% to 15% of the oil sold. The net capital invested in the oil industry accounted for only 4% of all investments in the 1870s. Mixed capital, with the participation of national capital, made up nearly 10%. In the late 19th century 49 out of 167 entrepreneurs operating in the oil sector were Azerbaijanis. The first oil stock company, Baku Oil Society, was established in Baku in 1874. The Swedişh Nobel brothers arrived in Baku in 1873 and witnessed the economic growth connected with oil. At that period they owned a number of oil fields, oil refineries, oil tankers in the Caspian Sea, barges, railways and hotels.

(b) 1920–1949

The second stage started in 1920 after the nationalisation of the oil industry in Azerbaijan and covers the period up to the opening of the offshore Neft Dashlary field. The production of oil had dropped to 2.4 million tons in 1921. However, with the expansion of exploratory activities, a number of new oilfields were discovered and brought into commission (particularly Gala and Buzovna-Mashtagha), and oil production reached the level of 23.6 million tons in 1941, making up 76% of the total volume of oil production in the Soviet Union.[1] Because of the removal of oil

1 The Union of Soviet Socialist Republics, abbreviated to USSR or the Soviet Union, was a constitutionally socialist state that existed between 1922 and 1991, ruled as a single-party state by the Communist Party with its capital as Moscow. It was a union of 15 subnational soviet republics.

equipment and oil specialists to eastern regions (including Tatarstan, Turkmenistan and Bashkiria) during the war, from 1941 to 1945 Azerbaijan accounted for just 11.1 million tons of oil production.

(c) ***1950–1969***

The third stage started with the commissioning of the Neft Dashlary field in 1950, heralding the development of an offshore oil industry in Azerbaijan, and continued up to 1969. During this stage offshore exploration activity expanded and a number of oil and gas fields were revealed and commissioned (Gum-Deniz, Sangachal-Divanni-Deniz-Khara-Zira island, Bulla-Deniz and Darwin pitcher). In addition, there were developments in offshore drilling, the technology for hydro-technological oil plant and the infrastructure of offshore oil production.

(d) ***1969–1991***

The fourth stage started in 1969 and was characterised by the rapid development of the oil industry. A new stage commenced in the development of offshore oil production at that time. The association Khazardenizneft was established in 1970, and realising the experience of Azerbaijan's oilmen in offshore work, the Ministry of Oil Industry of the Soviet Union empowered the Azeri oilmen to carry out all the geological, drilling, operating and other works across the whole of the Caspian Sea.

An Azerbaijani crane boat with a capacity of 2,500 tons started operating in the Caspian Sea. As a result, eight new oil and gas fields were discovered in the late 1960s. Total production of oil and gas reached 27.1 million tons (standard fuel) in 1975. The number of drilling plants reached 11 in the 1980s, and as a result of their operation, fields rich in oil were discovered in the Azeri sector of the Caspian Sea at depths of 80 to 350 metres.

(e) ***1991 to the present***

The fifth stage began with the collapse of the Soviet Union and independence for Azerbaijan, and encompasses the creation of a new oil strategy and a new history for the country.

One of the economic policy priorities of the new Republic of Azerbaijan was preparation of an oil strategy appropriate to an independent state. Implementation of this strategy, the main author of which was Azerbaijan's leader Heidar Aliev,[2] started in September 1994 with the signing of a 30-year contract between SOCAR and 12 large oil companies (Amoco, BP, McDermott, Unocal, LUKoil, Statoil, Exxon, Turkiye Petrolleri, Pennzoil, Itochu, Ramco and Delta) from a number of countries of the world (the United States , the United Kingdom, Russia, Turkey, Norway, Japan and Saudi Arabia). The contract concerns joint exploitation of the Azeri, and Chirag wells and the deep part of the Guneshli well in the Azerbaijan sector of the Caspian Sea, and is in the form of a production sharing agreement. This contact, 'the contract of the century', is a clear reflection of the implementation of the new oil strategy.

---

2 Heidar Aliev was the third president of Azerbaijan, representing the New Azerbaijan Party from October 1993 to October 2003.

2.2. Current reserves and production

Azerbaijan has been a world leader in oil production and refining, and at one time produced half of the world's oil. By 1994 Azerbaijan had produced nearly 1 billion tons of oil from its onshore and offshore deposits. The experience of the Azerbaijani oilmen gained from oil production made Azerbaijan famous in the world oil industry in the 20th century. In 1918 2.96 million tons of oil were extracted from 3,287 wells; in 1919 3.6 million tons from 2,066 wells; and in 1920 2.8 million tons from 2,037 wells.

Before the signature of the contract of the century in 1994, the reserves in three deposits (the Azeri, Chiraq and Gunashli fields) were estimated at 511 million tons of oil, but the latest research shows that the capacity of these deposits is nearly 1 billion tons of oil. Early oil production from these three deposits started in November 1997. So far, 123 million tons of oil has been produced from them. Since Azerbaijan began to produce oil within the framework of its new oil strategy output has begun to increase. International experts estimate that Azerbaijan's reserves of oil total 6 billion tons. There are 30 prospective deposits to be delivered through joint operations. There are 15 agreements relating to offshore fields on the Caspian Sea and 12 that concern onshore deposits. Under these agreements 43 companies representing 21 countries of the world are partners of Azerbaijan. It is estimated that $60 billion will be invested for the exploration, extraction and transportation of the country's hydrocarbon reserves.

In 2006, Caspian oil production totalled about 2.3 million barrels a day. Sizeable oil production growth has come primarily from the north Caspian states of Kazakhstan and Azerbaijan. Development of the region's oil resources has been led by three major projects: Tengiz and Karachaganak (in Kazakhstan), and Azerbaijan's Azeri, Chirag and deepwater Gunashli fields. Development of these decade-old key projects has given rise to an influx of new investment and infrastructure development that constitutes a second Caspian oil rush, the first having occurred in the late 1800s. Following these discoveries, major new finds were announced in Azerbaijan at Shah Deniz in 1999.

Oil production in Azerbaijan amounted to 23.8 million tons in the first half of 2011. That was a drop of 1,445,000 tons or 5.6% compared to the same period of the previous year, according to the State Statistical Committee of Azerbaijan. Production amounted to 4.1 million tons of crude in January, 3.8 million tons in February, 4.1 million tons in March, 3.9 million tons in April, 4.1 million tons in May and 3.88 million tons in June.

3. Petroleum legal regime

3.1 Petroleum law and relevant provisions

In accordance with the Law on the Subsurface, the subsurface, without impairing the rights of legal entities and physical persons, be owned by Azerbaijan.

Under Presidential Decree 200 on the Creation of SOCAR of September 13 1992, Presidential Decree 844 on Improvement of the Structure of SOCAR of January 24 2003 and SOCAR's charter (approved by Decree 844), SOCAR owns all petroleum produced, and is vested with the authority to carry out the exploration, discovery, preparation and development of all on and offshore oil and gas fields in Azerbaijan, the transportation, processing and sale of oil, gas, condensate and products obtained from them, the stable and sustainable satisfaction of consumers' demand for fuel and other works and services, and profit generation.

Under Presidential Decree 1089 on Exploration, Development, and Production Sharing in the Shafag-Asiman Offshore Block in the Azerbaijan Sector of the Caspian Sea of September 7 2010, SOCAR is authorised to prepare and execute an agreement on behalf of the Republic of Azerbaijan in respect of this block, and to represent Azerbaijan as a party to the agreement on all matters related to the agreement throughout its entire term.

The Presidential Decree on the Establishment of the State Oil Fund of the Republic of Azerbaijan (SOFAR) of December 29 1999, and the Statute of SOFAR of December 29 2000 are also relevant to Azerbaijan's petroleum legal regime.

(a) Regulatory bodies

The Ministry of Industry and Energy: The ministry is the executive body charged with drawing up state policy and regulating activities in the fuel and energy sector. These activities include upstream and downstream activities, exploration and development of fields, the operation of oil and gas refineries, power and heat generation, power supply and distribution through the networks, and so forth. The main functions of the ministry are:

- determination of prospective areas of production, preparation of the state and regional programmes to develop them and ensuring the realisation of those plans;
- forecasting the production of various energy products;
- participation in international cooperation agreements in certain areas of the energy sector;
- supervision of activities in order to enforce laws and regulations applying to the energy sector;
- creation of attractive conditions for external and domestic investment in the sector;
- issuing of licences (eg, for the sale of some oil products);
- ensuring an adequate supply of energy products to the domestic market;
- research and development in the sphere of energy;
- application of international standards and expertise within the country;
- preparation of activities aimed at decreasing potential losses during production, transportation, distribution and exploitation of energy resources;
- preparation of programmes ensuring energy security in Azerbaijan;
- ensuring the energy sector complies with ecological safety rules.

The majority of the tasks envisaged in the programmes prepared by the ministry are executed by SOCAR and the rest by AzerEnergy JSC. The forms in which they are executed and relevant competences are set out in presidential decrees.

SOCAR: SOCAR is the state-owned oil and natural gas corporation of Azerbaijan. It produces oil and natural gas, operates the country's two oil refineries and runs oil and gas pipelines throughout the country. SOCAR oversees the international consortia that are developing new oil and gas projects in Azerbaijan. SOCAR is ranked the 68th largest company in the world and is worth $20 billion.

SOCAR employs between 59,000 and 70,000 people. It is involved in exploring oil and gas fields, producing, processing and transporting oil, gas and gas condensate, marketing petroleum and petrochemical products on domestic and international markets, and supplying natural gas to industry and the public in Azerbaijan. Three production divisions, two oil refineries and one gas processing plant, an oil tanker fleet, a deep water platform fabrication yard, two trusts, one institution, and 22 subdivisions all operate as corporate entities within SOCAR.

SOFAR: SOFAR is a special-purpose state organisation in which Azerbaijan's revenues from its oil and gas agreements are accumulated, efficiently managed and preserved for future generations.

SOFAR was founded in order to manage oil and gas income efficiently as well as to invest it in the development of socially and economically important projects.

(b) Types of agreement

On September 20 1994 the first agreement was signed on the development and production sharing of the Azeri, Chirag, and Gunashli (deepwater) fields in the Azerbaijan sector of the Caspian. This agreement paved the way for foreign companies to sign new contracts in Azerbaijan. So far 27 contracts have been signed between SOCAR and foreign oil companies with regard to exploration, production of hydrocarbons and production sharing. SOCAR owns numbers of licences for exploration, production and other activities for which presence of a licence is a mandatory condition. These are issued by the Ministry of Industry and Energy, since otherwise SOCAR would not be able to function. Being a state body, SOCAR is the only company which is permitted to explore for and produce of oil and gas, which is why it is a mandatory party in all oil and gas production sharing agreements in Azerbaijan.

As an illustration, an agreement on exploration, development and production sharing for the Shafag-Asiman offshore block in the Azerbaijan sector of the Caspian Sea was signed in Baku, on October 7 2010, between SOCAR, on behalf of the Azerbaijan government, on the one hand and BP Exploration (Azerbaijan) Ltd, a company incorporated in England, and SOCAR Oil Affiliate, a company to be formed and wholly owned and controlled by SOCAR, on the other hand.

This contract was signed within the framework of Azerbaijan's oil strategy for the development of the Azeri, Chirag, and Gunashli fields in the Azerbaijani sector of the Caspian Sea through agreements with the foreign companies.

BP and SOCAR had signed a memorandum of understanding regarding exploration of the Shafag-Asiman structures on July 13 2009. It was the first official document regarding this block. The memorandum was followed by the signing of heads of agreement on basic commercial principles on joint exploration and development of the fields. The production sharing agreement itself runs for a period of 30 years with potential extension of up to five more years, and includes detailed regulatory provisions.

(c) *Acquisition of acreage*

Rights to use of the subsurface are granted following tenders, auctions and direct negotiations. The use of direct negotiations, however, occurs only in exceptional circumstances in accordance with a decision of the relevant executive authority. Depending on the actions intended to be undertaken with regard to the subsurface, the relevant authority could be the Ministry of Ecology and Natural Resources, the State Committee for Geology and Mineral Resources, the State Committee for Mining and Technical Supervision, the Ministry of Emergency Situations, or another body. The Ministry of Industry and Energy grants the rights relating to oil products.

A special permit grants the right to use the subsurface for geological exploration, development of proven reserves of mineral resources, storage of wastes from mining associated processing operations, establishment of specially protected geological facilities, or the collection of mineralogical and other geological materials. Where use of the subsurface encompasses activities falling within several of these categories, legal entities or physical persons may need several special permits.

A fee is payable for the issue of a special permit. The amount of the fee is established by the relevant executive authority.

(d) *Qualification requirements*

The Law on the Subsurface specifies the following principal requirements in relation to operations related to use of the subsurface:

- access to works will be granted only to duly qualified persons;
- persons engaged into mining and drilling works must be supplied with special clothing and protection devices;
- machinery, equipment and materials must comply with safety and sanitary norms;
- radioactive and explosive materials and related equipment must be properly recorded, stored and operated;
- supervisory activities must be carried out for the purpose of ensuring that work abides by normal technical standards and that any dangerous situations can be predicted;
- there must be regular control of the atmospheric state within the mine, as regards volume of oxygen, harmful and explosive gases and dust; and
- measures must be prepared and implemented to ensure the protection of the population in the areas affected by the operations.

The relevant executive authorities and subsurface users must ensure compliance with these standards in relation to works relating to use of the subsurface. So all exploration and production agreements must set out these rules or refer to this law. No agreement can exist if it does not respect these standards.

The law also sets out the following principal requirements in relation to geological exploration of the subsurface:

- there must be a scientific explanation regarding the effectiveness of the geological exploration of the subsurface;
- there must be full research into the conditions to be faced by the mining – technical, hydro-geological and ecological – in relation to the geological structure of the subsurface, the development of the discovered field, and the construction and operation of any facilities unrelated to the extraction of mineral resources;
- there must be a correct assessment of the reserves of mineral resources, their quality, volume, their components and their valuation;
- norms and standards prescribed by the legislation in relation to the protection of the subsurface and environment must be complied with;
- the geological exploration of the subsurface must be carried out using methods and procedures eliminating unnecessary loss of mineral resources and ensuring the quality of those recovered;
- materials and mineral resources must be extracted from the subsurface with the aim of causing no harm to the environment;
- fields should be developed, exploratory excavations and wells suitable for other business purposes should be maintained, and unusable excavations and structures should be abandoned following proper procedures;
- geological and technical documentation should be duly maintained, along with duplicate mineral samples acquired in course of the geological exploration of the subsurface and suitable for future use.

These requirements concern only the geological exploration of the subsurface. The Law on the Subsurface does not explicitly differentiate the stages of the project; it merely sets out requirements that can be attributed to the different project stages.

(e) *Duration*

In accordance with the Law on the Subsurface, sections of the subsurface may be transferred for use for the purpose of construction and operation of underground facilities, establishment of specially protected facilities and other purposes not related to the extraction of mineral resources for a certain period of time or on a permanent basis.

Subsurface rights may be granted for the following periods:

- for carrying out geological exploration – up to five years;
- for extraction of mineral resources – up to 25 years;
- for carrying out geological exploration and extraction of mineral resources – up to 30 years.

The period of use of the subsurface for the purpose of extracting mineral resources is established by reference to the outcome of development operations, efficient use of the subsurface and technical-economic studies ensuring protection thereof. The duration of rights to use the subsurface are calculated from the date of awarding the right of use. Where the subsurface user complies with the requirements of the special permit, the period of use of the subsurface may be extended upon agreement of the parties. An extension depends on the stage for which the subsurface user has a special permit and will be agreed only if he has respected all the requirements of that permit. The law does not require any additional conditions to be respected. A subsurface user cannot obtain extension for an activity not covered by the permit.

(f) ***Minimum work programme***

Before the beginning of each calendar year during the development and production period, the contractor must prepare and submit to the steering committee[3] for approval an annual work programme, together with the related budget, showing the petroleum operations that the contractor proposes to carry out in that calendar year. The steering committee must meet within 30 days of receipt of the annual work programme and budget to consider them and any revisions thereto, and to approve the annual work programme and the budget in their final form. If it is necessary to carry out the annual work programme, the contractor is authorised to make expenditure during the relevant calendar year in excess of the budget adopted there for so long as the aggregate of such excess expenditure does not exceed 10% of the budget. Extra expenditure exceeding 10% has to be approved by the steering committee, which approval shall not be withheld where the expenditure has been demonstrated to be reasonable and necessary. In the event that the annual work programme and budget have not been approved by the steering committee in the case of the first annual work programme and budget within 60 days of the formation of the steering committee, and in the case of each subsequent annual work programme and budget by the first day of the calendar year to which it relates, the contractor shall be entitled to carry out petroleum operations in accordance with some or all of its proposed annual work programme and budget until such time as the annual work programme and budget is agreed by the steering committee, or any dispute relating to the annual work programme and budget has been resolved by reference to arbitration in accordance with the arbitration procedure.

(g) ***Assignment and encumbrance***

No assignment, mortgage, pledge or other encumbrance shall be made by a contractor party of its rights and obligations arising under the agreement other than in accordance with the agreement. Any purported assignment made in breach of the agreement shall be null and void. Except where a contractor party is assigning all of its participating interest, no contractor party may assign its participating interest without SOCAR's approval.

---

3 The steering committee comprises an equal number of members from SOCAR and contractor. Initially the steering committee consists of 10 representatives appointed by SOCAR and 10 representatives appointed by contractor. If at any time the number of contractor parties increases or decreases the number of representatives to be appointed by each of SOCAR and contractor shall be increased or reduced, as the case may be, to equal the number of contractor parties, provided however that the number of representatives to be appointed by each of SOCAR and contractor shall never be less than four. The conditions of the steering committee's appointment can differ from one production sharing agreement to another.

A contractor party is entitled to assign all or part of its rights and obligations to any third party which:

- has the technical and financial ability commensurate with the responsibilities and obligations which would be imposed on it by the assignment;
- as to the interest assigned, accepts and assumes all of the terms and conditions of the agreement;
- is an entity with which SOCAR can legally do business.

Contractor parties have the right freely to mortgage, pledge or otherwise encumber their interests in the agreement or any property in or outside Azerbaijan which is used for petroleum operations, provided that any such mortgage, pledge or other encumbrance shall be made expressly subject to the terms of the relevant agreement.

Any proposed assignment, mortgage, pledge or other encumbrance by a contractor party to a third party requires the prior approval of SOCAR, which approval shall not be unreasonably withheld. If within 90 days following notification to SOCAR of a proposed assignment accompanied by the relevant information and the draft deed of assignment, mortgage, pledge or other encumbrance, SOCAR has not given its decision, then the assignment, mortgage, pledge or other encumbrance is deemed to have been approved by SOCAR.

(h) Local content

Local content requirements in Azerbaijan are generally contractual rather than legal, as most originate from the production sharing agreements rather than legislation. Production sharing agreements tend to have clauses on local content that acquire the status of binding law by ratification in the parliament. These agreements are generally not published. However, BP has made available for public scrutiny the production sharing agreements relating to both the Azeri, Chirag, and Gunashli fields and the Shafag-Asiman fields. These show that the contractor, its agents and subcontractors have the right to import into, and export from Azerbaijan, free of any taxes and restrictions and in their own name, goods and supplies that in the contractor's reasonable opinion are required for the proper conduct and achievement of the petroleum operations, provided however, that the contractor shall give preference to Azerbaijani suppliers in those cases in which such Azerbaijani suppliers are in all material respects competitive in price, quality and availability. The contractor and its subcontractors, and the joint operating company[4] and its subcontractors, are free to employ such personnel as, in the opinion of the contractor, are required for the purpose of carrying out the petroleum operations.

---

4 All production sharing agreements require that the contractor shall, as soon as practicable after the effective date, form a joint operating company, which may be incorporated or created outside of Azerbaijan but shall be registered in Azerbaijan in accordance with Azerbaijani law. The contractor has the right to substitute or to establish additional entities to undertake some or all of the responsibilities of the joint operating company with respect to petroleum operations. For the purpose of this chapter we use the term 'production sharing agreement' on the presumption that a joint operating company will be created.

The contractor has to require the joint operating company to give preference, as far as is consistent with efficient operations, to employing citizens of Azerbaijan for the performance of the petroleum operations to the extent reasonably practicable, provided that such citizens have the required knowledge, qualifications and experience. The contractor agrees to provide training (including retraining) for Azerbaijani citizens employed with respect to the petroleum operations.

(i) ***Environment***

The contractor develops jointly with SOCAR the safety and environmental protection standards and practices appropriate for the petroleum operations being undertaken under the agreement. These standards must take account of the specific environmental characteristics of the Caspian Sea and draw, as appropriate, on international petroleum industry standards and experience in exploration and production operations in other parts of the world and on existing Azerbaijan safety and environmental legislation. The contractor undertakes to conduct the petroleum operations in a diligent, safe and efficient manner in accordance with the agreed environmental standards. The order of priority for actions is the protection of life, then the environment and only finally property. The contractor has to implement an integrated management system covering all health, safety and environmental aspects of the activities carried out in relation to the petroleum operations.

The contractor must comply with present and future Azerbaijani laws or regulations of general application with respect to public health and safety and protection and restoration of the environment, to the extent that such laws and regulations are no more stringent than the agreed environmental standards.

(j) ***Governing law and dispute resolution***

All disputes arising between SOCAR and any or all of the contractor parties, which are not amicably resolved by the parties shall be finally settled by a sole arbitrator appointed by the unanimous decision of the parties or, in the absence of a unanimous decision within 30 days of the submission of a request for arbitration, by a panel of three arbitrators under the Arbitration Rules of the United Nations Commission on International Trade Law (UNCITRAL). In the event that these rules fail to make provision for any matter or situation, the arbitration tribunal may establish its own rules to govern such matter and procedure and any such rules so adopted shall be considered as a part of the UNCITRAL rules. For the purposes of allowing such arbitration and for the enforcement and execution of any arbitration decision each party waives any and all claims to immunity, including, but not limited to, any claims to sovereign immunity.

The arbitration shall be held in Stockholm, Sweden. The language used during the procedure shall be the English language and the English language text of the production sharing agreement will be utilised by the arbitrators.

3.2 Government take

(a) *Royalties*

The law provides that a royalty must be paid with a view to ensuring rational use of subsurface resources in the territory of Azerbaijan and on the Caspian shelf. The royalty must be paid by the physical entities and enterprises extracting the minerals from subsurface strata of the earth on the territory of Azerbaijan (including the sector of the Caspian Sea belonging to Azerbaijan). The rate of the royalty is established according to the type of natural resource being extracted; the royalty rate for crude oil is 26%. The royalty is calculated for each cubic metre produced.[5]

For oil, natural gas and all types of metals the appropriate tax rate is applied to the wholesale price of the resources extracted, and for other natural resources the appropriate tax rate is applied to each cubic metre of minerals mined from the subsurface. The wholesale price for the purposes of taxation is the actual output (sale) price (which may not be less than the market price) determined by the taxpayer for the natural resources extracted, but if these prices are determined by the state the wholesale price is the regulated price.

Royalties must be paid on a monthly basis, no later than the 20th day of the month following the accounting month. Taxpayers must also submit tax returns on a monthly basis no later than the 20th day of the month following the accounting month to the tax authorities, detailing the taxes to be paid.

(b) *Bonuses*

As a result of the implementation of Azerbaijan's current oil strategy and the conclusion of oil contracts with international organisations, foreign oil companies have paid Azerbaijan bonuses totalling $800 million during 1994 to 2000. In addition, more than 30,000 jobs were created in the Azerbaijan oil industry, which has led to an increase in employment.

One of the largest series of production bonus payments received by the Azerbaijani government is thought to have totalled $300 million, arising from the production sharing agreement for the Azeri, Chirag and Gunashli fields. The major sources of income for SOFAR are bonus payments made by foreign investors to SOCAR or other relevant government authorities as a result of the signature or implementation of oil contracts.

According to the SOFAR's annual reports for 2010 and 2011, the fund received a total of Am1.6 million ($2 million) in bonus payments in 2010, and Am15.7 million (US$20 million) in 2011.

(c) *Land tax*

Persons and enterprises who own or use land plots on the territory of Azerbaijan are liable to a land tax irrespective of the results of economic activity.

---

5 Taxpayers should bear in mind that, when calculating the tax, the volumes of oil and gas re-injected back into the well due for technological reasons are deducted from the volumes of oil and gas produced in accordance with regulations established by the relevant authorities.

The land tax is determined based on the documents that confirm the right of ownership and use of plots of land. Land on which structures and facilities are located and land necessary for the sanitary protection of facilities are all taxed.

Tax applies to land used for industry, construction, transportation, communication, commercial-consumer or other special purposes and housing. The tax is imposed on each 100 square metres of land in a plot at rates determined in multiples of the conventional financial unit specified in the following table:

Location	Land used for industry, construction, transport, communications, services and other special purposes (in manats)
Baku	10
Ganja, Sumgait	8
Other towns (except where subject to regional subordination), regional centres	4
Towns, districts and villages subject to regional subordination (except the districts of Baku and Sumgait)	2

Payment for the use of the subsurface may be taken as:

- money payments;
- part of the mineral resources or other products of the user (payment in kind);
- the provision of services.

The accounting period for the tax on land is determined on the basis of the calendar year.

Enterprises that have land in the territory of Azerbaijan must calculate their liability to the land tax annually and submit such tax returns to the relevant tax authorities not later than May 15 of each year.

The tax due is to be paid, in equal portions, before August 15. If the land tax was not paid by a previous owner of the land, it shall be paid by the new owner by that date.

(d) Special participation

SOCAR is likely to continue its involvement and participation in nearly every upstream hydrocarbon exploration and production agreement in the country in the coming years. International oil companies, most notably British Petroleum, Norway's Statoil Hydro, Turkish Petroleum Corporation and France's Total, are likely to increase their upstream activities in Azerbaijan due to their recent successes in the country, their upstream activities in the country over the past 15 years, and their declared strategic intent to increase upstream activities in Azerbaijan. Other international oil companies that are less likely to increase their activities but whose involvement should be mentioned are ExxonMobil, Lukoil, and Nations Petroleum. For the next five to 10 years it is highly likely that production sharing agreements will continue to be the format for upstream hydrocarbon investments in Azerbaijan.

(e) Corporate taxes

Profit tax has been lowered to 22% and the value added tax to 18%. The accounting period for profit tax is determined on the basis of the calendar year.

Resident and non-resident enterprises with permanent establishments in Azerbaijan, taxable income of which is generated from Azerbaijani sources and specified income of which is not taxed at the source of payment, must submit a tax return no later than March 31 of the following year.

If a legal entity that is a taxpayer ceases operations in Azerbaijan, it must make a declaration to the tax authority of the date of its liquidation or, for the permanent establishment of a non-resident, within 30 days from the date of the endorsement of the decision by the representation of the Azerbaijan Republic in a foreign state. Tax is then assessed to cover the timeframe from the beginning of tax year until the day of the taxpayer ceased activities.

4. Current issues

SOCAR and KazMunayGaz[6] of Kazakhstan announced a tender to prepare a feasibility report on exporting Kazakhstan's oil supplies across the Caspian Sea to Azerbaijan. Azerbaijan and Kazakhstan agreed on the project in June 2007. The project is to be implemented during 2013 to 2014. The volume will be 23 million tons a year initially, but it will be raised up to 56 million tons later. The oil will be exported by pipeline to coastal terminals in Georgia or Turkey or by railway to Georgian terminals.

BP has announced that Azerbaijan's parliament has ratified the new production sharing agreement, between BP and SOCAR on joint exploration and development of the Shafag-Asiman structure in the Azerbaijan sector of the Caspian Sea.

The ratification follows the signing of the agreement in Baku in October 2010. Under the agreement, which is for 30 years, BP Exploration (Azerbaijan) Ltd will be the operator, with a 50% interest, while SOCAR will hold the remaining 50% of the equity.

The block lies some 125km (78 miles) to the southeast of Baku. It covers an area of some 1,100km^3 and has never been explored before. It is located in a deepwater section of about 650–800 metres with a reservoir depth of about 7,000 metres.[7]

---

6 KazMunayGaz is the state-owned oil and gas company of Kazakhstan and was founded in 2002 by merging Kazakhoil and Oil and Gas Transportation.

7 On May 6 2011 the Law on the Confirmation of and Permission for the Production Sharing Agreement Between BP and SOCAR on Joint Exploration and Development of the Shafag-Asiman Structure in the Azerbaijan Sector of the Caspian Sea was adopted. There have been no further regulatory developments so far.

5. Conclusion

Azerbaijan oil policy has attracted foreign organisations and investors to get involved with the country. Azerbaijan wants to use their financial support and exploit the country's oil resources together, making it beneficial for both parties.

Azerbaijan is one of the key oil centres of the world, and is a country which has used the enormous energy potential in the Caspian to form a new economic model for the development of the region, and which plays an important role in the Caspian and Caucasus region in strengthening political and trade relations between Europe and Asia through INOGATE[8], TRACECA[9] and other enormous projects.

8 INOGATE is an international energy co-operation programme between the European Union, Turkey and countries of the former Soviet Union, with the exception of the Baltic states and the Russian Federation. Formally it describes itself as supporting "international cooperation between the European Union, the littoral states of the BlackandCaspian Seas and their neighbouring countries."

9 TRACECA (Transport Corridor Europe-Caucasus-Asia) is an international transport programme involving the European Union and 14 states of the eastern European, Caucasian and central Asian region. It has a permanent secretariat, originally financed by the European Commission, in Baku, Azerbaijan.

Iraq

Ahmed Mousa Jiyad
Iraq/Development Consultancy & Research, Norway

1. Introduction

Iraq's upstream petroleum sector witnessed three unprecedented interrelated developments post-2003: an opening to foreign direct investment; the offering of the most prized petroleum fields in a rather short period of time; and formulation of the basic model for long-term service contracts.

I would argue that if things go as planned and contracted, Iraq will become a major contributor to the world petroleum market; a magnet for foreign investment through the involvement of international oil companies, specialised service companies and other related activities; and could introduce a new but significant element in the legal and governing framework, which might have wide and lasting implications for the relationship between host developing countries and international oil companies. However, reality seldom coincides with expectations.

This chapter discusses the long-term service contracts in place for upstream petroleum development in Iraq. Due to the need to limit the extent of the analysis, the corresponding matters in the Kurdish region of the country are excluded, though a few references to the region are made. The analysis is based on the model contracts and, for verification purposes scanned copies of the signed contracts were consulted. However, because of non-disclosure commitment, no formal references will be made to any signed copies of these contracts. Also this chapter does not address matters relating to subcontracting, or to contracts for front-end engineering and design, engineering, procurement and construction or other types of contract. Finally, limitations of space has prevented the use of data, statistics, annexes, maps and charts that are available on matters covered by this chapter.

Part 2 provides an updated review of petroleum upstream activities in Iraq with regard to exploration, development and production. Because of the importance of exports, a few paragraphs are also included on the expansion and diversification of export outlets.

The complexities, components and interconnections of the petroleum legal regime are addressed in part 3. This part elaborates on three major issues: petroleum law and relevant provisions, government take and payment to and privileges of international oil companies.

Part 4 sheds lights on the main features of and new development in Iraq's long-term service contracts. Further insight is provided in Part 5 on three critical current issues: the legality of concluded contracts, the situation of international oil companies who concluded contracts with the Kurdistan Regional Government, and the reduction of production plateau targets and the renegotiation of contracts. The chapter ends with a few conclusions.

2. Upstream activities

The petroleum upstream sector constitutes the main pillar of the Iraqi economy. The national development plans, state budgets, the balance of payments and trade balance depend largely on oil production and consequent export revenues. Hence, the level and prospects of all economic activities in the country are affected by developments in upstream petroleum.

Ministry of Oil plans provide detailed information on the main components and direction of various activities within the upstream petroleum sector, while signed contracts illustrate the actual methods by which these plans are being implemented.

2.1. National Exploration Programme

Official Iraqi data issued in October 2010 shows proven oil of 143 billion barrels from known 66 oilfields, and this represents only 28% of the estimated oil in place, and proven gas reserves are estimated at 127 trillion standard cubic feet (tscf). Probable gas reserves are estimated to be 275 to 300 tscf.

The Ministry of Oil's plan for 2011 to 2014 aims to, "attain significant increase in the oil and gas reserves". Sources quantify these objectives as aiming at adding around 29 tscf of gas and 10 billion barrels of oil.[1]

The National Exploration Programme with funding of $644 million,[2] has three components: to hold a fourth bid round (which took place on May 2012); to launch massive exploration activities using national efforts and capacities; and finally to drill 12 exploration wells across Iraq.[3]

During the fourth bid round, 12 exploration blocks were offered: seven were gas-prone and five oil-prone. Only four blocks were contracted, three of which are classified as oil-prone.[4]

In the immediate aftermath of the fourth bid round the oil minister promised a new fifth bid round, stating that Iraq has more than 60 blocks ready for offer, and that preparations would start in few months for launching the round in which 10 to 15 oil and gas blocks would be offered. It is worth mentioning that Dr Shahristani, the Deputy Prime Minister for Energy, has reportedly asked the Ministry of Oil, "to sweeten the terms of the model contracts" for the new bid round.[5]

---

1 www.upstreamonline.com/live/article253707.ece.

2 Original data in Iraqi dinars converted at $1= ID1168. See Ministry of Oil *Summary of the Four-Year Plan* 2011-2014 for the Oil and Gas Sector (February 2011) .

3 See www.upstreamonline.com/live/article253707.ece. However, the plan refers to 10 not 12 exploration wells.

4 For analysis of the fourth bid round pre and post the bidding event, see Jiyad, "The Forthcoming Exploration Blocks Bid Round in Iraq: Issues for Consideration" *Middle East Economic Survey* Volume 54 Issue 23, June 6 2011, also posted on iraqog.com/oil/oillaw/jiyad62011.pdf and on www.iraq-businessnews.com/2011/06/06/the-next-iraqi-oil-round-issues-for-consideration; and Jiyad, Ahmed Mousa "Iraq's Fourth Bid Round: Assessment of The Outcome" *Middle East Economic Survey* Volume 55: Issue 25, June 18 2012, also posted on www.iraq-businessnews.com/2012/06/19/iraqs-fourth-bid-round-assessment-of-the-outcome.

5 www.iraqoilreport.com/politics/oil-policy/baghdad-re-asserts-itself-8522/?utm.

2.2 Expansion of development, production and export capacities

The second pillar of upstream activities comprises development, production and export capacities.

Most of Iraq's highly prized oilfields and three gas fields were offered to international oil companies through bid rounds and one by direct negotiation. International oil company involvement began through direct negotiation with the Chinese CNPC to convert the production sharing contract in respect of Alahdab oilfield, which had been concluded in 1997, into a long-term service contract, which was concluded in November 2008. The other oil and gas fields were awarded through three bid rounds between June 2009 and October 2010. A total of 15 contracts were signed covering 17 fields, including three gas fields and 14 oilfields.

The total oil production from oilfields offered under the first two bid rounds and from Alahdab will amount to 12.215 million barrels per day (mbd) when the contracted plateau targets are realised. Total oil production in the country would be even higher if oil production from other oilfields and those from Kurdistan are added.

Oil production also results in proportional volumes of associated gas. Technical information reveals that each million barrels per day of Iraqi crude oil produces 0.8 billion cubic feet per day of associated gas.[6] Moreover, the development of three gas fields has a strategic importance independent from oil production.

Oil production is intended mainly to satisfy world demand as domestic demand for oil is limited, and any future expansion in domestic economic activities and improvement in the standard of living would not absorb even 20% of the projected plateau production. Therefore, most of the crude produced has to be exported. As a result expanding and diversifying export outlets are prerequisites to realising any level of production capacity expansion.

Without going into too many details on the likelihood of success, the Ministry of Oil adopted the Iraq Crude Oil Export Expansion Project to expand and diversify export facilities through the Arabian Gulf (8.5 mbd), Turkey (1.6 mbd), Syria (4.5 mbd) and even Jordan (1 mbd). There is also a plan for a pipeline to deliver surplus gas to Syria and the Arab Gas Pipeline with a possibility of a connection to the port of Ceyhan (in Turkey) on the Mediterranean, or through Egypt and then on to the European network. To optimise the pipeline network and attain its export targets the Ministry of Oil signed a $13.3 million contract in May 2011 with the Canadian consulting firm SNC-Lavalin.[7]

3. Petroleum legal regime

3.1 Petroleum law and relevant provisions

Legal regimes governing the petroleum upstream and midstream sectors are both complex and multi-layered, and some of their components are ambiguous.

---

6 This was based on an average gas to oil ratio for Iraqi crude after discussions with Dr Thamir Uqaily in September 2012.

7 www.iraqoilreport.com/oil/production-exports/iraq-moves-forward-on-strategic-pipelines-5673/?utm.

In Iraq, the pyramid of legal and regulatory frameworks governing the petroleum sector and its development (impacting its formulation and execution) is composed of many levels and each has a distinct authority and role within the framework of legal and legislative instruments.

At the top of the pyramid stands the Constitution, which provide the basic principles and constitutes the heart of the mandatory framework. Collective ownership (Article 111) and 'highest benefit' (Article 112:2) are the most powerful core principles; participatory co-management (Article 112:2) is a basic operational principle; encouraging private sector involvement, both domestic and foreign (Article 112: 2), is a necessary promotional principle; finally, existing laws remain in force until they are annulled or amended (Article 130), which is an important transitional validation principle.

The second level includes instruments specific to the petroleum upstream and midstream sectors comprises three broad categories of laws. The first comprises laws that existed prior to the Constitution and that remain valid such as Law 80 of 1961, Laws 97, 123 and 130 of 1967 on the Iraq National Oil Company (INOC), Law 101 of 1976 on the Ministry of Oil, Law 84 of 1985 on the Preservation and Protection of Hydrocarbon Endowment, Law 3 of 1997 for the Protection of the Environment; Law 113 of 1983 on Income Tax (and its amendment by Law 19 of 2010) and Law 22 of 1997 on Public Companies.

The second category comprises draft laws that have been stalled by political deadlock since early 2007, and therefore not actually enacted. This includes the proposed Federal Oil and Gas Law,[8] the Iraqi National Oil Company Law,[9] the new Ministry of Oil Law, the Revenue Sharing Law and the Public Commission to Audit and Appropriate Federal Revenues Law.

The third category comprises other laws which could have direct and indirect implications for petroleum related projects. Among them are Law 13 of 2006 on Investment, Law 64 of 2007 on Private Investment in Oil Refining, and Law 21 of 2008 on Provincial Powers.

There are a number of legal uncertainties, ambiguities and disparities that could affect the legal predictability of upstream arrangements, especially those involving international oil companies. Ambiguities and imperfections and different interpretations of certain constitutional provisions have generated daunting uncertainties on one hand, while reference has also been made to older, though still valid, laws on the other. This has caused some serious rifts between the legislative and executive branches with regard to their respective roles in the development of the upstream petroleum sector.

The principles enshrined in the Constitution have caused serious differences of

8 For further analysis of the Federal Oil and Gas Law see Jiyad, "Iraqi Federal Oil and Gas Law Revisited". *Energy & Geopolitical Risk*, Volume 2, Issue 1 (January 2011); and Jiyad, "Federal Oil and Gas Law: Viability, Coherence and Functioning Perspectives", paper sent to Iraqi Institute for Economic Reform as a contribution to the workshop on the Federal Oil and Gas Law, Baghdad, December 17 2011, and published at www.mees.com/en/articles/3496-federal-oil-and-gas-law-viability-coherence-and-functioning-perspectives and at www.iraq-businessnews.com/2011/12/20/federal-oil-and-gas-law-viability-coherence-and-functioning-perspectives.

9 More analysis on INOCL is available from Jiyad (2009: May 2011)

interpretation, opinions, and generate ambiguities to the extent that observers find it necessary to resolve these ambiguities and make the required constitutional amendments.[10]

The most apparent and lingering problem is the legal status of contracts. While the executive branch – the Council of Ministers and the Ministry of Oil – considers that control of these contracts falls within its mandate and authority, others within the legislative branch – the Council of Representatives (Iraq's parliament) – and outside think the government is illegally intruding on the parliament's prerogatives. Informed legal and professional opinions tend to support the position taken by the Council of Representatives.[11] Furthermore, international oil companies have expressed concerns about the legality of their contracts in the absence of a clear legal framework, although they accept the risk associated with such legal uncertainty. But many are worried that future governments and parliaments might cancel or radically modify these contracts, which might affect their economics. Indeed, during the March 2010 election campaign and in the immediate aftermath political parties and groups declared their dissatisfaction with these contracts, and called for revision of them once the new government assumed office. That has been proven to be only election rhetoric this time.

(a) Regulatory bodies

Under the Constitution all legal instruments of the types referred to above are usually proposed by the government through the Council of Ministers (the executive authority), approved and enacted by the Council of Representatives (the legislative authority), and enter into force upon publication.

Accordingly, both the executive and legislative branches of government have their regulatory bodies, each with defined or assumed roles and responsibilities.

The regulatory bodies within the executive authority begin with the relevant sector ministry, the Ministry of Oil. The Ministry of Oil prepares draft laws and refers them to the Energy Committee of the Council of Ministers, and the Council of Ministers approves the draft law after the State Consultative Council has confirmed that the proposed law is in conformity with the Constitution. Once the Council of Ministers approves the draft law, it formally refers the draft to the parliament for enactment according to the constitutional process.

This demarcation between the authorities, roles and functions of both the executive and legislative branches is not without its ambiguities. The cause of such confusion is the wording and terms used in Article 60 of the Constitution. That article, in its first subparagraph, mandates the President of the Republic and the Council of Ministers to present "draft laws", and in its second sub-paragraph authorises "ten members of the [Council of Representatives] or ... one of its specialised committees" to present "proposed laws".

---

10 Almost all Iraqi politicians express regularly and repeatedly the needs to address the ambiguities in the Constitution, especially with regards to the provisions pertaining to oil and gas issues.

11 Such opinions were expressed by three Iraqi lawyers, dated June 4 2009 and issued through the Iraq Energy Institute, and by Dr Akramulhaq Baker, an Iraqi lawyer, circulated by an email message dated August 13 2009.

The terms "draft laws" and "proposed laws" create rifts and different interpretations between the executive and legislative branches, which camouflages the positions and attitudes of the main political blocs in the country. The differences in interpreting Article 60 became apparent in July and August 2011 when two different versions of the Federal Oil and Gas Law were submitted. One was suggested by the parliamentary Oil, Gas and Natural Resources Committee and the other by Ministry of Oil as adopted by the Council of Ministers.[12]

More often than not, the relationship between the two most important regulatory bodies – the Ministry of Oil and the Oil Gas and Natural Resources Committee – is affected by the political situation in the country, since the chairman of the latter should, according to the established political order, not be from the same political bloc of the former. Therefore it has become normal to hear very different views among the members of Oil Gas and Natural Resources Committee on the same issue, reflecting their political affiliations.

(b) *Types of agreement*

Between 2004 and 2008, the Ministry of Oil concluded some 50 memoranda of cooperation with many international oil companies to provide, according to Dr Ibrahim Al-Olom, a former Minister of Oil, support in three major activities: joint technical studies, training and development, and technical consultancy. The international oil companies covered costs related to these memoranda, and their overall assessment is positive.[13]

The memoranda of cooperation helped the formulation of the technical support contracts, which were devised for implementation by the international oil companies during 2008 and 2009. These contracts focus first on halting the production decline of the major oilfields (Rumaila, Zubair, West Qurna 1, Missan and Kirkuk), and then increasing production by 400,000 to 500,000 barrels per day. The Ministry of Oil pays for both investment requirements and the international oil companies' fees to achieve that target. Negotiations on these technical support contracts lasted from the fourth quarter of 2007 to mid-2008 without conclusion because of differences on serious issues.[14]

The Ministry of Oil then reduced the duration of the technical support contracts to one year. After that time they would overlap with the timing of bid rounds. The international oil companies refused the one-year duration as too short for such contracts. Accordingly, the ministry abandoned the contracts to focus on the bidding rounds.[15]

---

12 For discussions of both versions, see Jiyad, "Brief Review of the Federal Oil and Gas Law Proposed by the Ministry of Oil" (August 2011) at www.iraq-businessnews.com/2011/08/30/new-draft-oil-law-expert-analysis. And Jiyad, "Preliminary Remarks on the New Version of Oil Law" (the version proposed by the OGNRC) (August 2011) at iraqog.com/oil/oillaw/jiyadaug2011.htm.

13 I am very grateful to Dr Al-Olom and Mr Abduljabbar Al-Waggaa (former Deputy Minister of Oil) for useful discussions and information through direct communication on these memoranda.

14 Abdul Mahdi H Al-Ammedi, "Cooperation Policies with IOCs", presentation made before the Symposium for Reviewing Iraq Oil Policy, Baghdad, Iraq, February 27 to March 1 2009 (in Arabic).

15 According to Jabbar Luaibi, former Director General of South Oil Co, it was "a grave mistake" to call the contracts off, and he had recommended a five-year duration, but the minister refused that; see interview of May 20 2009 at www.iraqoilforum.com/?cat=7.

Based on the previous experience with the technical support contracts and the expected bid rounds the ministry began formulating and drafting the model contracts that would constitute the contractual framework governing the relationship with the international oil companies.[16]

This all contributed to the development of long-term development and production service contracts for oil and gas fields and exploration, development and production service contracts for exploration blocks. The first step was to convert CNPC's contract regarding Alahdab oilfield from a production sharing contract (which had been signed in 1997) to a long-term service contract, which was signed in November 2008. The model contract for each of the four bid rounds was based primarily on Alahdab contract in structure, composition, main principles and clauses. The variations pertaining to some components across these models are identified and explained in different parts of this chapter.[17]

(c) Acquisition of acreage

All existing development and production service contracts and exploration, development and production service contracts were awarded through bid rounds except, as mentioned above, the one relating to Alahdab oilfield.

For Alahdab contracts and all the contracts concluded as a result of the first three bid rounds, the acreages were defined by the area of the related field as provided for in the contract's Annex A "Description of contract area" and Annex B "Map of the contract area". As for the exploration blocks offered under the fourth bid round, the acreage of each block is defined in square kilometers in addition to the annexes of the service contracts concerned.

The four bid rounds followed similar procedure comprising the following steps:

- announcement of the fields and exploration blocks offered in the round;
- a request for international oil companies to apply for pre-qualification;
- specification of the parameters for pre-qualification and announcement of the qualifying companies;
- preparation of a profile and data package for each offered field or block, and sale of that information to the interested qualifying companies;
- workshops for the companies to discuss the data package and the draft model contract, and to review the bidding process and parameters. These workshops are usually open for the media and attended by senior officials from the ministry. The fourth bid round was attended also by representatives from local authorities in the areas of the offered blocks;
- the holding of bidding events in Baghdad with full publicity and TV coverage, with the bids being opened and announced in public with full competitiveness and disclosure; and
- approval of each contract by the Council of Ministers.

---

16 Al-Ammedi, "Service Contracts", presentation made before Symposium for Reviewing Iraq Oil Policy, Baghdad, Iraq, February 27 to March 1 2009 (in Arabic).

17 Earlier versions of my assessment based on the model contract were posted on many websites such as www.iraq-enterprise.com/rep/jiyad62009.htm (posted June 22 2009), and published as Jiyad, "Preliminary assessment of the GSDPC", in *Middle East Economic Survey* Volume 52 issue 30, July 27 2009.

The Final Tender Protocol for each bid round specifies the bidding parameters and the formula for calculating the bidding scores. For the first three bid rounds the bidding parameters were the plateau production target and the remuneration fee bid, while for the fourth bid round there was only one parameter, the remuneration fee.

For all bid rounds the Ministry of Oil has accepted the highest scoring bidder provided the remuneration fee proposed by the highest scorer does not exceed the maximum remuneration fee acceptable. This maximum is disclosed only if the highest scorer's proposed remuneration fee exceeds the maximum, in order to give the opportunity for the bidder(s) concerned to revise their proposed fee downward to that of the maximum remuneration fee. The Ministry of Oil has not disclosed the maximum remuneration fee it had set on many occasions when the highest scorer's proposed remuneration fee was lower than that maximum.

In the case of tied bids, whether the remuneration fees proposed are equal to or less than the maximum set, and where the tie is between a consortium and a single company, the consortium bidder is preferred and declared the winner. In practice this has not yet happened. What did occur was a tie between two consortia competing for West Qurna 1 in the first bid round. The ExxonMobil/Shell consortium, with a proposed remuneration fee of $4, and the Lukoil/ConocoPhillips consortium, with $6.49, both refused in June 2009 to come down to the maximum remuneration fee of $1.90. However, in late October Lukoil accepted that maximum fee, and that prompted ExxonMobil/Shell to do the same. Since the latter offered a higher plateau production target, they won the deal.

(d) Qualification requirements

The Petroleum Contracts and Licensing Directorate (which is part of the Ministry of Oil) announces the timeline and criteria for the pre-qualification process. Interested international oil companies provide detailed information in more than 20 tables covering at least the last three years on each of the five evaluation criteria: technical, financial, legal, health, safety, environment and training. Minimum and maximum marks are given for each criterion, and a company is considered to have qualified by scoring at least the minimum marks for each criterion. For each bid round the Petroleum Contracts and Licensing Directorate announces the number of the companies that participate in pre-qualification and the qualifying companies.

For every bid round the Ministry of Oil encourages the formation of consortia, and within each consortium the operatorship is usually given to the partner which has the highest participation interest in the consortium.

(e) Duration

All the service contracts concluded under the first three bid rounds have a common clause "Article 3 – Term of Contract". This article stipulates the contract's duration to be 20 years with a possible extension of a maximum period of five years, subject to new terms and conditions.

As for contracts concluded pursuant to the fourth bid round, Article 3 is more detailed and complex. Moreover, the article makes clear distinctions between oil and gas prone blocks and discoveries.

Briefly, the term for all contracts in the fourth bid round is a maximum of 30 years for an oilfield and 40 years for a gas field, excluding any possible extension, holding period or suspension period. The term consists of two periods: an exploration period and a separate development period for each development area within the acreage of the block concerned.

(f) ***Minimum work programme and minimum expenditure obligation***

Article 6 and Annex E in all the contracts concluded so far, regardless of the bid round, deal with the minimum work programme. In format and wording Article 6 and Annex E are identical in all the contracts. However, they differ in substance pertaining to three major items: what is to be executed, when, and how much should be spent. Taking these three items into consideration there seem to be common requirements for each bid round, resulting from the nature of the fields offered.

For contracts from the first bid round, the minimum work programme includes the following:

- preparation of rehabilitation and enhanced redevelopment plans;
- conduct of 3D seismic surveys, including processing and interpretation thereof;
- conduct of detailed geological and reservoir engineering studies, including 3D simulation for the reservoirs targeted for enhanced production;
- drilling of appraisal and/or development wells with the aim of further appraisal of the relevant reservoirs (defined in Annex D to the contracts), and achieving planned production in accordance with the rehabilitation plan;
- conduct of detailed laboratory and reservoir engineering studies to evaluate the most suitable secondary and/or enhanced recovery mechanisms for the reservoirs targeted under the rehabilitation plan and the enhanced redevelopment plan; and
- performing engineering studies and building or upgrading all necessary surface installations required under the rehabilitation plan, and the initiation of engineering work and infrastructure facilities expected to be incorporated in the enhanced redevelopment plan.

However, each field has its own minimum requirements, in terms of, for example, the area of 3D seismic surveys, the number of new production, new injection and work-over wells, and the rehabilitation of existing water intake plants and supply pipelines.

The minimum work programme should be executed no later than 36 months from the approval of the rehabilitation plan. The minimum expenditure obligation is $200 million each for the West Qurna 1, Zubair and Missan fields, and $300 million for Rumaila.

As for the second bid round, the minimum work programme includes the following:

- preparation and submission of the preliminary and final development plans;
- conduct of 3D seismic surveys, including processing and interpretation thereof;
- conduct of detailed geological and reservoir engineering studies, including 3D simulation; drilling of wells for appraising, developing and producing

relevant reservoirs (again defined in Annex D), and achieving the plateau production target;
- drilling of exploration wells or deepening other wells with aim of discovering new potential reservoirs (as defined in Annex D);
- conduct of detailed laboratory and reservoir engineering studies to evaluate the most suitable development approaches for the reservoirs programmed to come into production with the final development plan and enhanced redevelopment plan; and
- conduct of engineering studies and related surface facilities and flow assurance studies.

Again, each field has its own minimum requirement, in terms of the area in square kilometres for the 3D seismic surveys and the number of appraisal and exploration wells, among other obligations.

The minimum expenditure obligation has to be spent within three years from the date of approving the preliminary development plan. This obligation is: $100 million for each of the Badra and Najma fields, $150 million for each of Garraf and Qaiyara, $200 million for Halfaya, $250 million for West Qurna 2, and $300 million for Majnoon.

The minimum work programme under the fourth bid round is much simpler, comprising:
- preparation of the exploration plan and work programme;
- conduct of 2D or 3D seismic surveys for the specified area in each block, including processing and interpretation thereof;
- drilling of one exploration well; and
- performing detailed geophysical and geological studies necessary for the proper exploration of the contract area.

The programme has to be executed within the first five years of the exploration period, and the minimum expenditure obligations are $90 million (block 9), $100 million (each of blocks 8 and 10) and $150 million (block 12).

(g) Assignment and encumbrance

Article 28 of the model contracts provides for the possibility of an international oil company assigning its rights and obligations. The company has to provide the Iraqi contracting party one month's prior written notice of its intent to assign any of its participating interest, shares, rights, privileges, duties or obligations to an affiliate or to a third party. The Iraqi party must consider the request and notify its decision within three months of receipt of the notice.

Before such an assignment takes effect the foreign assignee must first provide the Iraqi partner with a guarantee in the form set out in a standard Annex F to the contract. However, the Iraqi side has the option to taking the interest to be assigned and instead assigning it to a nominated Iraqi entity on the same terms and conditions offered to the third party.

For financing purpose the international oil company may pledge, or otherwise encumber totally or partially, its rights to an internationally recognised bank and/or financing institution acceptable to the Iraqi party, provided that the pledge or encumbrance shall not in any way affect the rights or interests of the Iraqi party. There are further provisions concerning rights and conditions of assignment in cases of bankruptcy and liquidation.

So far Article 28 has only been invoked once, when Statoil withdrew from West Qurna 2 and Lukoil assumed all its participation interests.

(h) *Local content*

The term 'local content' covers many components which are all related to the use of local capacity to meet the demands of upstream petroleum operators. Four basic components of local content are considered: employment, training programmes, sub-contracting, and procurements of supplies and services.[18]

For employment, Article 9 of the model contract obligates the international oil company to give "first priority to Iraqi nationals" provided they have the required qualifications and experience; and to:

> *adhere to employment and training programs which shall aim at the Iraqization of manpower; all pursuant to a plan to be submitted for approval no later than six years from the Effective Date.*

In addition, Article 26 asserts that the company must "to the maximum extent possible, employ, and require Sub-Contractors to employ, Iraqi nationals having the requisite qualifications and experience."

Further, Article 9 requests the company to prepare and submit for approval:

> *employment procedures and personnel regulations for locally recruited personnel including scales of salaries, wages, benefits, and all allowances applicable to the respective grade of staff and employees, together with employment requirements such as standard job descriptions and qualifications to fill the jobs, all in accordance with the Law and local market conditions.*

The same article calls for equitable treatment of all employees, Iraqis and non-Iraqis, of similar qualification and experience.

Finally, Addendum Three (Article 8.6) stipulates that the company shall have the right to fill up to 15% of positions with secondees from the contractor, the remaining 85% to be filled by secondees from the contracted regional (Iraqi) oil company and/or directly recruited through the related field operating division.

The second component of local content is related to the development of local human resource capability through professional education and training. In this regard all contracts provide for the establishment of a Training, Technology and Scholarship Fund to offer and facilitate for an agreed number of Iraqi nationals, as designated by the Iraqi contracting parties in consultation with the international oil companies, the opportunity, both inside and/or outside Iraq, for on-the-job training and practical experience in petroleum operations and academic education. The fund

---

18 A United Nations Conference on Trade and Development (UNCTAD) study defines local content as the "total value added to, or created by the local economy through the utilization of local human and material resources and services at all stages of the value chain"; see Claudine Sigam and Leonardo Garcia, *Extractive Industries: Optimizing Value Retention in Host Countries* (2012), UNCTAD, New York and Geneva.

is also to be used for supporting local oil and gas related technology and research, including the establishment or upgrading of research institutes inside Iraq.

The Training, Technology and Scholarship Fund is funded by annual minimum contributions, which are not recoverable as petroleum costs, but are accounted for in the calculation of the R-factor (discussed below). The amount of the contribution varies according to the contracts: for Alahdab it is $200,000, for contracts from the first two bid rounds it is $5 million each, and for contracts from the third and fourth bid rounds it is $1 million each. Hence the annual income for the fund is $62.2 million during the duration of the contracts.[19]

The third component is local sub-contracting. Article 30 gives preference to Iraqi entities and firms, or foreign firms in association with local ones, provided their relevant capabilities and prices are competitive with those available in the international market.

The fourth component is procurement of local supplies and services, which as is the case with local sub-contracting, receives preference only if they are competitive internationally.

Such conditionality of international competitiveness in practice works against Iraqi firms, which are uncompetitive. Moreover, there are no real compliance mechanisms provided.

(i) National reservation

Since the contracts concluded to date are service contracts and the international oil companies receive remuneration fees for their services, national reservation does not apply to these contracts.

(j) Health, safety and environment

The environmental issues in upstream petroleum are governed by many provisions and guidelines enshrined in the Constitution, the Environment Law, related international instruments and in the contracts themselves.

Article 33 of the Constitution obliges the state to protect and preserve the environment and its biodiversity. Also Article 114 asserts the shared competencies of the federal and regional authorities:

To formulate environmental policy to ensure the protection of the environment from pollution and to preserve its cleanliness, in cooperation with the regions and governorates that are not organized in a region.

The Ministry of Environment is responsible for the proper implementation and enforcement of the Law for Protection and Improvement of the Environment (Law 27 of 2009).

In addition to its general provisions, Article 21 of this law relates specifically to upstream petroleum. All exploration, production and transportation activities are under the scrutiny of councils for the protection and improvement of the environment in each province and a ministerial council (comprising 20 ministries). The law requires an environmental impact assessment to be included in the

19 In Alahdab contract it is called "training budget", with "the purpose of training a number of personnel from the national oil company in various specialties related to oil industry" (Article 26.4).

economic and technical feasibility assessment of any project as a priority before it is implemented. Violation of the law can lead to temporary work suspension, to financial penalties, and to imprisonment. There is to be a special Environment Police Division, and an Environment Protection Fund. Iraq is also a signatory to many international legal instruments pertaining to a variety of environmental issues, which the international oil companies are obliged to observe.[20]

The model service contract gives considerable attention to environmental issues. At least two environmental impact assessments have to be carried out before the commencement of the final development plan of the oilfield to which the contract relates. Companies are required to adhere to "best international business practices", and there are provisions for addressing the consequences of "gross negligence and willful misconduct". The cost treatment of related activities are elaborated further in Annex C "Accounting Procedure".

(k) Governing law and dispute resolution

All contracts shall be governed, interpreted and construed in accordance with the "Law", which is broadly defined.[21] The dispute settlement mechanism has many phases with specific procedures and timelines, but eventually has to be settled under the Rules of Arbitration of the International Chamber of Commerce. The seat of the arbitration is Paris, unless agreed otherwise by the parties.

3.2 Government take

By their nature service contracts imply that the government bears all the risks, has full equity and acquires all income generated from upstream petroleum after paying investment and operating costs, remuneration fees and other expenditure to the contracting international oil companies. The government also receives payment from the oil companies in the form of bonuses, taxes and other deductibles as elaborated below.

(a) Royalties

No royalties are paid under Iraqi service contracts.

(b) Bonuses

The service contracts concluded so far include only a signature bonus. Payment of a signature bonus is a normal practice in the oil industry, especially in developing countries[22] and is intended to provide up-front income. Generally they are non-recoverable.

---

20 For a list of these international instruments see Thomas W Donovan, "Iraqi legal regime protects environment" (January 2011) www.iraqoilreport.com/business/companies/analysis-iraqi-legal-regime-protects-environment-5318/?utm.

21 As follows: *"Law" means any constitution, law, decree, resolution, statute, ordinance, rule, directive, order, treaty, code or regulation and any injunction or final non-appealable judgment, as adopted, enacted, issued, promulgated or ratified by the Republic of Iraq or, unless otherwise provided for herein, as such from, time to time, be amended or repealed.*

22 UNCTAD *Comparative Analysis of Petroleum Exploration Contracts* (1995) UNCTAD/DTCI/21, UN, New York and Geneva.

The signature bonus in the model contracts differs in substance, reflecting a rather inconsistent attitude by the Ministry of Oil in deciding the magnitude, form and rationale for this issue.

For Alahdab contract the signature bonus was only $3 million. This is, in comparison with such bonuses under other oil-related model contracts and what has been paid elsewhere, unreasonably low.

Contracts for the first bid round initially called for high signature bonuses: for the Rumaila contract it was $500 million; for West Qurna 1, $400 million, and for Zubair and Missan, $300 million each. However, instead of being non-recoverable payments, they were considered as interest-bearing loans payable with interest at the London inter-banks offered rate (LIBOR) + 1% over five years in quarterly installments commencing two years after the contract's effective date.

The second bid round generated $850 million of unrecoverable signature bonuses.

However, the Ministry of Oil agreed, in April 2010, to reduce the signature bonuses on the contracts for the West Qurna 1 and Zubair oilfields from $400 million and $300 respectively to $100 million each, but converting the bonuses from loans to unrecoverable upfront payments. This was a response to criticisms levelled at the way in which bonuses had been handled under the first bid round.

As for the gas fields offered under the third bid round, the Ministry of Oil abandoned the signature bonus as one of its concessions to induce international oil companies to bid. The ministry attracted criticisms for this unexplained u-turn on the issue of signature bonuses, and in the fourth bid round it re-imposed signature bonuses at $15 million each for blocks 8 and 12, and $25 million each for blocks 9 and 10.

The signature bonus is payable within 30 days of the effective date of the contract. The Ministry of Oil has generated $1.333 billion in signature bonuses from all the service contracts concluded so far. By way of comparison it is worth mentioning at this juncture that the Chinese company Sinopec paid a record high signature bonus of $2.2 billion in 2006 to outbid its competitors to get the exploration rights in two blocks in Angola.[23]

(c) Rental fees

The government receives no rental fees. On the contrary, the contracts oblige the contracting Iraqi oil company to provide the international oil companies with all available pertinent technical data, inventory and equipment in its possession used in maintaining petroleum operations prior to the effective date of the contract, and use of all existing wells and facilities related to the field within the contract area.

(d) Special participation

For each of the contracts concluded so far, excluding the fourth bid round, there is an Iraqi 'state partner' as part of the foreign contractor. The share or participation interest of the state partner is fixed at 25% without any up-front payment from the

23 UNCTAD *World Investment Report – Transnational Corporations, Extractive Industries and Development* (2007).

Iraqi side since this share is carried by the international oil companies in the consortium. The implications are that one quarter of the remuneration fee will be earmarked for the Iraqi state partner, and the state partner has one of four representatives on the foreign contractor's side.

All state partners are companies within the structure of the Ministry of Oil, but they should not be the contracting party itself.

(e) Corporate income tax

All international oil companies working in Iraq pay unified corporate income tax according to Iraqi income tax laws and regulations. The 2010 Income Tax Law (Law 19 of 2010) has three articles: an increase in corporate income tax for international oil companies from 15% to 35%; a provision linking this new law with the still valid 1983 Income Tax Law (Law 113 of 1983); and finally a provision mandating the Ministries of Finance and Oil to issue operational directives to facilitate implementation of the law. The model contract provides protection, through a stabilisation clause, from any:

> *change to the Law ... or ... revocation, modification, or non-renewal of any approvals, consents or exemptions granted to the Contractor ... in order to maintain the Contractor's financial interests under this Contract reasonably unchanged.*

3.3 Payment to and privileges of the international oil companies

A thorough examination of the Iraqi model contract will indicate a complex fiscal regime comprising many important variables that play a part in determining the final direct revenues received by the international oil companies. Significant indirect benefits, such as long-term secured access to oil resources, the possibility of further business opportunities through contractual provisions on exclusive or first rights, the establishment of strategic alliances and partnerships, and so on, are referred to, but no attempt has been made to quantify them here.

Payments to the international oil companies are calculated and made in US dollars only, but the companies have the right to buy crude oil using their recovered investments and the remuneration fee.

(a) Remuneration fee

The remuneration fee is the fee paid to the contractor (composed of the international oil companies and the Iraqi state partner) per barrel for the incremental or improved production above the baseline initial production rate (for the first bid round), or upon reaching the commercial production level as quantified in the contract (for the second and third bid rounds), as stipulated and calculated in the clauses therein. Each oilfield has its remuneration fee that was agreed upon during the bidding event. Moreover, for the second bid round, the international oil companies are entitled to receive the same remuneration for a barrel of oil and for the processed associated gas from the same field, based on barrels of oil equivalent. For the fourth bid round, the contractor is entitled to separate remuneration for each development area (if there is more than one), which it shall receive only from the date of first commercial production for that development area. The remuneration fee is the same for all development areas in a particular contract. The fee is determined by field/block and was one of the two bidding parameters in respect of which the international oil companies had to compete against each other, with their bids needing to be below a pre-determined maximum remuneration fee that the ministry was willing to pay. For the fourth bid round, the remuneration fee is the sole bidding parameter.

(b) *R-factor*

The R-factor is the ratio of cumulative cash receipts to cumulative expenditure in the conduct of petroleum operations as defined in the contract. Unlike the remuneration fee, which varies depending on the field covered by a particular contract, the R-factor is unified and fixed for all fields offered under the model contract in a bid round, meaning there are structurally different R-factor tables.

The R-factor is a sliding-scale method according to which the value of the remuneration fee declines as cumulative cash receipts increase as a function of the incremental oil and gas production (and also higher oil prices).

A serious criticism of the R-factor is that it encourages 'gold plating' by the international oil companies at the expense of cost-effectiveness in order to keep the R-factor at the upper range for as long as possible to ensure receiving a higher proportion of the remuneration fee.[24] There is some validity in this view, though the contracts provide sufficient protection against cost inflation if they are implemented efficiently and managed effectively. The issue then is not the R-factor itself but, as has been recognised earlier, the capabilities of the national bodies responsible for the oversight and administration of the contracts.[25] The application of the R-factor eventually leads to significant reductions in the remuneration fees actually realised by the international oil companies.[26]

(c) *Performance factor*

The remuneration fee could be reduced further due to the effects of the performance factor. As mentioned earlier there were two bidding parameters for the first three rounds: the remuneration fee and the production plateau target. The performance factor formula imposes a reduction in the remuneration fee corresponding to the percentage deviation of production below the production plateau target.

The inclusion of this condition was to prevent international oil companies from artificially inflating the production plateau target to gain a higher score and outbid their competitors. The performance factor is applicable only during the production plateau period.

(d) *Net remuneration fee formula*

After deducting the effects of the R-factor and the performance factor the remaining

---

24 See www.iraqoilreport.com/politics/oil-policy/ministry-unveils-tough-terms-for-4th-bid-round-6172/?utm.

25 UNCTAD, *Administration of Fiscal Regimes for Petroleum Exploration and Development* (1995) UNCTAD/DTCI/20.

26 For a calculation the R-factor's impact on remuneration fees for each of the companies in the first and second bid rounds, see Jiyad "Remuneration Fees Are Measured In Cents, Not Dollars", *Middle East Economic Survey,* Volume 53 Issue 11 (March 2010).

amounts of the remuneration fee are divided between the international oil companies and the Iraqi state partner, split 75% and 25% respectively. Moreover, the international oil companies have to pay 35% tax on their income (their earnings from the remuneration fee). The combined effect of the fee split and the tax, since both are constant percentages, is a formula dividing the remuneration fee between Iraq and the international oil companies at 51.25% and 48.75% respectively. The result of this is that for each dollar paid in remuneration fees Iraq retains at least 51.25 cents.

(e) *Cost recovery and remuneration fee payments: commencement and caps*

Many factors have to be considered with regard to cost recovery: payment caps, categories of cost, the interest rate for unpaid entitlements, and the conditions for commencement of cost recovery and remuneration fee payments.

International oil companies are entitled to recover their costs and fees, including the state partner's carried interest, and to receive their remuneration fee according to the provisions of their contracts. The contracts governing the deals are not unified on these matters. Some of the provisions are the same and applicable to all, while others are different. The major differences are addressed below.

For Alahdab contract, the fee is paid up to 100% of deemed revenues from the actual production. Unpaid fees carry annual interest at LIBOR + 3%.[27]

For the contracts arising from the first bid round, service fees (comprising 'petroleum costs' and the remuneration fee) are paid without interest, and the payable amount is limited to 50% of the deemed revenue from the incremental production, while supplementary fees are paid to the extent of 10% of the deemed revenue. Unpaid supplementary costs and fees bear annual interest at LIBOR + 1%.

The remuneration fee and petroleum costs are payable only after the net production rate reaches 10% above the initial production rate, with petroleum costs having priority over the remuneration fee where the total payable amount exceeds the allowable cap.

The same provisions apply for the contracts resulting from the second bid round, but each contract has its own commercial production level, attainment of which decides when payment commences.

For the contracts relating to gas fields offered under the third bid round, the commencement of cost recovery and the remuneration fee is subject to attaining 25% of the contracted production plateau target. Other conditions remain effectively the same as for the second bid round.

The model contract for the fourth bid round is more complex since there is provision for a holding period in the event of an oil discovery. However, payment starts once the commercial production rate reaches 25% of the specified production plateau target. The payment cap for cost recovery is fixed at 50% of deemed revenue, and for the remuneration fee at 30% of the remaining deemed revenue.

---

27 The condition for the commencement of payment was not clearly stated, however it is assumed that it is linked to attaining the commercial production level of 25,000 barrels per day referred to in the contract.

(f) ***Administrative overhead charges***

These charges are calculated at 1% of the incurred 'petroleum costs' and 'supplementary costs', and are shared equally between the contractor and Iraqi oil company. The corresponding percentage for Alahdab contract is 2%.

(g) ***Conditional rights for international oil companies to additional possibilities***

For each contracted field under the first three bid rounds the related international oil companies have the rights for further business opportunities.

Contractually, there are two economically significant additional possibilities: the first is discovered but undeveloped reservoirs, which the companies may develop and bring into production under the same contract, but subject to a new remuneration fee. This should be done within six years from the approval date of the enhanced redevelopment plan, or nine years from the effective date of the contract. The second possibility is to explore for and develop undiscovered potential reservoirs, in respect of which the companies have the right to negotiate a new agreement within six years from the effective date of the contract.

The significance of the first possibility is in its deadline, which falls in the middle of the production plateau period. If both parties agree on a new remuneration fee, the development of these discovered reservoirs proceeds and therefore a new level of production emerges. Since the development of these new reservoirs will be governed by the same contract, then the maximum duration the contracting companies could have to utilise them would be confined to 15 years only, assuming a five-year extension is granted to the contract's original duration.

As for the second possibility, it occurs at the commencement of the production plateau period. If the contracting parties agree on a new separate agreement, this could have totally different provisions leading to a new production target and probably a longer contract duration.

If the contracting parties fail to reach agreement, or the international oil companies fail to meet the stated conditions, the Iraqi oil company can invoke the relinquishment clause.

4. Main features of and developments in the model service contracts

4.1 Main features of the model service contracts

This analysis of all versions of the model service contracts identifies the nature and main characteristics of the contracts concluded so far, which were considered as "unknown in the oil industry" when they were introduced.[28]

First, all the contracts have similar structures in terms of equal number of articles, annexes and addenda, except those for the fourth bid round which have more addenda. Almost all the articles are identical or could be considered as common clauses, except those reflecting the specifics of the field or block.

Second, the contracts could be considered as being in a hybrid category of their

28 Fadhil J Chalabi, *Oil Politics Oil Myths – Analysis and Memoir of an OPEC 'insider'*, p 258, IB Tauris, London (2010).

own since they include components from production sharing contracts and components from conventional service contracts. Among the main features taken from production sharing contracts are: the long duration; the privileges of first/exclusive rights; the payment of a signature bonus; the R-factor as a sliding scale remuneration fee; and restrictions on sovereignty through consensus-based decision-making within the joint management committees.

Third, all the contracts are premised upon the principle of take-or-pay/now-or-later even when the government decides to exercise its sovereign rights to curtail production.

Fourth, all payments to the international oil companies (costs and the remuneration fee) are denominated in US dollars not in barrels or barrels of oil equivalent. This implies that any economic rent (windfall) belongs to the Iraqi side, and the international oil companies do not have any claim on rent in the event of oil price increases. The international oil companies benefit from higher oil prices by expediting the recovery of their capital and operating expenditure and by receiving greater volume in remuneration fees through the operation of the payment caps when there are higher revenues. This however also calls for the application of the R-factor, which reduces the remuneration fees.

Fifthly, for each of the concluded contracts there is a carried state partner participation interest of 25% with no up-front payment from the Iraqi side. The international oil companies in the consortium cover, proportionately, this participation until they recover it. The model contract for the fourth bid round does not have a state partner participation interest since the risk of exploration is taken on fully by the international oil companies should there be no commercially worthwhile discovery.

4.2 New provisions in the model contract for the fourth bid round

The current version of the fourth bid round model contract exhibits many new components, reflecting the still evolving development of the model contracts and the Ministry of Oil's learning curve in contract formulation.

A pre-development holding period is introduced, subject to certain rather complex provisions, in the event of an oil discovery. The rationale for this is that Iraq has too much oil to manage if all the contracted fields are developed as planned in addition to the existing production from other fields.

Also for the first time there is a transitional state partner. Initially the state partner is Oil Exploration Co, but once the value of the R-factor exceeds 1 then a new state partner takes over. This reflects the different phases of the contracts arising from the distinction between the exploration and development phases, and this distinction lead to the removal of the state partner's 25% interest, as mentioned above.

The third development is the absence of a performance factor, because with only one bidding parameter (the remuneration fee), and therefore no production plateau target, there is no reason to include the performance factor.

An important fourth new element was introduced to reduce the cost-inflating tendencies of international oil companies. A new term, 'cost production', is included to reduce the remuneration fee entitlement in such a way as to induce the international oil companies to pursue cost effectiveness and refrain from exaggerating costs.

The fifth new development is related to the application of take-or-pay/now-or-later principle. The contracting Iraqi oil company's obligation is confined to 80% of the produced gas if circumstances call for application of the take-or-pay/now-or-later principle. It is worth noting that the application of this principle remains as it was in the previous bid rounds in the event of an oil discovery.

The sixth new component is provision for dry gas export, subject to a separate contract and marketing arrangement. This is an option for the international oil companies to pursue, but does not constitute an obligation on them. No such option was or is offered for oil.

Another new provision gives the Iraqi oil company the right to terminate the contract if the international oil companies conclude another contract with any regional or provincial authority without Ministry of Oil approval.

The final new development is the establishment of an infrastructure fund to finance infrastructure projects in the province where the contract area is located. During the term of the contract the contractor will pay 10% of the annual budget for the fund.

5. Current issues

The development of upstream petroleum activities and the implementation of the contracts that have been concluded face many serious and formidable challenges. However, three issues of particular importance are discussed here because of their direct relevance to these contracts.

5.1 Legality of the contracts in the absence of the Federal Oil and Gas Law

The Federal Oil and Gas Law is a very complex and persistent issue for many reasons, as testified by the fact that debate on it has gone on since early February 2007. Iraqi oil professionals, among others, have written extensively on various aspects of the law,[29] and the debate continues unabated.

First, there are many versions of the Federal Oil and Gas Law: four pre-July 2011 and two after that date. The differences between these versions are very substantive in terms of contents, coherence, functionality and implications.

Second, all these versions have been based on the February 2007 draft, but between that date and now many serious developments had taken place, rendering the 2007 formulation obsolete, overtaken by events and dysfunctional. The Ministry of Oil has signed 19 long-term service contracts, while the Kurdistan Regional Government has signed 48 production sharing contracts covering most of Iraq's

---

29 Fouad Q Al-Ameer, "Remarks on the draft of the oil and gas Law – part one" (2007) www.albadeeliraq.com/new/showdetails.php?id=51&kind=dangerous (in Arabic); Tariq Shafiq, "Iraq Petroleum Law: Problematic Issues And its Fate (2/2)", *Middle East Economic Survey*, Volume 51 Issue 11, March 17 2008; Jiyad, "Key questions over the Oil and Gas Law in Iraq", *International Journal of Contemporary Iraqi Studies* (IJCIS) Volume 2, Issue 1, pp 7–30, (2008) (Intellect books, UK); Walid Khadduri, "Iraqi Oil Reconciliation Faces Challenges", *Middle East Economic Survey*, Volume 55, Issue 39, September 21 2012.

highly prized fields and many of the exploration blocks (in Kurdistan), and these contracts deviate seriously from those envisaged in 2007.

Third, the Federal Oil and Gas Law implies the enactment of many other laws, and the creation of some sort of organic links between these laws. This in turn implies an all-or-nothing situation, making it infeasible to promulgate any of them.

Fourth, the text of the Federal Oil and Gas Law (in any of the versions) is full of ambiguities pertaining to authorities, functions, procedures and the operation of many entities mentioned in the law, particularly those related to the Federal Oil and Gas Council and its jurisdiction.

Fifth, a 12-member joint special committee was formed, in late August 2012, within the Iraqi parliament from the Oil, Gas and Natural Resources Committee and the Legal Committee. The composition of this special committee was based purely on political affiliations from the main three political blocs. Two weeks later a new six-member committee was formed to review three different versions of the Federal Oil and Gas Law and decide which one the parliament will use as the starting point for debating the law. Another five-member committee was formed on September 17 2012 to "negotiate the oil and gas draft law to be referred to the cabinet, and come out with one formula, under the supervision of the Presidency [of parliament]". Obviously there is much confusion, as this series of special committees indicates.

Finally, as a result the legality of all contracts concluded by the Ministry of Oil and the Kurdistan Regional Government remains questionable and subject to a good degree of legal uncertainty and unpredictability.

5.2 Situation of international oil companies which concluded contracts with the Kurdistan Regional Government

The federal government considers all the Kurdistan Regional Government's production sharing contracts to be illegal and, thus, does not recognise them. International oil companies who concluded these contracts are usually blacklisted and prevented from participating in any upstream petroleum project in the rest of the country. For example Sinopec was excluded from the Zubair oilfield consortium; while Repsol, Chevron and Hess were excluded from participating in bidding rounds after qualification.

This blacklisting policy had some initial success in keeping major international oil companies away from the Kurdistan deals, but this policy faced serious challenge in October 2011 when ExxonMobil signed production sharing contracts for six exploration blocks.

The application of the blacklisting to ExxonMobil, Total and Gazprom could have direct effects on the development efforts in the three oilfields where they operate, and in the absence of an amicable solution the matter may have to go to international arbitration.

5.3 Reduction of production plateau targets and contract renegotiation

For the first three bid rounds, the production plateau target was one of two bidding parameters, as mentioned earlier. This prompted the international oil companies to inflate their production targets to out-bid their competitors. Consequently, plateau levels in all the resultant contracts came out much higher even than the Ministry of Oil had envisaged. Hence, euphoria began to surface at the prospect of crossing the threshold of 12.5 million barrels per day (mbd), and this then became a sacrosanct target for some within the ministry and outside it. But many oil professionals[30] doubted the feasibility of attaining these plateaus within the specified timeframe, and questioned the justification of constructing expensive production and export capacities based on these figures.

However, the Ministry of Oil and the government are now more receptive to the revision of the plateau targets, especially after thorough studies by the Word Bank and the International Energy Agency came to similar conclusions to those expressed by many Iraqi oil professionals on the probability of lower production levels, which will most likely impact the formulation of the forthcoming national energy strategy.

Accordingly, three main parameters could be revised compared with those envisaged under the signed contracts:

- lower plateau targets (probably a maximum of 9 mbd instead of 12.5 mbd);
- longer development periods (completion in 2020 instead of 2017 for first bid round fields);
- longer plateau production periods (over seven years for first bid round fields).[31]

6. Conclusions

- The long-term service contracts could become important milestones in shaping future political and economic relationships between international oil companies and host governments of developing countries.
- The fiscal terms of these contracts indicate Iraq has, undoubtedly, made good deals. However, if cost control is not properly monitored and professionally audited, costs could escalate to unprecedented levels. Accordingly there is an urgent need to bridge gaps in skills and capacity through a multiplicity of measures comprising specific crash-course programmes, short-term training, professional development and specialised capacity-development education. It is vital to create a special unit within the Ministry of Oil to ensure good management of the Training, Technology and Scholarship Fund in collaboration with other entities within the sector and outside it.
- Considering the importance of upstream petroleum and the number and

---

30 Including, among others, Faleh HM Al-Khayat, "Iraq oil output to hit 6.2 million b/d by 2017", *Platts Energy Economist*, Issue 370, August 2012; Jiyad, "Oil upstream development: the feasibility of a fast-tempo, big-push strategy", *International Journal of Contemporary Iraqi Studies* (IJCIS), Volume 5 Issue 1, pp11-46 (2011) (Intellect Books, UK); Sadad Al-Husseini, "Perspective: Assessing Iraq's Oil Expansion", *Energy Compass*, Energy Intelligence Group Inc, March 5 2010; Issam Al-Chalabi, "Iraq's Oil Export Outlets", *Middle East Economic Survey*, Volume 52, Issue 48, November 2009; and Thamir Al-Ghadhban, "Iraq's Crude Oil Production Capacity: The Way Ahead", speech given on December 7 2009 at the CWC Iraq Petroleum Conference 2009, London.

31 In January 2013, the Ministry of Oil began the process of revising downward the contracted plateau targets by amending the contracts for West Qurna 2 with the Lukoil consortium. While the remuneration fee was left unchanged, the contract was extended to 25 years with reduced plateau production from 1.8 to 1.2 mbd, sustainable for 19 and a half years, up from 13. Moreover, IOCs operating on Rumaila, Majnoon, Zubair and West Qurna 2 are involved in active negotiations with the ministry to arrive at lower plateau targets.

long duration of the service contracts, it would be advisable to formulate a national strategy pertaining to local content. The suggested strategy could involve creating a specialised agency with a clear mandate, auditing, monitoring and verification procedures, and institutional and legal frameworks.

- All international oil companies who signed the service contracts asserted, initially, a satisfactory internal rate of return despite what they considered to be tight fiscal terms. But the wide deviation between the bid and final remuneration fees would lead one to question the validity of the companies' economic model and its main assumptions. Such unexplained but significant deviations could make one suspicious of the companies' integrity and conduct.
- There are increasing indications that production plateau targets could be reduced thus requiring revision of contracts resulting from the first two bid rounds. The Ministry of Oil has to formulate its renegotiation strategy to ensure the best interests of the Iraqi people as enshrined in the Constitution.
- Finally, there is a high degree of uncertainty surrounding the legality of all the long-term service contracts agreed by the Ministry of Oil and all the production sharing contracts agreed by the Kurdistan Regional Government.

Grateful thanks are extended to Issam Al-Chalabi (former minister of oil), Ibrahim Al-Olom (former minister of oil), Walid Khadduri (MEES consultant) and Kim Talus (Professor, University of Eastern Finland), for their comments on this chapter. Any errors or emissions are the author's own responsibility.

Kazakhstan

Yerzhan Yessimkhanov
Grata

1. Introduction

Subsoil resources such as oil and gas are the exclusive property of the state. However, rights to use the subsoil may be granted to local and foreign individuals and legal entities on the basis of a subsoil use contract concluded with the Ministry of Oil and Gas (for the oil and gas sector) or the Ministry of Industry and New Technologies (for the mining industry) following an investment tender.

The Law on Subsoil and Subsoil Use (June 24 2012) sets out the basic framework for oil and mining operations in Kazakhstan. The legal regime governing the development of natural resources has evolved significantly over the years.

2. Upstream activities

Kazakhstan ranks as the 12th nation in the world in terms of proven reserves of oil and gas condensate, and comes 23rd in the list of the world's leading oil-producing countries. The Tengiz, Karachaganak and Kashagan fields constitute 70% of oil and 85% of gas production in Kazakhstan. Activities at Kashagan were begun in 2000 by the North Caspian Project Consortium.

KazMunaiGas Exploration and Production has taken a major role in upstream activities. It is the largest public oil and gas company in Kazakhstan. The national company KazMunaiGas JSC owns 61.36% of the shares in KazMunaiGas Exploration and Production.

Kashagan is one of the world's largest oil and gas fields. The parties to the North Caspian production sharing agreement estimate that the Kashagan field has 7 billion to 9 billion barrels of recoverable crude oil. The project involves building artificial islands in shallow water, with land rigs to drill wells, rather than conventional platforms. The experimental phase of the project has been completed, with the construction of five artificial islands in the Caspian Sea and 40 wells, including 32 production wells and eight injection wells. Production is expected to start in March 2013.

Karachaganak is a giant oil and gas condensate field in northwest Kazakhstan, discovered in 1979. The Karachaganak project is a production sharing agreement originally signed in November 1997 for a term of 40 years between the Republic of Kazakhstan and a group of foreign contracting companies: BG Group (32.5%), Agip (32.5%), Chevron (20%) and Lukoil (15%). Under the terms of the agreement, BG and Agip are the sole operators of the project. In 2011, the state and the contracting companies reached an agreement on the transfer of a 10% share of the Karachaganak project.

The Tengiz field was established in 1993 and is operated by Chevron, with KazMunaiGas JSC owning a 20% stake. Crude oil reserves there are estimated to be 245.8 million tons.

JSC KazTransOil is the natural monopoly oil pipeline operator in Kazakhstan, which operates three transportation companies: North-West Pipeline Co MunaiTas JSC, Kazakhstan-China Pipeline LLP and KazTransOil – Service JSC. JSC KazTransOil's major asset is the Uzen-Atyrau-Samara pipeline (which connects to the Russian Transneft pipeline). KCP is a 50:50 joint venture between JSC KazTransOil and China National Oil and Gas Exploration and Development Corp for the development of a pipeline to China. MunayTas is a 51:49 joint venture between JSC KazTransOil and China National Petroleum Co International in Kazakhstan. Following the completion of the Kenkiyak-Kumkol pipeline (one of the three sections of the pipelines to China) in October 2009, JSC KazTransOil is now able to transport crude from western Kazakhstan to China.

KazTransGas JSC operates the largest gas pipeline network in Kazakhstan. Its major asset is the Central Asia-Centre gas pipeline from Turkmenistan to Russia.

3. Petroleum legal regime

3.1 Petroleum law and relevant provisions

(a) Regulatory bodies

The Ministry of Oil and Gas is the competent body with regard to the preparation and organisation of calls for tenders for subsoil use rights, the conclusion and registration of subsoil use contracts, and the monitoring and supervision of compliance during the implementation of subsoil use contracts. There are many other regulators overseeing various aspects of operations, from labour to environment.

(b) Types of agreement

The Law on Subsoil and Subsoil Use provides for the following types of contract:

- exploration contracts (contracts for exploration for natural resources for a term of up to six years);
- production contracts (contracts for production of natural resources, normally based on the results of an exploration contract);
- combined exploration and production contracts;
- contracts for construction and/or exploitation of underground facilities not connected with exploration or production; and
- contracts for state geological research of subsoil.

Production sharing agreements were concluded with regard to certain major deposits, but this form of contract is no longer available for investors, having been withdrawn in 2009.

(c) ***Acquisition of subsoil use right***

The state awards subsoil use rights either through direct negotiations (in certain limited cases) or on the basis of a tender (open or restricted).

In order to pre-qualify, tenderers have to submit an application accompanied by a set of documents and information. The relevant state authority releases geological information on the subsoil plot to be allotted. Based on this geological information, tenderers prepare investment programmes and bids. The preferred tenderer is selected on the basis of such criteria as the starting date, the intensity of exploration/development, projected profitability of the development, the amount of the subscription bonus, the amount of the estimated initial and further payments to the state budget, investments, the terms and conditions of project financing, participation in social development of the region, compliance with laws and regulations on subsoil and environment, as well as safety and other factors.

Once the tender board (a board consisting of representatives of various state bodies) selects a winner, the latter is obliged to enter into a contract with the competent authority (the Ministry of Oil and Gas).

A subsoil use right is deemed to have been granted and acquired only from the time when the contract is registered. In the event that the winner of a tender fails to submit a draft contract for the performance of subsoil use operations within one year, the tender board shall abolish the decision made previously to award the applicant subsoil rights.

As regards direct negotiations, the following contracts can be concluded without a tender:

- contracts for the performance of production operations in association with a person who has an exclusive right to obtain subsoil use rights for production following a commercial discovery on the basis of an exploration contract. Assuming no major violations during the exploration stage, such exclusivity is normally granted to a subsoil user;
- contracts for the performance of operations associated with the construction and/or operation of underground facilities not connected with exploration and/or production; and
- contracts for the performance of exploration and/or production operations in association with the national oil company.

(d) ***Qualification requirements***

There is no clear list of qualifying requirements for obtaining subsoil use rights, however, based on certain provisions of the law, the following basic requirements may be identified:

- Applicants must be Kazakh or foreign individuals or legal entities.
- Applicants must possess technical, managerial, organisational, and financial resources.

(e) ***Duration***

Exploration contracts are concluded for six years. For offshore oil deposits, this term may be extended for a two-year period, if the contractor applies for an extension no later than six months prior to the contract's expiry. No such extension is available for onshore contracts.

Production contracts are concluded for 25 years. A contract for production at a deposit with large and unique reserves may be concluded for up to 45 years. The period of agreement may be extended in some specific circumstances, such as a reasonable necessity to spend more time in exploration of a deposit, if the contractor applies for an extension no later than six months prior to the expiry of the effective period of the contract and provided that there have been no breaches of the contract.

The specific terms of the contract are determined by an agreement between the parties in accordance with applicable laws. Every subsoil use contract must reflect certain conditions listed in the Law on Subsoil and Subsoil Use.

Before a contract is signed, it must undergo, among other things, expert economic, ecological, and legal examination and must be approved by the executive agencies responsible for sanitation, health and safety, geology and subsoil use. The contract must also be registered with the Ministry of Oil and Gas (the competent authority for oil and gas) or the Ministry of Industry and New Technologies (the competent authority for solid minerals), and becomes effective from the date of registration.

(f) Work programme

The work programme is an obligatory part of the contract. It is drawn up on the basis of documents that are developed and approved in accordance with the established procedure for project documents, in coordination with the competent authority for the study and use of subsoil. The work programme is agreed with the relevant authority as the draft contract is being examined. This process must be completed within a maximum of one month of the competent authority's receiving the work programme. The work programme is then added to the project documents. Any changes to the work programme as a result of alterations to the project documents are carried out at the same time as the approval of the project documents by the competent authority. These changes are incorporated into the work programme by signing an additional agreement appended to the contract between the subsoil user and the competent authority or local executive body no later than 30 calendar days from the date of approval of the work programme by the competent authority.

(g) Assignment and encumbrance

It is possible to transfer subsoil use rights and/or associated objects. The first prerequisite is permission from the competent authority. The application for permission must be made in writing in both Kazakh and Russian, and must contain the information specified by legislation.

However there are certain instances when permission is not required:

- In transactions involving shares, it is not necessary to obtain the permission of the state if one subsoil user alienates shares or securities in favour of another subsoil user that can directly or indirectly control or influence the decisions of the former subsoil user, providing that the latter subsoil user's core activities are associated with subsoil use in Kazakhstan.
- No permission is required when a transfer of shares in a subsoil user results

in a situation where a legal entity is able to dispose of less than 0.1% of the participatory interests of this subsoil user, or in a situation where the entity is able to make or influence decisions of this subsoil user if the core activities of the legal entity are associated with subsoil use in Kazakhstan. In the case of transferring (in full or in part) actual subsoil use rights (or objects associated with subsoil use), it is not necessary to obtain permission if rights are transferred by a subsoil user to a subsidiary that is 99% owned (directly or indirectly) by the subsoil user, provided that the subsidiary is not incorporated in a state with preferential tax treatment.

- No permission is required where rights are transferred between legal entities where 99% of the participatory interests are held by the same legal entity, provided that the acquirer of the subsoil use rights or objects associated with subsoil use rights is not incorporated in a state with preferential tax treatment.

It is especially important to note the third exception, where the crucial point is possession of 99% by one person. That is, if 99% or even 100% belongs to two or more entities, this exception will not apply, and the process of getting permission for the transaction from the competent authority must be followed.

In the process of transfer of subsoil use rights, the state has a priority right (see Section 3.1(i) below).

(h) Local content

Kazakh legislation requires all oil and gas companies operating in Kazakhstan under licences (awarded under the now abolished licensing regime for subsoil use that existed before the contractual regime, but which are still effective) or contracts to organise tenders for most goods, works, and services that they procure in the course of their oil and gas operations in Kazakhstan, and to give preference to local goods, work and services. In accordance with the Law on Subsoil and Subsoil Use, local content requirements for personnel, goods, works and services must always be contained in the subsoil contract, expressed in specific percentages and ratios, with due consideration of competitiveness criteria.

(i) National reservation

The Republic of Kazakhstan has a priority right over other parties as regards the acquisition a subsoil user's minerals at prices (as of the date of a transaction) not exceeding those set by the subsoil user, minus transportation and selling costs. In the absence of information on prices of minerals set by subsoil users in transactions, current world market prices (as of the date of the transaction) apply. The volume of purchased minerals and the type of payment are determined by contract. The procedure for exercising this pre-emptive right is to be determined by the Kazakh government. The state also has a priority right over any other party to the contract (including other participants which have the subsoil use right as well as other persons) to acquire any alienated subsoil use right (or part thereof) and/or objects associated with subsoil use right, for consideration or free of charge. The person that intends to alienate his subsoil use right (or part thereof) and/or associated object must submit to the competent authority an application for alienation of the subsoil use right (or part thereof) and/or associated object.

The application for alienation of the subsoil use right (or part thereof) and/or associated object must be made in both Kazakh and Russian and contain certain information required by the Law on Subsoil and Subsoil Use.

(j) *Environment*

The main state body for environmental monitoring is the Environment Ministry, which operates through departments in all the provincial capitals and large industrial centres. State monitoring of soil is executed by the Land Resources Management Agency. The content of harmful matter in edible crops is monitored by the public health authorities under the Ministry of Health.

Subsoil use processes must comply at all stages with the environmental requirements set out in the Kazakh environmental legislation. The contracts and project documents must pass state ecological and sanitary-epidemiologic appraisals. This, together with obtaining an ecological permit, constitutes the ecological basis for carrying out subsoil use operations. The subsoil user is obliged to submit all pre-project and project documentation, which must include an assessment of the impact of the proposed activity on the environment and a section entitled "Environmental Protection", for the state ecological and sanitary-epidemiologic appraisals.

A fee must be paid in respect of emissions into the environment, under the regime for "special use of natural resources". Special use of natural resources, as a term, encompasses several different types of resource use. Special use of natural resources is carried out on the basis of an ecological permit, which is awarded by the state authority in the field of environmental protection, but this does not cover emissions of polluting substances from mobile sources.

(k) *Governing law and dispute resolution*

The law which governs the rights and obligations of transactions involving the transfer of subsoil use rights, is that of the Republic of Kazakhstan.

Disputes relating to the performance, amendment or termination of a subsoil use contract must first be settled by negotiations. If such a dispute cannot be resolved within six months of negotiation, the parties shall have the right to resolve the dispute in accordance with the laws of Kazakhstan and international treaties ratified by Kazakhstan, in local or other courts depending on the conditions of the specific agreement.

3.2 Government take

(a) *Subsoil use taxes*

Minerals extraction tax: For mining companies, the minerals extraction tax is generally payable on the average exchange price of extracted minerals (as quoted by specified publications). The rates of minerals extraction tax for mining companies currently range from 0% to 22% depending on the type of mineral. For oil and gas companies, the taxable base is generally the average world price of crude oil and gas condensate (as quoted by specified publications). The rates of tax for oil and gas companies currently range from 5% to 18% depending on the amounts of oil produced. If oil is sold in Kazakhstan for specified purposes (eg, to local refineries or refineries in China subject to a customs procedure for processing outside the customs territory), the amount of tax payable will be reduced by 50%.

Signature bonus: A signature bonus is a one-time payment to the state for the right to use the subsoil. The initial amounts of this tax are determined in accordance with a formula in the Tax Code based on estimations of reserves, the economic value of the deposit, and certain other factors. The final amount of the signature bonus must be set out in the subsoil use contract.

Commercial discovery bonus: A commercial discovery bonus is a fixed payment that is payable by subsoil users when a commercial discovery is made in the contract territory. The rate of the commercial discovery bonus is 0.1% of the value of proven extractable reserves.

Rent export tax: Rent export tax is payable by exporters of crude oil, gas condensate and coal, except for companies operating under production sharing agreements and in certain other cases. The rates of rent export tax range from 0% to 32% of the world market price of exported oil (as quoted by specified publications).

Property and land taxes: Legal entities annually pay a property tax in Kazakhstan at the rate of 1.5% of the average annual balance sheet value for accounting purposes of real property (eg, buildings) owned by them. Owners of land pay a land tax in Kazakhstan on an annual basis. The rates of the land tax depend on the category of a particular land plot, its location and quality.

Reimbursement of historical costs: Subsoil users are supposed to compensate the state for expenses related to geological exploration and establishment of deposits, to be defined following the results of negotiations with the competent authority.

Excess profits tax: An excess profits tax is payable annually in respect of the net income under a specific subsoil contract exceeding 25% of cumulative deductions (for corporate income tax purposes) and certain other expenses. The tax rates range according to a sliding scale from 0% to 60%.

(b) General

Corporate income tax: The corporate income tax rate for tax residents is 20% of their worldwide income. The tax base is gross annual income after allowable deductions and adjustments. Deductions may be subject to specific limitations. Losses can generally be carried forward for tax purposes for up to 10 years. A non-resident who has formed a permanent establishment in Kazakhstan is liable for 20%

corporate income tax in relation to income which is attributable to the permanent establishment. In addition, it would need to pay the so-called 'branch profit tax' at a rate of 15% of the difference between the annual taxable income of the permanent establishment and the corporate income tax paid to the state budget.

Value added tax: Value added tax (VAT) is charged on the sale of most goods and services in Kazakhstan and on the importation of goods into Kazakhstan. The current rate of VAT is 12%. VAT is chargeable on turnover that takes place in Kazakhstan, based on the place of turnover rules. An export of goods is generally subject to a zero rate of VAT.

The VAT on sales must be paid by Kazakhstani legal entities, independent contractors and by foreign companies that have a branch or a representative office in Kazakhstan, provided they are registered as VAT payers. The obligation to register is triggered when the taxable turnover of the taxpayer in Kazakhstan exceeds approximately $325,000 during a calendar year. However, it is always possible to register to pay VAT on a voluntary basis.

Under the Tax Code, VAT is not imposed, among other things, on the lease and sale of land underlying residential buildings and residential buildings themselves (with limited exceptions), certain types of financial services, charter capital contributions and the sale of shares (participatory interests).

Generally, an excess of input VAT over output VAT should be refunded to the VAT payer. Until 2016, most taxpayers have to undergo a tax audit in order to obtain a refund (although certain large taxpayers are entitled to an automatic refund). From 2016, a tax audit will no longer be required for taxpayers whose VAT returns do not give rise to objections from the tax authorities. From 2017, a tax audit will not be necessary for any taxpayers who do not fall within a risk category established by a risk management system maintained by the tax authorities.

Withholding tax: A non-resident which does not have a permanent establishment in Kazakhstan is generally subject to withholding tax on income derived from Kazakhstan at the rates illustrated on the next page.

Personal income tax: With certain limited exceptions, the personal income of individuals is taxed at a flat rate of 10%. Residents pay income tax on their worldwide income (residents are generally defined as individuals who spend not less than 183 days in Kazakhstan during any consecutive 12-month period). Non-residents pay income tax on their income from Kazakhstani sources (but in certain situations this tax does not apply).

Employers are required to withhold income tax and pension fund contributions (except for non-residents who do not permanently reside in Kazakhstan) from salary payments to employees, and transfer them to the budget (see below).

Double tax treaties: Many categories of non-residents' income from Kazakhstani sources are exempt from both corporate and individual income taxes under double tax treaties to which Kazakhstan is a party. Treaty benefits generally apply only where

Witholding tax rates

Item	Rate (%)
Capital gains, dividends, interest and royalties	15
Service income and other income from Kazakhstani sources of entities registered in countries which have a preferential tax regime	20
Insurance premiums payable under risk insurance agreements	15
Insurance premiums payable under risk reinsurance agreements	5
Transportation services in international traffic	5
Service fees and other income	20

income from Kazakhstani sources is received by residents of countries with which Kazakhstan has double tax treaties, and where such income is not related to a Kazakhstani permanent establishment formed by such residents.

Kazakhstan has entered into bilateral treaties for the avoidance of double taxation with 45 countries to date.

The application of double tax treaties in Kazakhstan ordinarily requires a submission by the foreign company to its Kazakhstani counterparty of a legally notarised (apostilled) certificate of its tax residency in the relevant treaty country on an annual basis.

Withholding obligations, social taxes and charges: An employer must withhold personal income tax (see above) and pension fund contributions (which are charged at the rate of 10% of salary, but do not apply to non-resident employees who do not permanently reside in Kazakhstan) from salaries payable to its employees. These payments are the employees' costs. An employer is required to pay a social tax for each of its employees (both local citizens and non-residents) on the salaries and other income payable to them. The social tax applies at a flat rate of 11%. In addition to the social tax, employers must pay contributions to the Social Security Fund for each of their employees. These social security contributions must be paid by the employer at a rate of 5% of the income payable to employees. The amounts of these social security contributions are deductible from the amounts of social tax. Both the social tax and the social security contributions are at the employer's cost.

4. Current issues

At the present time, certain changes are being proposed to the Law on Subsoil and Subsoil Use. These are intended to eliminate contradictions and introduce other ways of granting subsoil use rights. In particular, legislators are considering dispensing with the need for the project documents to be examined by the state authorities, because of the risk of corruption inherent in that process. In addition to this, a number of changes are being contemplated in the area of exploration.

5. Conclusion

Oil and gas production is the backbone of the economy of Kazakhstan and its most rapidly developing sector, generating a substantial portion of the gross national product and providing a large part of budget revenues and hard currency earnings for the country.

Analysis of recent legislative developments in the area demonstrates that the state is willing to increase its role in regulation of the industry, in particular with regard to stricter control of transfers of subsoil use rights and related objects.

Pakistan

Muhammad Arif
Energy Lawyers Association of Pakistan

1. Introduction

Oil and gas play vital role in the economic development and national prosperity of every country. Its role for energy-starved countries like Pakistan is even more critical. Pakistan's primary energy supplies during the year 2010 to 2011 amounted to 64.522 million tons of oil equivalent. The share of natural gas in primary energy supplies was 47.6% with a total of 30.683 million tons of oil equivalent, while that of oil was 32.1% with a total of 21.014 million tons. Oil and gas together contributed 79.7% in primary energy supplies.

While energy demand in the country is increasing exponentially, supplies are decreasing due to depletion of indigenous reserves, slow exploration activity and increasing population, as well as the country's weakening economic health caused by lack of good governance. As a result during the current year (2012), the country is encountering average electricity load shedding of as long as 12 hours per day and the complete suspension of gas supplies to the industrial and commercial sector for two to three days a week. The government announced a new Petroleum Exploration and Production Policy 2012 on August 30 2012, with which the fiscal terms have been further sweetened to accelerate the pace of exploration.

It may be pertinent to point out that when the country came into being in 1947, it enacted the Regulation of Mines and Oilfields and Mineral Development (Government Control) Act 1948 and promulgated the Pakistan Petroleum (Production) Rules 1949, on the basis of which exploration licences were granted through direct negotiation on a case-by-case basis until the late 1980s. The last decade of the 20th century, however, saw a new era of petroleum policies in Pakistan. As democracy resumed, every government tried to bring in at least one new petroleum policy. Various petroleum policies were announced in 1991, 1993, 1994, 1997, 2001, 2007, 2009 and now most recently 2012. Every petroleum policy introduced a new set of fiscal system and provided stability to the terms previously offered without affecting rights and obligations that had already been granted. This was ensured through revisions in the model petroleum concession agreement (for onshore), the model production sharing agreement (for offshore) and new sets of rules to provide a regulatory framework to enforce the various policy incentives.

This chapter focuses on the fiscal terms offered under the Pakistan Petroleum Exploration and Production Policy 2012, which was formally notified in the *Gazette* of Pakistan SRO 1078(I)/2012 on August 30 2012.

2. Upstream activities

At present, a total of 37 exploration and production companies are operating in Pakistan. Foreign exploration and production companies include, BHP, United Energy, ENI, MOL, OMV, POGC, Premier, KUFPEC, Tullow, IPR, MND, Niko and OPL, all of which acts as operators except Premier and KUFPEC. These two companies are however fully poised to bid for new blocks as operators in the bidding round announced in October 2012.

Oil and Gas Development Company Limited is predominantly a public sector flagship company followed by Pakistan Petroleum Limited, both having a strong asset base and major exploration acreage in Pakistan. Government Holding (Pvt) Limited is 100% federal government-owned exploration and production company that is currently the caretaker of the government's share in exploration and production assets and aims to assume the role of operator in the future. Other major local companies are Pakistan Oilfields Limited, Zaver Petroleum Corporation Limited, Petroleum Exploration Limited, Dewan Petroleum Limited and Saif Energy.

The country's average domestic production was 65,866 barrels of oil and 4,032 million standard cubic feet of gas per day, during the year 2010 to 2011, while its total consumption of oil and petroleum products during the year was 385,700 barrels per day. The difference is met through imports. There are a total of six refineries in the country (PARCO, ARL, NRL, PRL, BYCO and ENAR), together having an aggregate refining capacity of 13.4 million tons per year or 259,300 barrels per day.

The first exploratory well, at Kundal, was drilled in Pakistan as far back as 1868. As of July 1 2011, a total of 785 exploratory and 1,066 development wells had been drilled/spudded, out of which 237 discoveries have so far been made (69 oil and 168 gas/condensate discoveries). The overall success ratio in Pakistan is 1:3.3.

Out of a total of 944.319 million barrels of crude oil reserves, 680.308 million barrels have already been produced, leaving only 264.011 million barrels of recoverable oil reserves as at July 1 2011. Likewise out of a total of known recoverable gas reserves of 56 trillion cubic feet, 28 trillion cubic feet have already been produced leaving another 28 trillion cubic feet of recoverable associated and non-associated gas reserves.

3. Petroleum legal regime

3.1 Petroleum law and relevant provisions

In the late 19th century, petroleum exploration activities first started in the areas now comprising Pakistan, with the grant of concessions to petroleum exploration and production companies by the governments of Punjab and British India. Attock Oil Company, Burmah Oil Company, Town Oil, IPS, IPBC and WPC were granted such early concessions. In addition, the government of British India and the British government of Punjab also drilled wells themselves. During that period, all minerals including petroleum were owned by the provincial governments and were accordingly regulated by provincial governments under the Crown Minerals Act which was comprehensive enough and constituted the entire regulatory framework for the concessionaries.

Article 156 of the Constitution of the Islamic Republic of Pakistan 1973 (as amended from time to time) provides for a National Economic Council which is constituted by the President and consists of:

- the prime minister, as chair of the council;
- the chief ministers and one member from each province to be nominated by the chief minister; and
- four other members as the prime minister may nominate from time to time.

The National Economic Council reviews the overall economic condition of the country and advises the federal government and the provincial governments, in formulating policies and plans, and ensures balanced development and regional equity in accordance with the policy principles set out in the Constitution.

Article 158 of the Constitution provides that:

The Province in which a well-head of natural gas is situated has precedence over other parts of Pakistan in meeting the requirements from the well-head, subject to the commitments and obligations as on the commencing day.

Article 161 of the Constitution provides for the treatment and payment of royalty and excise duty on natural gas and electricity, and specifies that:

(a) the net proceeds of the Federal duty of excise on natural gas levied at well-head and collected by the Federal Government, and of the royalty collected by the Federal Government, shall not form part of the Federal Consolidated Fund and shall be paid to the Province in which the well-head of natural gas is situated;

(b) the net proceeds of the Federal duty of excise on oil levied at well-head and collected by the Federal Government, shall not form part of the Federal Consolidated Fund and shall be paid to the Province in which the well-head of natural gas is situated.

Article 161 also provides that the net profits earned by the federal government, or any undertaking established or administered by the federal government, from the bulk generation of power at a hydro-electric station shall be paid to the province in which the hydro-electric station is situated.

Article 172 of the Constitution relates to property and provides that:

- any property which has no rightful owner shall, if located in a province, vest in the government of that province, and in every other case, in the federal government;
- all lands, minerals and other things of value within the continental shelf or underlying the ocean beyond the territorial waters of Pakistan vest in the federal government;
- mineral oil and natural gas within a province or the territorial waters adjacent thereto vests jointly and equally in that province and the federal government.

Soon after its creation, Pakistan enacted the Regulation of Mines and Oilfields and Mineral Development (Government Control) Act 1948, which was subsequently amended in 1955, 1964 and 1976. This act provided a framework for granting petroleum rights, and empowered the federal government to make rules for the day-to-day administration of upstream exploration and production activity. All petroleum found within the territorial jurisdiction of Pakistan is owned by the government of Pakistan. Furthermore, under the Regulation of Mines and Oilfields and Mineral Development (Government Control) Act 1948, the federal government is designated as the appropriate government in relation to mines of nuclear substances, oilfields and gas fields, and the development of these substances. It has power under the act to make rules governing, among other things: applications for, and the conditions and prescribed forms of the granting and renewal of exploration licences and mining leases; the rates and conditions of royalties, rents and taxes to be paid by licensees and lessees; the control of production, storage and distribution of minerals and mineral oil; and the prices at which petroleum is sold to the government. The act also empowers the federal government to enter into petroleum concession agreements and production sharing agreements with petroleum companies.

The most important laws regulating upstream oil and gas sector in Pakistan are as follows:

- Mines Act 1923;
- Regulation of Mines and Oilfields and Mineral Development (Government Control) Act 1948 (as amended from time to time);
- Pakistan Petroleum (Production) Rules 1949;
- Oil and Gas (Safety in Drilling and Development) Regulations 1974;
- Territorial Waters and Maritime Zones Act 1976;
- Pakistan Petroleum (Exploration and Production) Rules 1986;
- Petroleum Policy 1994;
- Petroleum Policy 1997;
- Pakistan Environmental Protection Act 1997;
- Income Tax Ordinance 2001 (Fifth Schedule);
- Petroleum Exploration and Production Policy 2001;
- Pakistan Petroleum (Exploration and Production) Rules 2001;
- Pakistan Offshore Petroleum (Exploration and Production) Rules 2003;
- Petroleum Exploration and Production Policy 2009;
- Pakistan Petroleum Onshore and Offshore (Exploration and Production) Rules 2009;
- Tight Gas (Exploration and Production) Policy 2011;
- Petroleum Exploration and Production Policy 2012;
- Pakistan Petroleum Onshore and Offshore (Exploration and Production) Rules 2012 (draft).
- Low BTU Gas Pricing Policy 2012;

(a) Regulatory bodies

Upstream activities in the oil and gas sector are administered and regulated through the Directorate General of Petroleum Concessions which is part of the Policy Wing in the Ministry of Petroleum and Natural Resources. The Policy Wing has three other directorates general namely, the Directorate General of Gas, the Directorate General of Oil and the Directorate General Special Projects, which provide support to the government in the formulation of policies for the midstream and downstream oil and gas sectors. The Oil and Gas Regulatory Authority regulates the midstream and downstream oil and gas sectors.

The Ministry of Petroleum and Natural Resources is responsible for the formulation of policies, monitoring, controlling, regulating and overall management of the oil, gas and minerals sectors in Pakistan. The Directorate General of Petroleum Concessions is the regulator of upstream exploration and production activity and reports to the Ministry of Petroleum and Natural Resources. It is responsible for implementation of petroleum policy and management of day-to-day regulatory functions relating to upstream activity. The Directorate Generals of Oil and Gas help in policy formulation relating to downstream oil and gas activity and also report to the Ministry of Petroleum and Natural Resources.

The Oil and Gas Regulatory Authority is an independent regulator and is mandated to regulate midstream and downstream oil and gas activity in Pakistan. It reports to the Cabinet Division.

The chief inspector of Mines is the relevant authority with responsibility for health and safety issues during drilling and oilfield operations under the Mines Act 1923. The Pakistan Environmental Protection Agency is the relevant regulatory body responsible for all issues relating to environmental protection under the Pakistan Environmental Protection Act 1997.

(b) *Types of agreement*

There are various agreements relating to the grant of petroleum rights in Pakistan, which include reconnaissance permits, exploration licences, petroleum concession agreements and development and production leases. An exploration licence provides exclusive rights for geophysical, geochemical and geological operations including the drilling of stratigraphic wells. At the same time as an exploration licence is granted, a petroleum concession agreement is also executed, providing the detailed rights and obligations applying to owners of a working interest. Concise details of the different agreements are set out in the table below.

Type	Petroleum right granted	Maximum acreage
Reconnaissance permit	Non-exclusive right for geophysical, geochemical and geological operations, including the drilling of stratigraphic wells. No rights to negotiate or convert into an onshore licence or offshore production sharing agreement.	Unlimited in open areas.

continued overleaf

Type	Petroleum right granted	Maximum acreage
Petroleum exploration licence – onshore	Exclusive right for exploration, including drilling and production testing, on terms specified in the licence, rules and related agreement.	Maximum 2,500km^2 with subsequent progressive area relinquishment of 30% of the original area after first phase of the initial term, 20% of the remaining area after the second phase of the initial term, and 10% of the remaining area on or before the start of the second one-year renewal.
Development and production lease – onshore	Exclusive right to develop and produce hydrocarbons from within a designated portion of an area covered by a petroleum and exploration licence, issued when the conditions laid down in the rules are satisfied.	Maximum acreage retained under the development and production lease as defined in the rules.
Petroleum exploration licence – offshore shallow water	Exclusive right for exploration, including drilling and production testing, on terms specified in the licence, rules and related production sharing agreement.	Maximum 2,500km^2 with subsequent progressive area relinquishment of 30% of the original area after the first phase of the initial term, 20% of the remaining area after the second phase of the initial term, and 10% of the remaining area on or before the start of the second one-year renewal.

continued on the next page

(c) *Acquisition of acreage*

Competitive bidding: The Directorate General of Petroleum Concessions publishes an invitation to bid in national newspapers and on the Ministry of Petroleum and Natural Resources website.

An invitation to bid remains valid for at least 60 days. The model petroleum concessions agreement, model production sharing agreement, applicable rules, policy

Type	Petroleum right granted	Maximum acreage
Development and production lease – offshore shallow water	Exclusive right to develop and produce hydrocarbons from within a designated portion of an area covered by a petroleum and exploration licence, issued when the conditions laid down in the rules are satisfied.	Maximum acreage retained for development and production as defined in the rules.
Petroleum exploration licence – offshore deepwater and ultra-deep water	Exclusive right and production sharing agreement for exploration, including drilling and production testing, on terms specified in the licence, rules and related agreement.	Maximum 2,500km^2 with subsequent progressive area relinquishment of 30% of the original area after the first phase of the initial term, 20% of the remaining area after the second phase of the initial term, and 10% of the remaining area on or before the start of the second one-year renewal.
Development and production lease – deep water and ultra-deep water	Exclusive right to develop and produce hydrocarbons from within a designated portion of an area covered by a petroleum and exploration licence, issued when the conditions laid down in the rules are satisfied.	Maximum acreage retained for development and production as defined in the rules.

and data package are provided to the bidders as part of tender document. All participating companies are required to furnish an undertaking to the effect that in the event that they are considered for the award of a petroleum right, they will not seek any change or modification or amendment or revision to the terms and conditions applicable to the invitation to bid, including those of the model petroleum concessions agreement and the model production sharing agreement. All the economic terms and conditions remain fixed for the term of the concession, unless otherwise mutually agreed by the parties and approved by the government of Pakistan.

All bids are opened publicly in the presence of authorised representatives of the bidders, should they chose to be present. If only one bid is received, the bidding company can be considered for an award in accordance with the rules, provided the company offers a reasonable work programme commensurate with the prospectivity of the area, and otherwise meets the eligibility criteria.

The award of petroleum rights to Pakistani state-owned companies is also subject to the same process.

The Directorate General of Petroleum Concessions makes every effort to conclude and sign a petroleum concession agreement or a production sharing agreement, as the case may be, based strictly on the model provided with the tender documents, within 15 days after the closing date of the invitation to bid, subject to completion of all documents to be submitted by the applicant companies.

The government reserves the right to exercise its powers to accept or reject any application and to cancel or annul the bidding process, on the recommendation of the Directorate General of Petroleum Concessions.

Each bid must contain the necessary information regarding work units to be carried out in the first phase of the initial term of the licence, which the bidder offers as a firm commitment. The work units concept and how it works is explained below in Section 3.1(f). The bid with the highest firm commitments on work units for the first phase of the initial term is declared the winner. Following a successful bid, either a petroleum concession agreement, for onshore acreage, or a production sharing agreement, for offshore acreage, is concluded between the government and the successful bidder(s).

Direct negotiation: Under the Petroleum Exploration & Production Policy 2012, the federal government may award selected onshore and/or offshore exploration acreage through a direct negotiation procedure to a strategic partner, which is to say a national oil company representing a foreign government. The strategic partner to whom a block is awarded remains the majority shareholder of that block. The block awarded to the strategic partner can only be farmed out to public sector companies of the same country acceptable to the government of Pakistan or to Pakistani public sector exploration and production companies including Government Holding (Pvt) Ltd.

Strategic partners are given privileged awards of petroleum rights, without having to go through competitive bidding, on mutually negotiated terms and conditions.

(d) Qualification requirements

All local and foreign companies presently operating in Pakistan are eligible to acquire petroleum rights. Foreign companies not operating in Pakistan but having operated concessions in other areas of the world are also eligible to acquire petroleum rights subject to proof of technical and financial capability.

Foreign and local companies not having any previous experience in the oil and gas sector can also participate in bidding as a non-operator in a joint venture with other companies. Companies having no previous experience in oil and gas can also bid as operator provided they either propose a strong management team or provide an operations and management agreement with an experienced company of repute acceptable to the Directorate General of Petroleum Concessions.

Every company interested in acquiring petroleum rights is required to furnish details of the nature and principal place of business of the company, the authorised, subscribed and paid-up capital of the company, the names and nationality of the directors and the names and holdings of the principal shareholders, and the financial and technical qualifications proving the company's ability to conduct activities under the petroleum right sought in accordance with good oilfield practices.

(e) *Duration*

Reconnaissance permit: The government of Pakistan grants non-exclusive reconnaissance permits for one year with possible renewal of one year.

Exploration license (onshore and offshore): The initial term of an exploration licence is five years (a first phase of three years and a second phase of two years) plus two possible renewals of one year each. For appraisal operations, a separate application can be made under the rules allowing a maximum period of appraisal renewal for one year, plus a possible additional five years retention period for gas.

Development and production lease (onshore and offshore): Following the discovery and proof of a commercial find, the government grants a development and production lease for up to a maximum of 25 years, with entitlement to a renewal for five years. There is a mechanism for further extension of the lease at the end of the total lease period of 30 years.

Upon written request by an operator, the Directorate General of Petroleum Concessions can, on a case-by-case basis, extend the term of the licence on the following grounds only:

- Seismic and drilling services are not readily available in the country for the timely discharge of the minimum work obligation. Proof to this effect will be required before the government considers accepting or denying a request for extension of an exploration licence. Such a request for extension can only be made after the holder of the exploration licence has exhausted all other options, including but not limited to pooling resources to undertake coordinated activities with other petroleum right holders, if possible.
- The holder of an exploration licence commits to undertake additional work which is equivalent to at least 10% more than the minimum work obligation of a subsequent phase or renewal.
- The holder of an exploration licence makes additional accelerated area relinquishment equivalent to 10% of the original licence area.
- The party was unable to perform work because of circumstances beyond its control (*force majeure*), such as a breakdown in law and order, or for unforeseeable reasons, including but not limited to a flood or earthquake and similar events.

However, in any event, the maximum period of extension is 24 months during the currency of an exploration licence. It is arguable, however, that a maximum extension limit of 24 months in the event of *force majeure* is not tenable as nobody can have any control over the duration of such events, so the extension period should not be limited.

(f) ***Minimum work programme***

Bidders are expected to offer their minimum work programme in the shape of 'work units' for the first phase, that is to say the first three years. Work units are defined in

Equivalency of work units for offshore operations (Zone O)		
Type of work		**Work unit equivalent**
One line-kilometre of 2D seismic survey (acquired, processed, interpreted and mapped)		0.3
One square kilometre of 3D seismic survey (acquired, processed, interpreted and mapped)		1.0
One exploration well with a surface location in shallow water (< 200m) grid area with the following well depths:	1,000m	300
	2,000m	550
	3,000m	1,000
	4,000m	1,800
	5,000m	3,200
	6,000m	5,800
	7,000m	10,000
One exploration well with a surface location in deep water (=> 200m and < 1,000m) grid area with the following well depths	1,000m	500
	2,000m	900
	3,000m	1,600
	4,000m	2,800
	5,000m	5,100
	6,000m	9,200
	7,000m or more	16,000
One exploration well with a surface location in ultra-deep water area(=> 1000m) with the following well depths	1,000m	700
	2,000m	1,300
	3,000m	2,200
	4,000m	3,600
	5,000m	6,400
	6,000m	12,000
	7,000m or more	21,000

Equivalency of work units for onshore operations			
Type of work		Work unit equivalent	
One line-kilometre of 2D seismic survey (acquired, processed, interpreted and mapped)		0.3	
One square kilometre of 3D seismic survey (acquired, processed, interpreted and mapped)		1.0	
		Zone I & II	Zone III
One exploration well with a surface location onshore with the following well depths:	1,000m	100	50
	2,000m	200	80
	3,000m	400	100
	4,000m	600	200
	5,000m	1,000	330
	6,000m	2,000	660
	7,000m	3,000	900

terms of kilometres of seismic surveying or numbers of exploration wells drilled. A work unit equates to an approximate expenditure of US$10,000 and the units defined for each zone and sub-zone are considered generic averages for those zones. The current value of US$10,000 is the 2012 base value for each work unit. The value is updated at a rate to be decided by the government from time to time before each bidding round. The value of US$10,000 (or the future equivalent value) is used where units have not been fulfilled to calculate the unfulfilled work programme obligations. The tables show the equivalency of work units to activities in different zones.

For the purposes of calculating work units only, 'well depth' means the well depth measured along the well bore from the seabed/ocean floor to the total depth for offshore wells; and the well depth measured along the well bore from the rotary table to the total depth for onshore wells. Where the well is a deepening of an existing well, the well depth is measured from the deepest point in the existing well to the new total depth. Where a well is side-tracked, the depth shall not include any depth drilled below the kick-off point of the side track, but shall include the re-drilled part of the well from the kick-off point to the total depth. Where a well is horizontally drilled or deviated, the length of the horizontal/deviated segment well shall be added to the vertical well depth.

(g) *Assignment and encumbrance*

With the priors written consent of the Directorate General of Petroleum Concessions, the owner of a working interest can sell, assign, transfer, convey or otherwise dispose of all or any part of its rights and obligations under a licence or lease to a third party, or to any of its affiliates. There is a mechanism for applying for such approval under the relevant rules.

Both petroleum concession agreements and production sharing agreements contain a provision on project finance whereby the owner of any working interest or a contractor can create an equitable charge on its working or participating interest to any reputable financial institution, in respect of any or all of its rights, to secure financing from that financial institution for the purpose of the agreement. This, however, does require the approval of the government.

(h) Local content

Although the Customs General Order 11/2007 dated August 28 2007 lists various engineering goods and equipment produced in Pakistan, in practice, apart from some liquefied petroleum gas and crude oil/condensate storage tanks, no major equipment is produced in Pakistan. There is a small manufacturing plant for the manufacture of wellhead Christmas trees.

The statutory provisions encouraging the use of local content are as follows:

- Imports of the equipment, machinery and plant listed in Customs General Order 11/2007, attracts a 10% import duty, plus a 16% sales tax in certain cases.
- Imports of equipment, machinery and plant which are not listed in that order attract only 5% import duty.

Under the Import of Engineering Goods (Control) Order 2001(SRO827(I)/2001 of December 3 2001), where engineering goods are procured by public sector agencies, they must give preference to locally produced goods by according them a price preference up to a specific percentage of the lowest quoted landed cost of an item of foreign origin with similar specifications to those mentioned in the tenders. The applicable percentage is determined according to the value added to the goods in Pakistan:

- where there is a minimum of 20% value addition through indigenous manufacturing the price preference is 15%;
- where there is 20% to 30% value addition through indigenous manufacturing, the price preference is 20%; and
- where there is over 30% value addition through indigenous manufacturing, the price preference is 25%.

(i) Local involvement

There are certain provisions which provide some specific incentives to local investors in the upstream industry.

- Exploration and production companies incorporated in Pakistan can have a 100% working interest in onshore petroleum concessions.
- There is a requirement for a minimum Pakistani working interest in onshore operations. Local exploration and production companies are entitled to a working interest of at least 15% in Zone I, 20% in Zone II and 25% in Zone III on a full participation basis. (The zones are explained In Section 3.2(a) below).
- Local exploration and production companies will, on a case-by-case basis, be entitled during the exploration phase to receive foreign currency against

payment in Pakistani currency to meet their day-to-day obligations under their permit, licence, concession or production sharing agreement. Once a commercial discovery has been made, local exploration and production companies are paid up to 30% of their sale proceeds in foreign currency to meet their day-to-day operational requirements.

- If a local Pakistani company does not have the requisite past operating experience, that company must either enter into an agreement with an internationally renowned exploration and production or services company acceptable to the Directorate General of Petroleum Concessions, or appoint a high calibre technical and management team with a proven track record of overseeing and managing operations in the international petroleum industry. However, this bar is not applied to exploration and production companies owned by the provinces.

(j) ***National reservation***

Pakistan is in a serious energy crisis. Every dollar invested in exploration and production is welcome. There are no national reservations in terms of repatriation of sales revenue or the like. Some foreign companies even have their sales invoices paid directly into their foreign accounts. There is only a good faith obligation on the foreign exploration and production companies with regard to training, development and employment of local manpower. However there is no bar on the employment of foreign nationals in technical positions whatsoever. The petroleum concession agreements and production sharing agreements do provide for the submission of annual training programmes and the progressive replacement of foreign experts with local personnel as and when local manpower is capable of undertaking such roles. This is again only a good faith obligation. However, foreign companies may find it more economical to utilise the services of competent local experts.

There is an enabling provision for export of crude oil, condensate and natural gas in the event that supply becomes greater than the domestic demand. With regard to natural gas, export can be allowed only if natural gas reserves amount to more than the country's aggregate gas demand for the next 15 years, a situation which is not likely to emerge in the foreseeable future. Currently some condensate is being exported due to refining limitations and no restrictions or conditions are imposed by the government on such exports whatsoever.

(k) ***Environment***

The Pakistan Environmental Protection Ordinance 1997 is relatively new environmental law in Pakistan under which the Pakistan Environmental Protection Agency is the regulatory authority. Under the model petroleum concession agreement, the companies are obligated to conduct petroleum operations with due regard to protection of the environment and conservation of natural resources. The companies are required:

- to employ advanced techniques, practices and methods of operation for the prevention of environmental damage in conducting petroleum operations; and

- to take necessary and adequate steps to prevent environmental damage and, where some adverse impact on the environment is unavoidable, to minimise such damage and the consequential effects thereof to persons, property or otherwise.

If a company fails to comply with these obligations or contravenes the provisions of the relevant laws, and such failure or contravention results in any environmental damage, the company must forthwith take all necessary and reasonable measures to remedy the failure and the effects thereof.

If the government has good reason to believe that any works or installations erected by a company or any petroleum operations conducted by a company are endangering, or may endanger, persons or the property of any person, or are causing, or may cause, pollution, or are harming or may harm wildlife or the environment to a degree which the government deems unacceptable, it may require the company to take remedial measures within a reasonable period to be determined by the government, and to rectify any damage to the environment. If the government deems it necessary, it may also require the company to discontinue petroleum operations, in whole or in part, until the company has taken such remedial measures or has repaired any damage caused.

Companies are required to carry out two environmental impact studies. The first study is to be concluded before commencement of any drilling in the exploration period. The second of the studies is to be completed before commencement of petroleum operations under an approved development plan and is submitted as part of the development plan. The specific approval of the relevant authority must be obtained before commencement of petroleum operations under the development plan.

Companies are required to ensure that:

- petroleum operations are conducted in an environmentally acceptable and safe manner consistent with good international petroleum industry practices, and are properly monitored;
- pertinent completed environmental impact studies are made available to its employees and to its subcontractors to develop adequate and proper awareness of the measures and methods of environmental protection to be used in carrying out the petroleum operations; and
- the contracts entered into between the company and subcontractors relating to its petroleum operations shall include the provisions stipulated in the agreement and any measures and methods for the implementation of obligations in relation to the environment.

Prior to conducting any drilling activities, the companies must prepare and submit for review by the government their contingency plans for dealing with oil spills, fires, accidents and emergencies, designed to achieve rapid and effective emergency response. The plans are discussed with the government and any concerns expressed must be taken into account.

In the event of an emergency, accident, oil spill or fire arising from petroleum operations affecting the environment, the companies must notify the government immediately and must promptly implement the relevant contingency plan and perform such site restoration and damage control activities as may be necessary in accordance with good international petroleum industry practices.

In the event of any other emergency or accident arising from the petroleum operations affecting the environment, the companies are required to take such action as may be prudent and necessary in accordance with good international petroleum industry practices in the circumstances.

(l) Governing law and dispute resolution

Under the model petroleum concession agreement, it is stipulated that any question or dispute arising out of or in connection with the terms of the agreement or the exploration licence or any development and production lease (regardless of the nature of the question or dispute) shall, as far as possible, be settled amicably through mutual negotiations between the parties in good faith within 30 days after the date the disputing party delivers written notice of the dispute to the other parties. Failing an amicable settlement within a reasonable period, the dispute is to be submitted to the International Centre for Settlement of Investment Disputes (ICSID) established by the Convention on the Settlement of Investment Disputes Between States and Nationals of Other States of 1965.

The venue of the arbitration can be in Pakistan or elsewhere as mutually agreed between the government and the companies. If such mutual agreement cannot be reached, the venue shall be decided by ICSID. The award rendered shall be final and conclusive. The judgment on the award rendered may be entered in any court having jurisdiction, or application may be made in such court for a judicial acceptance of the award and an order of enforcement as the case may be. The official language of arbitration is English.

It is also stipulated that if, for any reason, the request for arbitration proceedings is not registered by ICSID, or if ICSID fails or refuses to take jurisdiction over the dispute, it is to be finally settled by arbitrators under the Rules of Arbitration of the International Chamber of Commerce and by three arbitrators appointed in accordance with those rules. The arbitrators are not to be nationals of Pakistan or of the country of the other party to the dispute, nor shall any of the arbitrators be employees or agents, or former employees or agents, of any of the parties to the proceedings.

However, in the event of any dispute between Pakistani companies and the government, the arbitration shall be conducted in accordance with the Arbitration Act 1940.

Under the model production sharing agreement (2009 version), all disputes, differences or claims of a technical nature are referred to an independent sole expert appointed by an agreement between the parties. Failing agreement on the expert, it is done by the International Centre for Expertise of the International Chamber of Commerce. The decision of the sole expert is final and binding and not subject to arbitration.

If any question, controversy, difference, disagreement or claim for damages or compensation between the parties involves at least one foreign company, and cannot be settled amicably, it is to be finally settled by arbitrators under the Rules of Arbitration of the International Chamber of Commerce. The arbitration award rendered is final, conclusive and binding. For disputes among joint venture partners, the joint operating agreement contains sufficient provisions to resolve such disputes. All off-takers agreements also contain provisions for resolving commercial disputes. Selection of the dispute resolution mechanism, arbitration form and venue are negotiable in all commercial contracts such as gas sale and purchase agreements, crude oil sale and purchase agreements and the like.

3.2 Government take

There are two distinct fiscal systems in Pakistan; one applies to onshore exploration and production activity which is governed by petroleum concession agreements, and the other applies to offshore exploration and production activity which is governed by production sharing agreements, and applicable rules and policies. The two fiscal systems result in different government takes.

(a) Producer pricing

For the purpose of gas pricing and for determining the relevant local companies with regard to participation, the country has been divided into different zones:

- Zone I –West Balochistan, Pashin and Potowar basins;
- Zone II – Kirthar, East Balochistan, Punjab platform and Suleman basins;
- Zone III – Lower Indus basin;
- Zone 0 (shallow)–offshore;
- Zone 0 (deep)–offshore;
- Zone 0 (ultra-deep)–offshore.

The gas pricing mechanism applicable to the gas sold to the government nominees, which is set out below uses a reference crude price (RCP) taken from a weighted average of cost and freight (C&F) prices of imported crude oil.

Sample wellhead gas pricing mechanism

	US$/barrel
Weighted average imported crude oil C&F price (assumed RCP)	120
– Floor price	10
– Ceiling price	110

Sliding scale discounts are applied to the C&F crude oil price above the floor and up to the ceiling, are shown on the table on the next page.

US$/barrel	Applicable % of C&F price	US$/barrel
0–30	100	30
Above 30 to 50	Plus 50 of incremental increase	10
Above 50 to 70	Plus 30 of incremental increase	6
Above 70–110	Plus 20 of incremental increase	8
Applicable C&F price		54
Marker price Zone III	63.33 of applicable C&F price	34.200
Marker price Zone II	66.5	35.910
Marker price Zone I	69.66	37.616
Marker price for Zone O (shallow)	73.5 of applicable C&F price	39.8952
Marker price for Zone O (deep)	84.44 of applicable C&F price	45.5976
Marker price for Zone O (ultra-deep)	95 of applicable C&F price	51.3
Zone III producer price for pipeline specification gas		6 million British thermal units (M MBTU)
Zone II producer price for pipeline specification gas		6.3/M MBTU
Zone I producer price for pipeline specification gas		6.6/M MBTU
Zone O (shallow) producer price for pipeline specification gas		$7/M MBTU*
Zone O (deep) producer price for pipeline specification gas		$8/M MBTU*
Zone O (ultra-deep) producer price for pipeline specification gas		$9/M MBTU*
Conversion factor: assumed 5.7 M MBTU/barrel		
*Plus a bonanza of $1 per M MBTU for first three offshore discoveries		

(b) ***Windfall levy on natural gas (onshore and offshore)***

For the sale of natural gas to parties other than the government of Pakistan, a windfall levy is applicable on the difference between the applicable zone price for government sales and the third party sale price using the following formula:

$$WLG = 0.4 \times (PG - BR) \times V$$

Where:

WLG = windfall levy on share of natural gas

PG = third party sale price of natural gas

BR = base price

V = volume of gas sold to third party excluding royalty.

The base price is the applicable zone price for sale to the government.

Where the third party sale price of gas is less than or equal to the base price, the windfall is zero. The windfall levy does not apply on sales of natural gas made to the government of Pakistan and provincial governments.

(c) ***Crude oil/condensate price (onshore and offshore)***

The producer policy price for crude oil delivered at the nearest refinery gate is equal to the cost and freight price of a comparable crude oil or a basket of Arabian/Persian Gulf crude oils (known as 'reference crude') plus or minus a quality differential between the reference crude and the local crude oil. No other adjustment or discount applies other than the windfall levy. The cost and freight price is arrived at on the basis of the free-on-board price of imported crude oils into Pakistan plus freight on an average freight rate assessment, which is the deemed chartered rate.

The producer policy price for condensate is the free-on-board price of internationally quoted comparable condensate delivered at the nearest refinery gate, plus or minus a quality yield differential, based on the value in the Arabian Gulf spot products market of the crude oil/condensate. No other adjustment or discount applies other than the windfall levy.

(d) ***Windfall levy on crude oil/condensate (onshore and offshore)***

The windfall levy applies to crude oil and condensate using the following formula:

$$WLO = 0.4 \times (N - R) \times (P - B)$$

Where:

WLO = windfall levy on crude oil and condensate

N = net production (petroleum produced and saved)

R = royalty

P = market price of crude oil and condensate

B = base price, which will is as follows:

- for crude oil and condensate, $40 per barrel.

This base price for crude and condensate will escalate each calendar year by $0.50 per barrel starting from the date of first commercial production in contract area.

The amount of windfall levy paid to the government is treated as an expense for corporate tax purposes.

(e) ***Royalties***

On all onshore petroleum produced and saved, a royalty is payable at a fixed rate of 12.5% at the field gate. The royalty is paid in cash or kind by the federal government to the provinces to the extent of their share of liquid and gaseous hydrocarbons and of substances including sulphur, produced in association with such hydrocarbons.

However, a progressive rate of royalty is applicable on offshore production as follows:

Period	Applicable royalty
First 48 calendar months after commencement of commercial production	No royalty
Months 49 to 60 inclusive	5% of field gate price
Calendar months 61 to 72 inclusive	10% of field gate price
Calendar months 73 and greater	12.5% of field gate price

(f) ***Production bonus***

A production bonus is payable for each contract area at the start of commercial production and on reaching certain cumulative levels of production measured in barrels of oil equivalent (boe) as shown in the table below.

Onshore cumulative production (million boe)	Offshore cumulative production (million boe)	Amount ($)
At the start of commercial production	At the start of commercial production	600,000
30	60	1,200,000
60	120	2,000,000
80	160	5,000,000
100	200	7,000,000

(g) ***Rental fees***

Holders of exploration licences are required to pay an advance rental charge at the following rates:

- in respect of the five years of the initial term of the licence, PKRs3,500 per square kilometre or part thereof; or in respect of each year of the initial term of the licence, PKRs800 per square kilometre or part thereof; and
- in respect of each renewal of the licence, PKRs5,000 per square kilometre or part thereof; or in respect of each year of the renewal of the licence, PKRs2,750 per square kilometre or part thereof.

During the lease period, the following annual advance rental charges will apply:

- PKRs7,500 per square kilometre or part thereof covering the lease area during the initial lease period; and
- PKRs10,000 per square kilometre or part thereof covering the lease area during the renewal period of a lease and further lease term extension.

For offshore, both during the exploration and development phases, the contractor is required to pay an advance annual acreage rental for the area covered under the production sharing agreement of $50,000, plus a further amount of $10 per square kilometre or part thereof every year.

(h) ***Performance guarantee***

In respect of both onshore and offshore areas, a performance guarantee equal to 25% of the minimum work programme obligations has to be submitted to the government at the time of signing of the concession or agreement. Parent company guarantees or corporate guarantees are also acceptable to the government on a case-by-case basis.

(i) ***Training***

For onshore operations, during the exploration phase, an amount of $25,000 per year must be spent on training Pakistani nationals. This amount is increased to $50,000 per year during the development and production phase.

For offshore operations, during the exploration phase, an amount of $50,000 per year is to be spent on training Pakistani nationals. This amount is increased to $250,000 per year during the development and production phase.

(j) ***Social welfare (onshore and offshore)***

During the exploration phase, there is a social welfare obligation of $30,000 per year, which amount is to be spent in the area of operations. However, during the development and production phase, the social welfare obligation is as shown in the table below.

Daily production (boe)	Amount/Year of lease ($)	
	Zones I & O (offshore)	Zones II & III
Less than 2,000	50,000	37,500
2,000 – 5,000	100,000	75,000
5,000 – 10,000	200,000	150,000
10,000 – 50,000	400,000	300,000
More than 50,000	700,000	525,000

(k) ***Corporate tax (onshore and offshore)***

Income tax on companies engaged in petroleum operations, is levied at the rate of 40% of profit and gains as determined and assessed in accordance with the provisions of the Income Tax Ordinance 2001 and the rules contained in Part I of the Fifth Schedule to the Income Tax Ordinance 2001.

(l) ***Depletion allowance***

A depletion allowance of 15% per annum of the gross receipts is allowed for corporate tax purposes.

(m) ***Ring fencing***

There is no ring fencing for the purpose of calculation of corporate tax for exploration and production operations in Pakistan. Losses or sunk costs are also adjustable as deemed costs, and can be carried forward for a period of 10 years or until they are fully recovered.

(n) ***Cost limit offshore***

In the production sharing agreements, the cost limit is 85% including the royalty of 12.5%. The contractor can recover 100% of costs from up to a maximum of 85% of the gross revenues.

(o) ***Profit oil and profit gas splits***

The profit split is set on the basis of a sliding scale for shallow, deep and ultra-deep water grid areas. The sliding scale is based on cumulative production, permitting a rapid recovery of investments and a higher net present value, as shown in the tables on the next page.

Profit oil and gas share for wells in shallow grid areas of less than 200m water depth and depth to reservoir shallower than 4,000m

Cumulative available oil/ available gas from contract area	Government holding's share of profit oil/profit gas in contract area		Contractor's share of profit oil/profit gas in contract area	
million boe	Crude oil/LPG/ condensate %	Natural gas %	Crude oil/LPG/ condensate %	Natural gas %
0 – 100	20	10	80	90
> 100 – 200	25	15	75	85
> 200 – 400	40	35	60	65
> 400 – 800	60	50	40	50
> 800 – 1,200	70	70	30	30
> 1,200	80	80	20	20

Profit oil and gas share for wells in deep grid areas of 200m or more but less than 1,000m water depth or deeper than 4,000m to reservoir in shallow grid area

Cumulative available oil/ available gas from contract area	Government holding's share of profit oil/profit gas in contract area		Contractor's share of profit oil/profit gas in contract area	
million boe	Crude oil/LPG/ condensate %	Natural gas %	Crude oil/LPG/ condensate %	Natural gas %
0 – 200	5	5	95	95
> 200 – 400	10	10	90	90
> 400 – 800	25	25	75	75
> 800 – 1,200	35	35	65	65
> 1,200 – 2,400	50	50	50	50
> 2,400	70	70	30	30

Profit oil and gas share for wells in ultra-deep grid areas of 1,000m or greater water depth

Cumulative available oil/ available gas from contract area	Government holding's share of profit oil/profit gas in contract area		Contractor's share of profit oil/profit gas in contract area	
million boe	Crude oil/LPG/ condensate %	Natural gas %	Crude oil/LPG/ condensate %	Natural gas %
0 – 300	5	5	95	95
> 300 – 600	10	10	90	90
> 600 – 1,200	25	25	75	75
> 1,200 – 2,400	35	35	65	65
> 2,400 – 3,600	45	45	55	55
> 3,600	60	60	40	40

(p) ***Depreciation***

The depreciation rates in the table below apply to both onshore and offshore operations:.

On successful exploration and development wells	33% on straight line basis
On dry holes (exploratory wells)	Will be expensed immediately upon commencement of commercial production or relinquishment whichever is earlier
Non-commercial wells (exploration wells)	Expensed upon relinquishment of licence
On facilities and offshore platforms	25% on declining balance basis

Any unabsorbed depreciation may be carried forward until it is fully absorbed.

(q) ***Marine research and coastal area development fee***

A marine research and coastal area development fee is applicable during offshore exploration and production, as set out in the table below.

	Annual fee ($)
Until first discovery	50,000
Thereafter until declaration of commerciality	100,000
During the development phase	250,000
During the production phase	500,000

Qatar

Dario Arias
Qatar Petroleum

1. Introduction

Qatar is a peninsula located halfway down the west coast of the Arabian Gulf. It has maritime and land borders with Saudi Arabia and maritime boundaries with Bahrain, the United Arab Emirates and Iran. The total land area of Qatar is approximately 11,500 square kilometres (km^2). The terrain is flat and rocky with some low-rising limestone outcrops.

Qatar is a monarchy and has been ruled by the Al Thani family since the 19th century. The Qatari state is formally organised under a Constitution enacted in 2003. This Constitution declares Qatar to be a sovereign Arab, Islamic state, ruled by an emir who is advised by a consultative assembly, the Advisory Council, and who appoints members of the Council of Ministers, the principal law-making body of Qatar.

The Emir is the principal executive officer in Qatar and appoints the prime minister, the deputy prime minister, and the members of the Council of Ministers and the Advisory Council. The judiciary in Qatar is expressly established as an independent body by the Constitution.

Qatar is a member of the Gulf Cooperation Council (GCC) and the Organisation of Petroleum Exporting Countries (OPEC), as well as numerous other international and multilateral organisations.

Qatar has taken steps to become more attractive to foreign direct investment in almost all fields of the economy. A very recent study conducted by the United Nations Conference on Trade and Development indicates that Qatar had, as at June 1 2011, concluded 45 bilateral investment treaties[1] of which 14 were in force.[2] In addition, Qatar is in negotiations to conclude free trade agreements with Singapore and the United States.[3]

Moreover, Qatar is signatory of the 1980 Unified Agreement for the Investment of Arab Capital in the Arab States (and instituting the Arab Investment Court) under

1 See the full list at www.unctad.org/templates/Page.asp?intItemID=2344&lang=1. In addition, the author is aware of bilateral investment treaties between Qatar and each of Azerbaijan and Tunisia. There are no such treaties between Gulf countries as the Gulf Cooperation Council has a self-contained system to promote and protect reciprocal investments.

2 These countries are Belarus, Bosnia and Herzegovina, China, Finland, France, Germany, India, Iran, Italy, Korea, Morocco, Romania, Switzerland and Turkey. For a comprehensive study on this matter, see Minas Khatchadourian, *"A Survey of Qatar Bilateral Investment Treaties"*, published in the *Transnational Law Magazine*, February 2012.

3 A trade and investment framework agreement has been in place with the United States since 2004.

the umbrella of the Arab League.

Qatar holds observer status under the Energy Charter Treaty.[4]

2. Upstream activities

The first oil well, Dukhan 1, was drilled in 1939. Development continued after World War II and in 1949 the first crude exports were made and the first offshore concessions were granted. In 1960, the Idd Al-Shargi and Maydan Mahzam fields were discovered. The largest offshore field, Bul Hanine, was discovered in 1970 and came on stream in 1972.

The first shipment of oil was transported from Dukhan on December 31 1949 through the Mesaieed port terminal. Dukhan crude is of high quality, with an American Petroleum Institute (API) specific gravity of 40° and sulphur content of 1.5%. Crude oil from three other offshore fields operated by Qatar Petroleum joint venture partners on a production sharing arrangement is processed, stored and exported at Halul Island. Occidental Petroleum of Qatar Ltd operates PS-1 (Idd El-Shargi field, north and south domes), TOTAL Exploration & Production – Qatar operates the Al-Khalij field, and Qatar Petroleum Development – Japan operates the Al- Karkara and A-Structure fields. The state revenue from the oil sector has increased as the result of the rising of a number of production sharing agreements with foreign oil companies.[5]

Qatar Petroleum, is a state-owned corporation created in 1974,[6] which has a far-reaching remit that not only includes upstream oil and gas operations, but also covers petrochemicals, metals, financial services and real estate through its various subsidiaries and joint ventures.[7]

The North gas field, with total recoverable gas of more than 900 trillion standard cubic feet (tcf), was discovered in 1971 and is considered to be the largest single non-associated gas reservoir in the world. It covers an area of 6,000km^2, equivalent to about half the land area of the state of Qatar. Using this field's massive reserves has become a primary national goal, enabling the continuation of the development and prosperity of the country.

In the middle of 1991, production of gas in the Qatar North field commenced. According to *Oil & Gas Journal*, Qatar's proven natural gas reserves stood at approximately 896 tcf as of January 1 2011.[8]

Joint ventures with companies such as Anglo/Dutch Shell, American ExxonMobil and Norwegian Maersk Oil, have helped transform Qatar into the world's largest exporter of liquefied natural gas (LNG). Qatar exports 77 million tons a year of LNG and about 1.5 million barrels a day of oil.

Hydrocarbon revenues are the mainstay of the country's economy, accounting for 60% of gross domestic product. While the search for more oil and gas deposits in

---

4 We see limited benefit to Qatar becoming a signatory at this time if its neighbouring states do not also become signatories.

5 See www.diwan.gov.qa/english/qatar/KhalifaBinHamad.htm.

6 See www.qp.com.qa.

7 See K Baxter, "Qatar Petroleum" in *MEED magazine* (February 12 2012), at www.meed.com/supplements/2012/qatar-projects/qatar-petroleum/3123592.article

8 Qatar has also 25.4 billion barrels of proven oil reserves, see www.eia.gov/countries/cab.cfm?fips=QA.

Qatar continues, Qatar has built an industrial base and financial assets diversification strategy in order to reduce dependence on the oil and gas sector.

More and more states are also seeking to diversify their energy sources, with LNG seen as a more secure resource. Europe has the infrastructure required for the transportation of LNG and there has been a significant increase in the number of LNG terminals being built throughout Europe to take LNG – mainly from Qatar.[9]

3. Petroleum legal regime

3.1 Petroleum law and relevant provisions

Qatar has a relatively simple legal framework that regulates hydrocarbons activity within its territory. The main pieces of legislation, related to the upstream phase of the industry, are as follows:

- Decree Law 10 of 1974, establishing Qatar General Petroleum Corporation;
- Decree Law 4 of 1977, concerning conservation of petroleum wealth;
- Decree Law 15 of 1988, amending certain provisions of Decree Law 10 of 1974;
- Decree Law 36 of 1995, amending certain provisions of Decree Law 10 of 1974;
- Decree Law 11 of 1998, increasing the paid-up share capital of Qatar General Petroleum Corporation;
- Decree Law 14 of 1998, amending certain provisions of Decree Law 10 of 1974;
- Decree Law 18 of 2001, amending certain provisions of Decree Law 10 of 1974;
- Decree Law 110 of 2005, increasing the authorised and paid-up share capital of Qatar Petroleum;
- Law 3 of 2007, concerning the exploitation of natural resources;
- Law 10 of 2007, amending certain provisions of Decree Law 10 of 1974; and
- Law 5 of 2012, amending a number or provisions of Decree Law 10 of 1974.

Decree Law 10 of 1974, as amended, is the cornerstone of the Qatari hydrocarbons legal regime as it establishes Qatar Petroleum's responsibilities and powers. The state-owned company can engage in all phases of the oil industry in Qatar and abroad, including: exploration, searching and prospecting for oil and natural gas and other hydrocarbon substances; production; refining; transport and storage of the aforementioned substances and any of their derivatives and byproducts; and trading, distribution, sale and export of these substances.

It can also establish companies either on its own or jointly with others and acquire participations in existing companies. Further, Qatar Petroleum can contract with other companies or bodies whose activities are similar to its own or which may help achieve its objectives. Qatar Petroleum may also participate in any manner with

9 See K Qureshi, "Energy and the law – an overview" article published in *Qatar Today*, available at www.explore-qatar.com/qatar-today/energy-and-law-overview.

such companies or bodies, or may purchase them or annex them to it, and carry out all legal dispositions that would be necessary for it to perform its work properly.

Qatar Petroleum has concluded exploration and production sharing agreements and development and production sharing agreements with the following major international oil and gas companies: ExxonMobil, Anadarko Qatar, Maersk Oil Qatar, Talisman Energy Qatar, Wintershall Consortium and Marubeni. These agreements have enhanced Qatari oil and gas reserves through new discoveries and the development of existing fields. Some of the fields included in the agreements are the Idd Al Shargi dome (north and south), the Al Shaheen field, the Al Khaleej field, the Al Rayyan field, the Al Karkara Structure A field, and El Bunduq.[10]

(a) *Regulatory bodies*

The Decree Law 4 of 1977, concerning conservation of petroleum wealth, regulated oil and gas operations in Qatar and vests power and authority in Qatar Petroleum and the Minister of Energy and Industry, respectively.[11] Examples of such powers and authority include, requiring the petroleum operator[12] to submit to Qatar Petroleum for approval:

- a detailed description of the proposed project showing, among other things, the plans, location, production capacity and estimated costs of the project;[13]
- detailed information on the implementation of the various phases of the project on a periodic basis; and
- all programmes, reports and data relating to the petroleum operator's petroleum operations in general.[14]

Qatar Petroleum also has the right to monitor, follow up and ensure that the operations conducted by the petroleum operator are performed in accordance with the provisions of the law, the decisions issued and the approved plans.[15] The staff of Qatar Petroleum, designated by the Minister of Energy and Industry, have powers to inspect and pursue records, documents and data in the petroleum operators' offices, and to conduct investigations and examinations of the petroleum operator's field, laboratory and administrative operations.[16] However, today most of the supervisory and control powers that allow Qatar Petroleum to exercise oversight over international oil companies are established contractually.

It is clear that the Ministry of Energy and Industry has the ultimate responsibility for administrating the petroleum industry within Qatar, while Qatar Petroleum has the responsibility for developing and promoting the petroleum and mineral industries within the general framework of the country's economic development

---

10 See www.qp.com.qa/en/Homepage/QPActivities/QPOperations.aspx.

11 Before the transfer of powers and authorities to Qatar Petroleum and the Minister of Energy and Industry, they were vested in the Petroleum Department and the Minister of Finance and Petroleum.

12 "Petroleum Operator: Any natural or legal person legally licensed to conduct any of the petroleum operations", (Article 1 of Decree Law 4 of 1977).

13 Article 6 of Decree Law 4 of 1977.

14 Article 7 of Decree Law 4 of 1977.

15 Article 7 of Decree Law 4 of 1977.

16 Article 8 of Decree Law 4 of 1977.

policy, including the implementation and administration of general petroleum projects within Qatar.

It is also interesting to note that the Minister of Energy and Industry is the chairman and managing director of Qatar Petroleum. This situation provides a cushion between the two bodies and strengthens Qatar Petroleum's negotiation position with foreign oil companies.[17]

More importantly, Article 4 of Law 3 of 2007 establishes that Qatar Petroleum has "the exclusive general concession to explore, and produce petroleum and natural gas and other hydrocarbons and their derivatives, and to invest and develop the resources of such substances". Moreover, it is authorised "to license any natural or legal person to undertake any of the petroleum operations, in accordance with the regulation of Qatar Petroleum".[18] Law 3 of 2007 is currently under review and will be amended shortly.

In August 2012, the state of Qatar enacted Law 5 of 2012 amending certain provisions of Decree-Law 10 of 1974. By this law, the Qatar petroleum's board of directors came under the supervision of the Supreme Council of Economic Affairs and Investment (previously having been under the supervision of the Council of Ministers). In accordance with this law, Qatar Petroleum's plans and programmes must be approved by the Supreme Council of Economic Affairs and Investment. The auditor of the corporation also submits his annual report to this body.

(b) Contractual arrangements

The fact that there are no bid rounds for the acquisition of rights to exploit hydrocarbons in Qatar has led scholars to suggest that Qatar does not have a comprehensive petroleum legislative regime, nor a unified oil policy, under which the conditions governing the granting of exploration and development permits could be known and fixed in advance.[19] The terms of any exploration and development rights are determined on an individually negotiated basis, between the government and foreign companies. The resulting agreements have taken different forms and have evolved over the years.

A number of agreements were put in place for the swift development of the Qatari hydrocarbon industry. Qatar Petroleum established a number of either fully or partially owned subsidiaries, and entered into different types of contracts with different investors, vendors and buyers, mainly through production sharing agreements and joint venture companies. As of today, there are various subsidiaries

17 See T Al-Emadi, "The Qatari Experience with Gas Joint Venture Contracts", *Oil, Gas & Energy Law Intelligence* (OGEL) online publication at www.gasandoil.com/ogel/ (Volume 3, Issue 1, March 2005), p5.

18 The term 'licence' is not term under 3/07; a 'licence' is not a type of agreement usually utilised in Qatar for oil and gas activities; and the term بالترجيص (read balrjees) gives room to interpret it broadly. However in Arabic, the term does not mean 'licence' or 'concession' as the industry usually understands this expression (ie, "development phase of a contract after a commercial discovery has been made", see Johnston, D, *Petroleum Fiscal Systems and Production Sharing Contracts*; or "exploration and development agreements by hosts nations and foreign companies", see Dam, Oil Resources, 14, cited by Kramer, M, in *Manual of Oil and Gas Terms*). Hence, the term 'licences' in Law 3 of 2007 can be interpreted broadly, and will embrace different ways of enabling private companies to perform exploration and production activities within Qatar's boundaries (eg, authorisations, consents, permission, approval).

19 See T Al-Emadi, above note 17, p 9.

in which Qatar Petroleum's ownership interest varies from 50% to 100%, a number of joint ventures and a substantial number of production sharing agreements.[20]

Qatar Petroleum's strategy is to conduct hydrocarbon exploration and development through exploration and production sharing agreements as well as development and production sharing agreements, concluded with major international oil and gas companies.[21]

Qatar Petroleum has not yet entered into any type of service contracts.[22] Development fiscal agreements,[23] land leases, port use agreements, shipping agreements and sales and purchase agreements are also forms of contract closely related to exploration and production activities.

Production sharing agreements: Exploration and production sharing agreements and development and production sharing agreements are very similar in terms of the scope and rights granted through them to companies. The main difference is that the former contemplate exploration, while the latter do not. In a nutshell, under exploration and production contract agreements companies can explore, drill for, appraise, develop, produce and collect petroleum from the formations specified in the contract, as well as treat, store, transport, sell and if applicable export for sale, or otherwise deal with or dispose of the petroleum.

Access to and use of new and existing infrastructure in the state of Qatar owned or controlled by the government or Qatar Petroleum, for petroleum operations is determined by the government or Qatar Petroleum, including the company's right to use and access land, marine and other services and installations, which will be made available on non-discriminatory terms. Use of the facilities (except in respect of shared project facilities, if any) may be given on a non-exclusive basis for the term of the contract. The company is required to market its share of petroleum in accordance with marketing arrangements set out in the contract. Further, the company may occupy and use offshore areas within the contract area, for the purpose of constructing and operating offshore drilling, production and processing facilities, and may import, subject to applicable law (including customs duty), any goods and services required.

Development fiscal agreements: Development fiscal agreements are signed by the government (together with its national petroleum company, Qatar Petroleum) and the joint venture company formed by designated affiliates of Qatar Petroleum and the international oil companies. A development fiscal agreement awards and grants to the joint venture, among other things, the right to produce and manufacture liquefied natural gas (LNG) and associated products, and establishes the fiscal terms for the project (the LNG train). Development fiscal agreements establish a maximum volume (in millions of metric tons) of LNG to be produced per year, during the term of the

20 See Qatar Petroleum, Annual Report 2011, at www.qp.com.qa/en/homepage/mediacentre/publications/10-2015054360.aspx.
21 See www.qp.com.qa/en/Homepage/QPActivities/epsa_dpsa.aspx.
22 Interview with Qatar Petroleum executives in October 2012.
23 The set of economic terms and conditions of these agreements are usually known as 'fiscals'.

agreement. If at any time the joint venture company determines that the facilities built are capable of producing LNG in quantities in excess of the specified maximum annual quantity, it must notify the government. Any increase requires the agreement of the parties to the contract, and is subject to the approval of the government in its sole discretion and on such fiscal and other terms as may be agreed.

Condensate and other petroleum can also be produced, collected and transported, from defined formations (under the terms of the production sharing agreement). The government reserves the right to produce substances other than petroleum and crude oil from formations and reservoirs, other than the formations covered by the contract, in the contract location. However, the rights reserved by the government have to be exercised in such a manner so as not to endanger, prejudice or otherwise hinder or interfere with the petroleum operations of the development fiscal agreement.

Under a development fiscal agreement, the joint venture company is required to pay the government a royalty on all gas obtained under the agreement. The royalty is paid in US dollars per million British thermal units (BTU) of gas measured, and calculated in accordance with a set of formulae. The volume of gas on which a royalty is paid is reduced for:

- the BTU content of any condensate, LPG or ethane recovered from the gas which is sold and on which payment of a royalty is made separately;
- gas flared; and
- gas delivered by pipelines for domestic use, the so-called 'emergency backup' gas supply for power projects.

With respect to sales of LNG, where the principal receiving terminal is located in the United States, the European Union or east of Suez (irrespective of whether such sales are made on a free on board, cost insurance and freight, cost and freight, or ex-ship basis) the royalty is calculated on a gross heating value basis, taking into account reference prices such as Henry Hub and Brent, respectively. Notwithstanding this, a minimum gas royalty is set in the development fiscal agreement.

For the sake of brevity only the main features of the most recent exploration and production sharing agreements and development and production sharing agreements, signed between Qatar Petroleum, on behalf of the government, and international contractors, are described in the remainder of this chapter.[24]

(c) *Acquisition of acreage*

As stated above, the preferred mechanism for granting rights over Qatar's natural resources has been through direct negotiations between the Ministry of Energy and Qatar Petroleum and international companies interested in developing Qatar's natural resources. The acquisition of rights to acreage is, therefore, concluded on a case-by-case basis.

(d) *Qualification requirements*

There is no public information regarding specific requirements established for

24 For confidentiality reasons no explicit data is exposed nor reference to specific agreements made.

companies interested in acquiring rights to explore and exploit the vast hydrocarbons resources of Qatar. However, only international oil and gas companies which are capable of providing a high standard of technical services and know-how and are financially capable of executing their contracts are operating in Qatar. Further, the international companies with activities in the Qatari hydrocarbon industry are those incorporated in countries with close relationships with Qatar and which have a long tradition in the hydrocarbon business.

(e) ***Duration***

Subject to any right of termination by the parties, the term of Qatari exploration and production sharing agreements is usually 25 to 30 years from the date of an emiri decree, ratifying the agreement, which is required to give it full force and effect.

The contractor can seek an extension of the agreement for a period of five years, upon at least one year's notice to the government before the expiry of the term of the agreement. Such a request shall be given due consideration by the government, and any extension of the term, if granted, which is in the government's sole discretion, would be on such terms and conditions as the parties may agree.

(f) ***Minimum work programme***

Exploration and production sharing agreements set out an exploration period structured in successive phases. The duration of each significant contract phase is generally as follows:

- exploration – three to five years plus possible extension;
- development – two to five years; and
- production – 15 years.

The company undertakes certain minimum work and financial commitments (eg, seismic surveys, drilling of certain exploration wells) within each phase. Any work performed in excess of the minimum work obligations is credited against the obligations for the subsequent phase, provided it is notified and is of a type required for that subsequent phase.

Any commercial discovery must be notified immediately. If such a discovery is deemed by the parties to have commercial potential, then an appraisal programme is submitted by the company to the government. The government approves (or observes) the appraisal programme and budget.

At the same time, the company is required progressively to relinquish portions of the contract area, except for those parts necessary for the development and production of petroleum, in accordance with an approved development plan.

If the company elects not to develop a discovery, the government has the right to do so at its own cost without any compensation or payment to the company. However, the company is entitled to recover the costs associated with that discovery as petroleum costs from any other commercial discovery that it elects to develop under any other development plan for the contract formations.

For development and production sharing agreements, the precise coordinates of the contract location are agreed in accordance with certain procedures and technical criteria detailed in the agreement. The company is obligated to drill one or more appraisal wells in accordance with an established procedure and timeframe. It also has the right to test each appraisal well, to complete them for the purpose of use as a production well, to plug any well temporarily for possible future completion, or to plug and abandon them. These tasks have to be performed in consultation with the government and in accordance with the approved work programme and budget.

(g) Assignment and encumbrance

Companies cannot assign their rights and obligations under exploration and production sharing agreements, development and production sharing agreements or development fiscal agreements without the prior consent of the government, to be provided in the government's sole discretion. However, companies may transfer such rights and obligations without such prior consent if the assignee is a wholly-owned affiliate, provided that the assignor remains severally liable, unless the government consents to another arrangement. The company may acquire additional shareholders, by means of accession. No taxes apply to any of these transactions. A change of control is subject to government approval and the government can object if the new controlling shareholder does not have the required credit rating, or for national security reasons. Breach of these obligations entitles the government to terminate the agreement.

(h) Local content

Development fiscal agreements require local goods, services (to be performed in Qatar) and transportation services to be preferred by the joint venture company.

The obligation to select individuals who are Qatari nationals or companies controlled by individuals who are Qatari nationals is subject to:

- the company's judgement, which must be exercised reasonably, that it is satisfied as to whether they are able properly to perform the work entrusted to them or as to the fitness of the goods to be supplied (on the basis of demonstrated ability, experience, reliability, quality, timely performance, workmanship and other relevant criteria);
- the cost of local services and goods not exceeding 110% for services or 105% for goods of the cost of equivalent or comparable services and goods available from non-Qatari nationals or companies; and
- other terms and conditions applicable to local goods or services being otherwise competitive with those available from non-Qatari nationals or companies that are controlled by non-Qatari nationals.

In the case of marine transportation, the second criterion (price) does not apply.

Development fiscal agreements, exploration and production sharing agreements and development and production sharing agreements also contain a specific provision requiring the companies to recruit, employ and utilise qualified Qatari nationals, when they are available for work, at competitive rates to fill its required staffing. The parties meet from time to time to define such staff positions, number and job descriptions. The companies are also required to prepare plans and programmes for the training of nationals that could be recruited, to improve their technical competence and management abilities.[25] In furtherance of these objectives, secondment, attachment and development agreements are commonplace between Qatar Petroleum and foreign oil companies.

Moreover, the oil companies are required to use all reasonable endeavours to ensure that these rights and obligations relating to national content flow down to and are complied with by the operating companies, contractors and subcontractors in Qatar.

Exploration and production sharing agreements and development and production sharing agreements require the oil company to hire a government-nominated Qatari national as deputy general manager and a deputy administration and human resources manager.

(i) *National reservation*

The Government owns and holds title to the reserves within the contract formation or the contract area and the hydrocarbons produced up to the delivery point. Contractors are required to refrain from creating any lien, mortgage, or other charge or encumbrance.

Additionally, under exploration and production sharing agreements, the government has the right to acquire up to a 65% participating interest in the company's interest under the agreement, before the approval of the first development plan.

(j) *Environment*[26]

The joint venture companies are required to comply with present and future Qatari laws and regulations with respect to public health, safety and the protection and restoration of the environment. These include environmental laws and regulations issued by the Ministry of Environment, as well as supplemental requirements and environmental protection standards issued by said ministry and Qatar Petroleum's guidelines applicable to offshore activities.[27]

---

25 These persons under training schemes are usually called 'developees'. The process of training young nationals and increasing the number of Qataris in positions across all industries is called 'Qatarisation'. Qatarisation is a vital component of the state's strategic development plan, enabling Qataris to hold key positions to support the state's business requirements; see www.gsdp.gov.qa/portal/page/portal/gsdp_en.

26 The Permanent Constitution of the State of Qatar contains some articles which refer to the protection of the environment, being Article 29: "Natural wealth and its resources are the property of the State; and the State shall preserve and exploit the same in the best manner in accordance with the provisions of the law" and Article 33: "The State shall preserve the environment and its natural balance in order to achieve comprehensive and sustainable development for all generations."

27 Decree-Law 4 of 1977 contains, in Articles 4 and 5, some environment and safety related provisions. In addition, the Minister of Energy and Industry on the basis of Article 9 of Decree Law 4 of 1977 concerning the preservation of oil wealth issued Decision 5 of 2005 giving the Qatar Petroleum Health, Safety, and Environment Regulations and Enforcement Directorate regulatory and enforcement powers for the hydrocarbons sector, responsibility for following up the implementation of Law 8 of 2004, which concerned protection of maritime oil and gas facilities, and the tasks, function and responsibilities assigned to Qatar Petroleum and the Ministry of Energy and Industry as executive bodies in implementing the provisions on environmental protection in Decree Law 30 of 2002 and all related health, safety and environmental legislation, conventions, treaties and protocols. In 2011, as part of a review of the relevant legislation assessment, the directorate issued a health, safety and environmental legal framework for the oil and gas sector, see www.hse-reg-dg.com.

There are other environment protection-related clauses in the contracts, requiring the undertaking of a risk and environmental baseline assessment and an environmental impact assessment as part of the development plan, as well as provisions regarding abandonment and decommissioning of installations, gas flaring (permitted under special circumstances) and the government's right to suspend activities when a breach of any provision of the agreement threatens the health or safety of persons or the environment. There are also provisions on exceptional conditions in the event of emergency situations.

Finally, the standard of internationally accepted petroleum industry practices has been adopted and is incorporated into exploration and production agreements in Qatar, meaning that the companies must enforce good oil and gas industry practice as accepted by the international petroleum industry (including oil and gas field conservation practices). However, this standard is qualified with the caveat that this standard has to take into consideration the local practices generally recognised and observed by the petroleum industry in Qatar, including those general practices applicable to the government's petroleum operations.

(k) Governing law and dispute resolution

Contracts between Qatari entities or individuals and foreigners may contain any choice of law and jurisdiction clause agreed to between the parties. English law is often the preferred choice of law, as Qatar laws and cases are not readily available in any language other than Arabic. Instead of a court jurisdiction clause, such contracts increasingly contain an arbitration clause as the method for the resolution of any disputes in relation to the relevant contract.

The Qatar Centre for International Arbitration,[28] which is part of the Qatar Chamber of Commerce, and the Qatar Financial Centre each offer alternative dispute resolution through arbitration and mediation. The Qatar Centre for International Arbitration applies its rules of arbitration and the procedure contained in the Civil and Commercial Procedure Law (Law 13 of 1990), while the Qatar Financial Centre applies its own dispute resolution regulations and procedures.

The Qatari courts will enforce the judgments of foreign courts according to the principles of international law. As regards foreign arbitration awards, Qatar acceded to the 1958 Convention on the Recognition and Enforcement of Foreign Arbitral Awards with effect from 2003. Qatar also acceded to the 1965 Convention on the Settlement of Investment Disputes between States and Nationals of Other States with effect from January 2011.[29]

In the absence of a choice of law clause referring disputes to another jurisdiction, Qatari production sharing agreements and any related dispute are governed and interpreted in accordance with the laws of the state of Qatar.

Regarding dispute resolution, an escalation clause is generally used, where negotiations and "other constructive discussions" for a period of 60 days are followed by arbitration. For certain matters regarding measurement methods, devices or

28 The Qatar Centre for International Arbitration was established in 2006 by Emiri Decree 5/8.
29 McNair Chambers dissemination paper, *Doing Business in Qatar – The Essentials*, March 2011, p 12.

records, the dispute may be referred to the non-binding determination of one or more expert(s) under a specific procedure that regulates their appointment and decisions.

When a dispute cannot be resolved amicably (and it is not referred to experts) it is settled by 'final and binding' arbitration conducted by three arbitrators, in London, in accordance with the arbitration rules of the United Nations Commission on International law, except that the costs of arbitration that are to be allocated by the arbitrators.

Notwithstanding these provisions, any dispute may be referred for binding settlement to an alternative forum such as an independent expert or to the Qatari courts if the parties so agree in writing upon terms and conditions governing the conduct of the proceedings.

These provisions cannot be applied to disputes regarding the approval of the development plan.

3.2 Government take

(a) Production share

Under production sharing agreements, from the total production, the company is entitled to a portion computed as 'cost oil' and another portion computed as 'profit oil'. Cost oil is capped and ring-fenced to the contract area. All expenditure is recoverable at 100% from the start of production, and the term for which losses can be carried forward is unlimited. Qatar's agreements contemplate a sliding scale system of sharing rates based on level of production and an 'R factor'.[30] The government is entitled to the residual balance of the total production after deducting the company's share of the cost oil and profit oil.

(b) Royalties

Development fiscal agreements contain a provision related to LPG, condensate and ethane royalties. These royalties are calculated as a percentage of the proceeds from the sale of such products. There are no royalties contemplated in exploration and development production agreements or development and production sharing agreements.

(c) Bonuses

Exploration and production sharing agreements provide for the payment of a signature bonus, to be paid within 30 days from the effective date. Additionally, there are another four non-recoverable (as they do not constitute petroleum costs) production bonuses as follows: the first upon commencement of production, and the other three when gas is sold at the relevant delivery point at an average sustained rate of at least 500, 1,000 and 1,500 million standard cubic feet per day, respectively.[31]

---

30 An R-factor is a ratio of cumulative receipts from the sale of petroleum to cumulative expenditure.

31 Signature bonuses: US$1.5 million; production bonuses: $5 million at the export commencement date; see P Van Meurs, fiscal inputs sheets: "QATAR, Offshore: Oil & Gas – Negotiated Contract (2010)" provided in the Advanced Production Sharing Contracts training course (CWC School for Energy), London, 2012.

The relevant rate is required to flow for at least 30 consecutive days for the bonus to be payable.

(d) *Rental fees; participation*

Upstream agreements in Qatar do not contemplate rentals of fees nor special participations.

(e) *Corporate tax*

International oil companies are subject to the Qatari income tax law and regulations, including the computation of tax, the filling of returns, the assessment of tax, the withholding of tax, the payment of tax and the keeping of records for audit purposes.

Qatar has signed double tax treaties with France, India, Pakistan, Russia, Senegal and Tunisia. Several countries, including Japan, the United States and the United Kingdom, allow some unilateral relief against their own taxes for Qatari income tax paid.[32]

(f) *Other provisions*

Among other provisions of upstream agreements in Qatar, there are the usual standard clauses found elsewhere such as those relating to unavoidable circumstances (*force majeure*), confidentiality and public announcements, annual work programmes and budgets, obligations to procure and maintain throughout the term, full insurance coverage, requirements to keep the government fully informed in writing and in a timely manner as to the progress and results of all petroleum operations, and to provide copies of all data pertaining to such operations.

It is also worth mentioning the commitment made by Qatar Petroleum to provide assistance free of charge to the companies to help it to obtain all the usual and customary approvals from the Qatari authorities necessary for implementation of the project and the emiri decree approving the agreement.

Companies are obliged to cooperate reasonably with other operators. This cooperation comprises joint utilisation of facilities and operations, and includes the sharing of information with the objective of optimising the effectiveness of exploration, development and production activities, including reservoir management, and the sharing of services and facilities. It is interesting to note that the agreements establish that the government shall resolve all conflicts regarding proposed usage, and its decision is final and binding.

4. Current issues

Qatar has brought in international firms and used the North field to become the world's largest exporter of LNG, whereas Iran's development of the Iranian side of the field, referred to as South Pars, has been hampered by protracted delays, in part because of international sanctions, contractual issues and, recently, politics. Changes in this country's regime to a more democratic political system may result, in the long run, in a government open to attracting hydrocarbon investors willing to release the

32 See www.tawfikcpa.com/dbq_tax_structure.htm.

untapped potential of the northern side of this giant field. Developments on the Iranian side would create the need for coordinated mechanisms of production or unitisation.

Despite the fact that Qatar maintains one of the world's highest carbon footprints per head of population, the government is making efforts to shift the country's development into more sustainable paths. In the hydrocarbons field, monitoring and control of emissions and pollution is one of the key focuses for management.[33] Implementation of clean development mechanisms projects in line with the United Nations Framework Convention on Climate Change is one example of the implementation of this strategy.[34]

In the long term, there could be some concerns regarding the growing popularity of shale gas as a competing source of energy. However, exploiting shale gas is expensive, has high carbon emissions and is a relatively difficult process compared with the easy access Qatar has to huge natural gas reserves. If unconventional hydrocarbons, in economically recoverable quantities, are found within Qatar's boundaries it is possible that the contract models would be revised and customised to reflect the specific development challenges of unconventional hydrocarbons. Contractual and regulatory frameworks would need to reflect the different nature of unconventional exploration and production.

5. Conclusion

Qatar's current legal and contractual regime has enabled this country to form close ties with international oil companies, and has quickly created a robust hydrocarbon industry over the past decade that it has helped it to achieve annual growth rates of more than double those of China.

Now that the infrastructure is in place, and with no plans to increase production on the North field until at least 2015, the short to mid-term strategy will surely be to focus on consolidation and diversification of the country's economy.

Despite the global financial turmoil, social unrest and economic downturn, Qatar enjoys increasing demand for its products, especially as key Asian markets move away from coal-burning power stations towards the cleaner natural gas liquids that Qatar can provide. Qatar should be able to handle any threat from other countries emerging as large suppliers in the coming years[35] and from alternative gas sources, with just a few adjustments in its legal regime and contractual scheme.

Qatar's political leadership in the region, its strategic vision and planning, an increasing awareness of environmental issues and a sustained strengthening of Qatar's local workforce are some of the factors that will maintain Qatar's status as a first class player in the energy arena.

---

33 See Qatar Petroleum, *Annual Report* 2012, p 13.

34 The Al-Shaheen oilfield gas recovery and utilisation project is one case, see cdm.unfccc.int/Projects/DB/DNV-CUK1162979371.3/view.

35 See *Advancing Australia: Harnessing our comparative energy advantage*, Deloitte Access Economics report, (June 2012), available at www.deloitte.com/view/en_AU/au/insights/browse-by-job-title/coos/056b751fa6128310VgnVCM2000001b56f00aRCRD.htm.

Australia

Tracey Greenaway
Anthony Patten
Allens

1. Introduction

Australia has experienced a relatively rapid rise in its petroleum production capacity during the last 30 years. Since first production in 1989, the historic North West Shelf project provided Australia's only source of liquefied natural gas (LNG) production. This was joined by the Darwin LNG project in 2006, and more recently, by the Pluto project in Western Australia in 2012.

An unprecedented number of other onshore and offshore gas projects are currently under development or construction. If successfully commissioned, this new capacity is expected to make Australia the world's largest producer of LNG by 2020.

Such an active petroleum industry has in part been fostered by a well-developed set of regulatory regimes. These regimes have provided project participants with the certainty required to proceed with the massive capital expenditures required to commission upstream petroleum projects in Australia.

2. Upstream activities

Australia currently hosts a number of major producing upstream petroleum projects, with a particular focus on gas commercialisation by way of LNG. These projects are primarily sourced from conventional reservoirs,[1] however several unconventional gas projects are also currently under development in Queensland.

Australia's petroleum reserves are located within a range of offshore and onshore reservoirs. Of these, the Carnarvon, Browse, and Bonaparte Basins account for the majority of offshore production and reserves, while the Cooper, Canning and Surat-Bowen Basins account for the majority of discovered onshore reserves.

Australia's LNG production is predicted to grow from 2.5 million tons per annum in 1989 to over 100 million tons per annum by 2020. This growth is primarily expected to come from a raft of new projects coming online in the next decade, and will result in Australia becoming the world's largest producer of LNG, surpassing Qatar.

---

1 However, Santos' Moomba-191 well in South Australia produced first gas for the Australian domestic gas market in October 2012. This well draws gas from shale deposits in the Cooper Basin.

3. Petroleum legal regime

3.1 Petroleum law and relevant provisions

(a) *Overview*

Ownership of hydrocarbons *in situ* is vested in the Crown (ie, the Commonwealth, state or territory governments). The right to conduct petroleum activities, such as exploration and recovery, is obtained through the grant of various forms of tenure and approvals from the relevant government department or minister responsible for administering the applicable legislative regime/s.

The Commonwealth and each Australian state and territory has its own applicable upstream petroleum legislative regimes. The application of these regimes is determined by geographical location in the following manner:

- onshore in a particular state or territory;
- in the territorial sea of a state or territory (being waters adjacent to the low watermark of the state or territory extending seaward three nautical miles and including islands and exposed reefs with their own surrounding waters) (the 'state offshore area'); and
- offshore in Commonwealth waters (being waters outside of the relevant state offshore area extending to the limit of Australia's continental shelf, excluding the Joint Petroleum Development Area;[2] (the 'Commonwealth offshore area').

The location of both the relevant petroleum reserve and the activities being conducted in respect of that petroleum reserve will determine which legislative regime applies. It is not uncommon for Australian offshore petroleum projects to involve activities across both the state offshore area and Commonwealth offshore area with an onshore processing facility. Such projects will be governed by petroleum legislation from all three jurisdictions.

Commonwealth offshore area: Upstream petroleum activities in the Commonwealth offshore area are principally regulated by the Offshore Petroleum and Greenhouse Gas Storage Act 2006 (Cth).

Upstream petroleum activities in the Commonwealth offshore area are conducted under a statutory licensing regime, whereby the states grant rights to project proponents to conduct petroleum exploration, appraisal, development and production activities. These licences are obtained through the grant of tenure from the state, with each type of tenure permitting the holder to undertake certain activities in relation to the field.[3]

Tenure is granted subject to a range of mandatory and discretionary conditions.

2 The Joint Petroleum Development Area (JPDA) is a disputed offshore territory between Australia and Timor Leste, subject to claims by both countries. Exploration and development of petroleum within the area is governed by the agreed terms and conditions of the Timor Sea Treaty (enacted in Australia through the Petroleum (Timor Sea Treaty) Act 2003) and the Treaty on Certain Maritime Arrangements in the Timor Sea. The treaties provide for the regulation of petroleum activities within the JPDA, but do not determine sovereignty or the maritime boundary between the two countries. In Australia, the Timor Sea Designated Authority is responsible for the administration of the JPDA.

Tenure may be cancelled for non-compliance by the tenure holder with any of these conditions.[4]

Responsibility for the grant and administration of petroleum tenure in the Commonwealth offshore area resides with the relevant Joint Authority and the National Offshore Petroleum Titles Administrator.[5]

State offshore areas: There is no national legislative regime applicable to the regulation of upstream petroleum activities in the state offshore areas. Rather, each state and territory has its own legislative regime regulating petroleum activities in these areas.[6] The types of petroleum tenure under which upstream petroleum activities are conducted under each of these regimes are broadly similar to those contained in the Offshore Petroleum and Greenhouse Gas Storage Act, except that responsibility for the administration of this tenure lies with the relevant state or territory minister, rather than the Joint Authority and the National Offshore Petroleum Titles Administrator.

Onshore: As with the state offshore areas, there is no national legislative regime applicable to the regulation of onshore Australian upstream petroleum activities. Each state and territory has its own legislative regime regulating onshore petroleum activities. Again, the types of tenure under which upstream petroleum activities are conducted under these regimes are similar to those contained in the Offshore Petroleum and Greenhouse Gas Storage Act, with responsibility for their administration residing with the relevant state or territory minister.

(b) Regulatory bodies

Joint Authority: Responsibility for administering the Offshore Petroleum and Greenhouse Gas Storage Act resides with the relevant Joint Authority. The Joint Authority is responsible for the grant and renewal of petroleum titles in the Commonwealth offshore area. The Joint Authority is a committee comprised of the relevant Commonwealth government minister[7] and the relevant state or territory minister.[8] The relevant state or territory minister is determined by reference to the

---

3 The procedure for the grant of each type of tenure is set out in Chapter 2 of the Offshore Petroleum and Greenhouse Gas Storage Act, titled "Regulation of activities relating to petroleum". Part 2.2 provides for the grant of petroleum exploration licences, Part 2.3 provides for the grant of petroleum retention leases, Part 2.4 provides for the grant of petroleum production licences and Part 2.10 provides for standard procedures regarding tenure applications.

4 Section 274 of the Offshore Petroleum and Greenhouse Gas Storage Act.

5 Details regarding these two statutory bodies are set out in Chapter 1, Part 1.3, and Chapter 6, Part 6.10 of the Offshore Petroleum and Greenhouse Gas Storage Act..

6 In Western Australia, the Petroleum (Submerged Lands) Act 1982 (WA); in New South Wales, the Petroleum (Offshore) Act 1982 (NSW); in Queensland, the Petroleum (Submerged Lands) Act 1982 (QLD); In Victoria, the Petroleum (Submerged Lands) Act 1982 (Vic); in Tasmania, the Petroleum (Submerged Lands) Act 1982 (Tas); in South Australia, the Petroleum (Submerged Lands) Act 1982 (SA); in the Northern Territory, the Petroleum (Submerged Lands) Act 1982 (NT).

7 Currently, the Commonwealth Minister for Resources, Education and Tourism.

8 In Western Australia, the Minister for Mines and Petroleum; in Victoria, the Minister for Energy and Resources; in the Northern Territory, the Minister for Primary Industry, Fisheries and Resources; in South Australia, the Minister for Mines Resources and Energy; in New South Wales, the Minister for Resources and Energy; in Queensland, the Minister for Natural Resources and Mines. Note that Tasmania has opted out of the Joint Authority arrangement.

geographic location of a particular petroleum field. For example, the Joint Authority in respect of a petroleum field located in the Commonwealth offshore area in offshore Western Australia would be comprised of the relevant Commonwealth minister and the relevant Western Australian minister.

In the event that the respective ministers are unable to reach agreement on a particular matter, the decision of the Commonwealth minister will prevail, and will be regarded as the decision of the Joint Authority.[9]

National Offshore Petroleum Titles Administrator: Responsibility for the majority of day-to-day petroleum regulatory operations in the Commonwealth offshore area (other than the grant of petroleum title) resides with the National Offshore Petroleum Titles Administrator, a branch of the Commonwealth Department for Resources, Energy and Tourism, and is charged with the following roles in relation to petroleum activities in the Commonwealth offshore area:

- providing information, assessments, analysis, reports, advice and recommendations to members of the joint authorities in relation to the performance of the relevant Joint Authority's functions;
- managing the collection, management and release of data relating to petroleum titles;
- approving and registering transfers and dealings with offshore petroleum titles; and
- overseeing the keeping of the registers of petroleum and greenhouse gas storage.[10]

State offshore area and onshore: There is no national regulator responsible for overseeing upstream petroleum activities in the state offshore areas, or onshore. These activities are regulated by the state or territory minister in the state or territory to which the petroleum field relates.

(c) ***Types of agreement***

The following types of petroleum tenure are provided for under the Offshore Petroleum and Greenhouse Gas Storage Act. The legislative regimes applicable onshore or in the state offshore areas contain tenure that is broadly similar in name and function to these types of tenure.

Exploration permit: Exploration permits authorise the permit holder to explore for petroleum within the permit area. Exploration permits also authorise the recovery of petroleum from the permit area on an appraisal basis, and any works associated with these purposes.[11]

Exploration permits are most commonly granted under a work-bid programme,[12] whereby the permit is awarded to the applicant who submits the work programme

9 Section 59 of the Offshore Petroleum and Greenhouse Gas Storage Act.
10 www.nopta.gov.au/about/index.html.
11 Section 98(1)(a) of the Offshore Petroleum and Greenhouse Gas Storage Act.
12 See Section 104 of the Offshore Petroleum and Greenhouse Gas Storage Act.

that is most likely to achieve the fullest assessment of the petroleum potential within the permit area during the permit term.[13]

It is also possible (although less common) to obtain an exploration permit via cash bidding[14] or to obtain an exploration permit over areas that have previously been surrendered[15] (as discussed below).

Exploration permits are subject to a number of mandatory conditions and conditions that are imposed at the discretion of the Joint Authority.[16] The most common of these discretionary conditions is the requirement for the permit holder to comply with a minimum work programme in relation to the permit (discussed further at paragraph (f) below).

The duration of the permit varies between state and Commonwealth legislation, however the Offshore Petroleum and Greenhouse Gas Storage Act allows for an initial permit term of six years and, in most circumstances, permits may be renewed for a further two terms, each lasting five years.[17]

Importantly, an exploration permit allows the holder to apply for a production licence or retention lease in respect of the permit area.[18]

An exploration permit holder that identifies a petroleum pool in its permit area is required to nominate the blocks in which that petroleum pool is located as a 'location' to the Joint Authority.[19] The Joint Authority will consider that nomination and then decide whether to declare those blocks as a location. A declaration will be made where the Joint Authority forms the opinion that the permit holder has correctly identified the presence of petroleum in the relevant area. A declaration of a location is publicly available.

The nomination and declaration of a location is relevant to the relinquishment regime applicable to the renewal of exploration permits (set out below). Further, applications for a production licence or retention lease can only be made with respect to blocks that constitute a location.

Provided an exploration permit holder has maintained the relevant exploration permit in good standing (by complying with all conditions and rents applicable to the permit), the Joint Authority may grant two renewals of the exploration permit for up to five years each following the expiry of its initial term.[20]

At each renewal, the permit holder is required to relinquish a portion of their exploration permit area. As a general rule, the number of blocks that must be relinquished at the end of each permit term is one half of the total number of blocks contained by the permit area.[21] This rule does not apply to blocks on which a location has been declared. Therefore, the declaration of a location protects an area

13 Fact sheet: "Bid Assessment Criteria" – issued by the Commonwealth Department of Resources, Education and Tourism.
14 Section 110 of the Offshore Petroleum and Greenhouse Gas Storage Act.
15 Section 115 of the Offshore Petroleum and Greenhouse Gas Storage Act.
16 Section 99(1) of the Offshore Petroleum and Greenhouse Gas Storage Act.
17 Section 122 of the Offshore Petroleum and Greenhouse Gas Storage Act.
18 See Section 141 of the Offshore Petroleum and Greenhouse Gas Storage Act in relation to applications for a retention lease, and Section 168 of the Offshore Petroleum and Greenhouse Gas Storage Act in relation to applications for production licences.
19 Sections 129 and 130 of the Offshore Petroleum and Greenhouse Gas Storage Act.
20 Sections 102 and 122 of the Offshore Petroleum and Greenhouse Gas Storage Act.

in which a petroleum pool has been discovered from the requirement to be relinquished in accordance with Section 122 of the Offshore Petroleum and Greenhouse Gas Storage Act.

Retention lease: A retention lease allows a lessee to retain tenure over an area containing petroleum until recovery becomes commercially viable. Similar to an exploration licence, a retention lease authorises the lessee to explore for petroleum in the lease area, recover petroleum on an appraisal basis, and carry on such operations as are necessary for those purposes.[22]

A retention lease will only be granted if the Joint Authority is satisfied that the area that is the subject of the application contains petroleum, and that the recovery of petroleum from that area is not commercially viable at the time of the application, but is likely to become so within 15 years.[23] It is important to note that a petroleum location cannot be claimed not to be commercially viable because of the inability of the titleholder to acquire proven technology, skilled personnel or financial resources.[24]

Applications for a retention lease can be made by the holder of an exploration permit over blocks constituting a location.[25] Applications must be made within two years of the day on which the relevant blocks were declared a location.[26]

Retention leases are granted for an initial term of five years.[27] Retention leases may be renewed for further five year terms if the recovery of petroleum from the lease area continues to be not economically viable and previous lease conditions have been met.

Production licence: Production licence holders are authorised to recover commercial quantities of petroleum from the title area and also to conduct further exploration activity in the title area.[28]

Unlike exploration permits and retention leases, production licences granted on or after July 30 1998 are granted for an indefinite term. The Joint Authority has a discretion to terminate a production licence where no petroleum recovery operations have been conducted in the licence area for a continuous period of five years.[29] The Joint Authority also has the power to give a production licence holder a direction regarding the commencement or rate of petroleum production from the licence area where the Joint Authority is of the view that such recovery is not currently being achieved by the licence holder.[30]

---

21 Section 123 of the Offshore Petroleum and Greenhouse Gas Storage Act. Modified rules apply for permits comprising small numbers of blocks. For example, an exploration permit comprising five or six blocks will only need to relinquish a maximum of two of those blocks upon renewal: Section 123(7) of the Offshore Petroleum and Greenhouse Gas Storage Act.

22 Section 135(1) of the Offshore Petroleum and Greenhouse Gas Storage Act.

23 Section 142 of the Offshore Petroleum and Greenhouse Gas Storage Act

24 *Guideline for Grant and Renewal of a Retention Lease*, Department of Resources, Energy and Tourism, June 2006.

25 Section 141(1) of the Offshore Petroleum and Greenhouse Gas Storage Act.

26 Section 141(3) of the Offshore Petroleum and Greenhouse Gas Storage Act.

27 Section 139 of the Offshore Petroleum and Greenhouse Gas Storage Act.

28 Section 161 of the Offshore Petroleum and Greenhouse Gas Storage Act.

29 Section 166 of the Offshore Petroleum and Greenhouse Gas Storage Act.

30 Sections 189 and 190 of the Offshore Petroleum and Greenhouse Gas Storage Act.

Production licences may be granted subject to whatever conditions the Joint Authority thinks appropriate, and these conditions must be specified in the licence.[31] However, a production licence must not be granted subject to a specific condition requiring the licensee to make a well, carry out seismic surveys or spend particular amounts on the carrying out of work in the licence area.[32]

The Joint Authority may also direct that multiple production licence holders in respect of the same petroleum pool enter into a unit development agreement in order to facilitate the more effective recovery of petroleum from the relevant petroleum pool.[33] Importantly, this power for the Joint Authority to give directions only applies to multiple production licence holders, and does not extend to other forms of tenure, such as retention leases or exploration permits.

Pipeline licence and infrastructure licence: Upstream petroleum project participants will also generally require pipeline licences and infrastructure licences in respect of:

- the pipeline between the production facility and the processing facility; and
- any associated infrastructure, including the processing facility itself.

Each of these licences is granted subject to a number of standard conditions,[34] and is generally granted for an indefinite term (subject to a right of the relevant administrative body to terminate the licence if the relevant pipeline or infrastructure has not been operated for a continuous period of five years).[35]

(d) Acquisition of acreage

Commonwealth offshore area: Each year, the Commonwealth government formally announces a number of potential areas in the Commonwealth offshore area for which petroleum exploration companies can place bids for exploration permits (usually within a six or 12-month time frame).

Acreage is released on the basis of graticular blocks which form an 'area'. Each applicant nominates the particular blocks within a released area in respect of which it proposes to obtain an exploration permit. Areas that do not attract bids during the initial release may be re-released for further bidding. The re-release of an area is at the discretion of the Joint Authority.

Assessment of bids is a competitive process based on a minimum work programme (discussed in paragraphs (d) and (f) below).

State offshore areas and onshore: A similar approach is commonly adopted in respect of acreage falling within the state offshore areas or onshore. For example, the

---

31 Section 162(1) and (2) of the Offshore Petroleum and Greenhouse Gas Storage Act.
32 Section 162(7) of the Offshore Petroleum and Greenhouse Gas Storage Act.
33 Section 191 of the Offshore Petroleum and Greenhouse Gas Storage Act.
34 For example, see Section 212 of the Offshore Petroleum and Greenhouse Gas Storage Act.
35 For example, see Section 215 of the Offshore Petroleum and Greenhouse Gas Storage Act or Section 60H of the Petroleum and Submerged Lands Act 1982 (WA).

Western Australian Department of Mines and Petroleum administers the release of graticular blocks within its area of jurisdiction on a annual basis. Like tenure granted under the Offshore Petroleum and Greenhouse Gas Storage Act, the grant of acreage is a competitive process based on a minimum work programme (discussed in paragraphs (d) and (f) below).

(e) ***Qualification requirements***

Generally, applications for petroleum exploration acreage in the Commonwealth offshore area, state offshore areas and onshore are assessed on the basis of a work programme bidding system, under which applicants set out a proposed work programme to be implemented should their application be successful.

The stated primary objective of the Joint Authority in assessing applications is to award acreage to the applicant whose work programme is most likely to achieve the fullest assessment of the petroleum potential within the permit area in the minimum guaranteed period. Further, work programmes that significantly advance the exploration status of an area will be preferred.

As part of the work bid process, applicants must satisfy the relevant regulatory body of the adequacy of their financial resources and technical expertise in order to achieve the works set out in the work programme. Importantly, an applicant's past performance in respect of other petroleum exploration tenure in Australia or internationally will also be a determinative factor.

(f) ***Duration***

As noted in paragraph (b) above, exploration permits and retention leases are granted for fixed terms, with the possibility of limited renewals, while production licences, infrastructure licences and pipeline licences are generally granted for an indefinite term.

(g) ***Minimum work programme***

Petroleum tenure is commonly subject to a condition that the title holder undertakes a prescribed minimum work programme. In the case of an exploration permit, this work programme will usually be based on the work programme submitted by the title holder as part of its application for grant of the relevant exploration acreage. In the case of a retention lease or a production licence, this programme will be based on the result of negotiations between the titleholder and the relevant regulatory body, and in the case of a production licence, on the basis of a field development plan submitted as part of the application for a production licence.

As compliance with a minimum work programme is a condition of the relevant petroleum title, any non-compliance (that is to say, a failure to undertake the relevant work requirements in a given year) can render a petroleum title eligible for forfeiture.[36]

---

36 For example, Section 274 of the Offshore Petroleum and Greenhouse Gas Storage Act states that non-compliance with a condition of a petroleum title is a ground for the Joint Authority to cancel that title.

(h) *Assignment and encumbrance*

In the Commonwealth offshore area, a transfer of a legal interest in a petroleum title, or a 'dealing' in a petroleum title will generally not be effective until it has been approved and registered by the National Offshore Petroleum Titles Administrator.[37] Generally, an application for approval must be lodged with the National Offshore Petroleum Titles Administrator within 90 days of the completion of the instrument evidencing the transfer or dealing. The application is in a prescribed form[38] and must be accompanied by the relevant registration fee.

A 'dealing' is broadly defined in the Offshore Petroleum and Greenhouse Gas Storage Act and includes the creation of an encumbrance over the relevant petroleum title. Other arrangements classified as dealings include farm-in or farm-out arrangements, joint operating agreements, unit development agreements, production sharing agreements and private royalty agreements.[39]

Similar approval requirements are contained in respect of petroleum titles in state offshore areas.[40]

(i) *Local content*

There are currently no state or Commonwealth legislative regimes mandating prescribed minimum levels of local content to be employed in the development or operation of upstream petroleum projects in Australia. In fact, there is a view that the imposition of any statutory minimum local content requirement on major resources projects may be inconsistent with Australia's international free-trade treaty obligations.

Instead of imposing statutory local content obligations on upstream petroleum participants, the Australian government seeks to encourage the use of local goods and labour through a raft of policy measures and incentives. The Australian Industry Participation National Framework Agreement (AIP national framework)[41] was signed by state and federal ministers in 2001. Under the AIP national framework, all signatory state and territory ministers have committed to incorporating the principle of full, fair and reasonable opportunity into their approach to local supply. In 2011 the Australian government announced it will tighten the administration of the AIP national framework and require publication of Australian industry participation plans and outcomes. An Australian Industry Participation Working Group was established and charged with advising the Australian government on the implementation of various changes to the framework.[42] As a result of these recommendations, the AIP national framework was scheduled to be updated by the end of 2012.

Each state government is responsible for formulating its own local content policy

---

37 For example, see Sections 472 and 487 of the Offshore Petroleum and Greenhouse Gas Storage Act.

38 Available from www.nopta.gov.au.

39 Section 486 of the Offshore Petroleum and Greenhouse Gas Storage Act.

40 For example, Sections 79 and 81 of the Petroleum (Submerged Lands) Act 1982 (WA)

41 Available from www.innovation.gov.au/Industry/AustralianIndustryParticipation/Documents/AIP Framework.pdf.

42 See, Australian industry participation working group, *Report to the Australian Government on implementation of measures to extend Australian Industry Participation*, February 2012.

in accordance with the AIP national framework. Generally, these policies are implemented by either:

- direct agreement between the relevant state or territory government and the project participant(s); or
- the provision of financial incentives under the Enhanced Project Bylaws Scheme (described below).

Neither method of implementation is mutually exclusive, with both methods having been used concurrently in respect of existing Australian upstream petroleum projects.[43]

Direct agreement with the state: Historically, some major Australian petroleum projects have been the subject of agreements between the project participant(s) and the relevant state or territory government. Where these agreements have been ratified by legislation, they are known as 'state agreements'.[44]

A state agreement will customarily include local content obligations on the project participant. Although the terms of a state agreement are the subject of commercial negotiation between project participants and the relevant state or territory government, it is common for these obligations to broadly reflect the 'full, fair and reasonable' principles contained in the AIP national framework.

Enhanced Project Bylaws Scheme: The most common method through which the Australian government encourages the use of local goods and services in respect of upstream petroleum projects is by the Enhanced Project Bylaws Scheme (EPBS).[45] The EPBS operates to give import tariff concessions to eligible companies in exchange for that company formulating and implementing an Australian industry participation plan. In this manner, the EPBS provides a financial incentive for upstream petroleum participants to use local goods and labour in respect of Australian projects.

The EPBS applies to mining projects that have a total project expenditure on eligible goods in excess of $10 million. 'Mining' is defined within the EPBS Policy and Administrative Guidelines to include activities to extract and recover gases or liquids such a crude petroleum or natural gas. Given the historically capital-intensive nature of upstream petroleum projects in Australia, it is difficult to envisage a project that would not satisfy this $10 million threshold.

In general terms, project proponents may receive duty concessions in respect of imported goods relevant to the project if they prepare and implement an approved Australian industry participation plan. In order to qualify for such duty concessions, a project proponent's Australian industry participation plan must show how the

---

43 See for example, the Gorgon project, which is subject to local content obligations under both a direct agreement with the Western Australian government and under an Australian industry participation plan entered into pursuant to the enhanced project by-laws scheme.

44 State Agreements have been entered into between project proponents and the Western Australian government in respect of the Gorgon project (ratified by the Barrow Island Act 2003 (WA)) and the North-West Shelf project (ratified by the North West Gas Development (Woodside) Agreement Act 1979 (WA)).

45 The EPBS is underpinned by Item 71 of Schedule 4 to the Customs Tariff Act 1995 (Cth).

project participant intends to provide full, fair and reasonable opportunity to Australian industry to supply goods and services to the relevant project.

(j) *National reservation*

As with Australia's local content regime, there are currently no broad-based state or Commonwealth legislative regimes[46] mandating the reservation of gas produced from Australian upstream petroleum projects for domestic use.

Western Australia: Since 2006, the Western Australian government has implemented a domestic gas reservation policy (the 'domgas policy'). The domgas policy applies to all gas projects operating from reserves located:

- onshore in Western Australia;
- within the Western Australia state offshore area; or
- in the Commonwealth offshore area that have onshore processing facilities in Western Australia.

Under the domgas policy, project participants are required to allocate 15% of annual production from the project for supply to Western Australia's domestic energy market.[47]

The Western Australian government has publicly stated that it will apply the 15% rule under the domgas policy flexibly and that the application of the domgas policy will be subject to a 'commercial viability' test.[48] The Western Australian government has not provided a clear explanation of what circumstances would and would not be regarded as commercially viable in relation to the provision of reserved domestic gas from a Western Australian project.

The domgas policy is not a legislative instrument and is therefore not enforceable by the Western Australian government as such. Historically, the Western Australian government has imposed the domgas policy on project proponents by including a 15% reservation requirement in an agreement between the Western Australian government and the project proponent. The exact mechanism for documenting this agreement has varied between projects, but has included:

- a state agreement containing domgas obligations;[49]
- an exchange of letters between the Western Australian government and the project proponent regarding domgas commitments;[50] and
- formal gas sale agreements between the Western Australian government and project proponents for the supply of gas from the relevant project to the Western Australian domestic gas market.[51]

---

46 Other than the obligations to do so under specific state agreements, such as the Barrow Island Act 2003 (WA) and the North West Gas Development (Woodside) Agreement Act 1979 (WA).

47 See, Department of Premier and Cabinet, *WA Government Policy on Securing Domestic Gas Supplies: Consultation Paper*, October 2006 and Department of Finance, *Strategic Energy Initiative Energy 2031: Building the Pathways for Western Australia's Energy Future*, August 2012.

48 See, www.domgas.com.au.

49 Such as that entered into in respect of the Gorgon project: the Barrow Island Act 2003 (WA).

50 Such as those letters exchanged between the Western Australian government and the proponents of the Pluto project.

51 Such as those entered into in respect of the North West Shelf project.

A summary of how the domgas policy has been applied to Western Australia's current and proposed upstream gas projects is set out in the table below:

Project	Domgas commitment	How imposed
North-West Shelf	Under a 1995 revision to the state agreement, the North West Shelf was obligated to supply 5,064 picojoules of gas to the domestic market. Provisions exist for further supplies to be negotiated.[52]	State agreement: North West Gas Development (Woodside) Agreement Act 1979 (WA). Under a memorandum of understanding between the Western Australian State Energy Commission and the project proponents (subsequently converted into formal gas sale agreements).
Pluto	The project proponent has agreed to market and sell the equivalent of 15% of the project's produced LNG to the Western Australian energy market, providing it is commercially viable. The proponent and the state have agreed to negotiate in good faith an appropriate test of commercial viability. The commencement date of the commitment will occur five years after the date LNG is first exported from Pluto, or the date on which the 30-millionth ton of LNG produced at the Pluto site is exported.	An exchange of letters between the project proponent and the Western Australian government.

continued on next page

52 Economics and Industry Standing Committee, *Inquiry into Domestic Gas Prices*, March 24 2011, at page 79.

Project	Domgas commitment	How imposed
Wheatstone	State development agreement, which sets out the agreement between the Western Australian government and the project proponents, is not publicly available, but is reported to contain domgas obligations.	State development agreement
Gorgon	State agreement contains a detailed domestic gas reservation regime, including commercial viability pre-conditions to reservation.	State agreement: Barrow Island Act 2003 (WA)
Buru Energy/ Mitsubishi Corporation	State agreement includes arrangements that facilitate and prioritise a domestic gas project, pipeline and associated infrastructure. It also includes a statutory framework to develop a domestic gas and a LNG pipeline facility.	State agreement: Natural Gas (Canning Basin Joint Venture) Agreement Bill 2012 (WA).

Nationally: No other Australian states or territories (including the Commonwealth) currently have a domestic gas reservation policy.

New developments in upstream petroleum technology have meant that some projects being developed off the coast of Western Australia, but in the Commonwealth offshore area:

- are able to be developed solely in the Commonwealth offshore area via floating LNG technology;[53] or
- have elected to transport gas long distances via sub-sea pipeline for processing in other jurisdictions.[54]

These development options do not involve any jurisdictional connection with Western Australia. Accordingly, the Western Australian government has no ability to impose its domgas policy on projects of this nature.

The Western Australian government has previously requested that the

53 The Prelude project will operate via a floating LNG facility, with no domestic gas reservation obligations attaching to it.

54 The Ichthys project will operate from reserves in the Browse Basin, located in the Commonwealth offshore area off the coast of Western Australia and will transport gas for onshore processing in the Northern Territory.

Commonwealth government consider imposing a domestic gas reservation policy in respect of projects developed from reserves solely in the Commonwealth offshore area. To date, the Commonwealth government has confirmed that it does not support the imposition of domestic gas reservation policies.[55]

(k) *Environment and safety*

Upstream petroleum projects are subject to Australia's environmental protection legislation. The applicable legislative regime is determined by the location of the relevant project, with operations in the Commonwealth offshore area being subject to the Environment Protection and Biodiversity Conservation Act 1999 (Cth). Projects with operations spanning both the Commonwealth offshore area and a state offshore area or onshore area may be required to comply with both state and Commonwealth environmental protection regimes.[56]

In addition, the National Offshore Petroleum Safety and Environmental Management Authority (NOPSEMA) has regulatory responsibility for occupational health and safety, structural integrity, environmental management, and day-to-day operations of offshore petroleum facilities in the Commonwealth offshore area, and in state offshore areas where state and Northern Territory powers have been conferred.

NOPSEMA requires the preparation and submission of a safety case for every offshore petroleum facility, and is authorised under the Offshore and Petroleum and Greenhouse Gas Storage Act to impose penalties and enforcement measures to ensure compliance.

3.2 Government take

(a) *Royalties*

Proponents of onshore petroleum projects will be liable for state and territory based royalties on their production. Generally speaking, the states and the Northern Territory levy a royalty of between 10% and 12.5% on the wellhead value of petroleum production.[57]

(b) *Rental fees*

As with royalties, petroleum proponents may be required to pay to the relevant state or the Northern Territory an annual rent (or an equivalent charge, for example a fee) on petroleum tenure. The amount of rent payable will be subject to the type of tenure that is held.

---

55 See Department of Resources, *Energy and Tourism, Energy White Paper 2012* released on November 8 2012. Available from www.energywhitepaper.ret.gov.au

56 For example, the Environmental Protection Act 1986 (WA) operates in respect of projects carried out in Western Australia.

57 See: Part III Division 7 of the Petroleum and Geothermal Energy Resources Act 1967 (WA); Chapter 6 of the Petroleum and Gas (Production and Safety) Act 2004 (QLD); Part 7 od the Petroleum (Onshore) Act 1991 (NSW); Part 7 of the Petroleum and Geothermal Energy Act 2000 (SA); Part 10 of the Petroleum Act 1998 (VIC); Part III Division 5 of the Petroleum Act (NT); and Part 4 Division 5 of the Minerals Resources Development Act 1996 (TAS).

(c) *Petroleum resource rent tax*

The Commonwealth's primary method of obtaining revenue from Australian petroleum operations is the petroleum resource rent tax (PRRT).

The PRRT is profits-based tax levied on the production of petroleum projects. Entities will be liable for the PRRT where they have an interest in a petroleum project and are entitled to receive receipts from the sale of petroleum, or of marketable petroleum commodities produced from the petroleum. The tax is determined based on the receipts of a project, minus certain prescribed deductable expenses (eg, eligible exploration expenditure). The tax that is then required to be paid is 40% of those profits.

The scope of the PRRT was expanded as of July 1 2012 to encompass all onshore and offshore projects, including those on the North West Shelf and unconventional gas projects. When the PRRT was originally introduced in 1987 it applied only to certain offshore projects (later encompassing the Bass Strait project in 1990).

(d) *Corporate tax*

Companies that are incorporated in Australia, or that carry on business and have their central management and control in Australia (or voting power is controlled by shareholders who are Australian residents), are required to pay taxes on their income as an Australian resident company. Non-resident companies will also be taxed in Australia on income that is sourced in Australia.[58] The company tax rate in Australia is set at a flat rate of 30%, which applies to the company's taxable income (its assessable income minus eligible deductions). The Australian tax regime provides for certain eligible entities (such as wholly-owned subsidiaries within a corporate group) to elect to be grouped for income tax purposes.

4. Current issues

4.1 Unconventional gas

Australia has significant unconventional gas reserves, estimated as including 396 trillion cubic feet of onshore shale reserves alone.[59] The development of shale gas reservoirs is a relatively recent movement in Australia, at least in comparison to conventional reserves. In Queensland, coal seam gas provides up to 80% of domestic gas supply.

At present, there is no unified regulatory approach to the regulation of unconventional gas exploration and development across the Australian states and territories. This fact is in part due to the relative immaturity of unconventional gas development in Australia.

The unconventional gas industry has also had to contend with environmental and land access issues. New South Wales previously imposed a moratorium on the extractive process of fracking, which was recently lifted and replaced with two industry codes of practice. Similarly, Victoria has recently imposed a moratorium on fracking.

---

58 Australia's taxing rights may be limited where the non-resident is resident of a country with which Australia has a double tax agreement.

59 Energy Information Administration, *World Shale Gas Resources: An Initial Assessment of 14 Regions Outside the United States* (April 2011) p XIV-2.

Australian unconventional gas regulation continues to undergo significant reform. Western Australia is in the process of introducing new regulation. The Commonwealth government is also seeking a harmonised national framework for, and a national partnership agreement on, coal seam gas. The Victorian government has stated that its moratorium will remain in place until such a national framework has been developed.

4.2 Floating liquid natural gas

It is highly likely that the world's first floating liquid natural gas (FLNG) project will be hosted in the Commonwealth offshore area. The technology will be deployed for use in the Prelude and Concerto gas fields, located in the Browse Basin approximately 500km off the Western Australian north-west coast, arguably areas that but for the FLNG technology would likely be economically unsustainable for development. The project is currently in construction and is estimated to produce first gas in 2017.

4.3 Carbon pricing scheme

In July 2011, the Federal government passed a suite of legislation it refers to as the clean energy legislative package. A key element of the package was the introduction of a carbon pricing scheme (CPS), which commenced operating on July 1 2012. The CPS will operate with a fixed price on carbon until June 30 2015 (starting at $23 a ton), and on July 1 2015 the CPS will transition to an emissions trading scheme with a flexible price determined by market. Broadly speaking, an entity will be liable under the CPS if it has operational control over a facility that emits more than 25,000 tonnes of CO2 equivalent, or supplies or uses large quantities of natural gas.

The future of the CPS and broader initiatives under the clean energy legislative package is uncertain as the federal (Liberal/National Conservative) opposition has indicated its intention to repeal the CPS if it obtains power at the next election.[60] If the opposition does take power at the next election, it may still have difficulty repealing the CPS through the upper house of Parliament.

5. Conclusion

Overall, Australia has a mature, transparent and sophisticated framework for the regulation of upstream petroleum activities. This regime will undoubtedly become more comprehensive if and when a bespoke national regulatory framework is developed in respect of unconventional gas operations. While initiatives such as the carbon pricing scheme have been suggested as imposing some degree of sovereign risk on to Australian petroleum operations, the relative stability and objectivity of the regulatory framework by international standards continues to underpin the unprecedented level of capital expenditure, now estimated at approximately $260 billion over the next four years alone, on Australian upstream petroleum projects.

The authors would like to thank Kieran Chute, Anthony Graham and Miranda Hicks, all of Allens, for their invaluable contributions to this chapter.

---

60 The next federal election must be held by November 30 2013.

China

Liang Peng
Sunshine Law Firm

1. Introduction

China has transformed into the world's second largest oil consumer and the fastest growing user of oil and gas. China's fast economic growth has resulted in continually rising demand for oil. According to the BP Statistical Review, China's oil consumption grew from 4.9 million barrels per day (mbpd) in 2001 to 9.1 mbpd in 2010, a compound annual growth rate of 7.2%. Despite the growth in energy demand, domestic oil production growth has been stagnant. Oil production only grew from 3.3 mbpd in 2001 to 4.07 mbpd in 2010, a compound annual growth rate of 2.3%. China became a net importer of oil in 1993. Since then, China's reliance on imported oil has been growing: in 2011, China imported 57% of its oil supply from beyond its borders. Looking ahead, the Institute of Economic Affairs (IEA) expects China's net imports to exceed 12.5 mbpd by 2035, up almost 8 mbpd from the current level. The IEA also expects China to import about 79% of the oil it consumes by 2030.[1]

Natural gas has not been a major fuel resource in China's past. In recent years, the government has focused on developing clean and renewable domestic energy with an intention to ease reliance on imported oil and curb the severe environmental pollution. In its 11th national five-year plan, the government set a target of making natural gas 5.3% of domestic energy consumption by 2010 from 2.8% in 2005.[2] Natural gas consumption has grown from 2.7 billion cubic feet per day (bcfd) in 2001 to 10.5 bcfd in 2010, representing a compound annual growth rate of 16.6%. While natural gas production in China has largely kept with demand, demand has outstripped production since 2007. Going forward, the IEA expects China to be one of the fastest growing natural gas consumers and account for 25% of global gas demand growth by 2035.[3]

To support domestic upstream oil and gas development, the government has encouraged major international players to pursue joint production with the domestic oil companies. In addition to Petro China and Sinopec, China National Offshore Oil Corporation (CNOOC) has been particularly active in sharing concessions with foreign companies that offer advanced exploration and production technologies in offshore locations.

1 IEA, *World Energy Outlook*, 2010
2 David Blumental, "Upstream Oil and Gas in China", *Doing Business in China*, Juris Publishing, 2009.
3 Deutsche Bank, *China Oil and Gas*, June 2012

Most recently, shale gas, which is believed to be abundant in China, has been a new focus for security of energy supply. Foreign companies are allowed to participate in shale gas bidding in the form of a Sino-foreign joint venture (controlled by Chinese parties) or to cooperate with Chinese companies in shale gas exploration and production. Shell has now signed a production sharing contract with China National Petroleum Company (CNPC) to develop a shale gas block in Sichuan province. This deal is still subject to government approval, but it is the first shale gas production sharing contract ever signed in China.

1.1 Oil and gas reserves in China

As oil prices surged between 2001 and early 2008, and with the increasing demand for oil products, domestic recoverable reserve achieved some modest growth. During the 11th five-year plan period (2005–2010), recoverable reserves have increased steadily, representing a compound annual growth rate of 4.8%, and standing at 3.14 billion tons by the end of 2010. In 2011, China made several new discoveries according to the news released by the Ministry of Land and Recourses, adding 1.37 billion tons of new proved reserves. According to BP's energy statistics for 2012, China has proved reserves of 14.7 thousand million barrels at the end of 2011, representing a share of 0.9% of the world total. The reserve to production ratio is 9.8 years.[4]

Natural gas resources are abundant in China, with estimated resources of 5.6 trillion cubic metres (m^3) of conventional natural gas and 3.68 trillion m^3 of coal-bed methane, and the exploration rate of China's natural gas is as low as 19.5%.[5] According to BP's Statistical Review of World Energy 2012, China has proved natural gas reserves of 3.1 trillion m^3 at the end of 2011, accounting for 1.5% of the world total.[6]

1.2 Distribution of oil and gas reserves

Oil reserves are distributed unevenly in China. The eastern region (including the Northeast, North China and Yangze and Huai river areas) accounts for nearly 40% of the total resources, while the western region (including Xinjiang Uygur Autonomous Region, Qinghai Province and part of Inner Mongolia Region) and offshore account for 26.5% respectively.

Gas reserves are mostly concentrated in three basins in the western region: the Tarim Basin, the Ordos Basin and the Sichuan Basin, together accounting for 70% of the total reserves in China. The rest are located in the Songliao Basin in the northeast region and the offshore basins in Baohai Bay, East and the South China Sea.[7]

1.3 Production of oil and gas

Following the Daqing oil fields being discovered in Heilongjiang province in 1959, China experienced a fast growth period of oil production (from the 1960s to the late

4 BP, *Statistical Review of World Energy* 2012.
5 Website of Ministry of Land and Resources of China.
6 BP, *Statistical Review of World Energy* 2012.
7 Nobuyuki Higashi, *Natural Gas in China, Market Evolution and Strategy*, 2009.

Figure 1: The remaining recoverable reserves of major national oil companies (2001-2010)

Unit: 100 million tons; 100 million m³

Companies	2001	2002	2003	2004	2005	2006	2007	2008	2009	2010
CNPC	15.01	14.98	15.75	15.76	15.80	15.92	16.03	15.37	15.43	15.45
Sinopec	4.53	4.68	4.59	4.60	4.64	4.64	4.26	4.17	4.11	4.06
CNOOC	1.70	1.76	1.83	1.85	1.86	1.84	1.93	1.92	2.05	2.06
Others	3.6	2.83	2.16	2.70	2.59	5.19	6.10	7.45	7.91	9.83
Oil total	24.84	24.25	24.33	24.91	24.89	27.59	28.32	28.91	29.50	31.40
CNPC	10,217	10,985	11,826	12,805	13,619	15,141	16,172	17,327	17,898	18,548
Sinopec	988	943	818	859	836	809	1793	1971	1909	1826
CNOOC	919	943	1,119	1,224	1,282	1,300	1,260	1,193	1,179	1,242
Others	176	7,298	8,526	10,404	12,448	12,759	12,898	13,559	16,089	17,384
Gas total	12,300	20,169	22,289	25,292	28,185	30,009	32,123	34,050	37,075	39,000

Source: China Economic Information Network

1980s), but since then the growth in production has slowed. Between 2001 and 2010, the production grew with a compound annual growth rate of only 2.3%. In 2011, China produced 204 million tons of crude oil in total. Given the limited amount of oil reserves that are recoverable under present conditions, further growth of oil production will be very difficult in the near future. The most productive regions are Heilongjiang Province, Shaanxi Province, Tianjin Municipality, Shandong Province and Xinjiang Uygur Autonomous Region.[8]

Production of natural gas has grown quickly since large gas fields in the Sichuan Basin, the Ordos Basin, the Tarim Basin and the Qaidam Basin were developed in around 2001. Between 2005 and 2010, production has grown from 50 billion m³ in 2005 to 95 billion m³ in 2010, a compound annual growth rate of 14.1%.[9] In 2011, China produced 102.53 billion m³ of natural gas, an 8.5% increase on the previous year. With some new natural gas projects coming on line in the west and central regions in 2011, natural gas production is expected to keep growing in China in the

8 China Economic Information Network, *Oil and Gas Report*, 2012.
9 Information from State Statistics Bureau, 2010.

next few years. The majority of the production comes from Shaanxi Province, Sichuan Province, Xinjiang Urgur Autonomous Region, Qinghai Province and Guangdong Province.

2. Upstream activities

2.1 Upstream oil and gas sector in China

China's upstream oil and gas sector is dominated by three national oil companies: CNPC, Sinopec and CNOOC. The birth of these companies took place in the 1980s during the process of economic reform in China. First of all, CNOOC was established in 1982 to manage offshore development, which seemed rather difficult to perform and required cooperation with foreign partners. Sinopec was established in 1983 to handle downstream refining. Finally, responsibility for inland oil and gas production was delegated by the Ministry of Petroleum to the new national oil company known as CNPC, in 1988.[10] In 1998, the sector underwent a broad-scale restructuring: both CNPC and Sinopec began to handle entire segments from upstream to downstream but their mandates were geographically demarcated. All three companies were listed on the international stock exchanges in Hong Kong, New York and London in 2000, and several western oil majors bought their stocks.[11] In addition, since the latter half of 2004, CNPC and Sinopec have acquired offshore exploration and development rights, and CNOOC has been given land-based exploration and development rights. China's government introduced land-based/offshore competitive mechanisms in order to strengthen its domestic exploration and development.[12]

In recent years, the three major Chinese national oil companies have become significant players in global mergers and acquisitions in upstream oil and natural gas. The US$18.2 billion spent on merger and acquisition deals by Chinese companies in 2009 accounted for 13% of total global oil and gas acquisitions (US$144 billion), and for 61% of all acquisitions by national oil companies (US$30 billion). In 2010, Chinese companies again spent approximately US$29.39 billion with more than half being invested in Latin American (US$15.74 billion).[13]

Other major players include Yanchang Petroleum, the fourth largest oil company in China, Sinochem, China United Coal Bed Methane Company (CUCBM) and China Zhenhua Oil, a wholly owned subsidiary of North China Industrial Group (NORINCO).

Chinese oil companies are now operating in 31 countries and have equity in production companies in 20 of these countries, though their equity shares are mostly located in four countries: Kazakhstan, Sudan, Venezuela and Angola.[14]

---

10 Higashi, N (2006), "Energy" in *Chugoku no Tochi Noryoku – The Governability of China*, edited by Kokubun, R, Tokyo.
11 IEA, *Overseas Investments By Chinese National Oil Companies*, 2011, p 1.
12 Facts Global Energy, *An Update of China's Overseas Oil and Gas Investment*, 2009.
13 CNPC Research Institute of Economics & Technology, 2010.
14 IEA , *Overseas Investments By Chinese National Oil Companies*, 2011.

2.2 Upstream activities of key players

(a) CNPC

CPNC is China's largest oil and gas producer and supplier by production and sales volume. CNPC is also a leading integrated energy company and a major oilfield and engineering services provider. PetroChina is the largest listed company within the CNPC group, listed on the Hong Kong Stock Exchange with a market capitalisation of US$262 billion (as at June 11 2012). The issuer, CNPC General Capital Ltd (incorporated in the British Virgin Islands), is a wholly owned subsidiary of China Petroleum Finance Company Limited (CPF; incorporated in China). CNPC has an indirect stake of around 93% in CPF.

CNPC owns and operates 14 oil and gas fields, mostly concentrated in the north and northwest, accounting for 65% and 73% of the total proved crude oil and natural gas reserves in China, respectively. It also has 26 refining and petrochemical plants, and more than 56,800 kilometres of oil and gas pipelines in China. CNPC produced 105 million tons of crude oil and 72.5 billion m^3 of natural gas in 2010, 52% and 75% of China's total respectively. Crude runs in 2010 were 135 million tons, 32% of China's total.[15]

CNPC was the first of the Chinese national oil companies to expand its operations overseas. In the early 1990s, CNPC started to invest in Sudan, Peru and Kazakhstan despite the government's focus at that time on self-reliance and increasing domestic oil output. Its presence in producer countries has been matched by the opening of offices devoted to trading, finance and other market activity in London, New York and elsewhere.[16]

CNPC's overseas petroleum investment activities are concentrated in Africa, South America, Central Asia, and the Middle East. CNPC's upstream, refining, and infrastructure investment in Sudan is by far the company's most successful overseas venture. Currently, the major projects in Sudan are the Blocks 1/2/4 project, the Block 6 project, the Blocks 3/7 project, the Block 13, the Block 15, the Khartoum refinery project and the polypropylene project. Altogether, CNPC has invested at least US$4 billion in Sudan since 1995. Currently, CNPC's equity oil from Sudan is nearly 225,000 barrels per day, accounting for around 40% of its total overseas equity oil production.[17]

(b) Sinopec

Sinopec is the largest integrated petroleum and petrochemical company and the largest refined oil producer in China. Sinopec is also the largest distributor of refined oil products in China by sales volumes. Sinopec runs the largest number of service stations in China. The largest listed entity within the group, Sinopec Corp (China Petroleum & Chemical Corp), is listed on the Hong Kong Stock Exchange with a current market capitalisation of $86 billion. The issuer, Sinopec Group Overseas

---

15 Deutsche Bank, *China Oil and Gas*, June 2012.
16 IEA , *Overseas Investments By Chinese National Oil Companies*, 2011, p 10.
17 Facts Global Energy, *An Update of China's Overseas Oil and Gas Investment*, 2009.

Development Limited, is a British Virgin Islands incorporated entity and is effectively a wholly owned subsidiary of the state-owned Assets Supervision and Administration Commission of the State Council (SASAC).[18]

Sinopec currently explores for, develops and produces crude oil and natural gas in a number of areas across China and Africa. As of December of 31 2011, Sinopec held 192 production licences in China, with an aggregate acreage of 20,325.98 square kilometers (km^2) and with terms ranging from 10 to 80 years, and 297 exploration licences in China for various blocks, with an aggregate acreage of approximately 966,800km^2 and with a maximum term of seven years. As of December of 31 2011, Sinopec also held two production licences in Africa (Anglo Block 18), with an aggregate acreage of 322.57km^2, but currently does not have exploration licenses in Africa.

In 2011, Sinopec produced an average of 1,067 thousand barrels of oil equivalent (BOE) per day in China, of which approximately 77.88% was crude oil and 22.12% was natural gas. Sinopec produced an average of 50 thousand BOE per day in Africa, all of which was crude oil.[19]

(c) *CNOOC*

CNOOC Limited is an upstream company focusing on the exploration, development and production of oil and natural gas. The company is the dominant oil and natural gas producer in offshore China and the third largest energy company in China following CNPC and Sinopec. CNOOC Limited is also one of the largest independent exploration and production companies in the world in terms of reserves and production. CNOOC Ltd is 64.45% owned by its parent, China National Offshore Oil Corporation (CNOOC), a wholly owned subsidiary of the Chinese government under the control of SASAC. CNOOC Limited was established in 1999 and listed in 2001 on both the Hong Kong and the New York stock exchanges. The issuer, CNOOC Finance (2012) Limited is a wholly owned subsidiary incorporated in the British Virgin Islands and is guaranteed by the parent, CNOOC Limited.[20]

In China's offshore waters, the company engages in oil and natural gas exploration, development and production in Bohai, the western South China Sea, the eastern South China Sea and the East China Sea, either independently or through cooperation with foreign partners by production sharing agreements. As of the end of 2011, approximately 71.4% of the company's net proved reserves and approximately 78.9% of its production were located in China's offshore area. In 2011, the company's net oil and gas production amounted to 331.8 million boe. Its growth in production has remained steady in recent years.[21]

As regards independent operations, in recent years, the company has been adding more reserves and production mainly through independent exploration and development in China's offshore waters. As of the end of 2011, approximately 77.7% of the company's net proved reserves and approximately 71.8% of its production in offshore China were derived from the independent projects.

---

18 Deutsche Bank, *China Oil and Gas*, June 2012.
19 Sinopec Annual Report, 2011.
20 Deutsche Bank, *China Oil and Gas*, June 2012.
21 CNOOC Annual Report, 2011.

As for operations under production sharing agreements, CNOOC, the company's controlling shareholder, has the exclusive right to explore and develop oil and natural gas in China's offshore waters with foreign partners through production sharing agreements. CNOOC has transferred to the company all its rights and obligations under all the production sharing agreements (except those relating to its administrative functions), including new production sharing agreements that will be signed in the future. As of the end of 2011, the company had 24 such agreements with 22 partners in force.

Overseas, the company holds interests in oil and natural gas blocks in Indonesia, Iraq, Australia, Nigeria, Uganda, Argentina, the United States, Canada and various other countries. As of December 31 2011, the company's overseas net proved reserves and production accounted for approximately 28.6% and 21.1%, respectively, of the company's total net proved reserves and total net production.

3. Petroleum legal regime

3.1 Petroleum law and relevant provisions

China's petroleum industry has been significantly liberalised in the past 10 years. However, the exploration, production, marketing and distribution of crude oil and natural gas, as well as the production, marketing and distribution of certain refined petroleum products are still subject to regulations issued by many government agencies including the National Development and Reform Commission (NDRC), the Ministry of Land and Resources (MLR), the Ministry of Commerce (MOFCOM), the Ministry of Environmental Protection and the State Maritime Bureau.

In China, oil and gas exploration and production rights are licensed by the State Council and currently, only CNPC, Sinopec, CNOOC and Yanchang Petroleum Group Ltd have exploration and production licences.

The government allows foreign companies to explore for petroleum in China, but only in partnerships with Chinese national oil companies through petroleum contracts or production sharing agreements. In these partnerships, the rights and responsibilities of each party are not equal. For the right to enter the Chinese market, the foreign party must assume much greater risks, as well as the initial investment costs.[22]

Under the applicable laws, CNOOC is responsible for negotiating with foreign partners in offshore upstream activities, while both CNPC and Sinopec have the right to negotiate production sharing agreements with foreign partners in onshore upstream activities.

(a) Regulatory bodies

National Development and Reform Commission (NDRC): The NDRC is responsible for formulating and implementing key policies in respect of petroleum and petrochemical industry, including: formulating guidance plans for annual production, import and export amounts of crude oil, natural gas and gasoline

22 David Blumental, "Upstream Oil and Gas in China", *Doing Business in China*, Juris Publishing, 2009.

nationwide, based on its forecast on macro-economic conditions in China; setting the pricing policy for refined petroleum products; approving certain domestic and overseas resource investment projects which are subject to NDRC's approval as required by the Catalogue of Investment Projects Approved by the Government (2011); and approving foreign investment projects that are in excess of certain investment limits.

National Energy Administration (NEA): Since 1993, when the Ministry of Energy was dismantled, regulatory oversight has been fragmented among different regulatory bodies. Authority has shifted with each subsequent restructuring of the government. The country's energy industry needs a single regulatory body with sufficient authority to carry out regulatory functions in formulating and implementing a national energy policy.

In an effort to manage the problem of fragmented authority over the energy industry, the NEA was established in 2008 to facilitate communication between practitioners and government bodies. The broad mandate of the NEA includes the drafting of energy strategies, proposing reform advice and implementing the management of energy sectors. However, the NEA is under the leadership of the NDRC.

Ministry of Commerce (MOFCOM): MOFCOM has the authority to grant the import and export volume quotas for crude oil and refined products in accordance with market supply and demand in China and China's WTO requirements, to issue import and export licences for crude oil and refined products to oil and gas companies that have obtained import and export quotas, and to examine and approve production sharing contracts in relation to oil and coal seam gas and Sino-foreign equity and cooperative joint venture contracts.

Ministry of Land and Resources (MLR): The MLR oversees the exploration and production of the mineral and oil and gas resources within the national territory. The MLR has the authority for granting, examining and approving oil and gas exploration and production licenses, and the administration of registration and transfer of exploration and production licences.

Ministry of Environmental Protection: The Ministry of Environmental Protection's role is to prevent and control environmental pollution, and to protect the environment and public health.

State Maritime Administration: This body ensures compliance with maritime safety, and also regulates oil spills in the offshore region.

State-Owned Assets Supervision & Administration Commission (SASAC): SASAC regulates state assets held by state-owned enterprises to represent the government shareholder in such enterprises, including the three national oil companies, and to promote the modernisation of state enterprises. All managers of the state oil companies are appointed by the government, with SASAC playing a central role and the State Council making the final decision on all management personnel nominations.

(b) *Types of agreement*

Petroleum production sharing contracts: A foreign enterprise can only participate in exploration and production activities in China by entering into a production sharing contract for a defined geographic area referred to as a 'block'. Such contracts are won by the foreign enterprise either through negotiation or following an invitation to bid from one of the Chinese petroleum companies, followed by approval from the Ministry of Commerce (MOFCOM).

Coal-bed methane production sharing contracts: This is the type of contract entered into between China United Coal Bed Methane Company and a foreign contractor for developing coal-bed methane in China. The terms of such contracts are basically similar to an oil and gas production sharing contract. Generally, only slight differences exist in the provisions governing contract term, relinquishment, minimum exploration commitments, operator, employment, price of coal-bed methane, ownership of assets and data, coal-bed methane destination and marketing.

Shale gas exploration contracts: China started its shale gas bidding scheme in 2011. The bidding is for shale gas prospecting rights, which will have a term of three years. Successful bidders are required to sign a contract with the Ministry of Land and Resources. The terms include minimum work commitments and investment, and compulsory transfer or relinquishment of exploration rights when the obligations are unfilled. Bidders are also required to incorporate local companies in the provinces where their blocks are located when transforming the shale gas prospecting rights to exploitation rights.

(c) *Acquisition of acreage*

The Mineral Resources Law of the People's Republic of China was adopted in 1986 (amended in 1996) by the National People's Congress. The Mineral Resources Law and its supplementary regulations provide the basic legal framework under which exploration licences and production licences are granted. The Mineral Resources Law authorises the Ministry of Land and Resources (MLR) to exercise administrative authority over the exploration and production of mineral and oil resources within China, including its territorial waters.

The MLR has the authority to grant exploration licences and production licences on the basis of competitive bidding or on any other basis it considers appropriate. Applicants for these licences must be companies approved by the State Council to engage in oil and gas exploration and production activities. Currently, only Sinopec, PetroChina, CNOOC and Yanchang Petroleum Group Ltd hold such exploration and production licences.

(d) *Qualification requirements*

The state oil companies and foreign partners enter into new production sharing contracts primarily through bidding organised by the state oil companies and direct negotiation with the those companies. During a typical bidding process, the state oil company determines which blocks are open for bidding and invites foreign enterprises to bid. Potential bidders are required to provide information, including minimum work commitments, exploration expenditures and percentages of share oil payable to the Chinese government. The state oil company evaluates each bid and negotiates a production sharing contract with the successful bidder.

(e) *Duration*

Licence terms: The Ministry of Land and Resources issues full production licences to applicants on the basis of the reserve reports approved by the relevant authorities. The maximum term of a full production license is 30 years unless a special dispensation is given by the State Council. In those circumstances, the maximum term of the full production licence could be 80 years. The full production licence is renewable upon application by the holder at least 30 days prior to expiration of the original term.

At the exploration stage, the exploration period is generally divided into three phases, usually lasting seven years in aggregate. An applicant can also apply for a progressive exploration and production licence that allows the holder to test and develop reserves not yet fully proved. The progressive exploration and production licence has a maximum term of 15 years. When the reserves become proved for a block, the holder must apply for a full production licence in order to undertake production.

Production sharing contract terms: Production sharing contracts typically last for 30 years. The exploration period is generally divided into three phases, of three years, two years and two years, respectively, thereby lasting seven years in aggregate. If there is no commercial discovery by the expiry of the first or second phase of the exploration period, the production sharing contract may be terminated by the contractor. During the exploration period, exploratory and appraisal work is conducted in order to discover petroleum and to enable the parties to determine the commercial viability of any petroleum discovery.

The development period begins when the relevant regulatory authorities have approved the overall development plan, which is prepared upon presentation of seismic evidence proving that the oil field is commercial, and ends when the design, construction, installation, drilling and related research work for the realisation of petroleum production as planned has been completed.

The production period begins when commercial production commences, and usually lasts for 15 years. The construction of large and complex facilities with multiple producing zones may lend itself to longer production periods. Subject to negotiation, options to renew or extend each period may be incorporated in the production sharing contract.

(f) *Minimum work programme*

The foreign contractor must complete a minimum amount of work during the exploration period, generally including drilling a minimum number of wildcat(s), acquiring a fixed amount of seismic data and incurring a minimum amount of exploration expenditure. The foreign contractor is required to pay all exploration costs, which can be recovered according to the production sharing formula after commercial discoveries are made and production begins.

Common appraisal work commitments include the acquisition or reprocessing of seismic images of certain areas, the drilling of wildcat and appraisal wells of specified depths, and evaluation of geological data. The minimum work commitments must be completed within certain timeframes and are enforceable by means of penalty clauses coupled with the state oil company's right of termination if the foreign contractor fails to fulfill such work commitments.

The state oil company and the Chinese government closely supervise all exploration activities. Approval from relevant government authorities may be required for the drilling of wells or for the adoption of the overall development plan. Additionally, the foreign contractor may not substitute wildcat wells with appraisal wells without the state oil company's consent.

Upon expiry of any phase of the exploration period, if any minimum work commitments are unfulfilled and the foreign contractor elects to continue to the next phase, the unfulfilled works shall be added to the minimum work commitment for the next phase, subject to the consent of the state oil company. Alternatively, if the foreign contractor elects to terminate the production sharing contract, regardless of whether the minimum work expenditure requirement has been met, the outstanding work commitments are cumulated, converted into a cash equivalent and paid by the foreign contractor to the Chinese government. On the other hand, the foreign contractor shall not be obliged to reimburse the government for the balance of the minimum work expenditure if the minimum work commitments are fulfilled.[23]

(g) *Assignment and encumbrance*

According to the model contract, the contractor may assign part or all of its rights and/or obligations under the contract to an affiliate with the prior consent of the national oil company in accordance with certain requirements, generally including, but not limited to, the following:

- The assigning company shall submit to the national oil company copies of a written agreement on the corresponding part of its rights and/or obligations to be assigned.
- The assigning company shall guarantee in writing to the national oil company the performance of the assigned obligations.
- No such assignment shall interfere with the performance of the petroleum operations.

---

23 David Blumental, "Upstream Oil and Gas in China", *Doing Business in China*, Juris Publishing, 2009.

Where the contractor wants to assign part or all of its rights and/or obligations under the contract to any third party, such assignment must be reviewed by the national oil company in advance and approved by the Ministry of Commerce. However, the national oil company shall have the right of first refusal in respect of such assignment provided that the conditions offered by it are similar. The national oil company has to exercise this right by means of written notification to the assignor within a specified number of days after the date on which the intended assignment to the third party was notified to the national oil company.

(h) Local content

Throughout the term of the production sharing contract, the foreign contractor is obliged to give preference to the use of Chinese goods, equipment, and services. Such use is often subject to the caveat that the Chinese goods, equipment and services must be competitive in price, quality and/or performance as compared to their international counterparts.

The foreign contractor is also under an obligation to employ and train Chinese personnel and to transfer petroleum technology (including patents, know-how and confidential technology) to the state oil company. With respect to the number of Chinese personnel employed, the foreign contractor must increase the percentage of Chinese personnel employed until the minimum percentage threshold required by the production sharing contract is reached.

(i) National reservation

In some production sharing contracts, the contract requires that all of the insurance items as approved in the insurance programme shall be insured with the Chinese insurance companies or insurance companies in China under the laws of China.

Unlike requirements in other countries, there are no domestic supply provisions in Chinese production sharing contracts. The foreign partners can sell the petroleum to Chinese parties or ship it elsewhere at their own discretion.

However, the destination of the crude oil lifted by the foreign partners may be restricted. In the model contract, it says that in accordance with the decisions of the Chinese government, the national oil company shall notify the contractor (the foreign party) of any prohibited destinations which infringe on the political interests of the People's Republic of China. The contractor must not deliver the crude oil to the prohibited destinations so notified.

(j) Environment

Both onshore and offshore activities are subject to increasingly tight environmental regulations following several oil spills that have occurred in recent years including the Penglai 19-3 accident in 2011, where Conoco Philips was the operator.

Operations must comply with various applicable environmental laws and regulations, including laws and regulations administered by the national and local government environmental protection bureau.

Government agencies set national and local environmental protection standards. The relevant environment protection bureau must approve or review each stage of a project. Project owners must file an environmental impact statement or, in some cases, an environmental impact assessment outline before an approval can be issued. The filing must demonstrate that the project conforms to applicable environmental standards. The relevant environmental protection bureau generally issues approvals and permits for projects using modern pollution control measurement technology.

The national and local environmental laws and regulations impose fees for the discharge of waste substances above prescribed levels, require the payment of fines for serious violations, and provide that the national and local governments may at their own discretion close or suspend any facility which fails to comply with orders requiring it to cease or rectify operations causing environmental damage.

In 2010, the government issued Provisional Measures on the Abandonment of Offshore Petroleum Production Facilities (*Fagainengyuan* (2010) 1305), requiring offshore petroleum developers to prepare an abandonment plan before commencing commercial production and to provide and allocate special funds for environmental protection and ecological restoration purposes. The abandonment fund has to be paid on a monthly basis after the commencement of commercial production.

(k) Governing law and dispute resolution

Generally, petroleum operations in China are governed by Chinese law. If there is no relevant Chinese law governing a disputed matter, the applicable laws widely used in petroleum producing countries will apply. If the adoption of a new law leads to a material change which alters the economic benefit accruing to the foreign contractor, the production sharing contract will usually provide that the parties will make the necessary revisions to the contract to maintain the level of benefit to which the foreign contractor was entitled prior to the change in law. Such a clause is commonly known as a 'stabilisation clause'. However, it has been reported that a recent change to CNPC's model production sharing contract has eliminated the stabilisation clause in it. Foreign companies should be aware of this change. In China, production sharing contracts are usually drawn up in both Chinese and English, with both versions having equal force and effect.

In production sharing contracts, an obligation for the parties to consult for a fixed period of time before commencing arbitration is usually included to promote an amicable and flexible relationship. If the parties cannot amicably resolve the dispute, they may agree to refer the arbitration to the China International Economic and Trade Arbitration Commission (CIETAC) in accordance with its arbitration rules, or to an arbitration tribunal in a mutually agreed location and in accordance with the rules of the United Nations Commission on International Trade Law (UNCITRAL).

Typically, each party may appoint an arbitrator and the arbitrators so appointed will appoint a third arbitrator who must be a citizen of a country with formal diplomatic relations with China.

3.2 Government take

Companies or Sino-foreign projects undertaking oil and gas exploration and development activities in China are subject to a variety of taxes, fees and royalty payments as the table below shows:

Figure 2: Tax Items in upstream oil and gas sector

Tax item	Tax base	Tax rate
Enterprise income tax	Taxable income	Effective from January 1 2008, the statutory corporate tax rate is 25%, but a statutory corporate tax rate of 15% is applicable to operations in certain western regions in China which qualify for certain tax incentives through to the year 2020.
Value added tax	Turnover	13% for liquefied natural gas, natural gas, liquefied petroleum gas, agricultural film and fertilisers and 17% for other items. Under production sharing contracts, the rate is 5%.
Business tax	Income from oil and gas transportation services	3%
Resources tax	Value sold	Since December 1 2010, for 12 provinces in western China the resource tax on crude oil and natural gas has been assessed on the basis of value instead of quantity, and collected at the rate of 5% of the value sold. This taxation method has been applied nationwide since November 1 2011.
Compensatory fee for mineral resources	Turnover	1% for crude oil and natural gas
Crude oil special gain levy[24]	Sales amount above specific threshold	From November 1 2011 , the threshold above which the crude oil special gain levy is levied on domestic crude oil sold was raised from US$40 per barrel to US$55 per barrel, with five progressive tax rates varying from 20% to 40% applying.

continued on following page

Tax item	Tax base	Tax rate
Exploration licence fee	Area	Rmb100 to 500 per km^2 per year
Production licence fee	Area	Rmb1,000 per km^2 per year
Royalty fee[25]	Production volume	Progressive rate of 0%–12.5% for crude oil and 0%–3% for natural gas
Export tariffs	Export value of petroleum oil	5%
City construction tax	Actual paid production tax and business tax	1%–7%
Education surcharge	Actual paid production tax and business tax	3%
Local education surcharge	Actual paid production tax and business tax	2%

(a) ***Royalties***

Chinese and foreign enterprises engaged in the cooperative exploitation of onshore and offshore oil resources must pay royalties according to the relevant regulations. Payment of royalties is stipulated in:

- the Provisional Regulations on the Payment by Sino-Foreign Cooperative Joint Ventures of Royalties for the Exploitation of Onshore Oil Resources (Onshore Royalties Regulations), promulgated by the Ministry of Finance in 1990 and amended in 1995; and
- the Regulations on the Payment by Sino-Foreign Cooperative Joint Ventures of Royalties for the Exploitation of Offshore Oil Resources (Offshore Royalties Regulations), promulgated by the Ministry of Finance in 1989.

24 Collected on a quarterly basis.

25 It must be paid in cash and is only applicable to Sino-foreign oil and gas exploration and development cooperative projects in China. However, from December 1 2011, the royalty fee payable by new Sino-foreign oil and gas exploration and development cooperative projects in western regions was replaced by the resource tax, while those cooperative projects operating under contracts signed before December 1 2011 continue to be subject to the royalty fee until the contracts expire.

Royalties are calculated based on annual gross production and are payable in kind by installments to the Chinese tax authorities. The amount of the royalties varies up to 12.5% based on the annual production of the relevant property.

The 1995 amendment of the Onshore Royalties Regulations raised the minimum amount of annual production under which enterprises are exempt from royalties from 50,000 to 500,000 or 1,000,000 tons, as an added incentive to foreign cooperation in oil exploitation.

The Chinese government has provided CNOOC with a royalty exemption in all its fields (both independently operated properties and properties operated under production sharing contracts) for up to one million tons, or approximately seven million barrels of oil equivalent (boe) per year for its crude oil production, and for up to 2 billion m^3 (approximately 70.6 billion cubic feet or 11.8 million boe) per year for its natural gas production.

In 2011, the Chinese State Council amended the Provisional Regulation on the Resource Tax. As a result, since November 1 2011, the royalties payable to the Chinese government have been replaced by the resource tax, currently levied at 5% on sales revenues from crude oil and natural gas. Production sharing contracts signed before December 1 2011 are not affected by the amendment of the Provisional Regulation on the Resource Tax and are still subject to royalties until the contracts expire.

(b) *Bonus*

Generally the foreign contractor will pay a signature bonus to the state oil company upon signing the production sharing contract or within a certain time period thereafter. This is a lump-sum payment for the right to exploit the petroleum resource. The amount may be defined by the government based on the volume of petroleum resources and the economic value of the field.

(c) *Rental fees*

According to the Mineral Resources laws of China, the holder has to pay an annual exploration licence fee of Rmb100 per km^2 for each of the first three years. Afterwards, the annual fee increases by an additional Rmb100 per km^2 per year up to a maximum of Rmb500 per km^2. A holder of a full production licence has to pay an annual full production right usage fee of Rmb1,000 per km^2.

(d) *Special participation*

The state oil companies have the right to take participating interests of up to 51% in any oil or gas field discovered in the contract area, and may exercise this right after the foreign contractor has made commercially viable discoveries. The foreign contractor retains the remaining participating interest.

(e)] *Corporate tax*

As from January 1 2008, the statutory corporate tax rate is 25%, although a statutory corporate tax rate of 15% is applicable to operations in certain western regions in China which qualify for certain tax incentives until the year 2020.

(f) *Payments, costs, and cost recovery*

In addition to the payment of the signature bonus, the foreign contractor is responsible for all of the appraisal costs and bears the risk of failure if the appraisal wells are found dry. Effectively, the foreign contractor is required to carry the state oil company through the appraisal period.

If the foreign contractor fails to enter into the development period after incurring appraisal costs, such costs shall be deemed its loss and shall not be reimbursed.

The development costs are paid by the parties in proportion to their respective participating interests (generally 51% by the state oil company and 49% by the foreign party), unless the state oil company decides not to participate in the development, or decides to participate to an extent less than its participating interest. In such circumstances, the foreign contractor will be liable for any shortfall in the development costs. The foreign contractor is permitted to use its participating interest in the production sharing contract as security, subject to prior notification to the state oil company and provided that the security over the participating interest does not adversely affect the interests of the state oil company.

In the phase of commercial production, production is allocated between the parties after various deductibles including the special gain levy, VAT (at the rate of 5%), consolidated industrial and commercial tax, royalties (or resources tax if the production sharing was signed after November 1 2011), and unrecovered costs are subtracted from the gross annual production of the oil field.

After VAT, royalties or resource tax and other levies are paid to the state oil company and/or the relevant Chinese government authorities, a fixed percentage of the remaining production is deemed 'cost recovery oil' and prioritised for the reimbursement of operating costs for the production period.

In general, cost recovery for offshore production sharing contracts is from 50% to 62.5%, and for onshore contracts from 50% to 60% (when recovery of deemed interest on development costs is included). Cost recovery mainly involves recovery of the following expenditure in the order given below:

- petroleum royalties (replaced by resource tax for production sharing contracts concluded after November 1 2011);
- production and operating expenses;
- exploration expenditure;
- development expenditure;
- deemed interest on development costs, currently 9%.

(g) *Production sharing*

The remainder of the gross production after the deduction of taxes and recovered costs is added to the pool for profit production. Profit production is shared between the government and the production sharing contract participants based on the allocation factor stipulated in the contract.

In some production sharing contracts, the balance of gross production after the above allocations is deemed 'remainder oil' and is divided into 'share oil' which goes to the Chinese government account, and 'allocable remainder oil' which is shared by the parties in accordance with their participating interests.

Depending upon the value of the allocation factor, which is in turn dependent upon the level of production, the percentages of the remainder oil shared between the state oil company and the contractor will fluctuate. A high allocation factor implies a small amount of share oil received by the Chinese government. As such, the value of the allocation factor is subject to considerable negotiation.[26]

Figure 3: Example of the production sharing formula under Sino-foreign production sharing contracts

Percentage of annual gross production	Allocation
5.0%	Production tax (VAT) payable to the Chinese government
0-12.5%	Royalty oil payable to the Chinese government[27]
5.0%	Resource tax payable to the Chinese government[28]
50% – 62.5%[29]	Cost recovery oil allocated according to the following priority: 1. recovery of current year operating costs by national oil company and foreign partner(s); 2. recovery of earlier exploration costs by foreign partner(s); 3. recovery of development costs and deemed interest by national oil company and foreign partner(s)based on participating interests; and 4. any excess, allocated to the remainder oil
32.5%[30]	Remainder oil allocated according to the following formula: 1. (1-X) multiplied by 32.5% represents share oil payable to the Chinese Government; 2. X multiplied by 32.5% represents remainder oil distributed according to each partner's participating interest

Source: Annual report of CNOOC 2011.

26 CNOOC Annual Report 2011

27 As a result of the amendment to the Provisional Regualtion on the Resource Tax by the State Council, as from November 1 2011, the royalties payable to the Chinese government have been replaced by resource tax for new production sharing contracts.

28 Assumes annual gross production of more than 4 million metric tons, approximately 30 million boe. For lower amounts of production, the royalty rate will be lower and the cost recovery will be greater than 50.0% by the amount that the royalty rate is less than 12.5%.

29 The ratio 'X' (the allocation factor) is agreed in each PSC based on commercial considerations and ranges from 8% to 100%.

4. Current issues

In recent years, China has focused on developing clean and unconventional domestic energy resources to fuel the country's expanding energy demand and ease its reliance on imported oil, natural gas, and liquefied natural gas. Since 2011, the government has focused on promoting shale gas commercial development through a block bidding scheme, supportive policies and pilot development areas. According to the survey released by the Ministry of Land Resources, China is estimated to have huge shale gas reserves, approximately 25 trillion m^3 of recoverable reserves. However, at the moments there is no commercial production of shale gas in China. It is still unclear whether China will be able to develop these reserves on a commercial scale due to geological and technological challenges.

In June 2011, China issued its first shale exploration tender with an offer of four blocks to a group of six blue-chip state-owned energy and mining companies. Although foreign energy companies were not permitted to participate directly in this first bid round, they are permitted to form joint ventures with and supply technology services to Chinese companies engaged in the exploration and production of shale gas and liquids.

On September 10 2012, the Ministry of Land Resources announced the commencement of China's second round of shale gas bidding. Bidders were invited to bid for 20 blocks located in eight provinces, with a total area of 20,002.16km^2. A significant change in the bidder qualification requirements compared to those in the first round is that Sino-foreign joint ventures (controlled by Chinese parties) are now allowed to participate in the bidding.

The development of shale gas opens business opportunities for specialised international oil companies and foreign oilfield service companies. Both CNPC and Sinopec have cooperated with international oil companies including BP, Chevron, Shell and Total in developing some shale gas finds. In addition, service requirements are much higher for shale gas developments, with specialised equipment, supplies and technical expertise needed (eg, higher-horsepower rigs for drilling long horizontal wells, using multi-stage hydraulic fracturing). The current Chinese oilfield service industry will likely need outside help.

5. Conclusion

Since China's accession to the World Trade Organisation, the oil and gas sector in China has been liberalised gradually. With the continuing growth of the petroleum sector, foreign companies will find opportunities in all segments of the industry. However, while the opportunities may be great, so will the challenges, and it will be those companies that can navigate the obstacles will reap the greatest reward.

India

Anupama Sen
Oxford Institute for Energy Studies

1. Introduction

India, a country of 1.2 billion people comprising the world's second most populous nation, is widely regarded as one of the world's fastest growing developing economies and largest emerging consumer markets.[1] Following the onset of the great recession[2] in 2009, while the economies of the OECD collectively entered recession, the Indian economy grew by a staggering 9%.[3] Yet it is also a country which contains the largest number of poor people living in any single nation.[4] These extremes are representative of the types of policy conflicts being faced in many economic sectors in India, including most significantly in energy and hydrocarbons – the struggle to move from a former centrally planned autarchic system of operating, to one that is more market-oriented and connected with international trade flows.[5]

India's stellar economic growth is arguably underpinned by energy, and by extension, the extraction of energy sources.[6] The oil and gas sector accounted for roughly 40% of the value of mineral production in 2009, and for 2.6% of GDP.[7] Of India's total primary energy consumption of 559 million tons of oil equivalent, coal comprised 53%, oil 29%, natural gas 10%, and other sources, including nuclear, hydro and renewable, 8%.[8] Although economic activity has historically been based on coal, which is indigenously mined, marketed and distributed, data shows that India's dependence on coal imports has been increasing – in 1980 about 99% of coal

1 The bulk of these consumers come from a rapidly growing middle class. There is no standard definition of this middle class and various estimates of its size have been made both on the basis of income, as well on the basis of ownership of assets; a World Bank estimate puts it at 250 million people and growing; other estimates put it higher: Sen, A and Jamasb, T "Diversity in Unity: An Empirical Analysis of Electricity Sector Reform in Indian States" *The Energy Journal*; 33 (1); 83–130 (2012).

2 A term commonly used to refer to the global economic downturn which began with the sub-prime mortgage crisis in the USA in 2007.

3 Jain, AK *Natural Gas in India: Liberalisation and Policy*, Oxford University Press (2011). Although this figure fell to between 6% and 8% by 2011, this was still a healthy rate of growth in comparison with the developed world, at the time.

4 Sen, A "A Study of Auctions for Hydrocarbons Exploration in India", Oxford Institute for Energy Studies Working Paper, forthcoming (2013).

5 Sen, A "A Study of Auctions for Hydrocarbons Exploration in India", Oxford Institute for Energy Studies Working Paper, forthcoming (2013); Jain, AK *Natural Gas in India: Liberalisation and Policy*, Oxford University Press (2011). India's upstream regime for exploration was liberalised in 1999, but these policy conflicts are still apparent.

6 Although a large part of energy requirements are met through imports, these represent a cost to the economy and hence a constraint to economic growth.

7 Directorate General of Hydrocarbons, Ministry of Petroleum and Natural Gas, Government of India, *Petroleum Exploration Activities in India 2010–11* (2010), available from www.dghindia.org.

8 BP *Statistical Review of World Energy* 2012, available at bp.com/statisticalreview.

consumption was met through indigenous production, whereas by 2011, this figure dropped to roughly 93%.[9] These developments signal a shift in the composition of primary energy which has gathered impetus over the last decade. Although roughly 75% of oil continues to be imported annually, there has at the same time been a growing emphasis on increasing the domestic production of both oil and natural gas, primarily through inviting greater private investment in exploration.

It has been argued that the Indian economy is in a state of gradual transition from central planning to market orientation, and that the unprecedented energy challenges it faces are a part of this.[10] This chapter aims to provide an overview and critical analysis of one crucial aspect of the transition – the struggle to transform India's upstream regime for oil and gas exploration from a formerly publicly owned and operated sector with very little competition to a more dynamic structure reflecting mixed ownership. It begins with a discussion of the evolution of the sector and upstream activities. Section 3 describes the main components of the exploration regime. Section 4 discusses current issues in upstream regulation, and Section 5 concludes.

2. Upstream activities

The evolution of India's upstream hydrocarbons sector has mirrored that of its post-independence[11] socio-economic trajectory.[12] The linchpin of policy making was laid down in a constitutional division of power between the federal government, and each of India's state governments, specifying separate lists or 'schedules' of areas subject to policy making by the federal and state governments, with residual powers largely resting with the federal government.[13] This remains extremely relevant for the hydrocarbons sector as, constitutionally, all royalties from offshore acreages flow to the federal government, and royalties from onshore acreages to the states.

As the distribution of most goods and services at the time was limited to urban agglomerations and carried out by a small number of private companies, the independent government set out to establish public sector enterprises[14] to expand the availability of what it considered essential goods and services (including energy), to the vast majority of the population who lacked access to them. These enterprises soon evolved into large, vertically integrated monolithic companies which tended to control all aspects of production and distribution.

A similar structure was put in place for the oil and gas sector. Prior to independence, exploration was carried out primarily through two private companies, the Assam Oil Company and the Burma Oil Company – which together accounted for the production of roughly 250,000 tons of hydrocarbons.[15] These companies continued operating after independence in 1947. In the decade following

9 Government of India (2007), Integrated Energy Policy Report.

10 Jain, AK *Natural Gas in India: Liberalisation and Policy*, Oxford University Press (2011).

11 India gained independence in 1947.

12 Jain, AK and Sen, A "Natural Gas in India: An Analysis of Policy"; Oxford Institute for Energy Studies Working Paper 50; Oxford, UK (2011).

13 As of 2012, the Republic of India is a federal union comprising 28 states and seven union territories.

14 These were referred to as 'public sector units' at the time, which reaffirmed their alliances with government ministries and distinguished them from corporations, in a sense.

15 Petroleum Federation of India (Petrofed) and Pricewaterhouse Coopers India, *Paper on Review of E&P Licensing Policy* (2005); available at www.petrofed.org.

independence, exploration began to be increasingly administered and carried out by the government of India, primarily through the Oil and Natural Gas Directorate, formed in 1955, which in 1959 became the Oil and Natural Gas Commission (ONGC) and effectively, India's first national oil company (much later, in 1994, it was officially reorganised to form a public limited company – Oil and Natural Gas Corporation).[16]

Oil India Ltd (OIL), a company owned two-thirds by the Assam and Burma Oil companies, and one-third by the federal government, was also established (in 1959) to develop discoveries and boost the pace of exploration in the north-eastern region (it was nationalised later, in 1981, becoming India's second national oil company).[17] In 1984, the government set up the Gas Authority of India Limited (GAIL), to develop a gas distribution network.[18] An upstream regulator, the Directorate General of Hydrocarbons (DGH) was established in 1993, and tasked with providing technical consultations to the Ministry of Petroleum and Natural Gas, as well as oversight on exploration activity. A downstream regulator, the Petroleum and Natural Gas Regulatory Board, was established much later, in 2006, to provide oversight on downstream issues. Other public sector companies were set up to operate in the refining and marketing sectors, which eventually[19] diversified into upstream exploration.

The operations of these public sector companies and the distributional objectives that they were meant to fulfil on behalf of the federal government were reflected in the way their products were priced and allocated, which was also representative of India's central planning approach. In hydrocarbons, as the entire chain of production, marketing and distribution was administered by the government, this effectively meant that the largest consumers of energy products were public sector enterprises in downstream sectors such as power and fertilisers. In order to keep the prices of products low, it became common practice to apply a subsidy to hydrocarbons sold from the national oil companies to marketing and distribution companies, and then again to the price of the final product sold by major energy consuming sectors such as power to the end-consumer. The subsidy burden was, at various periods of time, shared between the federal government, the national oil companies and marketing companies. This created a chain of distortions in energy pricing, which over time added to the budget deficit and to a significant loss of revenues for the national oil companies and marketing companies.[20] Pricing has remained a controversial issue in the upstream sector, and it is generally carried out according to the fiscal regime governing each producing field.

16 *Ibid.*

17 *Ibid.*

18 GAIL later diversified into joint ventures in upstream exploration.

19 These companies included Hindustan Petroleum Corporation Limited, Oil India Limited and Bharat Petroleum Corporation Limited.

20 It has been argued that the lack of transparent pricing mechanisms have created a situation where the true level of demand for hydrocarbons remains unknown, and that it is very likely that excess demand has been created at very low prices; see Jain, AK and Sen, A "Natural Gas in India: An Analysis of Policy"; Oxford Institute for Energy Studies Working Paper 50; Oxford, UK (2011). Public sector oil companies also continue to suffer from the effects of prolonged subsidies despite an unprecedented policy decision by the federal government in 2010 to liberalise the prices of petrol at the retail level and end the subsidy regime for petrol. For instance, in 2011, Oil and Natural Gas Corp reported a loss of nearly US$900 million; see Jain, *AK Natural Gas in India: Liberalisation and Policy*, Oxford University Press (2011).

The national oil companies were relatively successful in their early efforts, evidenced by large discoveries in the western offshore (the Bombay High fields) by the mid 1970s. The Oil and Natural Gas Commission and Oil India Ltd dominated exploration from the 1950s to the late 1970s, with all activity carried out within the public sector. Although their early discoveries sustained production up to the 1990s, targets set by the federal government relating to the accumulation of reserves under each of the five-year plans following these large initial discoveries consistently failed to be met (the impact of this began to be felt in the early 1990s, when it was clear that the Bombay High fields were beginning to plateau and no significant new discoveries had been made).[21] This reason, combined with factors relating to capital and technology constraints, led to the launch of the earliest bidding rounds for exploration acreage, based on production sharing contracts, beginning from 1980.[22]

Prior to the liberalisation of the upstream sector in 1998, the federal government carried out nine bidding rounds for exploration acreages between 1980 and 1995 (table 2.1). In addition to these, there were two rounds of auctions of small and medium-sized fields that had been discovered by the national oil companies, but which they lacked the resources to develop (table 2.2).[23] Further, the government attempted to upgrade the information on the country's hydrocarbons potential in 1993, 1994 and 1995, by inviting bids from specialised companies for the conduct of speculative surveys within a fixed two-year period.[24]

These pre-liberalisation era bidding rounds were characterised by the role of the national oil companies – which were heavily involved in the identification of blocks for auctioning, in bid evaluation, and which were also able to participate in exploration ventures, initially through a 30% carried interest and in later rounds through a 25%–40% working interest.[25] The main criteria for evaluating bids under these pre-liberalisation rounds were the technical and financial capability of companies, work programme, and commercial terms offered to the government.[26] The fiscal terms of contracts tended to vary under each of these rounds. Very few contracts were signed under the pre-liberalisation regime.

Pressure to reform and liberalise the upstream regime came from both the private and public sector. Private companies argued that the incentive structure was flawed – given their independent exploration activities, national oil companies had an incentive to hide information on prospectivity – and therefore, the selection of acreage for the bidding rounds was subject to moral hazard. A similar argument was made in relation to the national oil companies' carried and working interest shares in exploration ventures – in the event of a discovery, the national oil companies were liable for the entire royalty – it was argued that this acted as a disincentive to them

21 Proved oil reserves steadily declined from 6.1 billion barrels to 5 billion barrels between 1991 and 1999, and oil production declined from 720,000 barrels of oil per day (bopd) to 590,000 bopd from 1989 to 1993, after which it rose again to roughly 770,000 bopd in 1995, and then appeared to plateau; *BP, Statistical Review of World Energy* 2012, available at bp.com/statisticalreview.

22 Petroleum Federation of India (Petrofed) and Pricewaterhouse Coopers India, *Paper on Review of E&P Licensing Policy* (2005); available at www.petrofed.org.

23 *Ibid.*

24 *Ibid.*

25 *Ibid.*

26 *Ibid.*

which created inefficiencies in the operation of the venture.[27] Arguments for liberalisation from within the government emerged following a slowdown in reserve accumulation, and a growing need to attract the capital and expertise needed to enter into deepwater activity.[28]

The upstream regime was eventually liberalised through the launch of the new exploration licensing policy on February 10 1999. A key statement from the policy resolution reads:

> *In order to attract private investment in [the] oil sector, [the] Government of India had been offering exploration blocks to private companies from time to time. There have so far been nine rounds of exploration bidding and [the] Government of India has entered into contracts for exploration by private companies through joint venture arrangements. The demand for petroleum is expected to rise rapidly and it is necessary to step up the level of investment in exploration to hasten the pace of reserve accretion, which can serve as a base for higher levels of domestic production.*[29]

Table 2.1: Pre-liberalisation exploration rounds, 1980–1995

Year	*Round*	*Number of blocks offered*			*Bids received*	*Contracts signed*		
		Offshore	*Onshore*	*Total*		*Offshore*	*Onshore*	*Total*
1980	1	17	15	32	4	1	0	1
1982	2	42	8	50	0	0	0	0
1986	3	27	0	27	13	4	0	4
1991	4	39	33	72	24	2	3	5
1993	5	29	16	45	15	4	2	6
1993	6	17	29	46	20	2	3	5
1994	7	17	28	45	12	2	3	5
1994	8	15	19	34	38	1	3	4
1995	9	10	18	28	22	1	1	2

Source: Petroleum Federation of India (Petrofed) and Pricewaterhouse Coopers India, Paper on Review of E&P Licensing Policy *(2005), p 87; available at www.petrofed.org/.*

27 *Ibid.*
28 *Ibid.*
29 Policy Resolution O-19018/22/95-ONG.DO.VI, Ministry of Petroleum and Natural Gas.

Table 2.2: Bidding rounds for developing small and medium discovered fields, 1992–1993

Year	*Round*	*Medium sized fields*		*Small sized fields*		*Bids received*	*Number of fields for which contracts signed*
		Offshore	*Onshore*	*Offshore*	*Onshore*		
1992	1	6	6	10	21	117	18
1993	2	2	6	4	29	54	12

Source: Petroleum Federation of India (Petrofed) and Pricewaterhouse Coopers India, Paper on Review of E&P Licensing Policy *(2005), p 92; available at www.petrofed.org.*

Nine rounds of the new policy had been carried out as of 2012; table 2.3 below summarises them in relation to the prevailing economic climate.

Table 2.3: Summary of upstream activities under the new exploration licensing policy bidding rounds

Bidding round	*Year*	*Blocks offered*	*Blocks bid for*	*Blocks awarded*	*Contracts signed*	*Oil price (nominal US$ per barrel)*	*Number of discoveries*[30]
NELP 1	1999	48	28	25	24	24.26	NA
NELP 2	2000	25	23	23	23	37.22	9
NELP 3	2002	27	24	23	23	31.29	14
NELP 4	2003	24	21	21	20	35.25	14
NELP 5	2005	20	20	20	20	62.80	26
NELP 6	2006	55	52	52	52	72.69	25
NELP 7	2007	57	45	44	41	78.53	67
NELP 8	2009	70	36	34	32	64.66	28
NELP 9	2010	34	33	33	13	82.00	33

Sources: Sen, A "A Study of Auctions for Hydrocarbons Exploration in India", Oxford Institute for Energy Studies Working Paper, forthcoming (2013); Directorate General of Hydrocarbons, Ministry of Petroleum and Natural Gas, Government of India, Petroleum Exploration Activities in India 2010-11*; available at www.dghindia.org; US Energy Information Agency (2012).*

The new exploration licensing policy, was a hybrid regime;[31] its main components included a provision for companies to recover 100% of their costs, profit sharing between the contractor(s) and the government based on a progressive pre-tax sliding-scale investment multiple[32] and a fixed royalty rate. The next section sets out these components of the regime, and of the scoring system that was put into place to invite bidding from prospective investors on blocks selected by the government. The new policy regime was only ever meant to be a bridge to a more flexible open acreage licensing policy, allowing companies to identify and nominate prospective acreage which could then be allocated or auctioned by the government. However, the new exploration licensing policy continues to survive more than a decade later, during which the open acreage licensing policy has repeatedly been postponed on the basis of the lack of a national data repository.[33]

Table 2.4 Summary of main terms of the new exploration licensing policy upstream regime of 1999

	Description
Competitiveness	• No mandatory state participation and no carried interest of the state • National oil companies compete on a level playing field with the private sector in bidding for acreage • Contractors (companies) free to market crude oil and natural gas in the domestic market[34]

continued overleaf

30 Refers to number of discoveries made in that year, and not to specific rounds.

31 It contained a mix of regressive and progressive features.

32 This is defined as the ratio of cumulative net income to cumulative investment, rounded off to the third decimal place.

33 At the time of writing, the government announced another delay to the launch of an open acreage policy in 2012, instead announcing that there would be a 10th round of the new exploration licensing policy.

34 This provision contained inherent policy conflicts; see Section 3 for details.

	Description
Fiscal Terms	• Royalty for crude oil set at 12.5% for onshore and 10% for offshore areas. Royalty for natural gas set at 10%. To encourage deepwater exploration, royalty charged at 5% for the first seven years of production for areas that lie beyond 400 metres bathymetry (deepwater). • No signature, discovery, or production bonuses. • No customs duty on imports required for petroleum operations. • A seven-year tax holiday from the start of commercial production.[35] • Fiscal stability during the contract period. • 100% recovery of exploration, development and production costs with unlimited carry-forward, applicable to the entire contract area. • Profit sharing based on a pre-tax investment multiple. • Companies, including the national oil companies, to be paid international prices for oil. • A model production sharing contract.
Administration	• Blocks to be carved out and offered on auction, with the Directorate General of Hydrocarbons continuing to play a key role in the identification of blocks. • An empowered committee of secretaries, comprising the Secretaries for Petroleum and Natural Gas, Finance, and Law, would look at bid evaluation criteria, negotiate with bidders when necessary, and make recommendations to the Cabinet Committee on Economic Affairs for the final award of blocks. • Half of the royalty from offshore blocks was to be credited to a hydrocarbon development fund to promote activities related to exploration, such as the acquisition of geological data, the building of institutions, and the advertisement of investment opportunities in the upstream sector. • The new exploration licensing policy was subject to the Conciliation and Arbitration Act (1996).

Source: Sen, A "A Study of Auctions for Hydrocarbons Exploration in India", Oxford Institute for Energy Studies Working Paper, forthcoming (2013); adapted from Comptroller and Auditor General of India, Performance Audit of Hydrocarbon Production Sharing Contracts (Ministry of Petroleum and Natural Gas), *Report 19 of 2011–12 for the period ended March 2011; available at saiindia.gov.in/english/home/Recent/Recent.html.*

The impact of the new exploration licensing policy in accelerating exploration is difficult to gauge accurately, specifically as there have been concerns over the implementation of contracts, including disputes over the extension of exploration phases (and relinquishment).[36] Table 2.4 summarises the official data on progress in exploration across India's 26 sedimentary basins, covering 3.14 million square kilometres (km^2).[37]

Table 2.4: Status of exploration in India's sedimentary basins

	1995 %	1998 %	2005 %	2010 %
Unexplored	50	41	22	12
Poorly explored	17	17	22	22
Moderate/ well explored	15	15	19	22
Exploration initiated	18	27	37	44

Source: Sen, A "A Study of Auctions for Hydrocarbons Exploration in India", Oxford Institute for Energy Studies Working Paper, forthcoming (2012); Directorate General of Hydrocarbons, Ministry of Petroleum and Natural Gas, Government of India, Petroleum Exploration Activities in India 2010-11*; available from www.dghindia.org.*

As of 2012, roughly 260 production sharing contracts had been signed under the new exploration licensing policy, and US$16 billion of investment committed. Approximately 600 million metric tonnes of hydrocarbons had also been added to reserves. The next section describes the main elements of the new exploration licensing policy.

3. Petroleum legal regime

The primary legislation pertaining to the upstream sector is the Oilfields Regulation (and Development) Act 1948, which provides for the regulation of oilfields and development of mineral oil.[38] The Petroleum and Natural Gas Rules 1959, drawn up under Sections 5 and 6 of the act regulate the grant of exploration licenses and

35 This was applied differently for oil and gas, due to disputes over the definition of 'mineral oil'. It was eventually withdrawn in the ninth bidding round.

36 Discussed in Section 4.

37 The basins are categorised by their prospectivity. Category I – 'established commercial production'; Category II- 'known accumulation of hydrocarbons but no commercial production'; Category III – 'considered geologically prospective'; Category IV – 'uncertain potential which may be prospective by analogy with similar basins in the world'. (DGH, 2010).

38 Comptroller and Auditor General of India, *Performance Audit of Hydrocarbon Production Sharing Contracts (Ministry of Petroleum and Natural Gas)*, Report 19 of 2011–12 for the period ended March 2011; available at http://saiindia.gov.in/english/home/Recent/Recent.html.

mining leases for petroleum and natural gas. These rules also specify the constitutional division of power on oil and gas:[39] the federal government has the power to grant exploration licences and mining leases for offshore areas, while the state governments hold this remit for onshore areas.

Grant of license or lease: (1) A license or lease in respect of

- *any land or mineral underlying the ocean within the territorial waters or continental shelf of India vested in the Union, shall be granted by the Central Government; and*
- *any land vested in a State Government, shall be granted by the State Government with the previous approval of the Central Government.*[40]

3.1 Petroleum law and relevant provisions

(a) Regulatory bodies

The Ministry of Petroleum and Natural Gas is responsible for the exploration and production of petroleum and natural gas, including the administration of the Oilfields Regulation and Development Act 1948.[41] On April 8 1993, the federal government established the upstream regulator, the Directorate General of Hydrocarbons, via a policy resolution.

The Directorate General of Hydrocarbons shall have the following functions and responsibilities:

- *To provide technical advice to the Ministry of Petroleum and Natural Gas on issues relevant to the exploration and optimal exploitation of hydrocarbons in the country and on the strategy of taking up exploration and exploitation of oil and gas reserves abroad by the national oil companies.*[42]

The Directorate General of Hydrocarbons is essentially the primary link between exploration companies and the government. Its functions include the selection of acreages for auction, conduct of bidding rounds, evaluation of bids, and assistance to the ministry on contract enforcement. It is arguably not an independent regulator, perhaps evidenced by the fact that it is staffed by employees seconded from the two national oil companies – Oil and Natural Gas Corp and Oil India Ltd.[43] The resolution also does not specify a separation of the technical function from regulatory oversight. Exploration activities are also subject to occasional audits by the Comptroller and Auditor General of India.[44] In addition, the legislative branch has indirect oversight through Parliamentary submissions by the ministry.

---

39 The Indian Constitution, Seventh Schedule, Union List, Item 53 and Item 54.

40 Petroleum and Natural Gas Rules 1959, Rule 5 (1).

41 Comptroller and Auditor General of India, *Performance Audit of Hydrocarbon Production Sharing Contracts (Ministry of Petroleum and Natural Gas)*, Report 19 of 2011–12 for the period ended March 2011; available at http://saiindia.gov.in/english/home/Recent/Recent.html.

42 Government of India Policy Resolution O-20013/2/92-ONG, D-III, Point 4(a); available at www.dghindia.org/pdf/Resolution.pdf.

43 This was meant to be an interim strategy when the Directorate General of Hydrocarbons was first established, but this practice has persisted.

44 In 2011, the CAG published an audit of a sample of 20 Production Sharing Contracts under NELP, alleging that the federal government's policy of granting extensions and its lack of enforcement of relinquishment clauses may in some cases have led to a loss of revenue to the exchequer (CAG, 2011).

(b) ***Types of agreements***

The primary agreement used in upstream exploration is the production sharing contract. The ministry publishes a notice inviting offers and a model production sharing contract setting out the main terms of the regime prior to the launch of each bidding round.[45] Contracts are signed between the federal government and exploration companies, which define profit sharing terms and give Indian officials a role in operations through participation on management committees;[46] in the case of onshore areas, clearances and licences have to be granted by the state governments. Rule 5(2) of the Petroleum and Natural Gas Rules 1959, specifically empowers the federal government to include "additional terms, covenants and conditions as may be provided in the agreement between the Central Government and the licensee or lessee", after consulting the state governments (for onshore areas). Production sharing contracts between the federal government and the contractor(s) are signed under this rule.[47]

(c) ***Acquisition of acreage***

Under the new exploration licensing policy regime, blocks are carved out by the Directorate General of Hydrocarbons. These are offered on auction through a first price sealed bid procedure.[48] Bids are evaluated against a set of predefined qualification and bid evaluation criteria and blocks are awarded to bidders that achieve the highest scores on these criteria. The bidding procedure is reasonably transparent: sealed bids are submitted by companies (both national oil companies and private companies) on a specified date, typically within a period of four or five months after the bidding round is launched.[49] Data packages are made available for purchase during this period. Estimates of production profiles and prices are provided for each block by the Directorate General of Hydrocarbons, which are used by potential bidders along with their own assumptions on geology, and operating and capital expenditure, to prepare their bids.[50] Bids are opened within a few hours of submission by officials in front of the auction participants, and are read out. This allows for very little discretion in the identification of the winning bids. However, the time period taken to progress to the actual signing of contracts has varied, often taking several months, and there is arguably room for some discretion in that process.[51]

---

45 The model contract for the ninth bidding round is available at petroleum.nic.in/nelp93.pdf and the notice inviting offers for the ninth round is at www.petroleum.nic.in/nelp91.pdf. The ninth round was the most recently concluded bidding round at the time of writing.

46 "Guidelines for the Management of Oil and Gas Resources", Section K, published by the Ministry of Petroleum and Natural Gas and available at http://petroleum.nic.in/ogmgmt.pdf.

47 Comptroller and Auditor General of India, *Performance Audit of Hydrocarbon Production Sharing Contracts (Ministry of Petroleum and Natural Gas)*, Report 19 of 2011–12 for the period ended March 2011; available at http://saiindia.gov.in/english/home/Recent/Recent.html.

48 Sen, A "A Study of Auctions for Hydrocarbons Exploration in India", Oxford Institute for Energy Studies Working Paper, forthcoming (2013).

49 *Ibid.*

50 *Ibid.*

51 *Ibid.* For instance, after the ninth round of bidding in 2010, although 33 blocks were awarded, only half that number of contracts was eventually signed a few months after the award of bids, signalling that there was some discretion exercised by the federal government.

(d) ***Qualification requirements and bid evaluation criteria***[52]

National oil companies and private exploration companies (domestic and international) are meant to compete on a level playing field under the new exploration licensing policy. Bids have been evaluated on the basis of four main criteria. These relate to technical capability, financial capability, fiscal terms and work programmes. Each of these is assigned a weight signifying its importance within the overall bid evaluation criteria. The relative weights assigned to each criterion have changed in successive rounds, reflecting the policy objectives of the federal government at the time. Within each of the main criteria, there are also a set of sub-criteria. Scores or points are assigned to each of the sub-criteria, which when added up, make up the total weight assigned to each criterion. Table 3.1 summarises the changes to these weights over the nine rounds.

Bids are evaluated by assigning marks out of the maximum possible score on each sub-criterion, and then summing up to obtain a total score on each of the four criteria. These are once again summed to obtain a composite score out of 100. Bidders that score the most points out of 100 are awarded the block (that is, the block is awarded to the highest bidder). No explicit reserve prices are used; instead, bids are evaluated relative to each other.

Technical sub-criteria have included the amount of acreage held by the bidder, the amount of reserves (of oil and oil equivalent gas) from previous exploration, the production from previous exploration, and additionally, for deepwater blocks, previous experience of the bidding company or consortium in operating exploration projects. Financial sub-criteria have included the net worth, the debt equity ratio and the profit before tax of the bidding company or consortium.[53]

The financial criterion became a 'non-biddable' component from the sixth round onwards, and the technical criterion, from the seventh round onwards (except for deepwater blocks) meaning that companies were only required to qualify on them.[54]

The third parameter is the fiscal criterion, which is biddable. Fiscal sub-criteria include the percentage of cost recovery bid by participants in the auction (which is permissible up to 100%), and the percentage of profits to be shared with the government at six different tranches of a pre-tax investment multiple.[55] The rationale behind cost recovery was that companies that opted to recover a lower amount of their costs each year received favourable scores (as this meant a potentially larger proportion of profits was available to share with the government).

The fourth biddable parameter is the work programme for the exploration

---

52 Summarised from Sen, A "A Study of Auctions for Hydrocarbons Exploration in India", Oxford Institute for Energy Studies Working Paper, forthcoming (2013).

53 A bidding consortium or group of companies is permitted under the new exploration licensing policy, on the condition that each participating company holds at least a 10% participating interest in the venture, and one company is the designated operator of the consortium. The operator is the company that leads exploration.

54 For the technical criterion, companies were required to obtain a non-zero score; for financial criteria, the net worth of the company was required to exceed the total value of the work programme (mandatory and biddable).

55 The investment multiple is the ratio of cumulative cash flow to cumulative capital expenditure. Six tranches of this multiple were set: 1.5 and below, 1.5 to 2, 2 to 2.5, 2.5 to 3, 3 to 3.5 and 3.5 and above. Companies were required to bid a percentage of profits to be shared with the government at each tranche.

Table 3.1: Bid evaluation criteria under the new exploration licensing policy rounds

Round	I	II & III	IV & V		VI				VII					VIII & IX		
			Onland and shallow water	Deepwater	Onland and shallow water		Deepwater		Onland and shallow water			Deepwater		Onland S-type	Onland and shallow water	Deepwater
Type of Block*	No Categorisation				A	B	A	B	A	B	Small Type	A	B	S-Type	No categorisation	
Technical	No Break up	6	6	9	15	15	20	20	Qualifying		–	30	30	Nil	Qualifying	25
Financial		4	4	6	Qualifying				Qualifying					Qualifying		
Work Programme		60	60	55	25	35	20	30	40	50	40	15	25	50	50	25
Fiscal		30	30	30	60	50	60	50	60	50	60	55	45	50	50	50
Total		100	100	100	100	100	100	100	100	100	100	100	100	100	100	100

*Based on geology, size and prospectivity.

Source: From Sen, A "A Study of Auctions for Hydrocarbons Exploration in India", Oxford Institute for Energy Studies Working Paper, forthcoming (2013); compiled from notices inviting offers for bids 1999–2010.

period, covering either seven or eight years, split into either two or three phases. The sub-criteria have included the number of line kilometres of 2D seismic surveys, square kilometres of 3D seismic surveys, and the number of wells (the depth of wells measured in metres also began to be taken into account in later rounds).[56]

(e) *Duration*

Article 3 of the model production sharing contract specifies details of duration.[57] The exploration phase for onshore and shallow water blocks is seven years, split into two periods of four and three years. For deepwater blocks, this is eight years, split into five and three-year periods. In order to retain the block after the first period of exploration, companies are required to drill one well per year in the case of onshore and shallow water blocks, or one well in three years in case of deepwater blocks. The development and production period is 20 years for crude oil and associated natural gas, and 30 years for non-associated gas.

(f) *Minimum work programme*

A mandatory work programme was established from the sixth round onwards, consisting of a stipulated number of line kilometres of 2D seismic surveys, acting as a notional reserve price. In addition to this, companies are required to bid a minimum work programme (bids on the minimum work programme are evaluated as specified earlier). Article 5 of the model contract outlines the details of the total work programme.

(g) *Assignment*

The federal government permits assignment of a participating interest, with prior approval (Article 28 of the model contract), with the exception of the smaller 'S' type onshore blocks (less than 200 km^2) for which the minimum work programme must be completed over the initial four-year exploration period. The assignee is also expected to provide relevant financial guarantees:

> *The amount of the guarantee referred to in Articles 29.1(a) and 29.2 above shall be an amount equal to seven and one half percent (7.5%) of the Company's Participating Interest share of the total estimated expenditure in respect of Minimum Work Programme including Mandatory Work Programme or Work Program as the case may be, to be undertaken by the Contractor in the Contract Area during the Initial or Subsequent Exploration Period.*[58]

(h) *Local content*

Unlike other developing nations, local content is not in itself one of the bid evaluation criteria. However, the model contract contains clauses relating to local content, in Article 22 "Employment, Training and Transfer of Technology" and Article 23 "Local Goods and Services":

> *Without prejudice to the right of the Contractor to select and employ such number of*

---

56 Details on bid evaluation and qualification for the ninth round are available at www.petroleum.nic.in/nelp91.pdf

57 This refers to the ninth round, which was the most recently completed round at the time of writing.

58 Article 29.3 of the model production sharing contract for the ninth bidding round.

personnel as, in the opinion of the Contractor, are required for carrying out Petroleum Operations in a safe, cost effective and efficient manner, the Contractor shall, to the maximum extent possible, employ, and require the Operator and Subcontractors to employ, citizens of India having appropriate qualifications and experience, taking into account experience required in the level and nature of the Petroleum Operations.[59]

In the conduct of petroleum operations, the contractor shall:

- *give preference to the purchase and use of goods manufactured, produced or supplied in India provided that such goods are available on terms equal to or better than imported goods with respect to timing of delivery, quality and quantity required, price and other terms;*
- *employ Indian Subcontractors having the required skills or expertise, to the maximum extent possible, insofar as their services are available on comparable standards with those obtained elsewhere and at competitive prices and on competitive terms....*[60]

(i) National reservation

Crude oil and natural gas produced under the new extraction licensing policy regime is subject to a domestic market obligation specified in the model contract.

Until such time as the total availability of Crude Oil and Condensate from all Petroleum production activities in India meets the total national demand as determined by the Government, each Company comprising the Contractor, shall sell in the domestic market in India all of the Company's entitlement to Crude Oil and Condensate from the Contract Area.[61]

As of 2012, there remained a supply deficit, and domestically produced crude oil and natural gas continued to be sold into the domestic market. It has been argued that the deficit is induced by artificially low prices and the system of allocation of natural gas where the government's gas allocation policy is used to determine priority consuming sectors, which has inflated demand.[62]

The marketing of gas has been a matter of frequent controversy. Specifically, a policy conflict has been highlighted in Article 21.3 of the model contract, which contains two contradictory objectives.[63] First, the clause assures gas producers the freedom to market their gas, and second, it simultaneously requires the prioritised allocation of gas to be carried out through the government's gas utilisation policy. It has been argued that this contradictory objective has in fact helped to maintain the status quo in the government's policy of rationing low priced gas to consuming sectors such as power and fertilisers where the public sector has a dominant presence.[64] Specifically, the contradiction is achieved by allowing gas producers to discover the price of gas through an arm's length procedure, but then requiring that they submit this to the federal government for approval, which if granted, would be

---

59 Article 22.1 of the model production sharing contract for the ninth bidding round.

60 Article 23.1(a) and (b) of the model production sharing contract for the ninth bidding round.

61 Article 18.1 of the model production sharing contract for the ninth bidding round.

62 Jain, AK *Natural Gas in India: Liberalisation and Policy*, Oxford University Press (2011).

63 *Ibid.*

64 *Ibid.*

a uniform price at which gas is then sold to the priority sectors specified under the gas allocation policy.[65]

(j) *Environment*

Article 14 of the model contract specifies environmental provisions including the requirements under a site restoration fund. Environmental impact assessments, including a social impact component are mandatory, but Indian law does not require them to be published. Environmental provisions are covered by the Environmental Protection Act 1986,[66] and the Environmental Impact Assessment Rules 2006.[67]

> *The Contractor shall cause a person or persons with special knowledge on environmental matters, to carry out two environmental impact studies in order:*
>
> - *to determine at the time of the studies the prevailing situation relating to the environment, human beings and local communities, the flora and fauna in the Contract Area and in the adjoining or neighbouring areas; and*
> - *to establish the likely effect on the environment, human beings and local communities, the flora and fauna in the Contract Area and in the adjoining or neighbouring areas in consequence of the relevant Exploration Period of Petroleum Operations to be conducted under this Contract, and to submit, for consideration by the Parties, methods and measures contemplated in Article 14.4 for minimising Environmental Damage and carrying out Site Restoration activities.*[68]

(k) *Governing law and dispute resolution*

Contracts under the new exploration licensing policy are subject to the Arbitration and Conciliation Act 1996, which is based on the United Nations Commission on International Trade Law (UNCITRAL) model. Article 33 of the model contract specifies related provisions ("Sole Expert, Conciliation and Arbitration"). It gives parties to the contract the option of referring a dispute to a sole, independent expert. Failing resolution through this channel, parties can refer the dispute to arbitration:

> *The arbitral tribunal shall consist of three arbitrators. Each Party to the dispute shall appoint one arbitrator and the Party or Parties shall so advise the other Parties. The two arbitrators appointed by the Parties shall appoint the third arbitrator.*[69]
>
> *The decision of the arbitral tribunal shall be pronounced within four (4) months unless otherwise extended by the Parties, and, in case of difference among the arbitrators the decision of the majority shall be final and binding on the Parties.*[70]

3.2 Government take

(a) *Royalty*

Article 17.4 of the model production sharing contract specifies fixed rates of royalty

---

65 *Ibid.* This contradicts the concept of freedom of marketing.
66 Clauses 3(1), 3(2) and 3(3).
67 Available at: www.moef.nic.in/legis/eia/so1533.pdf.
68 Article 14.5 of the Model Production Sharing Contract for the Ninth Bidding Round.
69 Article 33.4 of the Model Production Sharing Contract for the Ninth Bidding Round.
70 Article 33.8 of the Model Production Sharing Contract for the Ninth Bidding Round.

for production under the new exploration licensing policy regime:

Companies (Lessee) shall be required to pay royalty to the Government (Lessor) for offshore areas at the rate of ten percent (10%) of the well-head value of Crude Oil and Natural Gas. In case of an onshore area, Companies shall be required to pay to the State Government(s) (Lessor) at the rate of twelve point five zero percent (12.5%) of the well-head value of Crude Oil and ten percent (10%) of the well-head value of Natural Gas. In case of an offshore area falling beyond four hundred (400) metre isobath, the rate of royalty payable by Companies (Lessee) to the Government (Lessor) shall be at the rate of five percent (5%) of the well-head value of Crude Oil and Natural Gas for the first seven years from the date of commencement of Commercial Production in the Field. The valuation of Crude Oil and Natural Gas shall be as per the Article 19 and Article 21 respectively. The royalty amount due to Government/State Government(s) shall be payable latest by the end of the succeeding Month.[71]

(b) Bonuses and special participation

There are no bonuses under the new exploration licensing policy regime. There is also no mandatory state participation and the state has no carried interest.

(c) Rental fees

The *Petroleum Tax Guide* published along with the model contract and notice inviting offers contains details of surface fees:

Deposits, Licence Fee, Dead Rent and Surface Rent:

10. (1) Before the licence is granted, the applicant for a licence shall deposit with the Central Government or where the licence is to be or has been granted by the State Government, the State Government as security for due observance of the terms, covenants and conditions of the licence, a sum of Rs4,00,000 ...

(2) The licensee shall pay yearly in advance by way of licence fee in respect of his licence a sum calculated for each square kilometre or part thereof covered by the licence at the following rates —

a. Rs200 ... for the first year of the licence
b. Rs400 ... for the second year of the licence
c. Rs2000 ... for the third year of the licence
d. Rs2800 ... for the fourth year of the licence
e. Rs4000 ... for each subsequent year of the renewal.

(3) The applicant for a lease shall, before the lease is granted to him —

a. deposit with the Central or the State Government, as the case may be, as security, a sum of Rs8,00,000 ... for due observance of the terms and conditions of the lease,
b. also deposit with the Central or the State Government, as the case may be, for meeting the preliminary expenses, such sum not exceeding Rs1,20,000 ... as the Central Government or the State Government with the approval of the Central Government, may determine.

(4) On the grant of a lease, the lessee —

---

71 Article 17.4 of the Model Production Sharing Contract for the Ninth Bidding Round.

a. *shall pay to the Central or the State Government, as the case may be, for every year a fixed yearly dead rent at the following rates -*
   Rs100 ... per hectare or part thereof for the first 100 square kilometres and Rs200 ... per hectare or part thereof for area exceeding the first 100 square kilometres provided that the lessee shall be liable to pay only the dead rent or the royalty, whichever is higher in amount but not both provided that the Lessee shall pay within thirty days dead rent of the grant of Petroleum Mining Lease and yearly dead rent in advance for every subsequent Year.
b. *shall also pay to the State Government, for the surface area of the land actually used by him for the purpose of the operations conducted under the lease, surface rent at such rate, not exceeding the land revenue and cesses assessed or assessable on the land, as may be specified by the State Government with the approval of the Central Government.*

(5) The deposits, license fee, dead rent and surface rents are subject to change in accordance with the relevant laws and rules by the Government or State Government, as the case may be, from time to time.[72]

Additionally, Article 17.9 of the model contract stipulates the requirement to make these payments.

(d) *Income tax*

Contracts under the new exploration licensing policy regime (specifically, the ninth round) are subject to the following tax legislation:[73]

- the Income Tax Act (Act 43 of 1961);
- the Income Tax Rules, 1962;
- the Central Excise Act 1944 (Act 1 of 1944);
- the Central Excise Tariff Act 1985 (Act 5 of 1986);
- the Oil Industry (Development) Act 1974 (Act 47 of 1974);
- the Customs Act 1962 (Act 52 of 1962);
- the Customs Tariff Act 1975 (Act 51 of 1975).

Domestic companies are subject to tax at a rate of 30% and foreign companies 40%. Additionally, a surcharge (10% of tax for domestic companies and 2.5% of tax for foreign companies) must be paid for income in excess of Rs10 million.[74] An education levy of 3% also applies. The effective tax rates are therefore: for domestic companies, 30.9% for net income up to and including Rs10 million and 33.9% for income exceeding this; and for foreign companies, 41.2% and 42.32%.[75]

A minimum alternate tax applies to a company if the tax payable on its total income as computed under the tax laws is less than 15% of its book profits.[76] If the

72 Point 10 of the *Petroleum Tax Guide 1999*; subject to the Petroleum and Natural Gas Rules 1959.
73 See Point 2 of the *Petroleum Tax Guide 1999*.
74 Ernst and Young, *Global Oil and Gas Tax Guide* (2010).
75 *Ibid.*
76 *Ibid.*
77 *Ibid.* This was increased to 18.5% in the 2012 budget.

minimum alternate tax applies, the tax on total income is deemed to equal 15% of the company's book profit.[77]

No ring fencing applies from a tax perspective, and all exploration and development costs are 100% tax deductible.[78] Costs are aggregated until the year of commercial production, after which they can be fully claimed in the year of commercial production or can be amortised equally over a period of 10 years.[79] Development costs (other than drilling) are allowable under the normal provisions of domestic tax law.[80]

No excise duty is levied on the production of crude oil.[81] There was significant controversy over the differential treatment of oil and gas with respect to the seven year tax holiday; however, this was eventually resolved as the tax holiday was withdrawn in the ninth round.

A new Direct Tax Code, which constitutes a major reform of the Indian taxation law (replacing the Income Tax Act 1961), was due to come into effect on April 1 2012, but was deferred in the 2012 budget to another (unspecified) time. The impact of this on the upstream sector had not yet been clearly specified at the time of writing.

4. Current issues

It can be argued that the new exploration licensing policy regime, contrary to its original aim of increasing the pace of production and inviting foreign capital and technology, has suffered some serious setbacks in this regard. Although the regime has been in place since 1999, as of 2012, which marked a period of approximately two full exploration cycles, only one giant discovery of natural gas had been made in the eastern offshore Krishna-Godavari basin in 2004 (referred to as the 'KG-D6 field') by Reliance Industries Ltd. Although this boosted production and enabled the private sector to overtake the stagnating production of natural gas by the national oil companies in 2009, this discovery was in 2012 revised downward to roughly 3.4 trillion cubic feet from its original estimate of 11 trillion. In 2011 the field achieved approximately 30% of its originally intended production target of 80 million metric standard cubic metres per day, with production continuing to wane in 2012.[82] It has been argued that future supply, and the sustaining of economic growth, is contingent on the efficacy of the new exploration licensing policy in bringing fields into production on schedule,[83] and there have undoubtedly been concerns in this regard.

These concerns can be traced to the implementation of the production sharing contract, as the auction procedure is itself relatively transparent.[84] There have been two specific areas which have given rise to dispute and debate. The first relates to

78 Ernst and Young, *Global Oil and Gas Tax Guide,* 2010.
79 *Ibid.*
80 *Ibid.*
81 *Ibid.*
82 Sen, A, "Gas Pricing in India", in Jonathan P Stern (ed), *The Pricing of Internationally Traded Gas,* Oxford University Press, 2012.
83 Jain, AK *Natural Gas in India: Liberalisation and Policy,* Oxford University Press, 2011.
84 Sen, A, "A Study of Auctions for Hydrocarbons Exploration in India", Oxford Institute for Energy Studies Working Paper, forthcoming (2013), however, points out some weaknesses in the auctions procedure, highlighting the fact that most blocks have been won by just two large companies – one state owned, and one privately owned – and that exploration has been largely dominated by them.

pricing, specifically of natural gas, under the new exploration licensing policy. As discussed earlier, prices are arrived at through a price discovery process conducted at arm's length by the exploration company. These are submitted to the federal government, and once approved, are valid for a five-year period, after which the pricing formula is meant to undergo a review. Prices fixed for the KG-D6 gas field in 2009 were being disputed as early as 2012.[85] The second relates to provision for cost recovery. Again, disputes arose over a proposed upward revision in capital costs by the contractor of the KG-D6 fields in 2012. A third and related concern arose from the results of an audit by the Comptroller and Auditor General of India into a sample of 20 production sharing contracts, including KG-D6, which alleged that large amounts of revenues may have been lost to the exchequer as a result of the poor enforcement of contracts. It also recommended the adoption of a royalty/tax system. These events are likely to trigger further changes to the regime. These changes began, in fact, to be seen in the second half of 2012, when the federal government published a draft policy on the fiscal regime for shale, which saw the potential replacement of the pre-tax investment multiple system[86] with production-linked payments based on a sliding scale linked to incremental production, as well as the elimination of the cost recovery provision. The draft shale policy also proposes the payment of a commercial discovery bonus of $0.3 million. At the time of writing, a bidding round for shale was due to be announced in December 2013; and a review of the fiscal regime for hydrocarbons exploration had been published by a government-appointed committee[87] recommending the adoption of fiscal terms similar to those suggested in the draft shale policy and a revision of the gas-pricing formula.

5. Conclusion

This chapter has attempted to describe and critically evaluate the existing upstream fiscal regime for oil and gas exploration and production in India. A compelling observation that emerges from the discussion is the fact that the regime is still evolving, and this chapter has argued that the changes associated with this evolution can be placed in the broader context of the economic transition.[88] Despite the general atmosphere of change, it can also be argued that the terms of the new exploration licensing policy have remained largely stable over a period constituting nearly two full exploration cycles, which is perhaps indicative of the robust nature of the legislative and constitutional framework which underpins all upstream activity. Regardless of the recent challenges faced in the implementation of upstream contracts, it remains an undisputed fact that India offers a huge potential future market, as a large proportion of its citizens that currently lack access to modern commercial energy will eventually be brought into the system as economic growth proceeds, signalling massive future additions to the consumer base.

---

85 For a detailed account, see Jain, AK *Natural Gas in India: Liberalisation and Policy*, Oxford University Press (2011) and Sen, A, "Gas Pricing in India", in Jonathan P Stern (ed), *The Pricing of Internationally Traded Gas*, Oxford University Press, 2012.

86 Similar to an 'R factor'.

87 Also referred to as the 'Rangarajan Committee Report on Production Sharing Contract Mechanism in Petroleum Industry'. At the time of writing, these recommendations were yet to be officially adopted.

88 Argued in Jain, *AK Natural Gas in India: Liberalisation and Policy*, Oxford University Press, 2011.

Indonesia

Madjedi Hasan
Petroleum Consultant

---

1. Introduction

Indonesia is a civil law country, which operates on the basis of a tiered hierarchy of legal norms, meaning in particular that a lower norm is based on a higher norm and so on up the tiers until the point where it meets the highest norm, which is considered to be the basic norm. The Constitution and the decrees of the People's Consultative Assembly (MPR) form the basic law of the state, but they are technically outside the hierarchy of norms, as neither of them are formally a law or regulation directly binding the public. The hierarchy of legal norms as regulated in MPR Decree III/2000 is as follows:

- Laws are at the top of the hierarchy of laws and regulations that can directly apply to and bind the public. A law can also determine applicable penal, civil or administrative sanctions. In a case of emergency, the president may issue a government regulation in lieu of a law. A government regulation in lieu of a law is only applicable for a fixed period of time and must be ratified by the parliament in its first session after the regulation's enactment. Should the parliament ratify it, a government regulation in lieu of a law will be re-enacted as a law; otherwise, it becomes void.
- For the implementation of laws, the government will issue government regulations and presidential regulations. Government regulations may contain provisions imposing sanctions, while a presidential regulation is issued in one of two forms, namely a declaration or a public order, the latter being considered as part of the body of laws and regulations.
- Also included in the list are regional regulations, which are issued by regional government based on the Autonomy Law, presidential instructions, ministerial regulations and circular letters.

2. Upstream activities

In Indonesia, oil and gas exploration, exploitation and refining activities have a long history and have seen fluctuating fortunes. Oil and gas have been found onshore, offshore and in deep waters. An increase in exploration activities at the beginning of the New Order Government (in 1966) resulted in discoveries of new oil reserves and increased oil production from about 600 thousands barrel per day in 1967 to 1.7 million barrels in 1977. In 1977 Indonesia also exported liquefied natural gas (LNG) for the first time. This made oil and gas the main source for development funding. This progress can be attributed to the conducive business climate created by the government in cooperation with multinational companies, assisted by technology.

These increases, however, did not last long; oil production has been declining since the end of the 1970s, which can be attributed to a decline in exploration activities, which was triggered by changing the production sharing formula. Oil and gas activities began to increase when the government provided incentives and revised the terms of the standard production sharing contract's terms, but the results were not able to reverse the decline in oil prodcution. The factors contributing to this continued decline include the fact that the commercial success rate of new wells has tended to decrease both in terms of the number of discoveries and the size of those reserves found.

In 2012 production averaged 840,000 barrels of oil per day and 6 million cubic feet per day of gas. Most of Indonesia's oil production comes from the western part of the country, where exploration to date has been focused. This area has accounted for 75% of Indonesian oil production (23 billion barrels).

3. Petroleum legal regime

3.1 Petroleum law and relevant provisions

(a) Regulatory bodies

All energy activities dealing with petroleum and gas fall under the Ministry of Energy and Mineral Resources, which is charged with drawing up and implementing Indonesia's energy policy. The Ministry of Energy and Mineral Resources is divided into several directorates, with the Directorate General of Oil and Gas (MIGAS) responsible for all aspects of petroleum industry development, including employee training, promulgating regulations and inviting tender for acreage acquisition.

In late 2001, Law 22/2001 was introduced to replace Law 44/1960 on Petroleum, and Law 8/1970 on Pertamina. Law 22/2001 on Oil and Gas differentiates between upstream business activities (exploration and exploitation) and downstream business activities (processing, transport, storage and commerce). To implement the law, the government has also issued a number of government regulations (GR), including GR 42/2002 and GR 67/2002 on the establishment of BP Migas and BPH Migas, GR 31/2003 on the conversion of Pertamina's status to that of state-owned enterprise, and GR 35/2004 and 36/2004 on oil and gas upstream and downstream activities, respectively.

Upstream activities are controlled through a joint cooperation contract between the business entity and Executive Board for Oil and Gas Upstream Activities (BP Migas), which is a non-profitmaking state-owned legal entity and acts on behalf of the government as party to cooperation contracts with business entities. BP Migas's main responsibilities also include providing recommendations to the minister in preparing and offering work areas and cooperation contracts and appointing sellers of the government's share of oil and gas.

In the downstream sector, activities are controlled through business licences issued by the Regulatory Board for Oil and Gas Downstream Activities (BPH Migas). Among BPH Migas's responsibilities are regulating and determining the supply and distribution of oil-based fuel, regulating the transmission and distribution of natural gas, allocating fuel to the national fuel reserves, overseeing the use of oil and gas transportation and storage facilities, setting tariffs for gas pipeline use, setting the price of natural gas for households and small consumers, making recommendations on pipeline levies and setting the price of pipeline rights.

(b) *Types of agreement*

Until 1960 Indonesia's petroleum activity was operated using a concession system under the Dutch East Indies Mining Law of 1899. Then the Petroleum Law (Law 44/1960) was introduced, which stipulated that petroleum operations can only be performed by the state, for which purpose the relevant activities will be undertaken by a state-owned enterprise. For upstream activities, that enterprise is allowed to act in cooperation with investors, in the form of joint operating contracts based on profit sharing.

For this purpose, the government established three state-owned enterprises (Pertamin, Permina and Permigan), which later were merged into a single company, called Pertamina. The type of contract allowed was later changed to be a production sharing contract, which is based on a sharing of actual production between the state-owned enterprise and contractor, rather than on the traditional sharing of net profit. In 2001, Law 44/1960 was replaced by Law 22/2001.

Under the new law, Pertamina transferred its role as a party representing the Indonesian government in the petroleum contract to BP Migas. The joint operating contract as defined under Law 22/2001 is a production sharing contract or any other form that could generate higher revenue for the state; however, the law is silent with respect to just what other contractual forms are acceptable.

The present terms and conditions of the production sharing contract are as follows:

- The contractor may be a state-owned enterprise, a company owned by a regional administration, a cooperative, a small-scale businesses or a private business entity. Foreign investors in the oil and gas sector must set up a branch of their foreign company as a 'permanent establishment'. Incorporation as an Indonesian domiciled limited liability company under the Company Law (Law 40/2007) is a possibility for Indonesian investors only.
- Upstream entities are prohibited from engaging in downstream activities, and vice versa, except where an upstream entity must build transport, storage or processing facilities, or other downstream activities that are integral to supporting its exploitation activities.
- All investment funds for exploration, development and production must be provided by the contractor and will only be recovered through product sharing in the event of commercial discovery. Therefore the contractor bears all the risks during the exploration phase.
- Under the production sharing contract, the contractor is responsible for the day-to-day operations, and is responsible for the decision-making process generally and in particular during the exploratorion stage. BP Migas has

exclusive control over the overall management of petroleum operations. In exercising of this control BP Migas, on behalf of the Indonesian government, is responsible for approving the contractor's budget, work programmes, manpower plan, expenditure scheme and procurement of equipment and services.

(c) Acquisition of acreage

The Directorate General of Oil and Gas (DG Migas) is responsible for planning and preparing which working area is to be offered for cooperation. DG Migas may appoint Indonesian companies, permanent establishments of foreign companies or other parties with the relevant expertise (such as universities) to undertake the tasks of reviewing and processing the necessary data. Based on DG Migas's proposal, the Minister of Energy and Mineral Resources will then determine the working area to be offered. He also sets the terms and conditions of the cooperation contract to be offered to companies or permanent establishments, on the basis of BP Migas' recommendations and following consultation with the governor of the province in which the working area is located. DG Migas offers the working area by issuing a call for tenders. The bid document contains the time limits for applications, the tender procedure, information on the working area, the procedure for accessing relevant data, a draft of the joint cooperation contract and other terms.

The tender will be announced in the mass media (newspapers and electronic media) in various forums (DG Migas may appoint a third party to make the announcement). Calls for tenders are issued every year (once or twice per year).

Acreage may also be awarded on the basis of a direct offer based on a proposal put forward by a company or permanent establishment, or by DG Migas jointly with a company or permanent establishment following a technical review. Such direct offers may only be made in respect of a working area that has previously been offered by means of a call for tenders. The terms and conditions attaching to successful direct offers will be the same as those that had previously been offered in the call for tenders, unless the minister determines otherwise.

In addition to individual companies or permanent establishments tenders or offers may also be made by a consortium.

(d) Qualification requirements

The tender document consists of:

- a completed form signed by the company's director or attorney;
- proposals for three-year and six-year year work programmes and expenditure in relation to exploration, the first three-year programme being considered a 'firm commitment';
- a geological evaluation and technical appraisal showing the proposed location of wildcat wells and other infrastructure;
- proof of financial capability supported by audited financial statements for the past three years (or those of its parent company if the company has just been established);
- a statement confirming that the company or permanent establishment will

agree to provide compensation in return for the award of a contract, in the form of material and equipment and production bonuses;
- a statement confirming that the company or permanent establishment will agree to sign the draft of cooperation agreement if its bid is successful;
- evidence of data purchased;
- a legal document evidencing the company's incorporation;
- a bid bond based on the amount of the signature bonus that the party is willing to pay.

The tender will be evaluated by a team consisting of five members, and the evaluation will use the following criteria in recommending the prospective winner: technical and financial commitment, and performance. The technical evaluation will be focused on the three-year work programme commitment based on a geological and technical appraisal. The financial evaluation will be focused on the compensation offered and the bidder's financial capability, supported by its audited annual financial statements and an economic analysis of the proposal. While evaluation of performance will be based on the bidder's experience in the oil industry and its history of compliance with Indonesian laws and regulations in the case of those which have worked in Indonesia before.

Within seven days following notification of a successful bid, the bidder must submit a letter confirming its agreement with the draft of the cooperation contract (winner successful bidder may lose its bid bond, if it withdraws or no final agreement is concluded). It should be noted that the existing regulatory regime does not specify a time limit within which notification of a successful bid must be made.

In the case of direct offers, the company or permanent establishment which first made the proposal will not automatically be selected; however that company or permanent establishment has the right to match the highest bidder.

(e) *Duration*

The term of the production sharing contract is 30 years from the date of its signature in the event of a commercial discovery. Otherwise the exploratory period runs for six years which may be extended for another four years, and the contract will automatically terminate if during this period no petroleum is discovered in commercial quantities. Under GR 35/2004, the production sharing contract may be extended for 20 years at a time, and a request for such an extension may be submitted at the earliest 10 years and at the latest two years before it is due to expire, but the Indonesian government has the right to refuse such a request. There is an exception in respect of gas producers having a long-term gas sales contract, in which case the request for extension may be granted earlier.

Mandatory relinquishment of areas is made in phases, generally 25% at the end of third contract year, another 25% at the end of sixth contract year, and finally 30% at the end of the 10th year of the contract if petroleum is discovered in commercial quantities.

Normally the contractor has the right to terminate the contract in its entirety three years after its signature. Also the production sharing contract provides the right to terminate the contract in its entirety by 90 days written notice in the case of a major breach of the contract. However such termination is not automatic, and can only be made following proof of the breach of contract in arbitration proceedings.

(f) ***Minimum work programme***

The production sharing contract stipulates the minimum programme to be carried out by contractor in conducting exploration operations during the first six years of the contract, consisting of geological and geophysical exploration and drilling exploration wells. If during any year of the contract the contractor should spend less than the amount stipulated, an amount equal to that shortfall may be carried forward and added to the amount to be expended in the following year without prejudice to the contractor's rights.

The planned work programme for the first three years of the contract is a binding commitment, which means that if, at the end of the third year, the contractor has not completed the work programme and elects to relinquish its rights and be relieved of any further obligations under the contract, the contractor must pay the outstanding balance of the proposed expenditure for the three-year programme to BP Migas. However, in the event that all the activities under the three-year work programme have been completed by the contractor, even though it has spent less than the proposed amount, the contractor shall not be obliged to pay the outstanding balance.

The contractor will be required to place a performance bond covering the first three years' work and expenditure commitment. If the contractor decides to withdraw before completion of the three-year work programme and has spent less that the expenditure committed to, it has to pay the difference between the firm commitment and the actual expenditure. No payment is due if the contractor has completed the work programme at less cost.

(g) ***Assignment and encumbrance***

The contractor has the right to sell, assign, transfer, convey or otherwise dispose of all or any part of its rights and interest under the contract to any affiliated company or to a non-affiliated company. The transfer of a right or interest to an affiliated company requires the prior written consent of BP Migas, while a transfer to a non-affiliated company additionally requires the written consent of the government. Under GR 79/2010 such a transfer of an interest is subject to a transfer tax (levied at either 5% or 7% depending on whether the production sharing contract is in the exploration or the exploitation stage).

(h) ***Local content***

Obligations to provide preference to domestic products and services are provided in both the contract of work and the production sharing contract. Originally this requirement was just a simple clause dealing with promotion of the national interest and employment and training of nationals. The local content requirement was later expanded, with an emphasis on promotion of increased use of domestic facilities, services and supplies. This was expressed in various policies and regulations on providing preferential treatment to economically weak groups in purchasing their products and services.

In order to ensure compliance with these requirements, the government established a bid review procedure. A procurement review team was formed with representatives of the Office of the State Secretary and the ministry, which reviewed proposals to award bids. In the review process, the team adopted the practice of negotiating with successful bidders for even lower prices. the government justified these policies and procedures on the ground of national development, as the government noted that it ultimately paid 88% of the costs.

Entering the new millennium, the government revamped this policy, which now focuses on the principle of self-assessment and a transparent audit. For example, the Presidential Decree 80 of 2003, which was later followed by decrees from the Ministries of Industry and Trade, stated that in any tender process for procurement, local content should be determined at the outset, based on the goods and service required and a list prepared by the Ministries of Industry and Trade. The presidential decree also provided for preferential prices and treatment for small and medium sized enterprises in supplying their product and services. Under the presidential decree, preference is to be given to domestic goods where they cost up to 15% more than the price of imported products (excluding import duty), and to imported services that cost up to 7.5% more than those offered by foreign companies.

The presidential decree also stated that bidders for certain sizes of contract are required to be from within a given class of bidders. Large firms are required to form joint ventures with or subcontract to small and medium sized firms domiciled in the locality (the province, regency or municipality). Implementing agencies are required to give priority to local small or medium sized firms for contracts up to IR10 billion (US$1.11 million) for works, up to IR4 billion (US$444,440) for goods, and up to IR1 billion (US$111,110) for consulting assignments. Foreign firms are allowed to bid for contracts above certain amounts, but they must either form joint ventures with or subcontract to domestic firms.

In relation to oil and gas upstream activities, BP Migas, as a contracting party representing the government in the production sharing contract, requires preferential treatment for domestic goods and services, to which end it refers to the value of the level of domestic components in goods and services, known as the (TKDN). Under BP Migas Regulation 007/PTK/VI/2004 the TKDN refers to goods and services produced in Indonesia or overseas but owned 100% by domestic suppliers, while domestic product that is supplied by a foreign supplier will be considered to have 75% TKDN.

Furthermore, under Ministry of Industry Regulation 11/M-IND/PER/3/2006, the TKDN must be included as one of the bidding requirements. The TKDN for a product reflects the degree of local content in the goods and services concerned, to be computed by comparing the value of local components to the total value of the goods and services.

(i) National reservation

Article 33 of the 1945 Indonesian Constitution states that branches of production important to the state and which affect the life of most people shall be under the jurisdiction of the state, and that the land, water and natural resources contained therein shall be under the jurisdiction of the state and are to be utilised for the greatest welfare of the people. Control by the state means that state assets should be utilised to the maximum for the welfare of all Indonesian people. Therefore, individuals, communities or businesses having a right to a plot of land on the surface have no right to control or own any petroleum and natural gas contained underground.

(j) ***Environment***

The contractor must conduct an environmental assessment at the beginning of its activities, and must also take the necessary precautions for protection of affected ecological systems, navigation and fishing, and must prevent extensive pollution of the sea, rivers or any other area as the direct result of operations undertaken under the work programme. After termination of the contract, relinquishment of part of the contract area, or abandonment of any field, the contractor must remove all equipment and installations from the area and perform all necessary site restoration activities.

(k) ***Governing law and dispute resolution***

The governing law of the contract is Indonesian law. It should be noted that no terms or provisions of the contract, including the agreement of the parties to submit to arbitration, can prevent the government from exercising its inalienable rights or limit those rights. Disputes which cannot be settled amicably, if any, shall be submitted to arbitration with three arbitrators and the decision of the majority of the arbitrators shall be final and binding upon the parties. The arbitration will be conducted under the International Chamber of Commerce Rules of Alternative Dispute Resolution and Arbitration. However, this has changed in the recent model contract, which calls for arbitration using the United Nations Commission on International Trade Law (UNCITRAL) arbitration rules. The Secretary General of the International Centre for Settlement of Investment Disputes will appoint the third arbitrator if the parties do not otherwise agree.

3.2 Government take

(a) ***Royalties***

The Indonesian production sharing contract is based on sharing oil and production, and does not provide for royalty payments.

(b) ***Bonuses***

The production sharing contract stipulates the payment of various bonuses, including a signature bonus, equipment and services, and production bonuses, the latter being determined by cumulative oil production. All of such bonuses are payable 30 days following the end of the month in which the obligation to make such payments occurs. Bonus payments bonus are not recoverable costs, but they are tax deductible.

(c) ***Rental fees***

There are no rental fees.

(d) ***Special participation***

There are no provisions on special participations, except that BP Migas has the right to demand a 10% Indonesian participation (to be exercised by a local government company or an Indonesian national company) in the event of a commercial discovery and if the development plan is approved by the government. If BP Migas intends to exercise this right, it must notify the contractor within one month after the contractor's notification of such a discovery. For the acquisition of this 10% interest, the acquiring local government or Indonesian national company shall reimburse the contractor an amount equal to 10% of the operating costs that the contractor has incurred up to the date of its notification of a discovery.

(e) ***Government revenues and corporate taxes***

The terms of the production sharing contract have evolved through five generations; the main variation between each being the production sharing split. The first revision made following the drastic increase in crude oil prices in 1973 increased Pertamina and the government's take from 65% to 85% for oil and 70% for gas (net after tax) and removed the earlier cost recovery cap of 40% of revenues. The revision also included an amended provision on companies' payment of Indonesian income tax, to allow US companies to meet the conditions of Internal Revenue Service rulings for tax credit. Subsequent revisions involved providing additional economic incentives, aimed at meeting the industry's need for improved terms. The second revision in the late 1980s (the third generation model contract) introduced the concept of first tranche petroleum FTP, which essentially restored the cost recovery cap, and offered incentives for frontier, marginal and deep-sea areas.

At present, for oil, the profit split after cost recovery, for a conventional area, is 73.2143% for the Indonesian government and 26.7857% for the contractor. For gas, the profit share split is 53.5714% for the government and 46.4286% for the contractor. For a so-called frontier area (such as a deep sea or remote area), the financial terms are improved with respect to the profit split, which now becomes 44.6429%/55.3571% for oil and 53.5714%/46.4286% for gas. The applicable tax rate is 44%, including 30% income tax and 20% tax on interest, dividends and royalties (final). This makes the net profit split after tax for a conventional area 85%/15% for oil and 70%/30% for gas, all in favour of the government.

The production sharing contract provides for first tranche petroleum (FTP) of 20% (in a conventional area) and 10% (in a frontier area), which would means that the allowable annual cost recovery is limited to 80% and 90%, respectively. This entitles the government to the first take of oil and gas production each year. Historically, each contractor was entitled to FTP in accordance its equity share, but recent contracts do not provide for the sharing of FTP (in other words, all FTP accrues to the government).

For marginal fields, GR 8/2005 provides contractors with additional cost recovery of 20%. For an oilfield to be entitled to this incentive it must meet the following criteria: it must be located in a working area where there is already production, and its development will generate a rate of return of less than 15%. The incentive is provided on a yearly basis and may be extended if the annual rate of return is below 15%.

'Ring fencing' applies (see Article 13 of Law 22/2001), whereby only one production sharing contract can be granted to each permanent establishment or company. Therefore, separate bodies must be set up for each work area. There are also no group or similar consolidation arrangements in Indonesia. This means that the costs incurred in respect of one production sharing contract cannot be used to relieve tax obligations under another. This provision is also applicable to Pertamina, which was required to establish separate subsidiaries and enter into production sharing contracts with BP Migas for each of its work areas.

Once commercial production has begun, the contractor is obligated to sell BP Migas part of its equity oil and/or gas for the domestic market (domestic market obligation). The maximum domestic market obligation in any year is 25% of total production multiplied by 26.7857% (or 6.6964% of total production). The price for this oil is 25% of the export price, except that for the first five years of delivery from each new field the price is the full export price. For gas, the price is the weighted average price. Consequently, including the domestic market obligation the net profit split after tax is 88%/12%, in favour of the government.

Recovery of investment in capital items is done through a declining balance depreciation method at annual rate of 50% for assets with short useful lives and 25% for those with longer lives, while non-capital items are fully expensed in the current year. Subject to first tranche petroleum, all production of the current year is available for the recovery of operating costs.

Under the production sharing contract, equipment purchased by the contractor becomes the property of the Indonesian government, however, the contractor retains custody and control to that property during the performance of the contract. The costs of non-capital items purchased for inventory is recoverable at such time as the items enter into Indonesia.

The contract also stipulates that, for the purpose of recovering the contractor's operating costs, crude oil sold to third parties is to be valued at the net realised price free on board. Because of large fluctuations in the price of oil, in the late 1980s the government and industry agreed to use a price index for Indonesian crude oil, known as the Indonesia Crude Price. Initially this price was determined by the government based on a moving average spot price of a basket of five internationally traded crudes, namely Minas (Indonesia), Tapis (Malaysia), Gippsland (Australia), Dubai (UAE) and Oman. However, as this value did not properly account for significant movements in oil prices it was considered deficient, and oil is now valued on the basis of a basket of average Indonesian crude prices published by RIM (50%) and Platt's (50%). The value is calculated monthly by BP Migas.

Interest on loans obtained from affiliates or parent companies, or from third party non-affiliates, at rates not exceeding prevailing commercial rates for capital loans may be recoverable as an operating cost. Details of any financing plan and amounts must be included in the annual operating budget for the prior approval of BP Migas.

4. Current issues

As mentioned previously, Indonesia's oil production has been declining since the end of the 1970s, which has made Indonesia a net oil importer. The decline was not attributable to investors' perceptions of the potential of Indonesia's resources, the decline in oil prices or political instability, but was mainly associated with uncertainty in the execution of contracts. Factors affecting investment in Indonesia arise from the new regulations that have been imposed on existing contracts, uncertainties regarding taxes and import duties and new laws issued by regional governments that may conflict with the terms of the production sharing contract.

There are also other issues affecting petroleum operations.

Conflicting rights: There are conflicts in respect of land for mining (including oil and gas) on the one hand and forestry and, community tights on the other. The Forestry Law (Law 41/1999 and its amending Laws 1/2004 and 19/2004) prohibit oil and gas activities in protected forest areas except where a government permit is obtained. This might force a contractor to cease its operation in a particular area when it is later designated as protected forest even though the contractor had undertaken a considerable amount of expenditure on exploration. In such a situation, the contractor may be forced to move its drilling operations if part of its working area is located in the protected forest zone, if the change in status only becomes known after the contract is signed. In order to resolve this issue, on February 1 2010, the government issued a presidential decree which will allow some projects, including oil and gas activities, power plants, mining, transport and renewable energy projects, to take place in protected forests where they are deemed strategically important.

New Environment Law: Law 32/2009 requires entities to comply with standard environmental quality requirements and to secure environmental permits before beginning operations. Sanctions can include the cancellation of operating permits, fines, and/or imprisonment. Other environmental management responsibilities include taking into account certified emission reductions as part of the Indonesian government's commitment following its ratification of the 1997 Kyoto Protocol (the clean development mechanism). The environmental quality requirements (which concern emissions and waste water temperature levels) have been the subject of recent industry concerns due to the time lag required in implementing new process technologies and increased production costs.

Status of ministerial regulations: The absence from MPR Decree III/2000 on the hierarchy of norms of ministerial regulations as a form of quasi legislation has sometimes been a contentious issue, as it has been interpreted by many regional governments as meaning that any ministerial regulation that is issued and purports to bind regional government is not effective. Consequently, regional government regulations hold a higher position in the hierarchy of Indonesian laws than do ministerial regulations. The persistence of this omission has resulted in some degree of disharmony between the central and regional governments with regard to legislation on several important matters, such as taxation, business licensing procedures and investment. However, despite this, in many instances ministerial regulations have been used as guidelines on the technical procedures to be followed by the regional governments, for instance in the case of tendering procedures for procurement of goods and services.

Interpretation of contractual terms: In some cases there has been inconsistency in the interpretation of some terms of the production sharing contract. Issues arising from the different interpretations of some terms have not yet been completely resolved, and as a result contracts have been inhibited from pursuing upstream oil and gas activities. For instance, there has recently been controvery associated with the repayment of costs that were claimed by contractors (cost recovery claims).

Cost recovery and other tax changes: In late December 2010 the government issued GR 79/2010 on recoverable operating costs and treatment of the contractor's income tax. The purpose of GR 79/2010 is to increase the government's revenue by providing tight controls on the reimbursable operating costs, as cost recovery is now included as a separate item in the state budget. GR 79/2010 is also applicable to existing production sharing contracts which were signed before the enactment of the regulation.

Under GR 79/2010, some operating costs are not recoverable; these include the costs associated with community development during the exploitation phase and the training of expatriate personnel. Also, the regulation provides authority to the Minister of Finance to determine the maximum salaries for expatriates, while the Directorate General of Taxation may determine the maximum recoverable costs of exploration each year upon receiving a recommendation from BP Migas, which is the party in the production sharing contract representing the government.

Additionally, under GR 79/2010, the income tax rate for production sharing contracts signed after the promulgation of the regulation will be that which prevailed at signing or that prevailing from time to time. This appears to breathe life into the provision in law 22/2001 that joint cooperation contracts may specify that the applicable income tax laws can be either those applicable at the time of signature or those in force. The new approach differs from the position under contracts signed before GR 79/2010, in which the income tax rate is that which prevailed when the contract was signed. This grandfathering is consistent with the retention of the uniformity principle.

Furthermore, GR 79/2010 requires that there be uniform treatment of cost recovery and tax deductibility. This is pivotal as it appears formally to enshrine the longstanding uniformity principle. To satisfy this requirement the amount in question should still have been spent on income producing activities, satisfy the arm's-length principle (for related party transactions), be consistent with good business and engineering practices (which is technically a new requirement) and be approved by BP Migas and included in the relevant work programme and budget. GR 79/2010 also outlines 24 items of spending for which cost recovery is not allowed.

Moreover, GR 79/2010 stipulates that the Indonesian government has a right to demand that the tax be paid in kind. While this may look like a new feature that will require detailed guidance for its implementation, it essentially returns the production sharing contract to the position prevailing before 1976 but with a different net profit split. The amendment in the mid-1970s was made so that the contractor could claim a tax credit in its home country in order to reduce losses resulting from the Indonesian government's demand for a higher share of production. Consequently, the government's demand for tax payment in the form of oil or gas may create problems for the contractor (especially those from United States) if it seeks to claim a tax credit, thereby making Indonesia's production sharing contract less attractive.

In addition, as mentioned previously, GR 79/2010 now imposes a transfer tax of either 5% or 7% depending on whether the contract is in the exploration or the exploitation stage. The 5% tax rate will be imposed on gross proceeds where the transfer is for purposes other than risk sharing. GR 79/2010 still protects partial assignments such as farm-outs during the exploration stage if the interest to be assigned has been held for more than three years and the transfer is not intended to generate a gain. The 7% tax rate is levied on gross proceeds of transfers during the exploitation stage, except where the transfer is to an Indonesian 'national company', as defined in the contract's clause regarding the contractor's obligation to offer a 10% participating interest to such a national company.

In summary, GR 79/2010 has considerably changed the commercial terms of existing contracts, which in the past had been the subject of negotiation between the parties. An application for judicial review of GR 79/2010 submitted by the Indonesia Petroleum Association (representing the petroleum industry) was not accepted by the Supreme Court. What the impact of GR 79/2010 on oil and gas activities will be remains to be seen.

5. Conclusion

In terms of substantive content, Indonesia's oil contracts are a mixture of private and public law. The private law elements are necessary consequences of the contractual and commercial nature of the transaction, while the public law elements cover government control, state participation, domestic supply obligations, safety, environmental protection, the local content requirement and taxation.

The main contractual issue relating to Indonesia's production sharing contract in essence deals with maintaining the sanctity of contract, which essentially means according recognition to the contractual framework which embodies the understanding reached between the parties within the appropriate legislative context, in order that the parties' rights are protected and enforceability is not eroded. While the legal principle of *pacta sunt servanda* (contracts are binding) has been challenged in the petroleum sector, the principle continues to be observed as embodying behavioural standards like acting in good faith. As in many civil law countries, the principle of good faith is recognised in Indonesian contract law.

However, Indonesia's production sharing contract does not contain a stabilisation or renegotiation clause, a provision requiring that any action altering the balance in the agreed fiscal arrangements be compensated by another action that restores the effect of the original provision (re-balancing). It should be noted that such renegotiation is usually only applicable to the commercial terms of a contract, as many governments will be reluctant to agree stabilising for non-fiscal areas such as environmental or health and safety matters. Coincidentally, these are areas where the risks to investors have grown considerably in recent years.

As a final note, on November 13 2012, Indonesia's Constitutional Court declared that the existence of BP Migas was unconstitutional because it degraded state control over natural resources. While one judge expressed a dissenting opinion, the majority of the court's panel of judges found BP Migas did not directly manage oil and gas and instead handed it over to state-owned companies or private companies through cooperation contracts. According to the judges, such a mechanism limited the state's ability to ensure that the maximum possible benefit from the use of natural resources goes to the Indonesian people's welfare, as required by Article 33 of the 1945 Constitution. Despite disbanding BPMigas, the Constitutional Court ruled that all contracts concluded by BP Migas will remain in force until their expiration dates, to avoid unnecessary legal uncertainty. As a consequence of the ruling, BP Migas has been disbanded and, pursuant to Presidential Decree 9 of 2013 all of its functions have been transferred to Satuan Kerja Khusus Minyak dan Gas Bumi (SKK Migas) or the Special Work Unit for Oil and Gas Activities.

The scope, responsibilities and structure of SSK Migas are quite similar to those of its predecessor. However, it is now overseen by a committee led by the minister of energy and mineral resources and including the deputy minister of finance (deputy chairman), the head of the Indonesia Investment Coordinating Board and the deputy minister of energy and mineral resources.

Conclusion

Eduardo G Pereira
STR Holding
Kim Talus
University of Eastern Finland

This book has examined upstream law and regulation in over 30 jurisdictions around the world. These jurisdictions share many similarities, but they also have their differences. For example, some jurisdictions rely on contractual arrangements that can at times be complex and involve a range of negotiable components. The government take can likewise be both negotiable and complex, as the Indonesian example illustrates. Other jurisdictions rely on administrative licences as a basis for upstream activities. As with contractual arrangements, the level of complexity varies. Some jurisdictions have opted for a simple system, where bidding is based on a bonus only (eg, the United States); whereas others have a range of biddable components, ranging from monetary items to local content-related issues (eg, Brazil).

In addition to individual national circumstances, historical and external factors help to explain these differences. Whether a jurisdiction is a new or established petroleum-producing country will have an impact on issues such as local content provisions or national oil company participation. Countries such as Norway have moved from significant local content and national oil company participation to a more level playing field, and national preferences have been abolished – although in Norway's case this is also a legal requirement due to its EEA membership. In countries such as Mozambique, it was considered – rightly or wrongly – that due to the absence of a national industry, a local content provision would make no sense in the immediate term. Other countries, such as Sudan, have emphasised local content in order to create a national industry base.

Areas or reserves can be mature or 'wildcat'; here again, the difference may be reflected in the legislation. The movement offshore is one example of this, and many countries (eg, India) offer additional economic benefits to companies exploring in offshore areas. Government or national oil company participation can also differ in certain valuable deep offshore areas, as in Brazil – but this is rather to secure the national interest.

Shale gas has similarly triggered dramatic change in the industry. Not only are joint operating agreements and other petroleum contracts being modified to accommodate this new type of unconventional gas, but national laws are also being revised or even enacted to respond to a change in status from non-producer to gas or oil-producing state. Poland is one such example.

While the emergence of national oil companies is nothing new (including in western jurisdictions), this has also driven change in international upstream operations. Most petroleum resources globally are now held by national oil companies, rather than international oil companies. However, a distinction must be made in terms of resources held with a national oil company's home state and those held abroad. Many national oil companies primarily hold national petroleum reserves. However, there are also several internationally active national oil companies – such as the Chinese national oil companies, Russia's Rosneft, Norway's Statoil and Algeria's Sonatrach. These entities – often with the political support of the home state – are actively bidding for new reserves or new acreage. This may further be supported by other state or state-company activities in the target country. Deals for petroleum reserves may thus include several side deals relating to infrastructure, education and other development projects. This seems to be particularly true of the entry strategy of the Chinese national oil companies.

As has been seen throughout this book, national oil companies have a wide range of responsibilities and roles. In some countries (eg, Mexico), they act as regulators; in other countries (eg, offshore Brazil), they act as national champions and mandatory partners; and in others they are active on international markets and act either as an arm of the state or as an international oil company.

Historical factors also have a strong influence on this area of national and international law and policy. The choice between the various types of host government contract or granting instrument is one example of this. Consider the choice between a production sharing agreement (PSA) or concession system. The original concessions, which were typical in the industry before World War II, were extremely unfavourable to the host state. The international oil companies controlled the government's revenue by regulating production, which severely compromised national sovereignty over resources and curtailed the wealth that these resources could generate for a country. In the post-World War II era – which was marked by growing nationalism in the post-colonial world – these contracts were associated with colonialism and seen as a *de facto* extension of Western powers exerting control within the host country. Claims over national sovereignty caused a shift away from this type of contract. Accordingly, the old pro-international oil company contracts were gradually replaced by other types of arrangement: modern-type concessions and, in particular, PSAs.

Modern concessions are primarily used in countries such as the United States[1] and the United Kingdom, where the growth of the petroleum industry is disconnected from the stigma of colonialism and foreign domination. However, other factors also affect the choice of contract form, such as historical familiarity with their use or the host government's desire to retain ownership and control over hydrocarbons produced from its soil; and concessions are also used in other post-colonial countries, such as Argentina or Brazil. In many countries, a mixed system of concessions and PSAs is in operation for onshore and offshore operations, respectively.[2]

---

1 In the United States, both private landowners and the government (for land owned by it or offshore properties) have the right to lease the right to exploit hydrocarbons in a given area to an exploration and production company.

2 This has been examined in detail in K Talus, S Looper and S Otillar, "*Lex Petrolea* and the internationalization of petroleum agreements: focus on Host Government Contracts", *Journal World Energy Law and Business* (5) 3 (2012), pp 181–193.

Largely because of these similarities, and the international nature of the petroleum industry, the issue of *'Lex Petrolea'* has attracted attention in recent decades. Initially, *Lex Petrolea* was considered mainly in relation to international dispute resolution in this area, and followed on from the 1982 *Kuwait v Aminoil* case[3] and Doak Bishop's article on the topic published in 1998. In his study Bishop concluded, after a thorough examination of 25 years of arbitral awards, that the precedential value of those awards had "not yet created a mature set of legal regulations, but it ha[d] developed the beginnings of a *lex petrolea* that serves to instruct, and in a certain sense even regulate – within broadly-defined boundaries – the international petroleum industry".[4]

Today, the possible existence of a specific *Lex Petrolea* is examined in a wider context, beyond international and national dispute settlement in the energy sector. Regimes such as national petroleum legislation, specific host government contracts and petroleum industry practices, as enshrined in model contracts, have been included in the discussion.[5]

Some have argued in favour of such regime, suggesting either that it is in the making or that its existence would "contribute to international investment and cooperation".[6] It has also been argued that "[n]otwithstanding the existence or not of a *Lex Petrolea,* certain international best practises are increasingly visible in international petroleum contracts regardless of the transaction location". These common practices and the internationalisation of host government contracts are largely a result of "the availability of models and the interest of States to learn from earlier examples, from the influence of international institutional and private actors and international education in this area".[7] Similar international best practices are also visible in national upstream regimes.

International influences can be detected in several areas. These include "local content programs to promote local industry and the use of R-Factor and other sliding scales that capture additional revenue for host governments while ensuring IOCs recover costs and an acceptable profit margin. Other common features would relate to cost recovery limits, operating committees, rights for secondment, the right to gain local real-time decision making capabilities and ultimately develop local talent

---

3 *Government of the State of Kuwait v American Independent Oil Co (AMINOIL),* Award of May 24 1982, 21 *International Legal Materials* (ILM) at 976 (1982).

4 RD Bishop, "International Arbitration of Petroleum Disputes: The Development of a Lex Petrolea", XXIII *Yearbook Comm Arb'n* 1131, 1207–08 (1998).

5 K Talus, S Looper and S Otillar, *"Lex Petrolea* and the internationalization of petroleum agreements: focus on Host Government Contracts", *Journal World Energy Law and Business* (5) 3 (2012), pp 181-193; T Martin, *"Lex Petrolea* in the International Oil and Gas Industry", in R King, *Dispute Resolution in the Energy Sector: A Practitioner's Handbook* (Globe Law and Business 2012), with references. See also A Timothy Martin and J Jay Park, QC, "Global petroleum industry model contracts revisited: Higher, faster, stronger", (3) 1 *Journal of World Energy Law & Business* (2010), p 7; and TCC Childs, "Update on *Lex Petrolea*: The continuing development of customary law relating to international oil and gas exploration and production", *Journal of World Energy Law and Business* (4) 3 (2011), pp 214–259; M Sornarajah, *The International Law on Foreign Investment* (Cambridge University Press 2010), p 301, arguing that "Lex petrolea, if it does exist, depend largely on contract forms, arbitral awards interpreting them and writings on the subject".

6 LE Cuervo, "OPEC From Myth to Reality", 30 *Hou J Int'l* L 433, P535 (2008).

7 K Talus, S Looper and S Otillar, *"Lex Petrolea* and Internationalisation of Petroleum Agreements: Focus on Host Government Contracts', *Journal of World Energy Law and Business* (2012) 5(3), pp 181–193.

and resources. Another important international development is national reservation or security, where the host state can require production to be used locally before it can be exported if needed for national energy policy".[8]

This conclusion picks up on some of these themes and examines how the jurisdictions included in this book have dealt with issues such as the creation of a national oil company, local content and national reservation. Additionally, the legal foundations of the ownership regime for petroleum are briefly examined.

2. Creation and role of national oil companies

Many petroleum-exporting countries have decided to create a national oil company. Even without a national oil company, the role of the state in upstream petroleum must be carefully considered. The creation of a national oil company is but one option. Moreover, the creation of a national oil company does not address all questions relating to the role of the state and the various conflicting interests within the jurisdiction. While the creation of a national oil company will often help in developing national know-how – sometimes very efficiently, as in the case of Norway – and might lead to greater efficiency, this is not necessarily the case. As always, the devil is the detail: the national oil company might have obligations that interfere with its commercial operations. Consider Venezuela, where PDVSA acts in areas that have little or no connection to upstream or downstream petroleum activities. Similarly, the national oil company might be very close to being a national governmental or regulatory arm – consider Mexico's PEMEX. Foreign policy, regulation of upstream and downstream markets and other similar roles conflict with the purely commercial role that other national oil companies might have.

China is both an interesting example and a special case, as it has several national oil companies with different roles in the petroleum sector. CPNC is China's largest oil and gas producer and supplier, by both production and sales volumes; it is also a leading integrated energy company and a major oilfield and engineering services provider. CNOOC Limited is an upstream company focusing on the exploration, development and production of oil and natural gas. The company is the dominant oil and natural gas producer in offshore China and the third largest energy company in China, behind CNPC and Sinopec. Sinopec in turn is the largest integrated petroleum and petrochemical company, and the largest refined oil producer in China. It is also the largest distributor of refined oil products in China by sales volumes and runs the largest number of service stations in China. Under the applicable laws, CNOOC is responsible for negotiating with foreign partners in offshore upstream activities, while both CNPC and Sinopec have the right to negotiate production sharing contracts with foreign partners in onshore upstream activities.[9] The role of the Chinese national oil companies is often perceived in the context of more general Chinese foreign policy. Here, the internationally active national oil companies are relevant. In certain areas, such as some parts of Africa, the

---

8 K Talus, S Looper and S Otillar, '*Lex Petrolea* and Internationalisation of Petroleum Agreements: Focus on Host Government Contracts', *Journal of World Energy Law and Business* (2012) 5(3), pp 181-193.

9 See the China chapter.

Chinese presence is overwhelming – not only in the petroleum sector, but in national economies more generally. In some places, this is starting to create tensions.

However, a single national oil company in a given country – either active in the upstream sector or with a wider mandate and role – is more typical. One example of a national oil company with a wider remit is Qatar Petroleum, a state-owned corporation created in 1974. Its role encompasses upstream oil and gas operations, but also petrochemicals, metals, financial services and real estate, through its various subsidiaries and joint ventures. In contrast, Egyptian General Petroleum Company (EGPC) is tasked with managing upstream activities and, in doing so, implementing government oil policy: this variously involves maximising declining domestic oil production, securing additional foreign direct investment and operating the country's large refining system. In addition to holding shares in the production through partnership with international oil companies, EGPC directly produces 20% of the production.[10]

Mexico's PEMEX, on the other hand, not only is a national oil company, but also acts much like a regulator – especially in the wake of the 2008 reforms. PEMEX also has the power to call its own bid rounds, can choose its contractors, can issue its own safety rules and still has many of the legal powers commonly held by regulators. In many ways, PEMEX may be regarded as akin to a law-enforcing government entity.[11]

A more traditional type of national oil company is Greenland's NUNAOIL, which was set up in 1984.[12] Today, the company is a non-operating oil company which is custodian of the Greenland government's ownership shares of licences. Under Article 17(2) of the Mineral Resources Act, a licence can prescribe that a company owned or controlled by the Greenland government is entitled to participate in the licence.[13] Similarly, Mozambique national oil company Empresa Nacional de Hidrocarbonetos, was established as a state-controlled with a monopoly over the petroleum sector. The national petroleum regime grants it the right to establish joint ventures with foreign companies for the exploration and exploitation of petroleum.[14] Azerbaijan's State Oil Company of Azerbaijan Republic (SOCAR) is similarly tasked with the exploration and exploitation of onshore and offshore oil and gas fields, as well as with the transportation, processing, refining and sale of oil, gas, condensate and other related products.[15]

The role of a national oil company thus varies significantly from jurisdiction to jurisdiction. However, regardless of its specific role, one common feature is some level of governmental intervention. This is particularly sensitive in countries such as Brazil (for the pre-salt area), as any investor will have to deal with two types of national oil company within the same consortium (ie, Petro-Sal and Petrobras).

3. Granting instrument: licence or contract?

Granting instruments or host government contracts are typically concluded between

10 See the Qatar chapter.
11 See the Mexico chapter.
12 Set up under Danish Act 595/1984.
13 See the Greenland chapter.
14 See the Mozambique chapter.
15 See the Azerbaijan chapter.

a host government authority, government, ministry or national oil company on the one hand, and an exploration and production company on the other. The contract establishes a basis for the international oil company to operate in the country, and sets out the parties' rights and obligations. In addition to provisions on the division of production or revenue – an issue which is crucial to the deal for both parties – other clauses on matters such as work commitments and other obligations of the international oil company, local content obligations and information-sharing obligations can be included in the granting instrument. These instruments can variously be categorised as licences, concessions, PSAs and service agreements.

Inevitably, however, international practice does not strictly follow these categorisations. As such, a hybrid model is widely used, comprising elements from two or more of these four general instruments.[16] Many countries also use more than one of these different instruments. One example is Tunisia, where two agreements are in use for upstream oil and gas: concession agreements, where the oil and gas company is the holder or co-holder of the permit/concession; and production sharing contracts, concluded between the national oil company – Entreprise Tunisienne des Activités Pétrolières, which is the holder of the permit and all concessions issued – and a service provider.[17] Uganda also uses a hybrid system, where the PSA is supplemented by an exploration licence for exploration activities and a production licence for production activities. Similarly, the Russian system encompasses both options, and subsoil rights can be awarded either through a licensing regime or through the conclusion of a PSA. To formalise the right of subsoil use, a subsoil licence is also issued within 30 days of execution of the PSA. In this case the licence agreement reflects the general terms and conditions of the PSA.[18]

Sometimes the legal label and the actual content of the agreement do not correspond to the general categorisations. For example, while still formally termed a 'concession agreement', the main granting instrument in Egypt is technically a PSA. The 'contractor' (ie, the international oil company) agrees that in exchange for recovering its costs and a profit to explore and develop a specified area, it will share future production with EGPC, EGAS or Ganope – one of which, along with the government, will also be a party to the agreement.[19]

PSAs are also widely used in Africa and the Middle East. Upstream activities in Sudan are based on an exploration PSA whose parameters might depend on the potential afforded by the geological area under consideration (although these are negotiable).[20] Qatar also uses exploration PSAs and development PSAs.[21] Other types of contract are also used in the region, however – for instance, petroleum operations subsequent to the enactment of the 2001 Petroleum Law in Mozambique are conducted on the basis of a concession contract, but this actually has features of a PSA.[22] Iraq uses service contracts, which have some similarities to PSAs.[23]

---

16 E Smith, J Dzienkowski, O Anderson, J Lowe, B Kramer and J Weaver, *International Petroleum Transactions* (Colorado: Rocky Mountain Mineral Law Foundation 2010), p 501.
17 See the Tunisia chapter.
18 See the Uganda chapter.
19 See the Egypt chapter.
20 See the Sudan chapter.
21 See the Qatar chapter.

Argentina uses concessions which are public law contracts, realised through administrative decrees, and supplemented by the applicable legal and regulatory framework. A decree granting a concession to a particular company authorises that company to conduct the relevant activities, with an annual fee payable for each square kilometre under concession.[24] Similarly, Norway uses a concession system: the state depends on private companies to conduct exploration and production activities, and grants concessions to groups of companies for this purpose. The main concession is the so-called 'production licence'.[25]

Denmark uses two types of agreement: prospecting licences and exploration and exploitation licences.[26] Following this model, the rights connected with the exploration and extraction of minerals in Greenland are based on a licence system, which in turn is based on a number of specific licences, with associated conditions. The Mineral Resources Act has separate rules for hydrocarbon licences and for other mineral licences.[27]

The Mexican regime is a classic example of a service contract-based system. As a result of the constitutional reforms of 1960, only a restricted range of service contracts may be used to hire companies in Mexico. While certain types of service contract allow contractors to be paid in kind or in cash equivalents, the Mexican contracts provide only for cash payments, which may not be representative of the value of hydrocarbon production.[28]

It is thus apparent that any contractual arrangement can achieve the goals established by a government or international oil company: the main issue is not the title of the agreement, but rather its content. As mentioned, most titles do not in fact reflect the reality of the agreement – for example, a concession-type agreement should not refer to cost recovery. The details of the agreement are thus the primary concern for both government and investor.

4. Local content

The role of local content provisions will depend on the country and its pre-existing knowledge and industrial base. Local content is a particularly significant issue for emerging petroleum-producing countries, as it promotes economic development, helping to advance national know-how and industry both in the petroleum sector and more widely.

In some countries, such as Norway, there has been a logical progression in this respect. In the early days of petroleum activities in Norway, the regulatory framework promoted the use of Norwegian contractors and suppliers. International oil companies were to a certain extent required to favour Norwegian suppliers, to the extent that they could be deemed competitive with international players. This allowed the country to build up significant expertise in the petroleum industry.

22 See the Mozambique chapter.
23 See the Iraq chapter.
24 See the Argentina chapter.
25 See the Norway chapter.
26 See the Denmark chapter.
27 See the Greenland chapter.
28 See the Mexico chapter.

Under the current system, the EEA agreement prohibits discrimination based on nationality.[29] As in Norway, the local content provisions in Denmark and Poland are restricted by those countries' EU membership. Although part of Denmark, Greenland is not part of the European Union and can thus apply local content requirements. Article 18 of the Mineral Resources Act provides that a licence for exploration and/or exploitation may stipulate the extent to which the licensee must use labour from Greenland, use Greenlandic enterprises for contracts, supplies and services, and be socially sustainable.[30]

A good example of a local content plan in developing countries (in terms of upstream petroleum activities) is the Sudanese scheme. This aims to gradually replace expatriate employees with local Sudanese, providing for on-the-job training, annual formal training programmes and more.[31] In Uganda, licensees must present a local content plan as part of the process. Local content provisions are also contained in the Ugandan PSAs: the law provides that the licensee must give "preference to goods which are produced or available in Uganda and services which are rendered by Ugandan citizens". There is also a supervisory scheme which requires a licensee to submit to the Petroleum Authority, at least 60 days before the end of the year, a report of its achievements and those of its subcontractors in utilising Ugandan goods and services. Similarly, 12 months after grant of the licence and on each anniversary of the grant, the licensee must submit to the Petroleum Authority a detailed programme for the recruitment and training of Ugandans in all phases of petroleum operations. A licensee must also have a clearly defined programme for training local employees, whether through scholarships or training within or outside Uganda.[32]

While local content provisions have become common over time, their precise content varies significantly. In some cases these variables seem to relate to specific national circumstances; in others they seem to reflect what the state regarded as most valuable in the negotiations, or what the international consulting team advising the state considered important – most likely a combination of the two.

In Bolivia, the law requires that certain clauses be included in all petroleum agreements, one of which is an obligation to give preference to local manpower. This includes providing internships to students or higher-level graduates and training YPFB personnel. Similarly, local goods and services must be preferred where these are equivalent in terms of quality, quantity, price and availability.[33] Some countries, such as Afghanistan, go even further, obliging investors to utilise local capacity even where this is more expensive, up to a certain limit.

The Egyptian PSAs also contains local content provisions to promote employment and training and the use of local materials. These must be prioritised wherever possible. There are also obligations to pay a certain amount of salaries in the Egyptian currency, and to favour local contractors and locally manufactured materials as long as performance corresponds to international standards and is no

29 See the Norway chapter.
30 See the Greenland chapter.
31 See the Sudan chapter.
32 See the Uganda chapter.
33 See the Bolivia chapter.

more than 10% more expensive than international equivalents.[34]

Tunisia also imposes an obligation to employ Tunisian personnel, as long as this does not create operational difficulties. If there is no Tunisian expertise in a given field, Tunisian personnel must be trained in the field and a training programme submitted and approved by the granting authority.[35]

The Mexican local content scheme is based on national value added, which cannot be less than 40% of the total goods and services utilised under the contract.[36]

In China, foreign contractors must give preference to the use of Chinese goods, equipment and services, provided that these are internationally competitive in terms of price, quality and/or performance.

The Indonesian scheme is somewhat complicated: different obligations apply depending on the size of the company, with the percentage of goods and services that must be sourced locally ranging from 7.5% 15%. Numerous other very precise obligations must also be fulfilled.[37]

The Russian requirements are less complicated, but also quite detailed and extensive. Among other things, they specify that:

- Russian legal entities should have a pre-emptive right to participate in the works under a PSA, in the capacity of suppliers, subcontractors and service providers; and
- at least 80% of the employees for the project should be Russian citizens or at least 70% of the equipment for the project should be of the Russian origin.

Many other requirements must also be fulfilled.[38]

In contrast, some countries – such as Mozambique – have no local content policy. While India does not include local content as a bidding criterion, its model contract does include provisions on the use of both local manpower and local goods and services. Other countries, such as Argentina, have no national requirements on local content, but such requirements can be imposed by provincial governments.

Pakistan is another interesting example in this regard: although local content obligations are in place, it has no domestic industry on which to rely for their fulfilment, as no major equipment is produced in Pakistan.[39] However, the local content requirements may perhaps be intended to further Pakistan's development in this regard.

Local content is thus a relevant issue for any developing or underdeveloped country. These countries should seek solutions that could enhance their economy as a whole, because oil and gas are non-renewable resources. Norway and Scotland have managed to leverage their local content requirements to establish a thriving new industry: today, they export technologies and expertise on the back of decades of local content investment. However, local content requirements should also be

---

34 See the Egypt chapter.
35 See the Tunisia chapter.
36 See the Mexico chapter.
37 See the Indonesia chapter.
38 See the Russia chapter.
39 See the Pakistan chapter.

progressive and moderate. They should be achievable in both the short term and the long term, as the ultimate goal is to produce oil and gas. A balance must therefore be struck between the economic realities in the country and the need for further investment; and it is often difficult to determine whether international prices and quality are consistent with the local market.

5. National reservation

One of the more recent innovations in the requirements that host states impose on international oil companies is a requirement to supply the host state market before selling the petroleum internationally. This requirement can take different forms: it can be absolute, or limited to emergencies or to supply shortages.

Sudan has a detailed national reservation policy. The contractor must give first priority to local demand for petroleum, on a *pro rata* basis with other petroleum producers in Sudan. This petroleum, over a period and of a certain type, grade, quantity and quality, is to be determined by the government. Prices will correspond to competitive international prices for oil or gas of the same type, grade and quality at the time of sale.[40]

The Egyptian scheme provides that the national oil company has the right of first refusal to dispose of all or part of the contractor's share, in order to meet local market needs. Similarly, in the event of a war or national emergency, the Egyptian PSA grants the government a right of requisition over all or part of the production, as well as the related facilities. The PSA provides for compensation in such cases, except where damage is due to an enemy attack.[41]

In Tunisia, the granting authority has a priority right to buy a share of the hydrocarbons produced by the concession holder or for its account, in order to meet national demand. For petroleum, this share is pro-rated at a maximum rate of 20% of the volume produced by each concession; for gas, the share will be specified in a gas supply contract.[42]

In Pakistan, natural gas exports are allowed only if natural gas reserves exceed 15 years of aggregate demand (this threshold is unlikely to be reached in the foreseeable future).[43]

Crude oil and natural gas produced in India are subject to a domestic market obligation, which provides: "Until such time as the total availability of Crude Oil and Condensate from all Petroleum production activities in India meets the total national demand as determined by the Government, each Company comprising the Contractor, shall sell in the domestic market in India all of the Company's entitlement to Crude Oil and Condensate from the Contract Area."[44]

In Pakistan, Article 158 of the Constitution provides that the province in which a well head of natural gas is situated has precedence over other parts of Pakistan in

---

40 See the Sudan chapter.
41 See the Egypt chapter.
42 See the Tunisia chapter.
43 See the Pakistan chapter.
44 See the India chapter.

meeting supply requirements from that well head, subject to the commitments and obligations as on the day of commencement.[45]

Mozambique has no domestic supply obligations, except in the event of a national emergency.[46] Equally, there are no domestic supply provisions in Chinese PSAs.[47]

There are no rules on national reservation. Some countries might provide for a call option in special circumstances; others might provide for a right of first refusal over a certain amount of production; still others may have no regulations whatsoever. However, the reality is that petroleum agreements will remain valid for decades, and demand for oil and gas tends to vary over time and from country to country. The United States is a good example: historically a net importer of oil and gas, it may now be seeking export capacity as a result of its unconventional activities. Conversely, Indonesia is now seeking import capacity, whereas in previous decades it was a reliable exporter.

6. Ownership of petroleum resources

Ownership of petroleum resources can be structured in a number of ways. The United States and, to a limited extent, Canada are the only two countries where ownership of minerals is vested in individuals: the surface owner also owns the subsurface resources, unless these are expressly separated. Of course, not all minerals are owned by individuals – the owners can also be trusts, local, state or federal governments, Indian tribes, corporations, partnerships, limited liability companies or other forms of business entity.[48]

More commonly, ownership of hydrocarbons is vested in either the state or the people. Sometimes the management of these resources is organised so that various government levels control different areas. The best example is the United States, where the federal administration controls certain offshore areas and the state administrations control onshore areas.

In Azerbaijan, the ownership of all petroleum existing in its natural state underground or in subsurface strata is under the authority and control SOCAR.[49]

According to the Ugandan Constitution, the entire property in, and control of, all minerals and petroleum in, on or under any Ugandan land or waters are vested in the government, on behalf of the Republic of Uganda. The Parliament has the right to regulate upstream petroleum exploration and exploitation, the sharing of royalties, the restoration of land and so on. The Constitution also specifies that any petroleum exploitation must take into account the interests of individual landowners, local governments and the state government.[50]

The Bolivian Constitution 2009 reflects a strong presence of the state in all activities relating to the exploration and production of natural resources – mainly

45 See the Pakistan chapter.
46 See the Mozambique chapter.
47 See the China chapter.
48 See the US and Canada chapters.
49 See the Azerbaijan chapter.
50 See the Uganda chapter.

hydrocarbons. It provides that hydrocarbons – regardless of the state in which they are found or how they are extracted – are the inalienable and imprescriptible property of the Bolivian people. The state, on behalf of the Bolivian people, holds ownership of all hydrocarbon production in the country, and as such only the state is authorised to undertake its commercialisation. Thus, while the resources belong to the Bolivian people, it is the state's duty to administer the resources and their proceeds on behalf of the collective interest.[51]

Under Norwegian law, all offshore petroleum resources are owned by the state, and the state has exclusive rights of resource management. This important principle is stated in Section 1 of the Petroleum Act. In practice, the state depends on private companies for exploration and production, and grants concessions to groups of companies for this purpose.[52]

Under the Mexican system, all hydrocarbons in the national subsoil – whether in solid, gaseous or liquid form – are under the direct ownership of the Mexican nation.[53]

As a general rule, it may thus be said that oil and gas belong to the people of each country. Sometimes, the federal government will assume responsibility for managing these resources. Other times, this will be delegated to a regulator or even the national oil company. However, the main concern arising from this principle relates to its application. Does it refer to the entire nation, or more specifically to the relevant areas within each country? How about autonomous regions, such as Kurdistan; or even non-recognised areas, such as Somaliland? Each nation is comprised of different regions, so the principle should arguably apply as broadly as possible. However, the affected areas should also be compensated in a different manner, as they bear the risks associated with the petroleum activities. For example, in case of an oil spill, they will be the first – perhaps the only – affected area. It is thus necessary to strike a balance between investing in the future of the country as a whole and promoting development in the affected areas.

7. Conclusion

The upstream regulatory regime for oil and gas must achieve several objectives, and ensuring international competitiveness features high on that list. It is clear to most host governments that competition is intense on the current market. Each country is keen to understand what others are developing, so it can not only gauge the attractiveness of its own system, but also learn from different experiences. A good idea in one jurisdiction might be an even better idea elsewhere – and the opposite may also be true.

While comparisons are relevant, they must be based on a risk-reward parameter. For example, it is not possible to compare Norway with Uganda. Norway has a stable legal, political and economic regime, a well-developed industry with local and international service providers, and extensive proven reserves and production. It is

51 See the Bolivia chapter.
52 See the Norway chapter.
53 See the Mexico chapter.

also close to international markets and has easy access to sea and pipelines. Uganda is yet to start production, has no infrastructure in place and is a landlocked country. It is also far more vulnerable to political and legal instability, as the recent case of Tullow Oil has shown. While comparisons are important for both host governments and investors, they should be based on similar conditions in order to have any relevance.

Ultimately, the legal regime should thus follow the risk-reward principle. Greater risks should yield greater rewards; lower risks should yield lower rewards. If a host government does not follow this basic rule, it will be punished for the lack of investment. This is exactly what Algeria has learnt: while a harsh government take might be acceptable up to certain point, beyond that it will stifle new investments. As a result, time and investment will be lost until the balance can be re-established.

About the authors

Ivar Alvik
Associate professor, Scandinavian Institute of Maritime Law
ivar.alvik@jus.uio.no

Ivar Alvik is an associate professor at the Scandinavian Institute of Maritime Law, Department for Petroleum and Energy Law, at the Faculty of Law, University of Oslo. Previously he worked as a senior associate with Norwegian law firm Thommessen, focusing on arbitration and litigation in the maritime and petroleum industries. He was a research fellow at the Institute of Public and International Law at the Faculty of Law, University of Oslo from 2002 to 2006, and received his doctorate in 2007 on a dissertation on contract claims in international investment arbitration (published 2011 by Hart Publishing). He received his Cand Jur degree from the University of Oslo in 2000 and a M Jur from Oxford University in 2001.

Dario Arias
Senior legal counsel, Qatar Petroleum
arias@qp.com.qa/darioarias@hotmail.com

Dario Arias is an Argentine lawyer and senior counsel in the Projects division of Qatar Petroleum Legal Department. He holds a LLM in business law from Austral University (Argentina) and a LLM in mineral law and policy of the Centre for Energy, Petroleum and Mineral Law and Policy, University of Dundee, Scotland.

Mr Arias has participated on a number of teams that have negotiated transactions in a variety of sectors for over 15 years, mainly in oil and gas law. He has also participated in the discussion and drafting of several oil and gas regulations in Argentina, Bolivia and Qatar. He worked as an exploration and production in-house counsel for YPF, Repsol, Petrobras, BG Group and QP, in South America and the Middle East and Africa region. He has been arbitrator and counsel in a number of dispute resolution proceedings involving international oil companies.

He also lectured and authored a number of oil and gas, mining and environment publications.

Muhammad Arif
President, Energy Lawyers Association of Pakistan
muhammad.arif@opl.com.pk

Muhammad Arif is president of the Energy Lawyers Association of Pakistan as well as a full-time manager of legal and commercial for an upstream exploration and production company in Pakistan. He has been a member of the Rules and Policy Committee of the Pakistan Petroleum Exploration and Production Companies Association of Pakistan for the past 12 years.

He has an MBA from the University of Strathclyde, an LLM from the University of Dundee and a postgraduate diploma in exploration and production economics from the University of Oxford, United Kingdom.

Mr Arif has over 22 years' practical experience in the commercial, joint venture, corporate, legal and management side of upstream business. He is the author of *Pakistan Energy Law*, published by Kluwer Law International, and a number of papers on petroleum law and policy issues published by Oil and Gas Energy Law Intelligence and local newspapers.

Mohamed Atabani
President, Al-Sudan Energia
mta@alsudanenergia.com

Mohamed Atabani is the president of Alsudan Energia, a subsdiary of STR Holding, an oil and gas operator in Sudan. He has 14 years of oil and gas experience in business development, corporate planning, strategy development, technology management and academia. He holds a degree in chemical engineering and a master's in technology applications to oil and gas, and has led several projects in the oil and gas sector in Sudan.

Mr Atabani worked for both operators in Sudan and for Sudapet, the national oil company of Sudan, where he developed several strategic and technical alliances with reputable international companies aiming at providing Sudapet with international presence. While in Sudapet he supervised the development of several petroleum economic models and several research studies to advance the thinking in making the structure of Sudan's exploration and production sharing agreements more attractive while maintaining a balance of adequate pay for both investors and the nation.

Raul A Baldivia
Managing partner, Baldivia Unzaga & Asociados
rbaldivi@entelnet.bo

Raul Baldivia is a Bolivian lawyer. He has almost 20 years' extensive experience advising foreign investors on oil and gas law, international arbitration and the nationalisation of assets by host states. He has participated in the drafting and discussion of several oil and gas regulations for pipelines, rates, gas reinjection, right of way and open access rules, and advised the government in negotiation of bilateral investment treaties. He is an arbitrator of the Bolivian Chamber of Commerce.

Mr Baldivia holds an LLM in International Legal Studies (Fulbright scholarship) from the Washington College of Law at American University. He has been a law school professor and a lecturer at several universities (*Universidad Privada Boliviana, Universidad Católica* and *Universidad Andina*) and a guest speaker at international seminars.

For several years Mr Baldivia has been named as a leading lawyer in Bolivia by Chambers & Partners' global and Latin American directories.

Nigel Bankes
Professor of law, University of Calgary
ndbankes@ucalgary.ca

Nigel Bankes is a professor of law at the University of Calgary, where he also holds the chair in natural resources law. He is the former editor of the *Journal of Energy and Natural Resources Law* and he has published widely in the areas of water law, oil and gas law, and the rights of indigenous peoples.

Jose de Barros
Attorney and consultant
jose.barros@inp.gov.mz

Jose de Barros graduated in law from Eduardo Mondlane University, Maputo in 2001. For more than 12 years he has worked as a legal adviser at the Ministry of Mineral Resources, and for the last eight years he has advised the petroleum sector. He is currently head of the legal department for the National Petroleum Institute in Mozambique, assisting on petroleum matters.

As a senior legal adviser, Mr de Barros has extensive and in-depth knowledge of petroleum law, energy law and international negotiations. He was involved in the reform of the Mozambique petroleum legislation and the drafting of several model documents. He has also assisted in negotiations related to upstream agreements.

As an independent attorney, Mr de Barros is a member of the Law Society of Mozambique and managing director of consulting firm Sigma Consultores, Limited, where he advises on corporate transactions and foreign investment opportunities.

Manel Bondi
Independent Tax Advisor
manel.bondi@actua.tn

Manel Bondi has a master's degree in tax and accounting and a postgraduate diploma in tax law. She was with PricewaterhouseCoopers for over six years, in the tax and legal services department. She is currently an independent tax adviser.

Ms Bondi works on a broad cross-section of clients. She provides various tax services, including tax advice, tax structuring, tax optimisation, tax audits, tax due diligence, tax compliance and assistance before the tax department in case of tax controls.

Ms Bondi is also a lecturer specialised in international taxation. She participated in drafting the Tunisian section of *Worldwide Tax Summaries*, published by PricewaterhouseCoopers in 2012. She also participates annually in the World Bank's publication *Doing Business*.

Justyna Bremen
Professional development lawyer, Ashurst LLP
justyna.bremen@ashurst.com

Justyna Bremen is a professional development lawyer in the energy, transport and infrastructure department of Ashurst in London. She has considerable experience in the energy sector, having advised on a broad range of transactions, including conventional and renewable energy power projects, upstream oil and gas, as well as downstream gas and electricity markets regulation.

In her current role Ms Bremen has written extensively on energy matters, contributing to legal and industry publications.

Loïc Conan
Legal counsel, PICO International Petroleum
lconan@pico.com.eg

Paris and New-York qualified lawyer Loïc Conan has been based in Cairo, Egypt since 2010 and is legal counsel at Egyptian energy group PICO Petroleum. He has also advised BG Egypt. His experience includes drafting and negotiating industry-specific contracts, as well as commercial transactions related to assets/corporate acquisitions and divestments. He has also been involved in settling and cooperating with the Egyptian national petroleum company in connection with the legal and financial issues that arose in the aftermath of the Arab Spring. Among the articles he has published, one covered the recent situation in Egypt: "Material Risk in the Oil and Gas Industry, the Case of Egypt in the Turmoil of the Arab Spring". Mr Conan is a member of the Association of International Petroleum Negotiators and a contributing author to the *Oil, Gas, and Energy Law Journal.*

Ludmilla Corkey
Senior associate, Pinheiro Neto Advogados
lcorkey@pn.com.br

Ludmilla Corkey is a senior associate at Pinheiro Neto Advogados. Before joining Pinheiro Neto's oil and gas practice, she worked for integrated oil companies for over 10 years, advising on regulatory matters, business development projects, M&A transactions, infrastructure projects and oil and gas marketing. Ms Corkey received her BA and MPhil from the Catholic University of Rio de Janeiro, her LLB from Candido Mendes University and her LLM from Columbia University School of Law in New York. Ms Corkey began her career in the Rio de Janeiro office of El Paso Corporation. She also worked in Statoil's offices in Rio and Oslo.

Andrew B Derman
Head of the international energy practice group, Thompson & Knight LLP
andrew.derman@tklaw.com

Andrew B Derman is a partner and head of international energy practice group for Thompson & Knight LLP and chairman of Thompson & Knight Global Energy Services. He represents public and private companies and host governments in strategic design, commercial execution, negotiations, contract preparation and legal interpretation. Recent experience includes: acquisition and divestment efforts in North America, South America, Europe, Africa, Asia and Australia; commercialisation of natural gas; the full-range of host government contracts and industry contracts; LNG, GTL and unitisation projects; and litigation and arbitration.

Mr Derman completed the INSEAD Advanced Management Programme, Fontainebleau, France (1991), and obtained his JD from Temple University Law School (1978), where he worked on the Law Review (1976-1978). He is admitted to and a member of the State Bar of Texas, Pennsylvania and New York. He is board certified by the Texas Board of Legal Specialisation in the field of oil, gas and mineral law. He is a frequent speaker at conferences and universities worldwide and has published five books and numerous articles.

Paolo Esposito
Counsel, RAGA Advogados and Studio Legale Esposito
p.esposito@rosarioabrantesgarcia.com

Paolo Esposito holds a master's degree in law (Naples) and an LL.M (London). He is an *avvocato* (Italy), a solicitor of the Supreme Court of England and Wales, and FCIArb (London). Mr Esposito has wide experience in both domestic and international disputes, and specialises in the resolution of a wide range of commercial and investment disputes through complex and multi-party arbitrations, including matters under bilateral investment treaties and the Energy Charter Treaty. He has also experience as a mediator and a member of arbitration panels.

Mr Esposito focuses on offshore oil and gas and mining issues, and is a business consultant for several mining companies and contractors operating in the Sub-Saharan region. In addition, he teaches international arbitration at the Chartered Institute of Arbitrators in London and has published articles on arbitration topics. He is co-founder of the Arbitration Africa Project (arbitrationafrica.com).

Julian Cardenas Garcia
Visiting assistant professor, University of Houston Law Centre
Doctoral fellow, CREDIMI Université de Bourgogne
jcardenasgarcia@uh.edu

Julian Cardenas Garcia is a visiting assistant professor and the Andrews Kurth energy law scholar at the University of Houston Law Centre, where he teaches the courses "Transnational Petroleum Law in Latin America" and "International Investment Law". He is a Venezuelan attorney and doctoral fellow at the Research Centre on Investment and International Trade Law at the University of Bourgogne, France. He has been retained as an expert on Venezuelan law in an American Arbitration Association arbitration seated in Houston, involving petroleum service contracts in Venezuela. He has participated as a speaker in different conferences and lectures on petroleum transactions and investment law. Before his academic career, he served as a career diplomat at the Ministry of Foreign Affairs for nearly six years, working on sovereign boundary issues and multilateral affairs related to the Organisation of American States and the United Nations.

Bent Ole Gram Mortensen
Chair in commercial law, University of Southern Denmark
bom@sam.sdu.dk

Bent Ole Gram Mortensen holds a chair in commercial law, with a particular focus on environmental and energy law, at the University of Southern Denmark. For the past 20 years, Professor Gram Mortensen has been engaged in the legal aspects of the energy industry, including both upstream and downstream. He has written and contributed to a large number of articles and books in English, Danish and German, dealing with legal matters on both national and EU level.

Professor Gram Mortensen has previously worked for the Ministry of Justice, as a lawyer in private law firms and as a legal manager for Maersk Drilling. At present, he is a member of the Danish Energy Board of Appeal and chairman of the Valuation Authorities in Southern Denmark in compliance with the Renewable Energy Act.

Tracey Greenaway
Partner, Allens
Tracey.Greenaway@allens.com.au

Tracey Greenaway is an energy and natural resources partner at Allens in Perth. She has extensive experience in the sector, with a particular focus on oil and gas, both in Australia and internationally.

Ms Greenaway has advised on the development, financing and commercialisation of oil and gas projects in Europe, Australia (Northwest Shelf, Prelude and Ichthys), Libya, Oman, Nigeria, Russia and Qatar. She has particular expertise in the LNG sector having advised numerous buyers, sellers and also aggregators on a variety of LNG sales agreements (long term, short term and spot).

Before joining Allens in October 2012, Ms Greenaway spent eight years as a senior in-house counsel of Royal Dutch Shell, based in the Netherlands and Australia. Before joining Shell, she was part of Linklaters' global project finance team, based in London and Bangkok, advising on the project financing of international energy and infrastructure projects.

Miriam Grunstein
Associate professor, Center for Advanced Economic Research & Learning
Miriam.grunstein@cide.edu

Miriam Grunstein obtained her law degree from the *Instituto Tecnológico Autónomo de México* and amaster's and PhD (*summa cum laude*) from the Graduate School of Arts and Sciences of New York University.

Her experience in the energy sector began as a personal adviser to a commissioner of the Mexican Federal Energy Regulatory Commission, where she worked in a team dedicated to the analysis and drafting of energy regulations, directives, orders, resolutions and model contracts.

Dr Grunstein is an associate professor of law at the *Centro de Investigación y Docencia Económicas*, where she leads the research area of energy law. She has written a number of publications regarding energy law and has participated in many energy forums and conferences, both domestically and internationally. She is also international counsel at Chadbourne & Parke, Mexico City.

Samir Hadjiyev
Director, Grata Law Firm
shadjiyev@gratanet.com

Samir Hadjiyev graduated from the Law Faculty at Tefekkur University and then completed a course at the London Chartered Insurance Institute and obtained an LLM in international law from Baku State University. He also successfully passed various insurance law and management courses and training.

Mr Hadjiyev has held key management positions in various insurance companies in

Azerbaijan. His scope of competence comprised legal support and business development. He was appointed legal adviser and participated in drafting the Azerbaijan Law on Insurance Activities. He acted as the representative of an international law firm in Azerbaijan, managed its Baku office and advised clients in Azerbaijan and Kazakhstan on various issues related to finance, corporate, investment, commercial, labour and sub-soil law and intellectual property.

Mr Hadjiyev specialises in finance, corporate, commercial and investment law. He is fluent in Azeri, Russian and English.

Madjedi Hasan
Master consultant, PR Pranata Energi Nusantara
mh98@centrin.net.id

Madjedi Hasan is a master consultant at PT Pranata Energi Nusantara, specialising in Indonesia's energy sector. He holds a master's in petroleum engineering from the University of Oklahoma, and a master's and a doctorate in law from the University of Padjadjaran, focusing on Indonesia's petroleum and geothermal power projects.

In 1961 he served as a lecturer at the *Institut Teknologi Bandung*. In 1966 he joined PT Caltex Pacific Indonesia (the largest oil producer in Indonesia) and held various key positions in the company in Indonesia and the United States. Before retiring in 1989 he was the vice president of special projects. He has written numerous articles for presentation in various seminars and has published three books on Indonesian petroleum contracts. Since 2006 he has been a fellow charter arbitrator at the Indonesia National Arbitration Institute (BANI) and serves as an executive editor in the BANI *Journal*.

Ahmed Mousa Jiyad
Founder, Iraq/Development Consultancy and Research, Norway
mou-jiya@online.no

Ahmed Mousa Jiyad is an independent consultant and scholar. He is an associate of the Centre for Global Energy Studies and a senior energy expert mandated by the European Commission. He holds a BSc in economics (University of Baghdad, Iraq), a postgraduate diploma in planning (University of Birmingham, United Kingdom), an MSc in development studies (University of Bath, United Kingdom) and an MA from Fletcher School of Law (Harvard and Tufts Universities, United States). Mr Jiyad has over 40 years' extensive international professional experience from Iraq, the United Kingdom, the United States, Norway, Sudan, Uganda, Eritrea and Jordan. In Iraq (1968-1988) he worked as a lecturer at Almustansiriya University, a senior economist at the Ministry of Oil/the Iraq National Oil Company, chief expert and director at the Ministry of Trade and chief expert for the Council of Ministers.

Mr Jiyad is an active professional who regularly participates in international conferences, workshops and seminars. Since 1976 he has published widely on energy and developmental issues. Mr Jiyad is an Iraqi-Norwegian citizen – he was born in Iraq in 1945 and has lived in Norway since October 1989.

Ghada Kaptan
Legal counsel, BG Egypt SA
ghada.kaptan@bg-group.com

Ghada Kaptan is a legal counsel at BG Egypt SA, a subsidiary of UK group BG. She holds a BA in political science, LLB in law, and has a doctorate degree in the field of international law. She specialises in banking and finance and has worked for law firms in Egypt, the stock exchange and US aid projects. Ms Kaptan participated in *Doing Business in the Arab World* in 2010 and has led legal teams conducting due diligence and project finance projects.

Elison Karuhanga
Advocate, Republic of Uganda
rubafunya@yahoo.com

Elison Karuhanga is an advocate of the Superior Courts of Record in Uganda and has audience before the East African Court of Justice in Arusha, Tanzania. He has an LLM in oil and gas from the University of Aberdeen, an LLB from the University of Kent and a Diploma in Legal Practice from the Law Development Centre. He has written a number of articles for the New Nation newspaper in South Sudan on oil and gas law and policy. He works for the Ministry of Justice and Constitutional Affairs in Uganda and has previously worked in the legal department of a local commercial bank. Mr Karuhanga is well conversant with legal and policy matters in East Africa. He is also a member of the Association of International Petroleum Negotiators.

Harm Kerstholt
Partner, Nauta Dutilh NV
harm.kerstholt@nautadutilh.com

Harm Kerstholt is the head of the energy and utilities industry group. He primarily works for clients in the energy and natural resources industry and focuses on mergers and acquisitions, (energy) contracting and litigation.

Mr Kerstholt has worked on many major transactions and projects in the Dutch oil and gas market, including advising the lenders of two LNG facilities in Rotterdam, an underground gas storage facility in salt caverns, the Bergermeer gas storage facility and various power plant projects. He publishes frequently and teaches energy contracting for a postgraduate course at the University of Amsterdam.

Mr Kerstholt became a partner in 2006. The *International Who's Who of Oil & Gas Lawyers* recognises him as one of the highest ranking individuals for oil and gas work in the Netherlands. Chambers Europe described him as "intelligent and creative" and quotes clients saying "he provided tremendous value to us not just as a lawyer but also, generally, as a local business adviser".

Dario Gerardo Lamanna
Legal counsel, CNP
dario.lamanna@yahoo.com

Dario Gerardo Lamanna is an Argentinean attorney. He has an MBA and completed postgraduate studies in oil and gas law. He holds degrees from the Senior Management Programme at IDE Business School and the Management Development Programme at IAE Business School, *Universidad Austral*. He has spoken at several congresses and conferences on oil and gas in Latin America. Mr Lamanna is a university professor and the author of diverse books and international publications, such as the *Oil, Gas and Energy Law Journal*, the International Bar Association, OGEL, *La Ley, El Derecho* and *Petroleum*. He also wrote *Regime of Hydrocarbons in Latin America*, published by Editorial Abaco de Rodolfo Depalma (Buenos Aires, Argentina, 2007, second edition in progress).

Mr Lamanna has extensive experience advising high-profile multinational corporations, with wide expertise in energy deals and M&A transactions across Latin America. He is legal manager and director of several international petroleum companies and a member of the board of different energy corporations, chambers and associations. He is also a board member of the Association of International Petroleum Negotiators.

Mabrouk Maalaoui
Tax partner, PricewaterhouseCoopers
mabrouk.maalaoui@tn.pwc.com

Mabrouk Maalaoui has a diploma from the French National Tax School and a postgraduate diploma from the Tunis College of Civil Servants. Before joining PricewaterhouseCoopers, he was the head of the Tax Legislation Department of the Ministry of Finance and headed the Tunisian Committee to negotiate double taxation treaties.

Mr Maalaoui is the author of several publications. He is currently a tax partner at PricewaterhouseCoopers in Tunisia and provides tax and regulatory assistance to clients in several industries.

Anselme Patipéwé Njiakin
Lawyer, Ernst & Young Chad
patipewea@yahoo.fr

Anselme Patipéwé Njiakin has long international experience as a tax lawyer. He now specialises in the extractive industry (mining and petroleum). He has extensive tax experience in the industry's production and sharing regimes. Mr Njiakin is an authorised Economic and Monetary Community of Central Africa tax adviser and is a member of the Association of International Petroleum Negotiators.

As a tax consultant he has carried out many assignments throughout central Africa; his recent projects include work in Equatorial Guinea, Cameroon and Chad.

For five years Mr Nijakin has worked as a tax consultant at Fidafrica, a member of PricewaterhouseCoopers in Cameroon and Malabo. He headed the tax department of audit firm ECA in Cameroon and Chad, and is currently senior manager at Ernst & Young Chad.

Mr Nijakin holds degrees in international business law and commerce from the University of Tours (France) and a certificate of the International Law Institute in Washington, DC for the 2012 International Oil and Gas Seminar.

Mwendia Nyaga
Lead adviser and chief executive officer, Oil & Energy Services Limited
mnyaga@oilandenergy.co.ke

Mwendia Nyaga is a seasoned professional with over eight years' experience in the oil and gas industry in Kenya. He has been chief executive officer of the National Oil Corporation of Kenya, and also served as an adviser to the Kenyan government on upstream licensing and downstream logistics and marketing. He is currently the lead adviser and chief executive of Oil & Energy Services, a boutique oil and gas advisory firm providing consulting services for individuals and firms with an interest in the upstream and downstream petroleum industry in the Eastern Africa region. Mr Nyaga is a certified public accountant of Kenya and an active member of the Institute of Certified Public Accountants of Kenya and the Society of Petroleum Engineers. He holds a bachelor of commerce degree from the University of Nairobi.

Waniss A Otman
Petroleum economist
o_waniss@hotmail.com

Waniss A Otman is a petroleum economist who specialises in the area of risk and uncertainty analysis. He holds a PhD, an MSc, an LLM, an MSc, a mini MBA, and a BSc. He has written many peer-reviewed articles and authored several books: *The Libyan Petroleum Industry in the Twenty-First Century; The Libyan Economy: Economic Diversification and International Repositioning; Libya Oil and Gas Resources; Oil and Gas Fiscal Review; Understanding Modern Libya; Africa's Energy and Natural Resources in the Global Economy;* and *Natural Gas Markets in the Middle East and North Africa* (contributor).

In his early career Dr Otman was employed by the Libyan Ministry of Energy as an analyst in the Investment and Economics Affairs Department. In 2004 he was appointed head of the Libyan Permanent Gas Committee, a member of the Higher Committee for Energy Strategies in Libya and a member of the Libyan Petroleum Agreements Evaluation and Studies Committee. He currently manages companies actively involved in the upstream oil and gas sector.

Anna Ovcharova
Legal counsel, TNK-BP Management
asovcharova@tnk-bp.com

Anna Ovcharova deals with M&A, integration and upstream projects, including large-scale international projects, at Moscow-based TNK-BP Management. She holds two master's degrees in law and is at the final stage of her PHD. Ms Ovcharova focuses on corporate, energy and natural resources law and has significant experience in M&A projects.

Ms Ovcharova has recently supported the acquisition of the concession rights on an oil and gas field in the Amazon, Brazil, including structuring and formalising the contractual joint venture relations with the partner and providing post-closing support (secondment and operational matters). She also deals with oil services companies based in Russia (Nizhnevartovsk and Orenburg), acquiring shares in several major gas producers in Russia, including structuring and formalising partnership relations with the project partner, and acquiring petrol stations in southern Russia.

Ms Ovcharova has had a number of articles published in Russian and international legal magazines.

Anthony Patten
Partner, Allens
anthony.patten@allens.com.au

Anthony Patten is a partner at Allens in Perth, specialising in corporate and project development work in the energy industry, with a particular focus on oil and gas. Mr Patten is responsible for the coordination of Allens' oil and gas practice. He is experienced in advising national oil companies, major international oil companies, trading houses, utilities and independents on all aspects of their businesses. He has worked on a wide range of upstream, midstream and downstream oil and gas projects and transactions in many jurisdictions, including from an upstream perspective Iran, Iraq, Nigeria, Oman, Qatar, Russia, Trinidad and Australia, and from a downstream perspective India, Indonesia, Italy, the Netherlands, the United Arab Emirates and the United Kingdom. He has particular expertise in the LNG sector.

Before joining Allens in November 2011, Mr Patten was a partner in London with another international law firm. He also spent six years as a senior in-house counsel of Royal Dutch Shell plc, based in London and in the United Arab Emirates.

Liang Peng
Senior associate, Sunshine Law Firm
pl@sunshinelaw.com.cn

Liang Peng is a member of the Energy, Resources, Environment (ER) group of Sunshine Law Firm in Beijing, supporting the energy and environment and shipping and logistics practices. He holds an LLB in law and commerce and an LLM in mineral law and policy from the Centre for Energy, Petroleum and Mineral Law and Policy, University of Dundee. He specialises in petroleum and mining projects and M&A transactions for seven years while based in Beijing, Dalian, Riyadh and London.

Mr Peng has advised foreign multinationals and domestic companies on onshore and offshore energy-related projects. He has participated in several M&A transactions in disposal of petroleum assets in London. He also has advised in Saudi Arabia a leading petroleum company in connection with an engineering, procurement and construction contract for building a refinery, and has extensive experience in charterparties and sale and purchase of vessels.

Eduardo G Pereira
Managing director, STR Holding
egp@strholding.com

Eduardo G Pereira has been active in the oil and gas industry for several years and is an international expert on joint operating agreements. His experience in this area – both academic and practical – is extensive. Dr Pereira is a managing director of STR Holding. He played a key role in assisting Petra Energia in becoming Brazil's leading onshore oil and gas company and he is now assisting STR to become a leading onshore player in Africa and Asia. He concluded his doctoral thesis on oil and gas joint ventures at the University of Aberdeen. He is a visiting lecturer at the University of Eastern Finland and an associated editor of the *Oil, Gas and Energy Law Journal (OGEL).*

Piotr Pszczel
Of counsel, Kawalko & Godlewski
pp@kpglegal.pl

Piotr Pszczel is of counsel at Kawalko & Godlewski, a Warsaw-based law firm. Mr Pszczel worked for several international law firms before joining Kawalko & Godlewski.

His professional interest is focused on energy and environmental protection law. In 2005 Mr Pszczel acted as an expert in a project for the European Commission, where he was responsible for preparing memos and analyses on the degree of transposition of the EU energy and environmental directives into the Polish legal system. The environmental workload consisted of environmental impact assessment matters, including special protection areas and their implementation into Polish national law.

Mr Pszczel also has extensive practical experience in natural gas-related matters, both upstream and downstream, with a particular focus on the trade and exploration of natural gas. He has published numerous articles and chapters in various books about energy law and environmental protection.

Peter Roberts
Partner, Ashurst LLP
Peter.roberts@ashurst.com

Peter Roberts is an experienced upstream and midstream oil and gas projects lawyer specialising in project acquisition and project structuring and development. He is a partner with Ashurst LLP in London and heads up the firm's oil and gas practice in Europe, Africa and the Middle East.

Prior to joining Ashurst, Mr Roberts was the general counsel of Centrica Energy, in London. He has also worked in Hong Kong and Singapore, and was previously in-house counsel with Exxon Corporation.

Mr Roberts is the author of several leading oil and gas law textbooks (*Gas Sales and Gas Transportation Agreements* (Sweet and Maxell, third edition, 2011); *Joint Operating Agreements: A Practical Guide* (Globe, second edition, 2012); and *Petroleum Contracts and English Law* (Oxford University Press, due May 2013)).

Mr Roberts is an honorary lecturer at Dundee University's Centre for Energy, Petroleum and Mineral Law and Policy (CEPMLP), and is the General Editor of the AIPN's *Journal of World Energy Law & Business.*

Patrícia Rosário
Counsel, RAGA Advogados
p.rosario@rosarioabrantesgarcia.com

Patrícia Rosário holds a master's degree in law (Lisbon) and an LLM (London), and is an *advogada* (Portugal). She focuses on foreign investment, oil and gas, public international law and international arbitration. Ms Rosário has extensive experience in complex cross-border commercial transactions across a variety of sectors, including oil and gas, infrastructure and construction, namely in several Portuguese-speaking jurisdictions (Portugal, Angola and Mozambique).

In addition to working on corporate transactions, Ms Rosário regularly advises clients on investment structuring for treaty protection, drafting contractual dispute resolution clauses and serves as lead counsel in litigation and arbitration matters. She is currently a PhD candidate at the School of International Arbitration's Centre for Commercial Law Studies at Queen Mary College, University of London and also collaborates with the Oxford Institute for Energy Studies at the University of Oxford . She is co-founder of the Arbitration Africa Project (arbitrationafrica.com).

Anupama Sen
Research fellow, Oxford Institute for Energy Studies
anupama.sen@oxfordenergy.org

Anupama Sen is a research fellow at the Oxford Institute for Energy Studies. Her areas of expertise include policy on pricing, taxation and regulation of oil, gas and electricity in India, with extensions to other developing economies. Her work explores these themes within India's energy sector, with a particular focus on the interconnectedness of these themes through factors such as energy pricing and the allocation of natural resources. Her work has appeared in *The Energy Journal* as well as in several of the institute's publications, such as *The Pricing of Internationally Traded Gas*. She has also consulted widely for international organisations working on the natural resources sector.

She holds an MSc from the London School of Economics and Political Science and a PhD from Cambridge University. She is also a visiting fellow at Wolfson College, Cambridge University.

Kim Talus
Professor of European law, University of Eastern Finland
kim.talus@uef.fi

Kim Talus is a professor of European law and director of the LLM diploma programme on international and European energy law and policy at the University of Eastern Finland. His research and other activities cover international, comparative and European energy law. More specifically, he focuse on oil and gas, international investment protection and EU energy law and policy. He has published widely on natural gas contracts and is a frequent speaker on this topic at international conferences.

He has held teaching positions at University College London, the University of Houston and Bonn University. He is the editor in chief of *Oil, Gas and Energy Law* (www.ogel.org) and a member of the editorial board for the *Journal of World Energy Law and Business.*

Paul Verkleij
Senior associate, Nauta Dutilh NV
paul.verkleij@nautadutilh.com

Paul Verkleij is a senior associate in the energy and utilities industry group. He represents energy companies and financial institutions in cross-border transactions, silent auction sales, restructurings and joint ventures. He has extensive experience in energy-related commercial contracting (eg, gas, coal, power and LNG) and project financing documentation.

Mr Verkleij joined NautaDutilh in 2004 and was based in New York for 2006-2007. In 2009 he successfully completed the postgraduate Grotius Academy on corporate law.

Debra J Villarreal
Partner, Thompson & Knight LLP
debra.villarreal@tklaw.com

Debra J Villarreal is a partner in the oil and gas section of Thompson & Knight LLP. Her practice focuses on the acquisition and disposition of onshore and offshore properties and federal offshore (outer continental shelf) interests. She counsels clients and prepares agreements in relation to acquisitions and exploration and production activities. Ms Villarreal also has expertise in oil and gas title due diligence in both acquisition and mortgaging of properties.

Ms Villarreal holds a JD from Kansas University Law School (1990), where she worked on the *Law Review* and was Order of the Coif, Phi Kappa Phi. She also holds a BBA from Washburn University (1981). She is admitted to and a member of the State Bar of Texas and Pennsylvania. She has been named in *The Best Lawyers in America* by Woodward/White Inc (oil and gas law) for many years and has an AV rating by Martindale-Hubbell.

Marcelo Viveiros de Moura
Partner, Pinheiro Neto Advogados
mvmoura@pn.com.br

Marcelo Viveiros de Moura graduated with an LLB from the University of Rio de Janeiro Law School (1988) and an LLM from the University of Cambridge (Hughes Hall, 1993). He is a partner in the corporate area of Pinheiro Neto's Rio de Janeiro office, having also worked as visiting associate at the London offices of Slaughter and May (1992). Mr Viveiros de Moura specialises in corporate law, with a focus on M&A and corporate restructuring; regulatory law in the oil and gas, capital markets and insurance areas; project and corporate finance; and government procurements and contracts. He is a professor of corporate law at the *Fundação Getúlio Vargas* Faculty of Law. He has served as chairman of the British-Brazilian Chamber of Commerce (2007-2009) and is currently a member of the chamber's board.

Yerzhan Yessimkhanov
Partner, Grata
yyessimkhanov@gratanet.com

Yerzhan Yessimkhanov graduated with high honours from Kazakh State Law University, International Law Faculty, in 2004.

Before joining Grata, Mr Yessimkhanov worked for the Kazakhstan Investment Fund Group, in major Kazakh development company Capital Partners and as an associate of international law firm Baker & McKenzie. He has extensive experience in the areas of real estate and construction, subsoil use and infrastructure. He acted as a consultant on a number of large infrastructure projects realised in recent years in Kazakhstan, including work as head of the legal department working on the Medeu and Chimbulak mountain resorts reconstruction projects for the Asian Games 2011.

Mr Yessimkhanov is the author of a number of articles and reviews relating to real estate issues, construction and environmental protection in Kazakhstan, including an overview of Kazakh environmental legal framework for the PLC *Cross-border Environment Handbook 2010/11* and of the Kazakh climate change regulations for *BNA Environment Reporter.*

He speaks English, Russian and Kazakh.